The Limits of Legitimacy

The Limits of Legitimacy

Political Contradictions
of Contemporary Capitalism

Alan Wolfe

THE FREE PRESS
A Division of Macmillan Publishing Co., Inc.
NEW YORK
Collier Macmillan Publishers
LONDON

The Free Press
A Division of Macmillan Publishing Co., Inc.
866 Third Avenue, New York, N.Y. 10022

Collier Macmillan Canada, Ltd.

Library of Congress Catalog Card Number: 76–51567

Printed in the United States of America

printing number

1   2   3   4   5   6   7   8   9   10

Library of Congress Cataloging in Publication Data

Wolfe, Alan
    The limits of legitimacy.

    Bibliography: p.
    Includes index.
    1. Liberalism. 2. Democracy. I. Title.
JC571.W84   321.8   76-51567
ISBN 0-02-935570-2

Contents

Preface   vii

INTRODUCTION: THE PREDICAMENT OF LIBERAL DEMOCRACY   1

PART I: SIX SOLUTIONS IN SEARCH OF TRANQUILLITY   11

Chapter 1: The Accumulative State   13
Chapter 2: Visions of Harmony   42
Chapter 3: Dilemmas of Expansionism   80
Chapter 4: The Origins of the Franchise State   108
Chapter 5: The Franchise State at Work   146
Chapter 6: The Rise and Fall of the Diarchy   176
Chapter 7: Globalizing Contradictions   214

INTERLUDE: THE EMERGENCE OF LATE CAPITALISM   245

PART II: POLITICS AND THE EXHAUSTION OF ALTERNATIVES   255

Chapter 8: The Reification of the State   257
Chapter 9: Alienated Politics   288
Chapter 10: The Legitimacy Crisis of the State   322

Notes   348
Bibliography   393
Index   418

Preface

IT WOULD APPEAR to be an act of either courage or folly even to think of writing a book about politics at the present time. When a political movement can generate itself, dominate the news, and then disappear as if it had never existed, all in the space of ten years; when a President can be elected with one of the largest majorities on record only to become within a year the most unpopular of his genre since the invention of the public opinion poll; when ideologies can be pronounced dead at the very moment they are being reborn; when writers will have to proclaim the arrival of the post-post society since everything else will have been superseded—is it possible to say anything valid about a form of human activity that has fascinated observers since ancient Greece? I think the possibility does exist.

In spite of a tendency for writers to hail every nuance as a revolutionary change, there are at least two things about political activity that have remained fairly constant over the last two hundred years, especially in the United States and Western Europe. One is that it has generally taken place within an economic system that encourages private property, is oriented toward making profits, follows the logic of accumulation, and consequently creates divisions between rich and poor, powerful and powerless. Before it became a term of opprobrium, such a system used to be called capitalism, a good descriptive word that I will continue to use. In so doing, I mean only to discuss a concept once proudly defended by an establishment that no longer dares call itself what it is. This thing called capitalism has changed from time to time, as the following chapters will make clear, but the existence of a class that demands from the political system help in the accumulation of capital has been a constant since the late eighteenth century. Second, for most of the time a series of expectations has existed in the capitalist countries about how political life should be organized. A word that describes these expectations is democracy, and while, as is true of capitalism, its modifiers may have altered (agrarian, industrial, liberal, mass, social), the term itself is still in use. Politics may appear to be under constant change, but the persistence of the parameters within which the changes take place is equally impressive.

In emphasizing the persistence of capitalist needs and democratic desires, I am taking a conservative stance, the only way I know to preserve my commitment to fundamental social change. The ahistorical urges of late capitalist societies has led to the puzzling paradox that those committed to the status quo preach the arrival of a new era (the *post*-industrial society, *beyond* freedom and dignity, the *new* industrial state) while those who want to overturn the present insist with equal vehemence that the class conflicts of Victorian England are alive and well a hundred years after their demise. In such an atmosphere, the revolutionary, let alone radical, act is to discover one's roots and to try to make them put forth shoots again. My intellectual roots, as I discovered in writing this book, are in two places: first, in a preoccupation, second, in a tradition of terminology.

By seeking to establish the effects capitalism has had on democracy and vice versa, this book joins a debate that for a long time was the core of political analysis. From James Madison to John Adams, the early theoreticians of the American system speculated about this question and then tried to put their speculations into practice. The French Revolution gave birth to radical notions about equality as it did to an emphasis on God's hierarchy. The history of British politics in the nineteenth century is the story of how this question was asked and how it was answered. For most of the life of capitalist societies, in other words, debates on the extension of the franchise rarely neglected the role of property, and, conversely, arguments about new forms of industrialization could not take place without reference to political changes. There really was such a thing as political economy.

Moreover, the mutual effects produced by capitalism and democracy influenced the scholarship produced as the nineteenth century turned into the twentieth; first J. Allen Smith's *The Spirit of American Government* and then the various writings of Charles Beard testify to an interest in the matter. And it took some time before this concern disappeared. The founders of modern American political science, men like Charles Merriam and Harold Gosnell, retained this preoccupation, and one can see its traces in the work of men of quite different political perspectives, such as Pendleton Herring, E. E. Schattschneider, and V. O. Key. When I was four months old, Robert Lynd noted that "the attempted harmonious marriage of democracy to capitalism doomed genuinely popular control from the start," * and one would have thought that the relationship between these forces would constitute the primary focus of both political science and economics after the conclusion of World War II. This, it turned out, never did occur.

As both economics and political science became ensnared in their own trivia, political economy disappeared in the shuffle. When, in addition, broader questions of political theory and philosophy were no longer seen as relevant to the human condition, statements like the one made by Lynd could neither be accepted nor refuted. They were instead just ignored, and consequently very little attention was paid to the question of the effects produced by the tension between capitalism as an economic system

* Foreword to Robert A. Brady, *Business as a System of Power* (New York: Columbia University Press, 1943), viii.

and democracy as a political one. I see this book, then, not so much as breaking new ground as inserting myself into an old tradition whose development has been temporarily interrupted. The question of the impact of social class and the still relatively unchecked desire for private aggrandizement upon those fragile arrangements that are designed to ensure individual freedom and growth with equality and community is still open. Certainly it is no longer shocking to conclude that the latter ideals have been corrupted by the former realities, but the situation is, I think, a bit more complicated. For one thing, the ideals are still believed in by many, and there must somehow be an explanation for this. Also, a simple accusation, no matter how eloquent, against the powerful and in favor of the powerless is no longer capable of producing much of a reaction; it is inconceivable that today, as in 1890, a socialist propaganda tract could be a best-seller, not because socialist ideas are currently alien but because they are too common. Equality, like virginity, is as honored in theory as it is violated in practice, a situation that frustrates both those who write about it and those who try to bring it about.

Polemical attack, then, is not my goal in what follows; understanding is. But what are we to understand? In order to answer that question, I was led back to a second root, this time a terminological one. I would like to understand more about the state, yet one of the most puzzling aspects of recent political theory and practice is that, as more and more aspects of social life become located within the province of the state, the term itself begins to disappear from the language of political discourse. One possible explanation of such a paradox is that the nonuse of the referent is a reflection of the reality behind it. Although the basis of state power is ultimately the behavior of ordinary human beings, that power often takes on alienated, imposing forms. Insofar as the expression "the state" conjures up visions of those forms—the pomposity of Louis XIV, the tradition of *raison d'état*, the Germanic preoccupation with *Machtstaat*—there is something direct and honest about using it. But when a dominant urge of the political system is to mystify power more than to glorify it, the use of a term with such images would clearly be counterproductive. In the Anglo-American countries, it would seem, the state has withered away—but only in speech, not in political life. If state power is ever to be understood, the term itself must be brought back into existence; to resurrect the state is to make a political declaration about the centrality of organized political power in modern societies.

The state has not always been as neglected as it is now. The term did play a role in all four of the traditions that have shaped the twentieth century: anarchism, conservatism, liberalism, and Marxism. Unfortunately, one finds in reviewing these traditions a direct correlation between consistency and irrelevance. By almost every criterion, *anarchism* would seem to be the one ideology most irrelevant in an age of organizational complexity; yet the anarchist tradition is the only one to have even approached a consistent position on the state. A wide variety of philosophies and styles of action is subsumed under the name anarchism, but what does unite idealistic nobles like Kropotkin, political activists like Bakunin and his followers, and even social bandits is a determined belief that any form of human activity can be better performed when compulsion is not the motivation behind it. The state, in other words, is bad, and that is all there is to be said. One is left with an approach that is as elegantly consistent as it is exasperatingly meaningless, perhaps the reason for anarchism's sudden flashes of popularity amid general disrepute.

Conservatism, which is almost as irrelevant to the modern world as is anarchism, seeks the same consistency but does not find it. There is a strain of conservative thought, running from Burke to Buckley, which is distrustful of state action. Political activity is best performed by gentlemen possessing the appropriate skills, and when the untutored are allowed to play, they invariably appeal to the state to compensate them for their weaknesses. Hence the *modern* state, in the conservative vision as in the anarchist, becomes, in the words of Albert Jay Nock, "our enemy," the symbol of a deplorable human condition. But at the same time the conservative quest is always for order, and the task of preserving order is inherently political. For all their elegance as logicians, conservatives such as deMaistre, Bonald, and Stahl were forced to glorify the state—if not the existing modern one, then a theocratic one, a historical one, or even an imaginary one. The Burkean tradition itself has faced the same ambiguity. When conservativism is faithful to its origins as a critique of the rise of the bourgeoisie, it can often claim some valuable insights into political life. But when it accommodates itself to that rise in the interests of maintaining political stability and order, then it is both no longer conservative and no longer insightful. (This has happened to the peculiar movement in America that calls itself conservative.) The brothers Buckley, vulgar Burkeites, have about as much in common with their mentor as Edward Bernstein, the master of revisionist Marxism, had with his, which is why one of them could serve the state while disdaining its existence, a tactic he seems to have learned from Bernstein's Social Democrats.

Yet the conservative inconsistencies about the state are minor compared with the liberal and Marxist traditions, the two that have most thoroughly transformed the modern world. In both, an original preoccupation with things political became sublimated, to use Sheldon Wolin's term, into other areas of social life, leaving citizens of advanced industrial societies with little insight into the one institution wielding the greatest impact on their lives.

The Hobbesian origins of modern *liberalism* testify to an original seriousness about the state. To Hobbes, there was an unbreakable link between his psychology and his political theory; it was because men were perpetually engaged in struggle with one another that there was such a need for a strong sovereign. When the classical political economists borrowed Hobbes' view of man but left behind his defense of sovereignty, they revealed an ambiguity about political power that has bedeviled liberalism ever since. The pursuit of self-interest through rational calculation might fuel the market, but can it be trusted to provide for the commonwealth as well? Classical liberalism never made up its mind. For all his belief in the primacy of self-interest, Bentham—the man who most epitomizes the contradictions of liberalism—felt the same need for order that motivated defenders of the old regime. Bentham had no trouble justifying the repressive use of state power in the Peterloo Massacre (the self-interest of those below the middle class was not to be trusted). His plan for a model prison, which, in its desire to exercise total control over all activity but to do so with a benign face, became a metaphor for all of liberal society, was further evidence of the same ambiguity. In the liberal view, as in the conservative, there developed a tendency to contradict basic principles when the conditions necessary for a stable order demanded it. The state became a *deus ex machina*, resolving the conflicts within the society and giving the political drama a happy ending. But this role of the state was artificial, arising not out of any consistent view of the nature of political action but out of the needs of the moment. Liberalism did not so much explain the state as defend its purpose.

To defend the state one must recognize its existence, and for this reason liberalism maintained an interest in the problem of the state until fairly recent times. In England, one of the most extensive discussions about the nature of the state occurred between 1890 and 1920, just as the liberal state was meeting what George Dangerfield called its "strange death." From students of Hegel, from a wing of guild socialism, from the emerging science of public administration, arose a wide variety of analyses of the modern state. Bosanquet's *Philosophical Theory of the State*, Hobhouse's *Metaphysical Theory of the State*, and Mary Follett's *The New State* are the best, but by no means the only, examples of this interest. While one cannot speak of a "school" (Hobhouse's book is an attack on Bosanquet's), what does emerge from this concern is the notion that one need no longer fear the state. For the first time outside of Hegel's Prussia the idea is developed that the modern state might serve a positive end, not, as in Hobbes, the positivity of a negativity (preventing something even worse), but as a good in its own right. Eventually, of course, these strains were tied together into the notion of the welfare state (a formulation that I will reject in this book for an alternative nomenclature), the one major attempt by the liberal tradition to come to terms with the nature of the modern state. But the fact remains that for quite some time liberals discussed, defined, and demarcated the state.

It is therefore most surprising that so viable a tradition disappeared in more recent times. Robert MacIver's *The Modern State*, published in 1926, is its last manifestation, and MacIver himself best symbolized the change when he published much later *The Web of Government*. Two words that were not synonymous became so; political science became the study, not of the state, but of something at a less rarefied level called government. Indicative of the change was the popularity of pluralism in its various guises. When it discovered pluralism, the liberal tradition found its excuse for ignoring the state. As Arthur F. Bentley said with typical candor, "the 'state' itself is, to the best of my knowledge and belief, no factor in our investigation." * His knowledge and belief were quite accurate, and those who followed his lead in other areas followed it here as well. With pluralism the state simply vanished. Though pluralists agreed that all the various groups with which they were concerned struggled for control of something, they were reluctant to inquire as to what that something was. Like a Victorian novel treating passion without sex, the pluralists tried to examine politics without the state, and consequently their picture of the public life of their time was about as accurate as Thackeray's of the private life of his. David Easton devoted five hundred pages to an analysis of "political life" and never once—as a point of principle, not ignorance— even mentioned the state. Profoundly apolitical in spite of its self-proclaimed love of conflict and diversity, pluralism dealt with the key subject matter of modern politics by pretending that it did not exist.

This attempt to conceptualize the state out of existence would not have been so serious were it not for an equally conspicuous failure of the one tradition that always understood the vacuity of liberal analyses—the *Marxist*. Marx, though often called an economic determinist, had, like Hobbes, a preoccupation with matters political. From his first newspaper articles through his first philosophical speculations to his mid-career political writings to his last letters, Marx attempted to develop a distinct political theory. Because Marx's approach to the state has been so misunderstood, this question needs greater examination. The important point to be emphasized here is that the Marxist tradition, like the liberal one, does have its roots in a specifically *political* theory.

The draining of the political content from Marx's writings began even while he was still alive, in the emergence of a Social Democratic movement that put all its faith in economic advancement. To men like Bernstein and Kautsky, political questions, both theoretically and strategically, were constantly derived from economic ones; the real origins of "economic determinism" lie here. What social democracy began, Lenin in his own way completed. Though Lenin's critique of men like Bernstein was vitriolic, he did in fact concede a good deal of ground to his adversaries, for Lenin

---

* *The Process of Government* (Cambridge: Belknap Press of Harvard University Press, 1967), 263.

never resurrected the political to the extent that it had existed in Marx. (To be fair, much of Marx's political writing was unknown during Lenin's lifetime.) *State and Revolution*, nonetheless, became to Marxism what Bentley's *The Process of Government* was to liberalism. Here too the state became a simple repository of forces, but now the forces were social classes rather than political interest groups. The state was a repressive force used by the bourgeoisie to keep itself in power, but all that was needed to change things around was a victory for the proletariat, who would grab the state and use it for its own ends. Once its repressive function against the former ruling class played itself out, the state would disappear and a new stage of human history would be ushered in. The state in this view again assumes a purely instrumental importance, defined by factors entirely outside itself. In this version, there is no need to say any more, except to repeat what is already known. Harold Laski's *The State in Theory and Practice* and Stanley Moore's *Critique of Capitalist Democracy* are examples of books doing exactly that. Like David B. Truman's *The Governmental Process*, they can add some modern examples that their mentors missed, but they remain derivative nonetheless.

The state did not roll over and play dead just because the two most influential political traditions of modern times chose not to deal effectively with this dominant political fact. Indeed, state power was if anything increased by this avoidance, for as Wolin has noted:

> To reject the state meant denying the central referent of the political, abandoning a whole range of notions and the practices to which they pointed—citizenship, obligation, general authority—without pausing to consider that the strategy of withdrawal might further enhance state power.*

Thus the growth of state power and the decline of explicit theories of the state became linked, each to some extent causing the other. Because political theorists no longer asked difficult questions about the nature of political power, the exercise of such power was facilitated. Because political power was exercised with such apparent ease, theorists no longer posed difficult questions about it. Theory and practice seemed connected in a cycle of escalating irresponsibility.

It would be incorrect to conclude from this that the decision of liberals and Marxists to avoid the state constituted a rejection of the importance of developing a theory of the state. Actually the opposite was the case. Just as the decision *not* to develop a political theory is a political decision, the avoidance of the state became the central proposition of the theory of the state. Those who were denying the autonomy and even the existence of the state were at the same time glorifying its power, praising its achieve-

* *Politics and Vision* (Boston: Little, Brown, 1960), 417.

ments, trumpeting its virtues. It is no easy task to avoid a phenomenon and to justify it at the same time, but this is essentially what occurred. While the concept of the state went unexplored, political power, the national interest, governmental decision making, public choice, foreign relations, domestic policy, bureaucracy, administration, the politician—these were exalted. Not analyzing the state, therefore, resulted in a most peculiar contradiction. As the theoretical core of modern politics became mystified, the area surrounding it took on added importance. Those who were denying the reality of the state, on the one hand, were contributing to its power, on the other. Political thought became a confused and contradictory affair, sweeping back and forth with abandon from a thorough disgust with political power to a passionate apology for its exercise.

The simultaneous tendencies of avoiding the state and glorifying its power can be seen in the contemporary legacies of both the liberal and radical traditions. American political science since World War II, to take one example, has proceeded in two seemingly contradictory directions: on the one hand, into an apolitical empiricism that pretends the real world is unimportant; on the other, into a frightening, apologetic *Realpolitik* that is all too preoccupied with the real world of power and exploitation. The point is that these tendencies are two parts of the same process, for each in its own way refuses to take the state seriously as an entity in its own right. Half the profession sublimates the state into some other form of activity and half reifies it beyond the bounds of recognition, but neither takes it for what it is. The Marxist tradition finds itself in a similar position. The popularity of a strict economic determinism leads to one of two consequences: either the state is dismissed as part of an irrelevant superstructure (the Marxist equivalent of behaviorism) or, in a more sophisticated fashion, fantastic powers of perception and superhuman abilities are attributed to the ruling class and its political organs as they ward off dissent and preserve their power (a form of reverse Machiavellianism). Again, the effect of this duality is to render the state unexaminable as an institution that possesses some powers and does not possess others. The conclusion should be self-evident: there is a need to develop a theory of the state that neither sublimates politics into nothingness nor places it on a pedestal beyond analytic reach. The state must be withered back into the consciousness of political theory and the reality of political action.

In attempting to revive this once active concern with political economy and with the state, I have found myself part of an intellectual community that discovered the need at roughly the same time. I was fortunate to have both financial and intellectual help in my efforts. The Institute for Policy Studies, for example, provided both, and I am most grateful to its co-directors, Marcus Raskin and Richard Barnet, for their interest in my work. While at the Institute I participated actively in discussions with members of the Political Economy Program, and I want to thank

Len Rodberg, Robb Burlage, and Saul Landau for the time they took to talk over some of these ideas with me. Additional financial help came from the Rabinowitz Foundation and the Nation Foundation. My thanks go to Victor Rabinowitz, James L. Storrow, Jr., and Carey McWilliams.

Intellectually, my first debt is to the Bay Area *Kapitalistate* group, which responded enthusiastically to my first public presentation of some of these ideas. In doing so they gave me the confidence to keep going. David Gold took a very special interest in my work, as did Clarence Lo. But also helpful in many ways were the other members: Erik Wright, James O'Conner, Sue Bessmer, Margaret Fay, Roger Friedland, John Mollenkopf, Jens Christiansen, and Kay Trimberger. Michael Wallace showed more love and attention to both the manuscript and myself than anyone has a right to expect, even from so close a friend. His support I acknowledge with respect and gratitude. Todd Gitlin also gave me much of his time and energy, for which I will always be in his debt. Arthur Vidich wrote a careful critique of the manuscript that was instrumental in eliminating its worst abuses. And in one way or another, the following people helped me formulate my thoughts, though they may be unaware of how much or in what way they did so: Michael Merrill, Claus Offe, Nancy Hartsock, Jean Elshtain, Bertell Ollman, Isaac Balbus, Robert Mutch, David Vogel, and Wolf Deider-Narr. My final thanks are to Gladys Topkis, Elly Dickason, and Lionel Dean at The Free Press for their editorial skills.

In writing this book, I came to understand what it meant to be part of a political and economic tradition. While the writings of Marx, Gramsci, Lukacs, and others of similar orientation are still not so welcome in the United States as they are elsewhere throughout even the capitalist world, to consider oneself a participant in attempting to answer the questions they asked is exhilarating. At work on the book, I would sometimes ponder the isolation caused by being a Marxist in the most bourgeois of cultures, but such feelings were ultimately counterbalanced by the thrill of participating in an uncharted quest with like-minded people toward some understanding that was as important as it was neglected. Between the time I started writing and the time I finished, a small but quite viable critical spirit had developed within the American social sciences, and I no longer felt so alone. It is to the growth of this spirit of committed but undogmatic inquiry that I wish to dedicate this book.

Introduction: The Predicament of Liberal Democracy

SOMETHING PECULIAR SEEMS to have happened to the politics of advanced industrial societies. Twenty years ago a select group of social scientists praised Western societies for having achieved the Platonic Good; class conflict, disharmony, and disruptive ideas had withered away in a paradise of permanent perfection. Yet, fads being what they are, it is currently fashionable to argue exactly the opposite. The world of Pangloss has become that of Céline, and in a strikingly effortless manner. Societies once praised for having solved their problems are now viewed as overwhelmed to the point of paralysis by those very same problems. The key terms are no longer harmony, growth, and reconciliation, but stagnation, *immobilisme*, limited options, closed circles, steady states, *la société bloquée*. The shift in emphasis from iridescent optimism to a militant, aggressive pessimism can be seen in almost every area of life, from social conflict to the consequences of technology. One of the places where it is most notable is the realm of political values, for there has been a marked shift in feeling about the prospects for liberal democracy. Under the old perspective liberal democracy had been achieved and perfected, representing nothing less than the good life, in Seymour Martin Lipset's famous phrase. Twenty years later, it has suddenly become an ideal that can no longer exist in reality. There is a strong feeling that liberal democracy is a hopelessly outdated mechanism for coping with really *serious* problems, such as, as one writer put it, the end of the European domination of the world.[1]

The new attitude toward liberal democracy has been expressed in many places, some of which I will analyze in greater detail in Chapter 10. One prestigious body, the Trilateral Commission, has publicly questioned whether democracy remains the most viable political structure if capitalism is to be preserved.[2] Social science has turned to issues like "conflict regulation" in what are antiseptically called "divided" societies.[3] Other writers have become fascinated with the "breakdown" of democracy, finding conscious and unconscious parallels in the triumph of authoritarian regimes with possible futures for liberal ones.[4] Corporatism, a device popular in the 1920s for bringing class conflict into an ordered and regulated pattern, has been taken up like the films of that era by a nostalgic avant-garde among political scientists.[5] One historian, with brilliant if somewhat bizarre logic, has suggested that since political liberalism was a product of laissez-faire economics, and since we no longer accept Adam

1

Smith's ideas about how nations become wealthy, why should be not abolish liberal democracy as well? "What we need," Robert Skidelsky suggests, "is an up-to-date political wisdom," one that would do for Madison and Mill what Keynes did for Smith. Since it is not true, according to him, that "any tampering with constitutions or parliamentary systems leads straight to totalitarianism," people—he does not say whom—should begin to tinker with new forms of state power that would be efficient, rational, and authoritative. Our present representative democracies naturally produce "dishonest" policies, by which he apparently means ones that are popular among large numbers of people instead of among corporation heads.[6] And, finally, a popularizer of economic ideas seems to have put it all together. Because the world's resources are scarce, and because Malthusian checks have failed to control population growth, the world faces a future in which the affluence of the white, metropolitan areas is over. Can liberal democracy survive such trauma? Not according to Robert Heilbroner. While a few such states may continue to exist, "for the majority of capitalist nations, however, I do not see how one can avoid the conclusion that the required transformation will be likely to exceed the capability of representative democracy." [7]

Are the reports of the death of liberal democracy premature? Tempting as it may be to accept the new pessimism, to do so would be as incorrect as subscribing to the optimism of the 1950s. Rather than being opposites, the old optimism and the new pessimism are quite similar responses to the same reality: class conflict. If the class struggle cannot be wished away, it can be whisked away; both attitudes express a desire to abolish social class, not in the real world, but in the study of politics and history. In addition, just as the stump preacher shifts his attention back and forth from the oppression of hell to the sublimity of heaven, every utopia must have its apocalyptic negation; as the mirror image of the end of ideology, the world of darkness painted by the political pessimists is also its logical conclusion. Third, both kinds of approaches are reflective of a fascination for the dramatic instead of the analytic, a preference for cliché over serious study. And, finally, the optimism of the 1950s and the pessimism of the 1970s are equally ahistorical. The former posited nothing less than an end to history; the latter suggests that history has just begun, that a sudden and unprecedented "crisis" has come upon the scene. Yet crises, whether of population, energy, legitimacy, budgets, or politics, do not manifest themselves out of thin air; they are, in Lukacs' phrase, "an intensification of everyday life," [8] a culmination, not a negation, of historical processes. The new pessimism may be for some an appropriate psychological mood, but as an analytic mode it is as limited as what it replaced.

This is not to suggest that the future of liberal democracy is a nonissue. The pressures it faces are great, from both disadvantaged groups who want to participate and advantaged ones who find that the system no longer serves their interests. The existence of powerful and secret cabals within the state, loyal to few besides themselves; laws that say one thing yet do another; parties that do one thing yet say another; popular attitudes that appear to change radically yet stay the same; managers who want to reduce all human behavior to simple laws; bureaucratic structures that foil beneficent intent; regular breaking of the rules by those sworn to uphold them; dedication to the rules by those pledged to destroy them; concentrations of power that are vast yet apparently impotent to bring about even slight change; changing definitions of the political; the increasing role of the state in more and more areas of civil society—these are just a few of the processes being faced by liberal democracies at the present time.

What I do wish to suggest is that the issue, which is serious, can be examined only in serious fashion. Neither an arcadian nor an apocalyptic perspective is the answer; an analytic one is preferred. To examine the future of liberal democracy, it is best to begin at the beginning, a cliché that in this case has a twofold meaning. First, it is necessary to try to make some sense out of the term "liberal democracy," to know what we are talking about before talking about it. Second, beginning at the beginning also means having a sense of historical sweep, some understanding of how the European and American liberal democracies came to assume their shape. It is to these two tasks that we must turn before making any claims, one way or the other, for liberal democracy's future.

Any important political theorist of the nineteenth century would have been puzzled by the expression liberal democracy. As late as World War I, it was generally understood that there was one political tradition, liberalism, with a unique set of ideas, a specific class to which it appealed, and appropriate historical traditions, and another tradition, democracy, with its own ideas, class, and history. One had to decide to which tradition he adhered, for it was extremely hard, if not impossible, to choose both. Many a writer—John Stuart Mill being perhaps the best example—thought he could and found that the price he paid was vacillation, ambiguity, confusion, contradiction, and befuddlement, a vain attempt, in Marx's words, to reconcile irreconcilables.[9] The reason a definition of terms becomes so important is that the meaning of both liberalism and democracy has changed, and that change in meaning may be at the root of the troubles liberal democracies are now facing.

As a variety of writers, the most important of whom are Hannah Arendt and C. B. Macpherson, have pointed out, classical liberalism and the bourgeoisie grew together. Thomas Hobbes, in Arendt's view, "the only philosopher to whom the bourgeoisie can rightly and exclusively lay claim," developed a psychology and a politics requisite to a new order based on capitalist accumulation. Since "only the unlimited accumulation of power could bring about the unlimited accumulation of capital," the

Hobbesian emphasis on the need for order, regardless of its justification of one-man rule, became the basis upon which the liberal tradition was built.[10] Building upon while modifying Hobbes' formidable achievement, John Locke, in Macpherson's words, "provides a moral foundation for bourgeois appropriation." In his writings, natural rights were transformed into property rights, individualism became the rationale for the buying and selling of labor power, community became the exercise of authority necessary to ensure the stability of civil society, individual differences became class distinctions, and the social contract became the primary justification for a market economy. In short, whatever his differences with Hobbes over the means of preserving bourgeois society, Locke also "has justified the specifically capitalist appropriation of land and money." [11]

This interpretation of classical liberalism, though first greeted with disbelief by the intellectual descendants of the men being analyzed, has by and large been accepted as plausible within recent political theory. The advantage of such an approach is that it gives a historical specificity and a precise context to a term that, in everyday usage, has come to indicate someone who supports the welfare state, who is in opposition to a "conservative." In this book, I will use the term *liberalism* to refer to the marketplace ideology that emerged in the seventeenth, eighteenth, and nineteenth centuries to justify the increasingly important capitalist mode of production. The opposite of a liberal, then, is not a conservative but a defender of precapitalist social relations, on the one hand, and postcapitalist ones, on the other. Though confusion will be inevitable because this usage departs from everyday vocabulary, it is essential to my preoccupation with the impact of capitalist economic relationships on democratic expectations to adhere to the original meaning of the term. Liberal political arrangements may be defined as those that attempt to facilitate the accumulation of capital by removing traditional encumbrances to the market in labor power, encouraging a conception of man based on self-interest, and creating a government structure that facilitates control over the system by those with ability in economic affairs rather than social standing. Not all capitalist societies are liberal, but all liberal societies are capitalist.

If liberalism is the philosophy par excellence of the capitalist mode of production, in contrast to popular usage, the term *democracy* has also taken on a dual meaning. Understood in its historical context, democracy was at one time a fairly thorough anticapitalist political ideology. Democrats generally stood for two things: participation and equality. Genuine participation in civic affairs traditionally had a subversive quality, which can be understood by comparing liberals like Bentham and James Mill with radical democrats like Rousseau. The former viewed participation, in Carole Pateman's words, as protective: "ensuring that the private interests of each citizen were protected." In contrast, "Rousseau's entire political theory hinges on the individual participation of each citizen in political decision making and in his theory participation is very much more than a protective adjunct to a set of institutional arrangements; it also has a psychological effect on the participants, ensuring that there is a continued interrelationship between the workings of constitutions and the psychological qualities and attitudes of the individuals interacting with them." [12] Thus, Rousseauian democracy leads to the abolition of hierarchical and oppressive structures, which would stunt those very psychological categories necessary for civic life. In this sense, if Rousseau is the first major democratic thinker in the West, Marx is the second, for it was in a sense the latter who developed the analysis that showed why the former's optimal conditions could not be realized under a system of private expropriation. In his essay on Hegel's *Philosophy of Right*, for example, Marx posits an ideal system that he calls democracy (the basis for his later conception of socialism) and, throughout his work, Marx continually comes back to Rousseau as though returning for a drink of water after too long an exposure to the desert of English political economy. Writers like Coletti and Berman, who have emphasized the similarities between the political theories of Rousseau and Marx, are on the right track.[13]

Besides participation, democracy has also generally stood for equality (the purpose of participation in the first place). Insofar as it did, it was opposed by a capitalism that promoted equality in the abstract but fought it bitterly in the real world. Twentieth-century writers often seem mystified by the fact that Marx and Engels spent so much time advocating universal suffrage as the first step in the development of socialism, but in the context of the time it made perfect sense. Equality in the political arena could not easily have been granted when the economic arena demanded the rigidity of class lines. It did not take much imagination for the typical bourgeois to realize that if working-class demands for the suffrage were granted, working-class demands to control the factory would have to be faced. When Marx and Engels said that "the first step in the revolution by the working class is to raise the proletariat to the position of ruling class, to win the battle for democracy," [14] they understood this connection, as did the conservatives who fought against the advance of universal suffrage. Even when Marx and Engels broke with bourgeois democratic movements after 1848, they did so not to reject the spirit of democracy, but to reaffirm it, on the grounds that those who professed democratic norms were rapidly abandoning them in the counterrevolutionary atmosphere of the 1850s. As Arthur Rosenberg, whose *Democracy and Socialism* is perhaps the best account of the connection between these two forces, put it, "As long as they lived, they [Marx and Engels] remained democrats in the best sense of the word and in the spirit of 1848." [15]

The gap between the popular meaning of liberalism and the traditional meaning also holds true for democracy. The latter is no longer viewed as a subversive term, one that would make ruling classes shake, mostly because ruling classes adopted the term for their own use. In the West, democracy has come to mean bourgeois democracy; it is now defined, not by standards of participation and equality, but by the existence of certain formal political features such as elections, a constitution, and agreed-upon rules of political discourse. A system with a democratic structure is presumed to be democratic, whatever the degree of psychological health and equality experienced by its citizens. In this book I will reject the everyday meaning of democracy for the same reason I rejected the ordinary use of liberalism; the traditional term is more historically accurate and also poses in sharper fashion the essence of democratic expectations. *Democracy* will here be defined as a political ideal that advocates the maximum participation of all citizens in order to create a community based upon the mutual and respectful interaction of all toward commonly agreed-upon goals. In this sense, the logic of participation and equality leads as surely to socialism as the logic of individualism and appropriation leads to capitalism. Not all socialist societies are democratic, but any genuinely democratic society would have to be socialist.

Although liberalism and democracy connote opposite meanings, there is one area in which they have historically strengthened each other. As part of its challenge to the *ancien régime,* the emerging bourgeoisie often found itself in the position of advocating what we now call civil liberties: freedom of thought and expression, of religious worship, publication, and conscience. Throughout the years, this has been the greatest contribution of the liberal tradition to the Western world, and one would be foolish to deny it. But although civil liberty sprang from the liberal tradition, liberalism never developed it further. The promised liberties were hopeless ideals until the democratic tradition came along to demand them for the majority of the population. Thus, freedom of speech, though part of the liberal tradition, did not became an issue before the U.S. Supreme Court until the twentieth century, *after* democratic demands forced it there. In short, in this one area it took the democratic revolution to give life to a liberal notion, and both traditions were better off for it. One hopes that democratic movements in the twentieth century, including socialist ones, will preserve this commitment to the tradition of civil liberty.

But with the exception of civil liberty, liberalism and democracy work toward quite contrasting goals. This means that societies that proclaim themselves liberal democratic are in a sense announcing that they will be torn by conflict, replete with contradiction, under continuous pressure, and unable to face the future without substantial change. Yet they cannot help themselves. So long as a society remains in any degree capitalist, the state will be called upon to engage in the accumulation process to some degree. But at the same time, in order for capitalist decisions to be acceptable to the citizenry at large, democratic desires must in some way be taken into account. Writers like Jurgen Habermas and Claus Offe have

emphasized that the capitalist state is caught between these two imperatives of legitimation and accumulation.[16] The symbolic political expression of this duality is liberal democracy, for liberalism becomes the ideology of and justification for accumulation while democracy upholds the importance of legitimation, of some kind of popular participation and some
equality of results. The predicament of liberal democracy is that liberalism
denies the logic of democracy and democracy denies the logic of liberalism,
but neither can exist without the other. Without a bourgeoisie there is no
liberalism; without a working class there is no democracy. Liberal democracy is the perfect political system for late capitalism because it captures
the central contradiction that structures it. Like many marriage partners,
liberalism and democracy are totally incompatible, yet cannot live apart.

Throughout the nineteenth century, the inherent and necessary contradiction between liberal and democratic principles formed the basis of
most political struggles, as I will try to show in the first part of this book.
Though it originated in protest, liberalism rapidly became a theory of
power. Ruling classes found in it the principles by which their positions
and policies could be justified. In Mannheim's terms, liberalism was an
ideology, just as, in his sense, democratic ideals became utopian.[17] These
were the rallying cries of groups that did not receive benefits from the existing order of things and, dissatisfied with this state of affairs, wanted some
participation and rewards. But first, like pledges rushing a fraternity, they
had to prove themselves; in Polanyi's words:

> The concept of democracy was foreign to the English middle classes.
> Only when the working class had accepted the principles of a capitalist
> economy and the trade unions had made the smooth running of industry
> their chief concern did the middle classes concede the right to vote to their
> better situated workers.[18]

And, one might add, only when the ruling classes accepted the socialist
implications of democracy in their late-nineteenth-century reforms did the
working class concede the right of rule to their better-situated leaders. It
is hard to say which is more important, that concessions on both sides
were made or that they had to be made.

Though the logic of liberalism and the logic of democracy lead in opposite directions, in other words, logic is of only tangential importance in
understanding specific political developments. Because a broadened suffrage was granted by conservatives like Disraeli and Bismarck rather than
won through popular struggle, much of the revolutionary content of the
notion was absorbed. Furthermore, democratic demands could, in a sense,
be channeled outside of politics; such nineteenth-century phenomena as
jingoism, racism, and the promotion of mass culture can be understood as
attempts to render democracy less threatening to those in power. From

the other side, political reforms seemed to make the liberal world order less foreign to those removed from power, as their demands did appear capable of bringing about some results, however meager. Thus reconciliation between the two traditions was achieved for a time, as the contradictions between liberalism and democracy were submerged in the great compromise that has since come to be called liberal democracy. Does it make sense, in view of this coming together, once again to split apart the terms at this late date? In what follows, making this separation becomes the key to an understanding of the political contradictions of late capitalist society.

There are three reasons why the time is propitious for again raising the differences that inhere in the liberal and democratic conceptions of the political world. First, it makes methodological sense to split liberalism and democracy analytically. Hybrid forms can often be best understood by separating them into their component parts in order to divine how they came together. Though there has never been either a "pure" liberal or a "pure" democratic state, making the theoretical distinction between them becomes a heuristic device for understanding the complexities of a system that aims to be both.

Second, the tension between the two philosophies is not some dusty historical problem but an aspect of fairly recent political struggle. Far from having completely solved the problem of democracy, many liberal societies are still pondering what to do about it. Switzerland, to take an extreme example, only recently granted the suffrage to half its adult population. And other countries that consider themselves mature liberal democracies reached that stage surprisingly late in life. As Lipset once footnoted:

> Many of the restrictions on direct democracy persisted in large parts of the Western world until after World War I; some, until after World War II; and some are still maintained today. The House of Lords' veto power on British legislation was not modified until 1911, and it retained considerable delaying power until 1948. Double votes for property holders and university graduates were abolished by the British only after the Labor victory in 1945. The three chamber system of elections, in which a government based on a lower-class majority was impossible, lasted until 1918 in Prussia. Direct election of United States Senators was not enacted until 1916. Similar restrictions remain, or were only recently abolished, in Australia, Canada, Belgium, Italy and other countries.[19]

But a final reason remains the most important for attempting to disassociate liberal and democratic conceptions of the state. It can be argued that the devices invented in the nineteenth century to quell these tensions were only temporary. From this point of view, the compromise known as liberal democracy was not an eternal truth but an expedient that has served its purpose and may no longer be relevant. This argument, which is the most controversial of the three reasons advanced for separating liberalism from democracy, will be the theme of the remainder of this book.

The implication of this analysis is that liberal democracy is neither the realization of the good life, as its defenders would have it, or a "sham" designed to keep the "masses" happy, as its critics often allege. Instead, it combines elements of both. Liberal democracy at one and the same time expresses the hegemony that capitalist ruling classes have maintained over the political system and also gives some expression to democratic demands for a more responsive state. It is the degree of each element that is essential, and that degree can be determined only by the struggle of various classes to realize their interests. Those who interpret the rise of democracy as a victory pure and simple for the little man against the big interests, as proof that democracy is possible in a capitalist society, focus on only one side of this dual dynamic and therefore have an incomplete understanding of political processes.[20] On the other hand, those who interpret every popular reform as a cooptive mechanism designed to preserve and even, in the most subtle of ways, to increase the power of a capitalist ruling class focus with the same result on the other side of the same dynamic.[21] To label a system liberal democratic, in other words, is to indicate that class struggle between the few and the many is taking place, not that it has been resolved. To make sense out of late capitalism, a political analysis must attempt to comprehend these struggles, not pretend that they have already been decided.

It is now possible to summarize in outline form the arguments that I plan to advance:

1. The history of politics in capitalist society is the history of the tensions between liberal and democratic conceptions of the state (Introduction).

2. Since the rise of an industrial bourgeoisie, a series of solutions have attempted to resolve, or at least mollify, these tensions. Though none has solved the problem permanently, for it is unsolvable, each has constituted an important temporary expedient. The six solutions that sought, found, and then lost social peace can be summarily described as follows: (a) the *Accumulative State*, a compromise between the new liberalism and the active, hierarchical state of the old regime, designed to ensure active governmental intervention in the early phases of industrial capitalist accumulation (Chapter 1); (b) the *Harmonious State*, the first specifically capitalist theory of legitimation, which posed the idea that all classes would benefit from the activity of the dominant class (Chapter 2); (c) the *Expansionist State*, which asserted that the way to postpone the disruptive conflict between liberalism and democracy was to extend the scope of the political system through expansionist devices (Chapter 3); (d) the *Franchise State*, which attempted to solve both intra- and interclass conflict by granting public power to private agencies so as to dodge thorny issues about compulsion and authority in the hope of delaying the coming ir-

repressible conflict (Chapters 4 and 5); (e) the *Dual State,* which created two faces of the same state, one responsible for accumulation and the other for legitimation (Chapter 6); and (f) the *Transnational State,* which extended all the previous solutions into a realm somewhere beyond the nation-state but not as far as a new world order, thereby merely intensifying the historical contradictions (Chapter 7).

3. At the present time, all six of these solutions seem to have exhausted themselves. A period of eclecticism has come about in which all six continue to exist as legacies but no single one dominates. As a result, the emergence of a late capitalist state is characterized by outmoded or hybrid forms that cannot satisfy the political needs they create. Late capitalism ushers in a period of political stagnation (Interlude).

4. One important consequence of the stagnation of late capitalism is a fundamental change in the way the state operates. Greater potential power is matched by greater actual impotency. A separation between the ends of governmental activity and the means for achieving it is lost. Finally, in the absence of goals for public policy, the state becomes reified by its worshippers, called on to solve problems at the same time that its ability to solve them is undermined. The late capitalist state finds itself trapped in its own contradictions (Chapter 8).

5. Changes in the nature of politics accompany changes in the operations of the state. Instead of the traditional concept of politics in the West, an alienated form of politics emerges that makes the pursuit of power for its own sake the goal of the political system. Caught between a need to be political and a conception of politics that cannot meet this need, citizens of late capitalism develop schizoid expectations about political life that render them frustrated and impotent. Institutions such as parties and interest groups also assume a dual character and as a result lose importance. Everyday life of late capitalist society suffers from the inability of a genuine politics to express itself in the absence of a solution to the tension between liberalism and democracy (Chapter 9).

6. With neither government nor politics able to overcome the blockage caused by the exhaustion of alternatives, a legitimacy crisis of the state becomes manifest. Late capitalist ruling classes reexamine their commitment to liberal democracy and begin to consider more authoritarian solutions. Whether they will abolish liberal democracy, however, is not up to them, but up to the people over whom they rule. Therefore, the major political struggles of the late capitalist period will involve conceptions of the political world as much as concrete benefits. The winner of the contest between liberal and democratic conceptions cannot be determined in advance, but the bitterness of that contest will certainly be reflected in the immediate years to come (Chapter 10).

One can get to the last step only by taking the first, and so it is to the origins of the tension between liberalism and democracy that I now turn.

I

Six Solutions in
Search of Tranquillity

"A social system based essentially on property
cannot proceed toward anything but the final
destruction of all property."
                                    Hannah Arendt

1 / The Accumulative State

"The powers reserved to the several states will extend to all the objects which, in the ordinary course of affairs, concern the lives, liberties and properties of the people and the internal order, improvement, and prosperity of the State."

James Madison, Federalist 45 (1788)

"It is a settled principle of every constitution that the legislature is not merely empowered but obliged to interfere at times with the private rights of individuals, where the general advantage of the community requires it."

London Times (1845)

"Nothing great, nothing monumental, has ever been done in France, and I shall add in the world, except by the State. How could it be otherwise?"

Lamartine (1848)

ALTHOUGH LIBERAL DEMOCRACY has been the dominant political ideology of Western capitalist societies for a considerable period, there was a time in the history of these societies when neither liberalism nor democracy could be said to exist. To trace the forms taken by the tension between these two modern political forces, one must begin with the rise of liberalism, with the emergence of an industrial bourgeoisie committed to winning political and economic power on the basis of a series of ideas that stressed the sanctity of private property, individualism, some degree of free trade, and a representative theory of government. This is not so easy as it seems, for the liberals' break with the tradition against which they rose is not nearly so clear cut as most schematic interpretations would have it. A liberal conception of the state did develop at the end of the eighteenth century, but it was a compromise with, not a foil to, the political practice of the *ancien régime*. The first form of capitalist state associated with the rise of an industrial bourgeoisie cannot therefore be understood without at least some consideration of the system it was replacing.

In this chapter I want to examine the impact of the rise of industrial capitalism on a state that had been shaped by the needs of a precapitalist order. I will argue that in the struggle between new and old political conceptions, a compromise which I call the Accumulative State came into existence. This can be considered the first significant state in which industrialists played a role. The eclectic character of this experiment, a result of the class compromise at its heart, was the strength but also the ultimate weakness of this early form. Before examining it in greater detail, however, it is necessary to add an important cautionary note.

Though it is common to speak of such entities as the "feudal" or "capitalist" state, actual structures are generally composed of elements from various types. Consequently, the fact that the first important form of government associated with the rise of industrial capitalism was a product of, not a reaction against, the old order means that there never was, for any significant length of time, a pure capitalist state. The earliest forms of bourgeois rule were the products of struggles between landed and mercantile interests, which themselves resulted in compromises. The later forms, after these struggles had been resolved, came at the moment when the first significant challenges from below were being launched. Like the French Army in Zola's Le Débâcle, the industrial bourgeoisie was caught in a pincers between the resistance of the old order and the potential power of the working class. And not having a state of its own, the bourgeoisie also possessed no theory of the state. If it could use government for its own ends, it would do so; if it could obtain those ends without the state, that would be all right too; if others demanded a share of state power and were judged capable of bringing about either a revolution or a counterrevolution if denied, then power would be shared. Rarely comfortable in the theoretician's role, the bourgeois was more interested in money and power than in ideas; the political structures he helped to create reflect this bias. Thus the two most outstanding characteristics of the first form of government associated with the rise of industrial capitalism are its compromise nature and its lack of consistent theory, as I hope to make clear.

The Political Heritage of the Old Regime

In the beginning there was no state, if by the beginning we mean European feudalism. "A long list could be made of the activities which we consider inseparable from the idea of the State, but which feudal states completely ignored," wrote Marc Bloch, and he continued by pointing out how education, public works, and the structure of obedience all took place outside the formal jurisdiction of government.[1] To build a unified whole out of the conflicting and multitudinous claims of feudal society required a couple of hundred years and the sacrifice of an uncountable number of lives. So formidable was the task that Jacob Burkhardt, admiring one of its early manifestations, could call the state a "work of art."[2]

If the state was a work of art, its builders, men (and a woman) like the Borgias, Richelieu,[3] and Frederick William of Brandenberg must be considered artists, for it was due to them that a fundamental change was effected in the European political universe. In the words of Hans Rosenberg, "An aggressive, methodical, and often oppressive machine of hierarchical state management by dictation and subordination came to prevail over the less elaborate, more slovenly, and infinitely personal medieval contrivances."[4]

The authoritarian monarchies created in the sixteenth and seventeenth centuries are generally called the *ancien régime* and it is assumed that, once the label has been applied, little more need be said about them. Yet, as the recent research of Pierre Goubert has demonstrated, the simple generalizations of earlier French Revolution historians appear questionable.[5] Far from being a rigid "traditional" order, the old regime was itself composed of diverse elements, existing in an uneasy compromise. During the so-called "second" sixteenth century, a powerful state structure had come into existence in what are now regarded as the more politically developed European states.[6] According to the usual interpretations, this structure supported and was supported by the landed, aristocratic, quasi-feudal interests that wished to preserve a strictly hierarchical and immobile form of social organization. Yet the social life of the late sixteenth century was hardly staid; there was in fact a class struggle raging between the nobility and a rising mercantile bourgeoisie, and the structure of the state was due, at least in part, to the nature of that struggle.

Much recent scholarship has emphasized the transitional nature of the old regime. Though Perry Anderson, for example, calls absolutism "a redeployed and recharged apparatus of feudal domination," he makes it clear that the force that made a redeployment necessary was the emergence of a mercantile bourgeoisie. Hence Western absolutism was "an apparatus for the protection of aristocratic property and privileges, yet at the same time the means whereby this protection was promoted could *simultaneously* ensure the basic interests of the nascent mercantile and manufacturing classes."[7] Because of the class compromise at its core, Nicos Poulantzas considers the authoritarian state to be an example of the "relative autonomy" of the state within the Marxist tradition; to him the authoritarian monarchies, while not technically capitalist, had a "capitalist character" owing to the needs of the commercial element for primitive accumulation.[8] This compromise was difficult to realize, since the aristocracy desired order and hierarchy while the merchants wanted trade expansion, mobility, and an end to stagnation. But two considerations brought the different parties together. On the one hand, both had an interest in repression, and the basic function of the absolutist state was, in Anderson's words, "the repression of the peasant and plebeian masses at the foot of the social hierarchy."[9] On the other hand, each side could, as

Immanuel Wallerstein had argued, obtain benefits from absolutism if it were willing to bend its principles slightly:

> On the one hand, the king sought the assistance of favored segments of the urban commercial bourgeoisie who supplied him with money and some political counterweight to the centrifugal tendencies of the old nobility. On the other hand, the king was the pinnacle of the system of traditional social status and was ultimately the protector of the nobility against the corrosive effects of the developing capitalist system.
>
> In terms therefore of the two social strata, the old nobility and the commercial urban bourgeoisie, the absolute monarchy was for each a lesser evil, and its strength grew on the basis of their lack of alternatives. For it served them both well by creating the possibility of enabling the country as an entity to get a disproportionate share of the surplus product of the entire world economy.[10]

As we shall see, choosing the lesser evil becomes instinctive for every ruling class as it comes to power; in a contest between ideology and survival, the latter invariably wins.

The compromise between a mercantilist bourgeoisie and an older landed nobility was theoretically shaky but practically strong. The two groups had a common interest in a powerful state. The focus of the aristocracy was by and large internal, although of course they had their own international world, which coincided with their family structures. The interests of the mercantilists were primarily external, in world trade, although of course considerations of domestic economy, including protectionist legislation and taxation, were vital to them as well. In the strongest states, the generation of the surplus referred to by Wallerstein permitted both needs to be satisfied. Internally, a repressive bureaucracy could be created whose main task would be the preservation of order and rank; externally, the interests of the commercial bourgeoisie could be given an assist through active state intervention in the economy, for everywhere "an attempt was made in the late sixteenth and early seventeenth centuries to have the crown regulate the whole industrial life of the nation." [11] These two tasks, internal repression and external expansion, solved the conflict between the two groups but it did so at a price: the creation of a state that was strong, active, and capable of developing an interest of its own. This was the state that, with few substantial changes, greeted the industrialists who came along at the end of the eighteenth century and adopted liberalism as their creed. The history of the political struggles of the nineteenth century is in many ways the history of how liberalism came to terms with this older order and how it revolutionized some of its aspects, but also, more important, how it preserved and even strengthened others.

The confrontation between an industrial bourgeoisie committed to political and economic liberalism and an older regime in which merchant and noble shared power must not be viewed as a head-on collision but more as an unavoidable sideswiping that could, through adroit manipulation, be made to work to the advantage of both parties. In broad terms, what the industrialists did not like about the older society was, first, the fact that the mercantilist and aristocratic conceptions of society were accompanied by a corporatist ideology, which emphasized the interrelationship and interdependence of all its parts in a Great Chain of Being. Insofar as the new bourgeoisie sought to share in the privileges of the old order, this notion caused no particular problems, for it emphasized the right of every group to belong to society. But insofar as the same notion meant responsibility for the poor, it was found wanting, for that was a responsibility the new group did not want. As we shall see, the necessity to create a free market for labor led the new ruling groups to abolish the old system for those below them while trying to preserve it for themselves. Or, in the more sardonic view of Orestes Brownson, "The middle class is always a firm champion of equality when it concerns humbling a class above it, but it is its inveterate foe when it concerns elevating a class below it." [12]

Second, the traditional theory of society was static and allowed little or no room for truly dynamic economic growth. Although mercantilism created a world system, its world at the same time "was defined as known and finite." [13] The full potential of world markets was not being achieved, and in order to obtain it, the new liberalism, after an initial opposition to colonialism, eventually came to accept foreign expansion in a form much more dynamic than under mercantilism.

Finally, the world of the *ancien régime* was too immobile, a situation anathema to those whose wealth was being produced by their own activity. Formal, juridical equality must replace the rigidity of rank. The problem is stated most clearly in German, for the term *bürgerliche Gesellschaft* means both civil society, emphasizing formal equality, and bourgeois society, emphasizing the rise of the middle class.[14] In the words of Otto Hintze, "In a constitutional sense, 'bourgeois' is equivalent to 'civic,' that is, it signifies the civic legal equality of all the State's subjects without respect to status by birth or occupation—in other words, it signifies abolition of the old feudal privileges, equality before the law." [15] Of course, the new class was not opposed to hierarchy as such, just that based on irrational criteria. As Tawney expressed it:

> The inequalities of the old regime had been intolerable because they had been arbitrary, the result not of differences of personal capacity, but of social and political favoritism. The inequalities of industrial society were to be esteemed, for they were the expression of individual achievement, or failure to achieve. They were twice blessed. They deserved moral approval, for they corresponded to merit. They were economically beneficial, for they offered a system of prizes and penalties.[16]

In other words, fault-finding with the old order was never complete;

the new class did not object to the principles of interdependence, world-system, or hierarchy, just to their application. Compromise was therefore possible, even inevitable. In addition, in two important areas the old order and the new class found themselves with similar perspectives. These areas were the very ones in which the merchants and nobles had found agreement: the need for a repressive apparatus and a state that played an active role in the economy. The administrative structure of the old order was so extensive that even the French Revolution, as de Tocqueville showed long ago, could barely shake it,[17] and much of the purpose of that structure was the preservation of internal order. If a centralized bureaucracy did not exist (as in Britain where as late as 1833 the Home Office, responsible for prisons, police, lunacy, turnpikes, and temporary commissions of inquiry, had a total of 29 full-time employees),[18] a rural infrastructure of obligations and expectations did. Such arrangements might be found useful, as Mr. Helstone of Charlotte Brönte's novel *Shirley* found them useful, against "the widespread spirit of dissatisfaction against constituted authorities." For him, and for his friends among the manu-facturers, "the cures he prescribed were vigorous governmental inter-ference, strict magisterial violence; when necessary, prompt military coercion." In addition, both the traditional order and the new class were committed to a state that would be a full partner in the economic life of the society. Although some mercantilist practices were antiquarian by 1800, others, such as protective tariffs and state subsidies for roads and canals, could and would be adapted to the new order. Although the idea that the new manufacturing class was a firm believer in laissez-faire is popular, it is also, as I plan to show in detail, inaccurate. As Eli Heckscher, the Swedish economic historian, has said, "On many points both mer-cantilism and laissez-faire were based on one and the same conception with regard to man as a social animal, and . . . both had the same point of view of what the proper treatment of this animal must be." [19] Just as the mercantilists had, in Dobb's phrase, shown a "readiness" to com-promise with "feudal society once its privileges had been won," [20] the capitalists who followed them two centuries later showed the same propensity.

The *prise de pouvoir* of the industrial bourgeoisie, then, did not necessarily presage either the abolition of a repressive state system or state guidance of the economy, even though liberalism in theory suggested the opposite in both cases. The question was not whether there was going to be an active state (for all parties agreed there would be) but, rather, *cui bono?*—that is, which social classes would be the beneficiaries of state activity? The political struggles of the early part of the nineteenth century were much more likely to be over concrete results, not abstract theories. It was only after the struggle had been won, after the industrial bourgeoisie had come to power, that theories of the state would be advanced in any coherent fashion. First things came first, and in this case first things meant compromises over political practice. Just as de Tocqueville, in his *Souvenirs*, could describe himself as "in between the alternative reactions of complete freedom and oppression," [21] political figures in the first part of the nineteenth century sought, in Guizot's favorite phrase, the *juste milieu* between one world of traditional loyalty and state action and another of dynamism and industrial freedom. The obvious solution was to retain the activity of the state from the absolutist period but to alter its form. The resulting structure can be called the Accumulative State, defined as the transformation of the political compromise between the nobles and the merchants in order to accommodate the rising industrial bourgeoisie, which could be done by involving the new structure in the task of capital accumulation. The legacy of absolution, in this sense, lasted into the nineteenth century.

It remains to account for the structure of the Accumulative State, but first it is important to emphasize the consequence of the struggle over the state just described. From the sixteenth to the nineteenth century, a fourfold conflict took place around the state: first, the traditional landed nobility was engaged in its contest with the mercantilist commercial interests, one which resulted in the compromises of the authoritarian state; second, insofar as these two groups could unite around a despotic state, they were in conflict with the rise of an industrial bourgeoisie committed in theory to liberalism; third, as it came to power, the new ruling class found that it had areas of agreement with the older ruling groups and it began to make compromises with its liberalism around them; and, fourth, the resulting three-way alliance between aristocrat, merchant, and industrialist faced a threat from below in the creation of a working class that would become devoted to its own conception of society.

The constant factor during the nineteenth century is the intensity of these struggles and the fact that all four could be taking place simultaneously. In Prussia the issues were not really settled until World War I; Germany's defeat in 1918 saw both the *coup de grâce* of the landed-commercial alliance and the initial revolutionary stirrings of the postbourgeois world. In a sense, then, the period of unalloyed capitalist rule in that country lasted for only one month, and even that was under a nominally socialist government. French political history in the nineteenth century was dominated by these conflicts to such a degree that three rapid shifts from revolution to counterrevolution were produced. It was not until the Third Republic that the industrial bourgeoisie came to power on its own terms, and when it did, the specter of the 1848 national workshops and the 1871 Commune continued to haunt it, even while symbols of the *ancien régime* remained in existence. (In January 1975 a baron was shot to death while defending his *château* from agents of a bourgeois state.) In England the liberal victory was achieved early, yet even there, as we shall see, laissez-faire never abolished an active role for the state. And in America, although the initial conflict between land and commerce was muted by the fact that the Virginia gentry were also mercantilists, America's past was never purely capitalist for the very same reason: middle-class rule could not come about until the mercantilist mentality was vanquished, and that did not occur until after the Civil War, just in time for a working class to be created. In short, to cut into political reality at any point during the nineteenth century is to see under the surface a series of class struggles taking place, a fact that makes generalization as difficult as it is essential. It is possible to discuss this complexity in general terms, but only to make sense out of its complications, not to ignore them.

THE MANY FACES OF THE ACCUMULATIVE STATE

Ironically, given the devotion that industrialists would one day profess toward laissez-faire, the first state in which they played a significant role was one that showed an active and aggressive tendency to intervene both in the economy and in the social life of the early nineteenth century. The truth of this point can be demonstrated only by cataloguing the multitude of activities undertaken by the Accumulative State. Surprisingly, there have been few attempts to summarize the various ways in which government was involved in the accumulation of capital. Though some, like Guy P. Palmade—who speaks of the state as customs agent, banker, producer, and preceptor [22]—have discussed this notion in general terms, studies of the role of government have usually been confined to specific places, such as Victorian England,[23] early-nineteenth-century France,[24] Prussia,[25] or the state of Pennsylvania.[26] The absence of a catalogue makes it necessary to assemble one; the role of the state during this aggressive period of capitalist growth was sixfold: defining the broadest parameters of economic activity, preserving discipline in order to increase production, adjusting macroeconomic conditions, providing direct subsidies to private industrialists, fighting wars, and engaging in a panoply of activities that did not fall within the proper jurisdiction of any other institution.

The most important functions of the state are often the easiest to pass over. The eye might be struck by public grants to private corporations, for example, but much more important, even if less striking, is the process through which some things come to be accepted as public and others as private. The first role for the Accumulative State in this regard is to establish the legal parameters within which business activity could take place, especially since those parameters were unclearly defined in such a transitional situation. Consider the definition of a corporation. While to present generations a corporation is understood as any group of people who obtain limited liability from the state in pursuit of their private advantage, earlier in modern society the term meant something quite different. For this reason, the question of how a corporation would be defined became, not a matter of dry legal debate, but an intense part of the class struggle, as conceptions from traditional society vied with the newer theories of the industrialists.

Originally a corporation had been a mercantilist notion, referring to an exclusive grant by the state to a private company for the purpose of providing something that was in the common interest of the whole society. A corporation, *by its very nature, by definition,* was a restraint on trade, which was the reason why Adam Smith, speaking as he often (but not inevitably) did as a spokesman for a new class, could conclude that "the pretense that corporations are necessary for the better government of the trade is without foundation." [27] Like populists of a later era, aspiring industrialists were against the corporation, and for two good reasons. First, in order for a corporate charter to be granted, the economic activity had to be, in the words of Lord Hale, "affected with a public interest." In return for their grant of power, corporations were not "free" to do what they liked but were seen as agents of the state, developing part of the economy, not for private gain (though that did occur in reality), but for the commonweal. In pre–Civil War America, the only significant corporations were in areas like banking and transportation, not manufacturing and distribution. In Peel's England, railroads were incorporated because of the general understanding that they had a public as well as a private nature.[28] Second, because of its exclusivity, a corporate charter was fiendishly difficult to obtain. In the United States, a state legislature had to pass a bill (a process that sometimes led to extreme bribery, as well as, in one case, to a famous legal opinion of Chief Justice Marshall in *Fletcher v. Peck,* in which Marshall was torn between his dislike for unmitigated greed and his respect for contracts), while in England a private act of Parliament was necessary. France under Louis Philippe was an extreme but illustrative case. After proving that his hard cash was plentiful and his outstanding debts were not, an applicant underwent three separate investigations, first by a committee of the Conseil d'État, then by the full body, and then by the Interior Ministry. If the applicant passed all three, the Minister of the Interior asked the King for a signature, and only when (and if) the King signed was a corporation deemed to exist.[29] No wonder that partnerships and individual ownership were the preferred forms of economic activity, or that Alfred Krupp struggled all his life to prevent "his" firm from becoming a joint-stock corporation. (It was not until after Alfred's death that the Krupp works became a legal corporation.) [30]

Because of these difficulties, the industrial bourgeoisie fought a prolonged battle against the mercantilist definition of the corporation. The results were as interesting as they were contradictory. Unable to vanquish the mercantilist conception, the industrialists settled for a redefinition, a preservation of the form but a change in the content. Beginning in 1811 in New York State and lasting until after the Civil War, the granting of corporate charters underwent a change. In the United States, because of federalism, states competed with each other for wealth; they became, in a sense, sellers of sovereignty. Like cheap manufacturers entering a market dominated by established firms making expensive products, parvenu states sold their authority for next to nothing, giving up control over corporate activity as they did so. By the end of the Civil War this form of Gresham's Law meant that the notion of the corporation as an agency of the public good was as dead as chivalry. France reformed its law of incorporation in 1867, Prussia in 1870 (leading to the popularity of the *Kartell*), and in England the forming of joint-stock companies was facilitated by legislation in 1855 and 1862. English trading companies started to become corporations in the 1870s and, as late as the 1880s, many manufacturers were just beginning to consider the virtues of incorporation.[31] Within forty years, in short, corporate charters were no longer difficult to obtain and no longer had to serve the public interest. At the same time, the popularity of trusts and cartels meant that exclusivity, which had once been guaranteed by law, was now guaranteed by economic practice. Unable to defeat the mercantilist tradition, the new capitalists joined it, and they found the compromise quite advantageous.

The effects of this change in definition were serious, especially from a political viewpoint. As Berle and Means noted, "The history of the nineteenth century in American corporation law is in fact that of a slow abdication by the state of control over corporations." [32] Since the individual states, as Louis Hartz has shown, were considered as extensions of the people in pre–Civil War America,[33] the victory for the new concept of the corporation was a substantial loss for the concept of popular sovereignty. Nor did it necessarily follow that removing the state from the process of scrutinizing corporate charters was a triumph of laissez-faire. Laws could be changed only if the bodies that passed them were controlled; this meant that, in order to take the corporation out of the public sphere and place it in the private one, the industrialists had to enter the public sphere themselves. Ironically, a political battle had to be fought in order to place an important—in the nineteenth century perhaps the most important—institution outside of politics. One had to have power in the state in order to make it impotent. Few clearer examples exist of how the struggle over legal parameters cannot be accepted as a given but becomes part of the activity of the state itself, how such struggles are often more important than the battles that take place after the parameters have been established.

A second important general function of the Accumulative State was the preservation of order. Even those who, like Smith and Ricardo, wanted minimal governmental activity were disposed to welcome a policing function for the state. What they apparently failed to realize, though, was that their era, the period from roughly 1776 to 1820, was one of revolutionary transformation, in which a sharp dichotomy between a police function and other functions was unrealistic and impractical. Periods of transition are not likely to be periods of tranquillity; the seemingly simple task of "keeping order," therefore, became a major focus of governmental activity, since few periods in modern history have been quite so turbulent as this one. Like the Prince of Parma in Stendhal's *Charterhouse*, who detested "the desire for liberty, the fashion and cult of the *greatest good of the greatest number*, after which the nineteenth century has run mad," ruling groups found themselves faced with revolutions in the United States and France, bourgeois dynamism and Luddite protest in England, and nationalist student fervor in Central Europe, which meant the Alien and Sedition Acts, Thermidor and Napoleon, the Six Acts and the Peterloo Massacre, and the Carlsbad Decrees. Would it be possible for the state just to "keep order" at such a time without expanding into other forms of activity as well? The need for an "ordered" society led to both direct political repression and the creation of a wide variety of forms of maintaining discipline indirectly.

Minimalist notions about state power were eagerly set aside by ruling classes in their desire to keep order through direct political repression. Demonstrations in Manchester and Birmingham in 1819 so frightened the leaders of British society that they passed the Six Acts, the most repressive legislation in modern English history. Public meetings were prohibited, the right to bear arms was restricted, freedom of the press was curtailed through a variety of ingenious circumlocutions, and seditious libel was made easier to prove. It did not seem to matter that such laws contradicted English customs, for, as the Duke of Wellington put it, "Our example will do some good in France as well as Germany, and we must hope that the world will escape the universal revolution which seemed to threaten us all." [34] Wellington, though, could not have been more wrong. First, the world did not escape the revolution. Second, France and Germany were in no position to learn from England. In both of those countries the absolutist state of the old regime was, as a bureaucracy, still in existence, and as a policing mechanism, far more thorough and repressive than anything the English could invent. As Richard Cobb has shown, the revolutionary police merely borrowed the tactics and operations of those they replaced; the major change was to strengthen the worst characteristics of the old regime: "The police of the old regime were much more permissive than the far severer, more bureaucratic police of the Directory and the Empire. The experience of the Revolution had come between the two." [35] And certainly both Metternich and the Hohenzollern absolutists had little to learn from England in matters repressive. Actually it worked the other way around; under the pressure of discontent from below, the

English system of keeping order began to resemble continental bureaucracies more and more. The story of how this came about is worth telling, because it reveals a great deal about the broad nature of the Accumulative State.

As was the case with the corporation, the police practices of traditional Britain could not simply be adapted to new conditions; it was generally necessary to improve on them.[36] The outstanding characteristic of the British system of keeping order around 1820 was the lack of activity by Parliament. It was generally felt that order was the responsibility of the locality, among other obligations and expectations of a small-scale rural social order. There followed from this commitment to the locality two important consequences: first, control over traditional mechanisms was in the hands of the gentry; second, the system was uncoordinated, inefficient, and not synchronized with the social milieu of an emerging capitalist society. Chief responsibility for police matters in most instances lay with the Lord-Lieutenants, who as late as 1850 were still extremely aristocratic as a group. They went about their business in amateurish fashion, refusing to learn new techniques of crowd control, to experiment with new weapons, or to hire full-time police operatives trained in their work. Furthermore, their control was based on a political system that was being changed by successive reform acts. Thus before the 1830s the largest towns, such as Birmingham and Manchester, had no police because they had no political representation in general. If a riot took place in one of those places, it was impossible to assemble a police force from the prosperous citizens because very few prosperous citizens chose to live in them. Areas with the greatest need for magistrates were the least likely to have them. Without reform the police system concentrated its strength where it was not needed, in the rural parish, and dissipated it where it was, in the new industrial towns. Under the rise of a manufacturing class, this aspect of the state would have to be changed, and changed thoroughly.

The first strategy of the new bourgeoisie was to infiltrate the ranks of the existing police system. They demanded that magistrates for the industrial towns be chosen from among themselves, not from the body of the gentry. They began to succeed: "Notwithstanding the prejudices of the Lord Lieutenants, a certain number of persons drawn from the employing and mill-owning class found their way into the commission of the peace for the manufacturing counties." [37] The Liberal Party took up the demand for more magistrates, making it a key part of their program by the late 1830s. Under their pressure, newly appointed magistrates in the towns were increasingly "open to the successful businessman and industrialist." Just as in France men on the barricades were within a few years giving orders to *agents provocateurs,* in England, in the words of F. C. Mather, "The agitators of '32 had become the conservators of the peace of '39." [38] As with the corporation, the body of an old form was being retained, but as it came under the control of a new class, it was also being transformed. Yet in this case a simple occupation of the old forms was not enough. Capitalism in England was unifying the nation, and since industrialization became a national phenomenon, political repression would have to do so as well. Finding the localized system, no matter how transformed, inadequate to their needs, the industrialists turned to Parliament and asked for reform.

Much of the early energy of the Accumulative State in England was given over to matters of direct social control. Hence it should come as no surprise that the major theorist of the new capitalism, Jeremy Bentham, was also the major theorist of police reform. While many of Bentham's ideas and interests changed throughout his remarkable life, his concern with matters of police never did. From his *Panopticon* to his *Théorie des Peines et des Récompenses* to his Constitutional Code, he was preoccupied, almost obsessed, by the need for a judicial system that, as Elie Halévy has pointed out, was as illiberal as his economic philosophy was liberal.[39] Bentham's notions were influential in the Prison Act of 1835, which reformed and centralized the administrative structure of the English prison system. The strengthening of the metropolitan police, the passage of the Rural Police Act of 1839, and the inclusion of police matters into the Municipal Corporations Act for Birmingham, Manchester, and Bolton were all due to the work of Bentham and disciples like Chadwick. Although the Chartists had demanded "to have no police whatsoever until the working classes had a voice in the making of the laws of the land," [40] those in power thought otherwise. While these reforms did not transform the police into a modern, urbanized, efficient system of control (that would come later), they did take some major steps in the direction of professionalization. And Parliament was now active in an area that a short time earlier it had tried to avoid, a precedent that would have major consequences outside the whole question of police reform.

The structure of the apparatus of repression, then, was not a given but was, like the meaning of the corporation, part of the class struggle between older and newer ruling groups. This had two important consequences. First, traditional debate in England had been between localized and centralized government as ends in themselves. To men like Burke, the local world was the center of the universe, not just because it was controlled by the gentry, but also because it was felt to have inherent advantages due to its small size and distance from the alien center. To the cosmopolitan thinkers who associated themselves with the industrialists, the periphery was old-fashioned, the center modern. But the issue of social control transformed the local-versus-central issue into one of means, not ends. The end became the control of discontent, and the means anything that would accomplish the task. If local constables could do the job, then, as Lubenow noted, "even the most severe critics of parochial government were aware of the importance of retaining some of the traditional mechanisms of social control." [41] On the other hand, when local means were not sufficient, then the need for control demanded centralized action, a point of view very popular among American civic reformers, for as T. D. Woolsey said in 1871: "The better classes of society need that the ultimate control of the police should be out of the reach of municipal politics as much as if not more than they need that the city budget should be kept safe from the same influences." [42]

The change in emphasis from ends to means suggests that ruling groups, when forced to sacrifice their principles for the sake of preserving their rule, would gladly do so. Second, as it emerged, police control became indicative of the role of an active state. Early Victorian social legislation—such as the factory acts, the municipal acts, the public health acts, and the railway acts—were pushed by those who urged police reform and resisted by those who opposed it. The same theory, or lack of it, that went into the one went into the others. The same administrative structure set up under the one was established under the others. In short, it did prove to be impossible merely to keep order without giving justification to an active state, and as a result, questions of direct political repression must be seen as part of the economic role of the Accumulative State. Without a repressed working class there would have been no working class.

Keeping order did not mean just maintaining peace among the classes. Quiet, passive people are not necessarily productive ones, and in order for capitalist industry to expand, indirect methods of encouraging a disciplined work force had to be developed. The police could lead people to the factories, but they could not make them run the machines. Of all the methods that might be used to accomplish the latter, by far the most successful would be the manipulation of hunger. If the alternative were starvation, then living in the new industrial towns—"fungeous excrescences on the body politic," Southey called them—and working in the "dark, Satanic mills" might not be so bad. There was only one difficulty. It was an accepted part of the *ancien régime* that starvation was not permissible in a Christian society. Traditional practices such as the Speenhamland system in England, workers' benevolent societies organized by the Prussian monarchy, or even slavery in America provided measures against starvation. Here no compromise with the *ancien régime* was possible. One of the most aggressive positive uses to which the state could be put would be the repeal of traditional customs. Members of the gentry who had adopted capitalistic values, such as Sir Charles Edward Trevelyan, had tested starvation as a social policy during the Irish potato famine and had discovered that, although massive numbers died, the world of England did not cave in.[43] As far as the poor and unrepresented were concerned, laissez-faire could be made their reality. But the replacement of Speenhamland with Chadwick, the Benthamite administrator of the new poor law, was hardly a victory for any genuine kind of laissez-faire practice; in this case it was the exact opposite, a triumph of an active state, *one whose activity was expressed by its choice of doing nothing*. This is no play on words, for the repeal of the traditions of the old regime could come about only through a highly organized political campaign that required control over the legislature. Inactivity could be produced only through activity; creating nothing where there once was something is, however bizarre, an act of creation nevertheless.

The only free market ever created by capitalism was the labor market. The repeal of the Elizabethan Labor Statute in 1814, as S. G. Checkland wrote, "withdrew the State from the wages bargain . . . from 1814 forward the free market was to be the determinant of the price of labor." [44] The LeChapelier Law of 1791, which prohibited French workers from forming coalitions, was a reflection of the same desire, even though it applied more to transitional artisans than to an industrial proletariat. Germany in 1810 adopted the *Gesinde Ordnungen,* which "gave to the employer (but not the workers) the right to break a contract and thus gave him the means of imposing pitiless discipline." [45] In America the ideology of the free labor market did not really blossom until after the Civil War, but when it did, the arrangement was impressive.[46] Creating a free labor market, however, was no easy task. First, the commodity had to be identifiable. For this purpose the French invention of the *livret* was ideal. If one purchased a used horse, one could never be sure how old it was or for how many different farmers it had plowed. But if one bought the labor power of another, this information was readily available. The *livret* was a little book that contained the work history of the "commodity" in question; without it, or with one that was incomplete or suspicious, work was unavailable. Second, regularized institutions for buying and selling had to be established. Here again the French led the way. *Marchandage* was, as its name implies, a system of labor brokerage, in which a middle man, called the *marchandeur,* bought and sold men, and their *livrets,* for the greatest profit. These practices, because they facilitated the operation of the market, lasted until the end of the nineteenth century. Third, the commodity had to be rendered passive, and this was the combined effect of the entire labor process. In England, for example, theorists made a careful distinction between poor people and indigent people. Those who could work were those who, it was assumed, should starve if they did not do so; those who could not work might be helped through state aid. (Children could also be protected, though some even fought against that, since as minors they were not "free" sellers of their labor power.) Consequently it was not that these theorists were vicious and cruel as much as they were logical; work discipline was the goal; hunger was the sanction; and everything else followed from there.[47]

If the same conclusion about removing the state from the wage bargain had been applied to other bargains, then one could make a case that laissez-faire really had meaning to the early industrial capitalists. That was not to be. For one thing the classical economists, men like David Ricardo and Nassau Senior, were never consistent in their adherence to the notion of the minimalist state, as Robbins, Prouty, Parris, Blaug, Brebner, and Kittrell have all shown.[48] In addition, no attempt was made in any serious way to create the same free market conditions for employers that were being created for employees. As Adam Smith had complained, "The masters, being few in number, can combine more easily; and the law, besides, authorizes or at least does not prohibit their combinations, while it prohibits those of the workman."[49] This late mercantilist double standard was adopted by early industrial capitalism. "Look not to parliament, look only to yourselves,"[50] Richard Cobden had told workers who sought state aid to better their lives, but little such advice was proffered to capitalists, and when it was, it could be ignored with all the blissful ease of those who have obtained political power. When it concerned government assistance to the buyers, rather than the sellers, of labor power, the state not only looked the other way when coalitions were formed, but often put its budgets and best minds to work for the benefit of those alliances. A combination of mercantilist practice and capitalist power resulted in socialism for the employers and capitalism for their workers.

Direct state aid to the new industrialists, then, becomes the third way by which the Accumulative State transformed a mercantilist custom into a capitalist practice. That custom had been the provision of direct subsidies to manufacturers, the Colbertian system of royal support for the makers of luxurious goods being the classic example. It is common to divide nineteenth-century government subsidies to private interests into two types, the continental and the British. According to this interpretation, Germany and France tended toward full étatisme, in which the state became essentially a competitor with private enterprise, whereas in Britain private manufacturers dominated the scene and the role of the state was minimal. Such a dichotomy gives the impression that a split existed when in fact what took place was a change in emphasis. There were differences between England and the continent, but they were ones of degree, not of kind, of means, not of ends. In both France and Germany, state activity was generally designed to help private interests, not to compete with them. Consider the experience of Peter Christian Wilhelm Beuth, one of the remarkable group of active Prussian officials, like von Motz, von Rother, and von der Heydt, who revolutionized German business in the nineteenth century. Though a state official, Beuth was a disciple of G. J. C. Kunth, who in turn was a follower of Adam Smith. Realizing that state aid to business was essential in Prussia, Beuth nonetheless "greatly admired industrialists who were able to stand on their own feet without help from the government." [51] When he died in 1853 the system he had devised in the 1820s of using the state to make business independent of the state was no longer necessary, and presumably he died a happy man. As the biographer of these officials pointed out, "The main reasons for State action in Germany were of a practical nature." [52] It was not because they were dogmatic statists but because they desired to bring about capitalism that Prussian bureaucrats were activists. Contrariwise, the British loyalty to private initiative was not clear cut. Studies by Prouty of the Board of Trade and Parris of the railroads have challenged the notion that the state did not intervene to help business; [53] furthermore, as Lubenow has shown, opposition to state action, when it was expressed, was not based on a principled stand in favor of laissez-faire but on the most practical of considerations. Ideological confusion was much more prevalent than dogmatic attachment to a minimalist state: "Victorian England possessed little confident certainty when it came to the issues involved in the role of government, the character of administration, and the responses to the problem of industrialization." [54]

All the expediencies of the period can be seen in the development of state aid to railways. In no country in Europe (except Belgium) was a consistent policy followed. During the July Monarchy in France, private companies were not building new lines fast enough, so bills to encourage state enterprise were introduced. These, however, could not be passed due to the power of vested interests, leading to the working out of a compromise. The state bought the land, built the bridges and tunnels, and arranged for geographical considerations, while private companies furnished working capital, rolling stock, and passenger stations. When this compromise of 1842 fell apart, others, such as the Freycinet Plan of 1879, were put together. Under this arrangement the state built the railroads while private companies made the profits, and a Rothschild advisor was brought into the cabinet to give "confidence" to investors. [55] To try to find a consistent ideological pattern in this chaos would be futile. In Germany a similar confusion was everywhere manifest. Long before Bismarck, an unsuccessful attempt was made to nationalize railroad companies. Instead a "mixed system" was developed, in which

> some lines were built and run by joint-stock companies without any help from the State. Others were built by private companies but received assistance from the State since the government purchased shares or guaranteed interest on shares or loans. There were lines which were built by companies but were administered by the State. And when a Parliament was called and larger funds were available for railways the government itself would build and run the important lines. [56]

The one sensible statement made on this question was by Count Heinrich von Itzenplitz, later Bismarck's Minister of Commerce, who "declared that it did not matter who built railroads so long as someone built them." [57]

Other countries experienced similar ideological confusion. The governments of Italy between 1861 and 1877, besides furnishing almost half the expenses involved in railroad construction, found themselves in an incredible administrative confusion. Railways were often built by the state, sold to private companies, and then bought back by the state when those companies could not operate them profitably. A law of 1884 provided for the state to own the roadbeds (as in France) but also the stations (as not in France), while private industry would assume responsibility for rolling stock and equipment (again as in France).[58] Besides producing ideological confusion, such periodic transfers from public to private hands also led, as we shall see in the next chapter, to frequent opportunities for the exchange of graft. Britain, supposedly the home of laissez-faire, saw the creation of a Board of Trade Railway Department in 1840, one that was considerably strengthened in 1854. Furthermore, the most thorough analysis of the active role of the state in the regulation of British railways concluded that the situation in that industry "was not an isolated incident, but part of a more general trend toward the intervention of government in more and more branches of national life." [59] If there were two sharply defined and contrasting models of state/industry relationships in nineteenth-century Europe, the experience of the railways does not show it.

America was not immune from this European mishmash. The role of the state, far from being minimal, could approach the gargantuan; a full one-fourth of all the land in two states (Minnesota and Washington) was given away to railways in a land grab that still leaves the head spinning.[60] Although economic historians have for some time been debating the extent of state intervention in nineteenth-century America,[61] of greater interest to the present discussion is not the amount of government activity but the political theory behind it. And on that question little debate need occur, if one accepts the conclusions of Salsbury's detailed study of one railroad, the Boston and Albany, in the early nineteenth century. Salsbury found that laissez-faire was a myth so far as railroads were concerned, but at the same time "the states did not follow well thought through plans for the guidance and stimulation of economic development." [62] The number of plans submitted to the Massachusetts legislature —some for total state aid, some for partial, some for none—was bewildering, and the story of how state initiative was finally rejected and a private charter issued was so complicated that it belies any consistent ideology, either statism or laissez-faire. Here, at least, was one area where "American exceptionalism" did not exist; confusion was as popular on one side of the Atlantic as on the other.

Railway policy—indeed, any policy involving transportation and communication—was justified on mercantilist, rather than strictly capitalist, grounds. Henry Clay had envisioned his "American system" designed to create a complete infrastructure of roads and canals that would link together America in a way that neither state governments nor private capital could. Clay's vision, moreover, was not unique, neither to the United States nor to Europe. At home it was a popularization, not only of Hamilton's earlier *Report on Manufacturers* and Marshall's opinion in *Gibbons v. Ogdon,* but also of the much more consistently mercantilist political economy of European-born Albert Gallatin.[63] Meanwhile, in Europe the same need was clear. When Voltaire had complained that when traveling in Europe one changed laws as often as horses, he was expressing the same frustration an American businessman felt in contemplating a bewildering variety of state policies. Standardization was a felt need, and no other agency could bring it about except the state; in some ways government sponsorship of the metric system may have been one of the most fundamentally important acts of state during the period.[64] Clay's kind of thinking was felt in other areas; Michel Chevalier, economic advisor to Napoleon III, copied Clay's very language in proposing his "Mediterranean system," which would not only link together the nations of Southern Europe, but would add Asia and Africa as well. Plans like this would do for the Old World what Clay's would do for the new.[65] Friedrich Christian Adolph von Motz, Prussian finance minister, devoted much of his time to the creation of the *Zollverein,* another variation on the same theme, while also engaging himself in road building and trade agreements.[66] The superstructure through which private capital would expand, in other words, was built with public money; if left to themselves, capitalists might still be trying to get from Liége to Munich.

From this point of view the question of state activity does not break itself into two pieces but forms instead a recognizable, and not all that long, continuum. On this line, it is undoubtedly true that Germany and Italy were toward one end and England toward the other. Continental Europe was much more likely to see direct state participation in strictly manufacturing (as opposed to transportation) industries, but the reason, ironically was Britain herself. Since England had already started modern capitalist manufacturing, the use of the state in those countries that began manufacturing later was due to the practical need to catch up as rapidly as possible. Ferriere Italiano, the iron and steel corporation of Italy, was given direct state subsidy in 1880 for that reason,[67] foreshadowing twentieth-century experiments with ENI and INI (see Chapter 4). The Prussian Seehandlung, an overseas trading corporation, is an even better example. It was founded in 1772 by Frederick the Great as a privileged state trading corporation, and its mercantile character was quite compatible with the early years of Prussian industrialization. It made loans, found markets for new industries, engaged in wholesale trade (woolens, linens, flour, salt), financed internal improvements, built mines, operated textile and paper factories, and owned seven river steamships and ten tugs. Toward the middle of the century, when English liberalism filtered into Prussia, opposition to the Seehandlung developed, and the King curtailed its activities in 1845.[68] But the ideas behind it would reemerge whenever Germany found itself in a catch-up position with England—for example, during Bismarck's colonial ventures and under the Third Reich. The importance of these arrangements involving the state, then, is not that they were the exception to the rule for the capitalist state (which is how generations of Anglo-American economic historians have pictured them) but that they were the classic expression of the rule; if there was an exception, it was England, and even there the difference was over means and not ends.

Just as the repressive function of the state had its direct police component and its indirect disciplinary role, state subsidies can be viewed as a form of direct state aid to business while the task of adjusting macro-economic conditions—the fourth general function of the Accumulative State—can be understood as a form of indirect aid. The two most important instruments for this purpose were the banking and credit systems and the protective tariff.

There cannot be, either in theory or in fact, any such thing as a "pure" private banking system. The issuance of currency, for example, if done by private interests, would lead to chaos; even David Ricardo had urged that issuance (and the profits on it), as well as minting, would best be performed by a state monopoly.[69] The question, at least theoretically, was not what activities in the area of banking would be allowed the state, but what activities the state would allow banks. As creations of mercantilism, banks were excellent proof of Colbert's dictum that an institution totally outside private interests is necessary to sustain those interests. It is for this reason that in general the state's role in the nineteenth century on questions of banking revolved around, not abstract matters of political theory (though there was some of that, especially in the United States), but attempts to strike balances between the specific needs of private interests and the general needs of an emerging capitalist system as a whole. England's Bank Charter Act of 1844 is a good example. Issuance of currency was even further monopolized in the Bank of England (which, although legally private, had been so intertwined with the state that Lord North in 1781 called it "part of the Constitution") [70] than it had been. At the same time the administrative structure of the Bank was bifurcated, with issuance in one department and other banking matters in the other. These reforms did not provide a completely satisfactory solution to the problem of public money in a society dominated by private firms (financial crises of 1857 and 1866 led to the temporary suspension of the Act), but they did create a pragmatic approach to the question, one which, as Asa

Briggs points out, lasted until World War I.[71] In fewer areas was the practical character of the state more sharply defined than in matters involving banking and currency.

In the United States banking was much more controversial; indeed, it was perhaps the dominant issue in American politics before the Civil War, as Bray Hammond's classic work on the subject makes clear.[72] Moreover, there was ideological content to the question; William Appleman Williams claims that it was around the issue of the Second National Bank that a laissez-faire theory of the state arose to challenge the mercantilist consensus.[73] This claim seems somewhat exaggerated. While it was true that those who favored a national bank (Marshall, Madison, Gallatin, Hamilton) were the *crème de la crème* of American mercantilism, arguing that only an active role for the state in matters of finance could guarantee the stability and predictability necessary to run a well-integrated economy, Andrew Jackson's attack on what he called "the Monster" did not take the banking business out of government hands but transferred it from the national to the state level. The issue, then, was as much about what the character of state participation (local versus centralized) should be as about whether there should be governmental participation at all. And, at that, the period of time in the history of the United States during which there was no national bank was much shorter than when there was, for the creation in the twentieth century of the Federal Reserve System testified to the popularity of a kind of neomercantilism.

If in both England and America the state played a role in banking matters, naturally it would play one on the continent as well. Although the Bank of France had been created, in good mercantilist fashion, by Napoleon, by 1830 its directors were quite conservative, opposed to any change in a structure that benefited them. Thus, when the Périère brothers, the epitome of the *haute banque parisienne*, proposed a vast new system of state banking, they were rebuffed by an already existing governmental interest. By the reign of Napoleon III, however, their ideas were no longer controversial. The Crédit Foncier (mortgages), Crédit Agricole (farming), and later colonial banks were all subsidized by the state. Although the greatest Périère project of all, the Crédit Mobilier, was not a state bank, the government supported it by careful purchasing of its stock. Before its fall, the Crédit Mobilier had built the state-subsidized French Line and financed a major public works project, the Société de l'Hotel et des Immeubles de la Rue de Rivoli. Furthermore, French banks overseas were as popular as French wine, which itself was once in such demand that it became a form of currency. The Crédit Mobilier concept, as well as the scandal surrounding it, was exported to the United States and also (without the scandal) to Prussia, Austria, Piedmont, Spain, Portugal, the Netherlands, Sweden, Switzerland, and Turkey. As Rondo Cameron put it, "The banking system of every nation in Continental Europe bore the imprint of French influence," [74] though here again, for some inexplicable reason, Belgium was the exception.

Whether it was reform in England, charter repeal in the United States, or direct state participation in France, the purpose of bank policy was the adjustment of macroeconomic conditions for the benefit of those who controlled the state. In this sense, the tariff was closely related to banking and currency matters, for its goal was the same. In most countries the political question was not whether tariffs should be high or low but whether they should be high or astronomical. Excessive protection was the most common course of state action.

France provides a clear example. The protective system created by the mercantilist alliance with the old regime seemed sure to be abolished by the Revolution, since one of the few goals on which all the revolutionaries appeared to agree was the necessity to reduce duties. Yet the anticipated reduction never took place. Revolutionary wars were accompanied by economic retaliation, which meant high tariffs. In this realm as in so many others, Napoleon, when he came to power, simply took what was presented to him, for, as Soubol has emphasized with regard to financial matters, "Bonaparte was content in many areas to use the instruments created by his predecessors." [75] His continental system was designed to prevent the importation of British goods, an economic policy that produced mixed results. The returned émigrés who dominated the government of Charles X were even more sympathetic to high duties, and the bourgeois King, Louis Philippe, did not have much impact in changing this structure. In fact, from 1789 until the fantastically high Meline tariff of 1881, the only significant attempt to lower duties came through the secret treaty negotiated directly between Napoleon III and Richard Cobden. The popularity of protection as a matter of state policy is indicated by the fact that in one country after another the highest tariffs came at the end of the century, not at the beginning. The notorious French *octroi* was not abolished until the twentieth century, Germany passed its highest tariff in a hundred years in 1902, and the Payne-Aldrich Tariff of 1909 in the United States set records for high duties that were superseded twenty years later by Smoot-Hawley.

Tariffs are not just matters of economic policy; as A. L. Dunham, a writer sympathetic to free trade, says in his analysis of France: "We must condemn the tariff as one example among many of class legislation, and a rather important one. As such it was a factor in producing the labor movement in France and such events as the great strikes of the silk workers in Lyons and the widespread disturbances of 1848." [76] What was true in France in the first half of the century was even more true in the United States in the second. High tariff policy was a Republican position, associated with the most conservative wing of the party. Traditionally, businessmen argued that tariffs were necessary to protect "infant" industries, but by the end of the century this argument could no longer be supported. Therefore, legislation such as the McKinley tariff was rationalized purely on the grounds of self-interest. The election of 1892 was excellent proof of the class character of protection. With the victory of a Democratic candidate whose platform pledged a reduction in the tariff (because of enormously strong feeling throughout the country in favor of reduction), some relief seemed in sight. Yet, as Henry Clay Frick wrote in a famous letter to Andrew Carnegie, the change from Harrison to Cleveland might not be a disaster:

> I am very sorry for President Harrison, but I can't see that our interests are going to be affected one way or another by the change in administration.

To which Carnegie replied:

> Well we have nothing to fear and perhaps it is best. People will now think that the Protected Mfgrs. will be attended to and quit agitating. Cleveland is a pretty good fellow. Off to Venice tomorrow.[77]

Under Cleveland, of course, tariffs continued to rise; the men who denounced state action as a violation of basic liberty when it involved their workers were quite willing to accept state aid for themselves in the form of ever higher protection.

It is this class basis of tariff policy that explains why England once again pursued the same goal in a different way. If any single act is generally hailed as the ultimate victory for laissez-faire, it is the repeal of the Corn Laws, which broke up the Tory emphasis on protection associated with Lords Bentinck and Derby.[78] There is no doubt that passage of the repeal was a most important event, but the ideological issues surrounding it are not as clear as most interpretations would have it. While businessmen elsewhere saw their interests associated with protection, England, because it was an island removed from the general patterns of European commerce, was in a unique position. Already having "geographic protection," the British had less need of economic protection; English prosperity, as Briggs suggests, was based on "a variety of economic circumstances many of which had little to do with either the positive or the negative actions of government." [79] Repeal of the Corn Laws was therefore a product of immediate practical needs, such as finding outlets for goods or lowering the costs of agricultural products (thereby also quieting pressures from the working class at little cost). Repeal of protection, in short, was just as much a class issue in England as enhancement of protection was elsewhere. Richard Cobden himself said, "I am afraid that most of us entered upon the struggle with the belief that we have some distinct class interest in the question," [80] and perhaps it was for this reason that Cobden refused to ally the Anti-Corn Law League with any of the progressive movements of the time, especially the Chartists. Though it is generally seen as a victory for economic liberalism, English tariff repeal was as practical as it was ideological, based as much on immediate considerations of gain and loss as on abstract theories of man and his relation to the state.

Because tariff matters involve the state in the affairs of other countries, they are related to a fifth general function of the Accumulative State: making peace and war. Of course all states make war, so formally there is nothing new here. But this truism passes over the fact that under the pressure of an emerging class of industrial capitalists the nature of war underwent important changes in the mid-nineteenth century, with decided economic consequences. Before that time warmaking was generally a detached preserve of aristocratic gentility; as late as the War of 1812—the last of the mercantile wars—wars could be fought without changing the basic structure of the state. Forty years later, as the mercantile-aristocratic alliance was yielding to the industrialists, this was no longer possible. Consider the Crimean affair. Here was a faroff adventure whose purposes were never clear to most Englishmen. The war itself was, by modern standards, a short one, and the number of British casualties was slight. Yet the Crimean War had important effects on the structure of the English state. On the one hand, debates were held about how limits on the freedom of the press could be imposed. On the other, serious changes in governmental administration were adopted. Since bourgeois faith in aristocratic traditions was severely undermined by the failure of the military—the remaining stepchild of the gentry—to produce glorious victories, groups like the Administrative Reform Association tried to extend their earlier preoccupation with the economic aspects of the Accumulative State into public decision-making as a whole. The major consequences of the rationalization of government include the replacement of the highly personalized cabinet politics of early Victorianism by ad hoc cabinet committees and the streamlining of numerous administrative departments. In short, the Crimean War hastened the transition from a state of amateurs to one of professionals; under its imperatives a new class was winning political power. The ultimate effect is described in Olive Anderson's detailed study of this period:

> Confidence in the existing machinery of government had received a ruder blow than any it had yet sustained in England. A perceptible stimulus had been given to a tendency which had hitherto been unobtrusive: the tendency away from the cult and practice of parliamentary governments.[81]

In England the effects of the Crimean War were tendencies that would not reach their full potential until World War I. Here the basic structure of the state was affected, but not fundamentally altered. In the United States, on the other hand, the Civil War transformed the basic nature of government. This occurred, not only because at stake was the existence of the nation-state itself, but also because the needs of war brought together a wide variety of statist tendencies. During the war, as Roy Nichols wrote, "Congress became, perhaps unconsciously, the patron of interests, the source of subsidies." [82] As Jay Cooke learned, through government contracts, war could be healthy for profitmaking. Furthermore, wars, like commerce, require road building, railroads, and other internal improvements, and the Civil War brought the complete realization of Henry Clay's dream. Yet, again, wars enhance the role of the state in matters of repression, as the Supreme Court, after the fighting was over, noted in dismay.[83] In addition to these three concrete areas, the more general effects of the Civil War have been described by David Montgomery as "a government-controlled currency, the end of legal subordination of one man to another so that all Americans became direct subjects of the government, universal obligation for military service, and direct taxation to sustain the bureaucratic and military machine of the central government." [84] It has been shown by writers like Hartz, Goodrich, Fine, and Broude that laissez-faire before the Civil War, particularly as far as the state governments were concerned, was a myth.[85] After the war this was true for the national government as well. Fighting wars, then, became not simply a matter of routine government duty, but part of the tendency by which the Accumulative State played a role both in the economy and in the relations between social classes.

Aside from all the activities of the Accumulative State discussed so far, it is necessary to include an eclectic category of miscellaneous functions that could not adequately be performed by any other institution. When English investors were revolutionizing industrial production and the French wanted to participate in the wealth being created, what institution other than the state could best furnish, train, and support a bevy of spies to cross the Channel and smuggle back the secrets of the new machinery? [86] When in Italy it was found that the lands owned by the Catholic Church could be a valuable resource in the development of industrial capitalism, who could best take charge of expropriation than government officials? Between 1866 and 1867, a government department called the Domain of the State was charged with the responsibility for disposing of about 1.7 billion liras' worth of Church land that had been seized by the state.[87] In good eclectic fashion, a private company, the Società Anomina per la Vendita dei Beni del Regno d'Italia, was given the right to profit from the sales of the land in return for financing its acquisition. Because it is symbolic of the transition from a somewhat aristocratic to an industrial society, land, particularly the buying and selling of it, became a major public concern in the nineteenth century. This was especially true of the United States not because of its aristocracy, which was minimal, but because there was so much land. With the acquisition of new territory, someone had to own the land, and two theories of ownership competed in the course of the century. The mer-cantilist position was that land, as part of the national wealth, should be distributed in a rational and efficient way, one that constituted a land *policy*. It was no coincidence that the major theorist of American mer-cantilism, Albert Gallatin, was also, as Secretary of the Treasury, for twelve years the superintendent of public lands. Yet the careful and precise methods he brought to his job were overturned with the rise of new wealth. Under an expanding capitalist economy, land was of value because it could make money and thereby be transformed into capital. There was a rush to give away land in as chaotic a manner as possible. In a frenzy of land speculation culminating in 1837, now part of world literature thanks to Dickens' *Martin Chuzzlewit*, the policy of the government be-came one of having no policy. The state owned the land by default; its only task was to get rid of it as soon as possible.

This struggle between different conceptions of the state produced, as it did with corporations or repression, a little of both worlds. On the one hand, the land giveaway did spur capitalist production. On the other, the mercantilist conception of an active state was brought over into the new order. Between 1789 and 1837, 370 different laws dealing with land were passed by Congress (and signed by presidents), a fact that does not say much for the existence of laissez-faire, even at the national level. The effect was, as Rohrbough noted, as follows: "Through control of the public domain, the federal government touched the lives of thousands of re-mote citizens, who had previously neither known nor acknowledged its existence." [88]

The most unusual miscellaneous function of the Accumulative State was the most contradictory. Because of the compromise with the old order, in some places remnants of the corporate character of the *ancien régime* persisted through the Accumulative State period. Consequently, not all the activities of this first form of the capitalist state worked to the exclusive benefit of the emerging capitalists. Public works could improve the lives of all, and the competence of the French *corps des ponts et des chaussées* was admired and copied by enlightened aristocrats throughout Europe. The Administrative Reform Association in England had an idealistic, missionary sense that led it into matters of social policy as well as into the concerns of the bourgeoisie.[89] In America, as Hartz's justly famous study of Pennsylvania has documented, such "welfare" state activities as labor laws, inspection systems, licensing, and charter super-vision were all part of early-nineteenth-century governmental practice. To be sure, much of "the objectives of economic policy . . . ramified into virtually every phase of business activity, were the constant preoccupations of politicians and entrepreneurs, and covered interest struggles of the first magnitude." [90] These "interest struggles" are precisely the factors that undid the *Gemeinschaft* character of the early state, for the total triumph of the bourgeoisie as the century wore on vitiated these experiments (see Chapter 2). Nonetheless, the Accumulative State, whatever its tasks, was at all times an activist state, even when it tried to represent the public welfare as best it could.

THE LIMITS OF PURE ACCUMULATION

For all its activity, the Accumulative State was inappropriate as a permanent form of government, as a fixed solution to the problem of the capitalist state. It was a compromise, the product of a transitional situation, and its eclectic character gave it both its strengths and its weaknesses. Its major strength was that it fulfilled a need that private capitalists could not fulfill for themselves, that of accumulation. The central contradiction of modern capitalism, whose effects are still being felt, is that a system of private initiative could never have come into existence without substantial public activity. A collective effort was necessary to unleash the phenomenal power of modern industrial production, and it was government that provided, to one degree or another, the core of that effort. Modern capitalism could not have existed without the state, whatever later mythological interpretations about its origins would be spun. At the same time, though, the active role of the state, and the effects of a transitional situation, yielded three limitations that eventually destroyed the effectiveness of the Accumulative State.

First, transition, as I have been emphasizing, meant ideological inconsistency. Since a struggle for control of the state was taking place, and since each party had its own conception of the relationship between man and society, the failure of either side to dominate produced enormous confusion and contradiction. One of the most illustrative portraits of this confusion is contained in Anthony Trollope's fictional account of the rise of Phineas Finn, the genial, somewhat naïve, but ingratiating parliamentary character who views the changing nature of English society between 1830 and 1850 with an open eye.[91] Elected from a rural district under the sponsorship of the old system, Finn arrives in Parliament to find a new world being created. His adjustment is slow and painful, for all he learned in the periphery does him little good in the metropolis. He makes his compromises, but he also has a streak of integrity, which leads him to break with the old order, symbolized by his decision to conduct an actual campaign for office rather than depend on aristocratic patronage. Not a member of the gentry himself, Finn finds living in London an expensive proposition, since there is no pay for his parliamentary work. Ultimately his position becomes one neither of the aristocracy (he cannot win the hand of Violet Effingham) nor of the bourgeoisie (he cannot work for a living). He supports the Reform Bill, but his most insightful political comment, when faced with contradictions from every side, was that "life is so unlike theory." Bewildered by the confusions of his age, Finn returns home to marry his neighborhood sweetheart, apparently making a choice in favor of the local world. But he has now seen too much of the world to be satisfied with that. His wife's death clears the way for a reentry into politics; his second marriage, to Madame Max, ensures his political success, and, having decided to live with contradiction, Finn, for all his lack of great intellectual qualities, rapidly ascends the ladder of English politics. Unable to resolve the contradictions of the time, he participates in them, and on that basis he can serve the state well.

Second, the Accumulative State was unable to uncover for itself a meaningful conception of legitimation. There had been, under the old regime, an emphasis on organic solidarity that related every individual to every other individual, but that had been shattered by nineteenth-century business practice. "With the supreme triumph of Cash," Carlyle wrote in 1839, "a changed time has entered; there must a changed Aristocracy enter." Carlyle longed for "a *real* Aristocracy," one that took the task of governing seriously. "Not mis-government, nor yet no-government; only government will now serve." [92] The problem was—as both Carlyle and Marx, as different as they were, understood—the rise of an industrial working class.[93] "The Working Classes cannot any longer go on without government; without being *actually* guided and governed; England cannot subsist in peace till, by some means or other, some guidance and government for them is found." [94] In actuality, there was no chance whatsoever that such a policy could have come about. Although much has been made of Tory paternalism, David Roberts' careful analysis of Victorian parliaments shows that on matters dealing with the working class the Tories, with one or two visionaries excepted (dreamers, like Richard Oastler, not politicians like Disraeli), were as callous as the Whigs.[95] In the absence of measures that would have responded to the "social question," the Accumulative State could have saved itself by developing some mechanisms of legitimation, some ideology that could have been offered instead of results. This it never really did, probably because of its multiclass character. A sharing of power confused class lines, and under such confusion the existence of a working class could be ignored—at least for a while. Thus the most that was offered in the way of legitimation was Guizot's second favorite dictum, *enrichissez-vous*, as inappropriate to the lives of most people as it was crass in its sheer materialism. Without a theory of legitimation, the Accumulative State could not survive the development of a working class, so that by mid-century new solutions to class relationships were being taken seriously.

Finally, the transitional character of the Accumulative State was revealed once the class compromise that formed its *raison d'être* passed into history. It made sense as a solution only because it expressed the inability of the bourgeoisie to vanquish completely either the power of landed families or the commercial character of mercantilism. But suddenly this changed; there was, it is generally agreed, a second industrial revolution in the mid-nineteenth century that rivaled in importance the invention of the spinning jenny. Before the success of this phenomenal mechanization, industrial capitalism had remained a vision, a revolutionary ideal destined to change the world. By 1870 that vision was becoming a reality, the revolution a counterrevolution, the dream a nightmare. Industrial success inevitably led to political success; the bourgeoisie found that it was no longer compelled to share power with vestiges of the old regime. With the basis of the class coalition broken, there was no longer a need for the particular character of the Accumulative State. Having used the state to their advantage, the new industrialists could now turn around and argue that the state was irrelevant, an evil thing that had best, for the good of all, be avoided. Yet, in doing so, it found that something new had arisen to replace the power of the old regime, for a popular class was being created that had its own ideas about state power. As the influence of the gentry waned and the power of the working class began to assert itself, the Accumulative State became a form without a content. The bourgeoisie found itself in need of a political vision that could match its industrial genius. New states, like new machines, were just around the corner.

2 / Visions of Harmony

"The interests of the capitalist and the laborer are . . . in perfect harmony with each other, as each derives advantages from every measure that tends to facilitate the growth of capital."

Henry Carey, Political Economy (1837)

"It was precisely by the very rigorous, judicious and steady pursuit of self-interest that individuals and companies benefited the public at large."

Sir Robert Peel (1844)

"If this assembly shares my views, we will refrain from all political dispute and thus avoid conflicts leading to disunion. . . . If we are successful, we can count on the approval of the broad masses of the population and of all propertied groups. . . . Let us work toward our goal harmoniously, actively, wisely, and boldly."

Ernst von Bulow, addressing the Prussian Society for the Protection of Property (1848)

FORMS OF THE capitalist state, unlike old soldiers, neither die nor fade away but live well past the time of their maximum utility. The Accumulative State had begun to lose its rationale by the mid-nineteenth century, but the notion that the state should play an active role in the accumulation process persisted through the latter half of the nineteenth century (when laissez-faire, in theory, was more popular than ever), during World War I, and, in an especially unique form, in the rise of twentieth-century experiments. Still, as a compromise between an old regime seeking order and a new one in search of wealth, the "pure" Accumulative State had become too conservative for a bourgeoisie that was revolutionizing everything it touched. Forms of government could be adopted and then abandoned without emotion or nostalgia like the replacement of soft, natural metals with new synthetics like carborundum. Furthermore, the great strength of the Accumulative State, its very *raison d'être*, was its eclectic character, its purely pragmatic and nonideological quest for any solution to the problem posed by the need for rapid capital accumulation. Expediency, though, could mean unpredictability; what Théophile Gautier had said of Napoleon III ("He turned to the right and then to the left and one could never tell where he was going")[1] could be said about the experience of the Accumulative State. Unpredictability resulted in confusion—about ends, about means, about expectations, about obligations. The very strength of the Accumulative State was, within half a century, becoming its most conspicuous weakness.

Ideological vacillation is probably inevitable when one class must share state power with others. The political triumph of the bourgeoisie in the latter half of the nineteenth century meant that, for a time, power no longer had to be shared. The result was a test period for this new ruling class, the first time and the only time that it was able to rule in its own fashion, to create a society in its own image. In this chapter I discuss what was produced with this opportunity.

At the level of practice, in the sphere of everyday governmental activity, the new class failed to take much advantage of its situation. Many activities of the Accumulative State were simply brought over unchanged into the new order, and insofar as changes were made, they had decidedly negative consequences for the creation of a reasonable system of government. A class so ingenious, so closely approaching brilliance, in the area of engineering and technology, had no particular inspiration to add to the much more difficult art of governing. But imagination flourished in the creation of a new ideology. Searching for a formula to justify its control over the state, the industrial bourgeoisie stood the corporate character of the old regime on its head. Earlier it had been accepted that everyone was part of the whole, that the commonweal could be defined as the sum of its parts. The new ideology posited exactly the opposite: that the action of one of the parts, the one devoted to industry, would define the character of the whole. For the first time a purely capitalist theory of legitimation was proposed: if the men who controlled the corporations were allowed to pursue their self-interest, the general interest of everyone else would be guaranteed. I will characterize the various conceptions of legitimacy that emphasized the harmony of interests among all classes as the Harmonious State. Developing alongside an Accumulative State that was beginning to reveal its weaknesses, the Harmonious State eventually superseded it, lasting in one form or another until the first decade of the twentieth century.

The importance of the justification behind the Harmonious State lies not in its internal logic but in its existence; the Accumulative State required no constant need to legitimate itself while the Harmonious State did. The reason was that capitalism created not only capitalists but also workers. The development of a potential majority class demanded a response, some recognition of its existence. It was this presence that led to the need for an ideology of harmony and, because it did, the Harmonious State symbolizes not only the triumph of the bourgeoisie but also the first indication that the exercise of its new-found political power would always be defensive.

The Harmonious State is best understood, not as a statement of what is, but as a theory of what should be; an analysis of it requires examination of thinkers more than of laws. In the real world, harmony could never be produced in a society where equality had come to mean, in Tawney's phrase, "equal opportunities of becoming unequal." [2] The world of the late nineteenth century, for most people, bore closer resemblance to L'Assommoir than to The House of Mirth. Nevertheless, the theory of the Harmonious State deserves examination, for it has continued to be used as justification long after its heyday has past. Doctrines emphasizing the harmony of interests between a dominant class and a dominated one, as E. H. Carr has shown,[3] are inevitably advanced by the former to justify its rule over the latter. Harmonious State notions should not be dismissed because they do not accord with the reality of industrial society; it is precisely the gap that makes them so fascinating. As the only ideology ever produced by the industrial bourgeoisie, the Harmonious State has a history as intriguing as it is contradictory.

Furthermore, the Harmonious State, a rationalization for the existence of class society, was at the mercy of class society. The completeness of the doctrine was at all times related to the political success of the bourgeoisie. Where this was most thorough, as in the United States and to a lesser extent in England, the "pure" theory of the Harmonious State obtained its ultimate expression. There a tradition of thought following a line of development from Adam Smith's "invisible hand" through John Stuart Mill's "On the Limitations of Government" to Spencer and Sumner asserted that harmony is produced only when the state does not intervene to destroy a "natural" homeostasis. On the other hand, where capitalist and aristocratic forces continued to share power with the industrialists—as in Germany, Italy, and to a lesser extent France—harmonious theories took a different form. In Saint-Simonian visions, the theories of solidarité associated with men like Leon Bourgeois, the Kathedersozialisten, or men like Fedele Lampertico around the Giornale degli Economisti, harmony is not produced automatically but must be created, and the state is a valid part of the creative process. The Harmonious State is not the same thing as laissez-faire. Since the publication of Dicey's Law and Opinion in the Nineteenth Century, which posited a radical duality between "individualist" and "collectivist" theories of the state,[4] it has been generally assumed that the most important question facing nineteenth-century political philosophers and economists was the matter of state intervention. Judged by this criterion, the two kinds of Harmonious State theories just outlined would have to be kept separate. But if their ultimate goal—the attempt to justify capitalist society by showing the natural or potential harmony of its social relationships—is kept in mind, then the two doctrines become expressions of the same purpose. From this perspective, the extent of state intervention is a secondary question, a matter of technique, a practical, not a theoretical, issue. The men of the time did *not* regard the whole question of the state as dominant, as we shall see, and their approach is the one adopted here.

A Brief History of a Doctrine

Harmony has existed as an ideal as long as discord has existed as a reality. Wherever there is conflict, someone is likely to propose Arcadian solutions, if not in this world, then in some other. Since mercantile capitalism gave rise to its own form of class society, harmonious doctrines can often be found among the thinkers of the Accumulative State, though rarely in a coherent fashion, as the centerpiece of the analysis. Both the defenders of the mercantile order and its critics, speaking a new language of individual initiative, had their concepts of harmony; where they disagreed was on the questions of which elements had to be harmonized and what agency should do the harmonizing. To the mercantilists the most important conflict was that between different sectors of production. Seeking balance, Matthew Carey, in his *The New Olive Branch*, advocated "an attempt to establish an identity of interests between agriculture, manufacturers, and commerce,"[5] and for this reason he condemned state aid to commerce as class legislation. To him, Hamilton's *Report on Manufacturers* was "the most perfect and luminous work ever published on the subject," while *The Wealth of Nations* represented "the road to ruin."[6] Yet Smith, in his own way, was all in favor of harmony, although to him it was the interests of classes, not sectors, that needed reconciliation (ironic in view of his later reputation as a spokesman for business pure and simple). "No society can surely be flourishing and happy, of which the far greater part of the members are poor and miserable," he wrote. Public happiness could be produced, not by the tinkering that men like Carey would later advocate, but only by economic growth. "The progressive state is in reality the cheerful and the healthy state to all the different orders of the society. The stationary is dull; the declining, melancholy."[7]

Smith relied on the invisible hand to guarantee harmony, while the mercantilists generally favored state action. This is a difference of means, not of ends, but even at that the means were not so sharply distinct. In England both Ricardo and Nassau Senior, let alone Bentham, often found themselves in favor of state action on specific issues because their goals could not be achieved in any other way. In France, J. B. Say was the spokesman for laissez-faire, a man to whom state intervention was not a casual error but stemmed "from false ideas of the nature of things, and the false maxims built upon them."[8] Yet Say specifically advocated state action in weapons building, internal improvements, communications, schools, libraries, science, patents, inventions, and, most important of all, he says, in domestic security. On the other hand, the principal spokesman for state intervention during the century was J. B. Say's grandson Louis, whose *Etudes sur la Richesse des Nations* was aimed at correcting the "fallacies" of classical political economy. While he pours out his venom toward Smith, Louis Say indicates his debt to his grandfather, whom he identifies as his best friend, and claims that he is building upon, not criticizing. J. B. Say's work.[9] There are elements of family pride and disingenuousness in this, but it is also true that a dichotomizing of liberal and statist theories covers up a similar emphasis on harmony in both schools.

In many ways the generation of political economists who came after the strictly classic writers fudged the question of the state even more. This is particularly true of the group that has come to be called the Utilitarians. Dicey had made utilitarianism in general and Bentham in particular the major advocates of laissez-faire in nineteenth-century England, yet to others Bentham and such disciples as Chadwick are the exact opposite, government activists who laid the foundation of the twentieth-century welfare state in early Victorian England.[10] A major reason for confusion of this sort is that Bentham was neither of these things, or that he was both. His philosophy aimed at promotion of the greatest good for the greatest number, a bit of a twist on the harmony-of-interests theme. If this goal could be accomplished without the aid of the state, so be it; if the state was necessary, then the state was necessary. Utilitarianism, in other words, deliberately and cleverly avoided the question of the state because the state's role was secondary to the search for public happiness. This is why specific positions about the role of government, when taken out of context, can appear to be contradictory, why a John Stuart Mill can at times seem a classical liberal and at other times appear to be a budding socialist. Mill, like Bentham, kept an open mind on the question of the state because he had a closed mind on the question of harmonious interests. The latter could be preserved only if the former was allowed to shift.

Utilitarianism, when exported to America, became Radical Republicanism. The post–Civil War Republican platform, according to David Montgomery, "united the Jacksonian Democratic belief in the unlimited role of the majority with the Whiggish conception of an active State."[11] Its ideological mixture was so close to the utilitarian compromise that not only Cobden and Bright but Mill as well endorsed the Republican plan for reconstruction.[12] If this movement had a theoretician, it would have to be Henry Carey, perhaps the most important economist ever produced in North America, certainly the only one ever to have been subjected to textual analysis at the hands of Karl Marx.[13] Son of Matthew Carey (political economy, like Huntington's disease, seems to run in the family; there were the Says, Mill *père et fils*, and now the Carey combination), Henry Carey organized the American Industrial League of 1867, whose purpose was to struggle against free trade and to show "the identity of interest of all classes of the people . . . in promoting American production."[14] Carey's voluminous writings contain few consistencies. As the spokesman for a contradictory philosophy, he changed his mind a few times on questions like state banking and free trade before coming down in favor of the former and in opposition to the latter. This inconsistency is true of his attitude toward the state as well. The summation of his thought, his *Principles of Social Science,* was a vast attempt to utilize biology in the study of the economy. A bodily metaphor allowed Carey to sidestep the whole question of government. On the one hand, "the government—representing, as it does, the intelligence of the body, physical and social—has a duty and a use, and therefore, a right to a place in the natural order." But bodies must be in balance if they are to function properly, and hence the government must also respect its place. "While ministering to the well being of the body, it may not, and, as we shall see, it does not, intervene in that sphere of life which is nearest its central movements."[15] It is clear from this work that Carey would prefer to avoid the whole subject, that he wished the state would just go away. In his writings, as Joseph Dorfman noted, "the form of government is not important.[16]

Henry Carey was closely read in Europe, so closely that Frederick Bastiat's *Harmonies Economiques* appears, as Carey charged in 1850, to be nothing more than a plagiarism of his own work translated into French. Whether the charge was literally true or not, to Bastiat more than Carey must go the title of supreme theoretician of the Harmonious State. Founder in 1841 of the *Journal des Economistes* and an active member of groups such as the Association pour la Liberté des Echanges, Bastiat was a free trader while Carey, when he finally made up his mind, became a protectionist. Further, Bastiat's position on the state's role was more consistent than Carey's; for the former, state action was inevitably dictatorial and should be avoided at all costs. Since neither laissez-faire nor free trade was popular in mid-century France, Bastiat was not particularly influential in his own time. But his amazing optimism—"My belief," he wrote in the *Harmonies,* "is that evil, far from being antagonistic to the good, in some way mysteriously promotes it, while the good can never end in evil. In the final reckoning the good must surely triumph"[17]—would express the spirit of the men whom Morazé has called *"les bourgeois conquérants."*[18] His epigrams and borrowings aside, Bastiat's optimism was more important than his analysis. As we shall see, when the Harmonious State lost its naïve utopianism, it also lost its major reason for existence.

With Carey and Bastiat, an interesting change in the nature of the Harmonious State doctrine becomes apparent. To the earlier generation, the question of the role of the State did divide into schools, not very precise ones, and ones whose importance has been exaggerated, but schools nonetheless; Smith and Matthew Carey did disagree with each other. With the younger men it seems clear, disagreements between schools coexisted within the same person; Henry Carey adopted both his father's position and that of his father's antagonist at the same time. The reason has everything to do with the growth of the working class, a term that was not even in use when Adam Smith wrote *The Wealth of Nations*.[19] By mid-century the working class could no longer be ignored; Bastiat lived long enough to see the creation of Louis Blanc's national workshops in 1848 and Carey, the Draft Riots of the Civil War. In placing the question of harmony, by any means necessary, at the center of their analyses, these writers were testifying to the power of class conflict in the nineteenth century, the same conflict that was pushing Marx in a quite different direction. Reconciliation, not exacerbation, became the goal; as Bastiat said, "If capital exists merely for the advantage of the capitalist, I am prepared to become a socialist."[20]

But this attempt at reconciliation was quite problematic. Because they were writing early in the history of industrial capitalism, neither man seemed aware of how difficult the struggle to bring about harmony was to be. Attempting to mollify class conflict while preserving a capitalist framework created a real dilemma for utilitarian thinkers. Bastiat died in 1850, too early to witness the full limitations of his hopes. Carey, though, lived on, and with him the Republican ideology he had shaped. As David Montgomery has shown in excruciating detail, the Radical Republican ideology, halfway between traditional conservatism and the emerging labor reform movement, ultimately had to swing one way or the other.[21] By 1870 most of the Radicals had made their choice; like E. L. Godkin of *The Nation*, they rediscovered laissez-faire and became advocates of a triumphant capitalism. Toward the end of the century, harmony was still the professed goal, but the position on state action had hardened, and the utopianism had been replaced by cynical "realism." What began as a point of view undecided on the question of state action had become one with its mind made up.

Another alternative was possible, at least theoretically. If the Radical Republicans in the United States went toward unvarnished laissez-faire, continental thinkers from the same tradition often became *étatistes*. Two excellent examples are the French notion of *solidarité* and the Bismarckian attraction to welfare legislation. The French Radical tradition had its roots in the same soil that produced the Utilitarians and Henry Carey; Clemenceau had visited the United States during the Civil War and firmly endorsed the Radical Reconstruction program.[22] Throughout his long political career, Clemenceau was known to change his mind more than a few times, but what never altered, besides his hatred of the Germans, was his attempt to seek a middle ground between bourgeois complacency and socialist revolution, which is why he could both condemn Thiers and his repression of the Paris Commune (in terms as strong as Marx), yet sponsor his own programs of repression against those to the left of him. A founder of the Radical Socialist Party, he headed a movement that was an attempt, in John A. Scott's words, "to reconcile the conflicting ideas of laissez-faire and state intervention in economic life."[23]

The articulated philosophy behind this party was a mélange of ideas, built on Saint Simonian origins, called *solidarité*, and its leading advocates were Alfred Fouilée and Leon Bourgeois. The former, like Henry Carey, was fascinated by biology and tried to adopt it to social theory. Since the popularity of Darwin among social writers was pseudoscientific, it was possible to utilize his ideas and come away with any conclusion one wished. Consequently, Fouilée used a Darwinian framework and even some of the writings of Spencer himself to justify an active state, while Spencer had, of course, used those same ideas to suggest the inevitability of a passive state. Bourgeois, a far more popular writer and also an active politician (see Chapter 3), adopted these ideas in a theory that emphasized what he called the "social debt." Stripped of legalese, this doctrine held that, in return for the wealth they had accumulated, the rich owed the poor a better life, which could be achieved through the state. His doctrine, says Scott,

> avoided both the pitfalls of laissez-faire liberalism and the commitments of revolutionary socialism; it provided for the amelioration of glaring social abuses while maintaining untouched the existing bases of capitalist society in private property and freedom of business enterprise. It put forth, in terms of the division of labor and men's interdependence, an idea of social peace and inter-class fraternity designed to mask social conflict, to wean the working class from revolutionary socialism and to win it to support a "practical" program of social reform.[24]

With *solidarité* the Harmonious State was given a new lease on life, a distinct alternative to a pure laissez-faire conclusion.

The working class was little more than a spectator during the bitter debates that led to the unification of Germany. Both the liberals and the traditionalists at one time or another sought the support of the "masses," but both feared that giving power to the many would detract from the power of a few. Consequently, both sides in the struggle would develop harmonious doctrines—the liberals emphasizing free commerce and the conservatives traditional, paternalistic obligations—but both, to a strikingly similar extent, refused to take actions that would implement these doctrines. "Neither was able to win the allegiance of the proletariat," Theodore Hamerow writes, "because neither was able to satisfy its basic needs."[25] Liberalism was in no way absent from Prussian territory; it was just less powerful. Writers like John Prince-Smith and organizations like the Congress of German Economists preached all the usual laissez-faire sermons but were unable to put them into practice because of their defeat in 1848. They should have turned to the working class for alliance, and their defeat was in part attributable to their failure to do so earlier. Afraid of what they might unleash, they opted for rhetoric instead, and doctrines of harmoniousness replaced concrete attempts to form alliances. As Max Duncker expressed it, the moderate liberals "want the harmony of classes, not the subjugation of one by the other; not only the subjugation of the opponent to reform, but also his good will for it."[26] On the other hand, German conservatism, traditionally anticapitalist—Bismarck once defined capitalism as a system in which "he who can starve best will starve his competitors into bankruptcy, he who produces the shoddiest goods will destroy his rival"[27]—often flirted with the working class through paternalistic practices, but this too was incomplete. After the failure of the 1848 revolution, men like Joseph von Radowitz had tried to implement a conservative-proletariat alliance à la Disraeli, but Radowitz was unable to win much support either from his colleagues or from the King. In the unification struggle Bismarck chose not to follow a paternalistic strategy, and instead sought to ally himself with the liberals around the goal of unification. The creation of Germany gave both sides a method of avoiding the implications of their harmonious doctrines, already exaggerated because they were overgrown with romantic and idealistic rhetoric.

With unification accomplished the problem was reposed. The persistent growth of the Socialist Party transformed the question of harmony from theoretical speculation to active political reality. Suddenly the problem of what to do with the working class could no longer be ignored. It is generally held that Bismarck's response was to pass the first important social legislation in Europe leading to the modern welfare state. This point of view mistakes the nature of the legislation. First, Bismarck's "welfare" state was a glance, not to the future, but to the past; it is closer in conception to Speenhamland than to the New Deal. Part of a traditional paternalistic concern of the old regime, these laws were the products of a need perceived from above, not a demand for social justice from below. If the term welfare state in the twentieth century has any meaning, it grows out of popular dissatisfaction, pressure from below. Bismarck's social legislation was the extension to practice of the conservative theory of the Harmonious State, not a path-breaking venture in social experimentation. Second, the Bismarckian legislation was part of a rambling and eclectic approach to one of the basic functions of the Accumulative State: social control. The same man who passed the most repressive antisocialist laws in Europe also passed the most "liberal" welfare measures as well; from his point of view both were directed at the same end, maintaining power in a situation of great social flux. It makes sense to view these laws as part of the mid-century confusion surrounding the question of the future direction that the Harmonious State would take. It is for this reason that the period from 1865 to after unification was characterized by almost surrealistic ideological inconsistency.

From this brief review it becomes clear that by about 1870 the notion of the Harmonious State was splitting in two, one school of thought emphasizing laissez-faire and the other the active use of the state in the promotion of social harmony. These conflicting directions were manifest not only between but also within countries. In both England and the United States, the movement toward pure laissez-faire did not go completely unopposed. Hegel, of all people, was rediscovered, and writers like Green and Bradley in England and Gronlund in the United States used the Hegelian emphasis on totality to justify a state that attempted, at least formally, to be responsive to all social classes. (One neo-Hegelian, Richard Burton Haldane, as Minister of War in 1914, declared that Britain's army, if the world came to war, would be a Hegelian one.)[28] Neo-Hegelianism advanced the by-now-common emphasis on harmony of social classes in a new format. T. H. Green sounded a good deal like the classical economists when he announced that "no action in its own interest of a state which fulfilled its idea could conflict with any true interest or right of a general society."[29] Gronlund's *The Cooperative Commonwealth*, published in 1884, cannot be taken seriously as a work of political theory, but it did, in its herky-jerky fashion, express a common sentiment to use the state for the benefit of all, not just of a few. The state's "whole sphere," he wrote, "is the making all special activities work together for one general end: its own welfare, or the *Public Good*."[30] At a less abstract level, Jevons's *The State in Relation to Labour* previewed an attack on pure laissez-faire,[31] while men like Richard T. Ely and the "young Turk" founders of the American Economics Association, to quote the initial charter of the AEA, regarded "the state as an agency whose positive assistance is one of the indispensable conditions of human progress."[32] In both countries, however, it was the other face of the Harmonious State, the one that viewed the state with hostility, that established the dominant political tone of the day. Though eventually it lost the war, laissez-faire won this battle, as its tenets became the height of economic, social, and political orthodoxy. The popularity of Sumner and Spencer, the judicial conservatism of the U.S. Supreme Court, the flirtation between Gladstone and Bright, and, a bit later, the rise of men like Bonar Law in the Conservative Party—all represented the full flowering of a doctrine that many had thought was already obsolete. Like a dying dinosaur, laissez-faire thumped its tail one last time before expiring, causing incredible damage to those trapped wherever it landed.

THE DANCE OF THE SEVEN CONTRADICTIONS

The blossoming of laissez-faire at the end of the century rewrote history; a philosophy so widely accepted must have been around for some time. Actually its life was deceptively short. Pure laissez-faire began its new popularity some time between 1870 and 1880; by World War I it was to all intents and purposes finished, never again to appear except in the nostalgic fantasies of a class in decline. Thus its total life was equal to that of one generation of jurists, politicians, and thinkers, in only two countries, and at a time when its theoretical precepts were matter of factly violated in practice; yet that one generation was able to produce a body of ideas whose influence was as deep as its underlying philosophy was shallow. Like the burst of a flash cube, the key ideas of laissez-faire burned with spectacular intensity before lapsing into dark nothingness. The very brilliance of the flash blinded people to its true nature, for during its lifetime the basic nostrums of the doctrine were accepted by workers as well as employers, religious leaders as well as atheists, moral men as well as immoral societies. But when it had burned out, it became clear that the doctrine embodied a series of rather severe contradictions that made it unworkable. Though men of the time thought they had found a secret formula that would preserve capitalism forever, their solution was in fact temporary, for it was marked by seven limitations, which danced their way through the doctrine, causing it to sacrifice either its internal consistency or its external relevance.

First was the question of nature. In their desire to prove the inevitability of class rule, ideologists then, as now, adopted a pseudo-scientific camouflage for what were essentially propagandistic and unscientific, in some cases even antiscientific, doctrines. The popularity of Darwin's work served this purpose, and could also be used to justify racism at the same time. It was nature, not men, that decreed the struggle for existence, which, if left to itself, would paradoxically produce harmony. Yet there were no logical, or any other, connections between Darwin's biological theories and laissez-faire; both Carey and Fouilée, as we have seen, used biological metaphors to reach quite different conclusions about the role of the state, and their reading of Darwin was just as faithful (or unfaithful) as Spencer's. Similarly, for Sumner the thrust of his political recommendations seemed to be based on a popularized anthropology that was part of the development of social science. In retrospect, however, *What Social Classes Owe Each Other* was not based on *Folkways*, but the other way around; the political prescriptions came first and the pseudoscience later, in Sumner's mind if not in the chronology of his output. Laissez-faire thinkers, in short, turned to science not because their ideas were natural but because they were so unnatural. The self-confidence with which these ideas were put forward, as if this was the way the world inevitably had to be, could exist only because the class that was propagating them had won total control of the state. It is almost a sociological law that those in power will deny that power exists and that those who control the state will argue that the state is unimportant, for such ideas will make control easier to maintain. Thus, laissez-faire at this time signified more than ever the importance of political struggle, not of the struggle of nature; for without the determined, conscious, ruthless, and highly successful attempt by an industrial ruling class to grab the state for its own ends, laissez-faire could never have been proposed. Far from being natural, laissez-faire, as Antonio Gramsci once wrote, was "introduced and maintained by legislative and coercive means. . . . Consequently, laissez-faire liberalism is a political programme, designed to change—in so far as it is victorious—a State's leading personnel, and to change the economic programme of the State itself."[33] Proof of this was the difficulty of establishing the ideal of no state intervention; even those who were most committed to the principle were willing to go along with some violations in fact. If laissez-faire had indeed been natural, it would never have needed the passion and eloquence of a Sumner or a Spencer to justify it.

Second, laissez-faire never solved the contradiction between its universalistic rhetoric and its particularistic appeal. It always seemed that the more narrow the vested interest being defended, the more flourishing the rhetoric used in its defense. "That only is a free government, in the American sense of the term, under which the inalienable right of every citizen to pursue his happiness is unrestrained, except by just, equal, and impartial laws,"[34] wrote Mr. Justice Field grandiloquently, but his ardor was defending, as Robert McCloskey has pointed out, the right of a few butchers to challenge a Louisiana statute governing the slaughtering of animals.[35] In such flights of rhetoric, the doctrine of the harmony of interests received its most complete, and therefore its most intellectually bankrupt, expression.

Although it had been asserted since early in the century that what benefits the smallest class benefits everybody, the conditions of life in capitalist societies spoke otherwise. More and more, inherent harmony of interests became recognizable class bias. Rarely was this more clearly seen than in the definition of class itself, for under the theory of laissez-faire only the working class constituted a class; the bourgeoisie was not a class, but all of society. Anything in the interests of the dominant group was in the interests of all, was universalistic, whereas legislation passed to benefit others—workers or farmers, for example—was class legislation and stood condemned as particularistic. Herbert Samuel, a pessimistic and business-oriented leader of the British Liberal Party, detested "the idea that the State can take from one class and give to other classes" because such a policy represented "the divorce of common interests that results from all this interference with social life."[36] Of course, all his life Samuel devoted himself to taking from one class and giving to another, for that is what capitalism and the capitalist state are all about. Governmental aid to manufacturers, under this peculiar logic, did not interfere with the harmony of interests but helped to realize it, while government aid to others had exactly the opposite effect. It was under a similar double standard that lawyers like Joseph Choate and George Edmunds asked the U.S. Supreme Court to strike down provisions for an income tax, arguing that any law taxing one group in order to support another was "class" legislation and therefore unconstitutional, a request with which the Court speedily complied.[37] Such analyses of what constituted a class may have satisfied the thirst for power of those who offered them, but they were so contradictory that they could not be offered for very long. If advocates of laissez-faire raised the issue of class legislation, they were bringing up an issue that would be used against them with increasing frequency.

This double standard worked in two ways. Since a state that actively aided business was not engaged in class-biased activity while one that aided the majority was, it followed logically—and these men were extremely proud of their logic—that nonactivity that benefited business could be overlooked while nonactivity directed to workers was being imposed. One irony of the triumph of laissez-faire is that some of its most famous statements against state intervention were not concerned with businessmen at all, but with workers. As had happened earlier in the century, it was the labor market that was upheld as the ideal "free market," not the commodity market. In defense of his butchers, Field had called "the right of free labor" "one of the most sacred and imprescriptible rights of man."[38] Members of the Court were ever watchful that workers would enjoy a laissez-faire state that their employers were trying to avoid. As the Court ruled in the infamous *Lochner* decision, workers "are in no sense wards of the State."[39] Freedom of contract must be upheld and regulatory legislation condemned. Yet if workers were not wards of the state, businessmen still were; indeed, they were both wards and masters, giving out largesse and then collecting it.

Basic propositions like these revealed that double standards were becoming a key element of the theory of the Harmonious State, leading its advocates into inescapable ideological *culs-de-sac*. On the very same day that the U.S. Supreme Court struck down income taxation as class legislation, it also ruled that the Sherman Anti-Trust Act did not apply to manufacturing monopolies but did apply to labor unions.[40] These three decisions of 1895 symbolized the year of contradiction for laissez-faire; the

Court was true to a class interest but for almost forty years it destroyed its own legitimacy as a spokesman for that most universal of documents, the U.S. Constitution, choosing the particularistic interests of its own favored class as more important.

Somewhat related is a third contradiction, between utopian longings and counterutopian actualities. Sumner was among the most pessimistic of all the laissez-faire theorists, yet even he could write:

> The modern industrial system is a great social co-operation. It is automatic and instinctive in operation. The adjustments of the organs take place naturally. The parties are held together by impersonal force—supply and demand. They may never see each other; they may be separated by half the circumference of the globe. Their co-operation in the social efforts is combined and distributed again by financial machinery, and the rights and interests are measured and satisfied without any special treaty or convention at all. All this goes on so smoothly and naturally that we forget to notice it.[41]

Sumner's words are indicative of the attraction of the doctrine of homeostasis, which was still popular a hundred years after publication of *The Wealth of Nations*. What makes Sumner's view more interesting than Smith's is that the latter had a basis for his utopianism; for all he knew the capitalist revolution might indeed bring universal happiness. But Sumner should have known otherwise. The passage's most striking characteristic is not what it says but when it was written, at a time of extended depression, when industrial violence was nearing its peak,[42] and Populist discontent was as high as it had ever been.[43] The worse social conditions in the world became, the more glorious became the industrial utopia that, according to these thinkers, modern capitalism was creating.

These writers were not blind. They understood that the world was not perfect; in fact, they generally pictured it as caught in a struggle for survival, a race that only the fittest would finish. How could the concept of struggle be reconciled with that of utopian harmony? The answer was generally decided upon by relegating harmony to the realm of the potential rather than the actual. Harmony is what would have happened had not one group after another sought special privileges from the state, especially workers. Thus the world of laissez-faire became utopian and counterutopian at the same time, preaching survival but holding out Arcadia. This was quite a contradiction to swallow, and most people chose not to do so. Faced with a choice between the fictitious harmony they were offered and the real counterharmony they lived, they found it not difficult to separate fact from fiction, and a full dose of the Harmonious State became that much harder to accept.

Fourth, the late theories of the Harmonious State were suffused with moral and religious overtones in order to achieve quite secular ends. It was no coincidence that two of the most popular American spokesmen for the new ideology, Bishop Lawrence and Russell Conwell, were men of God, for who can better ensure the utopianism of a perfectly harmonious potential future than Him? God wanted capitalists to make money, of course, but it also appears that He wanted everyone else to accept that state of affairs. Both the ultimate emptiness of laissez-faire's theory of legitimation and its pseudoreligious quality (being a hodgepodge doctrine, laissez-faire could be both pseudoscientific and pseudoreligious at the same time) can be seen in these words of Mr. Justice Field: "It is only by obedience that affection and reverence can be shown to a superior being having a right to command. So thought our great Master when he said to his disciples: 'If you love me, keep my commandments.' "[44] Field never made clear exactly what role God played in a controversy involving legal tender, but perhaps this was not necessary. A social system of divine inspiration speaks for itself. Unfortunately for Field, the exact position of God was not so clear to others; reformers like Ely discovered in Him a defense of positive state action equally sanctimonious: "God works through the State in carrying out his purpose more universally than through any other institution."[45] Divine intervention was thus neutralized; both Field and Ely would have to face the fact that God was neither a classical liberal nor a utilitarian reformer, that His message was irrelevant to the world of political action. Both men wanted earthy, secular goals: in the one case pure bourgeois rule, in the other social reform. Basing their espousal on divine intervention did not help either to achieve his objective.

Fifth, untrammeled laissez-faire was developing a purely materialistic theory of society just when material values were being called into question. Classical political economy had always been committed to "economic determinism," for the conception of the good citizen whose every move is based on an economic calculation of profit and loss is a legacy of Smith, Ricardo, and Malthus. By the end of the century this tendency to make material considerations the definition of proper conduct and all other considerations secondary to it reached a culmination. While Bentham's utilitarianism did not make an explicit connection between "the greatest good for the greatest number" and material welfare (there was always an implicit one), Sumner did. Material values—which he generally labeled as "industry, frugality, prudence, and temperance"[46]—were the ultimate values. So intense was Sumner's commitment to materialism that he could say, with a perfectly straight face, "The savings bank depositor is a hero of civilization, for he is helping in the accumulation of that capital which is the indispensable prerequisite of all we care for and all we want here on earth."[47] The equation of a depositor with Odysseus may have given a rosy glow to the cheeks of the former, but such inspirational faith in materialistic values was incompatible with growing working-class consciousness. Struggling for their rights as citizens, workers, becoming a majority class, were beginning to discover such things as politics, culture, recreation, education, literature, and family life. To meet these needs, laissez-faire offered them just what they wanted to escape from: political economy. Through its inability to transcend the strictly materialistic world it had created, the Harmonious State was once again unable to respond when response was needed.

Sixth, the apotheosis of laissez-faire thinking at the end of the century posed more clearly than ever, before or since, the contradiction between liberal and democratic thought. The idea of the minimalist state comes straight out of liberalism and remains one of its most consistent contributions to political discourse. The unresponsive state brought with it a dual conception of citizenship since, if the workers were considered a class that would use organized society only for their own ends, they could not be trusted with political power. Industrialists, on the other hand, were entitled to hold power because what was in their interest as a group would benefit everyone. The result of this duality was that the only way the liberal state could be preserved was by protecting it against the influence of a democratic element. "Industry," wrote Sumner, "may be republican; it can never be democratic,"[48] and the same could be said of a state that worked for the benefit of industry. Fortunately for the ruling class, at least in the United States, one branch of government was explicitly undemocratic, and it is therefore not surprising that the Supreme Court should become the most ardent champion of purely liberal values. The more removed and insulated government was from the public, the more it championed classical liberalism; conversely, the more democratic and popular the institution, the less sympathy it had for the very same dogma None of this was particularly mysterious to the men of the time. As Harold U. Faulkner has observed, "That the Supreme Court knew, when it robbed the [Interstate Commerce] Commission of all power to enforce the [Sherman] Act, that it had nullified an overwhelming desire on the part of the people to regulate interstate commerce and eliminate long-standing abuses there can be no doubt."[49] Advocates of laissez-faire based their position on a "higher law" than that of political democracy; they knew that they had to choose between democracy and liberalism, and they made their choice explicit. The one ideal could be preserved only if the other's potential was blunted.

The same contradiction, to the chagrin of the industrialists, worked the other way around. If a genuine democracy was ever going to be created, the pure liberal state would have to be abolished. Hence even the slightest reform had to be fought, for as the champions of laissez-faire pointed out in brief after brief, a particular piece of reform legislation might look innocent, but accept it and who knows where the line would ever be drawn. If a simple income tax proposal were to be adopted, George Edmunds had argued in the *Pollock* case,

> This would be followed by further invasions of private and property rights, as one vice follows another, and very soon we should have, possibly, only one per cent of the people paying the taxes, and finally a provision that only the twenty people who have the greatest estates should bear the whole taxation, and after that communism, anarchy, and then, the ever following despotism.[50]

Most legal briefs of the time were like this; it was always a future nightmare, not a present need for remediation, that was argued against. Because of its fear of democracy, laissez-faire painted itself into a corner. Being unable to concede even the smallest point in its world view, it could stave off change through the ruse of dire prediction for a time, but this strategy also had the effect of making change more complete when it finally did come. Faced with the prospect of democracy, a judge with the Dickensian name of Peckham defiantly asked in 1905: "But are we all, on that account, at the mercy of legislative majorities?"[51] The question was as rhetorical as it was defiant, for his clear answer was no. As a result, because it would not bend, laissez-faire eventually broke. Because liberalism would not accept democracy, democracy would eventually turn against liberalism, not with finality, but with enough strength to put to rest both the minimalist state and the notion that businessmen have an absolute right to do as they please.

All these contradictions can be summarized through a seventh, the conflict between an offensive and a defensive strategy for the state. Laissez-faire, when it was first formulated, had been part of a militant crusade to transform the world. The rising bourgeoisie knew few limitations to its vision. As Emile Périère said in 1835: "It is not enough for me to lay out great programs on paper; I want more—to write my idea into the earth."[52] And he did, too, for men like Périère transformed the earth as we know it. In total contrast, in the twentieth century members of the same class who share minimalist ideas about state power are as defensive as those of the earlier group were aggressive. Laissez-faire, when embodied in the platitudes of a Barry Goldwater or a Margaret Thatcher, seems like an apology for some awkward and admittedly unrealistic ideas. In this transition of laissez-faire from an offensive strategy to a defensive reaction, the period under discussion falls somewhere in the middle. This transitional character gives its espousal of laissez-faire doctrines two characteristics. First, transition led to complacency. Neither Périère nor Goldwater was complacent, the one wanting to bring about a new world, the other to restore an old one. *Fin-de-siècle* advocates of laissez-faire held an attitude of neither reform nor reaction; for them the world was just fine. As Andrew Carnegie

said in 1886: "If asked what 'important law' I should change, I must per-
force say none; the laws are perfect."[53] Because their world was harmonious, the new philosophers assumed that everyone else's was also, and their
complacency in the face of the wretched social conditions they tried to
ignore was due as much to parochialism as to callousness. Aware that they
were moving from the offensive to the defensive, advocates of the Harmonious State saw an aura of fatalism and pessimism creep into their
ideas. No longer assured that the future was theirs, writers began to ponder
what E. L. Godkin had called the "unforeseen tendencies"[54] of democratic society. Conceptions of human nature changed from generous, open
ones, to narrow, closed, venal ones. But, whatever the result, during this
period a dialectical link was established between the increasingly offensive
strategy of those who were excluded from power and the defensive tone
of those who had monopolized it. The strength of one was closely tied to
the weakness of the other, and an ideology that had begun as a revolutionary manifesto was rapidly becoming a reactionary rationalization.

As a theory of legitimation, that particular form of the Harmonious
State advocating pure laissez-faire, the true orthodoxy of the most successful industrial elite, reached the point where it faced equally unpalatable
alternatives. If it remained faithful to its origins as an antistate doctrine
it became eloquent and consistent in theory while irrelevant to industrial
reality; if, on the other hand, it adapted itself to new conditions and
justified positive state action, it had a better chance of survival, but with
no consistent ideological content and therefore with no excuse for existence
as a theory of legitimation. Faced with this Hobson's choice, the Harmonious State, as a system of ideas, failed, despite its original promise,
to assuage the class tensions within capitalist societies, though harmony-
of-interest echoes can still be heard throughout Europe and in the United
States.[55] But what fails in theory can still have a partial *raison d'être* if it
succeeds in practice; the ideological flaws of the Harmonious State would
have been serious but not fatal if in the realm of ordinary politics it had
built something solid. Yet when we turn to concrete state action during
this time, we find little of solid value, and it is this double failure that
ultimately consigned the Harmonious State to nostalgia.

THE STRUCTURE OF POLITICS UNDER THE HARMONIOUS STATE

The ideology of the Harmonious State, in its purest form, reached the
pinnacle of its popularity in the period between 1890 and the outbreak
of World War I. This was the period of H. Gladstone's greatest influence
on the Liberal Party, and also when the Conservatives were dropping their
Tory paternalism; when the U.S. Supreme Court held its breath and delivered its "opinion" in *Lochner v. New York;* when the Third Republic

was being transformed from a republic without republicans to one with them; and when Giolitti brought laissez-faire liberalism to an Italy caught between the most conservative and the most revolutionary classes in Europe. At the very same time, however, these were also the years when the foundations of a post–Harmonious State solution were being laid. Modern welfare legislation was slowly being passed; men like Hobhouse, Brandeis, and the Fabians were showing the limitations of traditional liberalism; socialist parties were achieving startling success everywhere from Oklahoma to Bavaria; conservative governments were sponsoring reform legislation; reform governments were showing their respectability; and foreign adventures were everywhere giving new life to the state. In other words, the period in which the Harmonious State reached its height was also the period in which its inevitable decline became obvious. No sooner had power been won than threats to the exercise of that power developed; no sooner had the transition from the *ancien régime* to the bourgeoisie been finally completed than a new transition came into sight.

The transitional nature of *la belle époque* meant that what appeared on the surface to be one thing might be something completely different underneath. In appearance the period saw the adoption, with little if any modification, of the governmental principles of the Accumulative State. One can go through the catalogue item by item and show a general process of expansion for each major activity of the active state that had dominated political life in the first half of the century. I have shown how protection intensified at the end of the nineteenth century in every country, and it even began to percolate into England. Matters of banking and currency were still on the political agenda and seemed as eclectic as ever. Within a period of only three years, the U.S. Congress first passed and then repealed the Sherman Silver Purchase Act, which does not say much for the consistency of the political theory of its currency policy (nor that of John Sherman, who voted to repeal the very law to which he had three years earlier given his name). The tendency of the state to assume more banking functions also increased during this period; these were the years in which the American Federal Reserve System was being thought out, when a banking crisis in Italy (1893) led the state to reorganize the system completely, when state aid to colonial banks in France was part of the "continual cry for government aid to business."[56] "Keeping order" was also increasing in importance as, for example, in the extremely repressive Italian Penal Code of 1871 or the even more repressive Exceptional Laws proposed in 1899.[57] In both England and the United States the increase in the repressive powers of the state between 1890 and World War I was drastic, as those in power tried to control demands for women's suffrage and workers' rights, as well as anti-imperialist sentiment.[58] Imperialist desire, on its part, led to a strengthening of the foreign policy apparatus of the state that was bound to, and did, have domestic repercussions (see Chapter 3). France, Italy, and the United States were all trying their hand at modern imperialism for the first time, and England's politics were overwhelmed by questions involving Ireland. Direct state aid to business in no way changed, even though the theory of laissez-faire seemed to condemn it. The search for a balance between public and private in the building of railroads went on by and large in the same manner that it had earlier in the century, and the same ups and downs were also extended to other areas of transportation, such as the Italian and French merchant marine. Finally, the state's role in the social life of the society continued to grow. In the area of education, in France these years saw bitter conflicts as the Church's control over the educational system was slowly and inconsistently transferred to the state,[59] and in England laws in 1870, 1880, and 1891, respectively, created nonreligious schools, made education compulsory, and made education free.[60] In short, whatever the blaring trumpets of laissez-faire were announcing, the orchestra as a whole was playing a traditional accumulative overture. Eclecticism remained the order of the day.

Under this apparent continuity, however, several important modifications to the Accumulative State could be discerned. Perhaps most significant was the rise of a new creature, the bourgeois politician. During the period of the Accumulative State, the beneficiaries of state power were the members of the alliance between elements of the old regime and the rising industrial bourgeoisie, yet the actual personnel of the Accumulative State was much more heavily weighted in favor of the traditional classes. It was estimated by *The Economist* that in 1864 a political career in Great Britain was open to only about five thousand individuals, not all of whom showed any interest in following one.[61] Successive generations of Lords gave a real continuity to British politics, even if they rendered political history confusing to later generations: Which Lord Derby is currently politicking with Disraeli, father or son? Which Russell? Which Grey? To the landed gentry, politics was an aspect of public service, something that came with leisure time, independent wealth, and the right connections. Decisions were made, as in Trollope's *The Prime Minister*, at the country estate of a man like the Duke of Omnium, then ratified in Parliament. There is not a specific date at which all of this changed, but the effects of a change can be seen through a glance at the backgrounds of members of Parliament. In 1874, landowners and rentiers constituted 32 percent of the MPs, declining in 1880 to 19 percent, and in 1885 to 16 percent, while the number of men whose major occupation was commerce or industry increased from 24 percent in 1874 to 40 percent in 1880 before evening off at 38 percent in 1885.[62] Clearly an era was passing.

What was true for England was also true elsewhere. Even as late as the first ten years of the Third Republic, politics as a vocation was still reserved for the men whom Daniel Halévy called the "notables," members of a patrician class who had direct ties to the old order, whose power was in the land, and whose ideas were rooted in a Christian view of society as a totality.[63] The Duc de Broglie who had arisen in 1872 to challenge Thiers was a direct descendant of all the de Broglies who had played their part in both the *ancien régime* and the Revolution, and for good measure was also part of the family that produced Benjamin Constant, the Neckers, and the de Staëls. A more systematic study of the class origins of French political leaders was undertaken by Jean Lhomme, in part to see whether Halévy's notion of the decline of the dukes was true. Lhomme found that during the 1830s political power in France was shared between the aristocracy and an *haute bourgeoisie* centered around banking families like the Périères and the Laffittes. Between 1870 and 1880 the changes produced as this coalition lost power were, in his words, "massive." Elections to the legislature in the Third Republic, after an initial victory for the established families, were decidedly Republican, but so were local elections, under Third Republic reforms that permitted local officials to be elected for the first time in modern French history; in one instance the Maréchal Canrobert, an imperial war hero, was defeated for a spot on a municipal council in Périgord by a veterinarian. But the change was not simply political. Administratively, the same years witnessed what has come to be called *"la valse des préfets."* In 1879 Leon Say, who was still active in French political and economic life, proposed the replacement of a number of hereditary treasury positions; a new head of the Bank of France was appointed; a new prefect for the Seine was named; and the Minister of War suggested the replacement of five generals. In short, as Lhomme noted, "Politics had become a career." While it was not yet *une carrière ouverte aux talents* ("If 1879 constitutes a turning point, if the Republic is composed, for the first time, of republican personnel, still one cannot speak of the arrival of true democracy, let alone economic democracy."),[64] the decision of men like Thiers to broaden the *pays légal* was having its effect on the kinds of men who found themselves holding political office.[65]

Italy was going through similar changes. In 1866, about 250,000 persons, less than 1 percent of the population, played any role in Italian politics, including voting.[66] Under the system of government established in Italy's first representative democracy, senators were appointed directly by the King and had to be, as a matter of law, from aristocratic family backgrounds. Between the depression of 1874 and the end of the century, Italian politics swung back and forth from the right to the left, with the latter emerging as the powerful force. But these were tendencies that could be distinguished from each other much more clearly by the background of their leaders than by the policies they followed. The strength of the right, according to Clough, was based on "landowners, rich bankers, wealthy merchants," while the left received its support from "new industrialists, lawyers, lesser bourgeois, and anticlericals."[67] As the latter group assumed more power in the *Camera*, or lower house, a political career became more of a possibility for the man who was successful in manufacturing and related enterprises. By 1911, Salvemini pointed out the political success of the *piccola borghesia intelletuale*, arguing that politicians had become, in Allum's words, "middlemen and fixers in a society of scarce resources," a situation that was found to exist in Naples well into the twentieth century.[68]

There were two significant exceptions to this pattern. One was Germany, where the Junkers, who were nothing if not a self-contained class, managed to hold onto political power longer than similar representatives of an old order did elsewhere. Bismarck, according to Arthur Rosenberg's interpretation, was creating a middle-class society without using the middle class. By both sponsoring an empire and encouraging the growth of state-supported cartels, Bismarck gave the bourgeoisie what it wanted in return for an all-but-explicit promise from the industrialists that they would leave political power in his hands. Finding their ideal produced by someone outside their own ranks, "the great majority of the middle class, especially the educated and academic elements, came to distrust their own political judgement."[69] For industrialists like Krupp, it became a matter of pride to call oneself "nonpolitical," even as one served the state in all kinds of ways. Parliamentary government did not exist in the Second Reich because middle-class political rule did not exist. Nonetheless, even in Germany, non-nobles were slowly gaining positions of power in the state bureaucracy.[70]

A directly opposite situation to this one, but one still in contrast to England, France, and Italy, was in the United States. For there the transition to middle-class politics had taken place much earlier. To most historians it was the election of Martin Van Buren in 1836 that signified the political triumph of the professional politician and this is as good a date as any.[71] The last half of the century saw, not a transition to middle-class rule, but a solidification of it. To the extent that there was an aristocratic class in the United States, many of its members outplundered the bourgeoisie in their approach to the state. Some of the most venal politics of the day was practiced by men who would claim to be "bluebloods." The "boss" of Pennsylvania politics was Boise Penrose, of the Philadelphia Main Line, and the man who presided over the United States Senate was Nelson Aldrich, a capitalist who was trying to become an aristocrat. These exceptions, however, are ones of tendency, not of kind; both in Germany and the United States, power struggles were taking place, if not at the same time and at the same pace as in the other countries just discussed.

The world of the aristocrats, of landed political power, was an undemocratic one, no question about that. The men who rose to power within it tended to be quite conservative and generally unequipped to deal with the severe problems of modern industrialization. Yet this system had a

certain compelling dignity. The task of rulership was assumed with seriousness and deliberate recognition of its importance; those who held political
power were really a ruling class, in the sense that they had definite notions about what to do with that power. To the "four hundred families,"
whatever the country, business was generally business and politics was
politics. There was a fairly rigid demarcation between the two, since one
required short-term acumen and the other long-range perspective. The
rise of new men—such as Jules Ferry, Léon Gambetta, or W. H. Waddington in France; Joseph Chamberlain, Herbert Samuel, or Henry Campbell-
Bannerman in Great Britain; Francesco Crispi, Giuseppe Zanardelli, or
Giovanni Giolitti in Italy; John Sherman or Mark Hanna in the United
States—signified a new politics, in which business was business, to be sure,
but business was also politics, and politics, business. For the first time,
the industrial capitalists had the opportunity to become a ruling class,
without having to share power with any other group. What did the bourgeoisie do with this chance? The results, from almost any angle, were dis-
appointing; the new men proved that they had the power to become a
ruling class, but not necessarily the ability. Greater numbers of voters, an
increase in the activities of the state, and a simultaneous tendency toward
immigration and emigration combined to produce under bourgeois leadership such new phenomena as professional party managers, systematic election campaigns, and the pursuit of public office as an end in itself, not as
a public service. All of this meant that the meaning of a political
career was undergoing a change and, with this, the meaning of politics.
The single most important consequence of the control of the state by the
bourgeoisie was also the most subtle, a change in definition (see Chapter
9). The bourgeoisie liberated politics from oligarchy and infused it with
democratic potential but, once having freed it, did not know what to do
with it. Politics was divorced from purpose, cut off from a vision, however grotesque, of the social order of the whole, and made the instrument
of class rule in the narrowest sense of the term. Just as the theory of the
Harmonious State asserted that what was in the best interests of those
at the top was in the best interests of all, political practice seemed to
suggest that if the new ruling class used the state to feather its nest everyone else had no right to complain. Never was a class so potentially powerful yet so actually parochial at the same time.

Another consequence of the political triumph of the bourgeoisie was a
decline in political theory, not the sort of thing to worry contemporaries
all that much, but of great importance in historical terms. For at least
two hundred years political theory had been part of political action. Both
advocates of a new order such as Locke and defenders of an old one such
as Burke had committed themselves to work for the principles they
espoused. When political life was in transition, moreover, there was a
tendency for significant works of political theory to appear. The class

struggle fought between liberal businessmen and those attached to the traditional world of the gentry was reproduced, on an intellectual level, in some of the most widely read and brilliantly argued political pamphlets of modern times, such as those of Burke and Paine. The eventual compromise between the landed-mercantile interest and the industrial one was received with mixed reactions but, whatever the greeting, it was usually expressed with insight. There were those who, by emphasizing the mercantile contribution, could justify the new arrangements in brilliant terms, such as the authors of the *Federalist Papers*, a classic of mercantile thought and of the most sincere, deeply reasoned, and, for lack of a better word, noble rationalizations for a political system ever written. For those who found the new arrangements intolerable—a Bonald or de Maistre in France, a Stahl in Germany—the ideas they put together to condemn it, while so conservative as to be almost ludicrous, were so well reasoned that they can still be read with admiration. It was this tendency to combine political passion with political theory that had been undermined by the rise and fall of the Accumulative State, which offered its citizens maxims rather than syllogisms and its defenders pragmatism rather than principles. Still, the tradition had been so well ingrained that even by the latter part of the century enough remained to produce a Mill or a Bagehot. But, reading their works, it also becomes clear that political thought was changing, that missing was a power of abstract analysis, an imagination, a passion, even a hatred of something. And they were the best; by the end of the century political theory, while it had not disappeared, was becoming an academic specialty, no longer the product of men whose vocation was itself politics and whose values and desires were incorporated into their work. Earlier in the century Madison was both a thinker and a President; had he lived at the end of the century, he would have had to make a choice.

The reason for this decline is not hard to find. There can be no political theory without a conception of the political.[72] One of the most significant accomplishments of the early philosophers of liberalism had been to posit a sharp break between the economy and the polity, one that was designed to enhance the role of the former but also had the consequence of strengthening the latter. Liberated from medieval mystification, a coherent conception of the political could develop in the struggles of the seventeenth, eighteenth, and nineteenth centuries. But liberalism always had an ambiguous attitude toward politics, and the full potential was never reached; instead, liberal writers began to apply the calculus of rational man to the political realm as well, thereby destroying some of the very autonomy of politics that they had created. Hence the merger of a separate conception of the political into an economic conception of society was completed. When William E. Seward could define a political party as "in one sense a joint-stock company in which those who contribute the most direct the attention and the management of the concern,"[73] he was speaking for this tendency of the new class to substitute metaphors from the economy for political analysis and political vocabulary. Having destroyed an independent and autonomous conception of the political, the new bourgeoisie found it impossible to develop a specifically political theory.

Without a political theory there could be no political standards, and hence a transformation resulted in what was considered proper political conduct. I have reviewed the situation in the U.S. land office as a change from the mercantilism of Gallatin to the more capitalist Jacksonians, in which land was no longer considered a valuable asset of the nation but had become part of the maximization of greed. This trend continued throughout all of American government, as a comparison of Leonard White's book on the federalist theory of public administration with that of the Jacksonians makes clear.[74] In a word, capitalism, at least in the United States had no consistent concept of public administration. (England was different; there the rise of the Administrative Reform Association, plus the Benthamite concern with a constitutional code, underscored the preoccupation of a new class with matters of administration.)[75] But in America the absence of a public administration was ideological; since the state was not supposed to be used, even though it was being used, it made little sense to professionalize the task of administering it. For the theorists of laissez-faire to have developed a conception of public administration would have been to admit that the state was indeed playing a role in the economy, and this they were unwilling to do. Consequently the promotion of uniform standards of justice, criteria for government service, and rules for dispensing public largesse had been passed over in favor of a spoils system that allowed the strongest to take control of administration for their own private ends. This was so clear in the United States because the victory of the bourgeoisie was so thorough; there was little of an aristocracy around to mute these tendencies in favor of a bureaucratic (and despotic) class trained one way or another to reflect some idea of the public interest. Having control of the state, the bourgeoisie allowed it to fall out of control. "There is no politics in politics,"[76] James Bryce had said about the United States, meaning that lack of a political theory and political standards had made the American state resemble a free market in which personnel, procedure, and policy were sold to the highest bidder. Given a free hand, industrialists had created a state exactly in their own image, and the few notables shuddered and wrote novels such as *Democracy*.

Having corrupted definitions, theories, and standards, it comes as no surprise that the most noteworthy legacy of pure capitalist rule was political corruption in general. Control of the state would facilitate the reaping of short-term plunder. Policies would be judged on the profits they made and the self-interests they advanced. The exercise of power would be unrefined, direct, and not particularly subtle. The idea was succinctly expressed by Frederick Townsend Martin in his widely read book, *The Passing of the Idle Rich:*

> The class I represent cares nothing for politics. . . . We are not politicians or public thinkers; we are the rich; we own America; we got it, God knows how, but we intend to keep it if we can by throwing all the tremendous weight of our support, our influence, our money, our political connection, our purchased senators, our hungry congressmen, our public-speaking demagogues, into the scale against any legislature, any political platform, any Presidential campaign that threatens the integrity of our estate.[77]

Martin makes clear that business and politics were to be merged on the terms of the former, so that the corruption inherent in the one—bribes, payoffs, cheating on contracts—would be extended in wholesale fashion to the other. As Lincoln Steffens confessed in his *Autobiography:* "What Boston suggested to me was the idea that business and politics must be one; that it was natural, inevitable, and—possibly—right that business should—by bribery, corruption, or somehow—get and be the government."[78] One of the most significant sources of state activity during this period, then, was not the laws passed but the bribes exchanged, not the decisions rendered but the payoffs made. The political practices of the Harmonious State were more under the table than over it.

Corruption has been part of politics as long as some can profit at the expense of others, so the industrial bourgeoisie was hardly discovering a unique thing. What was new during this period was not the existence of corruption but the form it took. As James Scott has argued, corruption is most likely to occur when a class has achieved economic power without corresponding political power.[79] Under such circumstances, denied access to formal government, such a group will create its own informal one that by its very nature is not the legal government, and such an informal system will be juridically defined as corrupt. It is for this reason, he argues, that the venality of office under the *ancien régime* was so extensive or that Stuart England was filled with corruption. The analysis is a good one, for it was precisely because this condition did not exist during the Gilded Age that its corruption was so unique. The industrial bourgeoisie, holding both economic and political power, had no complex need for an informal system of government. Its corruption was for one reason only: pure plunder, the sheer profit of the thing. Thus, the scale of corruption accompanying the triumph of the bourgeoisie was unprecedented in modern history. The same expansionary vision and engineering genius that could lead a group of men to realize that it was possible to build a canal right through the center of Central America led those same men, in France, to develop a system of illegal plunder vast in scope, impressive in its ramifications, brilliant in its complexity.[80] This was genius, corruption with a vision, not the parochial selling of office characteristic of precapitalist society. The corruption of boroughs had become the corruption of empires and rotten boroughs had become rotten states. A class that was revolutionizing the factors of production was also revolutionizing the structure of graft.

Laissez-faire and vast corruption go well together; the periods of the greatest success of the one also saw the greatest amount of the other. Just before the Panama Canal scandal the new bourgeoisie had shown that nothing was as sacred to it as money, not even national honor, when it was discovered that the French Legion of Honor had been bought and sold like an ordinary piece of merchandise. Deputies, in a popular saying of the day, came to Paris *"moins pour servir que se servir"* (less to serve than to be served). This was even more true of Italy, where the record is outstanding:

> 1892: The Bank of Rome scandal, called by Hentze "the worst known scandal in the history of Italian public life";[81]
>
> 1902: The Merchant Marine scandal, which revealed almost as much graft as the Bank of Rome affair;
>
> 1903: The selling of the state-run railway lines (part of the perennial Italian search for a solution to the railway problem) for enormous sums, lining the pockets of private investors with money from the public treasury;
>
> 1904–1907: The affair of ex–Education Minister Nasi, in which the entire Education Department was found to involve "an intricate and permanent system of . . . corruption";[82]
>
> 1912: The Rome Hall of Justice scandal, in which the foundations of an important public building were lined with graft.

Capitalism had arrived late in Italy but with it came corruption on so great a scale that the traditional family-based crime in the villages was made to seem like child's play. The system of *trasformismo*—rewarding political opponents by allowing them to share in the rewards of holding office in return for their support—had, as Whyte suggests,[83] inevitably led to new depths of corrupt politics, that still exist in Italian political life.[84]

Political corruption in this period seemed to be a world-wide affair. The financial scandal known as the *Gründungsschwindel* was a product of large-scale profit taking at the expense of the petite bourgeoisie, so that it not only was a German variant of the new corruption, but it also fueled middle-class resentment against "Jewish" bankers.[85] The rule of Salisbury and Chamberlain in England was marked by frequent scandal: the Liberty Building Society affair of 1893, the New Zealand Loan Company fraud of 1898, and the Hooley affair of 1898 all involved the direct purchase of political influence.[86] Not much need be added about the scale of corruption in the United States, where graft and politics became synonymous. Aside from the ordinary daily life of local political machines, there was a direct line between Grant and Harding that tied together the Republican

Party, large capital, and political scandal. Crédit Mobilier and Teapot Dome are two peaks at each end of the period, but the hills in between were steep in their own right. Having won a legal battle to obtain state power, the new bourgeoisie proceeded to use it in the most illegal ways.

It is important to emphasize that the concurrence between laissez-faire and political corruption was not accidental but in fairly strict accord with the theory and practice of the Harmonious State. First, since the state was theoretically supposed to do very little, but since it was actually doing a great deal, a situation of mystification was established in which a gap between political appearance and political reality came into being. This gap would have tremendous consequences (see Chapter 5), but for the moment it became impossible to develop a reasonable and coherent set of standards of honest political conduct. The lack of a theory of public administration and the existence of corruption were two sides of the same process. Or, phrasing the same point another way, corruption *was* the theory of public administration. In the absence of formal mechanisms, informal ones became the rule, and the latter, not the former, became a guide to the theory and practice of the state. Thus the wisdom of a George Washington Plunkett can be read as a textbook in the public administration of the period, a more accurate account of what was taking place than the academic writings of a John W. Burgess or a Francis Leiber. There was, however, at least one man who understood all this at the time, the Russian-born, French-speaking political scientist Maurice Ostrogorski. Concluding his analysis of the system of political machines, Ostrogorski explained their success by noting that in the United States a dual set of standards and expectations had developed. Capitalism had been so successful that its view of the world invaded, and then triumphed in, the political realm. "The stronghold of the general interest, the State was invaded on all sides by money." As a result,

> in all the States where the industrial and financial corporations are numerous, the Machine and the boss, fed with their money as with a sap, flourish like a luxuriant plant that overshadows the whole public life. In these States, where the machine is supreme, republican institutions are in truth but an idle form, a plaything wherewith to beguile children.[87]

Relegated to the status of a "form," cut off by the formality of laissez-faire from a healthy recognition of its own potential, the state was a government in name only. In the gap between what it could be and what it was, corruption was allowed to flourish, for illegal activities grow best when expectations are unclear.

A second general reason for the coincidence between political corruption and the popularity of laissez-faire lay in the changing political strategy of the bourgeoisie. The political thrust of the Accumulative State had been an aggressive one, the active search for methods of utilizing the public treasury to facilitate the accumulation of capital. This direction was continued under the Harmonious State but added to it was a new tone, that of preventing any other group from using the state for the same purpose. In a letter to Burke Hinsdale explaining the problems he was having as an advisor to President Grant, James Garfield expressed it this way: "We had somewhat of a struggle to keep him from drifting into that foolish notion that it was necessary to make large appropriations on public works to give employment to laborers. But the Secretary of the Treasury and I united our forces in dissuading him from the scheme, insisting that the true remedy for the finances at present was economy and retrenchment, until business restored itself."[88] It is no coincidence that a President so easily manipulated on questions of social policy would be so easily manipulated on questions of graft, for the structure of a political system like the American was much more oriented toward concentrating preventing power in one person, just as it dispersed facilitating power to many; that is, in order to pass laws, one must be able to influence many legislators, and it is not always possible to bribe every one of them. But in order to prevent laws from being passed, one need control only a single person, so long as he occupies a crucial position, and if that person is weak, like Grant, or corrupt, like many legislative committee chairmen of this period, controlling him becomes that much easier. Thus there has been a correlation between periods of active state energy and little formal corruption, and another between negative action and gargantuan political corruption. Since the period of laissez-faire was part of the latter tendency, its corruption should not be surprising.

Finally, the contradiction between liberal and democratic political conceptions facilitated the growth of corruption. What was perfectly appropriate behavior for maximizing profit, the ultimate justification for liberal society, could be nefarious if done in the public sector where the public interest, the ultimate justification for democratic society, became a factor. Much of the bewilderment voiced by businessmen as their corrupt practices were publicized was probably genuine, for they could easily become confused about which set of standards were being applied where. Since the country was great, and business was what made the country great, one should expect to be rewarded, not pilloried, for using the state to make profit. But as democratic values began to advance during this period, as conceptions of morality changed, there were few guidelines about what was proper and what was not. Thus another of those gaps was created that permitted corruption to grow. Because the high point of the Harmonious State was both the ultimate victory of the liberal state but also the first stage in its decline, it was likely to see both high levels of political corruption and a strong revulsion against those very levels.

The net result of all these tendencies was a contradiction in the political practices of the Harmonious State that matched its theoretical contradictions. Corruption, in a word, began to undermine the very capitalistic values it was designed to fulfill. If profit by any means necessary was one part of business enterprise, order, predictability, and reliability were others, and they were being discarded for a system of graft. The more corrupt some elements of the bourgeoisie became, the more serious became other elements about eliminating graft and creating a "clean" system. An active group of industrial statesmen came into being who believed that business-men should indeed control the state, but in order to serve everyone, not just themselves. In the long run, industrial values would be preserved if the political system were reformed to ensure its honest and relatively im-partial administration. Consequently the new industrialists, having won state power, slowly began to split into two groups on the question of re-form. As early as 1868, for example, the National Manufacturers Associa-tion had supported the Jenckes Civil Service Reform Bill in the United States:

> Resolved, that for the integrity and permanence of our Government, it is indispensable that public affairs be conducted on business principles, and that the dangerous custom of giving public posts to political paupers and partisan servants, regardless of their fitness, should be discontinued, as such custom absorbs a large share of the public revenue, and thus imposes a useless and grievous burden on the people, tends to growing demoraliza-tion in public and private character, destroying true freedom and bringing ruin at last.[89]

While some were plundering the Treasury in the Crédit Mobilier scandal, others were reforming executive departments: Wanamaker in the Post Office, Whitney in the Navy, Elkins in War, Hitchcock in Interior. Around men such as these, and their allies in the university, an active public administration and civil service reform movement finally did begin. "The government does not govern,"[90] Henry Adams had said in 1870, and for that reason some of the more farsighted businessmen decided to dress up the state rather than to rape it. For these eminently practical men, who knew that the Harmonious State was a myth, the issue was simple: if they were going to use the state in order to preserve the legitimacy of their rule, they had better make sure that government could function. And since laissez-faire and corruption were so well linked, the elimination of corrup-tion became tied to an anti–laissez-faire perspective, one that wanted to use the state in order to alleviate class tensions as well as corruption. Thus a split in the ranks of the industrialists[91] corresponded with an intensifica-tion of class tensions throughout the society. The question of political re-form became an issue; the rise of an interest in reform and the decline of the Harmonious State were interconnected. Corruption and class bias, which had given the Harmonious State its life, became responsible for its death.

THE PASSING OF THE ACTIVE RICH

The same years (from 1890 to World War I) that witnessed the triumph of laissez-faire thought also saw the first sustained attempt to bring about reform under the political rule of the bourgeoisie. An attempt must be made to assess the character of this reform before a discussion of the Harmonious State can be concluded, for political reform was to become one of the most pressing issues of twentieth-century politics, and its origins can be traced to the decline of laissez-faire. Some very important events took place at the beginning of the new century. "The first decade of the [twentieth] century saw a great increase of State interference in economic and social life in Germany, Great Britain, and even the United States, no less than in Europe," David Thomson has written.[92] Yet his perspective, which is a common one, would seem from this analysis to be incorrect. Since under the Accumulative State governmental activity was omnipresent, and since the accumulative tendencies of the state increased throughout the last half of the century, political reform hardly meant an "increase" in state "interference." The state had always interfered with the economy, through all the devices listed above. But in another way this legislation was unique. For years other groups "below" businessmen had been trying to obtain state power in order to realize themselves as a class. Though the industrial bourgeoisie had fought these attempts, by the first decade of the century reforms were beginning to be realized nonetheless. Even a serious consideration of them, such as the sweeping Clemenceau proposals of 1907, was a victory for a new kind of politics, whether they were actually passed or not. Thus political reform meant a change, not in the object of state action but in the subject, not in character but in consistency. It was the same state, but it was being pointed in a new direction. Its class character was not being abolished but extended, its bias not eliminated but broadened.

The question of how much reform implied a new direction for the capitalist state is one of the most controversial points in contemporary historical research. The more orthodox position, that there was "an age of reform,"[93] in which disadvantaged groups used their greater numbers to win genuine changes in their lives, has been challenged by people like Gabriel Kolko for the United States and O. C. Moore for England, who argue that reforms were generally in the interest of some segment of the dominant class and only for that reason could have been passed.[94] The debate has been a vigorous one, yet both sides seem more interested in winning points for their own political perspectives than in understanding the politics of the period. The key point about fin-de-siècle reform is that for so long no reforms had been passed. What Agostino Depretis had said about international affairs could apply equally to the domestic politics of the Harmonious State: "When I see an international question on the horizon, I open my umbrella and wait until it has passed."[95] Insofar as there was an approach to reform under the Harmonious State it was based on what Italians called the *morphia* theory of social policy, giving the body enough injections to keep it barely alive; the relevant cliché was *prevenire per non ripremere,* or "anticipate in order to avoid repression." Yet, with all this delay, it followed that when the moment social conditions became so bad that they could no longer be ignored, Depretis' umbrella would be trying to hold back a flood. So much reform legislation was passed during these years only because to little was passed in previous years. Two consequences followed: first, the reforms of 1900–10 were a response not to social conditions of that period but to the period 1860–80; second, the passage of reform legislation was inevitably eclectic, responsive to many different kinds of problems. There was, in short, no political reform but many political reforms, each of which had a distinct character. The class basis of legislation cannot be analyzed in the abstract but must be based on the kind of reform in question. In order to facilitate an understanding of the meaning of political reform during this period, I will divide the legislation into three fairly distinct categories: rationalizing reforms, repressive reforms, and responsive reforms.[96]

Rationalizing reforms are those that attempt to improve and make workable the structure of the state. They do not shift the relative power of social classes within the society, nor do they alter the class that benefits from state activity. The conflicts over laws of this sort are within, not between, classes, though one faction or another may turn outside its immediate class for support. The reform of the civil service, a major political issue in the United States in the latter half of the nineteenth century, is a good example. Since some businessmen benefited from the "spoils system" while others fought for its abolition, the struggle over the passage and enforcement of laws like the Pendleton Act (1887) was part of the developing split within the new industrial ruling class. Those who favored laissez-faire were often the most tolerant of the kinds of corruption that the Pendleton Act and later the Hatch Act tried to eliminate. For example, Richard Olney, the Attorney General who personified the ideal of the state official creating a government of, by, and for the large corporations (it was Olney who had urged railways to control rather than oppose "regulatory" commissions like the ICC),[97] ruled in 1902 that letters by party officials "requesting" contributions of up to 2 percent of salary from post office employees was not "solicitation" as defined by the Pendleton Act.[98] To maintain that such solicitation was not solicitation was as difficult as the attempt by the Supreme Court seven years earlier to maintain that manufacturing was not commerce. If mass loyalty to the system was to be won, such flights of rhetorical imagination had to be curbed. A younger generation of reformers had been challenging perspectives like Olney's in organizations such as the National Civil Service Reform League or, within the state, in the Civil Service Commission. In fact, this latter body became notorious for its zeal when its effective leadership passed into the hands of a young man who symbolized everything that laissez-faire, and Richard Olney, was not. Theodore Roosevelt stood for presidential rather than congressional leadership, reform rather than reaction, long-range rather than short-run perspectives, and a class rather than a parochial perspective for those who were to run the society. The passage of power from the Olneys to the Roosevelts was indicative of what was taking place.

It has been suggested that "the government could not have supported the tasks that the country imposed on it in the twentieth century without the stable, competent, and responsible public service which the Pendleton Act made possible."[99] Herein lies the importance of rationalizing reforms during this period. There was active government during the Accumulative State, but its activity was often spontaneous, unplanned, even chaotic. This pattern continued through the Harmonious State since the ideology of laissez-faire did not permit the imposition of standards. But in the twentieth century the character, if not the amount, of state activity underwent a change. The development of large monopolies, each with control over some particular sector of the economy, suggested a "standoff," a situation where each one accepted the legitimacy of the other's control over its sector in return for an exclusive right to control its own. (All this will be developed in detail in chapters 4 and 5.) The key term that men like Roosevelt used in the struggle over civil service reform was the "political neutrality of the State," and it is an excellent expression of the major issues involved in reforms of this kind. Given a standoff, the optimal role for the state is a neutral one; it could operate only in the general interests of all if it no longer represented the specific interests of any. To be a class state, it could no longer be the state of any specific group or of individuals within the class. Rationalizing reforms, by streamlining the state in this direction, were part of the growth of a class perspective on the part of the industrialists. They are the classic example of reforms that serve the interests of a dominant group, even if some formerly powerful individuals have to lose something.

Much more complex are repressive and responsive reforms. Unlike rationalizing ones, both of these involve inter-, as well as intra-, class relations. Both are products of the development of a working class, since both raise the question of what reaction those now in control of the state would have toward this large mass of people who suddenly began to fill up the cities and the industrial towns. But from this point they differ. *Repressive reforms* are those passed over the protests of the majority class, designed to keep them members of a dominated class, even though they may contain monetary or other "benefits." *Responsive reforms*, though not altering in a major sense the political-economic framework of the society, are those that the working class managed, through their control over the democratic aspects of the state, to have passed over the delaying tactics of those un-accustomed to sharing state power. What sounds simple is in fact complicated, for both kinds of reform could often be embodied in the same, or very similar, laws. Thus, Maurice Bruce includes both education and wages and hours as examples of the "coming of the welfare state."[100] Yet these two kinds of laws cannot conceivably be discussed under the same rubric; although both appear to be "progressive" changes that improved the quality of life for large numbers of people, one was repressive, the other was essentially responsive.

There was a veritable flood of laws concerning education in the last years of the nineteenth century, as one country after another established state-run schooling systems, made education required, and reformed curricula to coincide with the needs of an industrial society. Although generally interpreted as meaningful change, because they gave "learning" to people who otherwise would not have obtained it, these laws were also likely to have had both repressive intentions and consequences. For one thing, in the United States, England, and France, passage of educational reform was opposed, and fought bitterly, by the few working-class organizations that existed. The reason was not hard to find. As Henry Pelling wrote about England, "There was nothing 'bourgeois' about this popular distrust of state intervention [into education]. On the contrary, it can readily be associated with the view of the state taken by Marxists, that it was an organization run by and for the benefit of the wealthy."[101] From the perspective of the working class, both the supporters of educational reform and the ideas they brought with them could only produce suspicion. Among those at the top of the social structure, educational reform was an idea whose time had come. In the United States, as Katz, Bowles and Gintis, Spring, and others have shown, earlier in the century men like Horace Mann had seen the link between "public education" and the need for work discipline, a link that was strengthened at the beginning of the new century.[102] England's Lord Percy could call elementary schools "finishing schools for manual workers."[103] while in 1905 a member of Parliament said to his colleagues:

> The future of the Empire, the triumph of social progress, and the freedom of the British race depend not so much upon the strengthening of the army as upon fortifying the children of the State for the battle of life.[104]

In France, Jules Ferry, the man who had won Indochina for France and who became the Third Republic's personification of the bourgeoisie in power, made educational reform his key issue. In an 1892 letter to all the primary school teachers, Ferry spoke of the need "to prepare a generation of good citizens for our country," and he included the following encomiums as his recommendations for the moral elevation of all children between eleven and thirteen:

1. The family: duties of parents and children; reciprocal duties of masters and servants; the family spirit.

2. Society: necessity and benefits of society. Justice, the condition of all society. Solidarity and human brotherhood. Alcoholism destroys these sentiments little by little by destroying the mainspring of will and of personal responsibility.

Application and development of the idea of justice; respect for human life and liberty; respect for property; respect for the pledged word; respect for the honor and reputation of others. Probity, equity, loyalty, delicacy. Respect for the opinions and beliefs held by others.

Applications and development of the idea of love or brotherhood. Its varying degrees; duties of benevolence, gratitude, tolerance, mercy, etc. Self-sacrifice, the highest form of love; show that it can find a place in everyday life.

3. The fatherland: what a man owes his country: obedience to law, military service, discipline, devotion, fidelity to the flag. Taxes (condemnation of fraud towards the State). The ballot: a moral obligation, which should be free, conscientious, disinterested, enlightened. Rights which correspond to these duties: personal freedom, liberty of conscience, freedom of contact and the right to work, right to organize. Guarantee of the security of life and property to all. National sovereignty. Explanation of the motto of the Republic: Liberty, Equality, Fraternity.[105]

Ferry's letter illustrates the complexity of educational reform. On the one hand, his recognition of the right to organize was a progressive step, a meaningful alteration of the unmediated class bias of traditional capitalist politics. But, on the other, his conception of education is one stressing obedience and respect for the order that men like himself were going to lead. For men like these, compulsory education run by the state was passed in part for the same reason that police forces were improved or radical agitation prohibited—to ensure class subordination.

To this point those who have argued that reforms were in the interests of the dominant groups have won the arguments, but their attitude does not apply to all the reforms, and to make it seem so is to engage in the most labyrinthic kind of reasoning. For it was during this period that the extension of democracy became a revolutionary idea, that the notion took hold that popular classes could use the democratic aspects of the state in order to further their class interests just as elites had used the liberal aspects for the same purpose. As a result, some reforms were passed which those in power did not want, which they fought hard to stop, and on which they lost. Such reforms were responsive to the democratic, not the liberal, element within the state. For that very reason, passage of them was neither smooth nor complete, yet they were victories for popular rule that fundamentally altered the beneficiaries of state action. This point can be made by an examination of wage and hour legislation, using the British case as the example where the issues were most clearly posed.

Unlike education the wage and hour question touched the businessman at the heart of his enterprise, his control over the wage bargain. Whereas state support for schools could be rationalized under the doctrines of the Harmonious State—education promotes mutual understanding between classes—minimum wages or maximum hours could not; instead, they grew out of a deliberate attack on the harmony-of-interests doctrine. When such laws were passed, they symbolized both the passing of laissez-faire ideology and the rise of a democratic element within the capitalist state. Unlike educational reform, the struggle over wages and hours was bitter, with industrialists opposed and workers in favor. A bill to limit the working day of miners—none disagreed that conditions were awful—was first introduced in the House of Commons as early as 1888, but it took twenty years before any legislation on this subject was passed.[106] It was finally passed during a strike that threatened the entire economy, sponsored by a prime minister who indicated his "great reluctance" to introduce such a bill, and it was then declared to be only "a provisional and . . . experimental measure to meet a special emergency in regard to a particular class of workers working under peculiar conditions in one great industry."[107] In spite of this caution, the law for miners eventually did become a precedent for other workers as well, and the eight-hour-day ultimately became a reality, although it "had to be won in England by those very piecemeal industrial methods which had earlier secured the nine hour day."[108] As difficult as it was to bring about, responsive reform was possible.

The Miners' Eight Hours Bill changed more than working conditions; it also provided the evidence for the bankruptcy of the Harmonious State. Businessmen in the 1906–1909 period were still committed to neoclassical orthodoxy; the reigning spokesman for industrialists was A. C. Pigou, who preached that a finite "wage fund" existed such that any raise for one group of workers automatically meant a decrease for others. Under this "iron law," Pigou argued, the only hope for labor was to increase its productive capacity, for only greater profits could mean higher wages.[109] Once again the interests of capitalists and workers were held to be the same, and on the former's terms, but now the earlier rhetoric of harmoniousness had acquired a "scientific" veneer, clothed with the precision of modern economics. Surprisingly, harmonious doctrines like this were subscribed to by labor leaders at the time. The Trade Union Congress had proven itself extremely wary of enforced collective bargaining in the first decade of the century, expressing the same distrust of the state that emerged in the realm of educational reform.[110] Furthermore, the Fabians, who originated many of the ideas contained in the Eight Hours Bill, wanted it applied only to a small number of industries, rejecting a counterproposal to include all workers except those who voted to exempt themselves.[111] The significance of the passage of hours legislation is that it changed both positions, that of the employers as well as that of labor. To be sure, some businessmen preached laissez-faire to the end, following the exemplary conduct of the legendary Colonel Sipthorp, who had refused to ride the railways all his life because their system of financing made them "socialist."[112] Rigid attitudes like his began to sound old-fashioned; the *Railway Review* spoke for a new generation: "To realize the full meaning of the miners' strike and to prepare ourselves for such changes in authority and practice as it implies, ought to be our first duties."[113] Labor leaders were changing as well. Aware that the power of the state could make real changes in people's lives, and under pressure from rank-and-file members and radicals in the labor movement, men like Ramsay MacDonald began to move ever so cautiously to the left, dropping their opposition to state-supervised collective bargaining. Even the Fabians changed; a 1911 pamphlet on profit sharing written by E. R. Pease explicitly rejected "harmony" as the basis of class relations.[114] It had become clear, as Sir George Askwith said in a 1911 memo to the cabinet on how to control labor unrest:

> The Victorian theories as to Capital and Labour have become obsolete, but no settled doctrine has taken their place. There is therefore a disposition to try to see things from the point of view of the workman, and to wonder not that he is discontented but that he has remained patient so long.[115]

It would take twenty or thirty years before new doctrines would emerge to replace the harmoniousness of Victorianism, a story to be told below (see Chapter 4).

After passage of the Miners' Bill, Sir Edward Grey expressed his unease that "a door has been opened with regard to the minimum wage which cannot be closed again."[116] The foot-in-the-door mentality of the British ruling class was a sign of the precariousness of their theory of the state, for, as we have seen, the Harmonious State could not admit even the slightest tampering before being revealed as class based and class biased. Thus political reform, whether rationalizing, repressive, or responsive, created nothing but pain for the Harmonious State. The industrialists, having only recently come to power, could choose one of two options. First, they could fight a last-ditch battle against change; the trouble was that if they lost, they lost completely. As an anonymous "Yorkshire liberal" had noted in 1908: "Once a wage is conceded beyond the economic value of the labour as a moral right . . . you cannot stop at any particular figure but give away the whole case against socialism."[117] The gentleman was undoubtedly correct, for by basing its rationale on the existence of an inherent social harmony that would be the unintended consequence of the pursuit of self-interest, theorists of the bourgeois state had become entrapped. If any role for the state in matters like wages were conceded, the entire justificatory apparatus of laissez-faire liberalism, like a house of playing cards, would fall with one, even very slight, modification. Given that, a second alternative was more feasible: to admit the need for reform but, as much as possible, to sponsor reform in the interests of the dominant groups. In *Die Hilfe*, written in 1904, the German liberal Friedrich Naumann had said, "The whole future of Liberalism taken in its widest sense depends on its frankly and openly acknowledging its class bias for only a class conscious liberalism has the strength to survive in these days of general class warfare."[118] Naumann's suggestion was, by and large, adopted in just about every country, but with it came a new problem. A class-conscious liberalism enabled the industrialists to remain in power, but it did so at the expense of sacrificing the Harmonious State ideology. Harmony of interest was based on the explicit statement that all classes had the same interests; to adopt an open class perspective was to put the final nail in the coffin of that system of ideas. It was the bourgeoisie that eventually lost faith in its own ideology of harmoniousness, just as workers had earlier. The Harmonious State served the bourgeoisie well as it tried to break into a political system dominated by prebourgeois elements; it worked passably well while no real challenges existed; but it could not work at all once the working class discovered that it too had a class interest which the use of the state could help satisfy. It was when both sides realized the truth of this, sometime around World War I, that the search for alternatives to the Harmonious State intensified.

3 / Dilemmas of Expansionism

"The question which now preemptorily challenges all thinking minds is how to create a foreign demand for those manufacturers which are left after supplying home demands. . . . This question appeals equally to the selflessness and patriotism of all our citizens, but to the laborer it appeals with tenfold force, for without work he cannot live, and unless we can extend the markets for our manufacturers he cannot expect steady work, and unless our manufacturers can undersell foreign manufacturers, we cannot enlarge our foreign market."

William E. Evarts, to the New York
City Chamber of Commerce (1877)

"The protective system is a steam engine without a safety valve if it does not have as a corrective and auxiliary a healthy and serious colonial policy. . . . The economic crisis which has weighed so heavily on industrial Europe since 1876 or 1877, the misfortune that has followed it and from which the frequent, long, and ill-advised strikes that have arisen are the most unhappy symptoms, has coincided in France, in Germany, and even in England with a notable and persistent decline in the figure of exports. . . . European consumption is saturated; one must move out into other parts of the globe for new classes of consumers, under pain of throwing modern society into bankruptcy."

Jules Ferry (1890)

"For us it is a question of life or death whether there awakens in the broad masses of our people a consciousness that in the long run only the expansion of German power can create employment at home and the possibility of further ascent. The fate of replacements from below is indissolubly linked to the rise of Germany to the position of a political and economic world power, to the power and greatness of the Fatherland."

Max Weber (1896)

TOWARD THE END of the nineteenth century a wave of expansionism broke out all over the capitalist world, as country after country sought to extend its influence around the globe. While foreign conquest is as old as the ancient Egyptian and Greek civilizations, there was something unique about this late-nineteenth-century burst of activity. On the one hand, neither simple accumulation nor spurious notions of harmony were able to justify the new capitalist order to all, causing real problems of legitimation. On the other hand, the contradictions between the liberal and democratic world views were reaching their peak around 1890, making it seem as if the polity were about to burst. Faced with this dual pressure, ruling classes turned to foreign expansion as a solution to domestic problems. A wide variety of experiments, collectively designated in this chapter as the Expansionist State, came into being, each designed to alleviate the conflict between the need to accumulate and the desire to legitimate. But these alternatives could be considered only at a price: a denial of some of the basic values of liberalism itself. In this chapter I will consider some of these expansionist alternatives and the effects that their adoption had on liberal ideology.

EXPANSION AND THE LIBERAL DEMOCRATIC CONFLICT

Late-nineteenth-century expansionism arose in a hostile environment. The mercantilist world order had been explicitly colonialist, and insofar as the original impetus for industrial capitalism was a critique of the mercantile mentality, there is truth in Schumpeter's contention that capitalism is anti-imperialist, at least in origin.[1] Certainly the liberal political thought that accompanied the rise of the new bourgeoisie was explicit on this question.[2] Adam Smith heaped scorn on the search for new markets in raw materials, calling policies based on the acquisition of silver and gold "perhaps the most disadvantageous lottery in the world" and damning the "folly and injustice" that characterized European colonial ventures. But the real problem for him was that colonialism was generally undertaken by state-regulated monopolies:

> The monopoly of the colony trade, therefore, like all the other mean and malignant expedients of the mercantile system, depressed the industry of all other countries, but chiefly that of the colonies, without in the least increasing, but on the contrary diminishing, that of the country in whose favor it is established.[3]

Ricardo saw fit to quote this passage in defense of his position that colonial trade would result in "a worse distribution of the general capital and industry," meaning that "less will be produced."[4] Even as late as John Stuart Mill some antipathy to colonialism remained intact. Mill recognized that colonies were a fact of economic life, and therefore he shifted the argument by concluding that policies concerning them should be undertaken by the state, since their existence should redound to the interests of all, not just of a few. Mill wanted a "self-supporting system of colonization," and he leaned toward emigration rather than further colonization as the solution to domestic pressure. Even more important, Mill defended the concept of a stationary state. Economic growth, as an end in itself, is part of the idea of expansion, since gains in productivity could be a substitute for growth abroad. But Mill did not see the necessity. No growth, a stationary state, would for him "be, on the whole, a very considerable improvement over our present condition." [5] Liberal political economy was not inherently, or even implicitly, in favor of expansion.

Given this tradition, to sponsor an aggressive system of political expansion required rejection of a system of beliefs that was supposed to be honored and respected. For many industrialist-statesmen, there was a veritable *cri de coeur* as they faced a contradiction between their liberalism, which professed free trade and a hostility toward colonies, and their sense of survival, which told them that only through protective tariffs and imperialism could the loyalty of the working class be won (at the same time ensuring that a surplus of manufactures could be absorbed). While the situation seemed difficult, precedent for a resolution was at hand. Liberalism, as we have seen, was both dogmatic and infinitely flexible; if a point had to be stretched in order to preserve capitalist hegemony, then a point would be stretched. Just as liberal theory preached the doctrine of a minimal state but accepted a goodly amount of state intervention, the anti-imperialist bias could be blurred by the simple device of changing one's mind. Jules Ferry, at one time an ardent free trader, came under the influence of Méline and eventually supported high tariffs. Joseph Chamberlain, whose growing discontent with the Gladstonian emphasis on free trade and opposition to colonialism was becoming more acute, broke with the Liberal Party and formed the Unionists, who became indistinguishable from the Conservatives. Although the ostensible issue that led to formation of the new party was the preservation of the union with Ireland, Chamberlain's sense that protection was necessary was a major issue as well. Even Bismarck, who was hardly a liberal, felt the same contradiction, since the program he was sponsoring was aimed at winning the support of the industrialists. Although he could say, in 1881, that "as long as I am Chancellor we will carry on no colonial policies," [6] he was at the very same time preparing the ground for German expansion into the Middle East and Africa. In this area, as in so many others, the liberals and those like Bismarck who adopted their programs showed their lack of a consistent theory of the state, their willingness to follow any policy, no matter how much it might contradict previous policies, if it appeared to be in their class interest.

Men like these changed their minds because they had gradually become aware that it was difficult for the state to act in liberal fashion vis-à-vis the accumulation of capital and yet also be responsive to the growth of a majoritarian working class. Two kinds of events crystallized this understanding. The difficulties of accumulation were symbolized by the first sustained capitalist economic crisis. The world-wide depression of 1873 was a preliminary indication that the rise to power of industrialists did not mean an economic paradise in which all classes would share harmoniously in the newly found prosperity. It would be impossible to overestimate the effect that the depression of 1873 had on the political leaders of the time, for it made clear to them that both their traditional economic and political analyses might be wrong. Desperate to find out what had happened, political elites everywhere experimented with new policies. Countries that were protectionist began to explore the advantages of free trade; others that were committed to free trade began to consider higher tariffs; still others that had no colonies sought to obtain them. A few examples can illustrate the breadth of this search. In the United States, the reigning orthodoxy was still that of Henry Carey, whose program of protectionism had been adopted in toto by the Republican Party. Overwhelmed by the effects of 1873, new ideas began to emerge. David Wells, who became for the Democrats what Carey was for the Republicans, argued that the surplus of production over demand could be reduced only through foreign trade, and hence tariffs had to be lowered in order to encourage other nations to do likewise.[7] While the depressions of the 1870s did not produce a full-scale demand for a British empire, they did, as Robinson and Gallagher point out, produce a felt need "to consolidate the existing empire of trade." [8] It was only after this attempt at consolidation failed that England experimented with protection with the same combination of timidity and boldness that the United States showed in flirting with free trade.

Other countries were also shaken up. Mary Townsend has pointed out that for Germany right after the struggle for unification, "The terrible crisis and panic of 1873 resulted. The necessity of financial recuperation was widely felt, and when conditions proved too narrow at home for capital and labor, the opportunity for expansion abroad was regarded favorably." [9] This point has been seconded by Hans-Ulrich Wehler, who has argued that the three depressions of 1873–79, 1882–86, and 1890–95 resulted in "an extremely difficult, structural crisis in the development of the modern industrial system," one that could be solved only through what he insightfully calls "pragmatic expansionism." [10] Finally, one year after the depression of 1873, Paul Leroy-Beaulieu published his widely read *De la colonisation chez les peuples modernes*. "The most useful function which colonies perform . . . is to supply the mother country's trade with a ready-made market to get its industries going and maintain it, and to supply the inhabitants of the other country—whether as industrialists, workers, or consumers—with increased profits, wages, or commodities," [11] he wrote, an assertion given extra force by the economic hardships of the period. The Tunisian expedition was one of the many results of the new attitude.

If depression stands as a symbol of the declining strength of the liberal promise that everything will turn out right in the long run, strikes represented the second series of events that led to a change of mind about expansion. The international development of working-class pressure became the symbolic representation of the rise of democratic demands. France had its Commune (1871) and the United States what Bruce called its "year of violence" (1877).[12] In Italy the number of strikes has been estimated as 132 in 1860–69, 553 in 1870–79, 752 in 1880–89, and 1,698 in 1890–99, a dramatic indication of the new sentiment.[13] Bismarck found he needed stringent antisocialist laws, and even in England, where the working class was not revolutionary in approach, its demands had a revolutionary potential; as Halévy has pointed out, they "amounted to a form of socialism. For they implied that the worker possessed a right to the produce of his labour before any claim by the employer could be entertained." [14] As depression produced new economic theories, in other words, strikes were responsible for new political ones. Thomas Power has pointed out how the Franco-Prussian War and the Commune "tremendously affected the outlook of men like Ferry. They were profoundly shocked. The crushing defeat of France in the War destroyed their hopes of a peaceful, liberal world; and the uprising of the Commune their confidence in the lower classes. Militarism was to be a key note of their generation, and to blight their bright hopes." [15] Walter Quintin Gresham, who during the violence of 1877 was a federal judge in Illinois, was devastated by the strikes of that year. "Our revolutionary fathers," he confided with great insight, "went too far with their notions of popular government. *Democracy is now the enemy of law and order*." [16] Sixteen years later Gresham would become Secretary of State and, more moderate in his politics, would urge a policy of free trade imperialism as a solution to class conflict. Sir William Ashley, while a student in the United States, witnessed the Homestead and Pullman strikes in the 1890s and returned to England so upset that he toyed with corporatist notions that would become quite attractive to ruling elites in the twentieth century (see Chapter 4).[17] The combined effect of economic depression and worker aggressiveness, one feeding the other, was enough to make any but the blindest aware of the need for new solutions to the tensions between liberalism and democracy.

There was little consensus about what to do as liberalism and democracy began to collide, because liberal political rule had been eclectic for so long. Thus, in reaction to the depression, some were convinced free traders and others protectionists, some imperialists and others anti-imperialists. In reaction to working-class militancy, some became paternalistic reformers, others believed in generous doses of repression, and still others, the majority, combined both. Yet, whether the politicians of the period moved to the right or to the left, what united free traders and fair traders, imperialists and anti-imperialists, reformers and repressors was their belief that expansion, of one form or another, was the solution to the increasingly urgent political contradictions of the period. Though differing on questions of technique, and sometimes allowing those differences to spill over into intraclass warfare, all sides within the ruling classes believed in the same ultimate goal, which was somehow to expand the universe of political action so that enough room could be provided for both liberal requirements (capital accumulation) and democratic expectations (legitimation).

Although an expanded system seemed to offer security, from the start this approach had its limitations. Expansion, despite its aggressive tone, was nothing else than a confession of failure. By going outside their borders, elites were confessing, even if unaware of it, that there were no answers left within them. There was no guarantee that what had failed at home could succeed abroad. As they began to understand that expansionism was a policy growing more out of weakness than out of strength, the ideologists of the Expansionist State became increasingly defensive and pessimistic in tone. The history of their solution is a series of attempts to avoid the inevitable, combined with a growing realization that the inevitable was about to happen.

TECHNIQUES OF EXPANSIONISM

Expansionism and colonialism are not the same thing; the search for colonies, the most dramatic form taken by the expansionist urges of the late nineteenth century, was only one option among many. Liberal rule was in general far too pragmatic to put all its faith in one form of expansionism only; solely in France was there a genuinely dogmatic attachment to the notion of colonialism as an end in itself. Everywhere else eclecticism was the rule or, to put it alternatively, dogmatic commitment to the idea of expansion combined with great flexibility as to means. Thus the empires brought into being in the period of imperialism were both formal and informal ones, and colonization was both a juridical category and a state of mind. The specific techniques adopted varied from one situation to another.

The eclecticism of expansion is illustrated by the fact that free trade, which theoretically should be the opposite of a policy of expansion, had, especially in England, been transformed into an imperialistic option. At one time early in the nineteenth century it was by no means taken for granted that the state would come to the aid of businessmen at home; one is reminded of the attaché to Sir Edward Law, who exclaimed with horror, "But, my dear Law, you are speaking of merchants; you don't seem to understand that we do not deal with such classes at embassies." [18] Under increasing pressure from an emerging industrialist class, the traditional rulers began to reconsider their position on questions of this sort; Lord Palmerston noted in 1841 that "it is the business of Government to open and secure the roads for the merchant." [19] Which was it to be: an international policy of laissez-faire or active state intervention into world affairs? The choice is a familiar one, part of the same dilemma at home. And if the dilemma was similar, so was the solution. As I pointed out in Chapter 1, it is the largest industries that urge a "hands off" policy in order to facilitate their hegemony; internationally, one would expect the most powerful nations to do so as well. So long as Britain was the major power in the world, it was able to maintain its attachment to free trade, but, as Robinson and Gallagher point out, such a decision was a form of "free trade imperialism" designed to preserve, not open access to a world system, but the preservation of British preference.[20]

The transformation of a nonexpansionist ideology into an expansionist practice indicates how wide were the options. Gallagher and Robinson show that expansion always involved a "variety of techniques," that "British governments worked to establish and maintain paramountcy by whatever means best suited the circumstances of their diverse regions of interest." From this point of view, the question of whether there would be an informal empire of "free" trade or a formal one of colonies was practical, not ideological. As they conclude, "One principle then emerges plainly; it is only when and where informal means failed to provide the framework of security for British enterprise (whether commercial, or philanthropic, or simply strategic) that the question of establishing formal ones arose." [21] This point is well taken, but what it suggests is not the emergence of a principle but the opposite, the triumph of a lack of principles. Here again, as so often with bourgeois rule, the end was seen as justifying the means. One must see free trade, fair trade, and colonization as possible options open to the shifting balances of power within the world-wide system that capitalism was creating. Countries adopted one or the other depending on their relative position in that world system.

Since it was Britain's position as the leading capitalist power in Europe (and therefore in the world) and not its attachment to free trade as such, which led to its international liberalism, it also follows that a decline in one would be accompanied by a decline in the other, that as Britain's power relative to other countries slipped, so would its attachment to the absence of protection. Between 1890 and 1895 a new approach to international relations began to be discussed in England under the impact of a relative decline in hegemony. First, the publication of John Seeley's *The Expansion of England* and then Charles Dilke's *Problems of Greater Britain* prepared the intellectual ground for an aggressive stance vis-à-vis the rest of the world.[22] Dilke's book is more interesting, though Seeley's was probably more influential at the time, because Dilke was a Liberal, and it was the Liberal Party of Bright and Cobden that had been most ideologically committed to free trade. But men like Dilke and Rosebery rejected traditional liberalism quite explicitly; they considered themselves

Liberal-Imperialists and sought to move the party closer to what was called a "modern attitude" toward colonies. Certainly both men were aware that their party was facing a crisis; though the Liberals had, with only a few exceptions, been the de facto governing party of England for fifty years, they lost the election of 1895 to Salisbury, a defeat that symbolized the passing of traditional policies. In their search for a new program, the Liberal-Imperialists received help from an unexpected corner, the Fabian Society. The Fabians adopted what Halévy has called "the Prussian solution"[23] to industrial society: social reform combined with colonial adventure. Describing the Webbs, Halévy wrote: "Convinced imperialists and looking to a national and militaristic state to realize their programme of moderate collectivism, they had never felt anything but contempt for every formula of liberalism and free trade."[24] The Webbs invited Rosebery and other liberal-imperialists to meet with them in a group called the Coefficients, aimed at creating a new party grouping that would advocate an imperialist solution. The only success of this group was that it formed the material for H. G. Wells's novel, *The New Machiavelli*; otherwise, the Coefficients failed for one simple reason. His name was Joseph Chamberlain.

Chamberlain, more than most figures of his time, was aware of the decline of British economic power. "I think I see, and I believe that every man of business sees, symptoms which, if not attended to in time, may lead to changes and disaster," he summed up in 1903.[25] This feeling that, unless vigorous action were taken to curb the British belief in free trade, Britain would "go under" motivated Chamberlain's actions both in power and in opposition. Like American policy makers after World War II who interpreted each Communist victory as part of a domino theory that was destroying the world as they knew it, Chamberlain saw free trade as sapping the moral underpinnings of British society: "Sugar has gone; silk has gone; iron is threatened; wool is threatened; cotton will go."[26] There were only two ways to stop this disaster looming just around the corner. One was to create a protective system: fair trade instead of free trade. The other was a healthy dose of "Prussian" social reform, which would win the allegiance of the workers to a protective system. The latter policy was pursued gingerly; though Chamberlain spoke a great deal about social reform and the need for all kinds of state policies to benefit the working class, his actual sponsorship of legislation was cautious, and his Unionist government did not bring forward a revolution from above.[27] But in the area of tariff reform Chamberlain was much more active. His wooing of Rosebery and the Liberal-Imperialists broke up the Coefficients group. His insistence on protection led to important modifications in the policy of free trade. The custom of the Board of Trade and the Foreign Office not to ally themselves with specific business interests but to guard the affairs of the "public"—which, though, generally meant business as a whole—declined ever so slowly under his leadership.[28] British manufacturers picked up the cry for fair trade so that they could achieve equality with foreign capitalists. Though his contemporaries judged Chamberlain's government a failure because his inflexibility on Ireland drove the Unionist Party out of office and out of existence, in a broader sense Chamberlain failed because he succeeded. "Pure" free trade was never again an issue in British politics; the Liberal Party had moved substantially in the direction of Chamberlain's analysis; many reformers, including labor reformers, adopted expansion as a goal; and eventually the problem of a formal empire was addressed. Chamberlain's policies mark a significant transition from one order to another; they constitute the birth of the modern British Expansionist State.

Within the United States developments strikingly similar to the British events took place, only in exactly the opposite direction. If economic decline leads to the popularity of protection, economic strength should lead to free trade. High protective tariffs had traditionally been the rule in America, but under the pressure caused by depressions the protectionist orthodoxy was under attack. Tariff reform (which meant tariff reduction; in England the same expression referred to a raising of duties) was popular throughout the country; periodically the House would pass lower tariffs, only to have them revised upward by the more oligarchic Senate. As was the case in Britain, there were class biases to the different positions. Higher tariffs were of immediate benefit to the specific manufacturers affected (and, a case could be made, to the employees of their companies) while lower tariffs were urged by reformers, who argued that they would stimulate demand overseas and therefore benefit the capitalist class as a whole (and therefore, through the harmony-of-interests doctrine, everyone else). For this reason, though free trade was the more "progressive" policy, the real difference between the two positions was over means. As *Iron Age* expressed it in 1890:

> Protectionists and free traders seem to have at last arrived at a common point, as both classes now profess to be desirous of enlarging our foreign trade. They are, of course, not in harmony with each other as to the means to be adopted in securing this purpose.[29]

Of the two approaches, there is no doubt that free trade, like Chamberlain's protective system, lost the battle, for the Dingley Tariff of 1897 revised upward the one moderate free trade victory, the Wilson-Gorman Act, and after Dingley, duties, like the temperature of a malaria victim, shot up to impressive heights. But just as Chamberlain had lost his fight for protectionism but won the larger war, the tariff reductionists were ultimately victorious, even as rates went up. In the context of the period, it was the assumptions underlying *lower* tariffs that were most compatible with expansionism. Tariff reduction was a farsighted policy of encouraging foreign trade in order to absorb the domestic surplus caused by overproduction, while tariff barriers constituted an old-fashioned attempt to seal the United States off from the rest of the world. The choice, in Thomas McCormick's apt phrase, was between closed doors and open markets, and when the United States committed itself to a foreign policy of expansion, the assumptions, if not the immediate policy objectives, of the reductionists were triumphant.[30] Although interest in tariff matters declined (the issue mysteriously disappeared from American politics for twenty years after the death of McKinley), interest in expansion, in one form or another, intensified.

In few other countries in the world was the connection between domestic contradictions and foreign expansion clearer than in the United States, for expansion had been seen as a solution to home pressures since the opening of the West and Madison's *Federalist Number 10*. For that very reason, as so many historians from Turner to the present have emphasized, the filling in of the West would mean, as James Bryce expressed it, that "a time of trial for democratic institutions" would be at hand.[31] Yet the real importance of the West was always as a symbol of escape, not so much an actuality, for the number of people who could flee poverty for land was always smaller than the mythology of the time would have it. Furthermore, it was not until the 1890s that a large, foreign-born, and class-conscious working class developed, and by then the frontier had already been pronounced closed. Consequently the pressure from below was severe. "In the three years of 1893 to 1895, almost everything occurred in the way of class conflict which conservatives and liberals alike had feared from the time of the Founding Fathers; almost everything, that is, except organized revolution," LaFeber has written.[32] Thus by 1895, the same year in which Salisbury came to power in England along with Chamberlain, the United States was preparing for the first major flexing of its expansionist muscles, the Venezuela boundary dispute. As LaFeber noted, "The timing is significant. Since this boundary dispute had simmered for over a half-century, it should be noted why the United States chose 1895 as the opportune moment to end the controversy and assert its control over the Western Hemisphere." [33] He attributes the timing to an industrial depression, which is certainly valid, but 1895, it should also be remembered, was the same year in which the Supreme Court, in the *Pollock, Knight,* and *Debs* cases, revealed that it was unable to solve the contradictions in political ideology presented by the simultaneous pressure of liberal and democratic demands. Those decisions made it clear that a state that chose to ally itself with the interests of the manufacturers yet turned a deaf ear to unions was one with no consistent mechanism for winning legitimacy. From this perspective, the Venezuelan intervention, followed so closely by the Spanish-American War, became a surrogate for democracy. Unable to win in the political sphere, the people were offered spectacular news stories, tales of rugged conquest, and foreign-islands instead. Cuba and the Philippines were the alternatives to control over monopolies and recognition of the right to organize.

The imperialists who pushed for an empire based on the British model never did achieve their goal. Just as in England the eventual form of the Expansionist State was shaped by compromises among the different factions pushing for an end to free trade, in the United States the adoption of the Open Door Policy was a halfway measure in between isolationism and empire. As Williams has characterized it, the Open Door was a form of "imperial anticolonialism," the creation of an informal American expansionism without the cumbersome weight of colonies. As such it was part of the world-wide search during this period for new, pragmatic solutions to the problem of how to create informal empires that would be more flexible and less expensive than the mercantilist empires had proven to be.[34] It was the search for solutions and not the result that constitutes the important constant. For example, during these years Germany did create a formal empire, which gives it the appearance of being dissimilar to the United States, which did not. Yet even formal German imperialism was not the product of a conscious and deliberate policy but more the end result of a series of failures. After the depression of 1873, which had hit Germany quite strongly, the industrialists demanded protection in the form of higher tariffs, which brought them into a state of agreement with the Junkers who had traditionally desired protection.[35] As in Italy, where northern industrialists had formed an alliance with southern landowners around a high tariff that impoverished small farmers in the South, the alliance between *Roggen* and *Eisen* became the basis of a protectionist policy.[36] Sensing the new forces at work, Bismarck, ever the realist, went along; his attitude, in the words of Hartmut Pogge von Strandmann, "had slowly been transformed from that of a modest free trader to a protectionist." [37] Such a policy demanded a role for the state, facilitated by the development of a repressive governmental apparatus during the antisocialist campaign. Yet Bismarck hoped that protectionism would be enough, that it would avoid the need for formal imperialism. His slogan *"nicht Regie, sondern Subvention"* (no imperial undertakings, but subsidies for enterprises) advocated indirect expansion, undertaken and administered by private corporations. The trouble with this approach was that it gave private advantage with no public responsibility; its limitations were symbolized by the ruthless suppression campaign undertaken in Africa by Karl Peters, the probable model for Conrad's Mr. Kurtz in *Heart of Darkness*, a man whose sadism was as great as his shortsightedness. In other words, "Bismarck's basic idea of having merchants and companies administer an informal colonial empire had failed. Now the *Reich* had been obliged to intervene, to take over more and more responsibilities, and eventually to build up an administrative system." [38] Germany became a colonial power, to be sure, but more by default than through conscious design.

The most important point that can be made about the various techniques of expansion adopted in this period is that they did not constitute rigid categories or options; each flowed into each other at some point, as ruling elites experimented with free trade, protectionism, and colonization in their desire to find workable solutions that would allow for international sublimation of domestic problems. Such eclecticism explains some of the amazing hybrid forms taken by the Expansionist State. The best example of a policy that attempted to combine the features of each approach was what can be called the *Zollverein* solution, tried out by both England and the United States. A pure compromise between free trade and protection, it involved a system of total free trade within a given transnational unit (for England, the Commonwealth; for the United States, the Americas of the Monroe Doctrine), combined with high protectionist walls between that unit and the rest of the world. The formulators of such an approach, William Evarts in the United States and Chamberlain in England,[39] hoped to use it to achieve the best of two worlds, though such structures were often far too cumbersome for the world of international trade. Such proposals are best seen as part of the lack of a policy rather than as the core of a consistent one. As Fieldhouse put it, "There really is no strong evidence that the politicians or senior officials of any major state drew up a prior blueprint for overseas expansion in the 1870s or 1880s on the assumption that the colonies would provide political benefits of these or other varieties." [40] Such a conclusion shows that the political elites of the period, who agreed on the need for expansion, had no inherent commitment to colonialism as the proper form for that expansion to take.

There are two exceptions to this eclecticism, France and Italy, and the latter is a weak one. As in Germany, Italians turned to expansion as soon as unification, an energy-absorbing activity of its own, was completed. "Having solved the problem of unity," Benedetto Croce wrote, "Italy began to talk of her need for colonies, and she did so more especially around the year 1878; for her, as for Germany, these could only be found in Africa." [41] Yet throughout this period Italians did not engage in a great debate over whether colonization represented the best means to achieve expansionist ends. To be sure, Francesco Crispi, faced with an economic crisis, had been arguing vigorously for colonies. They are, he said, "a necessary part of modern life. We cannot remain inert and do nothing so that other Powers occupy by themselves all the unexplored parts of the world . . . we should [if we did that] be guilty of a great crime towards our country, in that we should forever close roadways to our ships and markets to our products." [42] Crispi's actual policies, though, tended to be disasters, and there was an outpouring of what in the United States would have been called "isolationist" disgust at his halfhearted African adventures. By the end of the century opposition to colonialism, which had always been based more on anger at Italian defeats than it was on principle, began to wither away. The publication of Alfredo Oriani's *Fino a Dogali* (1889) and *La Lotta Politica in Italia* (1902), the polar expeditions of the Duke of Abruzzi (1899–1900), Marconi's invention of the wireless (1902), Labriola's shift from orthodox Marxism to enthusiastic expansionism, and the fact that Italian foreign trade increased by over 100 percent between 1890 and 1907—all these were signs of a new awakening of interest in areas outside the Peninsula. The burgeoning of nationalistic sentiment around writers like D'Annunzio and the Futurists was one sign of the new imperialism; another, more significant, was Giolitti's attempt to replicate the Chamberlainian synthesis of foreign expansion and domestic reform. By 1910 Italy had become a modern capitalist nation and had joined the imperialist powers; the Libyan adventure and then World War I were the immediate results. In short, colonialism was the result, but it had not occurred after an intensive national debate; by the time modern Italy had been created, the other European powers had already joined in the scramble for Africa, and Italy, which wished to be part of this world, had no choice but to go along.

France had always eyed the East, which for most of its history meant the Rhine. Faced with a hostile Europe, Danton used to refer to the "natural" borders of France as the Atlantic, the Pyrenees, the Rhine, and the Channel. But with Bismarck blocking any move in that direction, the intensification of working-class pressure at the end of the nineteenth century was bound to cause visionaries to try to reconstitute the overseas empires of old. In this sense France, more than any other country, took the view that expansion and colonization were synonymous. As was their wont, the politicians of the Third Republic were brutally open about their concerns; making no attempt to conceal their desire for colonies, they made the connection between capitalist contradictions and the need for expansion better than most Leninists could. The problem was self-evident: "Is not the colonial policy one of the great facts, one of the universal factors of our time?" Ferry asked, not really expecting an answer. "The policy is . . . a necessity like the market itself." [43] Since colonialism was "the daughter of the industrial policy," those active in the one were naturally active in the other. Ferry approached the acquisition of colonies with the same zeal he used in transforming education (see Chapter 2). Freycinet, who was active in the construction of railway plans within France (see Chapter 1), was also building new lines in Senegal. The French bourgeoisie adopted imperialism in the same manner that it took over the Opera: assertively, but always with a touch of suspicion that it had no right to be there.

Unlike the situation in Italy, there was a debate of sorts over French colonization. From the right conservatives fulminated; Jules Delafosse pointed out in 1881 that "every colony is a cause of weakness during war and an expense during peace." [44] From the left, such as it was, Clemenceau, whose patriotism could not be faulted, attacked France's Tunisian policy, undoubtedly because that policy had the tacit support of Bismarck (who wanted the French to forget Alsace-Lorraine); anything that was good for this man, Clemenceau reasoned, must be bad for France. Such debates were not very effective in altering policy. As the United States would find out in the twentieth century, it is most difficult to conduct an open and searching debate in the course of an imperial adventure. War credits for Tunisia were voted by 429 to 0 in the Chamber and 244 to 0 in the Senate. Debate was also hindered by the tendency of Ferry to lie about what was happening in Tunisia, fabricating stories that were both fantastic and transparent in his attempt to ensure French involvement. The adoption of a French colonial policy was a decision made by an elite, many of whom would profit directly by such adventures, in a demogogic atmosphere. Their actions made them seem in retrospect more like desperadoes than enlightened leaders of public opinion, a situation reflecting, not a defect in their character, but the fact that, faced with severe domestic contradictions, they grabbed at a policy that seemed to promise relief. Unfortunately for them, the policy did no such thing. As Kanya-Forstner has shown, French African expansion was based on a series of myths about the prosperity that would result, none of which were true. [45] It was always gold to be discovered or some magic kingdom around the next bend in the river, which would somehow yield fantastic profits and the support of all the French. Ferry should have listened to Adam Smith for, as it was, France's colonial policy was a disaster. There comes a time in the history of every ruling class when its cruelty, irrationality, and self-delusion all come together around the pursuit of irresponsible, illusory goals; such was the colonial policy of the Third Republic. As Félix Faure commented during the Fashoda crisis: "We have acted like madmen in Africa, surrounded by those irresponsible people generally called colonialists." [46] Devoted colonialists that they were, the French were no further along toward discovering the domestic happiness that England, Germany, and the United States were also trying to find.

THE INS AND OUTS OF EXPANSION

The theory behind free trade, protectionism, and neocolonialism was that they would in one way or another bring about prosperity, thereby avoiding the depressions that characterized the latter part of the nineteenth century. Escaping depression, however, was only one half of the dilemma that faced ruling classes in this period; they were also preoccupied by working-class militancy. To be sure, prosperity would alleviate this latter problem indirectly, for it would make the claim of a harmony of interests seem more genuine. But did such an important matter have to be handled indirectly? As part of the Expansionist State, ruling classes needed some way of directly relieving the pressure caused by a growing and active working-class movement.

One answer lay in neo-Malthusian population theories that had once again become popular among social thinkers. Unlike starvation, the eighteenth-century remedy for overpopulation, and genocide, the twentieth-century solution, thinkers of this period envisioned a better way, a more "civilized" approach to lighten the burden caused by the existence of too many people. Since labor power was a commodity, and since the basic capitalistic law in commodities is that they must be free to be bought and sold,[47] exchanging human populations could absorb the pressures of late nineteenth-century social change. Because the task of shifting populations around the world became so much a feature of the political life of this time, emigration must be considered as an important form of the Expansionist State. In a world of uneven development, where the factors of production were not in equilibrium, it was possible to ship, not capital (which was needed at home) or land (which could not be moved, Chopin's pocketful of Polish soil notwithstanding), but labor (which would remove domestic pressure at the same time). Emigration societies sprung up, motivated by that peculiar combination of charity and profit, generosity and self-interest, which characterized so much of the nineteenth-century bourgeoisie.

Emigration, of course, was not invented in the 1890–1914 period. Specific political developments, such as the Irish potato famine (which was only in the smallest measure a natural disaster) or the failure of the 1848 German revolution, led to large numbers of emigrants. In 1847 alone, it has been estimated, more than one hundred thousand Irish left for North America.[48] Some observers put the number of Germans who emigrated during the 1840s at close to 1 million.[49] Yet what took place at the end of the century, though in apparent continuity with 1840, was quite different under the surface. There was, for one thing, the simple fact of an intensification, which can be seen by a glance at the United States. The foreign-born percentage of the population in the United States was 9.7 percent in 1850 and 6.9 percent in 1950, but in between it was much higher:[50]

1860	13.2%
1870	14.0
1880	13.3
1890	14.7
1900	13.6
1910	14.7

Of the four great waves of European emigration to America during the century—1844–54, 1863–73, 1881–88, and 1903–13—it was the last that was far and away the greatest, with about 10 million arrivals from all of Europe in those years alone.[51] In 1903 there were 70 ships sailing the Atlantic, making 200 crossings, and carrying a minimum of 200,000 passengers.[52] Much of this movement involved peasants from Russia and Eastern Europe, but that does not alter its importance as a safety valve mechanism. Technical improvements in agriculture were forcing people off the land; if America had not been available, these people would have become city dwellers in their own countries or, more likely, in Western Europe, where they would have added their numbers to the rising discontent. Urban proletariats generally come from dislocated peasants; at issue was not whether these emigrants would be added to the labor force, but only the country in which they would be added.

It was not just numbers that made late century emigration unique; a second factor was just as important. While in the 1840s sending peasants to America was simply good business (agents received commissions on how many they could pack onto ships, and then could turn around and sell remaining belongings to make a double profit; steamship companies made fortunes by crowding people into the tiniest possible spaces), by the end of the century the matter had become too important to be left in private hands. Active state intervention became a sign that emigration was of increasing concern within official circles, that it was becoming a matter of public policy as well as private profit.[53] Through a series of Passenger Acts, England rationalized its emigration process, culminating in the Merchant Shipping Act of 1906, which brought emigration within the province of the Board of Trade. Germany in 1907 passed a law that coordinated the divergent policies of the German states into a unified system. Italy went furthest. Between 1888 and 1900, the most thorough system of inspection anywhere in Europe was established, one that became a model for other countries. So much has been written about what happened to the emigrants when they arrived in the New World yet little has been written about the zeal with which European societies went about the business of unburdening themselves of an unwanted reserve army of the discontented. Malthus was alive and well in Europe, as governments actively participated in the exchange of human beings to protect themselves against what is, after all, the essence of democracy: numbers of people.

A third distinct characteristic of *fin-de-siècle* emigration was the way it became intertwined with all the other forms of the Expansionist State just discussed. This interlinking can be illustrated through the German experience, which was fairly typical of Europe as a whole. Traditionally, those who were liberals, who professed free trade, were also opposed to too much state interference when the exchange was in human beings; protectionists, often basing themselves on Friedrich List, welcomed intensified government efforts to speed the flow of people. By the 1870s, the latter position was gaining popularity in Germany, reflected in writers like Ernst von Weber, whose *Vier Jahre in Afrika* (1878) argued that emigration would be the ideal solution to German overpopulation (which does not mean that Germany was overpopulated, just that leading thinkers thought that it might become so). Emigration, just like protectionism and colonization, became an option for a class facing a domestic crisis; the point was well expressed by Frederick Fabri in 1879:

> Every mighty polity [*staatlicher Bestand*] needs in the time of its flowering room for expansion, into which it may not only release its surplus energies, but from which also it may steadily receive back their productive achievements and multiply them in vigorous reciprocity.[54]

After 1879, when Bismarck was shifting his position from free trade to protectionism, there was, in Mack Walker's words, a "startling abrupt" intensification of German interest in emigration, and this renewed interest "was part of the same change" that was taking place in the area of international trade. Emigration, as it became official policy, led to further activity on the part of the state, for "the slowing of economic growth, the bogies of over capitalization and over production, the closing of foreign markets—these propositions made the future of the German economy everybody's concern, the state's business, to which the state ought to respond." [55] The response was twofold: on the one hand, both the anti-socialist laws and social legislation, like state sponsorship of emigration, were designed to alleviate class conflict; on the other, once Germans had emigrated, a formal colonial policy became necessary to guarantee their safety. Both the Congress for Commercial Geography and the Promotion of German Interests Abroad argued the link between emigration and colonialism, just as in Italy where men like Corrandini and Maraviglio were making the same point. Thus there existed a series of links, among which was emigration, all designed to achieve the same expansionist ends.

The question of whether emigration worked—that is, whether it did alleviate class conflict at home—must be answered ambiguously. Since American sociology was just being invented—one of its founders, Edward A. Ross, was in fact obsessed by these "hirsute, low-browed, big-faced persons of obviously low mentality" [56]—no survey samples of the new arrivals were taken to see if they would have been likely to engage in militancy in their country of origin. Probably they would not have, at least not directly. But that is not the important point, for there were two kinds of emigration taking place that must be specified. The first was essentially middle class, as Germans, English, and French, unable to make their fortunes at home, decided to emigrate, usually to Africa or Asia, in order to begin again. The other was the generally involuntary mass migration of poor peasants to the Americas. Of the two, it was the former that was better able to articulate its discontent. From the children and grand-children of these emigrants—writers like Orwell, Lessing, and Camus—have come the most vivid pictures of the rebelliousness of those who set off for other parts of the world. In a fascinating scene, Lessing recalled the arrival of British troops to Martha Quest's home colony, thereby contrasting some of those who had remained behind in England with those who, previous to World War I, had decided to move to Africa:

> Suddenly, overnight, the streets changed. They were filled with a race of human beings in thick, clumsy, greyish uniforms; and from these ill-fitting cases of cloth emerged pallid faces and hands which had—to people who above all had always enough to eat and plenty of sunshine—a look of incompleteness. It was as if nature had sketched an ideal—that tall, well-fed charming youth, so easily transformed into a tough hero—and, being starved of material to complete it with, had struggled into what perfection it could. That, obscurely, was how they felt; they could not own these ancestors; their cousins from Home were a race of dwarfs, several inches shorter than themselves. They were not burnt and brown but unhealthily pale. They were not glorious and rebellious individuals—for, above all, emigrants to the colonies had been that—but they had the look, as they stayed cautiously and curiously about the shallow little colonial streets, of a community whose oneness was emphasized by the uniform.[57]

Rapid social change generally comes about when rebels within the middle class ally themselves with mass movements; in part the emigration of people like Martha Quest's parents, stuffy as they were in Africa, deprived England of some potential agitators.

As far as the emigration of peasants and workers was concerned, even though the road to exotic colonies in Africa may have been blocked, it remained, like the American West, a symbol, one consciously exploited by the brand new development of the mass media (the first issue of the *Daily Mail* was published in 1896) to "prove" the possibility of escape. In addition, as far as the massive emigration of the poverty-stricken was concerned, it is important to remember that what upset the bourgeoisie in this period was not specific people but numbers. This was the time when the term "the masses" was being developed by writers like Gustave LeBon as a conscious alternative to theories of class. The fear was of size, not of militancy per se. Ruling classes were counting population statistics more avidly than profits; the popular image of an hourglass, whose sand was slowly running out, dominated their thoughts. Any policy that would stop, or even slow, the loss of sand was welcome, and emigration was designed to do exactly that.

Emigration cannot exist without immigration; unlike either starvation or genocide, which reduce the number of chips in the game, emigration simply shifts them from one player to another. In nineteenth-century-European politics, as some policies and trends resulted in sending large numbers of people overseas, others brought different people in to replace them. Cinanni, one of the few writers who dealt with the relationship between emigration and imperialism, estimated that of the 15 million people who left Italy between 1876 and 1920, almost half settled not in the Americas but elsewhere in Europe.[58] On balance, it is quite likely that more people entered France than left during this period; 57 percent of the increase in the French population between 1891 and 1901 was due to immigrants.[59] In Germany, 4.1 percent of the labor force in 1907 was foreign-born, mostly Poles and Italians.[60] In that contradictory manner so characteristic of capitalism in this period, fears of overpopulation were leading political elites and those concerned with a long-run perspective to encourage emigration, while the need for cheap labor in the short run was leading others to sponsor immigration. The balance between the two was determined by the strengths of the different forces, and for Europe as a whole there is no doubt that the direction was toward outflow.

The United States likewise pursued both policies simultaneously, as some were encouraged to seek their fortunes elsewhere while others were arriving in hopes of finding work. The fact that the West was still open absorbed many potential emigrants, however, so that for most of the century, the policy of the United States was in the direction of inflow. Because of the existence of the frontier—combined with a youthful capitalism that had difficulty finding people for all the jobs it was creating, let alone a surplus to keep the price of labor power down—American leaders sought actively to promote the absorption of potential workers from other countries. "After political security, there is nothing that the Republic needs as much as bone and sinew," one business periodical noted in 1865.[61] With the eclecticism characteristic of the Accumulative State, both public and private attempts were undertaken to achieve this end. Since the labor force had been drastically reduced by the Civil War, Congress, responding to appeals from men like Henry Carey, passed in 1864 an "Act to Encourage Immigration," the most startling feature of which was its exemption of imported laborers from the draft; they were needed in the factories, not on the lines. (In the twentieth century, women, not foreigners, would "emigrate" into the work force to play this role.) After the Civil War this act was repealed, but repeal did not signify an end to state action as such, just a shift from the federal to the state level. Individual states promoted immigration, usually in two ways. First, they advertised all over Europe, painting attractive portraits of the quality of life within their borders, at a time when private companies were forbidden by law from advertising for immigrants abroad. Second, states actively assisted private companies such as railroads and mines plus various voluntary associations in their promotional campaigns. Importing labor was one of the many areas where private goals were pursued with public aid.

This experience suggests that the desire to rid oneself of, or to acquire, labor power occurred neither from feelings of rapacious calculation nor from idealistic hospitality but simply as part of the market mentality of trade. Self-interest governs trade, and since self-interest can change as circumstances do, in the United States the growth of the Expansionist State and the decline of active immigration were interactive forces. With the depressions and strikes of the 1870s and 1880s, the idea of restricting immigration became more popular. If ever there was published in the United States a manifesto for the Expansionist State, it would have to be Josiah Strong's *Our Country*. This book, which contained an argument for expansion in the strongest possible language, used equally strong words to denounce immigration.[62] The promotion of one was linked to a critique of the other. In these situations of conflicting needs many businessmen became quite confused. They wanted immigration for the cheap labor it offered, but new workers also brought with them militancy, discontent, and depression. "Caught between growing trepidations and a lingering appreciation of the immigrant's usefulness, employers often sounded querulous, uncertain, unready to espouse a definite line of action." [63] Slowly a position of restriction came into being. Higham has called the change in attitude of businessmen on the question of immigration "remarkable," indicating a "full-circle" conversion from the early policy of encouragement.[64] Thus, as Congress responded to the new expansionist sentiment, it also began to respond to the new nativism. A law of 1882 was the first step in the direction of restriction, while another of 1891 brought the question under federal control and began to rationalize the process. The formation of organizations like the American Protective Association and the Immigration Restriction League indicated that political elites had decided that, just as tariffs in goods might be necessary to protect American industry, restrictions on labor power were needed as well. A new policy was emerging: an open door in the Orient, a closed door at home. Even though a return to prosperity after 1896 softened the need for a rapid change in the immigration law, the end was in sight. The restrictive legislation of the 1920s simply codified the new attitude that had appeared in the 1890s.

Immigration and emigration, I have been arguing, had the same non-ideological character as the other expansionist devices—trade, protection, and colonies. No matter what noble sentiments might be expressed in favor of opening the door, and despite the venal sentiments displayed in closing it, neither were believed in for their own sake, and people who favored one approach could easily, when economic conditions changed, turn around and favor the other. It is prosperity, not idealism, that leads to immigration, and depression, not xenophobia, that produces restriction, a dynamic that can be seen as late as the post–World War II experience with Common Market immigration policies.[65] Such flexibility undoubtedly gave the elites of the period an advantage, for it enabled the state to be responsive to changing economic conditions. But at the same time, such ideological inconsistency, which had been the problem with the Accumulative State, does not make for adequate long-run legitimacy mechanisms. Expansion of all forms, which then seemed the only way out, was a solution that, in time, would give rise to as many problems as it would solve.

EXPANSION AND THE GLOSS OF DEFEAT

The one obvious limitation to expansionism as a solution to the contradictory needs of accumulation and legitimation was that the world was, after all, a finite space. At some point all the available niches would be occupied, making confrontation inevitable. Expansion became, therefore, a policy of the highest irresponsibility, for political leaders in the Ferry-Chamberlain era simply bought time, passing on to future generations intractable dilemmas that they chose to avoid. The generation that came to political maturity in the 1970s is paying the price for the cowardly option that expansion represented in the 1890s. Furthermore, expansionism, far from alleviating class conflict, raised the possibility that such conflicts, when they surfaced, would do so with a much greater intensity than if they had been resolved at first appearance. But these limitations remained for the future. What was the success of the Expansionist State at the time it came into existence? Even as these men put their expansionist solutions into practice, contradictions arose that presented them with real difficulties. For the adoption of expansionism was a declaration that liberalism had failed, that the ideology urged on the world by the industrial bourgeoisie had for a century reached the point where it could no longer be taken seriously, even by ruling classes themselves.

First, the Expansionist State brought with it the pursuit of protectionism as an end in itself. Not only did Chamberlain violate fifty years of British faith in free trade, but in the immediate period, as Fieldhouse has noted, it is "a fact that the age of the 'new imperialism' coincided with the resurgence of protectionism in France and Germany and its intensification in Russia, the United States, and other countries such as Portugal, Spain, and Italy." [66] Previous to the Expansionist State, protectionism, as we have seen, was plentiful, but it was always viewed as the exception to the rule, as a temporary measure that would be rescinded as soon as "normality" (which generally meant economic hegemony) was achieved. The age of imperialism saw this rationale dropped, as tariff barriers became matters of permanent policy. Though the economic consequences of this change were minor, the implications for liberal ideology were not. Liberalism had, like Marxian socialism later in the century, presented itself as an internationalist movement; even the term "liberal" had been adopted from the Spanish as a symbol of solidarity with rebels against Iberian autocracy. Therefore, protectionism constituted for the liberal bourgeoisie what the voting of war credits in 1914 symbolized for Social Democracy, a consciously taken repudiation of its own internationalism in favor of a crass assertion of self-interest. For this reason the break with free trade, even if only as ideology, deserves Polanyi's label of a *great* transformation, for as he has eloquently shown, the tariff barriers of the late nineteenth century were also, in a sense, barriers against liberalism's own past.[67] There is no more certain symbol of the change from one world to another as the protectionist policies adopted by capitalist nations in the years preceding World War I.

A second confrontation between liberal theory and the politics of expansion concerned the role of the state. Although liberal ideology had bequeathed to the world the idea that state action was inherently bad, political practice and economic necessity throughout the century indicated otherwise. Both the Accumulative State and the Harmonious State saw active government intervention into the economy and civil society, as the previous two chapters have shown. Though state action was always plentiful, the demands of expansionism intensified it even further. There was no better way to establish tariffs, populate colonies, or sponsor emigration than through government action, which is why the most ardent expansionists were also theorists critical of laissez-faire, willing to justify, for the sake of expansionism, an active state. T. H. Green, who became, almost in spite of himself, a spokesman for the critique of pure Manchester liberalism, could, in Semmel's words, "be said to have laid the philosophical foundations for Liberal-Imperialism." [68] Many of the political leaders who pushed England toward imperialism, such as Asquith and Milner (the latter vowed never to marry so as to serve the state better), had been Green's students at Oxford. In France it was no coincidence that Leon Bourgeois, who in the 1870s was the most popular critic of laissez-faire in the country (see Chapter 2), was holding an important position in the colonial office in the 1880s. In the United States William Graham Sumner, the highest priest of laissez-faire thinking, was never comfortable with modern expansionism; it remained for others, like John Fiske, to argue the link between social Darwinism and modern imperialism. Among policy makers, men like Theodore Roosevelt (who would break the Republican orthodoxy toward laissez-faire in favor of an active state) at the same time became the most aggressive expansionists around. In Germany both Hegel and List had been expansionist critics of liberalism; by 1890 their legacy had influenced a generation of policy makers, for German imperialism, as Wehler has suggested, can best be understood as an aspect "of the growing interventionist state, as an attempt on the part of the ruling elites to create improved conditions for the stability of the social and economic system." [69] Finally the Italian nationalism of men like D'Annunzio was explicitly linked to an attack of liberalism, especially in its Giolittian form; the ultimate form of the Expansionist State in Italy became fascism, a clear rejection of the liberal theory of the state.

The break with laissez-faire by the ruling class meant that its last line of defense against working-class pressure had been abandoned. If an active conception of the state was admitted, there was no logical reason why the working class should not also benefit from government. Understanding this, many imperialists sought to anticipate the obvious consequence by sponsoring extensive programs of social reform. Bismarck's legislation became the model everywhere—a combination of "welfare" legislation, political repression, and imperialism. In England the Fabians were attracted to Bismarck's program, while Liberals like Sir William Ashley found inspiration in the ideas of Gustav Schmoller and the Kathedersozialisten, which combined a Harmonious State theory with the need for colonies.[70] Not to be outdone, Italian reformers also borrowed the Schmoller model, Francesco Crispi used Bismarck's antisocialist law as the model for his repressive campaign, and Giolitti, pointing out to his colleagues that "it is necessary . . . to re-evoke the affection of the lower classes for our institutions,"[71] borrowed his reform program from Chamberlain, who had in turn been influenced by Bismarck. John W. Burgess, the founder of American political science, was a reformer, a racist, and an imperialist, and he had been trained in Germany where a synthesis of all three positions had been accomplished. In short, once traditional liberalism had been rejected, reform had to be admitted. But the social reform of the imperialists tended to be paternal and not, despite its rhetoric, sufficient to relieve the pressure that rapid capital accumulation had generated. Having obtained some, the working class wanted more, and the twentieth century saw an intensification, not a diminution, of its demands for participation in the state.

Third, the drive toward expansion signified an underpinning of the philosophical foundations of traditional liberalism. The most given assumption of the liberal world view was that through the rational calculation of self-interest the general good would be produced. Imperialism denied this at every point. T. H. Green "had turned against the Benthamite utilitarianism which had supported the atomistic individualism of Cobdenism and had preached a new concept of the organic nation."[72] Bernard Bosanquet glorified the state in a mystical fashion totally at odds with the politics of rational calculation. Everywhere the concrete lost ground to the abstract: the *volk, solidarité,* manifest destiny, the imperial idea, even the general strike. Furthermore, even self-interest was negated. It was a national, a racial, a world interest that was at stake. As Halévy has pointed out, imperialism condemned the Benthamite doctrine of the "morality of self-interest." Analyzing the rhetoric of men like Rosebery and Chamberlain, he concluded: "Far from appealing to the self-interest of their audience, they call upon them to sacrifice their private interests, even their very lives, in pursuit of lofty national ideals." [73] The concept of individual self-interest, which had served the bourgeoisie well for over a hundred years, was discarded without apparent remorse when it no longer seemed needed, but with its demise also went the last strand of philosophical consistency left in the liberal tradition.

The worship of the spontaneous and the irrational—a decided feature of social thought during the Expansionist State—was accompanied by racism and xenophobia. The attacks on Jews and people of color, consequently, illustrate a fourth rejection of liberalism: the idea of an inherent, if not actual, equality of all people. As Hannah Arendt has shown, the connection between anti-Semitism and imperialism, especially in France, was a direct one;[74] the Dreyfus case can be understood as a form of internal imperialism, an assertion of cultural superiority against a domestic "colony." In England, Benjamin Kidd's *Social Evolution*, a bitter attack on rationality, laid the framework for a new racism, one that was completed by Karl Pearson, whose combination of racism and paternalistic sexism anticipated Nazism by thirty years.[75] A generation of imperialists—Milner, Chamberlain, Asquith, Rosebery—based their politics on racial theories, even proposing a Union of Teutonic Peoples, an alliance between England, Germany, and the United States against the inferior Latins of the Mediterranean. The idea received strong support from the other "Teutons." Leading American expansionists, like Alfred Thayer Mann, Brooks Adams, and Theodore Roosevelt, accepted the racial superiority of Northern Europeans as self-evident, since at this time a gentlemanly kind of superiority complex was part of the patrician approach to politics.[76] The German fascination for de Gobineau's *Essai sur l'inégalité des races humaines* hardly needs comment, except that Gobineau was French, necessitating restatements of the same idea by "Aryans." It was also at this time that a specifically Italian race was discovered by those most avid in their defense of Italian expansionism. Neoclassical thinkers suggested that the Roman Empire was about to be reborn and perhaps Africa was the place to do it. The suppression of people abroad seemed to require the elevation of those at home but the consequences were severe. Not only did racism prepare the ground for genocide, it unleashed a force that those who propagated it could not control. When liberals turned racist, they created a monster that destroyed liberalism as ruthlessly as it did people of color. The idea of juridical equality contained in the term "bourgeois" was replaced with the contrary notion that the majority of the people in the world were of inferior stock.

Finally, and perhaps most important, the Expansionist State, in spite of its aggressiveness, marked the transformation of liberalism from an optimistic to a pessimistic outlook. Although jingoism, as it was called, would seem to require an enthusiastic mystique in order to work, underneath the imperialist drive for expansion were strong feelings of doom. Comparing the scramble for Africa with earlier English experience, Robinson and Gallagher have captured this. "What stands out" in the English African policy of the 1880s, they conclude, "is its pessimism. It reflects a traumatic reaction from the hopes of mid-century; a resignation to a bleaker present, a defeatist gloss on the old texts of expansion." [77] Optimistic liberalism lost the intellectual offensive as new pessimistic doctrines were avidly understood by a bourgeoisie in decline. The transformation from bright to dark was best expressed in the culture of the period. The exuberance of early Romanticism—seen in Delacroix's discovery of the primitive, Berlioz' revolution in form, or Hugo and Bizet's attempts to shock bourgeois complacency—had turned into a naturalism that became increasingly nihilistic. There appeared a loss of faith, which was at root a fear of the "ignorant armies" of Arnold's "Dover Beach." Maurras, Daudet, and Barres, who were both artists and political reactionaries, developed the ideas that would become Acción Française, while a generation of Italian poets celebrated virility and doom with equal facility, glorifying the future yet simultaneously preaching decay.[78] "Doctrines of decay," Arendt has written, "seem to have some very intimate connection with race-thinking." [79] And, one might add, with the need for emigration and the search for colonies. The pessimistic core at the heart of the new expansionism broke one more link to traditional liberalism. By 1914 any resemblance in the political thought of the bourgeoisie to the spirit of Adam Smith was purely coincidental.

"Hope? Impossible! How can I go on hoping when I no longer believe in that which roused me, namely, democracy?", Clemenceau is reported to have said near the end of his life.[80] The pessimism of the elites was caused by the fact that, having rejected traditional liberalism, they were simply unprepared to welcome democracy, and therefore had nowhere to turn. It is difficult to recall exactly how fearful ruling classes were of the advance of democracy, of how revolutionary the democratic idea remained as late as the eve of World War I. One reason for this fear was that working classes remained, for quite some time, opposed to the imperial designs of the Expansionist State. In spite of the virulence of "yellow" journalism, ordinary people were unimpressed by the need to annex Cuba as a U.S. colony. As the American consul in Santiago noted in 1898: "Property holders without distinction of nationality, and with but few exceptions, strongly desire annexation, having but little hope of a stable government under either of the contending forces. . . . [B]ut such a move would not be popular among the masses." [81] The more extreme the expansion, the more antidemocratic the urge. One British Under-Secretary for the Colonies argued that expansion into Guinea and Zanzibar should continue, no matter how unpopular, "until the vulgar prejudice which is nowadays dignified by the name 'Public Opinion' veers round to a common sense and unsentimental view of this question." [82] Because of such "vulgar prejudices," planning for the Expansionist State often had to be isolated from democratic government. As Power has written of France, "Much of the planning and the important action in Tunisia thus was undertaken by men not directly responsible to the people or by ministers who did not consult with the elected representatives of France." [83] Both the contempt for public opinion and the preference for nondemocratic political structures would reemerge in twentieth-century attempts to create and maintain imperial designs (see Chapter 6).

Unable to be liberal yet unwilling to be democratic, bourgeois society found in expansion a temporary expedient to its limitations. Yet if the working class was unwilling to accept the expansionist alternative, foreign adventures would remain only that. Consequently, considerable energy was shown by expansionists on the problems of the working class, especially to its "moral" improvement. The connection between imperialism and educational reform discussed in Chapter 2 is worth reemphasizing here, for every country had its own Jules Ferry, its own advocate of both foreign expansion and educational change. Those imperialists who had studied at Oxford with T. H. Green heard his *Lectures on the Principles of Political Obligation*, which urged, in an uncharacteristically direct manner, that "education should be enforced by the state." [84] Green was active in the National Education League, the pressure group urging passage of the 1870 law that reformed English schooling, a law that saw the political triumph of young Joseph Chamberlain.[85] In America the ubiquitous Josiah Strong also urged new approaches to education and was a founder of the American Patriotic League, whose magazine, *Our Country*, borrowed its title from Strong's book. The APL advocated the creation of student governments to prepare young men and women for their proper role in the industrial system, and its roster reads like an honor roll of American expansionists.[86] In one country after another, those who wished to see the state expand abroad were also in favor of a system of compulsory education, enforced by government, and directed toward the working class.

The reason for the connection between imperialism and educational reform is not hard to find. Just as the former required a system of control in the dependent country, the latter, as Edward A. Ross—another expansionist, racist, and educational reformer—argued, must be viewed as part of an "economical system of police." [87] If the working class was opposed to expansionism, then a little expansion would be practiced on them. Manipulated through the new psychology of men like Stanley Hall or Hugo Münsterberg, the majority of people would come out sanitized, "morally improved," ready to assume the role of citizens of an imperial power. This was especially a need in the area of immigration, for one simply could not trust the ideas that Europeans brought with them. As late as the 1920s, when the Lusk Committee of the New York legislature issued a comprehensive report on the problem, the fascination of middle-class society with racial doctrines, educational reform, imperialism, and immigration could be seen.[88] In later periods the language of educational reform changed, but education remains until the present an area of great concern for those who desire an imperial role for their country.

In this context, educational reform was seen by important political leaders as a way to handle the working class without giving them democracy. One other method of achieving the same goal also seemed possible, the manipulation of everyday culture in order to win compliance to the legitimacy of an expansionist political order. Mass culture, in other words, did not just spring out of nowhere; it had to be created, and it is significant that many of the leading imperialists were also active in sponsoring various forms of spectacles for public consumption. The yellow journalism of Hearst and Pulitzer is only the most conspicuous example. Less blatant but equally interesting is the case of mass sporting. Cecil Rhodes, the archetypal imperialist-sportsman, was only one of a breed. There was also Robert Blatchford, one of the more important reformist spokesmen for imperialism, who sponsored a nationwide campaign for Sunday sports for workers in the industrial cities, in part so that they would not spend their newly acquired free time thinking.[89] Before 1850, as Robert Malcolmson has shown, English working-class games were not only participatory, but also could be the occasion of resistance to civil authority; by the end of the nineteenth century, a generation of imperialist-sportsmen had attempted to turn sports into either a spectator activity or an affair of "gentlemen" designed to ensure respect for rules and fair play.[90] In the United States as well, as Joel Spring has shown, the movement toward physical education as a necessary part of the school curriculum was most actively urged by those whose business interests gave them a preoccupation with expansion.[91] Mass culture—such as athletics and popular journalism—is indicative of the attempt by the Expansionist State to offer the working class anything except power—the one thing that might have changed its life for the better.

Neither educational reform nor the development of mass culture can seriously qualify as alternative ways out of the dilemmas that expansionism tried to solve. Neither should be seen as options but as a sign of the paucity of options, of the intractability caused by the irrelevance of traditional liberalism and the refusal to accept democracy. If the reaction of elites to the decline of liberalism was one of resigned acceptance, their reaction to democratic pressure continued to be a combination of resistance and fear. Caught in this no-man's-land between two political philosophies, ruling classes floundered in search of a workable theory of the state. Saved, for a time, by World War I, the contradictions that emerged in the 1890s were not directly addressed again until the postwar prosperity of the 1920s began to wane. Halfhearted measures like educational reform filled a thirty-year gap in which the search for new solutions to the problem of the state was unfulfilled. It was only after experiments with war economies, corporatism, and fascism—all to be discussed in the next chapter—that a unique form of granting public power to private groups became the way out of the contradiction between liberalism and democracy that revealed itself in the expansionist era.

4 / The Origins of the
Franchise State

"Scattered until now into usually autonomous organizations, the industrialists have not asserted themselves as a ruling class. They have fought for the future of their industries on economic grounds [but] they have been absent from public life as a tightly organized group with an active and united leadership. New times now summon the industrialists to play a larger role in public affairs."

Dante Ferrais, first president of
Confindustria (1919)

"The bourgeois state . . . is decomposing into the two parts that constitute it. The capitalists are forming their own private state just like the proletariat. . . . The state is vainly attempting to maintain the contest within the framework of its own legal order."

Antonio Gramsci (1920)

"I suggest therefore that progress lies in the growth and the recognition of semi-autonomous bodies within the state—bodies whose criterion of action within their own field is solely the public good as they understand it, and from whose deliberations motives of private advantage are excluded, though some place it may still be necessary to leave, until the ambit of men's altruism grows wider, to the separate advantage of particular groups, classes, or faculties—bodies which in the ordinary course of affairs are mainly autonomous within their prescribed limitations, but are subject in the last resort to the sovereignty of the democracy expressed through parliament."

John Maynard Keynes, The End of
Laissez-faire (1926)

The Wonderful School

WORLD WAR I imposed a superficial unity on the struggles over the state that had so dominated political life in the last years of the nineteenth century. Yet the euphoria produced by total war could not hide forever tensions that had still to be resolved. The most important were those emerging within the ruling classes and those that still existed between the

ruling classes and everyone else. While engaged in their ultimately successful effort to shape the state for their own ends, businessmen had certainly
become aware that within their own ranks were important differences:
large capital versus small, industry versus agriculture, finance capital versus
manufacturing, even conflicts among capitalist nations. Their temporary
unity was bound to fall apart once the state was won and these traditional
schisms reasserted themselves. Furthermore, the capture of the state itself
seemed, after all the shouting was over, a tenuous booty. The paradox of
laissez-faire, even as ideology, was that in order for the state to profess *not*
to act, one particular group had to control it. Could that control be
maintained in the face of even stronger pressures from below, which was
sure to be a political fact of life in the twentieth century? This question
would dominate public discussion at a time when sheer accumulation, the
assertion of a harmony of interests, and foreign adventure had all failed
or revealed serious limitations.

The twin factors of intraclass competition and interclass struggle did
serious damage to the classic liberal arrangements of a self-regulating market and a state that did something by doing nothing. To make the point
even more emphatic, the arrival of World War I had brought the last days
of the liberal world even closer. The war symbolized change, both in the
nature of industry and in the relationship between classes. The successful
prosecution of a modern war required industrial coordination for ends
higher than simple profit and at least some attempt at democratic structure and legitimation, so that large numbers of people would be willing
to give up their lives for something that was not necessarily in their best
interests. The war, in other words, saw the transformation of one kind of
world into another, and, as Karl Polanyi pointed out, "Nowhere has
liberal philosophy failed so conspicuously as in its understanding of the
problem of change."[1] The first casualty of this war was not truth but
liberalism.

The immediate problem that had to be solved once war broke out was
the tension within the new industrial ruling class: between the self-interest
of any one industrialist and the common interest of the class as a whole.
This was not a new phenomenon but a source of permanent difficulty
within capitalistic arrangements. But war gave the problem both a sustained intensity and a field of maneuver. The fact that lives were being
lost and national borders were being threatened transformed what to many
businessmen was an abstract and suspiciously philosophical problem into
an everyday concern. If businessmen did not cooperate with each other,
the process by which raw materials became implements of destruction
would be left haphazard until the enemy might appear at the factory gate.
All the profit in the world would mean little if a foreign power occupied
both country and plant. At the same time, cooperation meant restrictions
on total freedom, and having just won the point that there was no power

on earth to stop them, many businessmen did not wish to concede that, in fact, there was. Something had to be done to still this intensity, and the second new element provided by the war furnished the solution, for a wartime situation, with its emphasis on both urgency and emergency, allowed a freedom to try out new arrangements that peacetime never would have provided. Hence the war, regardless of the country that was fighting it, became a vast laboratory for experiments in the relationship between self-interest and common interest. It was, in the words of Grosvenor Clarkson, the former director of the Council of National Defense in the United States, a "wonderful school."[2]

School is a place for both teaching and learning; in this case the industrial bourgeoisie discovered that it had to do far more of the latter than of the former. The lessons varied somewhat from country to country, but every party to the war discovered similar maxims to problems posed by intraclass competition. What was learned, in brief, was that traditional political structures were inadequate to deal with class tensions, and that a new solution for the problem of the capitalist state had to be found. The experiences of both the United States and Germany indicate the breadth of the search.

Though it entered the war later than any of the other major parties, the United States is a good place to begin, for here the fear of the state was stronger than in the more statist continental countries. American businessmen were simply horrified, mostly from ideological training, at even the thought of the positive use of the state.[3] The state had been won so that it would not be used, not so that it would. The ideal solution to any problem involving a class interest, as opposed to an individual one, was for businessmen to meet in private and to work out, in a parody of civility, their conflicts. This ideal served as the first solution to the problem of wartime procurement. Bernard Baruch, who saw the need for cooperation more clearly than many of his colleagues, had himself appointed commissioner of the Munitions Standards Board, an agency of the state with little real power except the power to suggest. Using his personal connections, Baruch approached copper magnate Daniel Guggenheim during his "at home" hour one Sunday afternoon and urged a talk. Baruch forcefully recommended that the copper industry sell its product to the government at roughly half price; any losses, he patiently explained, would be more than made up for by the good public relations that would follow from such a generous contribution to the war effort. Guggenheim, convinced, called the four other oligopolists in the industry and a deal was worked out. The whole procedure was, in the words of its historian, "an exercise in business connections," in which "the role . . . personal friendships played ought not to be overlooked."[4] If cooperation like this could be achieved so easily at every turn, businessmen could have both their individualist cake and their collectivist feast.

The copper agreements became the model for the first systematic attempt at war mobilization in twentieth-century America. Baruch established "cooperative committees of industry" between April and June of 1917, charged with the responsibility of ensuring that intraclass conflict did not interfere with the goal of mobilization. Unlike the Guggenheim deal, though, these cooperative committees failed. The problem was that the spirit of Frank Cowperwood was still alive; Dreiser's fictional portrayal of the industrialist who damns all cooperation when it is a question of maximizing his profits was based on a real magnate, Charles Yerkes, and many industrialists preferred Yerkes to Baruch. As a result the chairmen of some of Baruch's committees, such as lumber, were unable to win any cooperation from recalcitrant manufacturers. Yet another problem existed: the military bureaus, composed of officers and civil servants trained to think in national terms, were unable to accept the extreme self-interest arguments of relevant business groupings. As voluntarism ran into one snag after another, only two alternatives became possible: a return to the principles and practices of the Harmonious State, which would satisfy individual businessmen but hurt the war effort; or a more centralized state that would salvage the interest of the class as a whole (by fighting the war efficiently) but that would necessitate compulsion against specific businessmen. Since both alternatives were anathema to someone, the War Industries Board, which was created to solve the problem, tried to satisfy both positions at once and thereby revealed its weakness.

The assertion that the War Industries Board (WIB) became the model of state-business cooperation in the twentieth century[5] is undermined by evidence indicating that it was more conspicuous for what it could not accomplish than for what it could. In its three most extensive areas of work—establishing industrial priorities, fixing prices, and structuring industrial planning—the Board was wont to take an aggressive and confident stance because of its private failures. Businessmen, so long used to the freedom to do anything they wanted, did not react favorably to what they saw as an alien imposition, no matter how often they were told that it was all in their ultimate interest. The vigorous assertion of vested interest continuously acted as a brake on the farsighted exponents of new economic arrangements. The ideological issues involved have been described in another context by Samuel P. Huntington, in his distinction between "business pacifism," which supported laissez-faire and was hostile to any form of militarist thinking, and the "neo-Hamiltonian compromise," which favored both an active state and an appreciation of military necessity.[6] Though the theory of the WIB—its assertion that state power can be used to preserve the national interest—supported the neo-Hamiltonians (who in turn supported it), the practice of the Board—especially its failure to stand up to vested interests—supported the business pacifists. The crucial question was the authoritative use of state power, and this was exactly the question that was fudged. Rather than make a flat assertion that it did indeed have the power to enforce its agreements, the WIB tended to deal with specific problems in specific ways. Though the more reactionary businessmen did not like the theory, they accepted the practice, just as the ideologists of an active state accepted the theory but shook their heads in dismay at the daily operations. The full implications of the problem were never resolved because the war ended, the country returned to the principles of business pacifism, and the WIB was dissolved at the end of 1918.

While these events can be read as a victory for those pushing for a minimal role for the state, who tended to be smaller, more parochial manufacturing interests,[7] other tendencies indicated that their victory would be a short one. For one thing, economic practices during the war tended to benefit the largest monopoly-oriented industrialists, and they were the ones who would be more likely to push for an active state.[8] Second, the vision of such a state now existed, even if only in theory. Vision in hand, more class-conscious businessmen were armed for the struggles that would take place after the war. Morris L. Cooke, a member of the WIB, had expounded this point of view in an address to the Frederick Winslow Taylor Society in 1917:

> Let us put our house in order. Let us build a democratic organization of these industries, let us build something that will at least compare favorably with the German structure; let us get our industry in such shape that it can be considered almost a part of the Government and the Government can come to us and do business with us feeling that we are almost a coordinate branch of the Government.[9]

What was "the German structure" that Cooke wished to emulate? It was the system devised by Walther Rathenau, a system that can be viewed as an alternative solution to the same problem that American capitalists had tried to solve.

Rathenau, subject of a painting by Edvard Munch and a novel by Robert Musil (*The Man Without Qualities*), was as quixotic and bizarre a character as one is likely to find in a chapter dealing with businessmen. In spite of his flights into fantasy, mysticism, and German Romanticism, Rathenau's more practical visions included a scheme for organizing the German economy during the war. As head of the Kriegsrohstoff Abteilung (KRA), the War Materials Administration section of the War Ministry, he initiated a process that was, in the words of his biographer, "an entirely original and typical idea of his own."[10] This idea was to bypass existing corporations, which Baruch had conspicuously not done, and to create new organizations, of an intentionally mixed public and private character, which would take raw materials commandeered by the state and transform them into industrial products. At all stages in the process, the state played a much more active role than it did in the United States. The state not only laid claim to the raw materials, it also extended a guiding hand in private exploitation of them and asserted the power to veto private plans when it felt that such a radical step was necessary. Even though Prussia had a long tradition of using the state in the economy, Rathenau's enthusiasm often got the better of him, and just as the U.S. solution ran into opposition from planners who objected to its minimal government role, Rathenau's plans were objected to by vested interests upset by its maximal role. By April 1, 1915, Rathenau had, under intense pressure, submitted his resignation as head of the KRA.

Freed from specific responsibility, Rathenau put down his ideas in the form of repetitious and generally vacuous books, but ones that nonetheless outlined some fairly radical notions. In *Von Kommenden Dingen, Die Neue Wirtschaft*, and *Der Neue Staat*, he envisioned a society in which class conflict was abolished and the entire economy was organized along strictly functional lines. Within each industrial sector, large-scale industrial unions, growing out of cartels and trade associations, would be created, charged with the responsibility of extracting raw materials, developing new technologies, planning expansion, organizing sales, and negotiating with workers and consumers. Anticipating a corporatist point of view, Rathenau's dream, like other corporatist schemes to be discussed below, never solved the problem of the state. In a strictly corporatist solution there would be no need at all for the state. Trade associations regulating their industries presuppose a harmonious balancing of the economy in which the exercise of state power is neither necessary nor desirable. From that perspective, Rathenau speaks of the state as being "behind" peak associations, giving it only "extremely self-restricting powers."[11] Yet the notion of the state as an active participant in the economy was also attractive to him, and he could at other times describe the state the way Nietzsche described the *Übermensch:* "The state will become the moving center of all economic life. Whatever society does will be done through the state and for the sake of the state."[12]

As these excerpts indicate, Rathenau was a contradictory thinker, and as such is symbolic of what would emerge as a fundamental truth in the twentieth century, that capitalists could survive only if they dropped their attachment to strictly liberal political ideas and accepted the notion of a form of state activity that would not only be noncapitalist but might even be anticapitalist. Though a product of the liberal tradition, Rathenau compromised with it on two points, centering around the two major forms of class tension in capitalist society. As far as the struggle between classes was concerned, Rathenau, as Walter Struve has pointed out, belongs in the company of liberals like Naumann and Weber who tried to refashion an elitist conception of liberalism that would protect those in power from what were seen as the irrationalities of the "mob."[13] Rathenau, like many intellectuals of his era, resolved the contradiction between liberalism and democracy on the terms of the former and against the latter. And as far as interclass conflict was concerned, Rathenau's advocacy of state action to ensure class cooperation, which his colleagues among the industrialists understood but detested, gave him such an ambiguous relationship to his class that the best description of it has been given by a novelist whose fascination lay with the phenomenology of human perception. Better than any historian, Robert Musil described fictionally the relationship between Dr. Paul Arnheim, an obvious portrait of Rathenau, and the men with whom he did business:

> He was notorious for quoting the poets at board-meetings and insisting that commerce was something that could not be kept apart from all other human activities, that ought, indeed, to be considered only in the larger context of all the problems of national life, including the life of the mind and even of the spirit itself. And yet, even though they smiled at these things, they could not entirely fail to see that it was precisely the fact that Arnheim junior adorned business with these qualities that made him of steadily increasing interest to public opinion. . . . They were all convinced that the world would be much better if it were simply left to the free play of supply and demand, instead of being run with the help of men-o'-war, bayonets, potentates and financial ignoramuses of diplomats. But the world being what it is, and there being an old prejudice to the effect that a life that primarily promotes one's own and only secondarily and indirectly the public advantage is less estimable than chivalry and loyalty to the State, and public commissions ranking, as they do, morally higher than private ones, they were the last people not to reckon with all this; and it is well known that they made thoroughly sound use of the advantages to the public welfare offered by customs negotiations backed up by armed forces or by using the military against strikers. But it is along this road that business leads to philosophy (for it is only criminals who presume to damage other people nowadays without the aid of philosophy). And so they became accustomed to regarding Arnheim junior as a kind of papal legate in their affairs. For all the irony with which they regarded his tastes, it was agreeable to them to possess, in him, a man who was capable of presenting their case just as well to a conclave of bishops as to a sociologists' congress; indeed he finally gained an influence over them similar to that exercised by a beautiful and intellectual wife, who looks down on the everlasting office work but is useful to the business because she is admired by one and all.[14]

It is precisely the contradictions embedded in Rathenau's ideas and his relations within and outside his class that make him such a fascinating representative of an era in transition.

Rathenau became an important public figure almost in spite of himself. His influence did not diminish after his 1915 resignation from the KRA; after the war, he once again worked his way into a position of power. Not only was the creation of a National Economic Council in the early

Weimar years a direct result of his ideas, but he also played an important role in the process by which the coal, potash, and steel industries were to be nationalized. As Minister of Reconstruction, and as a member of the second Socialization Commission, he drew up the plans for the nationalization of those industries in such a way that all subsequent debate centered on his draft. But still he could not make up his mind. Rathenau called the socialist plan for noncompensation of industrialists "impractical and unfeasible under present circumstances." "Coal production," he continued, "would collapse if you eliminate the mine owners suddenly."[15] This sensitivity to vested interests was further intensified when Rathenau's proposals were revised by the National Economic Council. Supporters of large industrialists shaped the nationalization plans so that they would be less harmful to their patrons. As David Felix views it, "They wanted a coal cartel under government aegis—capitalism with all the advantages of socialism."[16] What resulted from the complicated negotiations that went into the nationalization drive was a far *less* independent role for the state than Rathenau had at first envisioned. Business in this case won a substantial victory. "The resumption and failure of efforts to socialize the German coal industry," Charles Maier has written, "marked the end of any fundamental attempt to alter the distribution of economic power in Germany."[17]

Thus a curious correspondence between the German and the American solutions emerged. In one country a minimalist solution showed the dangers that could result if the state were not given enough power, and in the other a maximalist solution indicated exactly the reverse. From opposite ends of the problem both countries saw the development of new arrangements that moved toward each other by avoiding the crucial question of state authority and asserting ad hoc regulations that would solve matters on a case-by-case basis. All the other parties to World War I experimented with solutions that were somewhere in between these two models. In Italy, where industrialization occurred rather late, the war formed the rationale for creation of the Confederazione Generale dell 'Industria Italiana (CGII, or Confindustria). Very quickly Confindustria came to support large capital over small, and it used its key position to further the interests of the one over the other. Men like Gino Olivetti and Dante Ferrais relied on the state to advance their class interests from their positions within CGII. As Roland Sarti expressed it, "Industrialists and government officials sat side by side on the same planning agencies where they learned to appreciate the advantages of economic planning and cooperation."[18] Similarly, in France, the war and industrial self-organization came (and went) together. Though there was strong opposition among French industrialists to the idea of cooperation (they were afraid that if they organized they could no longer claim that the CGT, the largest labor union, was an illegal conspiracy), Etienne Clementel, the Minister of Commerce, who "came fairly close to the prototype of the politician who first as a deputy and then as a senator all but openly represented the interests of organized business in parliament,"[19] pushed the idea, and eventually, in 1919, the Confédération Générale de la Production Française (CGPF) was formed. Nor was England immune. Programme Committees were formed in each industry, modeled on the work of Sir Arthur Salter in shipping.[20] The Ministry of Supply, as Samuel Beer notes in passing, was nothing more than a trade association made into a government agency.[21] By the very end of the war, industrial organization reached its highest peak when all the national transport ministries, each the product of a trade association or cartel, merged across national lines into the Allied Maritime Transport Council, based in London. The partnership between private capital and the state had become transnational, the ultimate experiment brought about by wartime conditions.

To summarize, the lesson taught by the war was a paradoxical and confusing one. Industrialists had come to political power on the basis of a dual dynamic that had become for them an unquestioned article of faith. One tenet held that the maximization of profit in the short run was the highest good and the other posited that through the vigorous assertion of selfish interest the common interest would emerge. The war raised questions about both; it indicated that an arrangement guaranteeing short-run expediency and private aggressiveness could be preserved only if an institution existed that was preoccupied with long-run vision and common cooperation. To understand the full implications of this lesson required subtlety and a taste for dialectical analysis, neither of which were likely characteristics of businessmen. It comes as no surprise that in three of the five countries just discussed the man who played the crucial role in advocating an active state was Jewish. Baruch, Rathenau, and Olivetti symbolized the peculiar insider/outsider dichotomy that became a necessary part of the struggle for the state. As successful businessmen they were legitimate, if not totally so, in the eyes of their colleagues, but as potential pariahs, they also had a perspective greater than that of immediate self-interest. Even where the religious factor was not important, there was a need for a new kind of spokesman for industry. Discussing the replacement of René Duchemin by Claude Gignoux in the CGPF after the war, Henry Ehrmann writes of French businessmen: "In a situation in which they felt that the authority of management, and perhaps even the institution of private property, were threatened, they preferred to see their interests in the hands of somebody who was not identified with any of the possibly conflicting subgroups of business and who could therefore rise more easily in the defense of employers as a class."[22] For businessmen in France even to recognize that they had an interest as a class was a significant change, just as in other countries the use of the state for more than accumulation represented a whole new way of thinking. They were important lessons, and it was lucky for them that such a wonderful school had been found.

THE CORPORATIST FLIRTATION

Most of the experiments, practices, and arrangements brought about by the war ended the moment it was over. In France and the United States, traditional business hostility toward the state reasserted itself, and bureaus that had rapidly been put together were just as speedily dismantled. In England those in power wanted nothing more than a return to the prewar years when, under the influence of new leaders like Bonar Law, who was born in America and brought with him American ideas about state power, the Conservative Party began to adopt for the first time a laissez-faire outlook. More businessmen than ever before had been elected to the first postwar Commons, and they went about the business of abolishing price controls, state control over raw materials, and public influence on industry. As losers, Germany and Italy tried to demonstrate their loyalty to their new world order, at least for a time. Rejecting their own historical traditions, including the use of the state in the economy, both countries saw a flourishing of classical economic liberalism before the joint victories of fascism. Everywhere businessmen seemed to want nothing more than a return to the balmy days of the Harmonious State.

They were never to get it. Social conditions had changed too drastically for laissez-faire ever to exist again. For one thing, the war had, as we have seen, indicated that the contradiction between self-interest and common interest was real. Attempts to return to the no-state situation did not solve the problem but only pretended that it did not exist, and at least some businessmen, chastened by the war, were no longer interested in pretending. But even more important, the war unleashed democratic pressures for change with sudden intensity. The victory of the Bolsheviks in Russia was one sign, but ruling classes within the capitalist world had enough evidence at home as well. German revolutions occurred all along the northern port cities, and even in the South, where conservatism was as popular as beer, a temporary triumph of working-class parties was witnessed.[23] In the United States 1919 was perhaps the most intently political year in that country's history. A series of strikes, culminating in an unprecedented general one in Seattle, racial disturbances, demands by unhappy veterans—all these combined to produce general fear among the dominant elites.[24] In England the abolition of price controls raised prices, and when the government threatened a wage cut in the nationalized mines, a strike broke out that spread to other important industries. Drastic increases in trade union membership, the publication of a socialist daily, and the formation of the Communist Party were all signs of discontent, which continued unabated until the famous "Black Friday" of April 15, 1921, when union leadership capitulated to employer resistance.[25] As Annie Kriegel relates in her massive *Aux Origines du communisme français*, a general strike of railway workers, a naval mutiny in the Black Sea, and gigantic May Day demonstrations in 1919 that led to extensive repression all indicated dissatisfaction with the state of the postwar world.[26] Reacting to the same unease, Italian workers in 1920 occupied factories throughout the country and created workers' councils in Turin. The Socialists, sometimes calmly, sometimes not so calmly, went about the business of debating how they were going to take power. From the viewpoint of the powerful and the privileged, something had to be done to restore order so that industrial production, stimulated by the war, could continue unhampered.

The forces of order, as Charles Maier has argued, were able to reassert hegemony in the face of this revolutionary outburst, but (and this Maier does not emphasize enough) they paid a price.[27] Caught between a reliance on the state and a refusal to acknowledge that reliance, businessmen found that in order to preserve the former they had to sacrifice the latter. During the 1920s bourgeois forces did not lose power, but they did lose command over their traditional ideology, which was almost as serious. A review of each of the major capitalist countries should show how this tradeoff took place.

Obvious methods of restoring social peace included either negotiation with the dissatisfied or political repression. Since very few in power were prepared to do the first, there was increasing resort to the second. Some repression could be carried out privately by vigilantes, such as the work of the American Legion and the German Friekorps during this period, but in general, either negotiation, which was tried in Italy, or repression, which was tried everywhere, required the use of the state in some capacity. Consequently, the postwar years saw the thinking of industrialists heading in two contrary directions simultaneously. On the one hand, nostalgia dominated their fantasies and they wanted to return to a minimalist state; on the other hand, continued intraclass conflict and the outbreak of overt class struggle dominated their everyday activity, and such realities demanded the use of the state as a mechanism for organizing themselves into a class. Because of the pressure from both of these forces in most countries after the war, elites, not yet prepared to endorse fully the use of the state, made one last search for a solution to their problems without it. The device that seemed to offer both the advantages of class cooperation and a technique for maintaining power in the face of demands from below, but did so without requiring a serious confrontation with both their ideological and practical fear of state intervention, was corporatism and, in one form or another, corporatist solutions became popular in every major capitalist country during the 1920s.

Corporatism can be defined as the self-organization of the various sectors of the economy in such a way that their harmonious interaction will guarantee stability and productivity without state intervention, or with as little as possible. Yet this definition only begins to capture a little of the diversity of the experiments that have been tested under the corporatist label. As Philippe Schmitter has shown in a comprehensive review article on the concept, corporatism can be applied not only to the experiments in Catholic Europe and Latin America, but also to Scandinavia and Great Britain, and even in the socialist countries of Eastern Europe.[28] To make sense out of this diversity, Schmitter adopts the distinction made by the Roumanian corporatist Mihail Manoilesco between societal corporatism and state corporatism. In the former (associated with liberal democracies), the role of the state is minimal, the organization of the sectors of the economy nonhierarchical, and participation in the arrangements voluntary, while the latter form, characteristic of authoritarian political regimes, contains an active, guiding state, strictly hierarchical organization, and compulsory membership. Because my focus is on the conflicts between liberalism and democracy, societal corporatism is of greatest interest, for many saw in such a solution a way out of that conflict. Yet "voluntary" corporatism raised as many problems as it solved, and a consequence was that societal corporatism during the 1920s failed. Given the contradictions inherent in it, countries that experimented with societal corporatism faced a choice: either they could attempt to preserve the corporatist apparatus, in which case they moved in an authoritarian direction toward state corporatism, or they could drop the corporatist flirtation and search for other ways out of their dilemmas. Italy and Germany tended toward the former direction, the other countries under discussion toward the latter.

Far from being explained away by the simple term "fascist," Italy during the 1920s was a society very much in flux, where class conflicts were intense and the attempts to resolve them serious. As everywhere else, after the war the first instinct in Italy was to reassert classical notions of economic liberalism. Giolitti had once again come to power in June 1920, and he expressed strong belief in traditional liberalism. Paradoxically, his most important act as head of state was to arrange a compromise with the workers in the factories, using considerable powers of persuasion to win acceptance of this compromise from conservative industrialists, who looked lovingly on the old days of unshared power. That longing was reflected by the businessmen, organized into the Parliamentary Economic Alliance of June 1922, who called for "the relinquishing of the state of every function which is not strictly necessary."[29] The program of Alberto de Stefani, Minister of Finance from October 1922 until July 1925, came straight out of Adam Smith. Public enterprises such as the telephone company were given back to private business groups. The Ministry of Labor and Welfare, whose creation was a concession to wartime pressures for legitimation, was abolished. Edmundo Rossoni, one of the most intriguing of the polyglot group who associated themselves with Mussolini, pushed for an active role for labor and lost, his defeat symbolized by the temporary return to untrammeled laissez-faire. Yet in spite of this burst of activity, more rooted in the nineteenth century than in the twentieth, something was different. First, one had to control the legislature in order to repeal laws, hence political activity by businessmen did not disappear, but actually increased during this period. Second, the experience of the war lingered, for tempered with economic liberalism were a series of policies by which business hoped to use the state for its own ends.

The creation of the Council of the National Economy, a body given the responsibility of debating broad measures of economic policy, indicated a trend away from laissez-faire. Two thirds of the seats on this body went to business, and while business was given the right to participate in decisions involving labor, labor had no such rights vis-à-vis business. Further, the business sectors, such as industry, agriculture, and commerce "were staffed almost exclusively by representatives of the business groups which would be directly affected by the ministry's policies, a clear example of regulation by the regulated."[30] On May 8, 1924, the private chambers of commerce were absorbed directly into the government, becoming part of the Ministry of the National Economy, under the name of Provisional Councils of the Economy. In September 1926 Confindustria was officially recognized by the state as the exclusive representative of industrial employers in all labor negotiations, confirming what has been established in practice. As Renzo de Felice makes clear in his L'Organizzazione dello Stato Fascista, this tendency toward the merger of private agencies with the state in the form of new (or simply newly named) agencies that became little more than fronts for leading industrialists in each sector of the economy, intensified in the middle 1920s.[31] Something new was taking place; Confindustria now, in Sarti's words, "enjoyed both the administrative autonomy of a private organization and the juridical authority of a public institution."[32]

In no way, however, did the absorption of "peak" associations solve the problem of the state. Business interests continued to be opposed to consorzi obligatori, compulsory cartelization laws, and even when such laws were later passed, business interests prevented their enforcement. As they saw it, the merger into the state was designed to neutralize it, not to strengthen it. The fact that such a process was, almost by definition, impossible did not bother them, for they were in desperate need of the state in order to avoid the state; that is, they wished to use the state in order to organize themselves as a class so that they would be stronger in fighting the desire of any other class also to use the state for the same purpose.[33] It is for this reason that they put up such resistance to the idea of anyone else sharing state power with them. Certainly, as Mussolini defined it, corporatism included all segments of the society, even labor. When in 1934 a Ministry of Corporations was established, with twenty-two separate sectors of the economy represented, including workers, and with equal representation of labor on public boards, it was done so over the vocal opposition of businessmen. By then the depression in America had had its effects on the Italian economy, and businessmen "had no choice but to accept the rise of a mixed economy in which private and public enterprise were inextricably linked."[34]

Thus it becomes clear that industrialists were more interested in a flirtation with corporatism than in an embrace of the real thing. They preferred a kind of truncated version that applied only to the self-organization of business, and not to anyone else. They found out, however, that the self-organization of business through the state leads directly to demands from all other groups for the same thing, and once the principle is admitted, there is no way, logically or practically, to prevent such an extension. Further, when corporatism is put into practice, the problem of the state reasserts itself. While in theory the role of the state should be minimal, in actuality that can only come about when the state itself defines the reality, when it permits corporatism to take place. Hence, no matter what is said, the state has the final authority, since it can remove the corporatist arrangements any time it pleases. As it developed in Italy, corporatism, instead of becoming the one final solution that would avoid the state, saw the growth of state power under fascism.

Fascism did not represent a total break with the past, nor would it signifiy one with the future. As one historian put it, "Fascism did not suppress the causes of capitalist strife and class rivalry; it encouraged the centralization and coordination of that conflict such as was developing in other societies."[35] Those who were active fascists clearly rejected liberal democratic principles for capitalist arrangements, but this was done because fascism was seen as a solution to problems raised by those principles. Fascism was undemocratic because rulers did not like what they saw produced by democracy; it was illiberal because those men had not achieved what they wanted from liberalism. Since my main interest lies in the contradiction between liberalism and democracy, the road to fascism is more interesting than what happened at the destination. The triumph of fascism proved that in at least two countries the delicacy required for a societal corporatist solution could not be achieved; fascism's victory was corporatism's defeat. By solving the contradiction between liberalism and democracy through the elimination of both, societal corporatism was transformed into a form of state corporatism.

In Germany as well as Italy, what began as societal corporatism ended as something quite different. Rathenau had a corporatist perspective, but both his desire that labor be allowed to participate and his notion of the state as "behind" corporations were violated by Nazi practice. Corporatism had been extremely popular in Germany, attracting men like Othmar Spahn, who found in it, in Lebovics' words, a "socialism for the middle class."[36] In its German form, according to this fascinating study, corporatism was appealing because it offered a panacea for the problems of the working class. Like the Papal Encyclicals *Rerum Novarum* and *Quadragesimo Anno*, German writers emphasized that corporatism meant both an organized capital *and* an organized labor. Further, the point of the enterprise was to provide stability and calm, neither of which were in great evidence under Nazi rule. For these reasons corporatism during the Third Reich became, in Neumann's phrase, a "myth": "the economic organization of Germany has, indeed, no resemblance to corporatist or estate theories."[37] The reason is that under Nazism businessmen found themselves forced to do things in their own interests, and to do them on terms established by the political leadership. The transformation of the Reichsverband der Deutschen Industrie into the Reichgruppe Industrie was not a simple change of name; the new organization, part of the state, had the authority to compel membership, while the old one, as a "private" trade association, did not."[38] This growth in the power of the state made Nazism both a highly unique form of capitalism *and* a rejection of corporatism as well. The Nazis, in other words, transformed a solution that was still within a liberal perspective (societal corporatism) to one that was completely outside of it.

If in Italy and Germany societal corporatism had led to state corporatism, thereby invalidating itself as a solution to the tension between liberalism and democracy, elsewhere corporatism was a flirtation that ultimately was dropped. In England, much as in Italy, the idea was the product of a meeting of the minds between writers coming from a leftist perspective and those whose traditional allegiance was on the right. The great value of the corporatist solution, according to its proponents, was that it abolished the class struggle (no small thing), and all those who wished to see this occur—whether left-wing industrialists or right-wing trade unionists—joined forces in advocating the idea. From the Fabian tradition, writers like G. D. H. Cole and the Webbs urged what came to be called "guild socialism." From the curious brand of aristocratic socialism embodied in John Ruskin came the widely read book by Arthur J. Penty, *Restoration of the Guild System* (1906). The attraction behind the restoration of guilds was that internal self-regulation woud make external compulsion unnecessary. World War I had shown some businessmen that this "socialist" idea was not so bad. The basically anti-ideological appeal of corporatism was reflected when the Conservative Party indirectly endorsed the notion through the Whitley Committee schemes of 1917, which had urged that the solution to class conflict lay in the creation of "industrial councils," joined by both industrialists and labor leaders, which would work out, without the direct intervention of the state, rules of procedure for each area of industrial relations.[39] Corporatist conceptions, if not corporatism by name, were advocated by important elements within both the Conservative and Labour parties.

Corporatism was distinct from the Disraelian notion of an active state helping both in the accumulation of capital and in reducing the misery of such accumulation among the working classes—for two reasons. First, the corporatist appeal, as opposed to its practice, was against the state and hence was not compatible with this kind of Toryism. Second, when Disraeli was in power, there were no nationally coordinated, powerful, cartel-like trade associations; the enormous growth in the size, power, and membership of private groups was, as S. E. Finer points out, a twentieth-century phenomenon.[40] It was the combination of a Conservative Administration, influenced by industrialists who at one time would have been Liberals, coming to power after World War I when large-scale associations existed that produced the conditions necessary for a new approach to the state. The Education Act of 1921, the National Health Insurance Act of 1924, and the administrative practice of earlier laws like the Trade Board Acts all embodied a new principle. These laws, according to Beer, represented "a general shift in the climate of opinion toward legitimizing the representation of groups—and more particularly the representation of the new organized producer groups of the modern economy."[41] This legislation coincided with a movement toward industrial rationalization—the elimination of the "waste" of competition through more efficient business arrangements—and rationalization was ideologically very close to societal corporatism. Consequently a major thrust of the National Government period (1931–35) was the encouragement of cartelization in private industry, as Arthur F. Lucas documents.[42] Ad hoc arrangements were made to control prices, output, sales, and capacity. The resulting structure, Beer notes, did not represent full corporatism, though some advocated as much; instead, he called it "quasi-corporatism" in which "the relationship was neither one of business pressure groups dictating to government nor of government agencies planning the activities of business. Decisions were made, rather, in a process of bargaining and negotiation."[43]

Just as in Italy and Germany, though for different reasons, participants in these developments discovered the inherent limitations of a societal corporatist arrangement. What bothered them was not the antidemocratic implications of cartelization, but far more mundane matters of self-interest. The problem of what to do about the state existed here as elsewhere, but the British were willing to attempt a new answer to such a vexing question. Instead of locating power either in private trade associations or within the government itself, an indirect system of controls was invented using the tariff. The passage of protectionist legislation during the period of the National Government enabled the state to win compliance from recalcitrant business by using the threat of force rather than force itself. So-called "mature" businesses could be given all the benefits of imperial preference, while those who held out for selfish gain could be denied them. In the words of Neville Chamberlain, who was an important planner of new state arrangements before he was discredited by his foreign policy, tariffs "provide us with such a lever as has never been possessed before by any government for inducing or, if you like, forcing industry to set its house in order."[44] British businessmen, somewhat more class-conscious than their counterparts elsewhere, understood the message, and such devices led away from the solidification of a corporatist solution. When Harold Macmillan, then a young and forward-looking MP, proposed straight-out industrial self-government in 1935, he was rebuffed, for "the Government was as reluctant to devolve large compulsory powers on industry as it was to assume the tasks of central planning."[45] Furthermore, pressure from below was not as strong in England as it was on the Continent, relieving another excuse for an authoritarian solution. A combination of a class-conscious elite and a non-class-conscious union movement made full-scale societal corporatism unnecessary in England. Though corporatist urges continued to have influence within the Conservative Party—and to attract men such as Macmillan, Alfred Mond, Sir Charles Petrie, L. S. Amery, and Lord Percy[46]—by the end of the 1930s most intellectuals had rejected corporatism in favor of an alternative solution that I will discuss shortly.

Corporatism had been a part of French social theory since the Revolution.[47] As elsewhere it was attractive both to conservative writers, who appreciated its concern with order and hierarchy, and those coming from a radical tradition, who saw in it an extension of unionization to all areas of life. Both la Tour du Pin, who tried to reconcile Catholic principles with industrial organization, and Georges Sorel, the *agent provocateur* of revolutionary social theory, can be seen as influential corporatist writers, just as reactionaries in Action Française and revolutionaries in syndicalist unions were influenced by them. Theory was one thing and practice another, and more than in any other country except the United States, businessmen in France resisted the need for cooperation as long as they could. This reactionary ideology, when combined with a strong tradition of paternalism among employers, meant that corporatism would arrive late in France, and even then in unique form. True, by 1930 it appeared as if French employers had become "politically modernized." The CGPF had reorganized itself, changing its name to the Conseil National du Patronat Français, and the new name indicated that the preoccupation of this peak association would no longer be with industrial production alone, but with all the problems of modern employers. With the accession of Claude Gignoux, a man very much committed to industrial cooperation, as head of the new organization, it seemed as if French business was going to take a new direction. But beneath these changes was the France of old. "In reality," as

Ehrmann writes, "the employers movement, as it existed before 1936, never convinced the masses of French businessmen that there were advantages in organization."[48] As soon as a huge strike in 1938 was broken by methods of old-fashioned resistance and repression, there was a reaction against Gignoux and he was replaced by Baron Petiet, a believer in classical liberalism. "The relations between government and business remained for many months uncertain and confused."[49]

It was in this atmosphere that French corporatism finally began to show some attraction. When class struggle was omnipresent (as during the Popular Front period), and when conflict among businessmen did not stop through divine intervention, what became attractive was precisely an approach that claimed to be above politics. Calling itself explicitly an "antipolitical" organization, the Comité de Prévoyance de l'Action Sociale had a certain following in the 1930s, as did the Comité Central de l'Organisation Professionnelle, both of which were corporatist. Each group advocated the principle that the state should allow its powers of regulation to be directed by private association, which in this case meant employers. Though such an approach would have given French businessmen the opportunity to cooperate without the forcible intervention of the state, most of them failed to appreciate this and instead chose to go their own way. During the 1930s corporatism remained more of an appeal than an actuality. Yet principles like the ones these groups advocated were put into practice under the Vichy Regime. The *loi Bichelonne* of 1940 created *comités d'organisation* in every area of French economic life, which incorporated trade associations into the state and saw the by-now-common fusion of public and private. Based directly on Rathenau's experiments, these committees were designed to "avoid the alternative evils of totalitarian planning and of a predominance of self-seeking special interests."[50] The secret of the success of the arrangement was to work out a balance between vested interests and the state that would be acceptable to both. Yet when it came, probably because French businessmen so long opposed cooperation, it came in a form they did not like.

Although twentieth-century corporatists "with few exceptions evinced as much apprehension as had earlier theorists over the prospect of complete creation of a corporative regime by state fiat,"[51] the COs turned out to be quite aggressive, using the state to extend themselves into all kinds of activities that many businessmen considered improper. Neither Marshal Pétain nor middle-sized industrialists liked the arrangement for that reason, but it was supported by important civil servants, large capital, and the Germans, quite a formidable coalition. The Germans, who were the most important constituency, appreciated the trend toward cartelization because it promoted economic efficiency and therefore, as Robert O. Paxton points out, could "release labor for Germany." The most important consequence was that "Vichy . . . afforded French businessmen and administrators the most substantial lesson in planning and state management of the economy up to that time."[52] In other words, societal corporatism again revealed itself as a chimera, an interesting idea, but one that brought about state intervention, the very problem it was designed to avoid. And because large capitalists benefited from it and small ones did not, corporatism could not solve the problem of cooperation within the capitalist class as a whole. It was an idea whose time had come, but whose time, also, had gone.

The country least influenced by corporatist conceptions was the United States, although that ideology was not missing from American shores. In a fascinating book on the subject, James B. Gilbert has traced the influence of corporatist theories on six prominent American thinkers, and here again we see the unique confluence of left and right. Industrialists like Edmund Kelly, former radicals like James Burnham, and others in between advocated the idea that "modern social organization ought to emulate the contours of industrial organization."[53] As Gilbert shows, these men also had to deal with the problem of the state, and the contradictions of corporatism emerged graphically when they did so. It was not so much that they worshipped the state as much as that it was given importance "by default—that is, from other elements of society."[54] The state became the mechanism for cooperation because no other mechanism existed. Whether their theories were called industrial democracy, civic reform, or American Fabianism, what united all these writers was a distaste for class struggle and a sense that if "politics" were replaced by efficient and rational administration, the world would be that much better a place in which to live. These men never had much impact on actual governmental arrangements at the time they lived, though some were influential in local government.[55] The emphasis in their theories on collectivism and cooperation simply ran into severe ideological obstacles at the national level.

While each of the five countries examined in this chapter briefly visited the principles of nineteenth-century liberalism after World War I, what occurred in the United States was more like an extended stay. What Hicks called "The Republican Ascendancy" swept aside the War Industries Board, the Committee on Public Information, the League of Nations, and any and all such notions that were based on the idea of cooperation and long-run considerations.[56] Only a protectionist and repressive function was left for the state. With a reactionary majority seated in the Supreme Court, a conscious attempt was made to turn back the clock to an era when businessmen did not have to worry about all those problems that seemed to plague their European counterparts. Nonetheless the problems were there, and all it took to see them were open eyes. Throughout this period the man whose eyes were opened widest was Herbert Hoover, and, interestingly enough (given his reputation), it was he who came closest to a European corporatist mentality. As both William Appleman Williams and Grant McConnell have shown,[57] Hoover envisioned three spheres of social activity: business (including agriculture), labor, and the public. Hoover proposed an ingenious solution to his less observant colleagues: let us, he said in effect, allow labor to organize in return for our right to organize. Long before John Kenneth Galbraith coined the term "countervailing power," Hoover defended public protection through the balancing of giant interests. As Secretary of Commerce under Harding, he had tried to turn his agency into a gigantic trade association for business, but he was rebuffed because his solution required similar developments in other bureaus and no one was willing to do it. As President, he embodied some of his ideas into the Reconstruction Finance Corporation (an idea that has reemerged in popularity in 1975),[58] but this came at the end of his presidency. What Hoover proposed required time, and this was exactly the commodity that was too valuable as the Great Depression rushed its way into American life. Hoover is best seen as a theorist who happened to become President rather than as a President who happened to have some ideas. His administration was the closest that societal corporatism came to power in the United States, but, as in England, it was ultimately rejected in favor of other solutions.

In sum, the success of societal corporatism overall was mixed, leaning toward the negative side. First, "voluntary" corporatism required a great deal of class consciousness on the part of industrialists, and during the 1920s a long-run perspective was still not popular. Contrary to the view that a form of "corporate liberalism" strongly emerged around this time, what is most impressive is the tenacity with which businessmen held on to their parochialism and outmoded ideas even as they worked against their interests. Their refusal to submerge their immediate concern with profit led societal corporatism to dissolve into one of its two alternatives. Second, corporatism never solved the problem of the state but simply posed it in a new form. As could have been predicted from Rathenau's writings, whether the state was "behind the scenes" or an active participant could not be decided a priori, but was bitterly fought out. Third, corporatism did not solve the problem of class conflict but instead tried to ignore it. Its strength everywhere was in appearing to provide a solution to conflict and to what businessmen derogatorily call politics. By giving everyone a place, it also sanctified hierarchical arrangements in which business would always be at the top. In defining normal practice as that which could be worked out without the need for compulsion, it promised a curiously similar version of Marxist and anarchist theories of the withering away of the state. In every way the major problem of societal corporatism was that it was utopian, expressive of a yearning for an end to intra- and interclass struggle at a time when those forces were more powerful than ever. In short, both the economic and social (let alone the political) conditions of the 1920s and early 1930s made societal corporatism an interesting, but flawed, solution that flourished for a time and then began to wane.

Under different conditions, the idea could become popular again, which is one reason why explicitly corporatist proposals have been advanced during the economic crisis of the mid-1970s, when they stand a better chance of being realized than fifty years earlier (see Chapter 10). In that earlier period, the contradictions of societal corporatism, where they did not lead to fascism, led instead to the development of alternative ways to organize the state.

THE INVENTION OF THE FRANCHISE STATE

The world-wide depression of the 1930s made the quest for some relief to the political contradictions of capitalism desperate, for revolution was in the air and the traditional excuse of businessmen for their special privileges —that they brought prosperity to all—would have been laughable were it not that conditions were so serious. The problem was to develop a structure that could provide for cooperation among businessmen without leading either to the growth of a form of state corporatism that was too rigidly authoritarian or to a form of nineteenth-century liberal anarchy that was not authoritarian enough; and, at the same time, any such solution would also have to be responsive to pressure from below for greater equity. The contradictions were so severe by this time that any permanent structure seemed impossible, but there could be found ways to delay their full impact through temporary arrangements. Almost by accident, the idea was advanced of encouraging cooperation among businessmen, not by forcing it on them through the state, and not by suggesting it in a way that would have no impact, but through a combination of the two. Specifically, state power itself could be delegated to a private agency that would then exercise it in the name of the state. When this was done by a trade association, all needs for inner class cooperation could be met. That public authority was being exercised could not be doubted, but at the same time the form of this authority came in the clothing of one's own colleagues, somehow making it all seem more acceptable. Compulsion, in other words, could be used if things came to that, but in all likelihood they would not, because a juggling of the distinction between public and private authority would allow informal negotiations to work out (privately) the conflicts. In turn, when protests from the disadvantaged became too severe, they could be brought into the arrangement by giving each segment that showed sufficient strength a small grant of state power for its own use. The leaders of such a group could then be called on to control internal dissatisfaction in return for their seat in the state. Though the idea did not emerge with the precision that a summary of it implies, a solution along these lines seemed almost too good to be true.

The new approach resembled corporatism in that there would be self-organization of private sectors, but its ideological basis was quite different. Corporatism, though antistatist in theory, became increasingly statist in practice. The new solution was the exact opposite; while it praised the state in theory, to distinguish itself from traditional liberalism, it tended to reduce the impact of the government in practice by vesting public power in private agencies. Because of this distinction, it makes sense to utilize an alternative name for the new arrangement. Since the structure that follows from it resembles a franchise business operation, with a central headquarters and a series of branches to carry out business in its name, the new solution can be called the Franchise State. In one form or another, the Franchise State dominated the politics of liberal democratic societies between the Depression and the 1950s.

Where corporatism is successful, franchise solutions are likely not to be, and vice versa; hence the United States, which showed the greatest hostility toward the one, had the greatest affinity for the other. The events surrounding the New Deal illustrate one example of how the Franchise State came into being. Just as voluntarism in the first year of American participation in World War I had led to the necessity of a War Industries Board (WIB) in the second, the failure of business acting alone to prevent the Depression swung the pendulum back to state action. The WIB, however, had been based on the existence of a war, and the question arose as to whether an activist state could be permitted in times of general peace. If a war unfortunately did not exist, one could fortunately be invented; as William E. Leuchtenberg has convincingly shown, the theme of war dominated the thinking of nearly all the planners of the first New Deal. When they developed their schemes of legislation, they continuously had in mind the ideology of war, and it was therefore not surprising that proposed solutions in domestic areas as diverse as public power, housing, agriculture, rural reconstruction, banking, and the National Recovery Administration (NRA) "rested squarely on the War Industries Board example."[59] Ironically a solution invented to cope with war might succeed, rhetoric aside, in a period of peace.

The agencies created during the New Deal, however, differed from the WIB in one crucially important respect. The WIB never developed a formal and legal approach to the question of delegation of power. Many businessmen had refused to cooperate with it because the theory behind it was so neo-Hamiltonian, so impervious to their immediate needs. By contrast, the NRA was from the beginning explicitly designed to work in cooperation with leading industrialists. The goal was established by Franklin Delano Roosevelt in his famous Commonwealth Club speech of September 23, 1932:

> The responsible heads of finance and industry, instead of acting each for himself, must work together to achieve the common end. They must, where necessary, sacrifice this or that private advantage, and in reciprocal

self-denial must seek a general advantage. It is here that formal Government—political government, if you chose [sic]—comes in.

The exact role of the state, then, was going to be far from coercive: "Government includes the art of formulating a policy and using the political technique to attain so much of that policy as will receive general support, persuading, leading, sacrificing, teaching always, because the greatest duty of the statesman is to educate." Business would learn; government would teach. Yet a cooperative arrangement, where politics would replace coercion, could guarantee industrial cooperation, but it could not, as Roosevelt himself recognized, compel obedience from "the lone wolf, the unethical competitor, the reckless promoter, the Ishmael or Insull whose hand is against every man's." [60] In an effort to steer between no state power at all, which might prolong the Depression (which these men saw as a war), and an active state, which would not please large industry, Rexford Tugwell and the other planners who dominated the early New Deal proposed the theory of delegated power.[61]

The National Industrial Recovery Act (NIRA) became the model for the new approach. Its details are familiar and need be only quickly summarized here. In each industry brought under the supervision of the NRA, codes of fair practice were to be established, which covered price controls, production quotas, and labor practices. Trade associations were to work out the codes within their respective industries. The government was given the right to compel obedience, but this right was to be used only as a last resort. Leuchtenberg describes the results of this legislation:

> By delegating power over price and production to trade associations, the NRA created a series of private economic governments. The codes, as Walter Lippmann observed, were, in effect, charters like those granted the East India Company. The largest corporations which dominated the code authorities used their powers to stifle competition, cut back production, and reap profits from price-raising rather than business expansion. Since Roosevelt, [General Hugh] Johnson, and [Donald] Richberg hesitated to use punitive powers, and had little intention of undertaking extensive national planning, the private interests of business corporations overwhelmed the public interest.[62]

The NRA was ultimately declared unconstitutional in the "sick chicken" case,[63] but, as Theodore Lowi rightly points out, the principle of delegated power not only lived on but was strengthened.[64] In the *Schechter* case the Supreme Court had found that the codes were unconstitutional, not because they delegated public authority to private institutions, but because the delegation was from one branch of government to the other, and because it was imprecise and sloppy. So long as Congress drafted legislation with care, the principle that the powers given to Congress could be dispatched elsewhere stood a good chance of being upheld. *Yakus v. United*

States validated price controls during World War II, and by the end of that war it had become clear that the Court would fully accept the principle of delegated power.[65] Although these cases dealt technically with the question of delegation of power to state governments or to administrative agencies, and not to private bodies, the lack of any legal challenges to the latter procedure meant that the notion of giving state power to private groups for purposes of self-regulation could grow after the overturning of NRA. By the 1950s, delegated power became the single most important principle of the modern capitalist state. NRA, itself highly unpopular, as Ellis Hawley has shown,[66] lived on, but without the formal name and structure; what was an extremely conspicuous failure during its lifetime became a model of business-government relations in later years.

The oil industry illustrates one reaction to the constitutional demise of NRA. During its existence, the American Petroleum Institute, a private trade association that had been formed in 1919 by the oilmen who were members of the WIB, was permitted to fix prices and regulate production. After the NRA's dismantling, Texas Senator Tom Connally, permitting no legislative hearings, won the passage of a law creating the Interstate Compact to Conserve Oil and Gas (IOCC) which *informally* created the identical price-fixing arrangement that existed under the Blue Eagle. Neither truly private nor truly public, the IOCC enabled the industry to avoid simultaneously "the twin horrors of competition and anti-trust action."[67] When World War II broke out, the oil industry sponsored the creation of a Petroleum Administration for War, sent over three thousand of its executives to Washington, and used the power of the federal government to make enormous profits. Then, after the end of this war, an Oil and Gas Division of the Interior Department was charged with bringing order to the industry, and the division was effectively controlled by a "private" organization, the National Petroleum Council. In other words, the delegation of public power to private industry was in no way impeded by the Supreme Court's reversal of the NIRA. The oil industry, to be sure, is atypical, because it is the largest in the United States, yet studies of any industry that go into great detail, such as Sidney Fine's of the automobile industry,[68] show the same pattern of trying to reproduce the principle of using delegated power in order to control competition. The idea was too good to permit Court decisions or popular expectations about both business and government to stand in its way.

It is not particularly surprising that a system designed to benefit private corporations by granting them the authority of the state worked out so well in the United States, given that country's love affair with the pursuit of private gain. The French case is much more unusual, for in France, since Napoleon, there has been a state bureaucracy jealous of its power and not likely to give it away.[69] Furthermore, French businessmen traditionally have been unable to cooperate with each other for the satisfaction of their mutual interests, and an active, large, and sometimes radical left has been a reality of modern French political life. If a franchise-type operation could be applied here, it probably could be applied anywhere. Hence the importance of a phenomenon noted by Andrew Shonfeld:

> What the French are discovering in this way has long been familiar to other democratic societies, particularly in Northern Europe and in North America. The characteristic procedure there is to start by looking for a consensus among the relevant interest groups and next to translate this into national policy and action with the minimal intrusion of official authority.[70]

During the Fourth Republic, and to a lesser extent the Fifth, not only did the National Assembly become, in the words of Prime Minister René Meyer, a "Chamber of Corporations,"[71] but Premier Pinay could cry out to *Le Monde* in 1955, as if life were in danger, "I am besieged by the special interests."[72] What both men realized from their position at the top of the state was that below them a vast system of special state privileges for powerful vested interests had been created.

The Vichy experience did not bode well for the creation of a postwar state along Franchise lines. The tendency during wartime occupation, as we have seen, was toward a corporatist ideology that paradoxically resulted in an extremely active role for the state. When this was combined with the tremendous hostility toward business after the war—"I did not see you men in London," de Gaulle told members of the *Patronat* in his first postwar meeting with them—the first attempts to create a new relationship were decidedly against the interests of large manufacturers. The *comités d'organisation* were continued under a new name, and the state was given the authority to enforce decisions made by them.[73] Yet business eventually managed to escape from hostile public opinion and work its way back into the public graces. In part, this was due to a full-scale debate within the *Patronat*. New leaders, like Pierre Riscard and Henri Davezac, and the men associated with the *Jeunes Patrons*, took the offensive and argued forcibly for an end to the belief in classical liberalism. Although they never took over the organization, their influence was so strong that their point of view generally prevailed. As President Georges Villiers said after the war: "We will try to make the employers of good will understand that any return to an excessive liberalism is impossible, and that they must accept the necessary discipline in the framework of organized business."[74] Those "of good will" did understand, and eventually they were able to prove the advantages of the new attitude to their colleagues.

The constitutional structure of the Fourth Republic reflected this change in ideology. Franchise-type principles were built directly into the Constitution; as one example, the National Economic Council, created by that document, called for membership from the "most representative" private associations, thereby elevating the Franchise State into the highest law of the land. Yet nothing is simple in France when it comes to the relationship between business and government. French political life has been marked by extreme shifts from *dirigisme* to laissez-faire and back again, reflecting the ambiguity of businessmen caught between their preference for smallness and a necessity for "modernization." [75] Neither principle is compatible with the Franchise State, resulting in a situation where what was taking place in reality was continuously being denied in theory. The Constitution forbade delegated legislation, which is an important aspect of any granting of state power to private groups. Yet in practice, as Philip Williams shows, there was a strong tendency for delegated legislation to become a modus operandi of the Fourth Republic.[76] Again, the drive toward nationalization revealed contradictory tendencies. The Constitution had been explicit, due to the fact that nationalization was a part of the platform of every resistance group (including even de Gaulle's): "Every good, every enterprise, whose use has or acquires the characteristics of a national public service or of a de facto monopoly must become the property of the community." [77] This principle was carried out between 1946 and 1948, when mines, power companies, banks, transportation companies, and other important segments of private industry were brought under state control. Yet unlike Britain, where, as Adolph Sturmthal pointed out,[78] administrative responsibility in nationalized industries was clear, in France nationalization took a form that made the principle of "community property" deliberately ambiguous. The boards that administered the new corporations were given a mixed character under the name of *tripartisme*, an experience that I will examine in more detail in the next chapter. Attempts were made throughout the Fourth Republic to restore formerly private industrialists to positions of control in the new industries; one intriguing example was a 1953 proposal (ultimately defeated) to make the boards operate under *quatrepartisme*, in which the new group would be "persons known for their industrial or financial competence." [79] Indeed, all the contradictions of the new structure were captured by the widely used slogan of the time, *"Nationaliser, ce n'est pas étatiser"* (nationalization does not mean state control), which reflected both the economic necessity of state direction and the fear of an active state that has always been part of the bourgeois world view.

In no way can the nationalization of industry, however imperfect, be considered part of the Franchise State, for its thrust is toward public control. But aside from this one area, the Fourth Republic saw the growth of, in the words of a Rand Corporation economist who studied this phenomenon, "a hybrid mixture of public and private law of a kind previously unknown to France." [80] Specialized parliamentary committees, which dealt with the minutiae of administrative life under little public scrutiny; the drastic increase in the importance of private member bills; the system of *pantouflage* (under which leading administrators would take jobs in private industry, bringing their contracts and their data with them)—all combined to reinforce the wielding of public power by private groups. Rarely has any political system seen the exercise of pure power by private pressure groups as has the French Fourth Republic. The legislative system, in Williams' words, "allowed one committee, packed by a few assiduous defenders of a pressure group, to obstruct a policy desired by the majority; or several, representing different interests, to join in mounting converging assaults on the public till." [81] It was not often that a policy escaped the clutches of such groups.

Tax reform is one example of the capture of the state by organized groups, for "the most serious obstacle to tax reform is the concerted resistance of interest groups protecting their acquired rights." [82] Planning is another example. The theory of *le plan*, according to its enthusiastic advocates, was that planning would provide a mechanism for avoiding the contradictions inherent in the capitalist mode of production, including the contradiction between specific interest and general interest. The Monnet and Hirsch plans, though filled with reference to Rousseau and the *volonté générale*,[83] gave much more to private interest groups than they took from them. The most important consequence of the planning mechanisms of the Fourth Republic, in the words of the Rand Corporation study of the French economy, was that "the government has given important encouragement and assistance to the extensive activities of trade associations, which have resulted in a collective organization of large elements of business operations." [84] Though there was a slight move away from this tendency in the Fifth Republic, for the immediate postwar years, in Stephen Cohen's words, "planning is done by big business for big business." [85]

The formal ideology of the Fifth Republic was more ambiguous. As a conservative, de Gaulle felt a certain sympathy for large-scale industry, but that sympathy was always counterbalanced by a great distaste. Consequently de Gaulle wished to see both a strengthening of *dirigisme*, in which the state would tend to direct the economy, and support from established interests for his foreign policy, especially in Algeria, which required exactly the opposite. The former aspect of the duality is represented in the writing of Michel Debré, the most important Gaullist spokesman in the early years of the Fifth Republic. Debré was given to making statements like this:

> It is the business of the State to choose, to command, to impose. . . .
> [The State] is the expression of the general interest, the rights of the nation
> and the needs of freedom. This lofty responsibility is matched by a power
> of dedication and intervention, which certainly has limits, but the principles of which cannot be challenged in any domain.[86]

In his 1957 essay *Ces Princes Qui Nous Gouvernent*, he pictured France as under the total domination of private interests acting in irresponsibly parochial ways. Yet the practice of the Gaullist Republic never followed up the antibusiness implications of this perspective. The proposal for an Economic Senate, which would include all the powerful private groups, was receptive to private power, as was the idea of *concertation*, the system used in the Economic and Social Council for making public decisions through extensive extraparliamentary consultation with private interests.[87] Furthermore, the Fifth Republic often bypassed the legislative branch, which meant that private groups "switched their main efforts from parliament to the executive." [88] What did they find after the switch? Though high-level administrators, such as those of the Grands Corps d'Etat, were supposed to be strong statists, hostile to private interests in the tradition of Debré, the situation was, as Ezra Suleiman shows, far more complicated. Through long interviews with public administrators, Suleiman discovered that the hostility toward private groups was directed nearly always against middle level, less powerful organizations. When it concerned peak associations, these same men often saw them as quite legitimate; peak associations were not, according to these administrators, engaged in politics, but in normal administration. In short, these men of state have a concept of legitimacy that "reveals an undeniable bias in favor of strong, representative organizations." [89] For this reason, the actual policy of the Fifth Republic has been, as McArthur and Scott conclude,[90] the creation of a state structure that benefits the largest firms and encourages economic concentration and cartelization. The hostility of the Fifth Republic toward the Franchise State was a temporary one at best.

What happened in both France and the United States took place everywhere else throughout the capitalist world, though the timing and the degree varied considerably. In the fascist countries, which had seen extensive increases in state power, franchise principles could not be applied until after the war. Nonetheless, a basis for them existed. In Italy, the blurring of public and private, the tendency to use ad hoc arrangements, and the process of applying ad hoc standards of public policy all carried over after the war, though they took a new form. As Sarti pointed out, "The Ministry of Industry and Commerce, the direct descendant of the old Ministry of Corporations, is today probably more solicitous of CGII [confindustria] interests than the Ministry of Corporations ever was." [91] The tendency of postwar Italy to rely on what has been called *il sottogoverno*—the underbelly of public policy in which important decisions are made, substantially in secret, by the private groups most directly affected by them—is part of the Franchise State. The full range of tactics used by private groups to maintain their privileges, so well described over ten years ago by Joseph LaPalombara, still exists.[92] In Italy the change from fascism to liberal democracy has not brought a decrease in the exercise of public power by private groups, but a probable increase.

Germany's postwar political arrangements were formed during some rather unusual circumstances. Since "the economic arrangements of the occupying powers reflected chiefly the thinking of the Americans," [93] the American fascination with the Franchise State found its way into Germany. The development of West Germany's postwar state can best be understood as a compromise between two opposing forces. On the one hand, there was the fact that the occupying powers wanted stability and economic recovery, best assured by keeping the economic machinery of fascism intact, just finding new people (who could be old people, like those who directed it before the Nazis) to run it.[94] Since the Nazi system relied on cartels and the principle of *Wirtschaftslenkung* (guided private enterprise), a continuation would have meant a strong role for the state. But at the same time the economic thinking of the Adenauer group was best reflected in Ludwig Erhard, who advocated, of all things, something close to laissez-faire. A nonideological solution like the Franchise State was perfect for walking between these two principles, one morally repugnant but highly practical, the other quite unpractical but morally correct.

Finally, examples abound in English politics of the granting of public power to private groups. In fact, the difference between a corporatist solution and a franchise solution was well illustrated by an article in *The Economist* in 1939. Noting that during World War I the administrative heads of major agencies were "selected in the main from outside the industry to be controlled," the article went on to point out how in World War II "industry is controlling itself." [95] There followed a long list of every commodity within the Ministry of Supply and the name of the principal business interest of the man chosen to head each. The following raw materials were coordinated by representatives of the industries most directly affected: aluminum, alcohol, flax, hemp, iron and steel, leather, nonferrous metals, paper, silk, chemicals, timber, and wool. In addition, the Ministry of Foods saw direct administration by representatives of the dairy, grain, tea, meat, fruit, sugar, potato, and cooking oil industries. No wonder that the *New Statesman* could lament that this form of organization represented "a continuation of the policy of handing over powers to . . . capitalist groups which have been given authority to control production and prices. . . . The present government is pre-eminently a capitalist Government, and almost its one idea in matters of economic policy has been to endow the big capitalist associations and combines with authority over the consumers." [96]

After the war the precedents established during it continued. In 1946 the Road Haulage Organization, a formal part of the state, was legally disbanded and its administrative functions turned over to a private corporation.[97] The consultative mechanisms worked out during the war between the Ministry of Food and the Cake and Biscuit Alliance continued when it was just a question of the butter without the guns. There was a veritable explosion of private arrangements, in some cases involving matters of life and death, such as when the Poisons Board, as part of its routine procedure, consulted with the Association of British Chemical Manufacturers before publishing its list of lethal substances.[98] Matters reached the point when an official inquiry into the whole question of private power was undertaken, and the subsequent 1950 report of the Select Committee on Intermediaries said what by now everyone knew: "Ministers tend to deal with the trade association in formulating the basis of their policy." [99] Also in that year, it was estimated that the Federation of British Industries had directly nominated some thirty-four members of important government bodies, and the Trade Union Congress another sixty.[100] To be sure, there was disagreement expressed between powerful interests and the state indicating that not everything was taking the direction that the former wanted. To some extent these disagreements reflected real gains for public accountability, such as in some of the nationalized industries. But public squabbles of this type can also, as Finer noted, be compared to a lover's quarrel. Just as a liaison may see its frictions, which often seem severe, there is still a common agreement that holds the relationship together: "for the closer the bond between the two parties, and the more permanent it appears to be, the more anguished are the quarrels that do arise." [101] Probably the most fascinating of these "marriages," since it concerns a matter involving everyone, is that between the British Medical Association and the Ministry of Health. In his comprehensive study of this relationship, Harry Eckstein showed how a law that appeared to be hostile to a private interest came to be administered by that very interest for its own benefit. "On important points the profession's leaders have been consistently able to get their way, save only for one conspicuous exception (remuneration), so that one can accurately say that the National Health Service in operation is to a large extent a joint enterprise of the BMA and the Ministry, however intransigent the Ministry was at its birth." [102] The idea advanced in the Conservative Party's Industrial Charter of 1947 that public powers should be delegated to trade associations had come to fruition.[103]

What emerges from this view of the creation of the franchise system, and becomes a crucial point in understanding its nature, is that the general principles (if they can be called that) embodied into the Franchise State were not the result of Manichean ruling class prophets who understood the way in which society was about to change and met the challenge head on. Instead the Franchise State was developed defensively and with almost no forethought; one can find almost no manuals for its operation, just after the fact rationalizations for its existence. It was the failure of any previous solution to work that brought it into being, and wherever it became the major form of organization of the capitalist state, it did so in an unpretentious and modest sort of way. It entered the house of monopoly capitalism, in short, through the back door and it would stay inside only so long as it continued to function in something resembling a satisfactory manner. But before it even had a chance to sit down it found others knocking, this time at the front door, and if it wanted to remain in the house, it discovered that those people had better be invited in, even if only into the foyer.

The Extension of the Franchise State

Delegating public power to private trade associations seemed to solve one major problem confronting the industrial ruling classes. It created a state apparatus that was neither coercive nor voluntary, and whose flexibility reflected quite well the ambiguity of leading businessmen toward government. The fact that coercion, when necessary, came in a form that businessmen could accept also meant that the bugbear of "socialism," which so worried them in their dealings with government, would not be raised. Some form of relief to the tensions that had dominated business classes since World War I had been found, and during the later 1940s and 1950s one could hear the collective sigh from all over the capitalist world. But permanent shelter had not yet been discovered, for there still remained one problem, pressure from below, and that threatened to blow the whole structure to rubble.

The combined impact of the Great Depression and World War II made that pressure, in general, stronger than it had ever been before. In every country in which freedom of expression had been won, the message was direct and blunt: businessmen were rapacious and it was their activities that had led the world into economic catastrophe. This hostility intensified after the war, for most workers had postponed their right to strike in the interests of victory, while businessmen were clearly making profits from their wartime activities. Not only did workers occupy the factories in France once the fighting stopped, but in the United States a wave of strikes that constituted, in Irving Bernstein's opinion, the most serious militant activity by workers in twentieth-century America, broke out in Minnesota, San Francisco, and Alabama.[104] The pressures long throttled by fascism led to strong electoral victories for the Communist Party in Italy, which threatened to disrupt the Marshall Plan and other U.S. proposals for a "stable" world. Communist victories throughout Eastern Europe gave the impression of a world in revolution, even though many of those affairs were in fact quite conservative in their ultimate implications. The combined effect of militant dissent at home and anti-capitalist gains abroad made it clear that, if the Franchise State was applied to business and business only, it could never succeed for long in a hostile world.

The solution to pressure from below, this time, was simple. When demands became too strident, the leadership of the sector making the demands, provided it could be reformed into "maturity" and "responsibility" (I will discuss the meaning of these terms in the next chapter), could be welcomed into the franchise arrangement by being given a little piece of the state for its own use. Under this notion the Franchise State could be preserved; business would be unable to obtain everything it wanted, but it still had the first franchise, and, as with a hamburger stand or a gas station, getting the preferred location is they key to making the system work as much as possible in one's interest. Hence the years that saw the invention of the Franchise State also saw its extension to other areas of political life outside industry; the fear of business under corporatism, that all of society would be organized, came to be, but under conditions less unfavorable than corporatism—with its growth of state power—had become in practice. A partial victory was preferable to a total loss.

One sector that everywhere won quick admission into the Franchise State was agriculture, for farmers could at times support movements of dissent, both of the right and of the left, and in order to prevent this, it was better to have agriculture "regularized" along franchise lines. Since farming was an industry that for many years had not followed the dynamics of the liberal marketplace, it was ripe for a solution involving the state. In Britain this took place through the Agriculture Act of 1947, which had been planned during the war within the Ministry of Agriculture, controlled by large farmer organizations. The Act was deliberately made vague, under the assumption that details could be worked out administratively. "However," the most thorough students of these events conclude, "the Act did indicate a method of settling such questions in the form of cooperation between Government and the principal agricultural organizations." [105] The National Farmers Union, which had recently taken on a more centralized structure than in the past, was informally represented in the Act through a general understanding that membership on county executive committees, created by the Act, would come from this organization. As a result, farm policies for the nation as a whole were worked out by the organization that stood to gain or lose the most from them. As Self and Storing note, "Even for a period in which Government and interest groups have been drawn closely together, this relationship has probably been unique in its range and intensity." [106]

The British method of incorporating agriculture into the Franchise State was an archetype of what took place in other countries. In the United States, the first piece of legislation that brought public power to farmer groups was the Agriculture Adjustment Act (AAA) of 1933, and this was actually written in the Washington office of the American Farm Bureau Federation (AFBF).[107] The second AAA, passed after the Supreme Court nullified the earlier one, in some ways went further in creating a piece of the state for the exclusive use of agribusiness, as the experience of the Farm Security Administration, retold in the next chapter, indicates. The Taylor Grazing Act of 1934 applied the principles of the NRA and the first AAA to cattle grazing, giving large landowners in the West their section of the state,[108] and the TVA, created in May 1933, was within two years an agency for the cooption of local southern elites into the operations of the Franchise State.[109] In France, where there has long been a tradition of support for the independent peasant, the miserly, suspicious spirit of Balzac's M. Grandet gave way to the reality of the need for cooperation, and, after World War II, the state became strongly involved in price supports, surplus disposal, and marketing, all within an interest group framework worked out in other countries.[110] The "Green front" in West Germany lobbied for the creation of a Bauernstand, a corporate state for farmers.[111] Finally, under the dynamic leadership of Paolo Bonomi, the private organization known as Coltivatori Diretti became responsible for the public administration of Italian agricultural policy. Through a system begun in 1944, which reached its peak around 1958, every rural area was given a consorzi, all organized together into a federconsorzi in each province. These organizations, remarkably similar to the county agent system of the American Farm Bureau Federation, took on a host of public functions, including credit, storage, and price fixing, with the sole difference being that Coltivatori represented smaller farmers than those in the AFBF.[112] Like scientists independently making the same discovery at the same time, agricultural entry into the Franchise State, wherever and whenever it took place, seemed like a repeat of the same process.

The entry of labor unions was far more complicated. Farmers, for all their expressions of discontent, were at least businessmen, but the same could not be said for workers. With almost no exceptions, the entry of labor unions into the state was fought, and fought bitterly, by business interests, and it is a torturous manipulation of the facts to see labor's victory as somehow anticipated and planned for by business leaders. True, once the handwriting was on the wall, some businessmen decided to accept the new reality and try to work with it, but that is a far different matter. Labor could not enter the Franchise State without a struggle, and when it did, the state could no longer be understood as a simple agent of those who live off the production of others but incorporated, even if to an imperfect degree, representatives of producers (that is, workers) themselves. In most places this struggle took two different forms. In one case the franchising of labor was accomplished outside the state itself; participants from unions and trade associations met in private and arranged a deal by which labor's participation would be assured. The most perfect example of this took place in Sweden with the Basic Agreement of 1938, and the Swedes try to renew this bargain each year, priding themselves on the degree to which they can avoid the state.[113] The other approach to actual incorporation is less dramatic and takes place through the passage and administration of a series of laws, the gradual effect of which is to ensure some share of the state for the private use of labor leaders. Britain and France are examples of the first form, the United States and West Germany of the second.

The Matignon agreement of 1936 is a fascinating example of how a series of private arrangements can permanently affect the structure of the state. In 1936, with a Popular Front government in power in Paris, and with more than a million workers on strike throughout all of France, the possibility that the economy itself might ground to a halt was real. In an effort to avoid such an eventuality, four representatives of industry, eight labor union leaders, and four members of the government met at the Palais de Matignon, and devised a program that called for reforms in the French wages and hours laws in exchange for an end to the strikes.[114] Though this agreement preceded creation of the Franchise State in France, it provided the first employer recognition of the *fait syndicale*, the right of labor to organize. Business tried to pretend that it was all a nightmare, that it never happened. Those who supported Matignon were purged from their positions within the Patronat. With characteristic paternalism, employers, right up to the de Gaulle republic, sponsored "partnership" schemes between labor and capital that never worked because businessmen wanted all the power on one side. In spite of all these attempts to roll back time, Matignon became a symbol of the new order. Its spirit could be seen almost thirty years later in 1965, when Gilbert Grandval, a left Gaullist Minister of Labor, won passage of a bill that made compulsory a system of work committees throughout industry on which capital and labor would sit together.[115] The Association Capital-Travail, about which business had talked but on which they rarely acted, had come into being, only this time with the authority of the state behind it. It was a small step, for the partnership for labor was a junior partnership by any reckoning, but it underscored labor's right to belong to that series of arrangements known here as the Franchise State.

An extraparliamentary meeting also incorporated British labor into the state in the crucial years following World War II. What Samuel Beer called the wage restraint bargain of 1948 involved protracted private negotiations between organized labor and organized capital.[116] The Federation of British Industries, the National Union of Manufacturers, and the Associated British Chamber of Commerce (all to merge with each other shortly thereafter into a superpeak association) selected from among their leadership a small committee that met with key labor leaders and representatives of the Attlee government to hammer out an agreement on wages and prices. In exchange for limitations on profits and an agreement to hold down the price of goods, the labor leaders agreed to a policy of wage restraint. The class war was thereby transformed into a disagreement among "gentlemen" who worked out the areas in which they had a common interest. This proved to the well born that both labor leaders and a Labour government could work for the preservation of capitalist arrangements, making participation by labor in affairs of state a legitimate thing. Paradoxically, the same agreement also indicated something that, to the rulers, was much more ominous. In Beer's words, "The old syndicalist thesis was validated. For it was initially not by their votes, but by their control over instrumentalities necessary to carrying out vital national purposes that the organized working class raised themselves from their old position of exclusion and inferiority." [117] It was the threat of that power being used for its own ends, and neither charity nor democratic principles, that guaranteed labor's participation.

"Government management of the economy has drawn the TUC [Trade Union Congress] from the fringes of power into the center of economic decision making," [118] one political scientist has written. Things being what they are today, to make economic decisions is to make political ones as well, and it is not surprising that labor has taken its part in the state. The entire system of industrial relations in Britain can be understood as a process by which the wage bargain of 1948 is being made into a juridical relationship.[119] With the change of the Ministry of Labor into a Department of Employment and Productivity, the institutionalization of industrial courts (following the Whitley Council plans), the adoption of a prices and incomes policy, and the participation of labor in economic planning (six members of the General Council of the Trade Union Congress are allowed to sit on the National Economic Development Council, the national planning agency), labor would appear to have gotten its way. To some extent that appearance is deceptive. For one thing labor became involved in planning just at the moment when it was becoming passé, at least in its traditional form. Ironically, as Shonfeld notes, of all the plans proposed, labor consistently supported ones based on franchise principles, while businessmen—or at least some of them—showed themselves more innovative. As new arrivals to power, labor leaders were highly possessive of it.[120] Half in and half out of the state, labor necessarily plays an ambiguous role, one that, as Dorfman points out, may hurt it in the long run.[121] For the moment, organized labor in Britain, as in France, is still in the process of making official bargains outside the authority of the state.

In Germany legislation came first and negotiations afterward. Codetermination, the system whereby labor sits on boards for each industry that are responsible for full industrial relations, is unique among the countries being discussed here in the degree to which it officially recognizes the right of organized labor to play a role in the state. The effect of codetermination, as Spiro has shown, is to restrict business paternalism and at the same time to encourage cooperation among the different unions.[122] Altogether, the impact has been one in which class conflict has been subject to a system of rules that makes it all seem so much more tame. As Dahrendorf notes, systems like the one embodied in codetermination create a sense of illusory harmony in which "the notion of contradictions and tensions may be avoided at all costs." [123] This "nostalgia for synthesis," while preferable to the paternalism of Imperial Germany, leads, as in England, to labor supporting franchise arrangements more strongly than does business. Repeating the World War I experience, Social Democrats have once again made a capitalist system work.

Events in the United States can be understood in terms of what happens when private agreements cannot be reached. Before the creation of the Franchise State, the American Federation of Labor (AFL) had operated *internally* on a franchise basis. "The Federation parcelled out territories, real as well as imaginary, to the internationals, which became inviolable. Thus, the International Association of Machinists possessed a chartered claim to all machinists regardless of whether the union actually represented them or they worked in nonunion industries and might have preferred another union or none at all," one historian has written.[124] Ironically, in order to enter the Franchise State, private franchises had to be abolished, which meant essentially that the narrow craft basis of the AFL would have to be altered in favor of industrial unionism. Since the purpose of the Franchise State was the smooth working out of class conflict, mass labor organizations, not narrow ones, had to be *represented*, even if only by a small group of leaders. Initially, therefore, participation in the new solution broadened and democratized labor's role in public affairs.

A review of the history of American labor's early involvement with the state seems like a *déjà vu* experience. Under section 7(a) of the NIRA, the National Labor Board (NLB) was expected to intervene in situations of class conflict in order to have the various parties settle their differences peacefully. Not only employers, but the union leaders as well, were committed to the ideology of the Harmonious State, and consequently they preferred not to use state machinery wherever possible. It was the AFL, not the NAM, that had said in 1923: "Industry must organize itself to govern itself, to impose upon itself tasks and rules and to bring order into its own house." [125] The first test of the NRA apparatus, the Berkshire Knitting Mills strike in Reading, Pennsylvania, was an outstanding vindication of a minimal state solution, comparable to the Guggenheim-Baruch copper deal, Matignon, and the British wage restraint bargain. All parties cooperated voluntarily because their self-interest pointed that way; agreements were reached, and both the employers and the employees accepted them. The state played the role of mediator, and no coercion was necessary. But just as reactionary businessmen had undercut the voluntary character of Baruch's cooperative committees of industry, forcing a coercive role for the state in the WIB, companies such as Weirton Steel and Budd Manufacturing flatly and arrogantly refused to deal with the NLB. Their defiance was so easily accomplished that voluntarism was discredited, and when President Roosevelt seemed to support employer defiance in the automobile industry, a serious wave of strikes broke out around the country. There was really one issue: the creation of a state machinery that would have the power to compel, not merely recommend, allegiance to collective bargaining agreements. As with business, an active state did not come about due to clever planning, but was the result of a failure of any other mechanism to control both inter- and intraclass conflict. The analogue to the WIB, a body with more than suggestive powers, here became the National Labor Relations Board, created both by executive order and by the Wagner Act of 1935, which made organized labor a junior member of the Franchise State. The state rushed in where private parties feared—or dared not—to tread.

With a somewhat firm foundation created by the admission of agriculture and labor, the Franchise State in all capitalist societies historically becomes the repetitious extension of the same principle—delegation of state power to monopolistic private organizations—in other areas of life; in the United States, for example, veterans' affairs are turned over to the American Legion (just as matters involving veterans are handled similarly in Britain);[126] housing is given over to real estate interests; airline matters to airline companies ad infinitum. The eventual result of this reversal in the nature of government is captured by Lowi's description of the departments of Commerce, Labor, and Agriculture; they "are not meant to be governing agencies except in some marginal way. They are and were meant to be agencies of representation. They were, in other words, set up not to govern but to be governed." [127] And just as de Tocqueville said that the only thing Americans find harder than starting a war is stopping one,[128] the granting of state power to private groups, once begun, spread like a Wyoming forest fire. Besides the cases already mentioned, one can see the Franchise State at work when Congress allows the National Rifle Association to dispense surplus army bullets. Bar associations and medical societies have public functions and even the Society for the Prevention of Cruelty to Animals came under attack in New York City in 1974 because it was misusing its public grant of authority for private purposes. In the health field, according to the recent work of Sylvia Law and her associates, a complicated series of financial arrangements has become a smoke screen behind which a private organization, Blue Cross, establishes the shape of the entire federal health system.[129] Movies are rated, food evaluated, commercials tested, young Christian and Jewish men and women exercised, amateur athletes "protected," morals and decency scrutinized, parades organized, libraries kept up, professional standards maintained, and historical landmarks preserved—all by private agencies wielding public powers. Most bizarre of all, so peculiar that it almost defies belief, even the state itself seeks to win part of the state. The armed services, already part of the government, have sponsored the creation of private lobbying associations (Navy League, Air Force Association, and Army Association) that then, on a typical franchise basis, wrest away public power to be used in support of those very government agencies.[130] When they lobby for funds for their respective service, these groups claim to be private. When they drive official service vehicles and administer official service activities, they claim nothing. From this point of view, the state has not been gaining power but has been rapidly losing it; one wonders if there is any authority left to be parceled out.

Perhaps Franchise State principles were carried a bit further in the United States than anywhere else. Nonetheless the general structure described here was, to some degree or another, an operating feature of politics in every one of the countries discussed in this chapter. While each country has its own unique historical traditions, the solution embodied in the Franchise State was too convenient an answer to the contradictions of the capitalist mode of production to be ignored for long. The intentional confusion between public and private, the use of powers delegated from the legislature to a sympathetic bureaucracy, consultation and clientelism, and extensions of franchise arrangements to head off discontent—all these became in the postwar period highly visible features of the political systems of France, Italy, England, and Germany, as well as Holland, Austria (where a system called *Proporz*,[131] under which proportional representation of the major interest groups is guaranteed on all public boards, carries the theory of the Franchise State to its mathematical conclusion), and Canada. Further evidence of the popularity of such arrangements is that experiments such as Italy's ENI and IRI—hybrids of public and private management and responsibility—became the explicit model for Britain's Industrial Reorganization Corporation, France's L'Institut pour le Development Industriel, Canada's Development Corporation, Australia's Industries Development Corporation, Sweden's Statsforetag, and West German holding companies like VIAG.[132] Why this appeal? In a sense there is no other choice. Political life in twentieth-century capitalist societies, under the pressure of demands from below, simply had to become democratized and, faced with that reality, the Franchise State appeared as the solution least in violation of capitalist and liberal principles. Hence the Franchise State becomes the first form of the capitalist state juridically to recognize the contradictions between liberal and democratic principles discussed in the introduction to the book. Contradictions that once existed in the society but not in the state from now on existed in both. From this moment on the state will be involved both in its traditional accumulation function but also actively in the process of real legitimation. Neither the realization of genuine democracy nor the simple class state of nineteenth-century socialist theory, the state must now be understood as combining elements of both, the mixture and proportion in specific situations being the most important question of all.

5 / The Franchise State at Work

"It is, it seems, politically impossible for a capitalist democracy to organize expenditure on the scale necessary to make the grand experiment which would prove my case—except in war conditions."

John Maynard Keynes (1940)

"Everybody here has private interests, some are directors of companies, some own property which may be affected by legislation which is passing and so forth. . . . We are not supposed to be an assembly of gentlemen who have no interests of any kind and no association of any kind. That is ridiculous. That might apply in Heaven, but not, happily, here."

Winston Churchill in the House of Commons (1947)

"The frontier between the public and the private sector has become uncertain."

André Siegfried, De la IIIᵉ à la IVᵉ République (1956)

WITH PERHAPS THE single exception of bodily functions, no other area of human experience has provided more imagery for describing the state than that of business organization. If Ferdinand Lassalle's "nightwatchman" corresponded to the era of competitive capitalism, and the idea of the state as a giant trust to the period of economic concentration ("The perfect form of trust is the state," [1] one American reformer noted in 1895), then it is not surprising that the popularity in the twentieth century of franchised business operations in the private sphere has had its effect on the public as well. Gasoline stations, automobile dealerships, and fast food hamburger stands have become a model for the organization of public power. The following are the organizational characteristics of a franchised business operation: there is a central authority that retains the right of making decisions; part of this authority is given over to a branch that exercises it in the name of and according to the rules of the central authority; each branch is organized hierarchically, with a manager being the only person in contact with central headquarters, passing its directives down to those under him, directives that are supposed to be standardized but allow, either contractually or informally, for local variation; on questions of jurisdiction, managers are to work out their disagreements with each other, appealing to the central authority only when hopelessly deadlocked; finally, the goal of the whole structure is to provide (for a price) a standardized product, generally of not very high quality, yet one that most customers consider a bargain, even though its sales make a substantial profit for those at the top of the hierarchy, reinforce a passive consumer role for those at the bottom, and support a substantial bureaucracy in the middle. Each of these characteristics, to a greater or lesser degree and with variation from place to place, has become a feature of the capitalist state in the twentieth century.

DELEGATION AND THE DOUBLE BIAS

The first important characteristic of the Franchise State—embodied in the American NRA, the legislation of the National Government period in England, the Fourth French Republic, and the postwar West German Basic Law—is a substantial delegation of public authority from the central headquarters of the state to quasi-private bodies. What determines when a delegation of power will be made? Clearly not everyone who applies will be accepted, or the solution will not make any sense. In order to understand who is eligible to participate in the Franchise State, then, one must begin by looking at those who are not. An example was provided during the New Deal, for then attempts were made by liberal bureaucrats to solve the problem of rural poverty so graphically depicted by John Steinbeck, James Agee, and Walker Evans. All the trappings of the Franchise State were created in the Bankhead-Jones Farm Tenancy Act of 1937, which brought the Farm Security Administration (FSA) into being. The FSA attempted to embourgeois poor farmers by loaning them money to become little capitalists, at which point they, like their bigger neighbors, could obtain grants of public authority for their own use. Called by one writer "an effective branch of government," [2] the FSA had a simple problem: it worked, and because it did, it was subjected to as unfair, vitriolic, and bitter an extinction campaign as any legislative program has ever faced, a story that is still capable of arousing indignation, even among those made callous by example after example of the bias of organized political power. Powerful farmers, already organized into the Franchise State through the American Farm Bureau Federation, waged a relentless war on the FSA, for the uncomplicated reason that they wanted their franchise all to themselves. Tenant farmers found themselves in the unenviable position described by William Leuchtenberg:

> The FSA had no political constituency—croppers and migrants were often voteless or inarticulate—while its enemies, especially large farm corporations

that wanted cheap labor and southern landlords who objected to FSA and to tenants had powerful representation in Congress. The FSA's opponents kept its appropriations so low that it was never able to accomplish anything on a massive scale.[3]

The obvious lesson is that the Franchise State cannot be understood as a juridical form only; the structure can be created with relative ease, but unless a constituency has some degree of organized economic or political power, the structure will be meaningless.

The American War on Poverty contains another conspicuous example of a group that was unable to obtain a working delegation of authority under the rules of the Franchise State. The "analogue of war" that first motivated the Franchise State during the New Deal was resurrected in 1964 when Lyndon Johnson decided to abolish poverty, thereby reaffirming the notion that the state can muster itself to solve a domestic problem only by seeing it in militaristic terms. (Ten years after Johnson's war, inflation became an enemy against whom the American people had to "win," instead of the economic maladjustment that it is.) One might think that a fairly easy way to abolish poverty would be to give away money to poor people, roughly like the administration of Social Security. But such an approach, which can be described as a simple welfare policy, was not in keeping with the new ideology of the Franchise State that had emerged in the United States. Instead of direct state aid to the poor— simple in conception and easy to administer—a cumbersome attempt was made to bring poor people into the Franchise State by giving them, not money, but organization.[4] The state attempted to establish the prerequisites without which participation in the Franchise State is impossible: structure, leadership, and correct ideology.

On every account save one the attempt failed. An intensive study of the creation of poverty boards in the Los Angeles area found that poor people there "did not gain power over decisions made by the board, or diminish the public agencies' predominant influence on the board."[5] In other words, the public sphere dominated the private, unlike the rest of the Franchise State. Leadership was created, but these new representatives of the poor seemed atrophied, leaders without followers, like a hamburger stand without customers. Torn between their expectations and the reality of their failure, many of them never did develop the correct ideology, becoming more radicalized by the failure of each program. The inability to create mass organizations with "responsible" leaders who understood and accepted the operations of the Franchise State meant that when the War on Poverty was enervated, there were few vested interests around to keep the franchise in operation. The one organized group in the "poverty" sector was social workers, and that group benefited from the experience. As Daniel P. Moynihan observed: "With astonishing consistency, middle class professionals—whatever their racial or ethnic background—when asked to devise ways of improving the condition of lower-class groups would come up with schemes of which the first effect would be to improve the condition of the middle class professionals." [6] Moynihan exaggerates (knowing, as he proudly claims, no interest but self-interest, he is incapable of finding idealism in others), but in general he is correct: while the poor were still poor, the organized group had bureaucratic strength. The situation is like our hamburger stand without customers being kept in business by its suppliers; they succeeded for a while, but even though they had that much power, they could not confront the laws of the market forever. The failure to build a clientele, due again to the power of existing franchises (urban political "machines," for example), meant that this venture would eventually be terminated by the central authority.

Clearly, then, participation in the Franchise State requires, as E. E. Schattschneider once pointed out, a bias in favor of groups that are politically well organized.[7] Such groups are able to muster a resource at their command and, by manipulating that resource, to obtain the grant of state power that they feel they need. Four resources appear to be most important. Of course, sheer economic power was—and still is—the first criterion of entry. It is no accident that the chief business planner of NRA was Gerald Swope of General Electric, representative of one of the largest and most strategic industries in the United States, or that Walter Rathenau's business background was in the German equivalent of GE, the Allgemeine Elektrizitäts-Gesellschaft. The Franchise State was conceived in order to deal, not just with the giants, but with the giants among the giants. But, as the last chapter indicated, in order that the tension between liberalism and democracy be softened, a second criterion was developed. Some attempts have been made formally to represent the working class in the Franchise State. Labor controls both the productive process in the most basic sense (without workers, nothing can be produced) and is also the basis of a large number of votes, no small matter of detail in a liberal democracy. Third, there is also a way in which a combination of moral purity together with ideological self-righteousness can become a criterion of admission, especially in areas that, though heavily politicized, are considered nonpolitical. Patriotic associations, professional athletic organizations,[8] religious groups,[9] temperance associations, and watchdogs of national conscience are all, at one time or another, exercisers of public power. Finally, a group may be admitted into the Franchise State through the manipulation of a scarce resource. There is only a limited amount of air through which radio and television waves can pass: in the United States franchises to control what passed through that air were given to private corporations, and once they were obtained, these grants themselves became a scarce resource.[10] The television industry has consistently opposed technological developments that would permit the existence of a greater number of channels, leaving cable television, an invention with phenomenal potential, underdeveloped and underutilized, for any incursion into scarcity would undermine the rationale for the franchise. Managerial genius is seemingly granted to those who can suppress invention, refuse exploration, and deny capability, in a reversal of an earlier capitalist ethos.

Whatever the reason—economic power, ability to command votes, ideological purity, or control over a strategic resource—each of the groups just discussed was able to wrest a part of the state for its own private use. Behind this first line of bias, however, exists another system of stratification, for when a grant is made to a sector that has demonstrated its power, it is made, not to the whole sector, but only to the powerful within it. When Robert Michels proposed his iron law of oligarchy—that private associations will inevitably be led by a few at the top—he was being quite accurate about the society of his time and not, as he himself thought, about all societies at all times.[11] Michels was aware that one of the reasons for oligarchic struggle was that private associations were in competition with each other for control over available resources. The Franchise State converts this struggle into a *raison d'être*. The party that Michels studied would be a model of democratic openness compared with the rigid structures that the rules of participation in the Franchise State have imposed on more recent private associations. In a political system offering the choice of fairness with impotence or rewards with oligarchy, who is to say that choosing the latter option is wrong? One of the most stultifying features of the Franchise State is not which choice is made but the fact that one has to be made at all.

Strict hierarchy is the most important organizational principle of the Franchise State. In Italy, to take a somewhat extreme but nonetheless suggestive example, the close contact between the Italian Banking Association and the finance committee of the national legislature has led to the development of a series of protocols in which only the president of the Association can talk to the chairman of the Committee, the vice presidents to the next in line in the legislative body, and so on down to the bottom.[12] At the highest levels of power, men of similar inclinations easily recognize each other. Elitism in the state seeks out and reinforces elitism within private associations and vice versa; those who direct monopolistic associations find themselves having much more in common with other directors than they do with people below them in their own organization. The situation that Ezra Suleiman found with respect to the French Grand Corps d'Etat applies substantially throughout the West: "The members of the Grand Corps thus benefit from an aura of elitism and from a reputation for impartiality; they occupy important positions in the administrative, para-administrative, and private sectors; they form part of a network within and beyond the administration, which enables them to arbitrate conflicts and coordinate policies—all of which means that they are profoundly involved in the decision-making process." [13]

What does differ from country to country is the form that the inter- action at the top takes. In France, movement from the highest reaches of industry to the highest reaches of the state tends to occur in one direction. *Pantouflage* is the term used to describe the process by which administra- tors at some point in their career renounce their service to the state and sell themselves (and their information) to the highest private bidder. In the United States, on the other hand, the interaction tends to be in the opposite direction: the state recruits its personnel directly from the seg- ments of the society affected by the area of administrative jurisdiction. Various studies of the Brookings Institution have documented this rela- tionship. One, a comprehensive examination of all the under and assistant secretaries appointed between 1933 and 1961, the quintessential years of the Franchise State, uncovered the surprising fact that businessmen were more prominently appointed during those years than they were during the administrations of Harding, Coolidge, and Hoover; that 75 percent of all the Department of the Treasury appointments during those years came directly from banking and law; that twice as many Defense and War Department appointees were from large-scale business as similar bureau- crats in domestic areas; that the appointment process to Interior and Agriculture (the two places where the principles of the Franchise State are probably most advanced) reflected the interests of the dominant group in the private sector, exercised through congressmen from the affected areas; that of the 15 high officials whom Eisenhower appointed to the Commerce Department, 13 were businessmen and 2 were lawyers; that Truman did the same, to a slightly less pronounced degree, in reverse in the Labor Department; and that in the State Department "recruiters relied strongly on a community of men, both in and out of the government—in universities, foreign policy association, law firms, and banking institutions— who had had a broad and active interest in international affairs." [14] A similar, and even more detailed, study of all federal executives appointed between 1933 and 1965 did, as the earlier study did not, break down some of the data along industry lines. This one showed that the trend of appointing men who worked for defense contractors to state positions in- volving matters of defense increased greatly under Kennedy and Johnson. Further, the proportion of regulatory commissioners appointed from the industries they regulate varies according to the four criteria of delegated power just discussed. The highest number of industry representatives were appointed either in economically powerful sectors like finance (to the SEC) or railroads (to the ICC) or in those that controlled a scarce re- source, such as airlines (CAB), or, less clearly, communications (FCC). The lowest percentage was in smaller industries (FTC) and those involving a strong public interest (FPC).[15] The authors of these two reports make no evaluative conclusions about their data, but the figures certainly do suggest the mutually reinforcing hierarchical relationships that come to play an important role in the Franchise State.

The interlock of powerful private individuals and high state officials, whatever the direction in which it begins, results in one of the most striking paradoxes of the Franchise State: that it renders civic life both more democratic and more elitist at the some time. On the one hand, more groups are brought into affairs of state for the first time and are therefore much better off under these arrangements. But at the same time, the price paid is that decisions come increasingly to be made in a semi-secret, informal manner, with all the important details being worked out by similar-minded elites. This paradox is illustrated by the experience of French planning. In its rhetoric, the plan is seen as the triumph of democratic ideology, a response to demands for greater participation by formerly deprived groups. Indeed, it would have been hard to predict in advance that a capitalist society could have adopted so many of the key ideas of socialism and remained relatively intact. Yet in operation the plan is notoriously undemocratic. Shonfeld, whose language is generally judicious, goes so far as to call the operation of the plan "a conspiracy." Pointing out that the planning process ignores politicians, small business-men, and the general public, he writes: "In some ways, the development of French planning in the 1950s can be viewed as an act of voluntary collusion between senior civil servants and the senior managers of big business." The result, he says, is a "conspiracy to plan," and for those who feel that the word "conspiracy" is too strong, he adds that it is valid "because the result depended on a recognition by private business that the government official personally disposed of considerable powers which could be used to influence the success or failure of individual business. It all depended, therefore, on a series of bargains between the main centers of public and private economic power." [16]

Thus the process by which power is delegated in the Franchise State reveals a double bias, first only to certain kinds of associations, and then only to certain powerful people within those associations. It will be obvious that the net effect of this procedure is doubly conservative. Not only are leaders of organizations likely to have a vested interest in existing arrangements, whatever the nature of their organization (labor leaders are consistently as committed to the status quo, often more so, than their capitalist counterparts in country after country), but in addition the tendency toward decision making by informal elites becomes difficult to reconcile with democratic principles. After discussing the experience of planning in six different countries, Shonfeld was struck most by the confusion in public expectations that had resulted. "Perhaps," he suggested, "this obfuscation of what is really going on, whether conscious or unconscious, derives from a deeper reluctance to recognize that some of it does not fit at all well with the existing structure of Western democratic institutions." [17] Similarly, in his analysis of the role of interest groups in Great Britain, S. E. Finer found democratic structures being bypassed: "The arrangements negotiated tend to be package deals to the exclusion of the wider public and notably of Parliament." [18] This is true elsewhere as well, and certainly one reason for the decline of the legislative public power is the rise of monopolistic private power. The growth of the administration is due, consequently, not only to purely technological factors (many of which could more easily be used to further democratization and legislative government), but to the balance of class forces within the society. The leaders of large cartel-like syndicates need an active bureaucracy composed of men remarkably like themselves; legislatures, which as Edward Shils pointed out, are composed of a whole different breed of men,[19] are highly "dysfunctional" to them and hence they try to undercut their power whenever they can, which is often. The decline of the legislature reflects the antidemocratic side of the use of the Franchise State.

In 1916 an American corporatist, of left-wing persuasion, wrote: "Socialism, then, stands for something of the nature of the extension of civil service to industry." [20] He could not have been more wrong. In continental Europe it was capitalism that extended the bureaucracy to the private firm, while the United States saw the extension of industry to the civil service. But in either case the close cooperation between a private and public elite goes far to abolish the distinction between the economy and political society, one that early theorists of capitalism tried hard to maintain. In some places the state, as Marx had prophesied, became the executive committee of the ruling classes; elsewhere, as in America, the ruling class became the executive committee of the state. But in both situations the state and the ruling class together divorced themselves more and more from the people without whose allegiance there would be neither a state nor a ruling class, and this was the ultimate consequence of the dual bias involved in the way power is delegated in the Franchise State.

KEEPING THE HOUSE IN ORDER

Defensive, as if he knew all along that what he was doing was not quite legitimate, even if it was perfectly legal, Dwight D. Eisenhower once responded as follows to a question on why he was appointing to the Department of Defense's important Division of Petroleum Logistics a general who happened to be on the payroll of Standard Oil of New Jersey: "It would be idle to employ as a consultant anyone who didn't know something about the petroleum business. He is bound to come from the petroleum industry." [21] (As an aside, a sign of the decline of the Franchise State is that when President Ford tried to do roughly the same thing, appointing as head of the Federal Energy Office a man who had received a "separation payment" from an oil company, there was so much opposition that his nominee, unlike Eisenhower's, could not be approved.) Examples like these, when combined with the double bias involved in the delegation of public power, reveal the existence of an elite that benefits from the new political arrangements, but says nothing about the nature of those benefits. Why do various sectors want to participate in the Franchise State? What are the advantages and disadvantages that accrue? Simple statements must be avoided at all costs, for the Franchise State is neither a haven for private aggrandizement (many powerful groups fought its creation and resisted participation in it) nor a clear victory for public accountability. Instead, the best approach would be to view the arrangement that establishes and extends the Franchise State as a deal, in which each party obtains something it needs but also gives up something it would rather have in exchange. While the specific conditions of the deal vary from place to place and from time to time, in general its terms can be expressed as mystification in exchange for self-regulation. By entering the Franchise State, a private sector seeks enough independence to make it, except in extreme cases, autonomous from the rest of the state and therefore from the public. Such autonomy becomes impossible to maintain, however, because the Franchise State requires interdependence among its parts. The promotion of autonomy in an era of interdependence results in a series of mystifications and confusions, and the resulting hodgepodge of expectations and assumptions, it turns out, becomes the major benefit received for participation. But in return for this advantage, each entrant pledges, in the words of the single most popular metaphor used in describing the Franchise State, "to keep its house in order," [22] to regulate itself according to certain agreed-upon criteria. An examination of first the terms under which self-regulation takes place and then the benefits of mystification should shed more light on the everyday operations of the Franchise State.

Self-regulation takes a number of forms. The crucial password that, when uttered reverentially, permits entry into the Franchise State is "responsibility," and it is in order to ensure this nebulous quality that self-regulation is justified. Within the business component of the Franchise State, the history of the term responsibility originates in the conflicts that broke out within the industrial ruling class around the time of World War I. In general the largest capitalists were the ones with the greatest class interest and the most foresight about the need for cooperation, and they took the lead in condemning the shortsighted pursuit of maximum self-interest characteristic of their more parochial colleagues. In the perpetual struggle between large and small capital, the former tended to justify its practices in terms of responsibility and "maturity," leaving the obvious implication concerning the latter. Few socialists were as denunciatory of short-run business practices as Rathenau, while in Italy the debates between organizations of small businessmen (like Confapi) and the large ones in Confindustria have often been bitter. An additional irony is that the very largest Italian industrialists, representatives of firms like Fiat and Montecantini, find even Confindustria too parochial for their tastes; leaders of Fiat go directly to the state without using the intermediate association at all, except when it serves their convenience.[23] In France this struggle often expresses itself between the CNPF and the Confédération générale des Petites et Moyennes Enterprises; in the debates over a national incomes policy, the latter took the lead in reaffirming opposition to state intervention in the economy, while the former was more hesitant.[24] As a result, a distinction is often made in French planning between "good" and "bad" monopolies, with only the former being expected to participate in the management of the national economy.[25] A similar distinction has been widely used in the United States, where responsibility came to mean "reasonable" monopolistic practices as opposed to "unreasonable" ones, enshrined by the U.S. Supreme Court in its interpretation of the Sherman Anti-Trust Act.[26] The terminology had been originated by the National Civic Federation, a body that played a major role in the development of a long-range corporate perspective, when it advocated passage of the Hepburn Bill, eventually the Federal Trade Commission Act.[27] The fact that the distinction between good and bad business practices originates in intraclass struggle means that when observers speak of the "soulful" corporation or, in a more recent study, the "mature corporation," that becomes "an arm of the State," [28] what they are describing is not qualities of character and good breeding but the rationalization of the business practices of the very largest firms.

Although the difference between reasonable and unreasonable business activity is at root ideological, standing as it does for commitment to the Harmonious State as opposed to the Franchise State, self-regulation has had its impact on real arrangements, both in the area of industrial and political activities. Price gouging, blatant cheating of customers, grossly exploitative working conditions, and rapacious mineral exploitation have in general been replaced by price fixing, public relations, joint union-management enforcement of working provisions, and professed concern for community affairs. To be sure, there are exceptions; when it concerns the poorest sectors of the society, those not integrated into the Franchise State —such as large areas of South London where refugees from the British Empire live, the Parisian *Bidonvilles*, rural poverty areas, and urban slums—old-fashioned business practice is still a characteristic of daily life. Nonetheless, within those groups defined as part of the Franchise State, a significant change has taken place in business practice.

Business has also tried to change its politics as the price of entry into these arrangements. There is a transformation in the nature of what Italians call *la busterella* (the little envelope), a general term for payoff and corruption. Bribery, as I pointed out in Chapter 2, was an important aspect of the Harmonius State, for, given the lack of explicit standards for determining the beneficiaries of public largesse, unofficial ones were quick to develop. A bribe became, in an interesting way, a foreshadowing of twentieth-century solutions, because with bribes industrialists were buying a piece of the state (personified in an individual legislator) for their own use.

The development of the Franchise State transforms the theory, if not the practice, of corruption. For one thing, overt bribery should have declined because it became part of the public policy process. Administrative regulation and bargaining between clients and clientele agencies perform many of the functions that bribery accomplished under the Harmonious State: selecting options, regulating the "market" of claimants on the state, proving rewards for good service. In the fashion of Vermont's Senator Aiken, who proclaimed that the way to end the war in Vietnam was simply to proclaim it over and leave, bribery was theoretically eliminated by preserving the same practices but making them legal. Powerful vested interests, having been granted a piece of the state, no longer had to buy one. Then corporate leaders could condemn bribery as a thing of the past, replaced by more genteel activities, such as grants-in-aid, subsidies, bonds, or campaign contributions. But theory never did accord with practice, certainly not in this case. Though the ostensible reasons for illegal bribery were eliminated, the market for government services still makes it far too tempting to violate the rules. The Aranda affair of September 1972 in France implicated officials of the Gaullist party in a process of distributing contracts that was unseemly at best. The donation of the Associated Milk Producers to Richard Nixon's campaign in that same year violated the already low standards of legality for such contributions. The interesting aspect of both cases was that neither was "necessary." Presumably, both the private and public officials involved could have obtained what they wanted if they had been more patient and less greedy. But since devotion to the free market is as praised as it is ignored, adherence to a free market for government services is also bypassed when self-interest is at stake. Bribery and corruption continue to dominate the state, even as legal alternatives to them are adopted.

The change from competitive to monopoly capitalism also transforms legislatures. The older form of assembly is the one described by Henry Adams in *Democracy*, characterized by its "under-handed and grovelling intrigue." [29] It resembled a marketplace, with individual legislators, committees, and laws on sale to the highest bidder, and with competition among the buyers intense and often vicious. Under more modern conditions, just as monopolies regulate and "tame" competitive markets, legislative affairs are rationalized and simplified, so that the buyers and sellers of legislation meet in an atmosphere of predictability and mutual self-interest. In Italy legislative committees frequently meet privately *in sede deliberante* (that is, able to pass laws directly, in committee, without referring them to the larger house), a system that, according to LaPalombara, offers "extraordinary opportunities"[30] for private groups to get their way. Under the Fourth Republic, the National Assembly's education committee included a majority of teachers and priests; the medical profession was half of the health committee; 38 out of 44 members of the agriculture committee were from rural areas; 13 out of 18 on the beverages committee were from wine-growing areas, and so on.[31] The Agriculture Committee of the U.S. House of Representatives is not only composed almost solely of men from rural districts, but each commodity subcommittee tends to be chaired by spokesmen for the relevant specific commodity producer.[32] Another example of the more rationalized relationship is the special member, the man who becomes a spokesman for a specific interest while serving in the legislature, thereby making it redundant for that interest to hire lobbyists. The Fourth Republic perfected this pattern into an art, with men such as Pierre André (steel), Marcel Anthonioz (hotels and bars), and André Liautey (wine).[33] In the United States, one senator and perennial presidential candidate came to be called "the Senator from Boeing" because of his close ties with that particular industry.[34] During the height of the Franchise State, an American journalist spoke of the existence within the U.S. Senate of a "club" of influentials,[35] a situation that was also found to be characteristic of the French National Assembly.[36] This, too, is part of the politics of the Franchise State, because these "insiders" invariably owe their seniority to the safeness of their seats, due in large part to the comfortable relationship with important local private interests that they have developed. The gentlemanly character of the club (senators who were too aggressive, even if they had the right politics, could never be members) was reflective of the gentlemen's agreements that had replaced aggressive competition in the private sector. Furthermore, both the Franchise State and the "club" disappear together; when the former was found wanting (in the United States in the mid-1960s), the latter became less important.

With legislatures becoming more "businesslike," businessmen could disdain the purchase of votes and appear as responsible and mature in their political dealings. This not only made further self-regulation less urgent, but contributed to the process so well described by V. O. Key. "The great political triumph," he noted, "of large scale enterprise has been the manufacture of a public opinion favorably disposed toward, or at least tolerant of, gigantic corporations, in contrast with an earlier dominant sentiment savagely hostile to monopolies and trusts." [37] Self-regulation was a small price to pay for that.

What is good for business is good for the other sectors that have won part of the state for their own private use. When labor was admitted into the Franchise State through extraparliamentary negotiations, what would become normal under the Franchise State was already being put into practice, for the labor union leaders who were permitted to negotiate were not only an elite but tended to be from the more conservative unions, the ones most likely to be seen as responsible. Just as responsibility came to mean the practices of the largest business firms, in the arena of labor responsible unions were those who most accepted business ideology and therefore had the greatest stake in preserving the series of political arrangements into which they were to be admitted.[38] Only leaders of such unions could be entrusted with the ticklish problem of self-regulation. Labor would have to purge itself of "irresponsible" behavior, including wildcat strikes, organized political dissent, and outrageous racketeering. The American experience offers the most complete version of this "purification" process.

The first indication of what self-regulation would mean for American labor occurred during the debates on the Wagner Act that resulted in its entry. After Senator Wagner first introduced his bill, President Roosevelt, who did not favor it and wished a rapid adjournment of Congress, asked that Public Resolution Number 44 be passed instead. This compromise measure gave the President the right to create labor boards where they were needed. His reasoning was that since the Wagner bill was so controversial, it had to be delayed, but since at the same time a full-scale strike in steel was ablaze, PR Number 44 could enable him to settle the latter without a radical breakthrough for labor in general. Before passage, however, FDR insisted that William Green, the head of the American Federation of Labor, put down the steel strike, which Green agreed to do, demagogically breaking the back of the strike by attacking it during an AFL convention. Due to his actions, as Irving Bernstein put it, "the rank-and-file movement within the Amalgamated [Association of Iron, Steel, and Tin Workers] had been put to rout." [39] The message was cryptic and clear: the price of labor's participation in the Franchise State was maturity, which meant no wildcat activity. Spontaneous rank-and-file action, of course, did not disappear after the Wagner Act, just as scurrilous business activity and right-wing individualism by businessmen did not disappear either, but now its discouragement could be justified as the reasonable position.

Labor also took it upon itself to purge its ranks of organized dissidents, since in the peculiar vernacular of American society, having a strong belief in social change is generally considered irresponsible. The most interesting aspect of the purge of Communists from the Congress of Industrial Organizations was that it was *not* an example of state repression; instead, leaders of the union took on this campaign themselves. At the 1949 CIO convention, with no noticeable help from the state (but with its silent encouragement), the United Electrical Workers were expelled, members of the Communist Party were forbidden to hold office, and a constitutional amendment was adopted that allowed future expulsion of Communist-dominated unions.[40] The question is why, at this time, did labor leaders purge their own house, when previously they were only too willing to allow Communists to organize some of the most difficult industries in the country? Clearly the answer is that labor's entry into the Franchise State was no longer secure. After World War II, conservative congressmen had sought to roll back the effects of the Wagner Act. The sloppily drafted Taft-Hartley Act of 1947 was imprecise, but its clear intention reflected a "bias against collective bargaining" that "could be used unreasonably to restrict union activities." [41] Unlike business, whose admission, once secured, was never in doubt, labor, as junior partner, had to prove its responsibility continuously. The purge of the left was a sign to the state, in a time of anti-Communist hysteria, that labor leaders would take care of their own, and consequently labor retained its membership in the Franchise State. A return to "business" unionism, reflected in the rapid growth of the Teamsters, was officially encouraged, Robert Kennedy's vendetta against James Hoffa notwithstanding. No serious attempts were again made to expel organized labor from the Franchise State.

The question of racketeering is more complex and ambiguous than those of rank-and-file activity and organized dissent. The received wisdom of American life condemned illegal violence, and just as business was curbing its flamboyant use of vigilantism, labor would be expected to pay tribute to this ideal of cleanliness. Attempts at self-regulation were made, such as David Dubinsky's campaign to put the AFL on record condemning racketeering, one of his prices for bringing the International Ladies Garment Workers Union back into the Federation. His resolution at the May 1940 convention contained all the ingredients of self-regulation: removal of officers convicted of "moral turpitude"; creation of disciplinary procedures as a condition for membership in the AFL; and provisions for investigation and publicity.[42] It being much easier to expel Communists than criminals, Dubinsky's resolution was soundly and decisively defeated and an innocuous substitute was passed in its place. Why? Part of the answer is that powerful economic interests in the United States benefit from racketeering: it keeps out Communists, organizes chaotic labor markets, controls rank-and-file discontent through intimidation, and encourages conservative business unionism.[43] The failure of self-regulation in this case led to active state intervention. The Kefauver Committee (1951), McClelland Commission (1959–60), Landrum-Griffin Act (1959), and the Organized Crime Control Act (1970) formally removed labor's self-regulation and provided for direct government control of racketeering. However, most of these hearings and laws were for show only; organized crime continues to be an active part of union life because the functions it serves are too important.

The prize that made self-regulation seem like a bargain was autonomy, the freedom of each sector to pursue its goals with as little governmental interference as possible. Yet from the beginning the search for autonomy posed a problem; because the Franchise State resulted in an increase in bureaucratic rule making, and because it extended itself into new areas such as collective bargaining, under its tenets society saw a rise, not in independence, but in interdependence. Could autonomy be a realistic goal when everywhere the search for it produced a greater need for cooperation and common interest? It could in one way only—if there resulted such a confusion in the political realm that self-interest could be realized behind a miasma of compromises and ambiguities. The quest for autonomy in a situation of interdependency produced three confusions that became features of the political landscape under the Franchise State: one between what was public and private; another between what was capitalist and what was not; and a final one between what was in the general interest and what was self-interested.

As every writer who has studied the politics of advanced capitalist societies seems to have concluded, a confusion between the public and the private realm is a major characteristic of twentieth-century relationships between government and business. Matters involving the public interest being decided directly by the private firms involved has become common-place. Agriculture is the most extreme example, for all five countries examined here saw the creation after World War II of new bureaucratic structures in which private landed interests would participate with little or no obstruction in the making of decisions involving prices, distribution, crop development, storage, transportation, and surplus. The American Farm Bureau Federation, so carefully studied by Grant McConnell,[44] became a model for this type of activity. Farmers cannot get their crops to the cities without an infrastructure of bridges, roads, and other such construction, and in these areas as well the domination of public decision making by private groups became extreme. In France, the *corps des ponts et des chaussées*, which in the eighteenth and nineteenth centuries was the stronghold of a class of public administrators who would rarely yield their prerogatives to representatives of private interests,[45] became, along with the *corps des mines* and the *corps des travaux publiques*, pockets within the bureaucracy where private parties could exercise great influence,[46] in a fashion very much like that adopted by the U.S. Army Corps of Engineers.[47] In Britain the connection of the County Councils Association and the Association of Municipal Corporations with the Ministry of Housing and Local Government provided for close cooperation between private and public interests.[48] West Germany, according to one writer, had a greater number of interest groups than perhaps any other capitalist democracy, and many are neither private nor public but somewhere in between.[49] The study of "public" administration necessarily must include private associations.

While the windfall profits and unnatural extensions of power to private agencies that result from these practices are enough to arouse anger, there is another consequence much more important than the short-run advantages that private corporations obtain from the ability to make public decisions. Concluding his exhaustive review of the activities of organized business in France, Henry Ehrmann wrote: "In reality organized interests are no longer merely 'represented' in the various branches of government, but, posing as defenders of a nebulous 'general interest,' tend to substitute their activities for those of the government. The boundary line between state and society frequently disappears." [50] The importance of the disappearance of this boundary can hardly be exaggerated, for it is the existence of such a demarcation that forms the justification for liberal democratic thought. Some areas of life are part of a private "right" that cannot be interfered with by any public power; others are a part of the common good that the people, through the exercise of their public power, control. If the distinction is abolished, not only does it become difficult for the "general interest" to have any meaning, but the sphere of private liberty is damaged as well. In other words, the mystification that results from the intentional confusion of public and private, a consequence of the imprecise and ad hoc nature of policy making in the Franchise State, undermines the very ideology that brought the Franchise State into being. Something conceived of as a solution to the tension between liberalism and democracy can easily wind up with neither.

A political arrangement that prides itself on its promotion of responsibility paradoxically furthers irresponsibility because of the confusion it engenders. The mystification between public and private means that when it is convenient, which is generally when the greatest profit is available, a sector of the Franchise State can claim to be simply a private organization going about its business. At other times, particularly when a failure occurs and responsibility must be assessed, this same organization can turn its other face and claim a public character. Examples abound, but two indicate the Janus-like nature of participation in the Franchise State. At one extreme, in 1953 a lawyer for Sullivan and Cromwell, which represented the leading American oil companies, refused to supply data to a government antitrust investigation. Even though the government insisted on having the material, Arthur H. Dean said the oil companies had decided that a national security issue was involved and hence they would not release the information.[51] Here, *in extremis*, is a private organization claiming that it knew better than the state what was in the best interests of the state. One is reminded of the so-called "energy crisis" of 1973–74, when public officials were unable to obtain data about supplies from private corporations who claimed that, because they were private, the data was their own. Yet over on the other side of the dichotomy, public status can be claimed when it suits certain groups to do so. If a firm has a public character, then a strike against it becomes a strike against the state, which civilized people cannot tolerate. General Hugh Johnson, supported by leading executives, interpreted the NRA in just such fashion, concluding that strikes against industries that accepted the NRA codes must be illegal.[52] Robert Engler's words about the oil industry apply throughout the Franchise States: "The nation's largest industry is increasingly public in every aspect except those of responsibility and profit." [53] The confusion between public and private, and the irresponsibility produced by it, are bound to have effects on public attitudes and the question of legitimacy, and in Chapter 8 I will discuss what some of those effects have been.

The search for autonomy in a situation of interdependence produces a second confusion with important consequences, a suspension of the laws of the market, again quite unusual since business corporations, benefiting from the Franchise State, are supposed to be in favor of the laws of the market. But, rhetoric aside, capitalists generally detest competitive capitalism and are the first to undermine it. A great advantage of the Franchise State for businessmen is that it allows them to be capitalists without any of the disadvantages of capitalism. Specifically, the Franchise State absolves participating industries from five processes that at one time were held to be central to any definition of a competitive capitalist economy; risk taking, capital accumulation, profit making, price competition, and reproducing the material conditions of the worker. The opposite of risk taking is planning and that concept, once considered with horror by big business, is now part of everyday life.[54] An activity that has been part of the European scene for some years, planning has even made its way to the United States, the last bastion of laissez-faire liberalism, both in the private sector (corporate planning) and in the public (forecasting, tax policy, banking regulation, federal standards). The degree to which planning has been welcomed varies, with the United States and West Germany rather cool and France on the warm side, but in all advanced capitalist countries the idea of uninhibited risk taking as the central motivation of business activity has declined substantially. The order and regularization imposed by the Franchise State has replaced it.

What is true of risk taking is also true of other competitive activities. The accumulation of capital, certainly the historic *raison d'être* of capitalism, has more and more become a governmental function. A consequence of this tendency of the state to become involved in the process of accumulating capital has been a demise in the Franchise State itself, and hence a full discussion of this process will await a later section of this chapter. Although profit making is still a central activity of business corporations, to turn to a third tendency, in many cases the most accurate description for the final line of the balance sheet would be "profit receiving." Public corporations need to justify their existence in terms of profits, but they do not "make" them by their own activity; in many cases the state literally guarantees profits to them, making up when the corporation messes up. An extremely bizarre example of this tendency occurs in the United States, where the Department of the Navy, *as required by law*, produces its own crude oil, then sells it to the highest private bidder, and then buys it back at the market price—a mind-boggling process designed to guarantee corporate profits, without corporate activity, all paid for by the taxpayers, the single most graphic case of what profit receiving has come to mean.[55] Fourth, price competition has been driven underground by the economic practices of the Franchise State. Monopoly capitalism discourages economic competition as much as it encourages social competition. Government practices, furthermore, nearly always benefit the largest business firms. As Shonfeld notes, "There is no doubt that the activity of planning as it is practiced in France, has reinforced the systematic influence exerted by large scale business in economic policy."[56] In the United States, as Murray Weidenbaum has shown, the system of defense contracting disproportionately benefits the largest industries in the field.[57] Antitrust laws notwithstanding, Franchise State practice encourages monopolization and thereby restricts price competition. Finally, the conditions that permit workers to work have increasingly been assumed by the public authority; education, unemployment insurance, public housing, and insurance for medical payments are all activities that were at one time private, left either to the worker, private charity, or the whims of paternalistic businessmen.

The general process of regularization, standardization, and private aggrandizement is a characteristic of all participants in the Franchise State, not just of business. Agriculture receives from its membership an avoidance of the danger of overproduction (lower profits, the only danger), and at the same time obtains the use of the public treasury for the benefit of the largest farmers. In no other area of capitalist life are the laws of the market, in country after country, more ignored than they are in farming. Agricultural policy has become a vast enterprise directed toward the goal of providing private profit at government expense. Labor unions also expect help from the Franchise State in destroying challenges to the domination of the largest; paralleling industrial concentration has been the growth of monopolistic unions that benefit from governmental practices in maintaining hegemony over collective bargaining arrangements. As monopolization in industry tempers the market effect for commodities, syndical concentration regulates the labor market, particularly in the monopoly sectors of the economy. In those areas of the economy that participate in the Franchise State, there exists a controlled and restricted labor market characterized by regularity and predictability. In areas that have not won entry into the Franchise State, the labor market is competitive and anarchic. Thus, what some economists have called the "dual labor market" [58] is dependent for its perpetuation on the rules of participation in the Franchise State.

To summarize, the most important political effect of business as usual under the Franchise State is the promotion of exclusiveness—the right of the largest group within a sector to determine the organization of that sector itself. If such exclusiveness is inherently in opposition to traditional notions about capitalism, this is just one of the contradictions that will have to be lived with. It is this exclusiveness more than any other feature that reveals the nostalgia for Colbert's France or Elizabeth's England; Walter Adams once described government contractors in U.S. defense industries as "a quasi-governmental, mercantilist operation, maintained in privileged position by 'royal' franchise." [59] We enter a world where internal autonomy is achieved through external guarantees, an unstable situation that ultimately had to, and in fact did, fall apart. The conditions giving rise to this solution immediately began to undermine themselves; a system designed to preserve capitalism denied all of its logic except private profit.

The final consequence of the contradiction between autonomy and interdependence characteristic of the Franchise State is the by-now-widely-discussed notion that state activity yields the appearance of public control without the actuality. [60] As a result, the Franchise State operates as a substitute for regulation that would be genuinely effective. The traditional response of any participants in the Franchise State when misdeeds come to light is to point out that mechanisms already exist for resolving the matter within the industry. In the United States, the Business Advisory Council, created in 1933, was one of those quasi-public and quasi-private associations that the Franchise State loves to sire. This one existed in the womb of the Department of Commerce, and before it miscarried it assumed the task of deflating popular control of business by advancing the notion that business was adequately policing itself. More recently the Business and Defense Services Administration has tried to do the same thing. [61] When it concerns those agencies that are unambiguously part of the state, a similar process takes place. State and federal regulatory commissions become fronts for the industries they are to regulate, as observer after observer has pointed out, and thus act to prevent more extensive control. No doubt such a system of mystified public control has its economic advantages, but, to continue a theme being developed here, there is also a serious political issue involved. For if, in order to preserve the appearance of control, such state agencies necessarily engage in mystification, in the manipulation of symbols, then one more untruth is added to the political process, one more way in which deception becomes part of ordinary political life. The accumulation of mystifications produced by the Franchise State (public versus private, free market versus regularization, control versus autonomy) has to be paid for at some point in time, and the large amount of public distrust for the state that exists in all capitalist societies (see Chapter 10) is a legacy of this three-tiered process of obfuscation.

On the Relationship between the Powers

Although autonomy was the goal of the Franchise State, interdependence was the result. Consequently, some method had to be developed for regulating interaction between the various participants. Just as a franchised business must guarantee that conflicts among dealers be resolved in a peaceful way (Standard Oil of New Jersey once set up a complete judicial system within the corporation in order to accomplish this goal),[62] some rules and procedures must be developed to control conflict between sectors. This task became a very important one, for it was the failure of the sectors to work out voluntary mechanisms of cooperation that led the state to intervene and play the role of umpire, and when it did, the logic of the Franchise State was itself undermined. Hence an examination of the relationship between private sectors is also the story of how the Franchise State failed to resolve the problems that led to its creation.

One method developed under the Franchise State for regulating relationships between the sectors was the concept of tripartism, in which business, labor, and the public would jointly resolve situations of class conflict. In the United States the tripartite board was first used as a protection for business against labor; when a business interest alone was involved, such as with the War Industries Board, there was no attempt made to include the other sectors, but when it was a question of labor's interest, such as with the National Labor Board and the National Labor Relations Board, the tripartite structure was effectuated. This formal bias came to an end, at least symbolically, in 1940, when Sidney Hillman was appointed to the National Defense Advisory Council, but an informal one continued, for while there he had little actual power.[63] This was a reflection of general experience in the United States, where public members seemed invariably to side with business against labor. Such biases, however, only intensify the contradictions that brought these boards into existence; since they were designed to give the appearance of fairness, decisions constantly favorable to one group undermined their rationale, while evenhandedness is contrary to the real powers of the various parties in a capitalist economy. Caught in this bind, tripartite boards never became an important reality in public decision making, though they preserve a limited symbolic significance.

The same contradiction existed in the European experience with tripartism, though the actual balance of forces was different. There decisions favorable to labor were not uncommon, and hence the business side of the boards found itself disenchanted. In Germany a 1951 law created codetermination, the system by which works councils were established in most heavy industry.[64] With six representatives of management and six of labor, leaving a "thirteenth man" who generally chaired, codetermination seems to have contributed to the process of regularization and smooth management of class conflict. Nonetheless, industrialists have frequently complained about the system and one out of every four workers interviewed by a team of German social scientists made statements something like this: "One only wants to pacify the workers. They are to think that now they are well off. But in reality they are only tolerated up there. . . . The works council has its people sitting on the board. But how are they supposed to open their mouths there? . . . In reality it is only capital that governs. Labor cannot compete." [65] If in Germany tripartism has been a mixed success, in France it can better be described as a failure. Originally the industries nationalized after World War II were to be administered on the basis of *tripartisme*. But when the Confédération générale du Travail and the Communist Party demanded to participate, which was their right, conservative groups denounced the arrangements. Then another problem developed, as for example in the Charbonnages de France: groups with varying interests brought those interests to the board, and instead of resolving them, the boards became simply a sounding place for them. Reviewing the experience, the Commission de Verification des Comptes des Enterprises publiques, a sort of government accounting office, said in 1952: "The experiment has not yielded the anticipated results. The conflict of interests, as previous reports have indicated, has been manifested in precarious delays and ineffective compromises." [66] In short, the French discovered that when class conflict is strong, *tripartisme* can only reinforce it, not ameliorate it.

Managerialism was another method of trying to work out accommodations between the various participants in the Franchise State. With the growth of the state's role, there tended to be a change in the nature of the civil service. Administrators were needed to work together with private interests, and it was hoped that the informal ties between similarly trained civil servants might facilitate the relationships between powerful private groups. Public servants who constituted a class in themselves could "manage" conflict and channel it into back rooms where it would not threaten to "disrupt" social peace and harmony. In France, the similar background and identical training of high civil servants yielded the core of such a class, and in Italy, where there was no equivalent to an *Ecole normale*, nonetheless a disproportionately large number of public servants came from similar backgrounds in the South.[67] Furthermore, the top-level Italian bureaucrats, taking a lesson from their colleagues in the private sector, organized themselves into an association called DIRSTAT,[68] thus enabling them to seek part of the state—that is, to seek themselves. The small world of the English tradition of public service also facilitated a class role and in the United States, where there was no important public bureaucracy until late in the nineteenth century, various reformers tried to create a class of patrician, forward-looking civil servants out of whatever meager material might be available.

The rise of an administrative class, as the rise of any class, was rationalized through the existence of an ideology and the administrative ideology, like all ideologies, was contradictory.[69] Thus managerialism was simultaneously about power but not about politics. The new managers, reformers for the most part, shared the patrician perspective that conflict was a dirty business unnecessary in a civilized world, yet at the same time they were coming to power in a state whose very reason for existence was social conflict. Similarly, managerialism emphasized neutrality, professionalism, and responsibility to all, yet it was an ideology consciously shaped to be useful to an elite. Not that these contradictions were perceived; to the managers, the notion of an underlying harmony of interests between all classes, which they would discover, obscured the political and class bias in their work. This permitted them to act, sincerely in most cases, as referees without ever realizing that the match they were judging was fixed from the opening bell. Managers could not be brokers between groups because they blended in too well with the leaders of those groups. They became parties to the conflicts that they had hoped to resolve.

A legacy of managerialism was a strong distrust of politics; the Franchise State tried to subdue politics in the same way that monopolies try to destroy competition. These new arrangements meant, according to their defenders, that contemporary problems could no longer be approached in terms of class conflict and millennial searches for a better life. The problems now, it was said, were technical, requiring a new kind of solution, one based on expertise and the avoidance of struggle. This feeling was reflected in a number of different places. The close cooperation between higher civil servants and representatives of powerful private groups certainly created an atmosphere in which cooperation had replaced conflict. In France, various *directions techniques* (technical offices) were established in the ministries, and it was their job to rationalize contacts with trade associations in such a manner that efficiency would be enhanced.[70] The term for this procedure, *tutelle*, indicates a relationship between teacher and student, that of a mutual learning process, instead of the more antagonistic relationship between claimant and claimee. Another indication of the distrust of politics is the profusion of expert committees that were everywhere established after World War II. The National Economic Council in France,[71] the Italian National Council of Economics and Labor, Britain's planning agency, the National Economic Development Council, and the U.S. Council of Economic Advisors are all examples of this trend. These high-level "experts" are expected to ensure that national "goals" are established with which all important groups can agree. While most are ostensibly concerned with economic planning, there is a heavy element of political planning involved as well, for the routinization of class conflict is designed to be antipolitical, and antipolitics is the most characteristic political response of advanced capitalist societies (see Chapter 9).

Tripartism, managerialism, and the proliferation of councils of experts, all designed either to eliminate or to render harmless class conflict, ran into the rather obvious problem that so long as societies are stratified by class in such a way as to reward disproportionately those at the top, conflict is likely to be omnipresent. The mentality that promoted solutions of this sort, then, was a paradoxical one in which the most extreme pragmatism was comfortably reconciled with the most naïve utopianism. The very same people who could pride themselves on their ability to avoid emotionalism, on their realism, on their concern with efficiency, could turn around and envision a social harmony that would have made both Saint-Simon and Fourier blush. This seems to be the triumph of what Antonio Gramsci called "Fordism," the engineer's dream of maximum efficiency combined with a puritanical and spiritual moral regeneration.[72] The constant attempts by a ruling class to delude others led to the ultimate irony, a form of self-delusion so strong that most of those affected by it are still not aware of its impact. In Chapter 8 I analyze this utopianism at greater length.

The simultaneous desire to eliminate politics and yet the inability to do so is in all likelihood responsible for the fact that "pluralism" came to be the dominant description of Franchise State operations. It is easy, in retrospect, to see how this came about. The normal operations of the Franchise State included the control of a sector by an elite working in conjunction with the revelant state agencies. Insofar as this process worked, which it did most of the time, it was not considered part of the political process and was therefore not a concern of political scientists, though economists and specialists in public administration could not ignore it. When normal conditions broke down, each sector was forced to bargain with the others; in those cases, since conflict was overt, politics was said to take place, and clearly it was all very pluralistic. This process of negotiation among the elites became a substitute for real politics, and insofar as pluralism was a description of that process, it was for a time an accurate perception of reality. Bargaining was the key: questions of power, welfare, community, and purpose—when not decided unilaterally by the affected party—were discussed, resolved, and administered in the atmosphere of a Middle Eastern bazaar. When decisions were made in this situation of conflict, they were based, not on which party was telling the truth, not on which party had a more consistent vision of the national interest, and not on which had the most democratic following, but on which was the strongest party to the bargain. To be a good trader and a good citizen are not necessarily the same thing. The qualities that make for the former include command over the supply of a commodity, inordinate wealth or power, disingenuousness, the ability to manipulate fear of brute force, dogged persistence, a passionate attachment to one's self-interest, and a detestation of sentimentalism, idealism, concern for human welfare, and other such "foibles." These became the most singular characteristics for success in the Franchise State. Those, like Charles Lindblom and Robert Dahl, who praised bargaining as the best way to preserve democratic values, seemed unaware that what was being bargained away was precisely those values themselves.[73] In the strongest irony of the many described in this chapter, the principles of the free market finally triumphed, not in the private sector where they were supposed to, but in the public sector where they were not. In the early days of the Franchise State, Thurman Arnold understood this reversal: "Our government," he said, "even when it moves along the purely humanitarian lines of distribution of food, power, or financial support of tottering institutions, must pretend that it is an individual buying and selling in a competitive world." [74] The smoothness of planning in the private sector was matched only by the competitive chaos in the public sector.

When it was discovered that conflict between the groups could not be eliminated by voluntary means—like those implicit in tripartism, managerialism, and councils of experts—the practical response was to turn to the state in order to enforce solutions on all the parties. To do this, however, is to undermine the logic of the Franchise State, which came into being in order to avoid excessive growth in state power. Insofar as it worked, the Franchise State did exactly that; its major flaw, from the point of view of fairness, was not its power but its lack of it. It conspicuously refused to take action when such action would interfere with the privileges of vested interests, and hence it tended to be a state in name only. If it were granted the power to regulate conflict among the parties, it might become a state in fact instead of a state in name; it might, in short, begin to use its coercive powers against the very sectors whose autonomy it was supposed to protect. This was the dilemma that ruling classes throughout the post–World War II world had to face. Conflict between sectors threatened to disrupt harmony; harmony was considered the most important value; therefore, the state was increasingly called in to restore harmony. As this occurred, the Franchise State began to meet its demise, for it was forced to call back its grants and reclaim its franchises. The potential power that the capitalist state always had but chose not to use was used, and with this, one more solution to the contradiction between liberal and democratic principles discovered its limitations.

One example of this demise lies in the European experience with planning. In the balmy days after World War II, planning often became a way through which vested interests could obtain whatever they wanted, justified in terms of the national interest. When the Rand Corporation sent an economist to France to study the planning process, this was his major conclusion: "On balance, the net effect of government action appears to have been to strengthen the forces, formidable enough in their own right, that restrain the competitive process and reduce its effectiveness in allocating resources or promoting growth." [75] Wherever he turned, this economist found powerful, cartel-like associations obtaining maximum benefit form the economic activities of the state—from tax reform through economic decision making to agriculture. Slowly, this began to change in the postwar years. The traditional intransigence manifested by private interests in France continued after the war. In spite of the rise of a technocratic ideology, the impact of private groups was still so strong that social scientists began to complain even more than they had in the past about *immobilisme*. France was described as a *société bloquée* [76] in which progress (which, as one political scientist has insightfully pointed out, meant the U.S. experience) [77] became impossible. Out of this morass, it is not surprising that many civil servants, given their training as a self-conscious elite, began to use the planning process to stimulate movement. Andrew Shonfeld describes what happened next:

> The state in other words found itself, frequently and willingly, in the posture of a bargainer—a powerful bargainer, it is true, but one whose whole approach is influenced by the probability that at some stage it will have to enter into a compromise . . . once the state has accepted the obligation to intervene intermittently in order to secure some desirable condition for society, it soon discovers that its actions exert a powerful influence, whether it likes it or not, on long-term trends.[78]

An active role for the state was the main feature distinguishing the first from the second plan. The former was, according to Cohen, minimal in its aims, while the second sought to make broad social policy, though it also failed to provide the resources to do so.[79] The shift from one to another is an indication of greater distrust of a "pure" Franchise State.

A very similar shift in the state's role took place in England. When the Conservative Party came back to power in 1951, a superficial attachment to laissez-faire came with it. Consequently, in Harris' words, "the general attitude of the Government—pragmatism on each separate industrial issue, with fairly heavy dependence on outside pressures to set the context of its own decisions (rationalized in a claimed adherence to 'balance')—rendered it subordinate to the trends in industry rather than the grand architect of those trends"[80] But the longer they remained in power, the more disenchanted the Conservatives became with the franchise system. Since, in the words of R. A. Butler, "We are not frightened at the use of the State. A good Tory has never been frightened at the use of the State,"[81] a second phase of Conservative rule reversed the priorities. By the elections of 1964, "all the elements of the economy were being more or less pieced together to form a single instrument of State."[82] In one more country, franchise principles were being undermined from within.

A final, and particularly fascinating, example of the demise of the Franchise State was the American experience with defense contracting. Just as it was a war that started movement in the direction of the Franchise State in 1917, it was another war, this time the cold war, that began movement in the opposite direction. The former required an active state to bring about rapid and extensive mobilization, and while there were the usual practices by which industrialists made large profits during war (executives working in Washington "without compensation," paid by their corporations; suspension of antitrust laws; stockpiling "scandals"), the sense of emergency was not conducive to long-range profits and stability. With the advent of the cold war, some businessmen saw a chance to have both the high profits associated with war without the urgency and state control. In this atmosphere the modern defense industry was born, and at first it conformed to the principles of the Franchise State, taking the form of what H. L. Neiburg called "the contract state."[83] When government required a service, it contracted out to some other agency for it— whether a private corporation, a state government (which then generally recontracted to a corporation), a regional body, or a quasi-public, quasi-private institution. Thus the Navy Department, which predated the Franchise State, did its own work, but in electronics—a new field—the Department of Defense contracted out a full 97 percent of its needs.[84] Before World War II the single largest item in the federal budget was salaries; after the war, it was contracted goods and services.[85] At first it appeared as if delegation of public power was to continue unabated.

Two factors intensified this assumption. First, expenditures for defense took off like a cruise missile, making the total sums being contracted out enormous. In the two decades between 1950 and 1970 the budget of the Defense Department went from $12.9 billion (32.7 percent of the budget) to $83 billion (56 percent).[86] Second, planners learned that contracting need not be limited to matters of defense. Just as the Rand Corporation, which received its fair share of this new money, was at one point called to New York by Mayor Lindsay to save the city, the principles developed for the defense sector were transferred to areas involving welfare. Besides DOD, government agencies spending 90 percent or more of their money on grants-in-aid (to state governments and private contractors) in the mid-1960s included NASA, HEW, OEO, HUD, and the Department of Transportation.[87] Under the Kennedy and Johnson administrations, the tactic of using intergovernmental grants and contracts to deal with domestic problems increased by over 1,000 percent, and with it, the tendency of the Franchise State to concentrate power in exclusive hands also grew. So important was the process that the Advisory Commission on Intergovernmental Relations devoted a major report to an analysis of its consequences.[88]

The result of this growth in contracting was not what its beneficiaries expected. They had seen a chance to grab money for themselves from the state, and so they grabbed, but as the amounts of money increased, the state began to increase its supervision of the process. There was a certain logic to this. Since a market metaphor had come to dominate the political realm, the laws of the market followed in its wake. One of those laws is that whoever controls the supply of a commodity controls its distribution; if public authority is considered a commodity—and public dollars were being spent—then the state was, by definition, the monopolistic dealer in the area. By turning the public treasury into their own private source of profit, government contractors were simultaneously creating a force that was larger than themselves and that eventually could control them. Defense, it turned out, was a dangerous business.

This process is best seen in the actual dynamics of government contracting. At first defense contracting was a sprawling and ad hoc affair, with corporations making proposals to the state as often as the state made them to corporations. Sealed bids were the rule and some attempt, even if minimal, was made to preserve the appearance of competitiveness and private enterprise. The idea was maintained that the private corporations controlled the process; they were the sellers of a product and the government was the buyer. This situation rapidly changed. For one thing, increasing technological sophistication and specialization meant that sealed bids had become ludicrous; when a contract was offered for a highly complex piece of equipment, it was negotiated directly with only one firm. (In the 1960s, 80 percent of the contracting for DOD and NASA was negotiated.)[89] Second, the sprawling character of the process was in part responsible for inefficiency and grossly inflated budgets, which became a problem only when it was discovered that the treasury well did have a bottom. Third, the cost of building equipment, which would in all probability be used only once, could not be supported by private contractors and was assumed by the state, particularly as such equipment began to cost unheard-of amounts of money. Finally, the various defense contractors found that they had a greater long-range interest in sharing the government market than in competing for it. Informal agreements left an "understanding" that General Dynamics would have a contract for one sort of weapon and Lockheed for another.

One way to describe what took place is to see a change in the state's role from buyer to seller. Instead of being on the receiving end, purchasing a product, the state switched to the initiating end, selling its needs. Significantly, this occurred under the Kennedy and Johnson administrations, when defense contracting multiplied. Kennedy's director of the Bureau of the Budget, David Bell, after a review of the messy nature of the system, had noted that "the major initiative and responsibility for promoting and financing research and development have in many important areas been shifted from private enterprise (including academic as well as business institutions) to the Federal government." [90] Under the new system, state decision makers determined what was needed. They would then ask one private contractor to carry out the task with the price being negotiated. The final product would always "overrun" the initial proposal, at which point there would be much well acted anguish and finger pointing. Then the process would begin all over again. Private contractors made a great deal of money, but they no longer had very much power. And even the money they made was problematic, for the inefficiency of the whole process meant that, without the state propping them up, they would have no reason to exist and would go the way of the Edsel.

The enhancement of the state's role in this process can be measured in a number of ways. One is its control over capital. Private contractors make the product but they do so on machinery owned by the state. A study by the Joint Economic Committee in 1967 indicated that 209,598 pieces of equipment costing over $2.5 billion were held and used by private defense contractors while being legally under government ownership. Over $14 billion in government property was also being used, and the government was purchasing computer equipment and other expensive and sophisticated devices.[91] In short, the state became a major source of capital accumulation for private firms. Second, attempts by the state to rationalize the procedure—from systems management contracting in the 1950s to planning-programming-budgeting systems in the 1960s—led to new controls.[92] Third, expenses for research and development, an important aspect of industrial growth, have been assumed by the state; 90 percent of the research in the aerospace industry is paid for by the government.[93] Fourth, the state establishes standards that the contractors must meet; the resulting contracts are notoriously unidirectional. As Weidenbaum points out, the Armed Services Procurement Regulations, specifying the conditions that private contractors must meet, is over 2,400 pages long.[94] Finally, the fact that the state is a formally democratic one that must appear to be responsive to the society at large means that contractors must pay allegiance to antidiscrimination statutes and other "political" requirements that the state sees fit to impose. The lack of autonomy experienced by business firms in this area is in sharp contrast to the golden days of the Franchise State.

Besides class conflict and war, another problem indicating weakness in the structure of the Franchise State was the social discontent breaking out throughout the capitalist world in the 1960s. This dissatisfaction took three general forms. First, a revival in left-wing politics was motivated in large part by the abuses of private power under the Franchise State. The attack on the university, on imperialism and militarism, and on the effects of racism were all, in one way or another, linked to the dominant corporate and government practices of the postwar years. Although the activist phase of the American and European student movement was relatively short, in one country it did lead to a near insurrection and everywhere else indicated that, at least for one segment of the population, the neutrality of the state and the beneficence of private power would never again be taken for granted. Over on the right, a second reaction was taking place. A viable Franchise State required high taxes, because of the guaranteed profits and unnecessary duplications it spawned, and higher taxes breed discontent. Middle-class revolt, with either a populist or right-wing basis, revived, and a form of intellectual conservatism, which saw the growth of state power as a negative thing, mushroomed in countries as diverse as West Germany and the United States. Taxpayer revolts, disgust with government "handouts," and attacks on self-interest were directed against Franchise State activities, making the right sometimes sound uncomfortably like the left and vice versa. A final reaction against the Franchise State was a rise in cynicism, the view that government and the rich scratch each other's backs and nothing can be done about it. Apathy, withdrawal from politics, and the celebration of precapitalist life styles were variations on this theme. While many people, if not most, had a tangible stake in the Franchise State, few, because of the contradictions it gave rise to, found it defensible—morally, intellectually, or politically.

The undermining of the Franchise State, in short, was produced by the very three conditions that helped form it: class conflict, war, and something resembling a social crisis. The impact of these three forces can be seen in the obverse of the tendency of the rate of profit to fall, which is the tendency of the state to grow. Its budget is one reflection of this. In the United States, public expenditures accounted for 12.8 percent of the Gross National Product in 1945–50, compared with 22.4 percent in 1966–70.[95] The number of people who work for federal, state, and local governments has increased drastically over the past twenty years.[96] When the total amount spent by the Veterans' Administration—not one of the very largest bureaus—began to exceed the annual budget of Belgium,[97] the state's new size was evident. Nor was America alone. A replication of the U.S. studies on GNP percentage and total number of civil servants for Canada found the same tendency, to a lesser degree.[98] In Britain, it has been estimated, the total number of civil servants *decreased* between 1914 and 1938 (when the Franchise State was being formed) and then *doubled* between 1938 and 1966 (when it faced its most severe contradictions).[99]

The percentage of GNP devoted to governmental activities hovers around 40 percent for West Germany, France, England, and Italy (27 percent for the United States), and a simple rank-order correlation exists between systems that have liberal democratic capitalism and those that have high state expenditures.[100] Reflecting on trends like these, James O'Connor argues that the state has become a full partner in reproducing monopoly capital, and there can be little doubt that, if this has not happened already, it is certainly in the process of occurring.[101] Capitalism had become both too large and too replete with contradictions to be left to the capitalists. The Franchise State, the last significant attempt to keep economic power in private hands, slowly saw that power slip away into a government structure that, although serving capital, was not itself capitalist.[102]

6 / The Rise and Fall
of the Diarchy

"In proportion as the nation's statecraft is increasingly devoted to the gainful pursuit of international intrigue, it will necessarily take on a more furtive character, and will conduct a larger proportion of its ordinary work by night and cloud."
Thorstein Veblen, Absentee Ownership (1923)

"The price of democratic survival in a world of aggressive totalitarianism is to give up some of the democratic luxuries of the past."
Senator J. W. Fulbright (1961)

"World opinion? I don't believe in world opinion. The only thing that matters is power."
John McCloy to John F. Kennedy (1963)

THE FASCINATION FOR DUALITY

THE SLOW DECLINE of the Franchise State as a solution to the social contradictions of advanced capitalism led some of the more alert state planners to consider their remaining options. In the years after World War II a seemingly insoluble problem faced them: no state structure seemed capable of simultaneously serving the needs of the many and the few; there appeared to be no way to have a state that was both liberal and democratic at the same time. Not yet willing to concede that their task was impossible, a few resourceful politicians and thinkers found that, with a little imagination, one more option was left. If the Franchise State could not reconcile irreconcilables—indeed, if no single state could—then why not have two states, one serving each need? Startling in its simplicity yet revolutionary in its application, the idea of two states—or, more precisely, a Dual State with two faces—began to emerge as Nirvana in the dreams of policy planners.

The notion of two states existing simultaneously but serving different needs has a variety of roots, in such places as the Augustan concept of two cities ("In the one, the princes and the nations it subdues are ruled by the love of ruling; in the other the princes and the subjects serve one another in love");[1] in the differentiation between state and society that emerged in Hohenzollern bureaucratic absolutism;[2] and in the general distinction between *Machtstaat* and *Rechtstaat*.[3] Fascinating as those examples are, they are not particularly relevant to the politics of advanced capitalism. Yet as the contradictions discussed in this book made themselves felt, diarchic notions took on modern dress. Three specific characteristics of capitalist development led to a resurgence of Dual State theories: the rise of a majoritarian working class, the contradiction between rationality and irrationality, and the problems of imperialism. The combination of all three, reaching a pinnacle after World War II, gave birth to the modern form of the Dual State.

The rise of a working class that wanted to share in the civic life of nineteenth-century Europe presented a tough problem for the writers of that period; men like John Stuart Mill, whose motives were generally noble, could not bring themselves to admit that such people were deserving of full citizenship. The most interesting reaction to this development came from the editor of *The Economist*, Walter Bagehot. He counseled his colleagues not to fear, for the common people, those "ignorant but respectful . . . miserable creatures" could be kept obedient by presenting to them a spectacle that would take their eyes off government and allow smooth administration to proceed. Bagehot began with the assumption that the governing class, because of a "life of leisure, a long culture, a varied experience, an experience by which the judgement is incessantly exercised, and by which it may be incessantly improved," is naturally fit to govern. For the rest there is "the theatrical show of society," since for them "the elements which excite the most easy reverence will be the theatrical elements." Using a metaphor that had instant meaning to a society undergoing rapid urbanization, Bagehot said of the ordinary man:

> As a rustic on coming to London finds himself in the presence of a great show and vast exhibition of inconceivable mechanical things, so by the structure of our society, he finds himself face to face with a great exhibition of political things which he could not have imagined, which he could not make—to which he feels himself scarcely anything analogous.[4]

Based on this class analysis is the famous distinction between the "dignified" parts of government, those that capture public attention, and the "efficient," less publicized places where the important decisions are made. According to him, "the public" will be preoccupied with the former, which is why in a democracy the latter can survive without injury. The solution to the liberal democratic paradox, therefore, becomes the creation of a two-headed form of government, a quiet and efficient one for the elite and a spectacular and theatrical one for the "masses." With its two parts in harmony, a condition that could occur only, he felt, in England, such a Dual State structure would solve the problem of majoritarianism. Ruling classes could have the benefits of elitism and democracy at the same time.

Another modern attempt to utilize the concept of a Dual State grew out of a concern with rationality and irrationality. If the modern world had seen an increasing tendency toward "disenchantment"—Max Weber's term for the replacement of magic and symbol by modern administrative rationality [5]—then any state calling itself a state would in all likelihood be one. But the triumph of Nazism convinced a number of political analysts that the role of the shaman had not yet disappeared from the modern world. In an important, and generally neglected, interpretation of the Third Reich, Ernst Fraenkel turned to Karl Mannheim. Mannheim had elaborated the distinction between substantial rationality—by which he meant "an act of thought which reveals intelligent insight into the inter-relations of events in a given situation"—and functional rationality, or "a series of actions . . . organized in such a way that it leads to a previously defined goal, every element in this series of actions receiving a functional position and role." [6] According to Fraenkel, Nazism can be understood as a product of the contradiction between these two directions: "The legal order of the Reich is thoroughly rationalized in a functional sense for the regulation of production and exchange in accordance with capitalistic methods. But late capitalistic economic activity is not substantially rational. For this reason, it has had recourse to political methods, while giving to these methods the contentlessness of irrational activity." In other words, to satisfy its concern with order in the realm of production, fascism is frighteningly rational, but to keep up frenzied mobilization and excessive obedience, it becomes highly irrational. The result is the creation, according to Fraenkel, of a Dual State, a "rational core within an irrational shell." Using a distinction embodied in German legal theory, he labels the two halves of the diarchy as the Prerogative State and the Normative State:

> By the Prerogative State we mean that governmental system which exercises unlimited arbitrariness and violence unchecked by any legal guarantees, and by the Normative State an administrative body endowed with elaborate powers for safeguarding the legal order as expressed in statutes, decisions of the courts, and activities of the administrative agencies.

The entire analysis is then summarized in the following sentences: "German capitalism requires for its salvation a dual, not a unitary state, based on arbitrariness in the political sphere and on rational law in the economic sphere. Contemporary German capitalism is dependent on the Dual State for its existence." [7] If Bagehot is right, ruling elites can have both liberalism and democracy; if Fraenkel is correct, they can have both rationality and irrationality as well.

When capitalist powers began to develop into imperial ones, responsible for the extension of their influence all around the world, a third usage of Dual State theories was discovered. Since an important rationalization for imperialism was the existence of racism, or at least of some form of cultural chauvinism, what was good at home was not necessarily good overseas. In domestic politics, there existed a state that was popular, democratic, constitutional, and, it turns out, increasingly impotent. Centered in the legislative branches of government, it was based on rules that were reassuring: executives executed, legislators legislated, and judges judged. Certain standards of conduct—like due process of law, democratic representation, and appeals to history and tradition—were expected to receive homage. Yet for the victims of empire a different set of standards and expectations existed. Control over their affairs would be exercised by a state designed to achieve its ends with as much dispatch as possible. Questions of propriety, morality, constitutionality, and legality were generally considered beyond its purview. Usually located outside the legislative process, this covert face of the state could keep its budget, personnel, plans, and procedures as secret as possible. Wherever there was an empire, there developed a Dual State in this sense—whether in India, Algeria, or Vietnam. The problem was, as Roger Hilsman noted, that such an arrangement could easily lead to a *Staat-im-Staat*, a situation hard to reconcile with traditional democratic theory.[8] Certainly this was the theme of an American best seller of 1964, which began with these dramatic words:

> There are two governments in the United States today. One is visible. The other is invisible.
>
> The first is the government that citizens read about in their newspapers and children study about in their civics books. The second is the interlocking, hidden machinery that carried out the policies of the United States in the Cold War.[9]

Revelations about the extent of this second government, which I will discuss in the course of this chapter, have led many concerned citizens to conclude that agencies like the CIA are incompatible with American political traditions. That is a half truth at best. Even though covert agencies are explicitly antidemocratic, they are by no means antiliberal; indeed, the CIA became in many ways the logical fulfillment of the liberal notion of the state. Throughout the world, its primary task has been to structure the conditions necessary for promoting the accumulation of capital. By bringing order where there might be chaos (i.e., communism), agencies like the CIA, in the fashion of Hobbes' sovereign or Locke's civil society, stand between civilization and the state of nature. The CIA is to the internal affairs of Third World countries what Hamilton's executive was to the thirteen states, a device for ensuring public order. Far from contradicting liberal principles, the rise of covert activities suggests instead that those principles have become so antithetic to democracy that they can be carried out only in secret. Allen Dulles and John McCone are correct to view themselves as the true heirs of the liberal tradition.[10]

In this chapter I will analyze the rise and fall of one particular form of the modern Dual State, created in the United States between 1944 and 1976. A plausible reason why a Dual State arose at this specific time is the conjunction of all three of the fascinations toward duality just discussed. First, democratization had led to a majoritarian electorate making political demands, the single most important political problem faced in the 1880–1920 period. Never really solved except by temporary expedient, the question of majoritarianism would arise whenever discontent became explicit. Second, the increasing monopolization of capitalist society intensified functional rationality, for the purpose of the elimination of competition was to make economic behavior regular and predictable. Yet at the same time, the replacement of competitive by monopoly capitalism stimulated a frenzy of irrationalism, as the techniques of modern advertising were developed to promote consumerism. This contradiction emerged around 1920, with the development of the "science" of advertising, and continues until the present time.[11] Third, the empires created during the period of the Expansionist State were proving difficult to hold together, and as demands for local autonomy were becoming more incessant, the need to repress such demands became more urgent. The problem of holding on to an empire in the face of both external and internal opposition emerged around 1945 as the crucial foreign policy problem of the advanced capitalist societies. All three conditions were necessary to the creation of a Dual State, and all existed in 1945. Advanced capitalist countries wanted to hold on to their empires as much as possible. Antidemocratic theories advanced to counter the growth of the working class formed the rationale for a semisecret state. And the irrationality basic to the economies of advanced capitalism prepared the ground for the demagoguery and mystification needed to make a Dual State work.

Thus, at the end of World War II, the advanced capitalist nations began to experiment with diarchic notions. The Dual State would have two faces: one, democratic and popular, would be concerned with democratic legitimation, winning support for the political order; the other, lean and hungry like Cassius, would be liberal (in the classic sense), responsible for the accumulation of capital and for the protection of the agencies doing the accumulating. There is evidence for the emergence of one or another form of a Dual State in a variety of places at this time. In Italy, nine years before *The Invisible Government* publicized the American CIA, Enrico Nobis had published his *Il Governo Invisibile*, an attack on the power of monopolistic corporations that, he charged, had created a government for their own use, while leaving a more impotent one for everyone else.[12] In France, the war in Algeria had revealed the existence of a cabal of reactionary generals, capable of defying the edicts of the central government and of carrying out their terroristic plans as if they were a state of their very own. Since that time, the amount of government secrecy has increased so substantially that sober analyses such as that of Gerald Messadie, have asked whether it is proper to speak of the end of private life in France.[13] For those who view Great Britain as the last refuge of democracy, it may come as a surprise to learn that under the Victorians an apparatus of espionage was created in order to control the relatively peaceful, though certainly not tranquil, Chartists.[14] Nor has this tendency declined in recent years; the Official Secrets Act, a law that, as David Williams has shown, went far toward creating a special set of rules for guardians of the "national interest," preserves an aura of secrecy until the present day.[15] So important was the British structure that, as we shall see, Americans who were in the process of building their own Dual State praised it time after time as a model of what should be adopted on their own shores.

In America, the theory and practice of the Dual State was carried to an extreme unknown anywhere else. In this chapter I will depart from the pattern of the preceding sections of this book and examine only the American version of the Dual State. In part, the reason is that this is the most fully developed form, against which the European ventures into secrecy are faint jabs at the head of democratic practice. But more important is the paradoxical fact that the American Dual State, though more committed to secrecy, is also more open to inspection. The accidents that surround the release of the *Pentagon Papers* and the *Watergate Transcripts* are a godsend to the political scientist, for they constitute the only sources available for studying state power while it is being exercised. The events taking place in the United States *cannot* be generalized to all advanced capitalist societies as a whole, but they can be used to highlight the general contradictions that will exist when an attempt is made to apply Dual State principles to the central problem with which I have been concerned: the irreconcilability of liberalism and democracy.

The American Dual State was created in a series of stages that at first glance seem unrelated to each other. First, certain preparatory steps had to be taken, including changes in both public attitudes and governmental structures. Second, the actual covert part of the state had to be created both at home and abroad, a process that was filled with half-starts and conspicuous failures. Third, the techniques, as they were improved, were finally successful and as a result were institutionalized, professionalized, and eventually used at home. Finally, overzealous proponents of the Dual State partially destroyed it by upsetting the precarious balance between its two halves. By following the story through these stages, I hope to show the advantages and also, from the perspective of those in power, the extreme limitations of this general solution.

PREPARING FOR DELIVERY

A covert and undemocratic state, even if it was the reverse image of an overt and democratic one, could not function without some fairly drastic revisions in traditional American assumptions about government. The United States was the home of liberalism and democracy to a greater extent than any other society except England, and, whatever the realities of political power, most people considered the assertion of liberal democratic values—freedom of choice, civilian control of the military, representative government, self-determination for all nations, and rights to privacy —a first step in any discussion of public affairs. These popular expectations, combined with a patrician sense of "propriety" on the part of the elite, created a framework in which any action that appeared to violate democratic standards was taken quite gingerly. As late as the presidency of Franklin D. Roosevelt, only thirty to thirty-five years ago, three indicative actions took place. First, in what was by any sober person's judgment an emergency, the President moved cautiously and conservatively to help arm Great Britain, without a congressional declaration, in the "fifty destroyer deal." Second, Secretary of War Henry L. Stimson, in a famous statement, refused to involve himself in the unseemly act of code-breaking, declaring that "gentlemen do not read each other's mail." And, finally, Vice Admiral Marc Andrew Mitscher spoke for a military that prided itself on its removal from the making of public policy when he stated: "Please understand me. I know nothing about how things are running in Washington." [16] In the face of such opinions and actions, before a covert state could be created, a prior step required the destruction of *both* popular attitudes toward democracy *and* patrician attitudes toward civility.

The formation of the anti-Communist consensus satisfactorily accomplished both goals. To be sure, a strain of anticommunism had existed in America even before there were any Communists; what was unique about the post–World War II period was that an opinion, one among many, became a consensus, one among one. When anticommunism became a religion rather than an opinion, an excuse for the revocation of democratic values was born. It is not important to show that subtle members of the ruling class deliberately and hypocritically used fears about communism in order to go stealthily about serving the interests of the powerful. Indeed, men like the Dulles brothers seemed to believe everything they said about the "Red Menace"; a touch of hypocrisy would have made them somehow less frightening. Whatever the motivation, the important point is that the resulting atmosphere contributed to a feeling of perpetual crisis that made the assertion of notions like free speech and self-determination seem antique—"luxuries," in Senator Fulbright's unfortunately chosen but quite realistic term. Turning Leon Trotsky on his head, the new men of state envisioned a permanent counterrevolution, many of them, in fact, mimicking Trotsky's analysis without realizing it. The surest method of preserving the advantages of war was to have one all the time, especially if it could be done with a minimal amount of actual fighting.

The ideology of permanent crisis became the key ingredient in the alteration of patrician values that accompanied this change in popular attitudes. Most historians agree that the crucial date in this transformation was June 19, 1940, when President Roosevelt appointed two patrician Republicans to his cabinet.[17] One of them, Henry L. Stimson, Secretary of War (the other was Frank Knox), was of the old-fashioned persuasion, but his importance was not in what he did but in whom he picked to do it. Through Stimson men like Robert Lovett, Harvey Bundy, and John McCloy came to serve the state, and these were bluebloods of a different color. They preached a newer morality, in which any actions held to be supportive of "national security" were justified, so long as they worked. It was the children of these men—literally in the cases of Bundy and James Forrestal, figuratively everywhere else—who carried the new morality to the furthest reaches of the earth. Without them the Dual State could not have existed, for their very aristocratic and proper mien provided the cover for their vicious and often murderous policies. Their double morality makes them fascinating, for, as Richard Barnet expressed it, "They stood their personal moral code on their heads when they assumed their public role." [18] If any one event captures this duality, it is Kermit Roosevelt, as patrician a man as the United States can produce, organizing thugs and wrestlers in the streets of Teheran to prevent self-determination for that country.

What explains this transformation? One reason, as I argue in the next section, was that the patricians in the period after World War II had been losing power to an alliance between New Dealers and reactionary Republicans, a conflict fought out during the debate over the unification of the armed services. In order to show that they still "belonged," that they would in fact open each other's mail, an aggressive anticommunism became their new badge of identification. In addition, the empire created by their parents and grandparents seemed, in the postwar atmosphere of national self-determination, to be crumbling. Here the rhetoric of national security is important. Although the constant reiteration of the language of national security has led some to describe the postwar government as a National Security State, those who are most likely to speak of security are most insecure; what emerged after World War II is really the "National Insecurity State." The patrician ruling class no longer had the optimism of the heady days of the Wilson Administration, when anything seemed possible. Robert Lansing, Wilson's Secretary of State, could endorse the notion of "open covenants, openly arrived at" in a way that his nephew, John Foster Dulles, never could, for Dulles had witnessed the single most important event in postwar history, the victory of a Commu-

nist revolution in the world's largest country. It was the "loss" of China
that made the rulers insecure. Interestingly, the domino theory is as strong
a statement of personal inadequacy as one is likely to find. *They* are
winning; *they* will keep winning; *we* must do something, even something
desperate, but we probably lack the will and character. In a veritable explosion of insecurity, the Communists were assigned strengths they must
have wished they possessed. And since secrecy and fantasy are the hallmark
reactions of the pathologically insecure, it is no surprise that the enormous
emphasis on covert activity was combined with the *macho* rhetoric of
espionage to produce the covert face of the Dual State. Far from being a
response to America's rise as an imperialist power, it was the first important
reaction to the realization that such power was in decline. The Dual
State is a product of defeat and limitation, not of triumph and expansion.

Changes in attitudes and values represent only a portion of the preparatory stage in the development of the Dual State. Just as a consciously
undemocratic state could not exist given democratic expectations, one
could also not exist given a democratic structure. Eighteenth-century em-
phases on harmonious balance and the virtues of smallness had resulted
in a governmental structure that Dual State theorists found cumbersome.
Much as they needed the democratic façade, they were also forced to alter
that façade in order to further efficiency. Rather than junk the whole
structure, which would destroy their cover, or keep it intact, which would
prevent their coming to power, they sought a readjustment of the structure
such that it would appear to retain its democratic character yet also
allow them the flexibility they needed. Like the settling of the earth after
a quake, the structure of the state during and after World War II underwent significant modifications. In most texts this is referred to as the
enlargement of the presidency, but such a description gives a false impression, for what actually occurred was not that the presidency usurped
power from the other two branches so much as the other two voluntarily
gave up their power without asking for a thing in return, except a few
perquisites of public offiice. The "enlargement" of the President was due
in large part to the increasing difficulty that a ruling class was facing in
trying to hold onto its power while making politically impotent larger and
larger groups of people. Concentration of power was a response to contradiction, not a product of "the increasing complexity of modern government," or other such explanations. The presidency, as the least democratic of the three branches, was the natural nest in which the Dual State
would be hatched.

Two incidents, one from each of the lesser branches, indicate the
groveling that took place. At present the notion that Congress should play
the major role in matters of war seems amateurish and naïve, but the men
who wrote the Constitution did not think so. Nor did the American
people, as late as 1937, before the doctrine of permanent crisis became a

reality. In that year a man named Ludlow introduced into the U.S. Congress a constitutional amendment that would have required a popular referendum before any declaration of war. Since war is the most traumatic matter of state, the idea is not as absurd as current "realists" make it appear, and 75 percent of the population indicated their approval, bringing the motion to the point where, by a change of ten votes, it would have mustered a majority in the House. The demagogic campaign whipped up against the measure was similar to the one that took place one year earlier in California, where Upton Sinclair proposed the equally simple-minded notion that poverty be abolished in that state. The Ludlow Amendment, which Arthur Schlesinger, Jr., who detested it, called "the democratization of the war power," [19] became in a sense a last-gasp attempt to assert the notion that the people might have a say in how they are to be killed. A sure sign of the poor health of America's politics is that a similar motion, introduced in the 1960s by a racist and reactionary from Louisiana, received no congressional support whatever. Despite rhetoric about instantaneous decision making, modern war, emergencies, and totalitarian aggression, the plain truth is that the progressive tradition in Congress had decided to yield its war powers to the President. The most democratic branch of government found the responsibility of declaring war too much of a bother, and the consequence was the removal of one impediment to the rise of the Dual State.

One year before the Ludlow Amendment the Supreme Court, not a popular branch but one that occasionally does claim to represent the conscience of the people, also decided that it wanted more power for the President. The very judges who were aghast at the idea of any federal activity in the domestic sphere gave a blank check to the President when matters of foreign affairs were involved.[20] Another decision of that year interpreted executive agreements in such a way that any President who wanted to sign what was in fact a treaty without congressional scrutiny could do so.[21] And to make the point emphatic, when the Court, in *Civil Aeronautics Board v. Waterman S.S.*, had to tackle the creation of a covert state directly, it said, just as directly: "It would be intolerable that courts, without the relevant information, should review and perhaps nullify actions of the Executive taken on information properly held secret." [22] Edward Corwin's fears that such decisions would abridge constitutional arrangements in peacetime as well as in war, over domestic issues as well as foreign, were realized; Corwin, speaking almost alone, knew that the doctrine of permanent crisis had altered the democratic structure of the state beyond recognition.[23]

Once it saw that no other branch would raise objections to its growth, the presidency, like some monster from a Japanese horror movie, grew and grew and grew. One reason is that in the area of domestic policy, most liberals and progressives saw the growth of presidential power as a good thing, and conservatives like Robert Taft, who opposed it, could not garner enough support to stop it. Thus the real beginnings of the covert state structure can be traced back to the New Deal; the notion of wartime emergency, plus the determination to use the presidency to arrest it, were both associated with that time. One vital piece of legislation was the Emergency Relief Appropriation Act of 1935, which, according to Leuchtenberg, "authorized the greatest single appropriation in the history of the United States or any other nation. The law, which permitted Roosevelt to spend this huge sum largely as he saw fit, marked a significant shift of power from the Congress to the President." [24] Another key development was the issuance of Executive Order Number 8248 of September 8, 1939, which further centralized presidential power, created administrative assistants for the President's staff and brought within the White House the Bureau of the Budget.[25] The staff system misused by Richard Nixon had its origins in the New Deal. Finally, as Franz Schurmann has pointed out, the rhetoric of security that dominated New Deal thought was the same rhetoric, broadened out to the world, that dominated cold war imperialism.[26] In short, the combination of avoidance by the other branches and the growth of the state in domestic affairs led to changes in the structure of democratic arrangements that would permit the Dual State to be created with much greater facility.

FOR UNTO US A CHILD IS BORN

These changes in both the structure of government and popular attitudes toward the use of power by themselves only prepared the operating table for the birth of the Dual State. The actual delivery took place, not during the New Deal, but at the end of, and immediately after, World War II. In order for a diarchy to function, two tasks would have to be undertaken: first, it was necessary to create a central structure, located in Washington, to be the brains and decision-making center of the operation; second, "in the field," strategies and a policy apparatus had to be established for carrying out those decisions. In both areas the lack of practical guidelines and the uncertain state of what was considered legitimate and what was not meant that planning would have to be tentative. In addition, since the ends for which the Dual State was being created were contradictory, the new solution would face imponderable difficulties no matter what form it took. The Dual State was not born an adult, but as is generally the case, achieved that status only through awkward and painful attempts to make sense out of the real world.

Aside from the minor difficulties involved in any new enterprise, the founders of the Dual State faced three major constraints that placed limitations on what they could hope to accomplish. These can be summarized as the contradictions between expectations and performance, between unified interest and vested interest, and between control and self-determination. The fact that none of them were eventually overcome limited the effectiveness of the Dual State from the start.

If a state were to continue to exist with two faces, one responsible for preserving the prerogatives of those in power and the other for winning consent for those prerogatives, the balance between the two parts would have to be rigorously maintained. The problem can be expressed as follows: If a perfectly workable covert state were created and backed by extensive military might, both its cost and the fact that it violated some key democratic norms might make it unacceptable to the people at large, once the postwar hysteria had subsided. On the other hand, if costs were to be held low and democratic expectations adhered to, it would be impossible to protect adequately the "national interest," a convenient expression for the interests of those in power. The seriousness of the dilemma can be seen clearly in the events that gave formal birth to the Dual State, the passage of the National Security Act of 1947. This astonishingly comprehensive piece of legislation unified the military services after years of debate, institutionalized the office of the Joint Chiefs of Staff (JCS), established the National Security Council (NSC), and brought together various agencies in forming the Central Intelligence Agency. The life of every American was fundamentally changed by the passage of this law, yet few studies about it exist.[27] Its passage linked all the contradictions involved in the Dual State.

At the very end of World War II, on June 19, 1945, Secretary of the Navy James Forrestal asked a businessman named Ferdinand Eberstadt to answer three questions: Is military unification a good thing? If not, what changes should be made? What should be the scope of postwar national security organization? Although Eberstadt was a friend of Forrestal's, and was expected to issue the suggestions that Forrestal wanted, particularly a recommendation against military unification (which he did), there is nonetheless a hint of chastisement in Eberstadt's letter of transmittal:

> Sir: Military efficiency is not the only condition which should influence the form of our postwar military organization. To be acceptable, any such organization must fall within the framework of our traditions and customs. It must be of such size and nature as to command public support. It must be aimed at curing the weaknesses disclosed in late wars. And finally, it must be conducive to fostering those policies and objectives which contribute to the service and protection of our national security.[28]

The issue had been posed; more than any other participant, it was Eberstadt who insisted that democratic expectations were an important factor to be considered, which makes his report fascinating reading, even if its most important recommendation, against military unification, was not accepted. The specific "traditions and customs" that became issues in the debate over the law were three: civilian control of the military, preservation of a democratic façade, and high efficiency leading to low taxes.

The concept of civilian control of the military should not be dismissed as some rhetorical nonsense of a ruling class; it may be worthwhile from its point of view to sacrifice a bit of efficiency in return for more faithful adherence to its demands. Furthermore, civilian control over military affairs softens interservice competition that can reach severe proportions; having a businessman heading the Defense Department suggests to the Navy that an army man is not and to the Army that a navy man is not. Consequently there is every reason to believe statements like this one from the Hoover Commission Task Force on National Security Organization, again chaired by Eberstadt:

> The completely efficient security system will not be economical. The completely economical security system will not be militarily efficient.... Civilian control over military affairs involves some cumbersome and dilatory procedures and may even lead to serious technical mistakes; yet military power freed from civilian control would lead to even more serious mistakes—perhaps irreparable ones.[29]

In furtherance of this principle, a number of steps were taken. It was agreed that the head of the newly created CIA would be a civilian. When a proposal was worked out to unify the services, it was agreed that a civilian would also be, in the words of Senator Styles Bridges,[30] the new "super-deluxe" secretary. Further, Congress, and more specifically the two armed services committees, were promised participation in all the important decisions to be made. Finally, the National Security Council was placed under the direction of the President, whose role as commander-in-chief was emphasized, and this body, composed of both civilians and the military, was expected to be a policy-making body. The scope of military activity in the government increased enormously, but the important point is that so much attention had to be paid to reaffirming the notion of civilian control precisely at the time it was being undermined. Popular fears about generals in power were not easily set aside.

A similar problem arose with respect to secrecy. While everyone conceded that covert operations, and a covert apparatus to carry them out, would be part of the postwar structure, others understood that this also might pose a legitimation problem for the state. Eberstadt's report, as usual, expressed a contradiction: "The [National Security] Council should render annual reports to the President and to Congress. To the extent that national security does not absolutely require secrecy, its reports should be published. Thus the public would be posted on these vital matters by an authoritative and dependable source. In this way, the Council could aid in building up public support for clear-cut, consistent, and effective foreign and military policies." [31] Clearly too much secrecy was seen as a problem not because these men were committed to open government as a point of principle, for they were not, but because an attempt at openness would result in public acceptance of the new reality. They were utilitarians, not idealists. But in spite of this concern, little attention was paid to the problem at this point in time. Harry Truman said that he never expected the CIA to become an independent, policy-making authority; in his words, it was supposed to be only a gatherer of information.[32] In Senate hearings on the 1947 law, the CIA came up only three times and only once was there a substantive discussion about it. Senator Tydings, a highly conservative Republican from Maryland who would later be a victim of Joseph McCarthy, expressed his fear that the vagueness of section 202 of the law, concerning the CIA, would allow no restraints on that agency once it came into existence. General Hoyt Vandenberg assured him that this was not the case, because a new bill would be forthcoming specifying those exact powers. Had the new bill been prepared, Tydings asked. Yes, was the reply, "but we do not want to submit that bill until we have reason for it." [33] Evidently they never had reason, for there was no serious legislative discussion of the CIA until after it had committed its most serious blunders. Floor debate was minimal; to be sure, one member of Congress said, Cassandra-like:

> We must avoid the risk of there ever developing in our government a military Gestapo. As we well know, one of the causes of the last costly war was the fact that the military took over the control of civilian governments. The ordinary citizen lived in constant fear of the military intelligence. He was afraid to express himself. He was even afraid of his own thoughts.[34]

Remarks like this, however, stood alone. Besides, for a law of this type, floor debate was only for show; any substantial legislative input would have to come from the two armed services committees, and there the role of the CIA was barely discussed. The military chiefs wanted it, and the men on these committees had been selected because they knew how to listen to the military chiefs—quietly and respectfully.

In most cases members of Congress chose to ignore the implications of an organization of professional spies within the state. They could not feign ignorance, because the issue was laid out for them with precise clarity by Vice Admiral Forrest Sherman on April 2, 1947: "I consider," he said, "the Central Intelligence Agency to be a vital necessity under present world conditions. *Its necessity will increase with our greater international responsibilities* and as the power of sudden attack is amplified by further developments in long-range weapons and in weapons of mass destruction." [35] In an unusual procedure, a private citizen, a lawyer from New York named Allen Dulles, was asked to give his opinion of the CIA. Since he was leaving for Europe, Dulles filed a deposition that the chairman of the Senate Armed Services Committee placed in the record. Dulles said, "The Agency should be directed by a relatively small but elite corps of men with a passion for anonymity and a willingness to stick at that particular job." He emphasized that the head of the CIA should be a civilian; like a member of the high judiciary, Dulles said, the head of the agency should have long tenure and be free "from interference due to political changes," by which he meant elections. Pointing to the British system as ideal, he called for the CIA to possess "exclusive jurisdiction to carry out secret intelligence operations." [36] In short, testimony like this indicated that secret intelligence would pose a problem to the maintenance of democratic structures; the fact that very few chose to recognize the contradiction did not mean that it did not exist. Sherman and Dulles were explicitly advocating a covert, antidemocratic state.

From the amount of discussion devoted to it, a third point was considered by the participants to be much more important than either civilian control or secrecy, and that was the question of economy. If a national military establishment were to cost a great deal of money there might be a taxpayer revolt, but if the funds were kept low, there would be serious damage to the imperial designs of those in power. Once again the first Eberstadt Report underlined the conditions involved: "The American people," it said flatly, "will not support a military establishment which they regard as extravagant in its demand upon their services or their pocketbooks." [37] During the Senate hearings on the National Security Act, no issue dominated the minds of these conservative gentlemen, most of them from the Middle West, other than the question of cost. There seemed only one way to hold down costs, but it was highly contradictory. As the Hoover Commission report of 1949 expressed it, one of the "basic criteria" was that the "elimination of wasteful duplication is essential to good government, but . . . the preservation, within sound limits, of a healthy competitive spirit and of service pride and tradition are basic to progress and morale." [38] What was it to be—competition, which would be wasteful of the taxpayers' money, or the elimination of duplication, which would harm vested interests? Thus posed, the question illustrates the general problem of conflict between unification and vested interests.

As the Eberstadt Report reiterated, the major disadvantage of U.S. military policy during World War II had been the lack of coordination, both between the military agencies and between the government and private manufacturers. If this was true, then one would expect the Report to argue that the separate military services be unified, but they did exactly the opposite, arguing that unification would be a mistake. In an extraordinary passage, which reveals the admiration that even liberal members of the ruling class had for both fascism and Stalinism, Eberstadt noted:

The processes of democratic government in this country have sometimes seemed cumbersome and slow, even under the urgent stress of war. We *have often longed for the one-man decision* and have been inclined to minimize the tremendous benefits that arise from the parallel, competitive, and sometimes conflicting efforts which our system permits. At times *we have looked with envy at those systems which we believed dispensed with these time-consuming processes.* It has been enlightening, however, to find on closer examination that they have suffered from similar disadvantages without enjoying the benefits of ours.[39]

This was the manifest reason for opposing military unification, but it was at best a half truth, since nobody was arguing for the installation of one-man rule. Really at issue was an intense conflict between the Army and Navy departments. While it is easy to get bogged down in the details of the struggle and to lose the points over which they were fighting, this conflict over military unification had at its root social conflicts that were much more important than the theories of public administration offered in support of each position.

In 1906 Otto Hintze, the German historian and legal theorist, had written that "the Army is an organization which penetrates and shapes the structure of the state. The navy is only a mailed fist which extends into the outside world. It cannot be employed against the internal enemies." [40] Hintze was trying to explain the existence of democratic institutions in England and the lack of them in Germany. His idea was that countries dominated by a navy will be more likely to adhere to democratic structures, while those dominated by generals will be more repressive. This analysis is helpful in understanding military affairs in the United States. Traditionally, the Navy Department had been the most patrician part of the American ruling class; for a time it had seemed that the position of Assistant Secretary of the Navy was an inevitable stage in the upbringing of any male Roosevelt; men like Elihu Root, a key member of the group that Huntington called the neo-Hamiltonians,[41] had ties to the Navy; and writers like Alfred Thayer Mahan, an important apologist for American imperialism, were identified with this department.[42] The Army, on the other hand, was rooted, not in New England, but in the South and West, in more peripheral areas of American society.[43] (This pattern of recruitment did begin to change in the 1950s.) Like the split within the industrial ruling class between a reform business aristocracy and a parochial manufacturing class, there was a similar difference in outlook in the military services. When James Forrestal, a perfect representative of the patrician class, asked Ferdinand Eberstadt, another, to argue the case against military unification, he was being loyal to the "progressive" tradition. The defeat of the Forrestal position, then, indicates not only a change in the structure of the state, but a change also in the balance of class forces. With the rejection of its flush-deck aircraft carrier in April 1949, it had become clear that the Navy was losing power fast, and with it the patrician ruling class. A combination of New Deal Democrats like Truman and conservative Republicans close to the army hierarchy joined forces in a victory for the new military establishment, one more parochial, more isolationist (yet, paradoxically, less pacifist), and more willing to suspend its attachment to democratic forms in the interests of a narrow definition of national security. This alliance is not as surprising as it first appears. As Schurmann noted, "The Democrats traditionally have been more partial to the Army than the Republicans, and generally this is ascribed to the popular democratic character of the Army as contrasted with the other two elite services. But the Army is also much more compatible with a powerful Presidency, which the Democrats have always advocated." [44] Besides strengthening the executive, the alliance represented a move in the direction away from an interest in democratic legitimation in favor of an "efficient" if undemocratic foreign policy apparatus.

Truman's role in the passage of the National Security Act began to be more decisive. Although at first he failed to realize the importance of the legislation, when he did he came out in the strongest possible terms for unification. One phrase in the Eberstadt Report irritated him. Eberstadt had written that the National Security Council, during wartime, would turn itself into a "war cabinet." [45] Similar to reform-minded political scientists of this period, who wished to replace the chaos of American political parties with a model borrowed from Britain,[46] men like Eberstadt regarded the British system of fighting wars as perfection on earth. But Truman was aghast at the idea: "In some ways," he stated in his memoirs, "a Cabinet government is more efficient, but under the British system there is group responsibility in the Cabinet. Under our system the responsibility rests on one man—the President." [47] The doctrine of executive supremacy was clearly in the making. Truman wanted, not a war cabinet, but a group of advisors who would work under him, and for this reason the unification of the various services into one department in his formal cabinet was preferred to three separate departments each pursuing its own vested interest. The final structure was much closer to Truman's point of view than to Forrestal's. It was to be unification. Trying to save face, Forrestal called it all sorts of things, like merger and incorporation, but, when Senator Tydings sarcastically asked him if he was maintaining that a rose by any other name smelled differently, the point was conceded.[48] Truman, however, did not win every issue. As Forrestal said on March 18, 1947, "I should be less than candid if I did not admit that this bill is a compromise." [49] Perhaps in return for being a good sport and testifying for the bill, Forrestal was named the new super-deluxe secretary, head of a department he did not want created. Truman, on the other hand, was given the power to ignore the National Security Council if he wished.[50] Further, a series of amendments brought forth in 1949 strengthened the office of Secretary of Defense, thereby contributing to the furtherance of both Truman's theory and Forrestal's power.[51] As with the Franchise State, policy was being made on the basis of political brokering.

It had become apparent to both sides that excessive conflict would seriously undermine the advantages reaped by cooperation. In 1949, now in his capacity as chairman of the Hoover Commission Task Force on National Security, Eberstadt indicated that he was willing to go along with the new solution. Noting that "one of our greatest needs is to elevate military thinking to a plane above individual service aims and ambitions," his new committee recommended strengthening the office of the Secretary of Defense, since "a greater measure of centralized authority is required within the military establishment." [52] If this represented a *volte face* for the Navy, army sympathizers also showed themselves willing to compromise. Truman, for one, tempered his opposition to the NSC in practice; before the Korean War he would not even meet with it, but during the heights of that "conflict," the NSC was allowed to function, if only in an advisory manner. [53] The biggest surprise of all, however, occurred under President Eisenhower. Although most people thought that Eisenhower would naturally adopt the Army view of national security matters since he had faithfully adhered to that position during his testimony on the National Security Act, [54] the new President listened sympathetically to advisors who spoke otherwise. A committee headed by Nelson Rockefeller, which may have set the all-time record for the greatest percentage of ruling-class types ever to serve on one committee, joined the Eberstadt group in its recommendations for Secretary of Defense. [55] Furthermore, Eisenhower, unlike Truman, tried to meet with the NSC every week, even calling it into session from Colorado when he was ill. [56] During the Kennedy years it was a popular activity for political scientists like Hans Morgenthau and Henry Kissinger to denounce the Eisenhower staff system as not lean and hardheaded enough, [57] but, like a rediscovered piece of art deco furniture, it has a certain attraction in retrospect. Its great advantage was that its very bureaucratic nature resulted in a cautious use of state power. In May 1954 the Eisenhower Joint Chiefs of Staff made a startling assertion of "their belief that from the point of view of the United States, with reference to the Far East as a whole, Indochina is devoid of decisive military objectives and the allocation of more than token U.S. forces in Indochina would be a serious diversion of limited U.S. capabilities." [58] This had followed Eisenhower's public statement that he could not "conceive of a greater tragedy for America than to get heavily involved now in an all-out war" [59] in Southeast Asia. In other words, the reliance on the NSC machinery, approximating the despised notion of a war cabinet, while clearly undemocratic, was not inherently militaristic. The willingness of the parties to compromise their differences in the face of their common desire to preserve an empire meant that the contradiction between unification and the vested interests of each military service had been temporarily resolved.

But another similar issue was just as important. What was to be done about the relationship between the new, unified military establishment and all of those outside of it? If individual businessmen pursued their own self-interest, the process of obtaining material for the cold war might be hindered. If labor unions in defense industries went on strike, the same thing could occur. If the general public continued its privatist ways and did not respond to patriotic appeals, the mobilization necessary for the new structure might not be forthcoming. In order to deal with these questions, planners turned to every solution in the repertoire. To Forrestal, the answer lay in the principles of the Harmonious State. The National Security Act, for him, "provided for the integration of foreign policy with national policy, of our civilian economy with military requirement." [60] All would have been well if that were the case, and for a time it was, but not everyone's interest is the same, and as military requirements expanded, the civilian economy was hurt, and hurt severely. And foreign policy, as in Vietnam, eventually disrupted national policy in one area after another. To others, the principles of the Expansionist State offered a way out; the wealth of the empire would create such abundance that only the misanthropic would complain about aborted civil liberties, high taxes, or the militarization of everyday life. The trouble here was that the empire was not holding, and within two years the optimistic rhetoric of expansion had been replaced by the defensive language of security. Finally, others saw the answer in the practice of the Franchise State; national defense, as any other area of life, could be subjected to the pursuit of private profit through public grants of power, in which discontent would be alleviated by the judicious use of the grants. Hence the Eberstadt Report envisioned a National Security Resources Board, to exist in peacetime as well as in war, and its underlying principles were clearly specified. Searching for "proper organizational units," the Report said that "an important objective of military organization must be the maintenance of close relations between the military services and the industrial establishments—including the workers—on whom they must rely for the production of most of their weapons." [61] Advisory committees composed of both industry and labor were to be brought directly into the state to help make important decisions involving national security. In fact, in their proposed organizational chart, the Eberstadt committee pictured a complete syndicalist organization of the economy, fully integrating public and private into a harmonious amalgam.[62]

On top of all these attempted solutions, each of which ran into difficulty, one other answer to the perennial problem of vested interest versus common interest was tried. Instead of bringing the military to the people, the people could be brought to the military. In other words, the militarization of everyday life would give everyone a common interest in supporting the new military establishment and thereby solve the problem. Furthermore, such a solution would also resolve the legitimation issue by giving people something that they could support. The idea was so appealing that it justifies a long quotation from the Eberstadt Report:

> Today the American people seem to have accepted the necessity of implementing our ideals for world order with the use of force against aggressor states. In these terms public support for international cooperation has a high relevance in any planning of military policy. If this public acceptance is to be fostered and made effective, due consideration must be given in organizational planning to the probable effects of various structural forms upon public understanding and public interest.
>
> Interest of the American people in our Military Establishment is not best obtained simply through appeals to public opinion. It can be based on more substantial grounds if means are provided for *active participation in various phases of military affairs by groups particularly concerned with aspects of military policy*. Thus the degree of public support will be greatly affected by the extent to which the representatives of labor and industry are called upon to cooperate in mobilization planning, and experts in many other civilian fields are provided with opportunities to contribute their knowledge as it is related to national security problems. *Educational institutions and scientific laboratories can serve as channels of communication between the military and civilians*. An arrangement with the universities and with industrial and scientific laboratories by which skilled men move back and forth between Washington and their own principal employment is needed. Such arrangements would have the very desirable effect of *breaking down the isolation from the currents of civilian life* that has tended to make the military a group apart.[63]

Aside from anticipating just about every aspect of postwar life under the Dual State, this proposed solution worked. For twenty years so many key groups—businessmen, labor leaders, scientists, and intellectuals—achieved so much advantage from the militarization of everyday life that no significant opposition existed to the extension of the Dual State. When disenchantment came about, toward the end of the war in Vietnam, it was so strong precisely because for so long it had been so weak. Without the "cover" provided by policies of this sort, the Dual State could never have become a reality.

Besides the contradictions between expectations and performance and unified interest and common interest, a third limitation on the potential success of the Dual State was that it was not being planned in a vacuum. The whole point of the enterprise was to control populations—first abroad and then at home. Some of the difficulties presented by this task were relatively minor. Principles of an earlier era regarding international morality—such as self-determination for all nations or the idea of open treaties—would have to go the way of the Bill of Rights and low taxes, but this could be easily done since events in faraway places were never of much concern to Americans. Another minor difficulty was the calming of domestic political opposition to an imperial role for the state, most of which, and it is a commentary on the times, came from the right and not the left. What is now pejoratively called isolationism then constituted the only significant source of domestic opposition to the Dual State, and the warnings of men like William E. Borah now sound more like insightful predictions rather than hysterical rantings.[64] Opponents of the Dual State had no rhetoric to match that of the new men of power, however, and as a result no serious domestic challenges to the new order existed.

Surprisingly—at least to those who plan these things—the political opposition to creation of the Dual State came from those living elsewhere who were going to be controlled by it. What was really at issue in this period was not the ability of the United States to stop the spread of communism, for as Gabriel Kolko has shown in detail, Communist movements throughout the world after World War II were consistently conservative and even, in some cases, counterrevolutionary.[65] The real goal was the prevention and, barring that, the channeling, of nationalist fervor in the Third World countries let loose by the war. The breakdown of traditional European hegemony meant that vast areas would be open for exploitation, but this could not be done in the accustomed colonial manner. The Dual State was an attempt to make those populations subject to American control in the face of the fact that many people in those countries, and even some of their leaders, wanted to be free of external domination. In short, the Dual State experienced a contradiction between its own rhetoric—making the "free world" safe—and its actuality as a perpetuator of an unfree old order, albeit in a new guise.

In order to explore the impact of this problem, I must shift the focus from Washington to "the field" and examine the difficulties faced by Dual State planners as they attempted to establish an American presence in places where one did not exist. The problem can be stated simply: What mechanisms should be used to extend the state into new areas?

By now it should be clear that many state planners were not the most imaginative of men, and that when faced with a new problem, they invariably tried to resurrect an old solution. Having witnessed the creation of the Franchise State during the New Deal, and not knowing what else to do, they attempted simply to extend the Franchise State abroad; what worked in Tennessee in 1932 could work in Africa and Asia in 1948, or so they thought. Yet in order for the Franchise State to function, as we saw in the last chapter, certain prerequisites had to exist: a sector that desired entry; leadership for this sector that could be considered responsible; principles that would prevent the infringement of one sector's territory by another; mechanisms that would work out conflicts between one sector and the central authority; and agreement by all parties not to disrupt the fragility of the arrangements. None of these prerequisites existed in the Third World countries. With missionary zeal (and its counterpart naïveté), planners in Washington decided to bring them into existence.

Political scientists were recruited to specify what was needed for modernization—that is, participation in the franchise system—and plans were developed to put their ideas into practice.

Defining the parameters of a sector was the first task. Clearly any country in the world could be analogous to a sector at home, at least conceptually; the problem was that many of the new countries existed in name only. It was extremely difficult for units to interact with each other when there was no agreement on where one unit ended and another began. Sometimes these difficulties became serious, as in what was then called the Belgian Congo (Zaïre), where the question of what constituted the nation was the single most important political question. In general, territorial issues were outside the control of the United States, since they predated European involvement in these parts of the world. All the Dual State practitioners could do was give their support to the factions that shared their own conception of where the nation began and ended, and hope for the best.

Other things seemed more manageable. Since mature and responsible leadership was a vital prerequisite for the Franchise State at home, it became a goal of U.S. policy makers to find leaders in the new states who would be willing to to go along with the new rules. Once found, they, like the heads of a farm bureau or union, could be granted power in return for controlling the internal affairs of their "sector." That a franchise-type notion was implicit in U.S. policy is revealed by the names given it: trusteeship, lend-lease, and, most important, the concept of a client state. In the turbulent atmosphere of World War II, the United States had begun to search for "responsible" leadership in Europe, giving power to men like Darlan in France and the anti-Communist Poles outside of Poland. Even under Roosevelt, then, it became clear that extreme right-wing views were not a barrier to U.S. conceptions of maturity.[66] While a man with as strong a fascist proclivity as Darlan would have been embarrassing to any but the most determined, the reason for supporting him was clear; de Gaulle, impeccably conservative and as anti-Communist as one could ever expect, was also independent. The United States did not want strong leaders, it wanted pliable ones, who would accept without challenge the fact that the central authority was a franchise operation that would remain in Washington. How to find leaders who were weak yet could govern, who were elitist yet could inspire loyalty, and who were counterrevolutionary yet could rule in a time of revolutionary ferment became a part of Dual State activity abroad.

It did not seem to matter that the requirements of the United States for its sector leaders were so contradictory that no person in the world could meet them. The search still went on with great enthusiasm. In one case a liberal Catholic, Senator Mansfield, combined with a New Deal jurist, William O. Douglas, in recommending a man who, they felt, would satisfy all these conditions in his own country. The man was Ngo Dinh Diem and the country was Vietnam. The fact that relatively sophisticated men like Mansfield and Douglas could be so wrong is an indication of how desperate the search for responsible leaders had become. The Diem case is a fascinating example of the problems of the whole approach. Diem turned the logic of the Franchise State upside down; those places with the most power were most impotent and those with the least power called the shots. The *Pentagon Papers* document how, on periodic occasions, Diem would obtain what he requested from the United States without meeting any of its conditions.[67] It was Diem, not Mao, who made the United States into a paper tiger, and he did so with ridiculous ease. For the fact was that the Franchise State model was totally inappropriate in a world context, which Diem understood and the United States did not. In order for the franchise solution to have worked, there would have had to be mutual expectations on the part of the participants, a recognition that in giving something up one gets something in return. No such understanding took place across cultures as different as the United States and Vietnam. Furthermore, the Franchise State is based on the assumption, often valid at home, that a leader of a sector controls it and can make it conform to his will. Diem had no such control over affairs in Vietnam. When the United States attempted policies based on the Franchise State model— such as its Strategic Hamlet Program, which the author of the *Pentagon Papers*, understanding its franchise nature, called "pacification by proxy" —they invariably failed.[68] Maxwell Taylor began to understand this, suggesting in one memo that the United States must "force the Vietnamese to get their house in order in one area after another," [69] thereby adopting a metaphor used time and again by earlier theorists of the Franchise State at home.[70] But the expected housecleaning never took place, and although the United States tried to stick it out with Diem in the interests of domestic appearances within the United States, as John F. Kennedy suggested in a November 1961 cable to Ambassador Nolting,[71] eventually a Franchise State model that attempted to "induce Diem to do the things that the U.S. thought should be done" [72] was discarded. The United States supported the violent toppling of Diem in a coup d'état.

These Vietnamese events were a microcosm of what was taking place around the world. In a nutshell, the failure of the Franchise State to work in the field led to the use of violent and covert espionage operations instead. The heyday of CIA operations in the 1950s resulted because options that did not involve the covert use of force—such as Franchise State methods—were not working. Use of force, in addition, led to an expansion of the Dual State's Washington headquarters, and since those in charge of espionage had become a vested interest, the new apparatus would be used that much more in the field. The resulting vicious cycle escalated—to borrow one popular term from that period—until the covert face of the Dual State had become a full partner, to borrow another, in affairs of policy.

Increased reliance on espionage was decided upon, yet there was no guarantee that cloak-and-dagger operations would achieve the desired results. While intelligence operatives liked to picture themselves as professionals—cool, detached, and thorough—the fact is that they were amateurs trying out new approaches. No wonder, then, that the first attempts to use covert power systematically had an air of clownishness about them, an air that would reappear later in the Watergate affair. Throughout the 1950s the use of the covert state abroad could have been the subject of a Marx Brothers farce, were it not for the fact that people were being killed and self-determination was being stymied. In Iran in 1953 a man who had appeared on radio in the "Gang Busters" series took charge of covert operations. In Guatemala in 1954 the involvement of the Dulles brothers in furthering their own corporate self-interest was revealed for all to see. In Suez in 1956 the CIA was caught unprepared by the emerging conflicts. In Indonesia in 1958 President Sukarno exposed CIA activity in his country and won popular support for doing so.[73] Considering the controversy surrounding its use, the CIA—and the covert face of the Dual State, of which it was a part—was off to an inauspicious beginning.

The period of amateurism ended with the failure of the Bay of Pigs invasion, probably the most important event in the history of the Dual State. "The impact of the failure shook up the national security machinery," [74] Arthur Schlesinger, Jr., wrote. It seemed as if strong controls were going to be exercised over the CIA. They finally were, but the story of how they came to be sheds more light on the instability of this general solution; the process by which the Dual State became professionalized deserves to be told by itself.

MATURITY

The three years of the Kennedy Administration saw the solidification and professionalization of the Dual State; no other three-year period in postwar history is of comparable importance. Kennedy's campaign theme— "Let's get this country moving again"—suggested an intensification of the theme of insecurity that had dominated U.S. politics since the end of World War II. We were sluggish, getting fat, much too satisfied. The world was changing and it was unclear whether we could change with it. In addition, Kennedy inherited and strengthened each of the tendencies that went into the making of the Dual State. He sought his advisors from that patrician elite dedicated to the ruthless preservation of its power by any means necessary. Because he was a Democrat, he was sensitive to the anti-Communist hysteria of the 1950s and bent over backward to deflect the charge. He was ideologically motivated by a Trumanesque conception of presidential power at the expense of war cabinets and staff systems. Like Joseph Chamberlain, he combined foreign adventure with domestic reform or, as an astute observer put it, his "progressivism and his imperialism were inseparable." [75] He was committed to professionalization, finding the "best" minds and avoiding excessive cronyism. He loved power for its own sake and surrounded himself with men who told him that the worship of power was the highest duty of a leader. And, politically ambitious, he, like his predecessors and successors, was not going to preside over the liquidation of the American empire, whatever the cost in lives, the damage to democratic forms, and the dangers of instability. With Kennedy the Dual State had found its natural home.

Yet Kennedy had contradictory attitudes toward the Dual State. On the one hand, he wanted very much to control it, to infuse it with a broad ruling class perspective through which it would not be subject to the embarrassment caused by an intense pursuit of narrow interests, such as the Dulles involvement in the Guatemala affair. At the same time, for all his rhetoric, Kennedy was the most cautious of presidents, continuously postponing innovations until his mythic second term. His inability to decide whether to promote vested interests or national coordination is reflected in the composition of the committee that he appointed to examine the failure of the Playa Girón invasion. The four-man group was neatly divided down the middle; Robert Kennedy and Maxwell Taylor told the President that he should control the CIA; Allen Dulles (the appointment of those who fail to find out why a failure occurred was a legacy of the Franchise State) and Arleigh Burke told him that the old structure was basically sound.[76] With such a group, mealy-mouthed recommendations were inevitable; Kennedy accepted its advice of allowing the CIA to continue as it had, but removing from its operations activities as unwieldy as direct invasions of other countries. And when he appointed John McCone, the get-rich-quick defense operative, as his Director of Central Intelligence, it appeared as if Kennedy leaned toward the parochial vested interests if he leaned anywhere at all.

Kennedy needed an event to help him make up his mind. The war in Vietnam, which became not only a testing ground for new weapons but for new conceptions of the state as well, gave him his opportunity. After the failures of the CIA, Kennedy had become convinced that the covert centers of power within the state existed off by themselves, responsible to no one but themselves, and therefore were capable of making blunders since they were unable or unwilling to check their view of reality with anyone else. At the same time the public and overt side of the governmental apparatus—the State Department, for example—was seen as sluggish and unable to govern. The decision was made to avoid both institutions and to develop instead completely new ones. Kennedy's antipathy to the idea of a war cabinet led him to favor what the author of the Defense Department's secret history of the Vietnam War called "informal" processes.[77] Agencies like the NSC were considered invalid because, in the words of one Dual State theorist, they "put still another layer between the President and the problems which only he could decide."[78] Since "only he" could decide them, the logical place to concentrate power was in "his" staff; during the Kennedy Administration the position of Assistant to the President for National Security Affairs became the home of the covert state. Here Kennedy was strongly influenced by Senator Henry Jackson, whose subcommittee hearings into the "national policy machinery" were a most comprehensive search for what was called a "single, small but strongly organized staff."[79] The one first created included McGeorge Bundy, Walt Rostow, and Carl Kaysen, plus some transitional holdovers from the former administration, and the Bundy group gave a strong imprimatur to Kennedy's general policy of bypassing existing machinery in favor of small groups intensely loyal to him. The appointment of Maxwell Taylor as Special Military Advisor to the President (a direct slap at the JCS), Bundy's emergence with his own staff (an obvious replacement for the NSC), and the use of the President's brother on a wide variety of missions (formerly the job of the State Department) were all examples of the new trend.

Theoretically, new institutions would avoid both the secrecy and the parochialism of the CIA and the bureaucratic lethargy of the State Department. Actually they did neither. Instead of controlling secrecy, the new arrangement became a victim of it, controlled by it. And, instead of bypassing bureaucracy, Kennedy's personal assistants became entrapped in a deadly bureaucratic game in which poor decisions inexorably led to more poor decisions. What went wrong? The problem was that all of Kennedy's surface changes simply altered the form of the contradictions at the heart of the Dual State, not their nature. A combination of political ideology that was near totalitarian ("Ask not what your country can do for you . . .") plus the press of events in a fighting war that the United States was losing led to a decision to resolve the contradiction between vested interests and national coordination solely in the direction of the latter. The thrust of both the second Eberstadt and Rockefeller committee reports, that centralization of authority was the answer to the obstacles in the path of the Dual State, reached its zenith under Kennedy. Bundy's thirst for power culminated in a process by which the enormous power available to the leaders of the state had passed from Congress to the cabinet to the war cabinet or NSC, to the President and his staff, to the President's favorite advisor. H. R. Haldeman's ability to govern the country while his boss dreamed dark fantasies of revenge was possible only because the Kennedys perfected the President's staff as the power base of the Dual State.

The process of centralizing power in fewer and fewer hands solved the problem of coordinated policy, but it did so at the expense of the immediate needs of invested centers of power. An active NSC and JCS had meant less power for individual service branches. But power to the Presidents' staff disenfranchised both of those centers, and it was not likely that they would accept their newly inferior status gracefully. Control of foreign policy by the President was fought by the CIA, which by this time had become another vested interest. The decision to bypass these agencies meant that they would have to be given something so that they would still play the game by the rules. They were given a war. The CIA could run its escapades; the defense contractors could build their weapons; the generals could issue dire warnings; the defense-oriented political scientists could invent strategies; the research institutes could play war games; the Air Force could have bombs to drop; Selective Service could have lives to disrupt; and patriots could have dissenters to castigate. Off there busily doing whatever they do, it was possible for these groups to forget the power that they were losing, since they never seemed to have it so good. In practice, then, and not through any plan, the contradiction between vested interests and national policy was solved; the answer was to create a Dual State within the Dual State. The covert half of the larger Dual State split into two halves. One was bloated and essentially powerless but was given lots of money and plenty of symbolic prestige. The other became an inner core within an inner core, even more clandestine, narrower in size, and, as it continued to lose the war it was fighting, more desperate and amoral. Just as the citizens were finding out the details of the Dual State, in other words, the formerly secret branch was becoming public and a new secret one was being created. It is not surprising, though it remains astounding, that the deputy director for intelligence of the CIA did not know of plans for the Bay of Pigs invasion [80] or that during the height of the war in Vietnam major policy makers were learning what policy had been made by reading the newspapers. Those who thought they had power suddenly found themselves bypassed and began to understand the nature of powerlessness in the modern state.[81]

These developments explain in large part the structure of the Dual State during the Kennedy/Johnson and Nixon administrations. In the former, as Ralph Stavins has shown, covert actions moved from the level of occasional necessity to the level of everyday reality. The Vietnam War was planned and directed by a tiny group of men using various covert mechanisms: Room 303, the Special Group for Counter-insurgency, the country teams. These represented "an expansion of the war-making powers of the Executive to a degree never before anticipated in the history of the Republic. For the first time, total command over the several national security agencies was concentrated in the Office of the President." [82] Similarly, the Nixon Administration created a covert apparatus around

Henry Kissinger. Plans to disrupt the democratically elected government of Chile were made by a group called the "Committee of 40," which met every week with Kissinger in an effort to coordinate strategy. Major decisions, affecting millions around the world, were being made by just a few men. The years 1962–67 saw the final construction of the Dual State structure that had grown out of the tensions and contradictions of the years 1947–61.

At some point during the 1960s, then, a fully developed Dual State had come into existence. Because it was secret, very few were aware of its creation, though a persistent reader of daily newspapers could have discovered that something important was taking place. Because it had no public accountability, it was arrogant and ruthless, seeking to impose its will wherever it had decided that its will should be imposed. Because it considered itself omniscient, it developed its own language, its own code words, its own rules of proper reality—in short, its own symbolic structure.[83] Because it was divorced from the consequences of its actions, it developed its own rules of rationality: body counts, number of missions, captured documents were used as indicators of something called "progress." Though each step leading to its creation followed logically from the one that came before, the whole thing—when finally assembled—was frightening. For an unprecedented amount of weapons of destruction had been put into the hands of an unprecedentedly small number of men, and meanwhile the business of politics was supposed to go on in its usual fashion. Elections took place, bills were passed, emotions aroused, and hopes defeated—all while a state within a state went blithely about its business, seemingly immune to all the events surrounding it. The enormous power at its disposal was being concentrated in one small country in order that a declining imperialist power could still prove to itself that it could control the world. Because it could not, the days of the Dual State, despite the power available to it, were numbered.

A full-scale Dual State existed for only about ten years, from roughly 1963 to 1973. During that time, the details of what belonged to the open side of the diarchy and what was reserved for the closed were worked out amidst great controversy. One example, the most important probably, was the Tonkin Gulf Resolution. Using all the by-then-tiresome rhetoric of emergency and executive decision making, Lyndon Johnson was able to obtain from Congress a resolution that basically declared Congress' own impotence and little else. If there was a time to question the creation of the Dual State, this was it, but Congress refused. Yet, in contrast to what came after Johnson, the importance of this event was that the inner core of the Dual State still felt that they needed a declaration from the public state; those at the very core were not yet prepared to ignore the existing institutions of government.[84] By the time Congress woke up to what it had done, this attitude was changing. When the Senate Foreign Relations

Committee held hearings on a resolution calling for participation of the
Congress in foreign entanglements, the then legal theorist of the Dual
State, Nicholas Katzenbach, who also happened to be Attorney General,
issued a startling new law, as follows:

> Chairman Fulbright: You think it is outmoded to declare war?
> Mr. Katzenbach: In this kind of context I think the expression of declar-
> ing a war is one that has become outmoded in the international arena.[85]

Katzenbach then went on to expound in its entirety the rationale by which
the Dual State would be operated. If Congress did not like it, he informed
them, they could impeach the President. (At that time it seemed like a
rather unlikely occurrence, like predicting the date on which the world
would end.) Frustrated, Congress repealed its Tonkin Gulf Resolution,
but the dilemma it faced was indicated later when, in passing a bill to
restrict the ability of a President to fight a limited war, it articulated for
the first time a legislative basis for Dual State wars, a point that only a
few senators, like Thomas Eagleton (D-Mo.), seemed to understand.

During the Johnson years, as one commentator put it, the "highest level
of Washington officialdom was made personally responsible for the
planning of covert activity." [86] Nonetheless, the mere fact that men like
Katzenbach justified this form of state activity, no matter how arrogantly,
was a sign that some balance still existed between the two halves of the
Dual State. That balance, however, was quite precarious, and one mistake
—such as too much involvement of the Dual State in domestic affairs—
could easily upset it. It did not take long for that danger to be realized.

The Young Old Age of the Dual State

Looking back, it seems inevitable that the secret, authoritarian, and
centralized state developed to control reluctant populations overseas would
also be used for similar purposes at home. Not that there was any one
sharp moment when this began; rather, the development of the Dual
State for home consumption was a gradual thing, a result of forces that
could not easily be stopped. First, the assumption that constituted the
rationale of the Dual State applied domestically. Anticommunism could
be resurrected when domestic radicalism broke out in the 1960s. The
emphasis on unanimity in the face of external threat was used as easily
by Lyndon Johnson as it had been by Joseph McCarthy. Second, the distinction between foreign and domestic affairs had become tenuous at
best. In order to direct its war the covert state required a draft, and hence
from the very beginning it exercised its influence at home. The suppression
of bad news, the intensification of ROTC programs, the shaping of the
labor force through Selective Service, the inflation produced by wartime

spending—all these were domestic consequences of foreign policy decisions. Third, the dynamics of politics in capitalist society led to an emphasis on efficiency; since a covert apparatus already existed, it made business sense to use it wherever possible, since it was presumably the most efficient mechanism. This last point was especially valid if a President could cast his domestic policy in wartime language, a tactic popularized during the New Deal. Since 1965 alone, there have been wars on poverty, smut, disease, complacency, and inflation, each requiring a wartime mentality. Randolph Bourne's prophecy that "war is the health of the State"[87] proved true in many more ways than he could have anticipated.

Manifestations of the use of the covert state at home were in general received with shock by the American people, as if the 1947 law, which prohibited CIA activity in domestic affairs (leaving that to the FBI), were a Social Contract, in danger of being broken. The CIA, it turned out, had been spending money in support of organizations that it had chosen to favor, like the National Student Association. Unlike political scientists, whose neat categories divide up a complex world into simple diagrams, CIA men knew that the distinction between domestic and foreign policy was a silly one and acted accordingly. Trying to defend himself against charges that his behavior in the Watergate affair was unseemly, President Nixon told the American people that CIA activity in domestic affairs— illegal breaking and entering, mail checks, domestic surveillance—went back to the 1950s and included Democratic as well as Republican administrations.[88] He was, for once, not lying. Funds for magazines and small-scale snooping, however, were nothing compared to what would follow. In late December 1974, as a Christmas present to its readers, long used to sensational disclosures but deprived of one since Nixon's resignation during the summer, the *New York Times* revealed the extent of CIA domestic activity.[89] At least 10,000 people were the subject of dossiers for the "crime" of being opposed to the war in Vietnam. Under the leadership of its then director, Richard Helms, the CIA became a full-scale domestic repressive apparatus. As one CIA official commented: "What you had was an insulated secret police agency not under internal security or audit."[90] The Dual State had come home, and it had done so with a vengeance.

Such periodic raids by clandestine organizations into the life of civil society were accompanied by other developments, equally important. The 1960s had shown that the Democratic Party had few qualms about using the repressive power of the state at home when it needed to do so. Since it needed to only when there was something around to repress, the development of domestic radicalism in the New Left and Black Power movements gave rise to an apparatus of repression within the state.[91] Sporadic attempts at repression led to demands on the part of "law and order" watchdogs for more professionalization, and with the Justice Department new programs were established for the control of domestic populations. These techniques necessarily became covert because they contradicted large portions of the democratic rhetoric of the society. What the CIA was supposed to be abroad, the FBI and local police forces would be at home. (Federalism had guaranteed that there would be as many distinct police forces as there were groups to control.) A series of covert operations were begun at all levels of government: red squads, political espionage, wiretapping, illegal breaking and entering, mail checks, general surveillance, and the use of *agents provocateurs*. In the name of checking the power of the police state, a police state had been created.

Then came Watergate. When Nixon came to power the centralized and authoritarian face of the Dual State already existed. While in the realm of foreign policy it would have been inconceivable to tighten its power further, there was more room to maneuver in the domestic area. The Democrats had begun the construction of the Dual State for home use, but had not finished their work by 1968. The Nixon men, in other words, did not make a choice to create a covert domestic state but simply picked up where the other men had left off. The naturalness by which this was done is captured in the after-the-fact reflections of one of Nixon's men. At the moment he learned that the existence of the covert state that he had helped to solidify was going to be made public, Jeb Magruder realized:

> My life had changed that day. For the first time I realized, and I think we all realized, that we were involved in criminal activity, that if the truth became known we could all go to jail. During the spring, when Liddy was presenting his break-in plan, I should have been aware that it was illegal, but somehow it seemed acceptable, perhaps because we were discussing it in the office of the Attorney General of the United States. But at some point that Saturday morning I realized that this was not just hard-nosed politics, this was a crime that could destroy us all. The cover-up, thus, was immediate and automatic; no one ever considered that there would *not* be a cover-up. It seemed inconceivable that with our political power we could not erase this mistake we had made.[92]

What is informative about this statement is not the disingenuous disclaimer by a criminal that he was unaware of his crime. Rather, two important things stand out. First, the notion of the coverup as "immediate and automatic" suggests that among state operatives the furtherance of secrecy had become a reflex more than it was a conscious act. Secrecy had so much become the *mode de vie* of the democratic state that it was no longer necessary even to discuss it; making a matter of policy public was the controversial option that became the exception. Second, Magruder makes clear that holding state power was by itself sufficient excuse for taking any action whatsoever. The Liddy break-in plan, as he describes it, was so bizarre that it would have been laughed out of existence by any rational group of people. But holding state power in a society dominated by what I call in Chapter 9 alienated politics (called "hard-nosed politics" by Magruder) does not lead to rationality. Nixon's men were scared—of foreigners, of dissenters, of ordinary people, and of themselves—and they consistently acted like frightened men, carrying out their fantasies in secrecy and passing the blame to others when they were caught.

Frightened people generally do stupid things, and its was the extraordinary blunders of the Nixon "team"—including the most frightened and therefore most stupid of them all—that eventually led to the publication of the Watergate transcripts. For the first time the deliberations of the inner core of the Dual State were made public, and even edited they caused the kind of shock that could occur only when reality is forced upon those who have been denying its existence. After the release of the transcripts there could no longer be any doubt about the fact of the Dual State; reasonable people could disagree only on its meaning. Since the transcripts provide enough material to keep political commentators busy for years, perhaps the most productive procedure here would not be to review the events surrounding Watergate, but to use those events as highlighting the nature of the Dual State. For Watergate, very much a logical product of the Dual State, also permanently altered its form by producing the one ingredient that makes covert operations impossible: publicity.

The Watergate conspirators were not men of fascist persuasion trying to bring about an end to democratic politics. Perhaps they would have liked to do that, but the transcripts show continuously how the expectations of a liberal democratic polity limited their "options" and altered their "scenario." Speaking directly to Nixon about his "investigation," John Dean talks of John Mitchell's appearance before the Grand Jury:

> Dean: I was under pretty clear instructions not to investigate this, but this could have been disastrous on the electorate if all hell had broken loose. I worked on a theory of containment—
> President: Sure.
> Dean: To try to hold it right where it was.
> President: Right.[93]

The metaphor is much more appropriate than Dean probably knew. Containment was a doctrine once preached against Communists—the enemy. In the old days, when Nixon was stoned in Caracas but cheered in Los Angeles, he knew who had to be contained. Yet when Cairo provided the cheering throngs and New York the cascade of boos, things were not clear at all. A new population needed to be dealt with, and here Dean only brings out an assumption rather than making a discovery, an assumption to which Nixon can only assent. The men of the White House were learning something that Dual State operatives seem to have a hard time learning: that democratic expectations are a two-edged sword. When Haldeman dismissed the problems posed by the Justice Department investigation by saying that "basically it is a PR job," [94] he missed the point. Law can be used as a method of social control only if there is some evidence that the lawmakers adhere to it as well. Haldeman himself said on March 27, 1973, "Now, no man is above the law and that is a basic principle we must operate on, but . . ." and he went on to propose a strategy for avoiding that very principle.[95] The Nixon men were so wrapped up in the reification of the state (see Chapter 8) that they neglected its own rules of conduct, and this was a significant part of their undoing.

A second contributing cause of the Nixon debacle was the way in which his administration was insensitive to the problem of vested interests. By 1968 both the CIA and the FBI had become established components in the outer ring of the Dual State. Kennedy had tried to control both and found that the way to do so was to give each something to keep it occupied and to avoid offending the sensibilities of each agency's operations as much as possible. In this context the behavior of Nixon's men is most peculiar; impeccably sensitive to the vested interests within the private sector, they tended to ignore the power of parochial interests within the Dual State. Relations within the state did bear great resemblance to a monopoly capitalist economy. When the FBI asked the CIA for information on one Lee D. Pennington, a CIA agent who was a friend of James McCord, the latter agency "withheld" the correct information by furnishing misleading data, very much as multinational giants try to fool each other about prices.[96] But also like the economy, such agencies tend to band together when under attack, and the consequence of the Nixon strategy was to push the vested interests into some sort of an alliance.

Nixon offended just about every entrenched interest within the Dual State that could have been offended. His Huston Plan, the ultimate in domestic repression, was sabotaged by J. Edgar Hoover because no one "stroked" him to get his participation in planning and implementing it.[97] The White House repeatedly lied to the FBI, such as the time it delivered the contents of Howard Hunt's safe without informing them that important matters had been removed.[98] Such manipulations led a series of agents to leak important information to reporters from the *Washington Post*, without which the full story of the coverup would never have been known.[99] "The FBI is not under control," Haldeman complained to Nixon on June 23, 1972,[100] apparently with no realization that it was their own fault. Similar tactics were tried with the CIA. With extraordinary gullibility, Nixon thought that the CIA would fall for the same rhetoric used against the American people. He instructed Haldeman to tell Richard Helms, the director of the CIA, that his agency should "lay off":

President: O.K. Just postpone (scratching noises) (unintelligible) just say (unintelligible) very bad to have this fellow Hunt, ah, he knows too damned much, if he was involved—you happen to know that? If it gets out that this is all involved, the Cuba thing would be a fiasco. It would make the CIA look bad, it's going to make Hunt look bad, and it is likely to blow the whole Bay of Pigs thing which we think would be unfortunate—both for the CIA and for the country, at this time, and for American foreign policy.[101]

The idea that Helms, a professional Dual State operative, would have been moved by a twelve-year-old event like the Bay of Pigs, that he would scare off because of threats to the sanctity of the public side of the state, is amazing. Actually Helms was much more sensitive to the fact that Nixon's men had continuously lied to his deputy, General Vernon Walters, and had asked the CIA to risk its own cover for the sake of the five men arrested in the Watergate. It was Helms who was in a position to make threats to Nixon, not the other way around, something that Nixon realized too late.

The remaining ingredient in the events leading to Nixon's resignation is the failure of the strategy behind Watergate. Just as the creation of a Dual State for use in controlling populations abroad ran into the twin problems of amateurish tactics and local resistance, the Nixon men won their immediate objective—victory in the 1972 election—but did so at a very high price, the discrediting of the entire Dual State operation. The sloppy job of espionage led to the whole business. Simple matters learned in Breaking and Entering 101 (the University of Pennsylvania used to offer courses in spying) were forgotten, making it easy for the burglars to get caught. Having a man with White House connections among them is more incredible, almost as if it were, as Magruder quite realistically thought, a Democratic Party counterplan. The clownishness of the early days of the CIA is recalled by these events. But more important, once the affair became known, the political problem became the control of the American population, and that job was also handled in clumsy fashion. Overseas, American foreign policy makers had traditionally assumed that what was in the best interests of America was also in the best interests of the countries that America sought to dominate. So here the men around Nixon believed that whatever was good for themselves was good for everyone else. All they had to do was utter the words "national security" and they would be left alone. But the stratagems put forward in the coverup plan did not stem the tide of public curiosity; they increased the size of the waves. Nixon and his associates began to understand how difficult it was to shape events in such a way as to benefit a few at the expense of the many. In frustration Nixon cried out, "I just don't know how it is going to come out. That is the whole point, and I just don't know." [102] A smarter man would have known; he would have realized that such a strategy could never win.

The Watergate episode, the revelations about the CIA's activity at home, the publication of the "Media Papers" [103] (FBI files on controlling dissent)—all made public for the first time extensive material about the domestic operations of the Dual State. What all three show is that the contradictions that faced Dual State planners in developing the 1947 National Security Act, contradictions that they had seemingly solved, had once again arisen in a new form.

First, there was the contradiction between performance and expectation. The covert face of the state could work only if it did not destroy public expectations about democratic government. When a CIA official, on learning that the facts about CIA involvement in internal affairs were to be made public, said, "This is explosive, it could destroy the agency," [104] he expressed the problem succinctly. It is too early to tell whether his fears are fully justified, but certainly the Dual State may never again be able to operate with the reckless abandon of the past. Ford's presidency suggests that the political leadership of the country would like to reestablish the harmony of the Dual State as it existed before the Nixon years, but whether they can or not is another question. Restoring the Agency's credibility is the first task of Stanfield Turner, Carter's head of the CIA, but he must also justify agency business as usual.

Second, the contradiction between unified and vested interest, apparently solved by the compromises of the 1947 law, was stickier than it seemed at first. It was this contradiction that led Kennedy to develop his own apparatus for foreign policy making, the single most important development in centralizing power within the covert face of the Dual State. The same problem led to the revelations of the Nixon years, for time after time it was the anger of one covert agency, jealous of usurpation of its prerogatives by another, that resulted in the release of damaging information. The American people owe what they know to the fact that various parts of the secret state were more loyal to their bureaucratic "turfs" than they were to their common interest in preserving the structure of the Dual State.

Finally, and most important, the contradiction between control and self-determination proved to exist at home just as it did abroad. Americans were not as pliable as Dual State theorists had hoped. There was opposition to a policy of repression, perhaps not as much as one might have hoped, but enough to make the task of the covert operatives more difficult. Defense committees, demonstrations against political trials, not guilty verdicts by juries under strong pressure to find political prisoners guilty—all these contributed to putting rocks in the smooth road envisioned by practitioners of domestic political repression. In short, the Dual State could not be brought home without the contradictions that come along with it;

what was true for Asia, Africa, and Latin America also turned out to be true for the United States, though in a different form than those in power had wished.

These three contradictions make it clear that attempts to attribute Watergate to the idiosyncratic nature of Mr. Nixon's personality misinterpret what actually took place. Watergate is better seen as part of a larger problem, the rise and fall of the Dual State, and that problem is a structural one involving social forces, not an individual one that could have been avoided if the President had consulted an analyst. Specifically, what took place in the United States in the postwar years resulted from the pressures that had brought the Dual State into existence in the first place. Political democracy had never been fully accepted by the U.S. ruling class. A rampant elitism had been a major characteristic of postwar power holders. Quite unique in American history, a generation of "realist" intellectuals had preached the message that power was its own justification, and that anything was permissible as long as it was in the "national interest"; the effects of their message could be seen in John Kennedy as easily as in Richard Nixon. Both men revealed by their actions a contempt for democratic government that would have made Walter Bagehot proud. The response of American power holders to the increasing political sophistication of the majority was first to offer them demagoguery and then to offer them impotence. But if the existence of a democratic majority brought the Dual State into being, the same force was also responsible for its partial undoing. The people, contrary to what the sociologists preached during the 1950s, had much greater respect for democratic forms than did the leaders, and it was only because of this respect that any attempt to preserve them was made.

Second, it is necessary to return to the contradiction between functional and substantial rationality. The postwar years saw not only a rise in an antidemocratic ideology within the ruling class; they also saw modern capitalism begin to undo the very Benthamite logic that had brought it into existence (see Chapter 8). Although the rise of capitalism had contributed, in its early days, to a decrease in superstition and magic, and to an increasing rationalization of the world, by the mid-twentieth century that very process of rationalization had turned into its opposite. Monopoly capital had rendered meaningless the one sensible justification for the existence of capitalism: efficiency and cheapness guaranteed through competition. Stripped of the only ideology that made sense, businessmen could hold onto their privileges by intensifying the irrational to heights of frenzy. Advertising increased in importance as substantial rationality declined. The tendency of the productive apparatus to become decreasingly rationalized was matched, in the realm of consciousness, by an emphasis on the basest and least sensible of human needs. As the political rulers, desperate because their rule was no longer an accepted fact, turned to cloak-and-dagger operations, the industrial leadership, facing a similar lack of legitimacy in their control over the means of production, turned to manipulation of the mass media. In the atmosphere produced by this change, anything became possible; critical faculties were suspended; fantasy became reality. Without such an atmosphere the secrecy necessary for the Dual State could not have worked; it is hard to exaggerate the importance of the contradiction between functional and substantial rationality as a structural cause of the Dual State. But the manipulation of desire cannot work forever; all of the people were not fooled all of the time. It was because of demands by people to know what was really going on that the Gordon Liddys and Howard Hunts ended up in jail. The miasma of confusion created by the Dual State had been broken through, not fully, but enough to cause dismay in the heart of every potential spy.

Finally, the rise and fall of the Dual State must be understood as part of the rise and fall of empire. All of the fears implicit in the creation of the "National Insecurity State" had come out in the failure of the United States to win yet another war in Asia. Everything short of nuclear bombs was tried and everything failed. The release of the *Pentagon Papers*, a direct result of that failure, publicized the existence of the Dual State. Sitting alone in his hotel room reading page after page, Neil Sheehan, the *New York Times* reporter assigned to write the first articles based on these documents, saw coming into being

> a centralized state, far more powerful than anything else, for whom the enemy is not simply the Communists, but everything else, its own press, its own judiciary, its own Congress, foreign and friendly governments—all these are potentially antagonistic. It has survived and perpetuated itself often using the issue of anti-Communism as a weapon against the other branches of government and the press, and finally, it does not function necessarily for the benefit of the Republic but rather for its own ends, its own perpetuating; it has its own codes which are quite different from public codes. Secrecy was a way of protecting itself, not so much from threats by foreign governments, but from detection from its own population on charges of its own competence and wisdom.[105]

What was apparent to Sheehan would seem to be clear to everyone else as well. With its "cover" rudely ripped off, the Dual State could never again be the same. The effects of the failure of the Dual State to "deliver the goods" in Vietnam could be seen elsewhere. The men of the Dual State failed to keep the *Pentagon Papers* out of the hands of the American people, in part because the war itself had made clear that the words of these men were not to be believed. They had lied because they could not come to terms with a new world order; countries throughout the world were insisting on their right to self-determination, and the more the leaders of the United States put themselves in opposition to that desire, the more the Dual State, which they had built to lead the counterrevolution, began to crumble. Created in response to an empire, the Dual State fell victim to its dissolution.

In short, the events of the Nixon years were the old age of the Dual State, which took place when it was still quite young. It was not Nixon who caused the major events of that period (though both his political judgment and his idiosyncrasies colored those events), but the combination of political arrogance on the part of democratic leaders, the development of intensive irrationality under conditions of monopoly capitalism, and the inevitable failure of a world-wide policy of counterrevolution. Does this mean that the Dual State is finished as a possible solution? Such a conclusion would be permature. A battle over the CIA is taking place at this writing, and its outcome cannot be predicted. The appointment by President Carter of Theodore Sorensen to head the agency indicated a desire on Carter's part to control the excesses of the agency in order to make it more legitimate within the confines of democratic theory. But the fact that Sorensen was forced to withdraw his name indicates that professional spies have not given up easily and will fight to hold on to their control over the agency. Sorensen's replacement, Admiral Turner, is apparently more upset about those who publicize Dual State abuses than those who commit them. Whichever side wins the immediate struggle—and it seems as if the CIA has been surprisingly successful in deflecting the criticisms which stemmed from the revelations of its hanky-panky—it is apparent that a new generation of dual-state operatives has been coming to power. A fascination for duality will continue to exist so long as domestic and international political contradictions exist, but in the future the Dual State is not likely to be as flamboyant in its operations as it was in its heyday.

7 / Globalizing Contradictions

"The record does not show that our foreign investments to date have been very profitable, except for those in Canada, which I do not regard as a foreign country."

Anonymous American businessman (1946)

"U.S. foreign aid is designed to stimulate the mobilization of private capital and not to replace it."

Dean Rusk (1964)

"The world's political structures are completely obsolete. They have not changed in at least a hundred years and are woefully out of time with technological progress."

Jacques Maisonrouge to the American Foreign
Service Association (1969)

JUST ABOUT EVERYTHING was tried, and just about everything was at some point found wanting. Pure accumulation and assertions of harmony, expansion, corporatism, franchise principles, and diarchy were incapable of permanently resolving the inherent contradiction between liberal and democratic conceptions of political life. The obvious conclusion is that as these options are used up, the tensions within the state are bound to intensify. Yet there is one possible exception to this conclusion. At the moment when the state is finally about to confront the contradictions within it, it could disappear as an important historical entity. It would be meaningless to argue that internal tensions were about to cause the state to burst asunder if it were no longer in a position to make decisions affecting the lives of individuals and groups. Propositions have been put forward based on the passing of the nation-state, seriously in many cases, and some attention must be directed toward them before I can end my discussion of the limitations of historical solutions.

The two most intellectually respectable arguments for the demise of the nation-state involve the rise of transnationality. In various guises, certain writers and politicians have suggested that the major decision-making units in the world in the latter half of the twentieth century are not individual states, which are the legacy of nineteenth-century nationalism, but supranational units to which power has been and will continue to be flowing. In this chapter I plan to examine two of these kinds of arguments with some care. The first involves transnational political units, such as the United Nations and the European Economic Community. While the initial fervor that greeted these experiments has subsided, an analysis of their accomplishments and limitations sheds light on the international aspects of legitimation and accumulation, which unquestionably have become more important in the twentieth century. Second, the growth in multinational corporate activity has replaced the earlier fascination with the UN among global visionaries. Multinationals, in Jacques Maisonrouge's term, render the nation-state "obsolete," implicitly making irrelevant the contradictions within it as well. My argument in this chapter is that neither transnational political nor economic units have transcended the historical impasse between liberalism and democracy, but they have raised it to a new level. Far from resolving contradictions, they have internationalized them and therefore made them more important than ever. With transnationality, contradictions that once affected only Europe and the United States now affect the world.

The Un-United Nations

When transnational political units are created, they are likely to face many of the same problems faced by national political units. On the one hand, their purpose is to preserve a structure in which some benefit from a particular economic system more than others, even though the system in this case is world-wide. On the other hand, that structure can be preserved only if all participants adhere to it, which they are likely to do only if they perceive its decisions as legitimate. The historical problem of liberalism and democracy becomes transformed into a tension between hegemony and legitimacy. If a new supranational structure is to be erected, compliance to its decisions must be universal or it will have no reason to exist. Yet decisions taken in the interests of the universe of nations are, for that very reason, not likely to be looked on favorably by those who are used to defining the nature of the world order in an unimpeded fashion. It is, in short, as difficult for a Transnational State to be simultaneously hegemonic and legitimate as it is for a capitalist state to be both liberal and democratic. This was the lesson learned by the United States as it prepared to experiment with transnational political units.

Both the vision of a Transnational State and the problems inherent in that vision had been revealed in the failure of the League of Nations. Nonetheless the Great Depression and the arrival of World War II made the dreamers dream again, for those events indicated that the selfish pursuit of national sovereignty characteristic of nineteenth-century politics was rapidly leading the world to disaster. Just as the unchecked pursuit of private interests by individual capitalists had led to national disarray, the unchecked pursuit of national interests would lead to world disharmony, incompatible with the dream of a world-wide capitalist economy. In the post–World War II period, the need for international cooperation was becoming clear to even the most pigheaded industrialists, and in addition the United States, conspicuous by its absence in the early efforts toward a Transnational State, seemed not only willing to participate in transnationalism but anxious to take the lead.

While the United States had indicated its interest in the rest of the world as early as the 1890s, it had never before been in a position of world leadership. In order to lead, as American businessmen had discovered in the nineteenth century, one needed a theory of leadership, an ideology to justify one's conduct. It had occurred to those businessmen that so long as they controlled the state, a policy of pure laissez-faire was the best guarantee of their interest, because it kept all other hands off. By the time of the New Deal, though, such hegemony had been lost, and with it pure liberalism; yet for the world as a whole, this need not be the case. Before World War II the United States had already emerged as the major world power, and consequently the very ideology discredited at home could still be used abroad. It is a striking paradox that while Franklin Delano Roosevelt and the New Deal were dismantling laissez-faire liberalism within the United States, Roosevelt's Secretary of State Cordell Hull was creating laissez-faire for the world at large. As Calleo and Rowland point out, the Trade Agreements Act of 1934—the same year as such antiliberal measures as the Securities Exchange Act—represented the triumph of Hull's principles, for it officially placed the U.S. stamp on the free trade ideology that had been Britain's claim to world leadership.[1]

What free trade liberalism meant for transnational cooperation could be seen in U.S. international economic policy, particularly as it culminated in the Bretton Woods Conference. Ironically, Britain, which had once preached free trade the way a fundamentalist preached redemption, sought to create trade restrictions in order to help its devastated economy recover. Symbolically, the British negotiator at Bretton Woods was the man whose name had become synonymous with the rejection of the classical liberal tradition, John Maynard Keynes, and he was there at a time when his own personal thinking was as far left as it was ever to go. Matching England's reversal, the United States, which had been a protectionist power throughout most of the nineteenth century, adopted the advocacy of free trade with all the vehemence of a sinner redeemed. The reason was not hard to find. On the one hand, the United States was now the dominant world power, and free trade liberalism was the classic way to preserve hegemony. Yet at the same time, American policy makers seemed afraid that a protectionist Europe and a socialist Russia would make that control ever so much harder to maintain. Charles P. Taft expressed the problem this way: "Free enterprise cannot be confined within even our wide borders and continue to exist. The destruction of free enterprise abroad like the destruction of democracy [i.e., liberalism] abroad is a threat to free enterprise and democracy [i.e., liberalism] at home." [2] Liberalism was thus designed to produce social peace at home ("If we have regimentation in our foreign trade, how long do you think free enterprise can continue in our domestic commerce?", Will Clayton asked rhetorically) [3] and the domination of other nations abroad. As part of the International Monetary Fund (IMF) and the International Bank for Reconstruction and Development, the United States demanded, in opposition to the British and the Soviets, that all member states, in Lloyd Gardner's words, "would conduct their trade in conformity with basic capitalist commercial standards." [4] No wonder that the final transnational economic units created at Bretton Woods were "far closer in their principles to the American scheme than any other." [5]

What happened at Bretton Woods is doubly important, for out of this experience came the idea for the United Nations. The original conception of the Transnational State, in other words, was that it would constitute the political equivalent of organizations like the IMF. And just as the new transnational economic units were based on classical liberalism, any new political structures would also have to be organized that way. Clayton made the connection between free trade and the proposals for a United Nations Organization (UNO) in this fashion: "Our task in restoring the world to a multinational trade basis is an extremely difficult one, and we don't expect immediate success, but we are convinced that we must succeed if UNO is to have a fair chance of preserving the peace." [6] The devotion to liberalism, however, presented policy makers with a major problem. Theoretically, classical liberalism required a minimal state, but the existence of an international economic order required some sort of referee. Thus the liberal vision inexorably led to the need for a state, in this case a transnational one, whatever the ideology claimed. Hull's political conceptions, as summarized by Calleo and Rowland, point this out:

> True to his federalist heritage, Hull believed no principle or agreement was safe without an organization to embody and police it. Hence free trade called for an International Trade Organization and free convertibility called for an International Monetary Fund. To cap off the whole edifice, there was to be the old liberal dream of a Parliament of Man; hence the United Nations. [7]

Thus to men like Hull the problem of hegemony and the problem of accumulation were the same, both resolving themselves into a liberal conception of a minimal state that adjudicates between big powers by persuasion and, as a last resort, coercion. As his model of the Transnational State, Hull borrowed the night watchman of the nineteenth century; liberalism may have been obsolete within nation-states, but perhaps it could play a new role among them.

Hull's economic and political liberalism was challenged in three crucial areas. First, American allies, particularly Churchill and de Gaulle, were not stupid men; they knew from their own experience as conservatives that behind the rhetoric of laissez-faire is self-interest, and they were hardly likely to give up sovereignty to an international body dominated by one sovereign power. Second, the Soviet Union, itself a society without a liberal tradition, was amazed by the Hullian vision. Stalin favored a power-bloc approach, creating a structure that would facilitate meetings among those who ruled the world so that their rule could continue. Third, and another example of the ironies and inconsistencies of this period, Hull's world-wide laissez-faire was bitterly attacked by those most committed to the exact same doctrine at home, the Republican "isolationists" from the Midwest. This three-tiered opposition was crucial because it destroyed the liberalism behind the United Nations even before the charter was signed, in a way that seemed like a replay of an earlier domestic disenchantment with liberal principles. The classically liberal state had been undermined by its unresponsiveness to new, plural centers of power on the left and, as it admitted the need to change, by its recalcitrant defenders on the right. As Chapter 4 has shown, faced with conflicts from all sides, the domestic liberal state underwent changes in form, emerging eventually as the Franchise State. Thus it seems like a broken record that, as Hull's vision underwent changes in response to criticism, the new compromise that emerged gave a distinct franchise-like tint to the supranational units being created.

Domestically, the Franchise State tried to do two things at once: provide a solution for intraclass conflict that would be neither dictatorial nor ineffective, and structure demands from below in such a way that the more "responsible" ones would be accepted into the political framework. Transposed to the world system, the problem became one of regulating conflict among the leading nation-states while at the same time allowing entry of those states that threatened to disrupt the arrangements if they were not allowed to participate. From this point on, though, the franchise tint blurs, for internationally a solution emerged in direct opposition to the domestic experience. At home the Franchise State failed because the grants of public power to private agencies were reabsorbed by the state as they failed to work; in the world at large, however, the individual units retained their power, as the supranational structures were denied the final say over almost everything. Nonetheless, it is still useful to see how Hullian liberalism broke down into a model based on concentrations of national, rather than transnational, power.

The basic problem of American policy makers after World War II was that the goals of world domination and anticommunism were, in a peculiar way, incompatible. The liberal solution of world domination through laissez-faire required an enormous faith in America's destiny, a confidence that the United States could win all the struggles in a neutral organization without rigging the rules. Those who felt that this could be the case were, in their fashion, idealists, willing to risk an occasional defeat in order to salvage an international order that would only preserve a greater dominant role for the United States in the long run. Anticommunism, however, suggested a quite different reading of the world picture. If the Russians were as ruthless as was claimed, they would rig the rules, and the only hope of America was to beat them to it. The victory of anticommunism in the postwar period, in short, doomed Hullian liberalism from the start. It is in this context that the crucial role of Senator Arthur Vandenberg becomes explicable. It is often suggested that Vandenberg's conversion from "isolationism" to internationalism guaranteed the success of the Truman-sponsored plan for a new world order. Actually the reverse occurred. It was the liberals who gave in to Vandenberg's anticommunism; though the form of the UN was kept, the philosophy behind American participation changed. Specifically, the United States did not enter the UN ideologically as liberals but strategically as anti-Communists. Vandenberg demanded that the U.S. State Department makes its primary objective the challenge to Soviet power. Slowly it came around to this point of view. "The American Delegation and the State Department," Vandenberg later wrote, "have *accepted* every demand I have made along these lines. It remains to be seen what happens when we collide with London and Moscow." [8]

The expected collison never really took place. Both England and the Soviet Union understood Vandenberg's *Realpolitik* much better than they did Hull's obsolete liberalism. The domestic victory of anti-communism ironically ensured a United Nations organized roughly along Stalin's idea of three-power cooperation rather than Hull's formally disinterested body. And once Hull's ideas were defeated, the way was clear to organize the UN along Franchise State lines. The problem became one of creating a structure with a global frame of reference but allowing for national sovereignty, a problem the Russians understood just as well as American senators. This twin goal could be pursued the same way the Franchise State sought freedom for businessmen and order for the economy as a whole—that is, by judicious compromise, ad hoc arrangements, day-to-day alterations, and a careful fudging of precise definitions. The UN Charter that came out of the San Francisco Conference reflected all these ambiguities. A Security Council as well as a General Assembly, the Great Power veto, formal Soviet control of 3 votes, informal American control of 20—compromises along these lines would be easily recognizable to a Franchise State planner. The best that could be hoped for was a world organization that would permit each powerful nation-state to pursue its self-interest while at the same time creating a structure that would resolve conflicts among those interests in a noncoercive but still meaningful way. Far from becoming a transnational political unit, the United Nations borrowed the one domestic model of the state that avoided the problem of sovereignty most explicitly. The ideology of liberalism gave way to the reality of hegemony.

In one other important way anticommunism led to the adoption of a structure resembling the Franchise State. In a classic liberal market, the disadvantageous position of a trader can be rectified only by the trader himself; if he is losing money he must either change his approach or go bankrupt. Europe was a devastated partner after the war; in this sense the Marshall Plan and the decision to upgrade the European economies, while perfectly sensible from an anti-Communist point of view, were incompatible with traditional liberalism (firms do not bail each other out when in trouble in *The Wealth of Nations*, even if they do in the U.S. automobile industry). The U.S. decision to create an international Franchise State came to be reflected in the popularity of regionalism, such as the Atlantic Community. Like a cartel of businessmen merging their grants of public power in order to dominate a commodity market, the strategic theory behind the Atlantic Alliance was that it would permit the United States and Europe together to fight off challenges from the Soviet Union and from the so-called emerging nations. This decision in favor of alliances instead of liberalism represented a break with the Hullian approach to transnational economic and political units, described as follows:

> The universalism of the UN and the IMF shrank to the Atlanticism of NATO and the OEEC. . . . The visions were . . . greatly scaled down from Hull's day. As the Third World proved increasingly intractable to any integrating order, the liberal system evolved more and more into an Atlantic bloc of the world's developed capitalist economies—a bloc justified not so much by the economic ideals of Cobden, Hull, and Morgenthau as by the geopolitical visions of Mahan, Acheson, and Dulles.[9]

By the early 1950s America's stance vis-à-vis the rest of the world was better expressed in regional pacts like CENTO, NATO, and SEATO, each expressive of a group of franchises organized together, than it was in a worldwide political equivalent of a free market.

Hegemony was only half the problem. Transnational political structures must not only solve conflicts among the most powerful states, they must also take actions that can be accepted by the less powerful ones. Yet experiences with organizations like the UN indicate that legitimacy was fully as difficult to realize as interdependence. In the first discussions about the UN, American planners enthusiastically endorsed a democratic structure: one nation, one vote. There was both an idealistic and a practical basis for this commitment. A harmony-of-interests doctrine has generally been part of the liberal approach to the state, and insofar as men like Hull adopted the one, they also adopted the other. Since liberal capitalism was good, democracy presented no problem. Other nations would simply love to be part of the capitalist world system if granted a free choice; let them have a vote and they will vote right. To the skeptics a more practical point could be made. Since Third World countries, particularly in South America, were led by men sympathetic to the United States, votes for each country were votes for America. The UN would resemble an urban political machine in which the downtrodden, exercising their genuine freedom of choice, would choose those who kept them downtrodden. The skeptics, perhaps intuitively understanding that a Batista could turn into a Castro, remained unconvinced; the San Francisco charter seriously compromised the one nation, one vote principle in a number of ways. Still, reasoning like Hull's made a quasi-democratic structure feasible, because it provided a mechanism for legitimation that constituted a minimal threat to hegemony and that could even further it if all worked well.

All did not work well. It is hard to pinpoint the exact moment when Third World countries began to develop their own interests, but any of the following might do: the Chinese or Cuban revolutions; the Bandung Conference; the emergence of Nasser and the concept of nonalignment; or the 1964 UN Conference on Trade and Development, when 77 Third World countries voted as a bloc. Sometime during the 1960s it had become clear that the Hullian solution to the problem of democracy had become as obsolete as the Hullian solution to the problem of hegemony. Just like working classes at home, other nations did not find the harmony of interest that the more powerful assured them would soon arrive. A combination of nationalist sentiment and socialist revolution was leading Third World countries—which had gradually, under the relentless democratic logic of universal suffrage, become a majority in the organization—to flex their muscles. New spokesmen were producing new policies, of which the 1975 decision to permit representation of the Palestine Liberation Organization was, though the most dramatic, only one of many. These challenges to American hegemony raised the same question that nineteenth-century ruling classes had to face: If democracy is in conflict with continued rule, which is to be chosen? The answer this time was the same as the answer that time: democracy would have to be sacrificed.

American policy makers, who were the most insistent proponents of a democratic organization for the United Nations in the 1940s, became leaders of the antidemocratic sentiment of the 1970s. As early as 1964, the year when the emerging new bloc had become clear, the U.S. Secretary of State, in his Hammarskjöld Lecture at Columbia University, suggested that the United States, because of its special responsibilities toward the UN, should have a special status.[10] The same sentiment can be discovered in the thought of Richard N. Gardner, one of the most enthusiastic supporters of the UN within the United States. After an exhaus-

tive brief in favor of a continued American commitment to the organization designed to counter conservative sentiment for withdrawal, Gardner
nonetheless concedes the main conservative point: "The United Nations
will be able to assume greater responsibilities for the peace and welfare
of mankind only if its procedures adequately reflect the world's power
realities." [11]

Until sometime around 1970, "reform" proposals of this sort in proper
diplomatic fashion did not touch the sensitive question of one nation, one
vote. But given the tendency in U.S. politics for the Republican Party
to carry out policies suggested initially by the Democrats, the last years of the
Nixon and Ford Administrations saw the logical culmination of the Rusk-
Gardner position. The United States decided to take a "get tough" stance
toward the Third World. A figure was needed who could be blunt about
dashing U.S. enthusiasm for world-wide democracy and, almost as
a stroke of genius, a figure was found who more than any other policy
maker was responsible for providing the ideological rationalization for dashing those same hopes at home. As U.S. Ambassador to the United Nations, the man who developed the notion of "benign neglect," Daniel
Patrick Moynihan, led the assault on international equality. And just as
the Democrats so often work to give a smooth rationale to policies carried
out by Republicans, accompanying Moynihan's threats toward the Third
World was a new emphasis on "realism" and "the art of the possible." In
1975 Gardner served as U.S. representative on a 25-member international
panel that proposed extensive changes in the structure of the UN. The
proposal seeks to transcend the contradiction between democracy and
hegemony, and in so doing, it is replete with compromises and ambiguity.[12]
On the one hand, the most democratic body within the organization, the
General Assembly, will be bypassed and made, like Bagehot's monarch, a
dignified symbol. But, on the other hand, Third World representation in
bodies like the IMF would be increased. In either case, the proposal comes
out against any revision of the Charter and places its faith in negotiation
as a solution to difficulties. In a way the main, though unstated, conclusion
of this proposal is that the political contradictions of the UN are so
benumbing that it is best to bypass formal procedures in the hope that informal processes can lead to the continued life of the organization. Whether
adopted or not, the proposal can also be read as the death of the notion
that a Transnational State can be formally organized along democratic
lines. Not even the appointment of Andrew Young as the U.S. Ambassador will likely alter this antidemocratic direction.

Another example of the new "realistic" attitude toward international
democracy arises out of suggestions for a new world order that would reflect the dominance of the multinational corporation. Men like Jacques
Maisonrouge of IBM and George Ball, formerly of the U.S. State Department, have been publicizing their plans for new transnational structures,

since the old ones are so insistently described by them as "obsolete" or even "ridiculous." Ball's ideas are important because he is a man regarded as something of a folk hero for his internal opposition to the Vietnam War, but in many ways his thought is in a direct line from Woodrow Wilson and Cordell Hull, with one important difference. Earlier international liberals were willing to experiment with democracy; Ball is not, and the raging elitism of his conceptions tarnishes somewhat his image of dissenter-in-power. Ball realizes that any proposal for a multinational world order faces two immediate problems. First, if it is democratic, the United States will be unable to control it, making it, to him, unacceptable. But if it is undemocratic, citizens of the Third World cannot be expected to consider it legitimate. Since the dilemma is the same one that brought the Franchise State into being, Ball adopts the franchise notion of gradual entry. If one has to make hard choices, he implies, one does so. Therefore he explicitly rejects any type of UN model for his version of the Transnational State. Ball's world order will be liberal, not democratic; only the major powers are allowed to join. The purpose is to rationalize the international economy, not to disrupt it. As other nations show their responsibility—that is, as they accept the principles of a multinational capitalist world order—they can be allowed to join. Though Ball is frank about his rejection of democracy, his proposal, for all its "realism," is inherently utopian; his suggestions amount to a recognition of contradictions, not a solution for any of them. Suppose countries adopt restrictions on multinational corporations within their borders; this is already taking place. What would a Transnational State do in the face of this? Ball, when faced with a concrete problem, can fall back on only the most meaningless of rhetoric: "The operative standard defining these restrictions would reflect the intention to assure the ability of host nations to defend their natural interests with minimal encroachment on the interests of other states, while still preserving the freedom needed to protect the central principle of efficient resource use." [13]

The rejection of international democracy by the United States does not solve the contradiction of the Transnational State but merely shifts it from one pole to another. Having chosen hegemony, the United States has sacrificed legitimacy. Unable to appear as the idealistic savior of mankind, the United States will be forced into a position where it can maintain itself only by force, either the force of guns or the heavy indoctrination of the television commercial. In 1945, working actively to create a new world order, John J. McCloy telephoned Secretary of State Stimson for a chat. McCloy urged that the United States defend its hegemonic interest in any way it chose, while Stimson argued for adherence to international principles. After discussing numerous problems, McCloy said, "However, I've been taking the position that we ought to have our cake and eat it too." [14] What the breakup of the U.S. postwar approach to international organization indicates is that in the long run one has to choose either the cake or the feast. Though the free trade liberals were, in Lloyd Gardner's apt phrase, "architects of illusion," [15] so, it turns out, were the anti-Communist realists like McCloy; the latter won the battle for an anti-Communist strategy but lost the war for international moral leadership. In so choosing, they helped to destroy the very Transnational State that they were instrumental in creating.

TOWARD AN ILLUSORY EUROPEAN COMMUNITY

No discussion of transnational political units would be complete without at least a brief mention of the European Economic Community (EEC), an experiment that has been praised so often as the example par excellence of the Transnational State. Unlike the UN, where the problem of accumulation had become the problem of hegemony, the Common Market's concern with sheer accumulation was a constant from the start. Those who were most active in formulating the plans for a new economic community were unabashedly capitalist, rooted in the Christian Democratic parties of Western Europe and firm in their belief that economic recovery was a prerequisite to the reemergence of Europe as a world power. Rejecting the tradition of national economics, which posited a strong role for the nation-state in the accumulation of capital, many of the most important EEC planners were sympathetic to classical liberalism. "European unity," Uwe Kitzinger wrote, "was advocated by free-trade liberals who worked to diminish the impact of political boundaries and the influence of national governments on economic life." [16] Typical of them was Walter Hallstein, the first president of the EEC Commission, who could pontificate as follows:

> The whole economic and social system of the Community is liberally oriented; the businessman, the *entrepreneur*, is free to make his own decisions . . . . Enterprises are guided by the conditions of the market, by the law of supply and demand. Free enterprise opens an infinitely greater market for their goods than they enjoyed previously. Employees choose the place where they want to work and are free to seek another anywhere in the Community.[17]

There would seem to be something contradictory in a group of continental Europeans urging unity for that part of the world, yet adopting in toto the rhetoric of Britain and America, neither of which belonged. Indeed contradiction was manifest, for though liberal in theory, these men were also creating a state, a transnational one, to be sure, but a government structure nonetheless. An antistatist philosophy was used to rationalize government participation in the accumulation process at a level much higher than ever before seen in the history of Western capitalism. The EEC was off to an auspicious beginning.

The liberalism of the EEC also ran into an immediate conflict with democratic traditions. Internationalism was as much a democratic rallying cry as a liberal one, and the ideal of a European community was bound to appeal to those who sought a more equitable world order as well as to those who sought only the internationalization of the means of production. The problem of democracy took two important forms. Participation in the EEC had to be accepted by people at home, for as Harold Macmillan had expressed it in rejecting British membership, "One thing is certain, and we may as well face it. Our people will not hand over to any supranational authority the right to close down our pits or our steelworks." [18] Having just won a measure of participation in the nation-state, workers and unions were unwilling to see their new power absorbed into transnational units. The Communist parties of Europe, and some of the Socialist parties as well, opposed any participation in the EEC, making democratic participation, given the size of many of those parties, problematic from the start. In addition, the legitimacy dimension suggested that any international political bodies be based on acceptable democratic principles, which the major powers, particularly France, were unwilling to do. The result was tortuous compromise: a three-stage process by which community was to be achieved; five different kinds of voting procedures in the Council of Ministers, and the weighting of votes in the European Parliament. The planners of the EEC, in short, faced the same problem that the planners of any capitalist state face: how to be liberal and democratic at the same time.

The history of the EEC therefore became a series of attempts to solve the contradiction between liberal and democratic principles. Article II of the Treaty of Rome is in this context a remarkable statement, because in one short sentence it manages to rely upon Accumulative, Harmonious, Expansionist, and Franchise State principles, all at once:

> It shall be the aim of the Community, by establishing a Common Market and progressively approximating the economic policies of member states, to promote throughout the Community a harmonious development of economic activities, a continuous and balanced expansion, an increased stability, and accelerated raising of the standard of living, and closer relations between member states.[19]

From the point of view of ideology, in other words, the EEC was not as experimental as its enthusiasts proclaimed, for its theory and practice were based on a series of concepts that were not only old, but that also had conspicuously failed; the EEC really represents a throwback to an earlier period of capitalist development. Its adoption of laissez-faire liberalism, its harmony-of-interests basis, its preoccupation with sheer accumulation and its promotion of undemocratic, nonrepresentative political structures are all much more suggestive of the nineteenth century than of the twenty-first. Though portraying themselves as men of the future, the planners of the EEC were more like phantoms from the past.

If none of the traditional forms of the capitalist state had been able to solve intra- and interclass conflict at home, they would hardly be likely to be solved in an international context where sovereignty was even more problematic. Faced with irreconcilable contradictions, the best the EEC could do was to develop ideas and structures that represented compromises between all of its constituent parts. Consequently the EEC, like Hull's vision of the UN, moved away from its original international liberalism toward that ideological mishmash so characteristic of twentieth-century capitalist politics. The mélange of notions dominating the EEC in practice has been described by Kitzinger:

> The European idea was thus originally neutral in foreign policy between a third-force concept and the Atlantic Alliance, undecided in trade policy between regionalism and multinationalism, ambivalent in its attitude toward the emergent nations in Africa and Asia, silent in cultural and educational matters between Catholicism and anti-clericalism, and neutral also in economic policy between laissez-faire liberalism and socialist planning.[20]

Nor was there much success in overcoming these divisions. In their discussion of what they appropriately call "Europe's Would-Be Polity," Lindberg and Scheingold discuss at length the compromises resulting from the conflicting demands on the EEC. Economically they make a distinction between laissez-faire liberals and state planners, politically between federalists and confederalists. This produces four logical models of European integration, the point being that the policies of the EEC resembled none of them alone but contained elements of all of them.[21] The EEC turned out to be as devoid of consistent governing principles as were the nation-states comprising it.

The compromises that have shaped the EEC, far from making the supranational state stronger through pragmatism, have made it much weaker through opportunism. National hegemony is still a real force, and de Gaulle's attempts to preserve that of France have transformed the EEC from a supranational ideal to an intragovernmental reality. This shift, though, was not due to the perversity of nationalist sentiment in an international age, but to dynamics internal to the development of world capitalism. Given the fact that the EEC was designed to strengthen capitalism in Europe, its very success was responsible for its failure. For as capitalism recovered so did the nation-state, which has always been part of its growth, and once that occurred the need for a Transitional State was undermined. Nicos Poulantzas, one of the few writers skeptical of the great claims made for supranationality, understands this:

It is not the emergence of a new State over the nations that we are witnessing but rather ruptures in the national unity underlying the existing national states. It is in the very important phenomenon of regionalism, expressed through the resurgence of nationalities, which shows that the internationalization of capital brings about splits in the nations as historically constituted more than it brings about the supranationalization of the State.[22]

By accomplishing its economic mission, in short, the EEC destroyed any possibility of realizing its political mission. European unity is a dream that must await another world crisis.

Over and above the conflict between nationalism and supranationalism is a second reason for the political failure of the EEC. Conflicts among nations can be likened to the intra-ruling-class struggles of a domestic political system, but much more disruptive of social harmony is the struggle between classes, one that takes place on a transnational level as well. Since the left had emerged as a very powerful force in Europe in the post–World War II era, much of the impetus behind the EEC was designed to counter it. From the European Payments Union of the Marshall Plan to the Community's adoption of social welfare measures, bridling the left has been a central preoccupation of EEC planners. Of all the tactics developed, the most interesting was the general policy of depoliticization, because it bears so much resemblance to one of the most important domestic effects of late capitalism (see Chapter 9). As Lindberg and Scheingold note,

> The tactics of M. Monnet and his supporters were clearly designed to reduce to a minimum the likelihood of an inflammatory public debate on the scheme. Thus the bargaining and brokerage that went into the supranational compromise served not only to satisfy but also to quiet major political forces.[23]

A political strategy designed to depoliticize is, of course, a contradiction, and for that reason it was bound to fail. Even though both the British Labor Party and the Italian Communist Party have officially reversed themselves on their earlier opposition to the Common Market, one has the feeling that the European working classes remain the major stumbling block to the creation of a Transnational State. The fear of working-class militancy, which is still capable of producing such undemocratic monstrosities as the *Notstandsgesetz* (a West German emergency law of 1968, which allows the state the right to limit trade union activity)[24] has led some EEC planners to use transnational units as a way of rolling back the progressive gains made by the working class in the 1960s.[25] In this atmosphere, workers' demands for protective tariffs and hostility toward the dubious "internationalism" of the EEC are hardly reactionary, but indicative of a realistic distrust of a fairly traditional capitalist strategy of control.

The fanfare surrounding creation of the EEC announced that a Transnational State would do for Europe as a whole what the nation-state had done for each European country. That dream has been shattered, but in one unanticipated way it may yet be realized. The Transnational State and the nation-state increasingly resemble each other in their *inability* to be authoritative when faced with severe social contradictions. The political failure of the EEC bears a resemblance to the political failure of the capitalist state in general. Scheingold's description of the limitations of the EEC should sound familiar to any student of domestic politics:

> Structurally the institutions of the European Economic Community are very nearly as Janus-like as the treaty that gave them birth. There is a legislature (the European Parliament) which doesn't legislate; an administrative organ (the Commission) which both initiates legislation and administers it; a cabinet (the Council of Ministers) which is responsible to no one; and a supreme court (the Court of Justice) which is supposed to act as if these glaring weaknesses and strange anomalies didn't exist.[26]

One could, in retrospect, hardly have expected a group of men who could not resolve their political problems at home to do so abroad. The Transnational State would seem to be going the way of all the previous attempts to solve social and economic contradictions by purely political means.

THE MULTINATIONAL COUNTERREVOLUTION

The failure of transnational political units to solve the contradiction between hegemony and legitimacy should have turned the global dreamers into cynics, but all it did was to lead them to search for a new agency for their internationalism. Like pantheists searching for the spirit of God in the next tree, globalists wished to uncover a form for expressing the content of their internationalism. They found the multinational corporations. A world order created by and for business could accomplish what transnational political units were unable to do; IBM would carry the flame dropped by the UN. But, as I plan to show in the rest of this chapter, a world order dominated by multinational corporations could only highlight previous failures, not solve them. Multinational corporations did not bring about a revolution in transnationality, but the opposite: an attempt to impose conceptions of the state that were already obsolete.

The dramatic development of multinational corporate activity in the twentieth century has been accompanied by claims that the nation-state no longer remains an important political reality. Predictions of its demise can be heard from every end of the political spectrum. George Ball, a leading pitchman for this latest form of corporate behavior, puts the proposition bluntly: "No longer does the nation-state remotely approach an adequate institutional structure to define the activities of a modern corporate enterprise, while small nation-states are, as economic units, ridiculous." [27] What is more, many who are as critical of the multinationals as Ball is fawning seem to agree with his assessment. "The World Managers are the first to have developed a plausible model of the future that is global," two recent critics of the multinationals have concluded, taking for granted the transnational rhetoric so popular among the leaders of these enterprises.[28] If this were true, and multinational corporations did symbolize the transcendence of the nation-state, then a whole new plateau in the development of the capitalist state would have been reached, which would transform the basic unit of analysis itself.

For some reason the most conservative men often like to claim that they are the "true" revolutionaries, and this may be the case here. A strong argument could be raised that multinational corporate activity, far from representing a startlingly new stage in capitalist development, is simply the logical extension of business as usual. As Stephen Hymer has argued, "Since the beginning of the industrial revolution there has been a steady increase in the size of manufacturing firms, so persistent that it might almost be formulated as a general law of capitalist accumulation." [29] From this point of view, the multinationals are doing what corporations have always done, engaging in a search for the maximization of profits, which takes them into new areas of exploration and generally results in an increase in size. The same logic that caused a New York firm to open a branch in St. Louis in 1860 causes an American firm to invest in Rangoon in 1960. Furthermore, even if this most recent phase of capitalist development were to become truly global, it would not be the first time that a capitalist world order had been created. Mercantile capitalism had a similar international vision and, given the poor technology of the sixteenth and seventeenth centuries (no international conference calls, Concordes, satellites, and cross-Atlantic cables), the internationalism of the earlier period is far more impressive. It is almost as if mercantilism became a world system in spite of poor communications and transportation while the multinationals in the 1960s became global only because of improvements in both. Once the "secret" of capitalist accumulation had been found, there has been little new except intensification and growth.

Nonetheless, the increase of foreign investment in the post–World War II period is impressive. Every writer has his or her favorite statistics, but all agree that a profound intensification of international business activity has characterized corporate behavior in the past thirty years, particularly for American firms. As Myra Wilkins points out, multinationalism has been an aspect of American business since the founding of the Republic,[30] but it was in the period between 1946 and 1970, when the percentage of foreign invested capital increased from .23 percent to 4.40 percent, that this kind of activity came of age.[31] Another study shows that while the number of foreign subsidiaries of U.S. companies has gone up steadily since 1901, recent years have shown the greatest increases of all. Between 1957 and 1968, the total amount of sales of foreign subsidiaries of U.S. companies doubled in Canada, tripled in Latin America, quadrupled in Europe, and went up nearly 500 percent everywhere else.[32] The Finance Committee of the U.S. Senate has estimated that some $200 billion in tangible assets is controlled by the multinationals.[33] International activity, always present, has still found room to expand.

The obvious questions are: What caused this sudden spurt? What is its significance for the state? To multinational spokesmen the answers are straightforward. Growth has occurred because growth is good. In the perpetual search for the most efficient way to bring the greatest number of commodities into the largest number of hands, multinationals represent one more step in a complex rationalization process. They grew because no other institution could do the job as well. Multinational corporations stand for a move from strength to strength; they are on the offensive and the world, in the favorite cliché of the new corporate heads, "is their oyster." Consequently the future seems bright, as people and states drop their prejudices and adapt themselves to these new developments.[34] Even some of the critics agree, at least in part. While not painting a bright blissful future, still they feel that global corporations are on the offensive, that they are the logical product of dazzling increases in technology and productivity. Attempting (and succeeding) to point out the negative consequences of multinational behavior, critics like Barnet and Muller have also unwillingly written a "Capitalist Manifesto," for the implication in their work is that the multinational phenomenon developed out of a strong hand.

There is, however, evidence indicating that the upsurge of multinational activity in the post–World War II period may be explained much more reasonably as the result of weakness, not strength. Certainly in the prewar period multinational agreements were, to use Schumpeter's phrase, an atavism, for they constituted attempts to restrict competition and to repress challenges from abroad. As Raymond Vernon has written:

> Between 1900 and 1940, international cartel agreements were developed in practically every important processed metal, in most important chemical products, in key pharmaceuticals, and in a variety of miscellaneous manufactures running the alphabetical gamut from alkalis to zinc. The object of these agreements was generally the same as that of similar agreements in the new materials industries: *to take the uncertainties out of the market.*[35]

The upsurge of postwar multinational activity can be interpreted in very much the same way, not as an "American challenge," an idea that has been devastatingly criticized by Hymer and Rowthorn,[36] but as a challenge to America. Rowthorn's econometric analysis concluded that Japanese firms showed the highest growth rates between 1957 and 1967, with Europeans second and Americans third. Only in the electrical field was American superiority manifest; in seven other important industries, U.S. growth rates were about equal to the British.[37] This foreign competition, Hymer argues, "combined with the slow growth of the United States economy in the 1950s, altered world market shares as firms confined to the U.S. market found themselves falling behind in the competitive race." [38] The gigantic growth of U.S. foreign investment between 1950 and 1970 can be attributed to the declining efficiency and power of U.S. capital, not to its strength. The conclusion that follows is self-evident: "One can easily argue that the age of the Multinational Corporation is at its end rather than at its beginning. For all we know, books on the global partnership may be the epitaphs of the American attempt to take over the old international economy, and not the herald of a new era of international cooperation." [39]

Whether multinationals represent a move from strength or weakness is relevant to an understanding of the capitalist state in the multinational era. For if writers like Rowthorn and Hymer are correct, and both their reasoning and evidence are impressive, then the nation-state has remained alive and well. The state, as I argued in previous chapters, is called upon to rescue capitalists when they cannot obtain their self-professed goals; in that sense, the growth of political power and the decline of the power of capital are related. If multinationals represent a new stage of capitalist strength, on the other hand, it would follow that the world would become one vast free market, laissez-faire for the universe, with national sovereignty, to use Vernon's phrase, truly at bay. The fact that multinationals are a response to weakness is the reason why this situation of minimal government has not come about. Harbingers of state activity still persist; the relationship between government and firms must still be understood as a response to the contradictions discussed in the previous chapters. A viable Transnational State has not been created by international business.

The contradiction between liberalism and democracy is felt more strongly by multinational corporations than it is by transnational political units. Rather than being transformed into hegemony, the liberal theory of accumulation is not only present but extended out into the world. Whereas in writers like Locke, "primitive" societies symbolized the state of nature and should be preserved as such in order to remain a foil to the beneficence of the liberal world order, under twentieth-century conditions the primitive must be incorporated into the "civilized." [40] Monopoly capitalism makes the search for capital world-wide, incorporating every part of the globe into the economic system it creates. As this occurs, the political solution to accumulation must also become global, and one response has been to export, literally, liberal ideology to Africa, Asia, and Latin America. As Robert Packenham has argued, U.S. foreign aid involved as much the export of a liberal ideology as it did specific goods and services; creating new infrastructures in the dependent countries was as important as extracting their resources.[41] Yet, once proclaimed liberal for purposes of accumulation, the accompanying problem of legitimation almost immediately arises in the dependent countries. Unless steps are taken to respond to pressures from the new countries for control over their own economies, revolution may replace accumulation as a way of life. (The shift in the thought of Ho Chi Minh from the American Declaration of Independence to socialism is one version of this move from liberalism to democracy.) The same pressures that led capitalists in the dominant countries to favor the creation of liberal states in the dependent ones make them as suspicious of democracy abroad as at home. As David Rockefeller summarized the problem, "Often the more democratic the country, the more hostile it is to foreign investment." [42] The Transnational State of the multinational corporations, like the nation-states out of which it grew, finds that if it is to be liberal it cannot be democratic, but if it wishes to be responsive to democratic pressure, it must compromise its liberalism. The historical contradiction is there, even if the scope has become international.

A GLOBAL PASTICHE

Though given to utter felicitous phrases about one world and a new international order that transcends the nation-state, multinational capitalists in the real world, like those who preceded them, show no hesitation in using the nation-state to further their own ends. The Accumulative State, in other words, is still in existence in the multinational era. In fact, multinational activity has given sheer accumulation a renewed importance, for the internationalization of capital investment has brought into being new functions that make the accumulative tendencies of the capitalist state all the more important. Speaking in 1972 to the National Foreign Trade Convention, Fred Borch, former president of General Electric, underscored this development:

> Our government must recognize and accept—as the Japanese and European governments have long ago—that business and its employees are practically the sole source of national income. ... The Congress and the Administration must screen every legislative proposal in terms of its impact on U.S. international competitiveness.[43]

Few better testimonials to the endurance of nineteenth-century relations between government and business as a model for twentieth-century conditions exist than this plea to reconstitute the Accumulative State.

Actually, the U.S. government recognized its "responsibilities" in this area some time ago. Multinational corporations would never have developed if it were not for active state intervention. The Webb-Pomerene Act of 1918 "allowed U.S. business to join together to export without fear of prosecution under anti-trust legislation." [44] The Edge Act altered the Federal Reserve Act in order to facilitate the international activity of U.S. banks. American business firms were given special tax advantages under the China Trade Act of 1922. Oil company investments abroad were made so advantageously because of State Department diplomacy. While there was a diminution of this trend during the New Deal (FDR refused to help the Firestone Company during its troubles in Liberia), by the time of World War II the government was active once more. Many of the most growth-oriented multinationals won their greatest profits simply by following U.S. armies throughout Europe and claiming German factories as their own. (ITT not only obtained free resources in such fashion but was also paid for its troubles by the U.S. government.) [45] After the war, the Economic Cooperation Act of 1948 gave private firms public guarantees on their investments, and this principle was extended to 78 countries by 1967. The Cooley Amendment to the Agricultural Trade and Development Act of 1954, the Foreign Assistance Act of 1969, and the development of the Export-Import Bank and the World Bank were all part of the pattern of state aid to private firms. Like continental Europe in the era of Bismarck and Chevalier, multinational corporations found that governments could do for them what they could not do for themselves.

If a catalogue of current nation-state aid to international business were developed, it would be *larger* than the one assembled by the Accumulative State. Jack Behrman, a former U.S. Under Secretary of Commerce, has already developed one, and its features include such familiar items as assistance, promotion, rule making, judicial processes, control, advice and planning, ownership and partnership, and protection. [46] Twenty separate U.S. government agencies are actively involved in promoting international business, including State, Defense, Commerce, and Agriculture. Within the White House such interagency organizations as the Committee on Foreign Economic Policy, the Trade Agreements Committee, and the Advisory Committee on Export Policy give public advice on theoretically private matters. A series of task forces, such as the Grey Report on foreign economic policies or the Clay Report on foreign aid, work to benefit private firms. The government helps U.S. businessmen obtain foreign contracts, intervenes in negotiations over expropriated businesses, protects industrial property rights, and supports the creation of specific infrastructures in other countries beneficial to U.S. firms (American cable TV conquered Europe because of State Department intervention). The list of state activities in the multinational era is so long that the best procedure for understanding the resurgence of sheer accumulation would be to look at one or two examples more closely. Import-export policy and foreign aid are indicative of the diversity of governmental assistance to international corporations.

The historic swings between free trade and protection that characterized nineteenth-century economic policy (see Chapter 3) have been reproduced in intensified fashion in the era of the multinationals. In general, multinational corporations have adopted the ideology of free trade. During the 1940s the internationally oriented Committee for Economic Development placed its prestige behind a campaign for lower tariffs, and that has remained the dominant trend. But, as was the case with the British dedication to free trade in the previous century, this policy grows more out of economic size than out of a philosophical distaste for government intervention; the largest corporations attract high protective tariffs because they benefit from a situation that allows them to determine price. In other areas involving exports and imports, the same companies do not oppose, and even welcome, a role for the state. Businessmen have been known to urge the taxation of foreign income in order to equalize the balance of payments, a shortsighted policy with great retaliatory potential. State-sponsored export drives, as under Eisenhower, combined with groups like the National Export Expansion Committee (composed of major U.S. businessmen together with the Secretary of Commerce) and the Export-Import Bank, are illustrative of how businessmen welcome government when it is advantageous to do so. And it is because self-interest is the basis of opposition to protection that one may soon expect a change; though large multinational corporations, as the previous section indicated, are not necessarily strong, and as weaknesses reveal themselves, so will a shift toward protection, in all likelihood. Already, by 1975, one can discern a Chamberlainesque movement away from free trade on the part of important U.S. multinational corporations. As Calleo and Rowland put it, "In the early seventies, the American protectionist mood in general and the popularity of Nixon's trade measures in particular revealed a surprising fragility in the whole liberal trade policy—a fragility which suggests a certain erosion of its foundations and a growing disenchantment with its fundamental assumptions." [47]

One can also see the active remnants of the Accumulative State at work in the issue of foreign aid. "There is probably no other area of foreign economic policy in which there has been more consultation of business by the U.S. government," Behrman noted.[48] It took American businessmen some time to realize the advantages in foreign aid (the ideology of low, balanced budgets and the spirit known as isolationism took a long time to disappear), but once they did, they adopted the new policy enthusiastically. Thus while most businessmen seemed uninterested in either postwar aid for European reconstruction or foreign aid to Third World countries, an intense campaign led by a business elite and by government resulted in a change of heart. The Committee for Economic Development and the National Planning Association took the lead in showing what could be done to promote "favorable investment climates" overseas. From the report of Gordon Grey in 1950 to the 1969 creation of the Overseas Private Investment Corporation (OPIC), 12 full-scale reviews of the question of foreign aid were undertaken. Business leaders made their opinions known. Nelson Rockefeller, for example, as chairman of the International Development Advisory Board, in 1951 urged President Truman to support the principle. So did J. Peter Grace of the shipping firm, whose Committee for the Alliance for Progress (COMAP) dedicated itself to finding out where foreign investment would work. COMAP, which received governmental support in the form of money from the Agency for International Development, was also accorded formal government recognition in the 1962 Foreign Aid Act. Eventually the idea behind COMAP was divided into a public half and a private half; the Business Group for Latin America continued to work as a private interest group, while the Overseas Private Investment Corporation centralized the governmental functions into an agency whose sole purpose was to benefit private capital. Grace and Rockefeller's brother David, meanwhile, moved on to the Council for Latin America, a group in frequent contact with AID and the State Department, and they also sponsored the creation of the International Executive Services Corporation, designed to "lend" American executives to underdeveloped countries. In a manner similar to the nineteenth-century experience, the financial infrastructure necessary for a capitalist economy was created by the actions of private businessmen and governmental officials working together.

These examples suggest that the rhetoric on the death of the nation-state remains rhetoric. George Ball's enthusiasm for new political structures notwithstanding, the multinational period has resulted in a giant step backward into the past, not a leap into the future. The governing principles of the state have been adopted from the national economics of nineteenth-century France and Germany. One must face the contradiction that the development of transnational forms of economic activity does not result in a decrease in state power, but an increase. As two Italian Marxists put it, "The possibility that . . . the national state might be superseded by something else in the performance of these repressive and integrative functions which have a vital importance for the survival of the capitalist system, seems to us rather remote." [49] The same conclusion was reached by Robert Gilpin:

> Contrary to the argument that the multinational corporation will somehow supplant the nation state, I think it is closer to the truth to argue that the role of the national-state in economic as well as political life is increasing and that the multinational corporation is actually a stimulant to the further extension of state power in the economic role.[50]

If the Accumulative State has lived on and even grown in the multinational era, the same can be said of the second historical form of the capitalist state. Harmony-of-interest doctrines seem to have been reborn, only the groups that can now expect to live in peace are world-wide. Lee Morgan, executive vice president of the Caterpillar Tractor Company, has suggested that multinationals represent a "win–win" solution; if left free to invest wherever they please, "everybody benefits" he concludes, both those in the dependent countries and those at home.[51] Raymond Vernon has given the same notion academic respectability. Do host nations object to the presence of foreign corporations by bombing ITT installations? Does U.S. labor try to organize boycotts of American firms that move their factories overseas? They both do, but Vernon, standing Karl Marx on his head, suggests that a kind of reverse false consciousness is at work. If both nations and unions could understand that ultimately they would benefit from multinational activity, what he calls "disruptive political tensions" (Allende, Castro) would disappear into a higher synthesis of mutual compatibility:

> The men who direct the U.S. controlled multinational enterprise find opportunity and choice through the multinational character of their operations. The nations in which these enterprises operate outside the United States probably receive a share of these benefits of the increased productivity that some of these enterprises generate. It is even possible, though it is less clear, that U.S. labor also shares in these benefits.[52]

It will be recalled that the nineteenth-century Harmonious State took two forms, one leaning toward laissez-faire and the other seeking state intervention in order to promote class harmony. So it is in the multinational period. There are those, like Carl A. Gerstacker, chairman of the Dow Chemical Company, who says that the public sphere "should do as little as possible as a government. . . . Dow is a growing boy. It needs freedom to find its way." [53] Such pleas, like those of the Social Darwinists, cannot be taken too seriously, for what Dow desires is not minimal government but minimal regulation; in every other sphere of life Mr. Gerstacker, like all of his colleagues, would support an active state. At the same time, the alternative approach to the Harmonious State is also popular. One cannot dismiss the views of men like James P. MacFarland, chairman of General Mills, who envisions a kind of neosocietal corporatism become international. Speaking to the White House Conference on "The Corporation in 1990," he outlined his position: "Government and business and labor— and in fact all elements of society—should be sitting down to plan the future, to establish national priorities and to agree upon objectives and strategy." [54] While the fear of a state intervention that would curb their power still haunts businessmen, there is recognition that the government can serve as a vast harmonizing mechanism, guaranteeing social peace through a policy of encouragement rather than coercion. The ideas of *solidarité*, T. H. Green, and the Socialists of the Chair still seem as relevant to the multinational elites who dominate the 1970s as they did to some of the national elites who came to power in the 1870s.

Since multinational corporations are by definition international phenomena, it would be easy to conclude that traces of the theory and practice of the Expansionist State would play a major role in their rise. This has been true, but only in an amended form that requires some elucidation. I pointed out in Chapter 3 that there were a variety of techniques of expansion, among which formal colonization was only one. If the term "imperialism" is meant to suggest the existence of a formal colonial empire, then the multinational corporations would have to be considered, like Schumpeter's classic capitalist, anti-imperialist. If, on the other hand, the term imperialist is used to convey the sense of any international system of control, including an informal one, then the multinationals are as imperial as can be. Interestingly enough, the multinationals arose, not at the beginning of America's attempt to create a world empire, but at the end; the intensified rise of the multinationals and the inglorious defeat of U.S. foreign policy in Vietnam can roughly be understood as two sides of the same coin. In this sense, the Expansionist State vision of the multinational chiefs is a *post*-imperialist vision, in which a system of indirect control through consumerism is substituted for a direct one of military force. Control of subject populations can be achieved the same way that Americans at home were rendered loyal, through the beneficence of capital, for, as the Council of the Americas once expressed it, "consumer democracy is more important than political democracy." [55] Expansion, in this case meaning economic growth along capitalist lines, will stifle democratic demands by swamping them in a sea of gadgets, or so the modern expansionists hope.

The newer form of Expansionist State does share one characteristic with its nineteenth-century predecessor; it is equally nonideological. The search of men like Chamberlain and Bismarck for a pragmatic solution to their troubles, no matter how such a solution might violate liberal philosophy, can be seen again in the multinational era through the rapprochement with the Soviet Union and China. As shortsighted and negative as it was, anticommunism was at least a set of principles. A foreign policy based on anticommunism contained assumptions and deductions that could be made from those assumptions with a certain predictability and regularity. It is one of the lasting achievements of the multinationals that they helped abolish the anti-Communist hysteria dominating U.S. politics during the Dual State period, a hysteria, incidentally, that they themselves created. The selling of Pepsi in the Kremlin, or the opening of relations with China, is the triumph of expansionism, the fulfillment of the principles of 1898. When the Open Door Policy, the first major statement of the U.S. version of the Expansionist State, was proclaimed, it was with China in mind. Almost eighty years later, and with Mao in power, the door was finally opened. The two biggest markets in the world, the only logical places left to expand, were both Communist countries. U.S. business, facing a contradiction between its ideology of anticommunism and its self-interest in expanding markets, did what it has always done, which is to sacrifice the former for the latter. The multinationals are as "anti-imperialist," in other words, as they are aggressively expansionist. In their vision this is no contradiction, but a necessary complementarity. They are correct, for the desire of multinationals to make the world into one gigantic market in which accumulation needs could be performed while legitimation would be satisfied through consumerism, requires stability and order; in that context guerrilla war and national resistance movements can only be seen as disruptive. Whether the new strategy of butter will be more effective than the old one of guns remains problematic, but in the meanwhile the multinationals have continued at least one of the traditions of the Expansionist State.

Conceptions similar in nature to the Dual State have also made their appearance in the multinational era. Just as a major task of the Accumulative State is the creation of a structure of political repression in order to facilitate within the working class those attitudes necessary for rapid capital accumulation, one of the most important functions that the nation-state can perform for multinational corporations is the gathering of intelligence and the creation of police forces in countries that suddenly find themselves part of a capitalist world order. Under twentieth-century conditions the task requires a covert apparatus, and hence the popularity of the Dual State. It is obvious that there will be resistance on the part of domestic populations to having their lives shaped by foreign governments and corporations. One way to make it slightly more acceptable is to recruit domestic elites to carry out foreign functions, and since the latter's position is often precarious, secrecy is required for their own safety. In addition, the stakes are so high and the participants so opportunistic that "cloak-and-dagger" operations seem to be adopted naturally. The business of controlling people is hard enough, and when it is done by foreigners for obvious self-advantage, the difficulty is doubled. This combination of the need for control and the impossibility of control results in a situation where effective decisions tend to be made by foreigners operating in clandestine fashion, whatever the political structure of the dependent country.

There is much more of a balance between private and public intelligence gathering in the multinational version of the Dual State than in the domestic. Through what are known in the trade as "commercial cover agreements," a large number of career CIA officials ostensibly work for multinational corporations while carrying out their governmental functions. In the most typical arrangement, the agent does "legitimate" work for his company (any profits he makes are split between the CIA and the company), while the agency also provides his salary and a contribution in the form of office and staff expenses. It is estimated that some 200 men are so employed in this unique version of the duality between private and public status.[56] Even those who have no such commercial cover and who work full time for the agency spend some of their time being of direct assistance to multinational corporations. Not only do taxpayers pay for this service, but actions of this sort can be defended as protecting the "national interest." Because, in Behrman's words, "political intelligence made available to U.S. business helps it in making longer-term decisions and avoiding short-term traps," agencies like the CIA can perform a vital corporate function.[57] Philip Agee, a former CIA agent in Ecuador, reveals in his diary that a goodly proportion of his time was spent predicting the anti-business moves of a Populist president that would affect the "attractiveness" of Ecuador for U.S. investment. One of his most trusted contacts was the Ecuadorian Secretary of the Treasury, who personally assisted him in planting illegal money on a prominent leftist whom the CIA wanted to embarrass.[58] Another of his activities included infiltration in Ecuadorian labor unions. Finally, the intense efforts by the CIA to curb leftist tendencies in Ecuadorian politics resulted in a coup sponsored by military officers. Agee's comments on this event implicitly suggest the whole purpose of CIA work: "From our standpoint the junta definitely seems to be a favourable, if transitory, solution to the instability and danger of insurgency that were blocking development. By imposing the reforms this country needs and by taking firm action to repress the extreme left, the junta will restore confidence, reverse the flight of capital and stimulate economic development." [59] Men like J. Peter Grace, who worked for the CIA in Latin America as chairman of the board of the American Institute for Free Labor Development, could only be thrilled that covert work had paid off so well. Agee's book demonstrates how thin (and often nonexistent) is the line between the gathering of information and political repression, for the knowledge sought was never neutral but part of a system of domination. His diary, because it avoids the dramatic and highly publicized CIA escapades, shows a different side of the covert state: the everyday, routine operations designed to ensure that a country remains available for private investment.

Besides formal government intervention into the affairs of other people and the kind of quasi-public, quasi-private intervention of the commercial cover agreements, the Dual State also engages in private spying. American corporations that, as Richard Eels indicated, have created fairly impressive espionage systems at home, continue the same kind of activity when they expand abroad.[60] Having even less respect for foreign citizens than they do for their own, multinational corporations feel the need to know everything they can. Though it would probably be more efficient to have only one intelligence operation in each country, corporations, exercising their distrust for the state and pursuing their ideology of self-interest, create their own networks. ITT officials, as Anthony Sampson relates, pride themselves on how much more workable is their corporate security apparatus than that of the CIA.[61] They may be right, but the proliferation of intelligence services is ultimately self-defeating for it produces not only disarray but also illegitimacy. As the most watched people in the world, citizens of Third World countries have come to develop a dislike for attempts to export the Dual State to their shores.

The persistence of such traditional forms of the state in a period proclaimed by its beneficiaries to be revolutionary is noteworthy. What does this political conservatism suggest about the role of the capitalist state in the multinational era? For one thing, it implies that a zero-sum approach to political power is not very helpful. Just because there is an increase in transnational political power, it does not follow that there will be a decrease in national political power. As Robin Murray has expressed the problem:

> Even if the growth of international corporations did require parallel international political organizations, nation states might well remain suitable units for the undertaking of certain economic functions .... The question, therefore, is not whether or not the nation state is compatible with international forms, but what functions the nation state is likely to continue to perform, in an era of international capital.[62]

Second, of the historical forms of the capitalist state, the oldest and most traditional have shown the greatest resurgence. An ultramodern technological revolution is accompanied by a political counterrevolution, in which conceptions of the state emerging between the sixteenth and nineteenth centuries seem to have more relevance than those of a more recent period. One of the most striking ironies of the multinational era is the tenacity by which men who see themselves transforming the world hold onto political ideas that were obsolete one hundred years ago. This has everything to do with the persistence of the contradiction between liberal and democratic principles into the multinational era. If they had put all their problems behind them, multinational spokesmen, like the early nineteenth-century bourgeoisie, could rightly consider themselves a revolutionary force. But because their major problem—the contradiction between liberalism and democracy—not only persists but intensifies, they are forced to dig into their past in order to arrive at a mélange of notions that, they hope, will enable them to preserve for as long as possible their already tenuous existence.

Charles Kindleberger once remarked that "the nation state is just about through as an economic unit." [63] This may be true, but only in the dependent countries, where planning by the multinationals has made a mockery of the autonomy of various Third World governments, as Lewis Turner has shown in detail.[64] The irony of the multinationals is that their internationalism is achieved at the expense of other people's nations, not their own. As far as the capitalist state is concerned, multinational corporate activity has not brought about its end but has given it a new lease on life.

TRANSNATIONALITY AND THE INTENSIFICATION OF CONTRADICTION

Transnational political and economic activity has pushed the historic contradictions of the capitalist state to new heights. In the earlier periods of capitalist rule, conflicts tended to be of a first order of complexity. While many different types of struggle were taking place, the basic and most system-defining conflict in both the Accumulative State and the Harmonious State was, as in a basketball game, one on one: new elite versus old elite in the former, and the resulting coalition versus the developing working class in the latter. By the time of the Expansionist State and the Franchise State, however, contradictions were raised to a second order. There were two simultaneous struggles taking place. On top of the traditional class struggle, splits within the ruling class intensified, yielding a new degree of complexity. Both the Dual State, and more important, the Transnational State, raise the stakes to a third order of contradiction. Splits within the ruling class intensify; the historical struggle between classes, though muted, continues to exist; and then a new struggle comes into existence between the elites of the dominant country and the emerging self-interest of the dependent country. The intensification of contradiction is the political equivalent of economic weakness; the Transnational State is not a response to an aggressive drive to bring more and more people into the capitalist world order, but is more a reaction to the inability of dominant elites to structure the world in such a way that they can combine both profits and political control.

In spite of the failures of political units like the UN and the EEC, and in spite of the conservative nature of multinational activity, there has been a tendency toward transnational capitalism after World War II. One example, cited by Kjell Skjelsbaek, is that the number of nongovernmental international bodies—such as the International Air Travel Association, the International Olympic Committee, and the World Council of Churches—has tended to increase from 1,012 in 1954, to 1,470 in 1964, to 1,899 in 1968.[65] It is clear that the needs of advanced capitalism have internationalized political and economic life. Yet, and this is precisely the reason why such internationalism is interesting, these movements beyond the nation-state, as I have tried to show, are more often the expression of consolidating urges than they are of revolutionary ones. Thus, the tension established between the need for transnationality and the conservative impetus behind it is responsible for a whole new series of contradictions that have not replaced earlier ones but have accumulated alongside and on top of them. The complexity of the class struggles of the transnational era solves few problems but intensifies many.

The confusions between public and private, autonomy and inter-dependence, and regulation and determination that emerged during the Franchise State are not solved in the transnational era. If anything, their effects multiply as the process of capital accumulation becomes a world-wide phenomenon. ITT activity in Chile raises again the specter of a pri-vate body making public policy, but this time those affected are the citi-zens of two countries, not one. Similarly, the creation of a world political economy makes both firms and states more interdependent than ever, yet also leads to increased demands by corporations for autonomy. The "energy crisis" of 1974 is a perfect example of how the pursuit of autonomy in an era of increased interdependence can cause havoc. Finally, corporate be-havior seems less regulatable as the need for regulation increases. As im-potent as bodies like the ICC were in regulating the railroads, they are powerful when compared with national attempts to regulate international air travel, where not even the form of an effective public regulatory agency exists. The political contradictions that emerged between the 1930s and the 1950s exist in an even stronger form in the 1970s.

Transnationality adds new dimensions to these conflicts and mystifica-tions. First, as Anthony Sampson has pointed out, a giant multinational firm like ITT has the best of two worlds; it can claim to be an appendage of the nation when it chooses, or it can claim to be an international citi-zen when that suits its fancy.[66] Like domestic corporations that claimed both public and private status depending on circumstances, multinational firms can walk in and out of the nation-state at their pleasure. The nation-state, the instrument through which both modern liberalism and modern democracy came to maturity, goes the way of all other obstructions to the accumulation of capital. Second, the Transnational State destroys its own reason for existence by taking advantage of the diversity of the world in order to impose upon it uniformity. The reason for going multinational in the first place is that certain parts of the world have something—raw mate-rials, cheap labor power, particular climates—that the advanced capitalist nations need. But as these uniquenesses are exploited they are destroyed. Raw materials are used up, workers awake, and ecological differences are disrupted. Politically, the extension of the Transnational State shapes the entire world in the pattern established by three centuries of European his-tory; the conflict between liberalism and democracy becomes a world phenomenon, not a Western one. Trying to escape that conflict, the Trans-national State winds up extending it.

Of all the implications of transnationality, the most important is that it escalates the incompatibility between liberalism and democracy. A cer-tain historical closure is brought about. While in the early nineteenth century, liberalism and democracy were understood to be contradictory, there was, as my introduction pointed out, a blurring of the distinction between them. The Transnational State retracts that blurring and re-establishes the original tension between the liberal and democratic conceptions of the modern state. On the one hand, this came about through an intensification of the accumulation function. The Transnational State, which emerges in response to accumulation needs of one type, interferes with accumulation needs of another type. State planning is in many ways one of the most important political developments in the history of capitalism because it constitutes an implicit confession by capitalists themselves that the market does not function properly as an allocation mechanism. Accumulation was found too important to be left to the anarchy of a system of purely private decision making. But the Transnational State undercuts the planning function by internationalizing the scope of the area affected by decisions. As Martinelli and Somaini note, multinational corporations interfere with state planning in four distinct areas: full employment, sustained rates of growth, balance of payments equilibria, and levels of public expenditure.[67] Just when it seemed that capitalism had transcended the problem of anarchy, the Transnational State brings it in through the back door. But this time there is a difference. Anarchy in the market was one thing in the nineteenth century when there were few other alternatives. Returning to it in the 1970s, when both state planning and socialist allocation mechanisms exist, is a dangerous move. An unplanned economy becomes twice cursed; not only did it fail once, but other experiences indicate that growth can be achieved in new ways. One can only wonder why so many businessmen, who were willing to violate their belief in classical liberalism when they adopted the Franchise State, are now so intent on violating the Franchise State and returning to classical liberalism. The reason must be that they were never very happy sharing power in the first place, and as the Franchise State began to develop real teeth, they saw the internationalization of capital as a way to escape through the cracks. By once again turning on a solution that they helped improvise, multinational businessmen see the chance to make large profits with very few checks.

Multinational corporate activity, in addition, escalates the contradictions between liberalism and democracy by transposing them to the world capitalist system. This direction will be intensified with the coming to power of the Carter Administration, for rarely has one President been so identified with multinationals. The Trilateral Commission, the creation of Carter advisor Zbigniew Brzezinski, understands full well what is at stake in the world system. Brzezinski, for example, has written that the multinationals represent the long tradition of liberty with which the United States has been identified, while Third World countries are more directly concerned with equality. The problem is that liberty and equality are often contradictory, so that the problem for American foreign policy becomes one of maintaining the credibility of the one in the face of the threats from the other.[68] Brzezinski issues a call for a return to liberal principles. If he succeeds in carrying out that idea as national security advisor, he will make the international confrontation between liberalism and democracy as direct as it can be.

A move toward liberalism is inevitably a move away from democracy. Profits will be achieved at the price of legitimacy, for the Transnational State is the least democratic, that is, the least subject to popular participation and control, of any of the six major forms of the capitalist state. "Transnational relations and other multinational processes," Karl Kaiser has written, "seriously threaten democratic control of foreign policy, particularly in advanced industrial societies." [69] One important reason why this is the case, as Barnet and Muller note, is that multinational businessmen prefer to deal directly with the executive branches of government, which tend to be more responsive to national and international elites, than with legislatures, which invariably are more in touch with local interests.[70] The reification of the executive branch in making foreign policy has been helped along by multinational corporations. But one also sees a decline in popular control over domestic policy. The complexity of the decisions that directly affect multinational corporations only indirectly affect the public at large, turning these matters into "administrative" rather than "political" issues. And, beyond that, the sheer size of the multinational corporations becomes a political factor. Bureaucracy is never an accident; the multinationals are large so that they cannot be controlled, either from within or from without. It is precisely their size that exempts them from all rules of responsibility. If they fail, they are not to be punished but rewarded, because their size makes them a "national asset" (see Chapter 8). If they deal directly with something of national concern, they must be permitted to shape public policy in that area, because they are so important to the economy. When one corporation in 1975 can exceed the size of the whole Republic in 1775, political conceptions about popular control had better change. The failure of political theory to keep up with economic practice has permitted the multinational corporations and the men of state who work for them to destroy democracy in both theory and practice. If it returns to the world of pure liberalism, the Transnational State will consciously forego the world of democracy. The 1970s will experience what the 1770s knew full well: that one cannot have both liberalism and democracy at the same time.

Interlude
The Emergence of
Late Capitalism

THE POLITICAL HISTORY of capitalist societies, as I have tried to show in the first half of this book, has followed a path neither linear nor simple. Before turning to the contemporary consequences of that history, which is the theme of Part II, it makes sense to pause to review from where we have come and to set out where we will be going.

Liberal democracy, I have been arguing, neatly symbolizes a contradiction at the heart of Western polities, one that has been expressed as an inherent, if not omnipresent, tension between the needs of accumulation and of legitimation. The demands of a private system of accumulation gave rise to a liberal ideology that structured public conceptions about the state; the desire for popular acceptance and obedience gave rise to democratic notions about political life quite at odds with the earlier liberal ones. Tensions between these contrary expectations were temporarily resolved through six different "ideal types" of capitalist states, each of which corresponded to a particular historical "moment" over the course of the past two hundred years. While summaries cannot do justice to the nuances and exceptions of actual historical periods, one may be in order at this point to facilitate the argument that follows.

The Accumulative State, which corresponded to the first wave of capitalist industrialization, made accumulation its own mechanism of legitimation. Since the end was held to be the accumulation of wealth, and any means necessary to that end was justifiable, the Accumulative State was not ideologically committed to laissez-faire but instead saw active government intervention into the economy and social order. The Accumulative State was responsive to at least six different public needs: defining the parameters of the emerging capitalist society; preserving discipline; adjusting macroeconomic conditions; providing direct subsidies; fighting wars; and supporting miscellaneous eclectic activities. A compromise between the active state of the mercantile period and the requirements of industrial capitalism, the Accumulative State had an eclectic character that was simultaneously its strength and its weakness. It possessed the requisite flexibility for a transitional era, but when the task of legitimation became necessary with the rise of a working class, it was too contradictory to work. Although traces of the Accumulative State persist today, the "pure" form disappeared by the middle of the nineteenth century.

In its place arose a preoccupation with legitimation, which resulted in the Harmonious State. Two different strands of thought came together to emphasize that under capitalism all classes had an interest in allowing the bourgeoisie to control the state. One such strand, a direct heritage of classical liberalism, promised ultimate harmony if matters were kept out of the hands of government; the other, which developed an ideological rationalization for state action, was a reform version of liberalism, developed in response to working-class threats from below. Though these two strands of thought are often seen as polar opposites, their common attempt to use theories of harmony to justify capitalistic arrangements makes them quite similar. But the first one internally was so contradictory that it could never last long as a legitimation mechanism, as an analysis of its manifestation in Social Darwinism indicates. At the same time, the latter, which led to concrete reforms, disproved the notion of a harmony of interests by having to sponsor reforms in the first place. Aside from these underlying theoretical problems, the Harmonious State was also having difficulties in practice. Politics in the last part of the nineteenth century was dominated by the bourgeois politician, who brought with him new definitions, new modes of organization, and new processes, all of which became corrupt. Theoretical weakness combined with practical corruption made harmonious doctrines seem shallow and led toward new solutions to the problem of the state in a capitalist society.

When the contradictions between liberalism and democracy seemed to reach the breaking point, foreign expansion, a notion at odds with classical liberalism, became more appealing. Although an imperial foreign policy seemed to relieve domestic pressure from below, it did so at substantial cost: the violations of liberal theory became so pronounced that liberalism began to be undermined by those who in the past had advocated it most vigorously. Far from being "futurist," expansionism symbolized the close of the era of classical liberalism. The end of free trade and unrestricted immigration were accompanied by attempts to control working classes in new ways, such as through education and mass culture. It would take some time before the full contradictions of foreign expansion would realize themselves, but even so, the justification of the Expansionist State as an end in itself was already sounding hollow by the end of World War I.

The war revealed that it was not only the struggle between social classes that was paralyzing the state but bitter conflict within ruling classes as well. Politics in the postwar period became a series of experiments designed to harness discontent in both of these areas. One of the most popular experiments was corporatism, but it ran into the twin extremes of being either too authoritative or not authoritative enough. Almost as an afterthought, the idea of delegating public power to private bodies for purposes of regularizing class conflict began to emerge. General solutions along these lines, which I have called the Franchise State, offered a fairly long period of stability, especially after the principles of the Franchise State were extended to groups outside of industrial sectors that had organized enough political power to make their claims on the state. Nonetheless, the Franchise State eventually began to cause as many problems as it was solving; mystification, for example, was necessary to its operation but became counterproductive when definite standards were needed. The state was supposed to give away power, not to exercise it, but with the failure of private agencies to regulate themselves effectively, the Franchise State began to decline. Although it had arisen out of the experiments of World War I, by the post–World War II period its contradictions were becoming too blatant to ignore. Defense spending in the United States and economic planning in Europe became areas in which the state began to assume the power that theoretically belonged to it all along; as it did so, the Franchise State became a thing of the past rather than a solution for the future.

Perhaps the most unusual attempt to resolve the inherent tension between liberal and democratic conceptions of the state was the general solution of a diarchy. Instead of one state trying to do two different things, two states were created, one charged with keeping order and the other with preserving a democratic façade. In order to work well, the Dual State required political leaders sensitive to its divergent functions, a most difficult balancing act. Early experiences with the Dual State made this clear, for rank amateurism in covert affairs was more common than subtlety. Although these difficulties were ironed out for a time, the covert face of the Dual State became smaller and smaller as the need for secrecy became larger and larger. In addition, the Dual State found itself caught between the vested interests of its component parts and its general interest in secret intelligence. These internal difficulties would have existed regardless of who was in power, but the Nixon Administration, through general ineptitude, exacerbated them. The fate of the Dual State is unclear at this time, but even if it successfully defends itself in the face of the publicity around Watergate and revelations about CIA, it will still confront internal and external contradictions that will limit its general applicability as a permanent solution to the contradiction between liberal and democratic principles.

Just as the contradictions of the polity were beginning to overload the nation-state, the internationalization of capital gave rise to multinational corporations that saw the world, and not any particular nation, as their market. But this development did not transcend the problems of nation-states, for, if anything, multinational corporations required government assistance in a way not seen since the heyday of the Accumulative State. In other words, prominent experiments in what I have called the Transnational State—such as the experiences of the European Common Market or the United Nations—do not resolve the contradiction between accumulation and legitimation but raise it to a new level. Because they extend the historical limitations of the capitalist state to a new plateau, transnational political arrangements are as much an expression of difficulty as they are a resolution of it.

An obvious question is raised by the attenuation of these six solutions: are there others waiting in the wings? Alternatively put, have Western liberal democracies reached the point where they are no longer capable of generating from within solutions to the social conflicts they create? The question is as important as it is difficult to address. In order to deal with it, I would like first to locate the answer in a tradition of political economy which seeks to understand the structural limitations and the historical impasse of late capitalism. The writers who have influenced my answer most are James O'Connor and Ernst Mandel, and it will help to say a few things about their approach before turning to the whole issue of whether liberal democracies have exhausted their political alternatives.

Many Marxist analysts of capitalist society are devoted to showing how impressively the system works, yet they ignore features tending toward disequilibrium. One who does not is James O'Connor, who argues that a work like *Capital* can be understood as an attempt to explain two simultaneous and contradictory processes.[1] On the one hand, the process of capitalist accumulation involves a transition from a system based on simple, petty commodity production to one involving modern, large-scale units and an intensification of the way the worker sells his or her labor power. The description of this process is what makes *Capital* famous, and there is little that can be added to it. But, O'Connor continues, a second element enters, for, by definition, the process by which one thing is accumulated is always the exact same process by which another thing disaccumulates. The theory of the rise of large-scale capitalist production can therefore be understood as at the same time a theory of the demise of what preceded it, which O'Connor calls commodity production. Following this logic, the argument can be extended to say that the accumulation of capital will also give rise at some point to its own disaccumulative tendencies, that the system created in the mid-nineteenth century will undo itself. According to O'Connor, Marx was quite aware of this, and some of his analyses, such as the tendency of the rate of profit to fall, anticipate the decline of the system that Volume 1 of *Capital* set out to explain. Since the process had just begun when Marx wrote, there is in his writings no complete theory of the disaccumulation of capital (and therefore, continuing the logic, of the rise of primitive socialism, which is the same thing), and this project is one that contemporary Marxists should be undertaking.

On the basis of this logic, O'Connor then offers an analysis of the economic contours of late capitalism. Late capitalist production, he argues, is disaccumulative because the conditions necessary for the production of surplus value become restricted. The proportion of unproductive labor, which does not contribute to surplus value, is going up, both because workers are hoarding their labor power through conservative resistance to technological change and because they are refusing to expend their labor power through strikes. Since the size of the labor force is relatively fixed, the capital and labor shares of national income steady, and the working day established, there is little room for new strategies of accumulation. Therefore, in contrast to the accumulation phase of capitalism, labor is less mobile, demand must be stimulated because otherwise it would not exist, greater discipline and control over the work force are needed or else workers would not work, and the class struggle takes a subtle, indirect, but very powerful and consistent form. Furthermore, the tendency of more people to work for the state than in industrial production and the increase in "guard" labor made necessary by worker resistance both contribute to the decline in the production of surplus value. O'Connor concludes that the stagnation and lack of accumulation that currently characterize late capitalist production are signs of the emergence of a form of primitive socialism in the body of a decaying capitalist mode of production.

Basing his analysis on some provocative passages from Marx's *Grundrisse*, Ernst Mandel has developed another explanation of the stagnation of late capitalist society. Mandel argues that the present period, rather than being characterized as "post-industrial," represents the expansion of industrial production to every sector of the economy for the first time in the history of capitalist societies. Under this pressure, a structural crisis emerges. On the one hand, increased automation, an increase in the organic composition of capital (that is, a greater emphasis on capital-intensive rather than labor-intensive investment), and a reduction in the man-hours engaged in productive labor lead to limitations on the expansion of the real wages of the working class. On the other, workers make constant demands for higher wages. The two pressures clash head on, and unless they can be diverted through such serious emergencies as fascism or war, late capitalist societies must face the fact that no permanent solution to this tension exists. Symbolic of both the growth but also the waste and decline of late capitalism is automation:

> On the one hand, it represents the prefected development of material forces of production, which could in themselves liberate mankind from the compulsion to perform mechanical, repetitive, dull and alienating labor. On the other hand, it represents a new threat to job and income, a new intensification of anxiety, insecurity, return to chronic mass unemployment, periodic losses of consumption and income, and intellectual and moral impoverishment.[2]

The term "disaccumulation" is coming into use to describe these various structural restraints on the capacity of capitalist societies to find ever increasing sources for the expansion of surplus value.[3] Disaccumulation has important political and social implications as well. In late capitalist societies characterized by disaccumulation there is a tendency for ruling classes to run out of political options—which bears a strong resemblance to the failure of late capitalism to generate the surplus necessary to its own reproduction. Considerable attention has already been given to this phenomenon. Jürgen Habermas, for example, has argued that late capitalism has been characterized by a series of inter-connected crises in all its spheres of existence.[4] The political system is no longer capable of resolving the tasks which the economy imposes upon it. As pluralism breaks down, the state becomes immobilized by the contradictory demands made upon it by groups with different interests who can no longer resolve their differences outside the state. Moreover, a crisis of meaning is generated by the fact that symbols are not as effective as they once were in compelling loyalty to the society. The result, according to Habermas, are serious problems of legitimation in late capitalism which rival the problems of accumulation discussed by writers like O'Connor and Mandel.

In the remainder of this book I will examine this legitimacy crisis of the late capitalist state in greater detail. My argument will be that the arrival of late capitalism has corresponded with what I will call throughout Part II *the exhaustion of political alternatives*. By this phrase I mean that each of the six major forms of the capitalist state created to resolve the tensions between accumulation and legitimation within the framework of liberal democracy has been found wanting. To suggest that the alternatives have been exhausted is therefore to suggest that the inherent tensions within liberal democracy will increasingly come to the surface. *In late capitalism, in other words, the major political issues will not take place within the parameters of liberal democracy but over them.*

The effects of the exhaustion of political alternatives can already be seen. The emergence of late capitalism gives the political systems of Western Europe and the United States their stagnant character; societies become dominated by frustration, blockage, political opacity, exhaustion, rigidification, mystification, and overall lack of direction and confusion. The remaining political history of late capitalism will be a contest between the desperate need to do something and the inability to do anything. Calls for drastic action will be accompanied by numbing inertia. Political thought will swing rapidly back and forth, from the apocalyptic to the cynical, from an intensive urge to change to a rigid preference for what exists. The state will be worshipped while state action will be denigrated. Politics will be praised as depoliticization takes its place. A precarious stability will characterize the late capitalist state, until the point where a full-scale legitimacy crisis pushes toward either great control over the population or greater control by the population. As the tensions between liberalism and democracy manifest themselves, in other words, resolutions may be sought in an authoritarian direction (toward the primacy of accumulation over legitimation) or in a democratic direction (the assertion of legitimation over accumulation). It is impossible to predict which will happen, but it is not impossible to predict that one or the other will happen.

In order that the thesis of the exhaustion of alternatives be properly understood, two words of caution are in order. First, the proposition that all the forms that the tension between accumulation and legitimation can take have been used up is an empirical observation, not a theoretical one. That is to say, there is no *necessary* reason why a seventh, eighth, or ninth form would not develop at some future time (or might be developing now). One could even invent, with little effort, some possible new options for different classes to consider. But while alternatives are theoretically possible, the concrete fact is that none is being put into practice. No solution along the lines of the six discussed in Part I has arisen, nor is any likely to arise, given the structural constraints to be discussed below. Indeed, the major thrust of political thought at the moment is a return to much earlier conceptions of the state rather than a concern with future ideas. Nothing symbolizes the vacuity of serious political thinking more than the resurgence of popularity of theorists as irrelevant to the modern world as Smith, Locke, Malthus, and Saint-Simon. The fact that a book that argues the case for laissez-faire could be taken seriously in 1975 is an impressive indication of the decay of political thought.[5] Nor is a highly publicized attempt to resurrect the social contract much of an advance, even if its politics are less barbaric.[6] A neo-Malthusian notion of triage that makes careful calculations about who shall survive indicates that a significant segment of bourgeois thought is far more comfortable in the early nineteenth century than in the late twentieth; Malthus, like an ancient talisman, is brought out whenever liberal society is in trouble.[7] The "futurists" who envision a postindustrial society reflect the same mood, for their science fiction is based as much on Saint-Simon as it is on the latest space age gadgetry.[8] Even among Marxists, the textual preoccupation that one finds in Louis Althusser represents the same kind of almost determined irrelevance.[9] As the worship of nostalgia in popular culture finds its equivalent in political thought, the six forms of the capitalist state tend to turn in upon each other instead of reaching out for new options, a sign that something is amiss in the political world. Not only politicians, but political thinkers as well, have become men of quiet desperation.

A second word of caution: The thesis of the exhaustion of alternatives in late capitalism is a historical development, not a sudden shift. Nothing will be or can be suggested here that indicates how long the period of late capitalism is likely to last. To posit that liberal democracy is disintegrating because its conflicting demands can no longer be reconciled is not to assert that either socialism or fascism will immediately and vengefully replace it. Contradictory systems can continue to exist for some time, and this one may (or may not) do so as well. The point is, rather, that, considered from a historical perspective, liberal democracy may be in its last stage, but that stage has an indeterminable length. Its future depends on calculations made by majority and minority classes as to when the precise moment to go beyond it will come about. Though I emphasize a theory of disintegration, in other words, I do not wish to imply a *Götterdämmerung* prediction of the end of the Western world as we know it. I mean instead that modes of production and their accompanying political forms come and go, and the one we have had for a while seems about to go. While it is in the process, some important political developments have been taking place that are very much within the scope of this effort. It is to those developments that I turn next.

II

Politics and the
Exhaustion of Alternatives

"What 'ought to be' is therefore concrete;
indeed, it is the only realistic and historicist
interpretation of reality; it alone is history in the
making; it alone is politics."

Antonio Gramsci

8 / The Reification of the State

"My idea is that when things are not going so well, the State should come in, but when things are going well, the State should keep out. In other words, it is a policy determined by the state of trade in the country."

Major Lloyd George (1946)

"There is mounting evidence that government is big rather than strong; that it is fat and flabby rather than powerful; that it costs a great deal but does not achieve much. There is mounting evidence also that the citizen less and less believes in government and is increasingly disenchanted with it. Indeed, government is sick—and just at the time when we need a strong, healthy, and vigorous government."

Peter Drucker (1969)

INCREASING POWER, DECREASING OPTIONS

IT HAS BECOME axiomatic to characterize the modern state by its increase in size, brought about by the adoption of a range of new policies. The expansion of government is, indeed, striking. In Great Britain, the percentage of the Gross National Product taken up by public expenditure was 12.7 percent in 1910, 25.7 percent in 1937, 44.9 percent in 1951, and 50.5 percent in 1973, if the capital expenditure of public corporations is included.[1] Excluding state productive enterprises, OECD figures for 1972 show similarly high percentages for all the late capitalist societies: 39.8 percent for the United Kingdom, 36.7 percent for France, 38.0 percent for West Germany, 40.0 percent for Italy, and 34.3 percent for the United States.[2] No other conclusion is possible but that government has become a central ingredient of modern capitalism.

The increase in public expenditure is a fact so self-evident that its true significance is easily missed. In a play suffused with dramatic tension, one is so often preoccupied with the theatrics that one can ignore changes taking place in the characters. Similarly, to focus only on the dramatic expansion of government is to pay less attention to changes in the character of public life that have been taking place at the same time.[3] Thus, it is not so much misleading as it is incomplete to conclude that "the power and scope of government has been vastly increased in recent years."[4] Nor is it sufficient to note, as did the Club Jean Moulin in France, that when compared to the absolutist monarchies of Louis XIV, the government of Charles de Gaulle has far more power, for its decisions "envelop the everyday life of all." To speak of the modern state as "the principal creator of wealth, the promoter of progress" [5] is to tell only half the story. Such idylls to growth, like a second-rate critic, focus only on the flashy and ignore the substance.

On its face, the idea of making a comparison between state power in 1660 and 1960 is foolish enough, given the transformation of society between the two periods. But even if the comparison is made, arguments like that of the Club Jean Moulin simply do not hold up; what was *la gabelle* if not something that "enveloped the everyday life of all"?; what was Colbert's sponsorship of industry if not "the principal creator of wealth, the promoter of progress"? Any assertion about the specific policies of the modern state faces a similar problem. If the cause of the expansion of the modern state is felt to be its welfare functions, then one must confront a three-hundred-year history of governmental policies toward relief. [6] If intervention into the wage bargain is the criterion, then we must explain the Statute of Labourers, which created a system of wage and price controls as early as 1351. [7] If state promotion of the economy is the crucial issue, then both Colbert's system as well as Elizabeth's were the precursors of the accumulative, eighteenth-century capitalist state. The closer one examines them, the more simple propositions about the uniqueness of the modern state begin to crumble.

It is neither size per se nor specific policies that are central to an analysis of the late capitalist state, but changes in the *character* of government. Although contradiction has been a part of bourgeois politics for over two hundred years, the failure of the six solutions discussed in Part I to resolve them has only intensified them. What happens to the character of government when the available methods of resolving the contradiction between liberal needs and democratic desires have been utilized? That is the question I want to address in this chapter. The activity of the state has increased to the point where it has become a major producer and certainly the major consumer, but often forgotten is that the growth in the potential power of the state is matched by a decline in the options that the state has at its command. For this reason the increased activity of the state reflects, not an expansion of alternatives, but the exhaustion of them. The enormous political power in the hands of the leaders of Western societies is accompanied by a generalized inability to use that power toward purposive ends. The more the state does, in short, the less it can do. As one group of social scientists expressed the problem, the "expansion of government activity was tribute not so much to the strength of government as to its weakness." [8] The single most important effect that the arrival of late capitalism has had on the structure of the state is this peculiar tendency for greater power to bring about greater impotence.

Class struggle is thus the root cause of the political stagnation of the late capitalist state. At home vested interests block reforms favorable to powerless groups while the majoritarian residue of liberal democracy formally prevents the state from serving as an unmediated arm of the ruling class. Internationally, struggles against hegemonic powers make the latter ineffective for all the weapons at their command, while a bureaucracy developed in response to political needs prevents those needs from being realized. In addition, political immobility creates its own contradictions. The decline in the ability of the private accumulation system to generate capital necessitates that the state play more of a role in the accumulation process, granting subsidies to giant corporations, helping multinationals subdue populations, supporting research and development costs, and warping the tax structure to help private companies increase their profits.[9] Then, if the balance between class forces is not to be disrupted, welfare and repressive functions must continue or be increased. And as hegemonic powers lose control, their arms budgets, searches for new weapons, and corresponding state expenditures go up also. Inertia pushes one way while necessity pushes the other. The late capitalist state is caught in a bind, in which the more functions government must perform, the greater the inability to perform them. Damned if it does and damned if it doesn't, the state approaches the point at which its utility for reproducing social relationships is nil.

After giving a few examples of this contradiction between increased power and decreasing options, I will examine the effects that this situation has had on the public life of late capitalism. First, the absorption of class conflict within the state gives the public bureaucracy an impossible task: to resolve political issues within the framework of a nonpolitical ideology. Second, these contradictions lead to a reversal of Benthamite rationality, in which administrators are no longer governed by reason but become victims of a world of illusions and untruths. As a result, political scientists and public officials develop contradictory expectations about state power, praising its ability yet despairing of its potential. The implicit point throughout this discussion is that the late capitalist state is incapable of working its way out of the contradictions that both the conditions of production and the expectations of political life have imposed on it.

"To govern," John F. Kennedy used to say, "is to choose." If the art of government lies in the creativity of the choice, then the rulers of late capitalist society have become copiers rather than creators, for the number of options from which they can choose has narrowed. Consider Kennedy's own experience. If any one event is cited as his finest hour, it was the Cuban missile crisis. Here was a case where maximum state power was at

Kennedy's command. The number of weapons of destruction he could control was fantastic. The emotionally charged atmosphere surrounding these events gave him substantial influence over the domestic political system. The development of the Dual State meant that the eventual decision would be made by a very small number of men, all sympathetic to him. The fact that U.S. power had not yet been successfully confronted by insurgent forces made foreign governments kowtow to American power. The Cuban missile crisis, in other words, came at a time when the potential power of the rulers of American society seemed to be at its pinnacle. Yet a careful examination of the crisis by Graham Allison reveals that in fact there was almost nothing Kennedy could do except what he did. The National Security Council presented him with six options, ranging from doing nothing to full-scale attack, but the extremes in either direction were spurious. As Kennedy surveyed his choices, they narrowed down to either a surgical air strike or a blockade. The former had the advantage of sweeping away the problem like a vacuum cleaner; in Sorensen's words:

> The idea of American planes suddenly and swiftly eliminating the missile complex with conventional bombs in a matter of minutes—a so-called "surgical" strike—had appeal to almost everyone first considering the matter, including President Kennedy.[10]

A surgical strike became a wish fulfillment for these men, a fantasy that what irritated them could be swatted out of sight and out of mind. But it was not to be, for the military could not guarantee the "cleanliness" of the strike. Thus six options had shrunk to one, the blockade, "a middle ground between inaction and attack." [11] And even when the inevitable decision was reached, there were still limitations. Kennedy's decision to remove U.S. missiles from Turkey, for example, was stymied time and again by the bureaucracy. The "most powerful man in the world" could not control his own State Department. Men possessing unheard-of power had made their decision, which was

> a mélange of misperception, miscommunication, misinformation, bargaining, pulling, hauling, and spurning, as well as a mixture of national security interests, objectives, and governmental calculations recounted in more conventional accounts.[12]

Despite the possession of unheard-of amounts of power, Kennedy and the men around him were limited in the options from which they could choose.

The contradiction between increased power and decreased options is neither confined to the making of foreign policy nor to the United States. One sees a similar process in the domestic area. Certainly the last forty or so years have provided extensive opportunities for domestic reform. Knowledge about social policies and how they operate has increased; a revised conception of citizenship in capitalist societies has condemned poverty and hunger as unacceptable; experts in public administration are plentiful; political majorities sympathetic to reform are (or were) the rule; and the technical ability needed to administer complex social systems is present. Yet, to begin with America, the minimal energy expended on new programs during the New Deal has not been matched since. There has been an almost total absence of effective domestic policy for forty years, a startling fact when contrasted with the potential power that the state seems to possess and with the obvious existence of unmet needs. Even the few new departures attempted prove the stagnation of the state. The Johnsonian War on Poverty, a significant attempt to construct a breakthrough, ran afoul of vested interests and was disbanded. The Nixonian Family Assistance Plan, which, as Daniel Patrick Moynihan has shown, was a deliberate attempt to transcend the conservative versus liberal debates that were a heritage of the New Deal, seemed to offer the promise of a new kind of reform, but it was also sacrificed on the altar of political expediency.[13] If a proposed domestic policy was stripped of vision and cast in the framework of a forty-year-old approach, it had a chance at implementation. If it was visionary in the slightest sense, and tried to use potential state power, it was sabotaged. The minimization of options was as acute on the domestic front as on the foreign.

This contradiction between increased state activity and decreased choices is also characteristic of European societies in the late capitalist period. It has become fashionable to describe France as a *société bloquée*, in which "the political process is bogged down in artificial conflicts through which no innovation nor institutional progress can be achieved."[14] Crozier's research into "the French bureaucratic system of organization" remains the classic example of what *immobilisme* means; in reaction to this stagnation, reforms like the *rationalisation des choix budgetaires*[15] can be viewed as the main attempt by French civil servants to "get their country moving again." Similar concern about whether Britain has become, in Shanks' terms, a "stagnant society"[16] led to a deliberate attempt to reform the British state along more modern lines. Both in the system of national planning initiated under the National Economic Development Council and in such civil service issues as the Fulton Report (1968), reform of government became a high-priority agenda item for British men of state. As Trevor Smith pointed out, "The extensive changes made to the institutions and personnel of government in the 1960s were unprecedented in British political experience—at least in times of peace."[17] Yet the most interesting consequence of this push toward change was that so little changed. The more England attempted to revise the outmoded structure of its government, the more outmoded that government seemed to become. Whether Conservatives or Labourites were in power, the tendency toward "big government" corresponded with a tendency toward impotent government. The lack of dynamism in the British economy found its counterpart in the state.

Italy has had its own variation on the theme of political immobility. Allum contrasts the economic dynamism of the postwar years with the lack of innovation in the polity. He attributes this stagnation to changes in the balance of class forces that occur with the emergence of late capitalism. Throughout most of the 1950s, Allum argues, the political system remained in the hands of a capitalist ruling class dominated by a cozy relationship between businessmen and bankers. For roughly fifteen years, the state was ideal from the capitalist point of view, mediating between the different forces within society to the benefit of high finance. But this system was put into jeopardy in the 1960s, as economic growth created social problems requiring state action. Trying to walk a narrow line between reform of the problems that they themselves created and fear of an articulate working-class movement, the rulers of Italy found themselves running out of options. In general, Allum notes, "it is not that the government has abdicated all responsibility, but too often, when faced with opposition within its own ranks, its measures become a case of too little too late." [18] The result pushed toward both the ideological and political bankruptcy of the Christian Democratic Party, in which corruption seemed to become a surrogate for the ability to rule.

Each of these examples suggests that, whether due to domestic class conflict or a decline of international hegemony, the political systems of late capitalism find themselves with fewer options. The lack of choices forces a reliance on state activity that, although it can act as a temporary palliative, further reduces options in the long run. This cycle in which stagnation results in decisions that stagnate further is bound to affect the way in which the public business is carried on in late capitalist societies, as a glance at the most conspicuous feature of that business can reveal.

PUBLIC LIFE IN LATE CAPITALISM

The single most noteworthy feature of the public life of late capitalism is the intransigence of bureaucracy. While bureaucracy is an old phenomenon it assumes a unique aspect in the late capitalist era due to the exhaustion of political alternatives. So long as the state was concerned predominantly with an accumulation function, government bureaus were small and easily managed, or in the case of the United States, easily mismanaged. The need to reconcile accumulation with legitimation changed this uncomplicated situation; out of this need the modern bureaucratic state began to grow. Because, in Lowi's words, "administration is a means of routinizing coercion," [19] the most important contributing factor to the growth of bureaucracy is the attempt by the state to manage and contain the class struggle. For example, when planners of the Franchise State tried to avoid reliance on the state by encouraging quasi-private bodies to make public decisions, they were also avoiding firm determinations that would be binding on all the parties. When it was discovered that coercive decisions were in fact required, there was no alternative but to turn a private association into a government bureau. Thus, the more the state was called on to regularize both intra- and interclass conflict by making authoritative decisions, the greater the inevitable bureaucratization that followed. Increases in bureaucracy stem from the tension between liberal and democratic conceptions of the state, which are channeled into public agencies that attempted to resolve it on an *ad hoc* basis.

The creation of new bureaus was tantamount to a confession that no solution to the basic contradiction of advanced capitalism existed within the sphere of private life, forcing the state to assume the role of conflict resolver of last resort. State intervention, however, did not solve the problem but transformed it in two significant, and contradictory, ways. On the one hand, each failure of a public agency to routinize class conflict with finality led to demands for new bureaus, intensifying the failure even more. There is no better symbol of the inability of the late capitalist state to extricate itself from its own dilemmas than the sprawling, irrational, contradictory, and wasteful bureaucratization it engenders. But while this was taking place, new demands on the state were *incompatible* with further bureaucratization. A distinction that Claus Offe makes between allocative and productive state activity is helpful in this context.[20] According to Offe, the capitalist state can act in two ways: distributing existing resources to all the contending parties, and creating new resources directly by participating in the accumulation process. Under late capitalism, there is a turn in the direction of state productive activity to generate solutions to economic and political stagnation. But productive activity, contrasted with allocative, is incompatible with a bureaucratic mode of organization. Productive activity, Offe notes, assumes a range of questions that bureaucracies are not equipped to answer: What is the end goal of the activity? What is the most efficient way of obtaining it? How should it be financed? For this reason, the emergence of late capitalism brings about new needs that bureaucracy cannot satisfy at the same time that it encourages greater bureaucratization. In other words, the most noticeable feature of late capitalism is the tendency of the bureaucracy to become caught in a bind between what it must do and what it is inherently incapable of doing.

An alternative way to express this situation is to suggest that, under conditions of late capitalism, public administration is called upon to resolve questions that at one time were left to the market. Habermas calls this tendency the repoliticization of the relations of production, as the state assumes the fourfold task of constituting and maintaining the mode of production, complementing the market, replacing the market when necessary, and compensating for the market under pressure from disadvantaged groups.[21] When the state assumes the task of allocating and even producing resources within a capitalist economy, a devastating contradiction emerges. If the state is to uphold the conditions necessary for capitalist accumulation, as Offe suggests, it must be organized according to a noncapitalist logic. If, on the other hand, it denies capitalist logic too strenuously, it undermines the capitalism that it is supposed to be supporting.[22] This central contradiction of the late capitalist state requires, in Habermas' words,

> the mutually contradictory imperatives of expanding the planning capacity of the state with the aim of a collective-capitalist planning and, yet, blocking precisely this expansion, which would threaten the continued existence of capitalism. Thus the state apparatus vacillates between expected intervention and forced renunciation of intervention, between becoming independent of its clients in a way that threatens the system and subordinating itself to their particular interests.[23]

Because of these polar imperatives, public life under late capitalism becomes a hodgepodge of conflicting urges. The late capitalist state supports certain bureaucratic alternatives that it must then suppress, only to find that the suppression of them causes once again a need for their existence. In the remainder of this section, I will argue that this simultaneous need for but despair of bureaucratization colors the public life of late capitalism and gives it a decidedly confused character. This can be done by examining four consequences of this ambiguity toward state action: politicization, centralization, decentralization, and rationalization.

Because the growth of new bureaus does not solve the problems for which they were created, the state faces an administrative crisis of which its much publicized fiscal crisis is only a part. Volker Ronge has shown how this administrative crisis is due to the conflicting needs of accumulation and legitimation, which push state policy makers in contrary directions. The major consequence of this duality, he argues, is to break down the traditional distinction that capitalist societies make between politics and administration. Since "more and more administrations must strive for specific support for their policies" when faced with contradictory expectations, the bureaucracy finds itself unable to resist building support for its decisions, thereby becoming as political as it is administrative.[24] But this politicization creates problems anew, as shown by the experience of the U.S. Bureau of the Budget (BOB) since the 1950s. The BOB could only carry out its important administrative tasks if it possessed what Hugh Heclo has called "neutral competence"—that is, devoted civil servants who pride themselves on their distinctly nonpolitical character.[25] The existence of this neutral competence made the BOB vital to the administrative process; but, as it became essential, demands to politicize it became intense. Nixon's decision to change the BOB into the Office of Management and Budget (OMB) was the most extreme form of this politicization: "The threat to neutral competence was not initiated by the Nixon Administration. Both the Eisenhower and Kennedy administrations came to Washington vowing vengeance against a Bureau of the Budget suspected of disloyalty to the new President."[26] Bureaus that serve crucial needs tend to become politicized in other words, and as they do, they can no longer serve crucial needs. Politicization arises out of a desire to control the bureaucracy, but destroys the very purpose for which control is being exercised.

A second consequence of the ambiguity of the late capitalist state toward bureaucracy involves centralization. For a considerable period of time, the monopolization in the private sector was not matched by a similar cartelization in the public. As firms eliminated competition and subjected the economy to a thorough rationalization, bureaus within the state remained parochial, competitive, and inefficient by capitalist criteria. This was the period when industrialists looked at the public sector with dismay, wondering aloud why government did not seem as efficient as monopoly capital. But given the monopoly sector's eventual reliance on the state,[27] such a disparity between the principles that were organizing the two sectors could not be tolerated, and the result was an attempt to organize public bureaus in monopolistic fashion. Centralization into superadministrative units became the public administrator's watchword. In the United States a liberal Republican, John Lindsay, created superadministrative agencies for New York City, while a conservative one, Richard Nixon, proposed dividing up the executive branch into four super-level departments, coordinated by OMB.[28] Throughout the 1960s in England, conglomerate departments became the rule, especially in domestic policy,[29] leading political scientists like Samuel Beer to wonder whether centralization had become a key feature of British politics.[30] The United States and the United Kingdom, despite different traditions of public administration, had become quite similar under the pressure of the imperatives of late capitalism, as Ian Gough has pointed out:

> The growth of state expenditure has led to a marked political centralization within the modern capitalist state. . . . Trends such as the removal of functions from local government and its reorganization into large areas, greater control over its current expenditure, centralization of public sector debt management, the setting up of new unelected and *ad hoc* bodies, the growth of regional planning institutions and the centralization of control over public expenditures within the executive: all these trends are as observable within the U.K. as much as the U.S.[31]

Other variations on the theme exist elsewhere, such as in France where U.S.-trained civil servants were seen as "commandos," coordinating information and attempting to overcome the parochialism of traditional bureaus.[32] Monopolization was found to be as necessary to public life as it was to private.

When competitive capitalism was transformed into monopoly capitalism, the market was destroyed as an allocation mechanism, replaced by administered pricing. Similarly, attempts to centralize bureaus within the state may eliminate waste and duplication (although the point is highly debatable) but they do so at the cost of eliminating self-generated standards of propriety. As Offe has pointed out, the firm and the state operate by different standards; because the latter is not a unit of capitalist accumulation, the criterion by which it makes decisions is not bounded by considerations such as profit or the market.[33] And with the adoption of Keynesian fiscal policies, not even a balanced budget constitutes a limitation on state activity.[34] Centralization under these conditions leads the state into an endless spending cycle, much as conservative economists charge, with limits established only by the political process.

At the same time, centralization has a serious effect on innovation under conditions of late capitalism. As Heclo and Wildavsky have noted, the fear of embarrassment is a major motivation of bureaucrats in the British Treasury:

> The desire to create and maintain trust explains the great dread of being caught by surprise that prevails among ministers and civil servants. To be surprised is no sin, but to seem to be surprised decreases confidence and nurtures distrust among colleagues. Avoiding embarrassment to ministers in public, and particularly in the House of Commons, is one of the driving forces throughout British government. Many failings of a minister may be overlooked, but misjudgement and error is far less damaging than to be seen as unsure, surprised, and out of touch with important events.[35]

In a situation where error is less of a taboo than surprise, it is no wonder that innovation is so rare. In the club-like community that Heclo and Wildavsky see as characteristic of the Treasury, one deliberately avoids taking risks if one wants to advance. This might be good for individual careers, but it also explains why the public bureaucracy of England is so stagnant.

Another example of the effects of centralization on risk taking is revealed by a study of resignations-in-protest undertaken in the United States. Weisband and Franck discovered a fascinating statistic: the percentage of those who resigned in protest from high bureaucratic positions and made their reasons public was 16 percent in the 1910–19 period, 10.5 percent between 1920 and 1929, 21.7 percent in the 1930s, and then 10.7 percent in 1940–49, 5.1 percent in 1950–59, and 6.3 percent in the 1960s, the time of the Vietnam War.[36] The more concentrated the decision-making apparatus, it would seem, the less likely policy disagreements are to be aired and therefore subject to debate. Besides making for less informed policy, this dramatic decline in publicized resignations-in-protest, according to the authors of the study, contributes to the lack of innovation in the public sector:

> The key executive posts in the federal government are now locked into a recruitment process that insures a population of yea-sayers, of men who speak softly and carry big, as well as small, secrets; who define themselves in terms of membership in a select "club" of eligibles; men who can be trusted by a President never to respond to higher loyalties to themselves or to the public.[37]

The consequence of this is that men of imagination and vision tend to avoid or fail the test of public service, while promotion and rewards go to those who deliberately refuse innovation. In the late capitalist state there exists a reversal of responsibility in which correct perception and judgment are not only unrewarded but deemed positively suspicious, a phenomenon that reached its heights during U.S. participation in the Vietnam War. Men who understood international events, like Paul Kattenberg, were literally ostracized from positions of responsibility, replaced by those who deliberately refused to see what the truth-tellers were expounding.[38] In the late capitalist state, as in the late capitalist economy, the tried and true is far more often adopted than the high risk, high gain.

Thus centralization of bureaus ultimately did little more than contribute to the further stagnation of policy making. As Crozier phrased it, "The state, as the main contractor, assumes responsibility for executing the program. It desperately tries to control this program, unaware that its methods of encouragement, subsidy, and control generally work against the goals it is pursuing." [39] Control is indeed the issue. Speaking, as they generally do, for the officials they have interviewed, Heclo and Wildavsky noted:

> The rise of huge, conglomerate departments, joining together several that used to be separate and independent, has made further delegation necessary but also has increased Treasury fears about the effectiveness of its control. . . . Treasury officials wonder if loss of internal knowledge of policy will not both defeat attempts to keep spending totals down as well as reduce its knowledge of what is going on.[40]

If centralization had become counterproductive because it could not provide a means of control, the obvious solution was to call for decentralization. The fact that this alternative was diametrically opposed to the one just tried was not a problem, for solutions to the difficulties of the capitalist state have traditionally been eclectic; if tariffs can go up and down rapidly, bureaus can be created and dismantled at the same rate. Decentralization eventually became as attractive as centralization as a way out of the *cul-de-sac* of contradictory bureaucratization.

Decentralized departments might be less "efficient" by the standards of monopoly capitalism, but their virtues were touted nonetheless. Political scientists like Martin Landau tried to show how duplication and overlap need not necessarily produce chaos; in his view, a certain redundancy works to foster coordination by encouraging extensive communication.[41] In addition, competitive departments, like firms in a competitive economy, must bargain with each other for scarce resources, and the bargaining process, like the market, could be relied on to produce policies that were the best available compromise among all the different interests.[42] In opposition to the centralizers, a school of thought developed holding that approximation to a marketplace system of allocation *within the state* was the best option. For every conglomerate department, there were calls for vouchers, local initiatives, creative federalism, and voluntary programs. Centralization and decentralization were even advocated by the same men at the same time; Richard Nixon, for example, would argue publicly for creative federalism while centralizing national power to new heights.[43] In this confused ideological context, one must see both solutions as not being answers in themselves. The fact that political thought could swing with such abandon from one pole to the other is testimony to how intractable the problem of bureaucracy in late capitalism was becoming.

Decentralization was as illusory as its opposite, another point these two poles have in common. This may have been understood by some of its advocates, for among those urging bureaucratic decentralization were those urging a retreat from social policy objectives;[44] to decentralize was therefore to cripple. But even assuming more charitable motives, the idea of competitive bureaus within the state would probably work as well as had competing units within the economy. In the words of Charles L. Schultze before the Joint Economic Committee's hearings on economy in government: "In the great majority of cases, it is probably true that we cannot provide competition as a means of introducing incentives for effective and efficient performance into public enterprises."[45] Schultze goes on to discuss other means, such as developing measures of performance and charging public enterprises for the "costs" they incur, but the weakness of his proposals reinforces the point that decentralization is as inadequate as centralization in solving bureaucratic problems. It is not the way the bureaucracy operates that is central, but the inherently contradictory tasks that the bureaucracy is called upon to perform.

A fourth indication of the ambiguous role of bureaucratization in late capitalism emerges out of attempts at rationalization. In the 1960s, new strategies designed to bring order out of the chaos of administrative procedure began to fascinate policy makers in one country after another. Planning-programing-budgeting systems (PPBS) in the United States, the

Public Expenditure Survey Committee, Program Analysis and Review, and Central Policy Review Staff in the United Kingdom, and the *rationalisation des choix budgetaires* in France all spoke a new mood, one in which criteria of rationality would be applied to the budgetary process, hopefully bringing order to all other processes as well.[46] Once again, the issues involved were not all that dissimilar from one that had emerged earlier in the private sector. At various points in the first half of this book, I discussed conflicts between vested interests and broader class interests, in which representatives of the latter would use the language of reform to attack the privileges of the former. Bureaucratic rationalization operates in a similar way, as reform-minded "cosmopolitans" seek to work their way around the entrenched privileges of "locals." For this reason, critics of reform like Wildavsky are correct to point out that such proposals are political, not administrative, for they involve not changes in procedure but in the distribution of power.[47] What appears to be a process of rationalization could just as easily be interpreted as a process of politicization.

Have reform proposals like PPBS been successful? In general, such ventures have not made many inroads into the vested power of bureaucratic elites; like recalcitrant businessmen before World War I, immediate interest was found to be more valuable than long-range gain. Such reforms had an impact only when they were tailored to, and did not try to counter, traditional methods of performing the public business, which is precisely what was supposed to have been reformed in the first place.[48] Without a rational allocation system, budgetary considerations were left, as O'Connor points out,[49] to the usual pattern of incrementalism, with consequences that I will discuss in the next section. What Helco and Wildavsky noted for Britain applies to the United States as well: "Despite recent talk about priorities, strategies, and rational allocation, the British Cabinet is unable to consider and decide upon any clear over-all allocation of expenditure resources."[50] In other words, the anarchy of the marketplace that businessmen found intolerable remains, but it is an anarchy caused by sprawling government bureaus and not one brought about by competitive firms. The late capitalist state operates by principles once thought to be appropriate, but later found wanting, to the nineteenth-century economy.

The problems associated with politicization, centralization, decentralization, and rationalization reinforce the point that in late capitalism public administration assumes many of the contradictions once existing in the economy. To phrase this another way, the process of absorbing the class struggle within the state means that the bureaucracy must confront within itself the irresolvable tensions that at one time lay within the province of the entire society. In late capitalism the bureaucracy becomes more than unwieldy—it becomes the one place to which the most impossible tasks are assigned. The class struggle and the political process once decided who gets what, when, and how; in late capitalism, the bureaucracy performs this function. But public life is not organized for this task; indeed, the formal ideology of bureaucracy is that it is nonpolitical, conflict-free, and concerned only with administrative rationality. Caught between its politicized tasks and its depoliticized rationale, public administration in late capitalism searches for answers to its intractable task wherever it can find them, only to discover that each possible option causes as many problems as it solves.

Bureaucratization is therefore symbolic of the closing of political options characteristic of the late capitalist state. One could generalize and say that the greater the class conflict in any late capitalist society, the more paralyzed will be the bureaucracy. Yet at the same time, the greater the amount of class conflict, the greater also will be the need for state intervention to keep it in check. In this double-bind situation, the nature of government undergoes a change, best described by Offe's concept of selectiveness.[51] Offe argues that the fundamental problem for the late capitalist state can be viewed, not as promoting certain activities over others, but as excluding from the agenda questions and policies that would disturb the class character of the state. Selective mechanisms, which he describes as a "system of filters," are created, designed to exclude claims and interests on a number of different levels. Whereas the early capitalist state served the interests of the bourgeoisie by acting in certain ways, the late capitalist state tends to serve that interest by not acting in others, which is why the literature on "nondecisions" has more applicability to the public administration than the literature on decision making as such.[52] Under late capitalism, selectivity may become so important that there is little left from which to select.

This politicization of administration is a most important development, given the tendency of the public bureaucracy to assume the consequences of class struggle and political conflict. But at the same time that administrative life becomes politicized, as I will argue in the next chapter, political life increasingly becomes administered, as the political process loses ts content and becomes subject to rules of predictability. Ever since Saint-Simon, radical writers have been fascinated by his vision that the government of men would be replaced by the administration of things, but under late capitalism the opposite occurs: the administration of men and the government of things. Because the attempt to administer more and more areas of social life can be understood only as part of the desperation of a state that is running out of options, government, to recall Kennedy's aphorism, means not to choose but to choose not to choose. As choices decline in a state of exhausting options, public life, as symbolized by the bureaucracy, becomes a swamp in which attempts to act are matched by the inability to act. Their enormous power tied up in knots, the rulers of late capitalism tend to decide what they will not decide, not what they will. The public administration of late capitalism becomes weaker the stronger it appears to be, a contradiction ultimately caused by the gap between its political requirements and its administrative ideology.

THE ECLIPSE OF BENTHAMITE RATIONALITY

The existence of great potential power in the state but substantial impotence in practice has implications, not only on the way bureaucracies operate, but also on the way bureaucrats think they should operate. At an earlier period, a science of public administration—based on Benthamite principles—permeated the capitalist world. Even in the United States, where, as Chapter 1 pointed out, no theory of public administration took hold, there was still a Benthamite influence in certain areas, such as the work of Henry Lloyd in creating a modern army.[53] This logic was extreme in its rationality; one simply established a need that was in the public interest, created a governmental machinery corresponding to it, and then set about solving the problem. In this section I will argue that the political contradictions of late capitalism have undermined and transformed this Benthamite rationality. The state becomes victimized by irrationality in a fundamental sense. The extent of this irrationality can be examined by tracing, on the one hand, the decline of problem solving as a bureaucratic approach and the disappearance of the public interest as a bureaucratic motivation, and, on the other, the rise of a world of illusions and falsehoods as operating governmental realities.

The procedure by which a problem is identified before it can be solved would seem basic to a system of public administration. Yet there is every reason to doubt whether under conditions of late capitalism the state is able to proceed in precisely this fashion, due to two separate trends. On the one hand, the exhaustion of options characteristic of late capitalism results in a political theory of resignation that I will discuss below. The reformist zeal that allowed the Benthamites to describe themselves as "radical" is replaced by a vision that avoids identifying problems because to do so would be to admit the need for action. Hence the anti-Benthamites of modern administration make their mark by *denying* the need for or possibility of reform in one area after another. Presidents hire advisors to tell them, not what to do, but what not to do, as in the case of President Nixon's fascination with Edward Banfield's *The Unheavenly City*. But while this is going on, state activity is going up, not down, as more and more aspects of both civil society and the class struggle are subject to government purview. From this point of view, the "problems" the state is expected to examine become so numerous that the identification of any one specific one is lost in the morass. Between one trend that leads to the recognition of no problems and another that suggests infinite ones, the rationality of the Benthamite approach to problem solving is undermined.

The consequences of the decline of problem solving are serious. Instead of trying to rid the society of its noxious qualities, a vested administrative interest in preserving them develops. One reason why air polluters are allowed to fill vacancies to pollution control boards is not simply the self-interest involved, but also the need for public officials to ensure that the justification for their existence is perpetuated. This, in turn, contributes to the reversal of responsibility described in the previous section; since the task of the administrator is to preserve problems rather than to solve them, those who can pinpoint what is wrong must be punished and ignored. Furthermore, administrators, not having any guidelines for action based on factors external to themselves, develop purely internal ones. A major criterion for government action becomes the precedent of government action in the past, which means that mistakes and mismanagement become cumulative. Why, for example, did the Lockheed Corporation, which freely gave away money to foreign states, receive money from its own state? The answer lies in the peculiar domino theory in which one error leads to another:

> Despite its inefficiency and mismanagement, Lockheed was subsidized by the U.S. taxpayers because of its very size. Too much was at stake to permit Lockheed to fail—24,000 jobs, $215 billion in outstandiing contracts, and $240 million advanced by airlines. (The collapse of Lockheed, the banks argued in support of the rescue operation, would lead to the collapse of TWA.) [54]

Without problem solving, decisions become incremental, locked into historical events, and as a result, to quote Wildavsky, "problems are not so much solved as they are worn down by repeated attacks until they are no longer pressing or have been superseded by other problems." [55] Without a problem-solving approach, the ability of the state to chart new courses of action is minimized, stagnation sets in, and the tendency to avoid new breakthroughs in favor of business as usual is reinforced.

Closely related to the irrelevance of problem solving is the disappearance of the public interest. This is not to argue that there is, or ever was, such a thing as the public interest, merely to point out that under the Benthamite approach administrators operated on the basis that one existed that they understood. Their perception of what the public interest was often corresponded to the interests of the emerging bourgeoisie, but nonetheless the possession of such an ideology gave their actions a purposive dimension. As Franz Schurmann has noted, every bureaucracy can be understood as a contest between vision and purpose, on the one hand, and entrenched, self-serving interests, on the other. Managers try "to turn all politics into matters of interest," while traditional politicians try to transform matters of interest into visions. Visions democratize; in Schurmann's words, "ideology is the door through which the people enter the closed room of the realm of interests." [56] The decline of problem solving and the disappearance of a conception of the public interest resolve this contest in favor of pure self-interest at the expense of general goals, a tendency reinforced by the antipolitical character of late capitalism (see Chapter 9). What happens when a bureaucracy operates without a conception of the public interest? An argument can be made that the replacement of politicians by managers contributes to the rigidification of the late capitalist state in a way similar to the absence of a model of problem solving.

Most significantly, the decline of the public interest has a negative effect on the ability of the bureaucracy to legitimate itself. A bureaucracy without vision is a bureaucracy dominated by what Lowi has called "interest group liberalism," in which "modern law has become a series of instructions to administrators rather than a series of commands to citizens." [57] Under these conditions, the administrative system becomes increasingly elitist, as popular participation is denigrated in favor of administrative consultation. As a result, "with each significant expansion of government in the past century there has been a crisis of public authority." [58] In addition, when private interest triumphs over public visions, the administrative system loses its Benthamite clarity, for as LaPalombara has argued, "interest groups thrive in administrative situations that are muddy and confused." [59] Goals become blurred, divisions between departments lose their rationale, and the purposes of government actions are no longer clear, even for those who take them. Between these two trends, the exhaustion of alternatives characteristic of late capitalism is reinforced. The "efficiency" obtained by the administrative system is illusory because it is applied to a world that has lost its connection to the people over whom it is supposed to rule. A bureaucracy without vision is, in the final analysis, a bureaucracy without power.

The irony of this development is that the Benthamites, for all their proclaimed liberalism, never really believed in laissez-faire. Although in the economy some thought that the "invisible hand" might apply, in the state, all were agreed, it did not; it was necessary to have a conception of the public interest because one would never be generated naturally. Among contemporary anti-Benthamites the exact opposite is true; willing to support government intervention in the economy, they would prefer that relationships between bureaus in the state would be regulated by an invisible hand of competition and compromise. Aaron Wildavsky, perhaps our leading anti-Benthamite, makes a case for pluralism within government:

> A partial adversary system in which various interests compete for control of policy (under agreed upon rules) seems more likely to result in reasonable

decisions—that is, decisions that take account of the multiplicity of values involved—than one in which the best policy is assumed to be discoverable by a well-intentioned search for the public interest by everyone.[60]

In the context of late capitalism, Wildavsky is correct; given a situation of exhausted alternatives, the best for which one could hope is interest group liberalism. For precisely this reason, any change in the bureaucratic structure of the late capitalist state toward effective coordination and vision would, as Wildavsky understands, "be tantamount to a radical change in the national political system." [61]

The disappearance of both problem solving and a conception of the public interest must be compensated for, and in late capitalism what emerges in their place is a preoccupation with the politics of illusion. To be sure, illusions have always played a role in affairs of state. During the Absolutist Period, it was common to speak of an *arcana imperii* in order to distinguish between the genuine motives of rulers and those they presented to the public. Some writers, such as Thurman Arnold and Murray Edelman, have discussed an up-to-date version of this old-fashioned practice.[62] In their view, political leaders deliberately try to manipulate symbols in order to preserve their hegemony. Edelman in particular shows how numerous regulatory commissions work to instill political quiescence, because in any controversy between big business and the public, "it is not uncommon to give the rhetoric to one side and the decision to the other." Thus, "the administrative system, as symbol and ritual . . . serves as legitimizer of elite objectives, as reassurance against threats, and sometimes as catalyst of symbiotic ties between adversaries." [63]

One can nonetheless question whether elites would have the flexibility that would enable them to manipulate symbols with the free hand that Edelman envisions. Under late capitalism decision makers, instead of creating illusions for public consumption, become consumers themselves. Having spun so many myths, they come to believe in their own rhetoric, to the point where they manipulate illusions, not to convince the public, but to convince themselves. With the exhaustion of alternatives, public administrators become entrapped in their own symbolic world, which is increasingly divorced from the needs and concerns of the society at large. One example of this tendency grows out of the contradiction between increasing power and decreasing options. When a bureaucracy is unable to obtain its wishes, despite its apparent power, a preoccupation with a more controllable symbolic fantasy life is likely to result. During the Cuban missile crisis, numerous generals and high state officials tried to block the removal of U.S. missiles from Turkey, while the President and his advisors supported their being dismantled. A fierce bureaucratic struggle was waged, astounding in its intensity. The literal future of the world seemed to be at stake. Yet, and this defies understanding, all sides to the controversy agreed that the missiles in Turkey were of very little, if any, strategic importance.[64] Men were willing to blow up the world in order to preserve the sovereignty, not of their nation, but of their symbolic belief structure, a sign that they had lost the ability to distinguish between their own "real motives" and those they presented to the public.

The decline of the public interest also contributes to the miasma of illusions. As the bureaucracy conducts its business as if it were operating in its own private world, it develops—as any isolated tribe would—its own rituals, language, and systems of indirect communication. And just as any isolated culture is likely to intensify its devotion to its unique rituals when it feels threatened by the external world, the bureaucracy, faced with something called the public looming over its shoulder, becomes more attached to its symbols and rituals as the public demands to know what is going on. A good example of this phenomenon is Schurmann's discussion of how hearings over weapons systems take place in a kind of code, "in such a way that the coded signals are understood by the actors and not by the viewing public." [65] Though they may think they are fooling everyone else, the players of this game are fooling only themselves, because if their talk must be conducted in code, it is only a sign of their isolation and irrelevance.

The greater the isolation of the bureaucracy, the more ritualistic will be the behavior of the men who occupy positions within it. The proof of this dictum lies in the development of the Dual State, for the covert face of that experiment was the most isolated case of government created in the history of capitalist societies. Here were men hidden from public view, making decisions on the basis of information that only they possessed, and accountable only indirectly for the consequences of their decisions. Theoretically, this removal from the mass public should have enabled these men to act rationally. Actually, to the extent that their behavior has been revealed, they operated in complete contrast to Benthamite standards of right reason. The Kennedy men, for example, betrayed the most noticeable characteristic of extreme adolescence. They were faddists; if guerrilla war was the latest trend among the *cognoscenti*, then they all went out and became experts, or so they thought, on guerrilla war.[66] They were susceptible to flattery; it became essential to bureaucratic advancement to flatter one's superiors as ostentatiously as possible, especially including the President himself.[67] They were preoccupied with trivia; small details would be scrutinized, while large assumptions went unchecked. These traits were, if anything, intensified by Kennedy's successors. The Nixon men were morbidly status conscious; Jeb Magruder has described how punctilious H. R. Haldeman could be about the status hierarchy of golf carts, a concern comparable to the way teenagers in the 1950s would fight over who would ride "shotgun" (next to the driver) when they went out cruising.[68] They were also visibly juvenile; one thinks of G. Gordon Liddy exposing his gun the way deranged derelicts expose their private parts. They were attracted to surface appearances; Haldeman would publicly berate his aides for wearing ties with too much color.[69] In the inner world of the Dual State political leaders were infantilized, and if it were not for the maturity and sophistication of the "masses"—who demanded an end to both Vietnam and Watergate—who knows to what greater dangers the illusory world of men of state would have led?

Lest one conclude that juvenile behavior is restricted to the United States, Heclo and Wildavsky's examination of the British Treasury reveals many of the same characteristics among high policy makers. One gets the distinct impression that faddism is a way of life for these men. Consider the plight of a person whose one "flaw" is that he is not from London: "In a hundred different ways, the provincial can reveal that he is not intimately acquainted with current wisdom. He is likely to be written off, for an important part of merit in the eyes of judges is an awareness of current modes, even phases of thought, that are the special preserve of those 'in the know.' " [70] It is not expertise that matters in this characterization, but the opposite: familiarity with the latest fad. The obvious effect of a preoccupation with whatever is *au courant* is that it discourages the formation of independent judgments. Administrative routine becomes other-directed: "For those engaged in the day-to-day control of public spending, the most important way of assessing climate is deceptively simple; they watch the run of decisions." [71] When faddism is strong, not only is rational decision making undermined, but the accompanying distrust of independent judgment reinforces tendencies toward stagnation. A politics of illusion is rarely a politics of dynamic movement.

Ultimately, the politics of illusion becomes a politics of falsehood. The decision maker learns that lies are more highly valued than truths, and the collective work of the bureaucracy becomes the ritualistic construction of myths that most men know to be false but that the conditions of their work force them to accept as true. When Daniel Patrick Moynihan argued for the adoption of a guaranteed income plan, he also proposed a strategy to avoid the negative implications of such a proposal: "But nothing required that a guaranteed income be *called* a guaranteed income. . . . Accordingly, the President declared that the Family Assistance Plan was *not* a guaranteed income." [72] Of course, as Moynihan goes on to say, both the President and his advisors knew perfectly well that what they denied was a guaranteed income plan was precisely that. In like fashion, Aaron Wildavsky has issued a series of guidelines to administrators in order to help them obtain their goals. Among the various suggestions—which read like a public administrator's version of Stephen Potter's *One-Upmanship* trilogy—is lying, which Wildavsky, following his own advice, calls exaggeration. "On balance, it seems desirable to accept the disabilities flowing from exaggeration in order to reap the benefits of quick response to emergent needs." [73] The isolation of the bureaucracy from the public under late capitalism, combined with the state of war comparable to a free market economy within the government, places a premium on untruth and makes myth weaving a virtue. Administrators internalize the message of Warren Avis: "It is unprofitable to be honest." [74]

If men of state were able to maintain the distinction between truth and falsehood, this whole matter would be Machiavellian and therefore neither new nor noteworthy. But it is unique, for just as officials believe their own illusions, eventually they accept as true what they had originally held to be false. Entrapped by their own lies, their ability to govern becomes hindered by the by-now-almost-instinctive tendency to hide the truth from themselves. Like hardened criminals, lying becomes so automatic to late capitalist officials that their sincerity could fool the best polygraph. Once again, the clearest example is furnished by those at the pinnacle of the Dual State, ostensibly those freest from any public pressure that would cause them to lie. Yet such "rational" men as Lieutenant General Paul D. Harkins regularly began falsifying intelligence reports after 1961. [75] Harkins and the military did not want negative information, which left them two choices: they could change the world itself or they could change reports of what the world was like. Unable to alter the former, they decided to manipulate the latter. And they were not alone. Ultimately, the entire policy-making machinery began to lie to itself, in a way graphically pictured by David Halberstam. Describing the policy makers' judgment that the Diem regime in South Vietnam could be popular with its own people, Halberstam wrote:

> They knew that this judgement was false, but they never challenged it, because of their own previous wishful thinking, because of their inability to control their own bureaucracy, and because above all, of a belief that telling the truth to the American people was unimportant. They—both Kennedys, Rusk, Lodge, Harriman, Hilsman, Truehart, Forrestal—knew the war was being lost, but they never got it down on paper or into their own statements, or into their briefings with congressional leaders. A lie had become a truth, and the policy makers were trapped in it; their policy was a failure, and they could not admit it. [76]

Lying, which in the Machiavellian tradition gives leaders flexibility, has the opposite effect when liar and victim become the same person. Rigidity and blockage triumph where flexibility fails. As Arendt has pointed out, "For the trouble with lying and deceiving is that their efficiency depends entirely upon a clear notion of the truth that the liar and deceiver wishes to hide. In this sense truth, even if it does not prevail in public, possesses an ineradicable primacy over all falsehoods." Consequently, "in the realm of politics, where secrecy and deliberate deception have always played a significant role, self-deception is the danger par excellence; the self-deceived deceiver loses all contact with not only his audience, but also the real world, which still will catch up with him, because he can remove his mind from it but not his body." [77] Just because the men who habitually lie become so isolated from the people over whom they are ruling, their ability to control the world is diminished. Thus, the politics of illusion and falsehood are caused by, and in turn cause, the trend toward the exhaustion of options so relevant to the political life of late capitalism.

Benthamite rationality, appropriate for the capitalist state when it was in its dynamic period, is counterproductive to a society in which the basic political options have been exhausted. Men of state substitute fantasy for reality and truth for falsity, not because they are bad men, but because the political contradictions of their society leave them no alternative. Although the rulers of late capitalism justify the eclipse of Benthamite rationality by claiming that the lack of firm standards allows them the flexibility to govern, in actuality the triumph of irrationality within the state becomes more an indication of how locked in the rulers are by the contradictions that they themselves played a role in producing.

REIFICATION AND RESIGNATION

The ambiguities, confusions, and irrationalities of the late capitalist state adversely affect the quest for legitimation. In order to continue to rule without challenge, late capitalist elites need an institution that can make it appear that the political contradictions of the society either do not exist or are being resolved. But where is such an institution to be found? The firm cannot be called upon, because it is ordered by the logic of private property, which, by definition, precludes a public role. The Church cannot do it, because the mode of production has rationalized the society in increasingly secular fashion. The family cannot perform the task because of its particularity. Consequently, the only institution that can be called upon to resolve the contradictions taking place within the state is the state itself, and each time it tries to do this, it further intensifies these contradictions, thus requiring even more state intervention. The state is called upon to prove that class tensions do not exist at the moment when the state is immobilized by those very tensions. Only the state, the object of class struggle, can appear to be above class struggle. The self-proclaimed spokesmen for each class, businessmen as well as labor leaders, wish the state to be both partisan and nonpartisan, to serve their specific interests and to serve the general interest at the same time. Hence the late capitalist state can satisfy its class interest only by being universal and can be universal only by fulfilling its class character. The state is part of the problem and part of the solution at the same time.

The task of the late capitalist state, in short, is an impossible one, to be both one thing and another simultaneously. Its Sisyphean character leads to a transformation in the way it is perceived. One would think that an institution charged with an impossible mission would be denigrated, and to some extent this is true. A school of thought, which I will call the political theory of resignation, develops, holding that state action is incapable of bringing about any fundamental change. But many of the members of this school once held the opposite position, and in their writings is a sureness of position that converts so often possess. The fact is that before disenchantment with the state set in, affirmation was the more likely reaction. The more common argument is that the state can do what no other institution is capable of doing, which is to ensure social peace in a class society. In general, defenders of public order ascribe more and more power and ability to the state, hoping that it can perform an alchemy that will magically quell all tensions and bring about a utopia within the existing class structure. Thus, the contradictions of the late capitalist state bring about, not unexpectedly, a contradictory response; the state is praised and the state is blamed; the state is the answer to all problems and the answer to none. In both cases, the state is no longer accepted for what it is but is assigned extrahuman powers, the sublimity of heaven or the intractability of hell. For this reason, both alternatives can be seen as similar responses to an identical problem, no matter how divergent their prescriptions.

A central political development of late capitalist society has been an increase in the tendency to view the state as capable of solving problems that lie outside its competence. As the ascription of ability and magical powers to the state fails to solve these problems, advocates of statization press their claim for even stronger potions, producing a cycle in which impotence results in calls for greater potency, which bring about higher levels of impotence. The more the state fails, the more it is worshipped, and the more it is worshipped, the greater will be its failure. I will call the process by which the state is assigned a wide variety of mythic powers the reification of the state.[78]

The reification of the state is a key aspect of the political life of late capitalist societies. To be sure, there has long been a tendency to worship the state by assigning it extraordinary powers, beginning with Plato, modernizing itself with Bodin, Machiavelli, and Hobbes, perfecting itself in the absolutist monarchies, and reappearing in contemporary fascism. These can be considered examples of a premodern form of reification, for in each case the state was ascribed greater power in order to satisfy an end outside of itself: in Plato, the search for justice; in early modern political philosophy, the idea of the nation; in absolutism, the will of God; and in fascism, the glory of *das Volk*. One of Max Weber's contributions to political sociology was to show how the process of rationalization stripped away these justifications, leaving the state naked as an instrument of power, the monopoly of the legitimate means of violence. In this context, reification takes place when state power is justified as an end in itself and not as a means to some other end. To defend the state because it promotes the preservation of order is to engage in this type of reification; since the definition of the state is that it alone preserves order, to justify it on this ground is tautological. The state is good because it is the state. The same kind of reasoning applies to those who defend the state as the embodiment of the national interest, when they also view that interest as codeterminous with the state. Such kinds of modern, secularized reification will most likely occur when two conditions are present: first, extensive social conflict forces a reliance on the state that makes questions of government authority important; and, second, an element of democratization requires a theory of legitimation. These conditions are associated with late capitalism, which is why the reification of the state is not a relic of feudal society but a matter of importance to modern capitalist life. The reification of the state can become the tangible expression of the exhaustion of political alternatives.

The modern forms of the reification of the state seem to have been developed in two stages. First, in the years when class conflict seemed so disruptive that capitalist societies were in danger of falling apart, political thinkers began to view the state as the answer to social cohesion. While one can detect this tendency as early as Hegel, and in mid-century followers of his philosophy like Matthew Arnold ("The state is of the religion of all its citizens without the fanaticism of any of them"),[79] the most important period in this first stage of development was just before and after World War I. Changes in both conservative and reformist thinking led to a reevaluation of the state. Within conservatism, the state was rediscovered to provide an organic whole that would ameliorate the anarchy and extreme parochialism of liberal society. Whether we consider Durkheim in France, Mosca-Pareto-Michels in Italy, Heinrich von Treitschke in Germany ("The State . . . is not only a high moral good in itself, but it is also the assurance for the people's endurance. Only through it can their moral development be perfected, for the living sense of citizenship inspires the community in the same way as a sense of duty inspires the individual"),[80] or Haldane (influenced by Bluntschli and Bosanquet of an earlier generation) in England, the conservative revival was a direct response to class conflict. Similarly, among reformers, whether of the liberal or socialist variety, there was a fascination with the state. Inheritors of *solidarité* like Clemenceau, plus the Webbs, the Socialists of the Chair, and men like Richard Ely in the United States seemed to join the conservatives in viewing the state as the answer to problems caused by class conflict. Not since the period of absolutism had the state enjoyed such a revival.

Because it grew out of a concern with either conservative organicism or liberal reformism, this first stage in the modern reification of the state was ideological, based upon explicit principles. But as various forms of the capitalist state began to reveal limitations, the justification for state action increasingly became nonideological. Holders of state power became concerned not with the ends of state action but with performance, state activity as a task in its own right. Coming to power at a time when ideology was discredited anyway, they argued that state power was good simply because it was state power. Some examples of the modern attempt to reify the state should give some indication of the importance of this development to the late capitalist state.

Three of the most common forms taken by the reification of the state are personification, objectification, and epicization. *Personification* represents a reversal in the ascription of power, for rather than viewing the state as growing out of the activity of people, its activity is personified, given human characteristics, while the activity of people is depersonalized and made instrumental to the state. The roots of personification lie in the approach of men like Durkheim, to whom the state was an "organism," charged with the responsibility of "thinking." [81] To the extent that people have any human characteristics at all, it is only because the state, the "prime mover" of society, gives it to them:

> It is the State that has rescued the child from patriarchal domination and from family tyranny; it is the State that has freed the citizen from feudal groups and later from communal groups; it is the State that has liberated the craftsman and his master from guild tyranny.[82]

One legacy of the Durkheimian personification of the state occurred during the Nixon presidency. As Jonathan Schell has noted, Nixon reversed the relationship between state and citizen.[83] Rather than the latter having rights and claims against the former, the former was given rights against the latter. To Nixon, the state was a person that had the right of free speech, the right to defend itself, and (in practice) the right to make substantial profits. The citizen, on the other hand, was at his best when "silent," for true freedom was realized by allowing the President, as the embodiment of the state/citizen, to speak for him. The basic tenets of eighteenth-century liberal philosophy were thereby reversed, all in the interest of trying to find a rationale for the exercise of power when most rationales had been used up.

In contrast with personification, the *objectification* of the state takes place when the state is assigned characteristics that make it seem a concrete thing as opposed to the instrument of the people's will. Mechanistic conceptions of society are generally associated with the objectification of the state, for if society is conceived of as a machine, then the state becomes a homeostatic valve, making adjustments here and there in order to keep the machine in operation. Technocracy has contributed a good deal to the objectification of the state, as has the "little black box" of the systems approach to political science.[84] In practice, one of the more common forms of this objectification is the ideology of the professional civil servant, particularly in places like the French Grands Corps d'Etat; higher civil servants often see themselves as perfecting that intricate mechanism known as the state so that society can operate more smoothly. Since the state becomes an object, they are clinical, neutral, and full of expertise, repairing the body politic the way an automobile mechanic would repair a car. The "thingness" of the state is rarely so well articulated as in the political theory of the professional administrator.

Finally, the *epicization* of the state refers to the process by which political figures, rather than being seen as public *servants*, are transformed into public *heroes*, generally of epic dimensions. There is something quaint and also positive about the notion of a public servant, for it expresses the idea that those who hold power do so at the bidding of the people who put them there. As subordinates, power holders should be grateful for whatever favors the public chooses to give them. With the reification of the state, the concept of a public servant undergoes a thorough transformation into its opposite. The power holder is the master, and the general public the servant. "We" should be thankful for whatever "they" give us, for we are at their mercy even though, in theory, they are at ours. Hero worshipping men of state is one of the primary ways that this tranformation takes place. One clear example was the coming of the Kennedy Administration, for those who took power in 1961 deliberately set out to write epic poems about their man. His untimely death, like that of Houseman's dying athlete, cut short his achievements but that stimulated the epicization even more. Arthur Schlesinger's *Thousand Days* is a contemporary *Chanson de Roland*, a vast song of praise to the conquering hero, as he sits in his oval office contemplating the future of mankind. During the missile crisis, the single most important event in epicizing the American President, Robert Kennedy looked at his brother and thought, "For a few fleeting seconds, it was almost as though no one else was there and he was no longer the President." [85] The joke was on the Attorney General, for his brother was not "the President"; he was simply a man doing his job, which became clear in a moment of crisis only to be lost again as events returned to "normal." The epicization of the state is a complex process that has taken place in many contexts, but a good deal of the conscious myth weaving associated with it can be attributed to the cynicism of the Kennedy presidency.

The reification of the state can also be viewed through the writings of some of its most representative advocates. One example from France and several from the United States should be indicative. In proposing a political program for the Fifth Republic, Michel Debré argued that the old state, located in the traditional ministries, was being superseded (*dépassé*) by a new one responsive to new needs, such as railways, automobile manufacturing, electricity and gas, and so on. These tasks create an opportunity "which no other collective organism can fulfill," but at the same time the administrative and financial responsibilities yield "a political problem whose seriousness for the future of France is just beginning to make itself felt." It is a good thing, Debré implies, that men like Debré are around to be "of service to the nation." [86] Debré has written voluminously about himself and the state (to some extent they appear inseparable in his mind), yet through all the words one cannot find a single rationale for his activity that is not either a cliché (the values preserved by the state are "order, justice and good administration") [87] or a tautology ("The State is, above all else, a political authority possessing an elevated sense of collective responsibility, and organizing, in order to meet this responsibility, those services and men which have constituted, throughout the centuries, the entity 'State' "). [88] It is almost as if, knowing somewhere in his heart that his defense of state power has no real rationale, he feels called upon, like the Flying Dutchman, to proclaim his message to any who will listen. Debré's various writings constitute an excellent example of reification in late capitalism because they contain a passionate defense of state action matched only by a general neglect of the purposes toward which that action might be directed.

In the United States, to take a second example, the Nixon presidency represented the flowering of the reification of the state. Not only did Nixon continuously personify the state, but he took concrete steps to make that personification a reality. Nixon's domestic policy represented nothing less than a brazen attempt to centralize all state power in his own hands, first through denigrating Congress (impoundment) and then by "reorganizing" the executive branch in centralized fashion (the Urban Affairs Council, the Ash Commission, OMB, etc.). In matters of internal "security," Nixon attempted to create a system of surveillance directed by the White House (the Huston Plan) while working toward the destruction of the independence of both the CIA and the FBI. Internationally, the making of foreign policy became a dialogue between the Secretary of State and the President, with the results sometimes announced *ex post facto* and sometimes never announced at all. Between an ideology that exalted the state (often in the name of freedom from it) and a series of policies that gave this ideology life, the reification of the state achieved a life of its own under Nixon.

Yet what Nixon attempted was not far removed from the theory and practice of his immediate predecessors. This is not the place for an extensive review of how the state came to be exalted in modern American thought, but a few important points can be noted. In foreign affairs, the post-Niebuhr "realists," holding that any action in defense of the national interest was justified, provided one ingredient. At home, the post-Schumpeter theorists of democracy, frightened by their studied misreading of the experience of European totalitarianism, developed models of state power that excluded mass participation.[89] Reacting to what Edward A. Purcell called "the crisis of democratic theory," [90] American political science on the one hand began to justify all existing political institutions and on the other began to write manuals in praise of organized political power. Two expressions of the new attitude, one academic and one popular, were indicative of the reification of the state. Richard Neustadt's *Presidential Power*, with its fawning, neo-Machiavellian style, counseled presidents that they would best serve the national interest by quenching their own insatiable thirst for power. Theodore White, chronicler, not of the court but of access to the court, and the man who probably had the single greatest impact in shaping popular notions about the presidency, engaged in his own form of epicization:

> I've been in the White House, in and out, now under five Presidents, and I'm always scared when I speak to a President. Some people go in there and freeze up and they forget what they're going to ask the President.... I always have that sense of awe, so that normally, if I do want to speak to a President, I will send a note in advance saying "I want to talk to you about this and this and this...." The White House is an eerie place. It's so quiet and so hushed and so beautiful.[91]

Attitudes like those of Neustadt and White were just as fervently believed in by the men who held power. Even better than Schlesinger-Sorensen raptures are McGeorge Bundy's Godkin Lectures, given at Harvard in March 1968. At a time when both Kennedy and Johnson, under Bundy's urging, had dangerously centralized power in ways from which Nixon would learn, Bundy wrote that "the American system of government is today far too weak to do the job now assigned it, let alone the job it ought to be doing." As presidential power was making representative government a sham, Bundy argued that "the Executive Branch is . . . dangerously weak in its own internal capacity for sustained, coordinated and energetic action." [92] Three years before Nixon announced plans to centralize the cabinet under his personal control, Bundy proposed a cabinet reform that would have accomplished the identical end. When it came to the purpose for which all this centralized power was to be used, Bundy stumbled. The aim of government, he announced, was to promote freedom, but freedom was never defined, except where he confused it with efficiency, the ability to accomplish things.[93] In short, power must be concentrated, though the reasons why are never provided. If, as I pointed out in Chapter 6, the enhancement of the Dual State under Nixon was based on the actions of men like Bundy, then to a significant extent the notion of the pursuit of power for its own sake, so embodied by Nixon, had its origin in Bundyism as well.

The ironic thing is that in many ways Bundy is correct; government is too weak to do its job, although the primary cause of that weakness is its apparent strength. For this reason, Bundy's proposals to strengthen government would make it weaker still. But more important than locating ways out of the *cul-de-sac* of late capitalism is the symbolic significance of the reification of the state. To praise a process rather than a result, which is what men like Debré and Bundy are doing, is to reveal an utter bankruptcy of political ideas. The reification is to the realm of thought what the exhaustion of alternatives is to the realm of practice. It is no surprise that men who possess vast apparent power but are impotent in using it are also men who glorify power without any sense of the purposes for which that power might be exercised. The reification of the state consequently signifies the process by which the late capitalist state has painted itself into a corner.

Eventually it became increasingly difficult to reify a state whose accomplishments were meager. Bundy's call for a strengthening of government was heeded, but with little practical results. Internationally, the centralization of the Dual State did not help America control the world; if anything, American hegemony declined as government was strengthened. Reforms designed to counter the sprawl of bureaucracy did not bring about cheaper government, more easily managed in the direction of rationality. Each reform, in fact, seemed only to increase government expenditures, culminating in the phenomenon of Republican presidents like Nixon and Ford presiding over the largest budgets ever submitted. Reified as it may have been, the state became, in Nixon's famous words, a "pitiful, helpless giant." Consequently, given the lack of principles so characteristic of bourgeois ideology, those who once advocated state action turned around and began to question their previous commitment. The reification of the state turned into its opposite, and public philosophers became as skeptical about government power as they once were enthusiastic.

In other words, with public policy in both Europe and the United States subject to increasing blockage and paralysis, there arose what could be called a political theory of resignation. Signs of the new mood are everywhere. In a dramatic policy reversal, perhaps the most important political event in the last thirty years, the British Labour Party announced that it was prepared to "roll back" the welfare state in an attempt to cut the role of government.[94] Likewise, in the American presidential campaign of 1976, politicians promised to be antigovernment, a contradiction if there ever was one, and those who had the greatest success divorced themselves most thoroughly from the state. As President, Jimmy Carter presides over a state apparatus he has been criticizing. Even in the Scandinavian countries, where welfare state principles have formed part of the political consensus, critics of state action are showing signs of success, such as Mogens Glistrup of Denmark. The state is no longer being accepted as the *deus ex machina* of social contradictions.

The new political mood has received its intellectual justification in the form of writers who are calling for "a retreat from objectives." [95] Reform, it is argued, is hopeless because government can never bring about fundamental change due to the inevitable tendency of vested groups to preserve their own power. Instead of vision, Daniel Patrick Moynihan argues, policy makers need the short-term management of crisis, or simply "coping." [96] Far better to "muddle through" with existing machinery than to create desires among the population that cannot be satisfied. Caution has become the watchword: "The polity must take care what it undertakes to provide, for failure to do so is likely to be attributed to malevolent purpose. This is not to say that expectations should not be raised, but only that they should not be raised indiscriminately." [97] Explaining what he called "the fiasco of the welfare state," Peter Drucker warned that "government is sick" and that reform might be better accomplished through "reprivatization" than through new public policies.[98] A significant body of opinion, ironically centered around a magazine called *The Public Interest*, took the lead in arguing the position that the limitations facing reform in domestic policy are such that resignation to the status quo was the only rational alternative.

It *is* extremely difficult to mobilize the energy of the late capitalist state in the direction of reform, especially when changes will conflict with vested interests. The major problem of the political theory of resignation is not its analysis, which is accurate, but its lack of a valid explanation of why government seems so locked in and unable to operate with panache. Sometimes what Aaron Wildavsky calls "fundamental facts about human perception" are felt to be the key; a budgetary process that is specialized, fragmented, based on previous allocations, repetitive, and sequential is, according to him, more in accord with those perceptions than one based on the public interest and standards of rationality.[99] Often the theory of veto groups is borrowed from David Riesman, and the blame is laid on the mutually canceling power that private groups exercise in a pluralistic, democratic society.[100] This is certainly better than human perception, for such groups do often exercise a veto power, but this only describes what occurs and does not explain it. The real question concerns the structural factors that gave private groups this veto power, for they did not always have it. Finally, the anomie of modern life is generalized to the point where cause is transcended. The sickness of government applies everywhere throughout the world, Drucker says, thereby ignoring not only the manifest public energy of Cuba and China (which can be accused of many things, but government inactivity is not one), but also that of British Columbia and Jamaica. In short, the political theory of resignation is a correct perception of the politics of exhaustion characteristic of late capitalism, not a theory of why stagnation is taking place.

As the opposite of reification of the state, the political theory of resignation also completes it. Both views of the state are reactions to the political contradictions of late capitalism, for both indicate how problematic the political search for answers to economic and social contradictions has become. So long as the late capitalist state is expected to resolve irresolvable tensions, the contradictions of its existence will produce contradictory expectations about its performance. A cycle of praise and blame for the state is likely to be a conspicuous feature of the political life of late capitalism, reflecting a cycle of increased power and decreased options. The modern state is indeed a unique phenomenon, but its particularity lies more in its contradictions than in its capabilities.

9 / Alienated Politics

"The degradation which has come up in the words 'politics' and 'politicians' in their American use marks a degeneration in political methods which deserves the attention of every lover of his country. 'Politics' has become simply the work of managing a party for its own advantage or that of its leaders; and the term 'politician' is applied only to the campaign directly; the local committeeman, the appointment-broker—in short, to men who manage parties and distribute the public offices."

American Century *magazine* (1887)

"One of the things I tried hard to keep out of the campaign was foreign policy. There should be no break in the bipartisan foreign policy of the United States at any time—particularly during a national election. I even asked that a teletype machine be set up in the Dewey train so that the Republican candidate personally could be informed on all foreign developments as they progressed."

Harry Truman, Memoirs (1955)

"The political rights of citizenship, unlike the civil rights, were full of potential danger to the capitalist system, although those who were cautiously extending them down the social scale probably did not quite realize how great the danger was."

T. H. Marshall (1963)

THE POLITICS OF POLITICS

IN DECEMBER 1973, as had happened every December for thirty-nine years, football buffs attended the ceremony at which the Heisman trophy —given to the college football player of greatest ability—was awarded to John Cappelletti, a halfback for Penn State. The ceremony, held at the New York Hilton, featured a speech by then Vice President Gerald Ford. Mr. Ford praised football because its "spirit of individualism" was a needed ingredient to the American character. "Show me a nation in which the spirit of individualism has been stifled," Mr. Ford said, "and I will show you a society in which the desire to excel has been extinguished." The event was routine, including the story in the *New York Times*, which noted that the Vice President's speech was "unpolitical." [1]

The clear implication of this little anecdote is that to many people the

288

term "politics" is reserved for the ways in which men compete for public office. Anything else—such as citizenship, ideology, values, legitimacy, and obedience, all essential ingredients of Mr. Ford's speech—must be called something else. Yet the decision to apply the definition of politics to some kinds of activities rather than others is bound to have important implications. If politics concerns only the struggle for office, then a man like Richard Nixon would have to be called, as he called himself, a political man par excellence. If, on the other hand, politics were to be defined as the sincere quest for a viable human community, then the same Richard Nixon would be considered one of the least political men ever to live in the White House, for his actions during his six-and-one-half-year occupancy indicate that forms of cooperative activity were not his *specialité*. The question must be asked, then, how a society comes to apply one particular definition of politics and not another. No given conception of the "political" should be seen as ideologically neutral, to be accepted as it appears on the surface with no questions asked. The process through which any society decides which acts, ideas, institutions, practices, and persons are to be called political and which are to be relegated to the nonpolitical is itself a political act. What is needed is a politics of politics; before the political dynamics of late capitalist society can be grasped, politics itself must be politically analyzed.

A politics of politics did exist at one time. As Hannah Arendt reminds us, the Greeks—who in a sense invented the modern notion of the political—specified very carefully what was included and excluded from its purview.[2] Any events that were the result of mere chance, which took place at a level lower than the state (like the family), which concerned the satisfaction of wants and necessities rather than ideals, which were preoccupied by questions of efficiency and means rather than ultimate ends, and which (surprisingly) dealt with the relationship between rulers and ruled were *not* considered part of what the Greeks meant by *politikē*. In short, the ancient Athenians offer an example of how deeply a particular definition of politics can affect the social life of a society. To them, a political community was one in which a group of people who were roughly equal, and who lived under conditions in which both internal needs and external security were satisfied, pursued in common fashion the attainment of the good society, one they defined as containing *eleutheria* (happiness or freedom) and *autarkeia* (self-sufficiency). Based as it was on a preindustrial slave-owning, small-scale world, the Greek experience is totally irrelevant to modern capitalism, but its process of defining politics does constitute a standard against which all societies can compare themselves.

How do modern capitalist societies stand up against the Greeks in the self-consciousness of their political conceptions? The answer is intimately connected to the nature and extent of class conflict. The emerging bourgeoisie had advanced its own theories of politics as it sought control over the state. In contrast to the organic philosophies of the *ancien régime*, the liberal conception of politics was primarily instrumental, emphasizing the secular ends that could be obtained through political action. For this reason, theorists like Locke went far, as Carole Pateman has argued, to transform the traditional Western meaning of politics into one more compatible with an individualist conception of order.[3] If the Greek definition is used as the standard of what constitutes politics, the triumph of liberalism was antipolitical; with liberalism what Wolin calls "the erosion of the distinctly political" becomes a feature of political life.[4] Although liberalism gave rise to important and articulate political philosophers, the position they were defending with rigorous logic and passion was a retreat from the most well defined politics of politics in the West.

If the instrumental character of liberalism gave it an antipolitical tinge, democratic theory began with a notion of political purpose that bore greater resemblance to the Greek ideal, even though the latter was notoriously undemocratic. A democratic thinker like Rousseau, for example, found in the city-state the ideal solution to the problem of community. But democracy was as much a political movement of the lower classes as it was a Rousseauian ideal, and with the making of a working class in the nineteenth century, a new, visionary energy was directed into the political process that conflicted with the instrumental, practical conceptions of the bourgeoisie. The working class made not only democracy possible, but politics as well, for the presence of a majority class forced the political system to confront questions of its ultimate direction and purpose. One important consequence of the class struggle in the nineteenth century was to pose anew the question of what kinds of activity were to be included within any conception of the political, as examples from a number of countries can illustrate.

One of the clearest examples of the energizing effect that the rise of the working class had on conceptions of politics took place in France. In the early part of the nineteenth century, village politics remained under the domination of local notables, who organized political life in paternalistic fashion; it was not uncommon for local landlords to win office by lopsided, even unanimous, margins. Under the pressure of urbanization and industrialization, the nature of political activity began to change, especially during and immediately after the revolution of 1848. Large numbers of people, writes Theodore Zeldin, "entered political life with enthusiasm. . . . Paris was alive in these days in a way which has only been repeated in two or three critical periods since." Energy was the dominant motif. "In the clubs and cafés also, they gave themselves up to interminable discussion, and some pretty effective organization."[5] In short, politicization had occurred, and consequently the relationship between social classes could never again be the same. Each expression by the working class of its political vision had to be met with resistance, and French politics became characterized by extreme swings between what Zolberg has called "moments of madness" [6]—liberating periods such as the Paris Commune when a new politics seemed possible—and the ordinary political life of a Second Empire or Third Republic. Moreover, a mobilizing conception of politics dominated the political left whatever the tendency of the bourgeois world. Despite his idiosyncrasies and flights of demagoguery, Jules Guesde possessed a conception of politics that was revolutionary in its approach to politics. In the Nord and the Pas de Calais, the Guesdists built a strong party organization, which ultimately "became the largest single socialist party in France in the late nineteenth century." [7] Moreover, the reason for this was that his party penetrated the

> local life of the textile towns to an extraordinary degree, and used traditional festivals and recreational societies for the service of the party. It organized balls, concerts, county fetes, competitions, billiards and card games, dramatic societies and shooting clubs, and in this way gave a new revolutionary content to traditional social activities.[8]

The urge to politicize was a creative urge, which challenged not only the rule of the bourgeoisie but its increasingly deenergizing conception of politics as well. So powerful was the urge that even explicitly nonpolitical movements of dissent like the Syndicalists wound up creating various *bourse de travail* that, in their promotion of collective social life, politicized in spite of their disdain for voting and elections.[9] In France the working class, democratization, and politicization all proceeded together.

Similar changes took place in England. In contrast to many interpretations, it was not the Reform Act of 1832 that revolutionized English politics; as Gash has shown, many of the nefarious prereform electoral practices continued until the 1850s.[10] By bringing the middle classes into an aristocratic political life, the Reform Act broadened the suffrage but did not change the fundamentally paternalistic electoral system that confronted a radical like Felix Holt. Intimidation, violence, and drunkenness remained aspects of village political life until the second half of the century. What did revolutionize politics in England was the organized power of the working class; in this context the most convenient symbol for the change was not the Reform Act, but the passing of power from the Liberal to the Labour Party. It was not the policies of the Liberals that made them increasingly irrelevant; in fact, many Liberals were prepared to go beyond some of the socialists in the name of reform. Of far greater importance was the fact that the Liberal Party was based on a conception of politics that was not compatible with the energizing effects of a politically emancipated working-class and feminist movement. In order for a politics from below to be expressed, liberalism had to be bypassed, either through unions (which formed the basis of the Labour

Party) or through the kind of extraparliamentary but highly politicized activities of the Pankhursts.[11] In short, as Henry Pelling has argued, "long-run changes involved in the transformation of politics"[12] were responsible for the demise of one party and the rise of another. Although the examples are less graphic than they were in France, Britain also experienced a conflict between bourgeois and working-class (or, in the case of feminism, dissenting) conceptions of politics.

In the United States, where democratization had been worrying writers since Madison and de Tocqueville, the potential liberating power of the working class was to some extent held in check by urban political machines. The "boss" depoliticized his followers, winning their passivity in exchange for benefits. A notion of politics that was as cynical as it was corrupt prevented any clear-cut challenge between one kind of politics and another. Nonetheless, class struggle over conceptions of politics was real enough to have an impact. For one thing the machines were, in spite of their depoliticized character, responsive to some of the social needs of working-class communities, and therefore they constituted a threat, however minimal, to bourgeois hegemony; as I will show municipal reformers found the machines in violation of their own conceptions of depoliticization. Second, late-nineteenth-century politics, in contrast with today's, was far more mobilizing. American politics then, according to Walter Dean Burnham, involved "an extremely full mobilization of the potential electorate."[13] With all its flaws, the character of this participation was surprisingly serious-minded. Elections tended to be organized around issues of importance to the community. Positions were distinct among the candidates and communicated to the voters. Some face-to-face interaction was achieved despite the great size of the country; 13 percent of those Republicans who voted for William McKinley in 1896 visited his home during the campaign, a fascinating example of a small-scale conception of politics operating in a large-scale political system.[14] The political rally, captured in the painting of Thomas Hart Benton, remained part of the social life of the community. Even for the political system at large, democratization had something of an energizing effect when compared with later periods. Finally, politicization was highest among those working-class parties most explicitly identified with the left. As the research of Charles Leinenweber has shown, the New York Socialist Party created and sustained a street culture in the early years of the twentieth century that included not only oratory, but community activities and cultural ones of a more general nature.[15] There may have been no "golden age" of American politics, but without question the emergence of an American working class stimulated political life.

In the first part of this book I tried to show how the divergent theories of government inherent in liberalism and democracy formed the character of the capitalist state. The same is true for a politics of politics. The conception of politics that society adopted was formed by the struggle between the energizing, politicizing tendencies within democracy and the instrumental, antipolitical strain within liberalism. In a liberal democratic system, in other words, one will likely find two contradictory conceptions of politics fighting with each other for hegemony. Consequently, the energy released by democratization at the end of the nineteenth century was found by dominant elites to constitute a threat, not only to their rule, but to their conceptions of politics as well. The resulting struggle over the *nature* of politcal action was fully as important as struggles over its results.

The liberal attack on democratic political notions toward the end of the nineteenth century has been extensively studied, particularly for the United States. Richard Jensen has argued that political campaigns changed from "militarist," based on highly mobilized electorates, to "mercantilist," based on coalitions of interest group leaders.[16] In this transformation to a *less* broadly based electorate, the legal reforms associated with Progressivism played a major role, as Arthur Lipow has brilliantly argued.[17] From the standardization of the ballot, which took the party out of the business of printing it, to the direct primary, which wreaked irreversible harm on minor parties, these reforms—issued in the name of "democratization"—succeeded in making party affairs the concern of a few. The tradition of civic reform that sought the elimination of both corruption and working-class militancy transformed the political system according to the same principles by which it was revising the corporate order. Just as both unruly workers and excessively rapacious businessmen were bad for an ordered system of business affairs, political parties and their accompanying democratic surges would harm a stabilized, well-ordered political world. Thus, according to Burnham, the factors leading to the transformation of active nineteenth-century politics "were, in the main, devices by which a large and possibly dangerous mass electorate could be brought to heel and subjected to management and control within the political system appropriate to 'capitalist democracy.'"[18] Burnham's insight has been extended in a fascinating essay by Samuel Hayes, who has argued that "the movement for political reform was an attack on the entire party system as it had developed in the nineteenth century, a rejection of community involvement in decision-making, and a demand that public discussion be made through mechanisms other than the political party. It stemmed from fear of rather than faith in community political impulses." Local party structures, because of their democratic base, were, according to Hayes, incompatible with an emerging corporate order based on "initiative from the top down, not from the bottom up or the middle out." Between parties that were politicized, activist, local, and colorful and business corporations that were impersonal, passive, national, and routinized, the choice for reformers was clear: "The reformer's model was the business corporation, not the political party." [19] The bourgeoisie found politics distasteful, even subversive, to its purposes. The businessman's distrust of politics achieves its "takeoff" point here.

Another reason for the decline of an energizing politics can be found in the transformation of work. Since Adam Smith and David Ricardo discovered the ideal political system in those arrangements bearing closest resemblance to the free market, there has existed a rather close link between the life of the worker and the life of the citizen; as T. H. Marshall expressed it, "Civil rights were indispensable to a competitive market economy." [20] It is not surprising, therefore, that the period in which genuine politics flourished was also one in which workers had some relative autonomy. As Katherine Stone and Stephen Marglin have argued, productive conditions in many nineteenth-century plants were far different than they are today.[21] Workers participated in a variety of decisions, had some choice over their daily activity, and led an active social life on the plant floor. While there is a tendency to romanticize the extent of this autonomy, it is still clear that the nineteenth-century steel worker, for example, possessed an individual autonomy and collective identity that has since been lost, in part by the same forces of "reform" that changed the political system. What Harry Braverman calls the "reduction of work to *abstract labor*" [22] is accompanied by a change from a genuine to an abstract citizenship. As the worker is degraded, cut off from the joys of his or her labor, the citizen is isolated, removed from the social life of the community. Braverman finds the key years in the development of abstract labor in the last decade of the nineteenth century; [23] in these same years civic reform was rendering a live political process into an increasingly lifeless conception of politics. The decline of politics and the degradation of work proceeded together.

Thus this period was one in which two conceptions of politics fought for supremacy. The managerial, antipolitical elements so crucial to solutions like the Franchise and Dual States indicate that most of the battles were won by the liberal conceptions. But the victory was a paradoxical one. In order to depoliticize effectively, the liberal conception of politics had to politicize effectively—that is, it had to rise to the challenge of democracy and vanquish it. Consequently, the struggle between liberal and democratic notions of politics constituted a basis for movement and direction. The struggle itself gave the period some maneuverability.

In more recent times, this basis for movement no longer exists. Under late capitalism, the antipolitical needs of liberalism conflict so strongly with the politicizing desires of democracy that there is a standoff. Politics, in its original sense, increasingly interferes with the solutions that are advanced to contain the contradictions inherent in capitalist society, and therefore politics must be suppressed. Given the exhaustion of political alternatives, the best hope for dominant classes to preserve their by-now-tenuous power is through an extensive depoliticization that attempts to ensure that opposition classes have no alternatives either. A situation of stalemate produces a fear of politics; Jürgen Habermas expresses the point this way:

> Because a class compromise has been made the foundation of reproduction, the state apparatus must fulfill its tasks in the economic system under the limiting condition that mass loyalty be simultaneously secured within the framework of a formal democracy and in accord with ruling universalistic value systems. These pressures of legitimation can be mitigated only through structures of a depoliticized public realm.[24]

In the depoliticized universe produced by an exhaustion of alternatives, the citizen becomes, in Habermas' perceptive phrase, "a participant and a victim" at the same time.[25] Late capitalism finds itself increasingly at odds with the politics that gave birth to it.

But if the elites controlling the late capitalist state are forced to be antipolitical, the ordinary people who are expected to adhere to the decisions of the state retain their political character. Attempts by ordinary people to participate in decisions affecting their lives inevitably confront the depoliticized character of late capitalism and give rise to new sources of political energy. In addition, without politics there can be no legitimacy; in order to ensure that people accept the given order, some politicization must be encouraged. Late capitalism, in other words, both requires and distrusts political vision. Faced with this approach-avoidance conflict, the political process becomes locked in in a way quite similar to the stagnation of the state described in Chapter 8. In this chapter, I hope to show how this contradiction between politicization and depoliticization contributes to the rigidification of late capitalist society by reinforcing the absence of effective alternatives. This contradiction is fought out and expressed in the so-called political process, which, rather than being the neutral arena within which struggle takes place (as it was earlier in history), becomes part of the struggle itself. Each part of the "political process" becomes, under conditions of late capitalism, subject to a tug of war between depolitical requirements and politicizing needs. In order to shed some light on this process, I will examine three arenas within which this contradiction expresses itself: arenas of individual action, institutions that mediate between the individual and the state, and matters directly involving the state.

The Schizophrenic Citizen

Caught between the democratic urge to be political and the tendency of liberal society to depoliticize, the late capitalist citizen develops a case of political schizophrenia. One side of his personality is victimized by the depoliticization process, leaving him withdrawn, apathetic, and sullen. The other side is filled with rage and can express itself at any moment through a political urge, ranging from a sudden burst of intense conversation to collective violence. Dual messages accost him at all times, and in order to pick his way through the confusion of symbols made available to him, the late capitalist citizen must come to terms with a political life that is simultaneously ambiguous and contradictory. The plight of the schizophrenic citizen can be illustrated in two important areas of individual concern: the development of political attitudes and the scope of political participation.

It is becoming increasingly apparent to political scientists how important are the early years of citizenship, when the first coherent political attitudes are formed. Based on a developmental model borrowed from psychological learning theory, the study of political socialization is a burgeoning one. Psychological developmental theories when applied to political science bear a strong resemblance to economic development theories. Early stages of childhood are seen as less mature than later ones, just as low economic development is associated with the lack of political sophistication. The perfectly socialized adult is one who accepts the "rules of the game" of liberal democracy, just as the perfect polity is one that honors those rules. The analogy between the two approaches is so striking that it introduces an immediate caution. Just as theories of political development seem to be riddled with value judgments that make their scientific objectivity suspect, recent research in political socialization has more to do with the values of the researcher than with the learning of political norms. In other words, the data uncovered by the plethora of studies performed on young people may lead to conclusions strikingly different from the model of increasing political maturity and sophistication.

In this section, I will offer an alternative understanding of the data collected on political socialization. If the essence of citizenship under conditions of late capitalism is schizophrenia, living with contradictory messages, then it becomes the responsibility of the socialization process to induce and make viable split personalities. Children do not go through a political socialization process; rather, they are born political, in a sense, and go through a process of *depolitical socialization*. Peer groups, family, and school—the troika of socialization research—become agencies of depoliticization, warping the inherently political values of the child into the antiseptic world of adulthood required for the smooth operation of the late capitalist polity. Thus the socialization process becomes part of political struggle, since it seeks to inculcate one conception of politics at the expense of another. As Easton and Dennis have noted, "Children just do not develop an attachment to their political system, in the United States, in some random and unpatterned way." [26] Three of the shifts uncovered by socialization research are particularly important in this depoliticization process: from the intimate to the impersonal, from authority to legitimacy, and from sporadic to systematic beliefs.

Research into the socialization process of every late capitalist society reveals a clear movement from the intimate to the interpersonal in the development of attitudes. In the words of Easton and Dennis, "The child's conception of government is, therefore, brought in stages from far to near, from one small set of persons to many persons, from a personalistic to an impersonalized form of authority, and toward an awareness of the institutionalization in our system of such regime norms as are embodied in the idea of representative popular democracy." [27] Among English schoolchildren a nearly identical move "from personalization to institutionalization of government" was uncovered.[28] Research among French children shows a high level of vague and abstract notions about politics that sharpens over time.[29] A crossnational survey of adolescents revealed that as children grow older, they develop "a more differentiated view of the individual's relationship to the community." [30] In short, the research findings all seem to agree that the child's political conceptions are undifferentiated, personalistic, moralistic ("There is some evidence in our interviews that younger adolescents do indeed utilize more advanced moral principles in political reasoning, but are limited to applying them to the face-to-face social situations"),[31] and simplistic. No system of representative government, the argument implies, could exist if such patterns were maintained into adulthood, and fortunately they are not—the mature citizen drops these inappropriate attitudes and develops ones requisite to the complexity of his society.

These findings can be interpreted in quite a different way. That children are more moralistic than adults could mean that they have a more finely developed political sense, a greater perception of right and wrong. Excessive moralism, though, runs counter to the ideological inconsistency of late capitalism and must be suppressed in favor of amoral relativity. Whether the latter is more "mature" than the former is an open question at best. Similarly, the child—like the ancient Athenian—understands politics in terms of face-to-face interaction. The substitution of a distant universe, far removed from the immediate community, reproduces in daily life the historical political shift from *Gemeinschaft* to *Gesellschaft* described by Samuel Hayes for the end of the nineteenth century.[32] While many social scientists prefer large, anonymous, differentiated societies to personal communities, the shift from the former as children become adults is not necessarily a victory for political sophistication, but can be viewed as a blow against a viable, community-based conception of politics. Finally, the tendency of the child to personalize politics—to identify with strong personalities and to interpret political events through those personalities—is an attempt to assess both blame and praise for the events taking place in the social world. Personalization implies causality and suggests that the child is capable of linking events with prominent figures. The replacement of personalization with an impersonalized view of the political system can suppress this causality in favor of political perceptions so differentiated that they lose a sense of accountability and responsibility. The evidence of the socialization research, in short, can be interpreted to indicate that the shift from the immediate to the impersonal may be regressive, depoliticizing, and harmful to community.

A second important transformation uncovered by the socialization literature is the shift from authority to legitimacy. Children, in the most common finding, identify politics with policemen and other authority figures, a tendency that declines as adolescence takes place. As Easton and Dennis' study revealed, from grade 2 to grade 8 the policeman goes down as a symbol of government while voting goes up.[33] Identifying government with police or negative authority figures is also a characteristic of "alienated" children, such as poor ones in Kentucky or blacks in the inner city.[34] The shift from authority figures to symbols of government is generally related to the shift from personal to differentiated conceptions of politics. In the words of Easton and Dennis, "Children move, in a sense, from a very personalized conception of government authority to one better characterized as 'legal-rational,' institutionalized, or impersonal political authority, to continue the Weberian parallel." [35] Once again a historical process —from traditional and charismatic authority to legal rationality—is reproduced through the growth of the child. This shift is facilitated, according to Easton and Dennis, because support for authority figures like policemen is generalized to the institutions of government as a whole; without the early identification with authority figures, later legitimation would be more difficult to accomplish.

If one accepts the view that one of the primary tasks of the capitalist state is the reproduction of an inegalitarian social order, then an identification with police is a normal and perceptive act. From this perspective, the replacement of this insight with legal-rational criteria represents not maturity but a mystification of the nature of political power. What this research uncovers, in short, is a developing process of false consciousness, not of political socialization. Evidence for this conclusion is clear from the research findings themselves. As both Rodgers and Taylor and Greenberg note, black children are far less likely to shift their conception of politics-as-police to one of politics-as-representative government than are white children.[36] The early experience of children who are forced by the conditions of their lives to view government as repressive cannot be overcome with ease. Blacks, as opposed to whites, tend to preserve the political sophistication of their childhood. Very similar conclusions can be drawn from the literature on political efficacy. An oft-cited study, again by Easton and Dennis, showed how a sense of efficacy increased dramatically between grades 3 and 8.[37] But the fact is that most people who feel a strong sense of their potential effectiveness in late capitalist society are deluding themselves, substituting wish for fact. As Easton and Dennis note, "This early acquisition of the norm [of political efficacy] may operate as a potent and critical force in offsetting later adult experiences which, in a modern, rationally organized mass society, undermine the political importance of the ordinary member." [38] In this context, it is interesting that while young boys and young girls have an equal sense of political efficacy, women have a lower sense than men.[39] This appears to indicate that deprived groups are less likely to develop a mystified sense of their power than those who delude themselves into a false sense of security. The implication of all this is that children who replace their identification with authority figures by legal-rational criteria and who develop a high sense of political efficacy are the most depoliticized because they are the most out of touch with the realities of power in their society. In order for politics to express the collective quest for a better life, the conditions inhibiting that quest must first be understood.

Finally, the literature on political socialization traces a change from a sporadic to a systematic conception of the political order. The research of Joseph Adelson, who has tried to uncover the attitude of children toward some basic questions of political philosophy, is interesting. Adelson found that while children are egocentric, in Piaget's sense of the term, as they grow older they become more familiar with complex ideas, such as the public good, civil liberty, and a sense of community (one defined by Adelson, though, as involving a national, not a local, collectivity).[40] Having learned these values, they become "better" citizens, more willing to live within the framework of democratic society. Political philosophy gives criteria for judgment—a sense of value, order, and propriety. In like fashion, Philip Converse has discovered that time is by itself an important political variable.[41] The older people get, the more stable become their political beliefs. The stability of democratic countries, Converse argues, must be attributable at least in part to this process of settling down. From childhood to old age, there is a tendency for the diffuse to become the specific, the random the ordered, and the unpredictable the standardized. The citizen becomes less volatile and more set in his basic political conceptions.

One person's stability is another's resignation. What the shift from the sporadic to the systematic may indicate is that the younger citizen is flexible, open-minded, and not committed to any particular ideological doctrine, whereas the older one becomes locked into definite positions, either out of boredom or out of exhaustion from trying to change the world. Thus Adelson's research findings can be interpreted to mean, not that the citizen becomes more politically mature, but that his awareness of the complexity of the community leads him to withdraw between clichés and slogans instead to trying to bring his political ideas into reality. And Converse's notion of a settling down over time could be due to sheer boredom. Uninterested in a spectacle with little relationship to their lives, people refuse to take seriously the professed values of political society and withdraw into rigid beliefs that make the contradictions of political life easier to accept. Converse's own research suggests that most citizens in late capitalist society prefer the "simple, concrete, or 'close to home'" to the "remote, general, and abstract." [42] Alienated from the latter, they focus on the former, a conclusion that makes perfect sense in the face of their general powerlessness. The shift from the sporadic to the systematic can therefore represent one more tendency toward depoliticization to the degree that it represents withdrawal and cynicism.

The findings of research on political socialization indicate that to a significant extent the process of socialization is a part of the class struggle. Easton and Dennis point out that "considerable societal efforts are probably being made to transmit a concept deemed appropriate to the American political system." [43] Why need the effort be considerable? The reason is part of the contradiction between liberal and democratic conceptions of politics. To dominant elites, a deenergizing notion of politics is consciously chosen for emphasis. In a study of civics textbooks, Edgar Litt found that working-class communities read books containing a notion of politics emphasizing passivity and a harmony of interests, while more affluent communities read messages emphasizing a conception of politics that was idealistic and active. [44] This finding expresses the nature of political socialization in late capitalism in a nutshell. A certain amount of politicization is required if the polity is to be accepted as legitimate, especially within the segments of the population from which elites will likely emerge. At the same time, for the rest of the population, passivity must be encouraged so that the state can be permitted to go about its functions of accumulation unimpeded by potential mobilization. What happens between classes, though, must be reproduced within every individual. Children in late capitalism are torn between their immediate moralistic ideals and the attempts to depoliticize them through abstract and alienated conceptions of the political. Possessing one set of notions from their democratic character and another from their society, their values become understandably contradictory, and the most important lesson they are taught is that as future citizens they will have to hold irreconcilable sets of values if they want to be "socialized."

The schizophrenia learned in childhood prepares the late capitalist citizen for the day when he must participate in the political process. Like socialization, participation has been exhaustively studied through the empirical techniques of contemporary political science, yet the facts uncovered often seem to bear little resemblance to the theories advanced to explain them. In a fashion similar to developmental theory, the most influential book written about citizenship in recent years—Almond and Verba's *The Civic Culture*—posits a scale of increasing sophistication, in which late capitalist societies come across as more mature and civic-minded than such relatively "backward" areas as Italy and Mexico.[45] Yet the data they present often do not support their conclusion, especially in the realm of participation. If a sign of the mature citizen is his willingness to participate in the political process, then Italy—where voter turnout is over 90 percent and where Italians working abroad regularly come home to vote—is far more mature than the United States, which has the lowest voter turnout of any advanced industrial society. Indeed, the contrast between these two countries suggests the hypothesis that the more totally capitalist a society, the *less* its degree of politicization, and vice versa. In order to explain facts such as these, Almond and Verba define the most mature form of civic competence, not as one that encourages participation as such, but one that encourages political schizophrenia. The most advanced "civic cultures" are also the most schizophrenic.

This surprising conclusion is presented in detail by Almond and Verba toward the end of their study. After making distinctions between parochial cultures, which are traditional, subject cultures, which are obedient, and civic cultures, which are democratic, they point out that the civic culture "sometimes contains apparently contradictory political attitudes" and that this is "appropriate for democratic political systems in that they, too, are mixtures of political contradictions." Hence,

> the civic culture is a mixed political culture. In it many individuals are active in politics, but there are also many who take the passive role of subject. More important, even among those performing the active political role of the citizen, the roles of subject and parochial have not been displaced. The participant role has been added to the subject and parochial roles. This means that the active citizen maintains his traditional, nonpolitical ties, as well as his more passive role as a subject.

It comes as no surprise, given all these contradictions, that "the democratic citizen is called upon to pursue contradictory goals; he must be active, yet passive; involved, yet not too involved; influential, yet deferential." [46] A better description of the schizophrenic citizen could hardly be found. The active–passive, involved–withdrawn, and influential–deferential citizen is a fit reminder of how, under conditions of late capitalism, political urges conflict with depoliticizing needs to produce ambiguity, confusion, and contradiction.

There is an obvious explanation for the emergence of the schizophrenic citizen so well described by Almond and Verba. As political philosophers from the Greeks to the present have understood, states and citizens bear a dialectical relationship to each other. Since the late capitalist state has contradictory functions, the late capitalist citizen will have contradictory expectations. Because of the dialectical relationship between state and citizen, an active state can exist only when given passive people, and vice versa. As Almond and Verba express it, "The inactivity of the ordinary man and his inability to influence decisions help provide the power that governmental elites need if they are to make decisions." At the same time, a legitimate state can exist only when given active citizens. Again, in the words of Almond and Verba, "The power of elites must be kept in check. The citizen's opposite role, as an active and influential enforcer of the responsiveness of elites, is maintained by his strong commitment to the norm of active citizenship as well as by his perception that he can be an influential citizen." [47] Because the state must serve both an accumulation and a legitimation function—a fact understood not only by Marxist writers but also by political scientists like Almond and Verba and, even more directly, Harry Eckstein [48]—the citizen must be both active and passive. Thus the schizophrenic citizen is an inevitable resident of the late capitalist state.

Participation means little until the object of participation is specified. In late capitalist society, citizens are urged to participate in a process that is ritualistic, alienated from real human needs, and incapable of generating sustained interest. The most essential features of American elections, for example, have been described as "the low emotional involvement of the electorate in politics; its slight awareness of public affairs; its failure to think in structured ideological terms; and its pervasive sense of attachment to one or the other political parties." [49] Each of these characteristics testifies to the depoliticized nature of American politics. Low emotional involvement follows from the alienating character of election campaigns; given their divorce from human needs, high emotional involvement becomes nearly pathological. Slight awareness of public officials reflects the common understanding that such men are not the major wielders of power and that the methods of selecting them are not the most important events in one's life. A failure to think ideologically is the heritage of two hundred years of ideological inconsistency reflective of the bourgeois state. Partisan attachments convey a sense of resignation, a feeling that the messages are so confusing that all one can do is grasp onto a party label and stick with it for better or for worse. Desultory voting, meaningless choices, illusory options, deenergizing campaigns—these become the dominant features of bourgeois politics. Under these conditions, the purpose of participation in the "political process" of late capitalism becomes depoliticizing. Politics becomes the means by which politics is displaced.

In the United States the depoliticizing nature of the political process is most advanced. Decades of schizophrenic messages and ritualistic elections have had their effect—over two thirds of the U.S. population can be classified as nonparticipants, voting occasionally and playing no other role.[50] Furthermore, even for those who do choose to participate, the structure of the depolitical process operates as a filtering mechanism, driving out political concerns at each step along the way. As I pointed out in the previous chapter, Claus Offe spoke of the late capitalist state as a selective mechanism, screening out options from the agenda of political discussion. The so-called political process operates in a similar fashion. A model developed by Cobb and Elder is helpful in this context.[51] They envision the political process as a series of steps in "agenda building," ranging from broad input at the level of the general population to narrower discussion at the level of the state. But what they really describe is not how agendas are built, but how they are dismantled. Each step in the process acts as a roadblock, detouring political concerns, until by the time an "issue" reaches the decision makers, nearly all of its political content has been stripped away and it is amenable to technocratic considerations. Like tonsils, institutions in the political process—elections, parties, interest groups—absorb politics, swelling themselves as a result, but passing on a clarified and bacteria-free version to the rest of the body. A well-functioning depolitical process becomes an important aspect of life in late capitalist society.

There is some evidence that European politics are becoming as depoliticized as the American. In West Germany, political scientists emphasize the notion of the "quiescent subject," the relatively passive citizen who accepts with few reservations a depoliticized role.[52] But political schizophrenia also exists in this country, as evidenced by a study which found that German youth intended not to participate in politics but at the same time indicated that they did feel a high sense of political efficacy.[53] If they did intend to participate, one is tempted to hypothesize, their sense of efficacy would probably *decrease*, since the political process encourages passivity. In France, in spite of a multiparty system, the electorate is no stranger to depoliticization, American style. "It is unlikely that the common French citizen devotes any greater portion of his attention to politics than his American counterpart, and he may well give less," Converse and Dupeaux have written. Alienated politics produces similar effects wherever it takes place:

> The data give no striking reason to believe that the French citizen either through the vagaries of national character, institutions, or history, is predisposed to form political opinions which are more sharply crystallized or which embrace a more comprehensive range of political issues than do comparable Americans. On both sides, opinion formation declines as objects and arrangements become more remote from the observer; and much of politics, for both French and Americans, is remote.[54]

No wonder there is so much concern about dissatisfaction and alienation in European politics. As di Palma indicates, those who are disaffected, alienated, and cynical do not participate in the political process, both in Europe and in the United States.[55] Although di Palma views this withdrawal with some alarm, I would argue that those who are alienated from an alienating process are potentially healthy; the nonparticipation of the disaffected in bourgeois politics may be an indication of a willingness to participate if an alternative and more genuine politics were available.

The one exception to this process of depoliticization occurs within those mass movements that political scientists often consider "extremist." Insofar as a party has as its goal the creation or replication of community, it may energize and politicize its members. The Italian Communist Party (PCI) is one example of a party that has remained genuinely *political*. Through its extensive workplace organizing, its promotion of a cultural *egemonia*, its journalism, and its active social life, the PCI has been an active force toward politicization. In a reexamination of the data collected by Almond and Verba on Italy, Donald McCrone found that members of the PCI scored higher than Christian Democrats on all the following scales: interest in public events, willingness to talk politics, feelings of subjective political competence, campaign interest, and support for the necessity of election campaigns.[56] As Timothy Hennessey commented on this data, "Those who identify with the parties of the left, particularly the Communist Party, are by far the most efficacious, involved, and supportive of the system of political parties." Moreover, "By contrast with the Communists, the Christian Democrats express attitudes which appear quite antithetical to the rules of the democratic political game." [57] Aside from the irony that nonbourgeois parties teach bourgeois norms better than their opposite, these findings suggest that depoliticization is not inevitable; democratic urges continue to energize. At the same time, there is evidence that the PCI, in its quest to assume state power along *la via italiana del socialismo*, may be losing its political character. Sidney Tarrow has shown how the increased effectiveness of the PCI in bourgeois politics inevitably shapes it with bourgeois culture, from which depoliticization will undoubtedly flow.[58] Indeed, because of what Tarrow calls the "dual nature" of the PCI,[59] it stands out as a model of schizophrenic politics, trying to preserve its unique politicization while the needs of its society demand increased depoliticization. The fate of the PCI is identical with the fate of the citizen in late capitalist society.

Because participation in the affairs of the late capitalist state is a contradictory business, emphasizing at one and the same time involvement and withdrawal, the effects are likely to be severe. The major effect is that paralyzing tendencies that emerge in the state are reproduced in the political process. As I pointed out in Chapter 8, the tension between liberal and democratic conceptions of the state reached its height in late capitalism, resulting in a public administration that must perform political tasks in spite of a nonpolitical ideology. But in the political process the reverse takes place, since socialization and participation must perform nonpolitical tasks in spite of a politicizing ideology. The former contradiction resulted in a reification of the state; the latter produces a paralysis of the citizen.

With political agencies depoliticizing and depolitical agents politicizing, the schizophrenic citizen discovers that his mental state approaches psychosis. "The actual and potential participant population has grown just when effective participation becomes more difficult," Verba and Nye have written. "Citizens may be participating more but enjoying it less." [60] Faced with dual messages and institutions that deny their own logic, the citizens of late capitalist society become as ineffectual as a state paralyzed by dual expectations. The rigidity that hinders the rational business of the latter also produces the withdrawal, cynicism, and alienation of the former. An immobility of government reinforces an immobility of citizenship, and together both contribute to the substantial legitimacy problems of the late capitalist state.

THE BREAKDOWN OF MEDIATING MECHANISMS

Both socialization and participation concern the citizen as he channels his expectations, desires, and demands up to the state. Before they get there, these "inputs" are met by a series of mediating mechanisms, such as parties, private associations, and interest groups. At least since de Tocqueville, intermediate associations have fascinated political observers, who view them as central to the stability of democratic society. In theory, mediating mechanisms work to the degree that they temper the excessive demands of the citizen and the authoritarian needs of the state, producing the happy compromise known as pluralism.[61] There is some reason to believe that for a time the theory did accord with reality, particularly in the immediate post–World War II period. But the experience with late capitalism as a whole raises some important questions. What happens to mediating mechanisms when there is a politics of exhaustion? If the state becomes locked in by declining options and the citizen is paralyzed by schizophrenic expectations, can mediating mechanisms continue to function in anything like their expected fashion? There is a need, in other words, to reexamine the theory and practice of mediating mechanisms in the light of the exhaustion of alternatives characteristic of late capitalism.

Changes in the nature and functions of political parties illustrate one way in which mediating mechanisms have become transformed. At one time parties had a clear mobilizing function, accumulating power and stimulating consciousness in the process. So long as questions of boundaries, citizenship, and the nature of the state were unsettled, parties sought to expand and broaden their base, incorporating new elements into the population and thereby politicizing them; an expanding and dynamic capitalist economy possessed a lively party system. As capitalist societies modernized and settled their territorial limits and class composition, the meaning of political power began to change. In the words of Reinhard

Bendix, "Politics ceased to be a struggle over the distribution of sovereign powers wherever the orderly dominion over a territory and its inhabitants is conceived to be the function of one and the same community—the nation state. Instead politics became a struggle over the distribution of the national product and over the policies and the administrative implementation which affect that distribution." [62] Distributive questions characterized the party struggle throughout the nineteenth and early twentieth centuries. Although the nation-state itself was not broadened, parties still had room to expand within the nation-state; competition for the votes of immigrants, workers, women, and dispossessed farmers enabled the parties, especially those of the left, to continue a politicizing function. Parties, as noted above, were very much alive by the last part of the nineteenth century, which is why reformers planned their execution. A capitalist class that found competition intolerable in the economic sphere was no less inclined to view it with disdain in the party sphere. The politicizing character of party systems began to disintegrate as capitalist elites no longer found it to their advantage.

Twentieth-century experience with parties is a history of depoliticization. As Burnham noted for the United States, between 1920 and 1950, electoral politics "tended toward a much tighter integration than had been the case earlier in the century." As elections lost their spontaneity, "the political parties are progressively losing their hold on the electorate." What Burnham calls the "onward march of party decomposition" [63] testifies to the depoliticization of the party. Similarly, observers of the European situation have commented on the transformation of party systems there. In recent years, according to the Rokkan-Lipset school of political sociology, parties lost their ideological character and became bargaining agents trying to win rewards for their constituent elements. [64] As left and right began to accept the legitimacy of each other, there was a greater concentration for the "centrist" vote. To the extent that parties try to assemble governing coalitions rather than preserve an ideological vision they become, in Otto Kirchheimer's suggestive phrase, "catch-all" parties. [65] According to Kirchheimer, a catch-all party is caught between its desire to hold state power, which pushes it toward moderation, and its need to legitimate itself, which requires that it capture and express indignation. "The very nature of today's catch-all party forbids an option between these two performances. It requires a constant shift between the party's critical role and its role as establishment support, a shift hard to perform but still harder to avoid." Wavering between these contradictory needs, the catch-all party loses its politicizing character:

> The party's transformation from an organization combining the defense of social position, the quality of spiritual shelter, and the vision of things to come into that of a vehicle for short-range and interstitial political choice

exposes the party to the hazards of all purveyors of nondurable consumer goods: competition with a more attractive packaged brand of a nearly identical merchandise.[66]

Thus, parties in a liberal democratic society are caught between two different functions. In order to win state power, parties must arouse expectations, but in order to hold state power, those same expectations must be dampened. In most cases, bourgeois parties have responded to this contradiction by suppressing expectations, so that with late capitalism one sees the emergence of *depolitical* parties, whose most fundamental principles are to prevent politicization as much as they can. Parties, in Offe's words, must "expel from the consciousness of their members as voters those opposing social interests which it had been the original purpose of parties to articulate and present to the public at large." [67] Depolitical parties are most thoroughly identified with the United States, which is, according to Kirchheimer, "still the classical example of an all pervasive catch-all party system." [68] For one thing, U.S. parties demonstrate by their behavior that they would rather nominate colorless candidates sure to bore the citizenry rather than dynamic ones who might stir up real political sentiment. In an insightful, if sloppily argued, book, Walter Karp makes this clear: "The whole purpose of party organizations at every political level is to sift out, sidetrack and eliminate men of independent political ambition, men whom the party cannot trust." [69] American parties also prove their devotion to depoliticization in a second way; if faced with a choice between preserving their local organization and holding state power, they generally sacrifice the latter in order to preserve the former. Contrary to the myth that parties desire to win elections above all else, parties by their actual behavior will, like a well-meaning prizefighter, "throw" the election in order to preserve their prerogatives. As Karp puts it, "Anything that stirs up the electorate, anything that rouses their interest in politics, is harmful to party organizations." Or, even more pithily, "*Not* winning elections is not always easy." [70]

The importance of depoliticized parties to late capitalism cannot be overestimated, since an active state requires a passive citizenry, and the party system, by default, becomes the best available means for ensuring that passivity. Yet, in spite of this importance, many writers continue to view parties as mobilizing, politicizing agents and therefore cannot explain what appear to be mysterious events. Thus, reflecting on the findings of *The American Voter*, Donald Stokes wondered, "In view of the fact that very few Americans have any deep interest in politics, it is a mild paradox that party loyalties should be so widespread." [71] This is no paradox at all. It is precisely because partisan identification was so high that the 1950s saw such a low interest in politics; a lack of excitement is exactly what late capitalist parties are supposed to encourage. Those who identify strongly with either party are probably the most depoliticized element of the population. A few years later, Samuel Huntington described what he called a "peculiar paradox, in which popular participation in politics was going up, but the premier organization designed to structure and organize that participation, the political party, was declining." [72] Huntington's puzzling paradox is no more mysterious than Stokes' mild one. If parties are agencies of departicipation, it follows logically that as they weaken, participation will increase. Both writers inadvertently point to the depoliticizing role of late capitalist parties.

Depoliticization runs its own risks. As the parties become responsible for ensuring the replacement of political concerns by technocratic alternatives, they shed their historical preoccupation with mobilization and take the chance of losing popular support. In other words, as parties drop their mediating role and move closer to the state, they inevitably move farther away from the citizen. A number of developments reflect this decreasing legitimacy of the parties. First, party identification and party voting have declined dramatically, especially among younger citizens. In the United States, 80 percent of the voters in 1950 cast straight party ballots compared to 50 percent in 1970. Furthermore, 28 percent of people in their twenties called themselves independents in 1950 compared to 43 percent in 1971.[73] Second, as Jack Dennis has shown for the United States, public loyalty to the party system has plummeted, and again this is especially true of younger people.[74] Some evidence of the lack of respect for parties is indicated by the Almond and Verba data; when asked what they would try to do to influence local government, only 1 percent of the people in the United States, Britain, and Italy said that they would work through a political party, about the same percentage as those who said they would engage in violence.[75] Third, faced with declining support, parties are increasingly unable to finance themselves, thereby requiring assistance from the state. In Germany, 35 percent of the party funds are supplied by government,[76] and in both Italy and the United States, recently passed legislation has provided for public support of the parties. Like the Lockheed Corporation and New York City, parties require state aid when they are in danger of bankruptcy, but, unlike them, their bankruptcy is as ideological and political as it is financial.

The delegitimation of parties makes them, not vehicles for the expression of conflict, but parties to conflict itself. Because they must depoliticize to serve the state yet mobilize to preserve legitimacy, parties, like citizens, have a schizophrenic character. The fact that parties in general sacrifice legitimation for depoliticization does not answer their most basic problems but shifts the weight from one problem to another. So long as the state serves contradictory functions, the parties serving the state will do so as well. Whether proposals to "reform" the parties will succeed in restoring to them a working depoliticization, or whether their delegitimation will constitute a breakthrough for genuine politics, are questions that are being fought out now. The undeniable reality is that in late capitalism political struggles take place not between the parties but over them.

Not surprisingly, some of the contradictions affecting parties have also transformed the character of other mediating mechanisms, such as interest groups. It is an axiom of nearly all political science research that interest groups preserve democratic values by encouraging "joining." As citizens band together to advance their interests, the theory runs, they form ministates, learning the rules of participation and democratic conduct. As Almond and Verba state, "Voluntary associations play a major role in a democratic political culture. The organizational member, compared with the nonmember, is likely to consider himself more competent as a citizen, to be a more active participant in politics, and to know and care more about politics. He is, therefore, more likely to be close to the model of a democratic citizen." [77] Yet, according to Almond and Verba, the democratic citizen has a Janus-like character, shifting back and forth from apathy to involvement. If this is the case, then we would expect interest groups to serve a partial depoliticizing function, "cooling out" members in such a way that their participation in the affairs of the interest group will guarantee their nonparticipation in the greater collective political life of the society.

These depoliticizing tendencies are strengthened by the fact that interest groups, more directly than parties, deal with the central class contradiction of capitalism: the struggle between capital and labor. Although the class struggle sometimes spills over into the party realm, especially in France and Italy, it more generally takes the form of direct conflict between corporations, trade associations, trade unions, and other such "interest" groups. In one sense, the battle over resources between these groups expresses the differences between liberal and democratic expectations, since corporations are a product of the former and labor unions of the latter. But at the same time, leaders of both kinds of groups find that they have a common interest in submerging these differences in favor of negotiation over questions of distribution. Thus interest groups, like parties, must simultaneously raise the hopes of their members and then dash those hopes through administered settlements. In such a contradictory situation, "business as usual" can take place only if negotiation is chosen over mobilization as the general rule; hence leaders of interest groups make a tacit agreement that the central issues of a capitalist society, all revolving around the struggle between capital and labor, will not be permitted to be aired in an interest group context. Highly publicized disagreements about how the product is to be carved up remove attention from the nature and character of the product itself. The political energy at one time generated by interest groups in the pursuit of their self-interest is lost as the quest by the interest group system as a whole to keep real political concerns off the agenda of late capitalism intensifies. Offe has described this transformation as follows:

> In the early, less organized period of bourgeois society, mechanisms of suppression and repression still required an explicit act of will on the part of the dominant groups of individuals. Today, this is no longer the case. The very manner in which political institutions function and the immanent conditions for their continuing stability have made these mechanisms automatic. To be sure, the functions are still equivalent: the pluralistic system of organized interests excludes from the processes concerned with consensus formation all articulations of demands that are general in nature and not associated with any status group; that are incapable of conflict because they have no functional significance for the utilization of capital and labor power; and that represent utopian projections beyond the historically specific system insofar as they do not unconditionally abide by the pragmatic rules of judicious bargaining.[78]

As was also the case with parties, the depoliticizing character of the interest group system causes a decline in legitimacy. The following Harris polls taken in the United States indicate what happens when the interest group system loses its political character:[79]

TABLE 1. Proportion of the Public Expressing a "Great Deal of Confidence" in Leadership of Institutions (Percent)

	1966	1971	1972	1973
Institution:				
Major companies	55	27	27	29
Organized labor	22	14	15	20
Higher education	61	27	33	44
Medicine	72	61	48	57
Organized religion	41	27	30	36

Similarly in Europe, according to Michel Crozier, all private groups are increasingly seen as illegitimate, including the Church, education, and the Army.[80] Interest groups, in short, cannot have it both ways. If they mobilize and express an "interest," they will be viewed favorably; if they suppress political interests, they will not. Mediating mechanisms are in serious trouble when they no longer mediate.

The breakdown of such mediating institutions as parties and interest groups is bound to have serious consequences for the political life of late capitalism. Of all the implications that could be discussed, two seem appropriate to the themes of this book: the nationalization of the legitimation function and the centrality of what I will call "alienated politics."

As parties and interest groups lose their mediating character they also lose substantial legitimacy. Some other institution must assume the burden created by this breakdown, and in most cases it is the state; in the history of capitalist societies, there is a tendency for legitimation to move upward, passing from family and region to parties and groups and eventually to the state itself. At the same time that the state becomes increasingly absorbed in the accumulation function, it finds itself participating more in the process of legitimation as well. The task of obtaining loyalty to the existing order becomes "nationalized" in roughly the same way that railroads become nationalized. Numerous studies have indicated the rising importance of the state in this regard. Hess and Torney found that schools, generally part of the state, assume a greater role in the socialization process than families, especially in the inculcation of specific values.[81] Another study has shown how important the mass media have become in shaping political attitudes; in most late capitalist societies, the media are part of the state, and even where they are not (as in the United States), they generally serve the same interest.[82] With the state involving itself more in political repression, assuming power once exercised by private police forces,[83] there results an intervention into civil society comparable in many respects to the more widely recognized intervention of the state into the economy.

The consequences of the nationalization of the legitimation function are contradictory. On the one hand, the increased activity of the state in areas of private life gives it an awesome appearance. An example is the increase in the public surveillance of private life, the subject of a recent book by James Rule. Although he warns against any simplistic Orwellian conclusions, Rule's analysis does "convince one that systems of mass surveillance are a fairly recent product of modern industrial society." The accumulation of power, it would seem, has been matched by an accumulation of data, in which "the over-all development of increased surveillance capacity" [84] is bound to weaken the viability of private life. Yet, on the other hand, the increase in state intervention into private life may, as in the case of the accumulation function, suggest weakness, not strength. The fact that the state assumes responsibility as legitimator of last resort means that all other institutions have failed in this regard. Like the failure of firms within the private sector to generate enough capital, the failure of nongovernment institutions like parties to generate enough loyalty constitutes a serious undermining of the bourgeois order. In this sense, the more important consequence of the nationalization of the legitimation function is that it constitutes one more aspect of the exhaustion of alternatives. State involvement in social reproduction becomes a vivid reminder of how the contradictions of late capitalism narrow the possible options of any given ruling class as it seeks to preserve its privileges. It is interesting to note that the growth of this state involvement took place when the legitimacy crisis of the state became acute. I will discuss this subject more in the next chapter; it is worth emphasizing here that the emergence of what Roland Inglehart has called "post-bourgeois values" [85]—those incompatible with traditional modes of capitalist accumulation—comes at a time when state activity is maximal. The nationalization of the legitimation function is a symptom of, not a solution to, the legitimacy crisis of late capitalism.

A second important implication of the breakdown of mediating mechanisms is the centrality of alienated politics. The depoliticization of the means of politics becomes responsible for some drastic changes in the meaning of political action. In late capitalist society, parties and interest groups are put in an awkward position, since in order to depoliticize effectively, they must absorb the political energy of the citizenry so that the state can go about its business without interference. Swollen with the political energy of others, parties and interest groups claim to be sources of political power in themselves, when in actuality whatever power they possess is the product of the members from whom it has been taken. If, following the Greeks, one conceives of politics as the common quest of equals for the just and happy society, then in late capitalism politics of this sort is replaced by a form of *alienated* politics, in which parties and interest groups become responsible for absorbing the common power that people possess and for using this power to rule over the people from whom it came in the first place.[86] Like a worker who sees the product of his labor transformed into a commodity alienated from himself, the late capitalist citizen finds that the source of his alienation lies in his own productive activity, in this case the production of community rather than commodities. Expropriation is no longer unique to the economy.

Alienated politics contributes to the rigidification of late capitalist society. Without genuine politics, substitutes must be offered. Power is conceptualized on the basis of the uses to which it can be put, for example, which denies or ignores the origins of the power itself.[87] Or it becomes popular to view power as an exchange process, in which people give it up in the form of a vote in return for favors received, a conception that also mystifies the popular basis of political life.[88] Both use value and exchange value theories of power, like their equivalents for the labor process, describe a certain reality in capitalist society while at the same time promoting conceptions of politics that are divorced from human action. This divorce is correlated with the fact that the world of political activity emerging in late capitalism increasingly loses its relevance to the everyday lives of citizens. Candidates for office address "issues" of far more interest to themselves than they are to the people who vote. Public office holders act according to rules of proper conduct that would be impermissible among ordinary people. To be responsible to other power holders, one must be irresponsible to everyone else, and to be responsible to everyone else is to disqualify oneself from a traditional political career. Politics takes on a desiccated quality, as if it were floating somewhere above society rather than being part of it. Like the robber barons of the nineteenth century, twentieth-century power barons accumulate as much independence from ordinary people as they can, only to find that the rarefied atmosphere in which they conduct their business has no solid support. In the early part of the twentieth century, popular attention was directed to John D. Rockefeller and his unprincipled pursuit of wealth; later on, attention was drawn to a man like Robert Moses and his unprincipled pursuit of power.[89] Moses, indeed, is the personification of alienated politics, the perfect picture of a power holder who divorces himself from the original source of the power he holds.

Together, the nationalization of the legitimation function and the centrality of alienated politics produce enormous confusion about the meaning and purpose of political life. The former process becomes responsible for the politicization of private life, in which increasing aspects of one's personal affairs are made the objects of state intervention. At the same time, alienated politics promotes the reverse, a privatization of public life, in the sense that the political process loses touch with any meaningful sense of community or common purpose. Ultimately the distinction between public and private, liberalism's greatest contribution to human freedom, becomes undermined by the liberal traditional itself. The result is doubly unfortunate. It is not just that privacy is lost, for one can conceive of circumstances in which a loss of privacy can be justified on the basis of some greater collective good. It is that the absorption of private life into the state is also matched by a failure of public life, that in late capitalism neither individual liberty nor collective goal achievement can be satisfied. This confusion about what belongs in the realm of the political and what does not make it extremely difficult to find ways out of the stagnation of the state. A society that has replaced genuine politics with a depoliticized opposite is one in which the capacity for transformation approaches zero, since the mobilizing energy that real politics produces is lost. Those who fear the subversive power of community become victims of their own fear. Thus, while rigid, the late capitalist polity is not stable; what the breakdown of mediating mechanisms signifies is one more indication of a lack of maneuverability. Depoliticization becomes, not a brilliant strategy of leadership, but a symbol of the lack of it.

THE UTOPIANIZATION OF THE RULING CLASS

The sometimes hidden, sometimes overt struggle between political urges and depolitical necessities is bound to have an impact on the men who occupy positions of power within the state. As products of the political process, the attitudes and predispositions of late capitalist elites will surely be affected by such phenomena as schizophrenic socialization processes, a contradictory conception of citizenship, and mediating mechanisms that "cool out" more than they "turn on." Men of power are likely to undergo important changes as they face a situation of political exhaustion, in which genuine politics is being continuously transformed into an antiseptic replica. I will conclude this chapter with some thoughts on what these changes might involve.

The most influential attempt to trace the impact of modern capitalism on the rise of a new kind of politician is Max Weber's essay "Politics as a Vocation." [90] Parties, Weber notes, were at one time associations of notables, restricted to an elite and possessing a definite common interest around a certain conception of society. With the rise of what Weber calls plebiscitarian democracy, capitalist, not aristocratic, conceptions of life begin to dominate the political process, best illustrated by the caucus system in England and by American political machines. Especially in the United States, the "boss" is to the accumulation of votes what the employer is to the accumulation of capital: "Who is the boss? He is a political capitalist entrepreneur who on his own account and at his own risk provides votes." Like the capitalist, "the boss has no firm political principles; he is completely unprincipled in attitude and asks merely: what will capture votes?" This does not mean, however, that these men who live off, rather than for, politics have no passion; rather, Weber suggests, their passion is over "the sense of matter-of-factness" that produces a valuable sense of proportion. "This is the decisive psychological quality of the politician: his ability to let realities work upon him with inner concentration and calmness. Hence his distance to things and men." The capitalist politician, finally, is not unethical. Weber speaks of two competing sets of ethics. One, the ethic of ultimate ends, is fundamentally religious in nature and seeks the attainment of the perfect life. The other, the ethic of responsibility, is less chiliastic and tries to pursue limited goals based on an awareness of the limitations and deficiencies of people and societies. Because "the decisive means for politics is violence," those who pursue the ethic of ultimate ends through politics, like syndicalists and revolutionary socialists, are a danger to civilized life; in comparison, the bourgeois politician, for all his lack of principles, has a certain virtue after all. The fragility of democratic societies can be preserved only if politics as a vocation is reserved for the political brokers who seek power rather than the salvation of men's souls.

Because the triumph of fascism seemed to confirm Weber's realism, his defense of unprincipled politics has had a major impact on twentieth-century political sociology. Daniel Bell makes the distinction between the ethic of ultimate ends and the ethic of responsibility the cornerstone of his analysis of "the end of ideology." [91] An Englishman who could write in the 1960s that "the man who treats everything as a matter of principle cannot be happy with politics" is paraphrasing Weber and coming dangerously close to plagiarism.[92] Another political scientist, ignoring the qualifications that Weber advanced in contrasting his two ethics, has used them as part of an attack on all political radicals.[93] There are Weberian undertones as well as Daniel Boorstin's argument that, in contrast with European societies, "the genius of American politics" is its thoroughly flexible and nonideological character.[94] Is pragmatism, as Boorstin argues, a work of genius? In many ways it is, for the ability of capitalist politicians to revise their positions by violating maxims that they once proclaimed sacred does approach an art form. But does such pragmatism, as its defenders claim, promise the preservation of democratic values? In theory, an absence of principles should permit men of power a high degree of freedom to make unrestricted choices. Not tied down by the obsolescence of ideology, such power brokers could counter the exhaustion of alternatives by developing unexpected, unencumbered, and unusual solutions to intractable problems. The question to be addressed, therefore, is whether the late capitalist politician can utilize the flexibility that his lack of principles is supposed to provide.

Those who argue the importance of flexibility for politicians generally make a distinction between the political attitudes of the elite compared to everyone else. Unlike the ordinary citizen, who in their view is intolerant, dogmatic, and moralistic, the leader is seen as open-minded and flexible; without leaders committed to democratic norms, their argument continues, the fragility of democratic structures would be easily ruptured.[95] Yet leaders are part and parcel of the society that produces them and will therefore be subject to the same pressures faced by everyone else. More careful examination would probably reveal what Norman Luttbeg discovered: that leaders are as confused and ambiguous about politics as the people who elect them, that they, too, "have difficulty in placing their opinions within the total context of their belief systems." [96] In short, if the essence of the so-called political process in late capitalism is the inducement of schizophrenia, then the leaders who emerge out of that process are likely to be the most schizophrenic people of all. The most distinguishing characteristic of late capitalist political elites may be their ability to live with contradictions that nonleaders would find intolerable.

The schizophrenic character of elites is most clearly revealed in the case of elected officials, for they have the closest relationship to the alienated political process. An insightful piece of research that investigated this problem is P. A. Allum's study of Neapolitan candidates for the Italian parliament.[97] According to Allum, the Neapolitian politician is caught between two worlds: the Mediterranean, almost precapitalist milieu of his district, and the *Gesellschaft* characteristics of the late capitalist state he serves. Adopting the role of middleman between state and society, the politician becomes, in a sense, paralyzed by conflicting expectations. If he "modernizes" himself by identifying with the state, he runs the risk of distrust at home. If he preserves the "folk" character of his constituency, he alienates himself from political power at the national level. The major effect of this duality, according to Allum, is that it leads politicians to engage in "sentimental rhetoric" rather than political analysis. Thus, Giorgio Galli's study of Italian parliamentary debates showed that representatives of all the parties spent most of their time spewing forth vague rhetoric or just pointing blame at others; there was remarkably little political content in the conduct of these "politicians." [98] As with the people who elect them, officials find that the contradictory nature of their life leads to a withdrawal from politics. An antipolitical kind of politician comes to dominate late capitalist society, one whose relationship to the Greek notion is minimal. No small amount of confusion is introduced because these antipoliticians are designated as politicians—indeed, they have preempted the term—but in truth there is very little of the political about them. The lack of politics within legislative assemblies accords with the depoliticizing tendencies of late capitalist societies as a whole.

In another study of politicians, this one based on a comparison of Italian and British legislators, Robert Putnam found that in both countries politicians who were ideological were also inclined to participate in the give-and-take of parliamentary life.[99] Rather than there being two mutually exclusive categories of ideologues and practical politicians, many of the men combined both roles into one. A possible explanation for this convergence is that the ideological role is directed to the constituency, where legitimation problems predominate, and the practical to the state, where efficiency vis-à-vis accumulation is a requirement. In other words, a duality similar to the one formulated by Allum could be said to exist in Britain as well as Naples. When it comes to the question of depoliticization, Putnam's findings indicate that Britain may be farther along this particular road. Just as was the case with parties and interest groups, legislators show a reluctance to recognize class conflict, the central ingredient of the political world:

> Many British politicians, but fewer Italians, feel that in society and politics harmony and consensus are the norm. Further along the scale, many politicians in each country emphasize conflict, but emphasize also its essential reconcilability. And many Italians and a few Britons stress nearly unbridgeable conflicts of interest in social relations. Among the Italians this spectrum of opinion is closely tied to traditional notions of social class relations, while in Britain class conflict is interpreted in a less malignant way and views of social conflict or cohesion are not so intimately linked to specifically class images. Substantial numbers in both countries, though more in Italy, call attention to a distinction between apparent conflict, which may be quite intense, and real conflict, which they consider relatively insignificant.[100]

Technocratic, as opposed to visionary, conceptions of politics are more pre-dominant among British politicians than among Italians, reflecting the correlation between late capitalism and depoliticization.

Political scientists who study elites have a preoccupation with the most uninteresting correlates of behavior—social background, age, occupation, and so on—and consequently it is difficult to generalize beyond the mate-rial collected by more interesting studies, such as those of Allum and Put-nam. If their data are accepted, it indicates a partial qualification of the idea that pragmatism yields greater flexibility. For one thing, it is often the more ideological men who are most flexible, especially those of the left, as Putnam makes clear.[101] But more important, the dual nature of the politician's role in late capitalism leads, not to flexibility, but to a partial immobility. Caught in a bind between a relationship with his constituents based on mobilizing tendencies and one with his colleagues based on de-mobilization, the politician must at one and the same time arouse and suppress political concerns. Since the road to political success lies more with the state than with the district, the parliamentarian will generally resolve his conflicts by suppressing politics in favor of rhetorical mumbo-jumbo, demagogic manipulation of symbolic issues, meaningless debate over trivialities, or publicity as an end in itself. The late capitalist politician is as contradictory as the process that chooses him, and the institutions in which he operates are as intolerant of political concerns as the parties and interest groups that interact with him.

Thus we can see that the late capitalist elected official is only demi-political, that only in his relationship to this constituency is mobilization likely to take place. Even this partial political residue is threatened by vari-ous tendencies characteristic of late capitalist society. For one thing, re-search findings indicate that younger politicians are less ideological in the traditional sense than are older ones. Putnam found that younger politi-cians are more likely to emphasize technical knowledge and to believe that the emergence of "postindustrial" society makes class conflict irrelevant.[102] If this trend were to continue, the political residue would shrink even more. Second, the passage of power away from electoral politicians toward administrators further weakens the political character of elites. Although there is some inclination to treat the bypassing of elected officials as a natural occurrence, like floods or earthquakes, this trend is brought about by the contradictions inherent in the late capitalist polity. Frank Myers finds the cause in the contradiction between accumulation and legitima-tion:

> The decline of legislatures ... is bound in closely with the basic develop-ments of society and its productive system. The continuation of emascu-lated representative bodies is essential to the resolution of the contradiction between an egalitarian and democratic ideology current in a system in which

industrial producers require the authoritative stamp of government to assure continued economic stability necessary for long range planning. Emasculated legislatures permit the corporate state to function smoothly in a way implicitly at odds with liberal theory even while liberal theory may receive rhetorical endorsement.[103]

In other words, depoliticization—this time expressed by the increased impotence of the one semipolitical institution left—again becomes the only solution to the paralysis brought about by class conflict.

Though depoliticized and without principles, the new men of state are by no means open-minded. Those who seek narrow goals along nonideological lines become so absorbed in the quest for power as an end in its own right that their political practice takes on the appearance of a religious crusade, while those interested in the salvation of souls, hankering after bourgeois respectability, adopt the stance of pragmatic brokerage, which they mistakenly believe is the hallmark of bourgeois politics. Thus in 1973 a televised debate between Georges Marchais, head of the French Communist Party, and Valéry Giscard d'Estaing, soon to be the head of France, revealed a strange reversal of traditional roles. Marchais was the utter realist, talking the language of concrete program and the steps necessary to come to power, while Giscard appeared to be the utopian, offering visions of a technocratic future in which both social and technological conflict would disappear, creating a better life for all. A similar reversal has taken place in theory. The "utopian socialism" of Saint-Simon and Fourier has been adopted, not by dissenting political activists (who seem preoccupied with making difficult decisions about logistics and strategy) but by self-proclaimed "realistic" sociologists who, following the technocratic consciousness that emerged in the French Third Republic, greet the arrival of a postindustrial society characterized by a general absence of strife.[104] To use Weber's terminology, the ethic of responsibility has itself been pursued through the ethic of ultimate ends, and vice versa. Fear of class conflict makes utopians out of pragmatists while the desire to share political power makes pragmatists out of utopians.

The deradicalization of formerly revolutionary movements has been much commented on, but less has been said about the gradual utopianization of the ruling class. The incorporation of one of Weber's ethics into the other is responsible for one of the most puzzling and contradictory aspects of the late capitalist state, the tendency of ruling elites to become more and more ideological as the basis of their rule becomes more and more pragmatic. Instead of the promised flexibility, the antipoliticians who come to power offer a blind commitment to the pursuit of power as an end in itself. What I called in the previous chapter the "reification of the state" is accompanied by a fawning worship of power itself rather than of the ends for which power might be used. Power is no longer to be feared but to be praised. Power is good. Power accomplishes. Power, it would seem, cleanses, and absolute power cleanses absolutely. Power, in the words of one neo-Weberian, becomes not a *sturm und drang* phenomenon, but "the generalized capacity of a social system to get things done in the interest of collective goals." Hence, "it can be positively asserted that power, while of course subject to abuses and in need of many controls, is an essential and desirable component of a highly organized society." [105] In such a perspective, the accumulation and distribution of power becomes the purpose of the political system, and those who carry out the task become its political elite.

Most belief systems capable of moving large numbers of people toward collective expression have involved the *ends* for which political action was being undertaken: justice, freedom, equality, the nation, socialism, and so on. The development of the late capitalist state, however, has been accompanied by an increasing suspicion of such goals. The fear of class struggle has tended toward the routinization and regularization of the state, not toward messianic mobilization, and the lack of principle has transformed the ends toward which people were working with such consistency as to undermine their legitimacy. Consequently, in late capitalism the reification of the state and the curtailment of the political imagination lead to the building of ideological conceptions over the *means* of action, not the ends. And since it is extremely difficult to motivate people over means, while ruling classes have destroyed the ends, the ideological tasks of the state and those who serve it become difficult to accomplish. Just as fear can make a person believe at one and the same time in inner strength and divine intervention, ruling classes, when faced with these difficulties, are simultaneously attracted to both a ruthless *Realpolitik* and an eleemosynary utopianism. Late capitalist society makes theory out of practice, a utopia out of cynicism, and a mission out of nihilism.

The coexistence of a ruthless practicality and a naïve utopianism can be seen in the realm of technology. Scientists and engineers, who have a reputation for the hardheaded investigation of facts in the most nondoctrinaire way, are not immune from utopianism, as Robert Boguslaw's interesting book *The New Utopians* documents.[106] In their preoccupation with cybernetic control processes, the new utopians become idealists not over the purposes of technology but over the process itself. In much of the science fiction literature, and also in books like *Walden Two*, the technology of control is more fascinating than the goals for which control is exercised. This technology, it is simplistically believed, will bring about the perfect feedback system, a veritable utopia of smoothly interlocking mechanisms. So it is among the cybernetic utopians of the political process. To them, the social control of the population, the harmonious integration of all disparate elements in a common pattern of deference and restraint, is the goal around which their ideologies are built. The reason for this new harmony is not a vision of a better life, but the pursuit of harmony and integration as an end in itself. Like the paternalistic father who is both loving and threatening, the new political utopians downgrade power as a motive for control while creating a system of power with devastating potentialities. Their conception of power is as cynical as it is myopic, a reflection of the contradiction at the heart of social engineering in a hierarchical society. For given a class society, attempts at smooth and harmonious integration are bound to have a utopian dimension. In this sense, the frustration of ruling in late capitalism, when immobilism blocks so much reform, is particularly conducive to the emergence of ruling class utopianism. The "downtrodden" who spin harmonious dreams out of whole cloth become the elite, and not the mass.

The simultaneous justification of existing power combined with a utopian longing for homeostasis exists in a variety of guises among political elites. The Oxford School of Industrial Relations in Britain, which hopes to still class conflict through the reform of industrial relations practices, is one example of this duality.[107] Others emerge in the technocratic ideology of Giscard and his followers,[108] and in the paternalism of a Henry Ford II or an Agnelli. Even the Nixon presidency, in its fashion, contained both elements. While it would be difficult to imagine anyone more cynical about power and more ruthless in its quest than Nixon and his top aides, their secret conversations reveal all kinds of hopeless utopian longings, symbolized by their belief that they could control the "scenario" and resolve the controversy to their advantage. The more ruthless the practicality, the more utopian the longing for order and control. The clearest example of this contradiction emerges from the administrator who most resembles Boguslaw's new utopian, Robert McNamara. His career illustrates the reversal of Weber's ethics. Weber's great fear was that the zealot would obtain control over the monopoly of the means of violence and then slaughter whole populations in pursuit of his apocalyptic vision. As Secretary of Defense, McNamara possessed control over means of violence much larger than Weber ever could have imagined. As a policy maker, he initiated a series of decisions that brought this violence into use in precisely the way Weber feared. Yet what was the end for which an attempt was made to destroy the populations of three countries? It was nothing other than to preserve the believability of power itself, not an "absolute end" like justice, human equality, or the Kingdom of God. In pursuit of this ideological nonideology, McNamara, the Martin Luther of late capitalism, toyed with all kinds of utopian ideas, like electronic battlefields that would replace actual soldiers or mechanically created boundaries that would stop "aggression." [109] Alternating between a fantastically naïve faith in technology and a thoroughly practical disdain for human life and the possibility of community, McNamara epitomizes the fear of politics and the consequent worship of power so characteristic of the elites of late capitalist society.

Unfortunately for the neo-Weberians—and, indeed, for the rest of us as well—the elites of late capitalist society have not given us the flexibility to counter the exhaustion of alternatives; they have given us instead Robert McNamara and Richard Nixon. The men who control the late capitalist state are as doctrinaire in their devotion to power as an end in its own right as they are pragmatic about the ends for which that power is used. One is left with the worst of both worlds: lack of principles *and* ideological rigidity. In this sense it is fitting that Richard Nixon, often considered the least principled man ever to hold public office in America, was also the most unbending and rigid, not only in matters of personality, dress, appearance, and style, but also in his conception of office. It was the single-minded rigidity of his pursuit of power that allowed the bending of his principles and the sheer transparency of his principles that facilitated his thirst for power. Nixon was the fulfillment of two hundred years of pragmatism just as he was the logical product of two hundred years of the fear of things being out of control. The schizophrenia characteristic of the political process of late capitalism produces men of power who are as locked in by contradictions as the system that sustains them.

In conclusion, the most striking political fact about late capitalism is the absence of politics. The rigidity of the late capitalist state, which I discussed in Chapter 8, would be a solvable problem if the political process were capable of generating new sources of political energy. But the opposite takes place. Citizens, who in early capitalist society constituted the source of republican virtue, become so paralyzed by schizophrenic expectations that they withdraw from political activity almost completely; the result is not a confusion in public opinion, but the lack of a *public* opinion. Without a public, the notion of representative government has no meaning. Nor do mediating mechanisms constitute a source of mobilization. Their energizing functions long in abeyance, mediating mechanisms have opted for the government pole of the duality composing them, making themselves as irrelevant to political change as they are illegitimate. Neither parties nor interest groups are political in any meaningful sense of the term. Finally, public office holders are the products of the depoliticized process. Cautious, unimaginative, and unspontaneous, the late capitalist office holder is anything but political; the one dominant fact of his life would seem to be the fear that he might have to act in a political manner, against which he guards. A politics of politics for late capitalism, in short, reveals more what is not present rather than what is, and shows once again how the exhaustion of alternatives has undermined the ability of societies to work out the political contradictions that they have generated.

10 / The Legitimacy Crisis
of the State

"Any objective analysis . . . can only conclude that a crisis of the most serious magnitude now exists in the response and assessment of the people to their government."

Louis Harris (1973)

"I believe we are coming to a watershed in Western society; we are witnessing the end of the bourgeois idea—that view of human and of social relations, particularly of economic exchange—which has molded the modern era for the last 200 years."

Daniel Bell (1976)

"To the contrary, liberal democracy on the American model increasingly tends to the condition of monarchy in the 19th century: a holdover form of government, one which persists in isolated or peculiar places here and there, and may even serve well enough for special circumstances, but which has simply no relevance to the future."

Daniel Patrick Moynihan (1976)

THE BREEZY OPTIMISM with which partisans of liberal democracy greeted the post–World War II years has, as I pointed out in the Introduction, changed to a desperate pessimism about whether liberal democracy has a future at all. It is no longer uncommon to hear political observers says things like "it would be no bad thing if the expectations of citizens of democratic states were somewhat reduced," [1] even though such statements were once considered too far to the right to be taken seriously. A new tone has crept into the usually placid language of political science, as represented by these musings of Anthony King:

> Although no one has produced a plausible scenario for the collapse of the present British system of government, the fact that people are talking about the possibility at all is in itself significant and certainly we seem likely in the mid or late 1970s to face the sort of "crisis of the regime" that Britain has not known since 1832, possibly not since the seventeenth century. [2]

The new mood is contagious. Willy Brandt's prediction that democracy in Western Europe will last no more than twenty or thirty years, the feeling among "cold warriors" that communism is about to triumph throughout the Mediterranean, and the defensiveness of Henry Kissinger are all based on the assumption that liberal democracy as we know it has seen its best days.[3] The most relentlessly pessimistic analysis of all has been offered by Robert Nisbet, who sees in the rise of mass democracy an erosion of political civility so extensive that militarism, bureaucracy, and unchecked power become the hopeless condition of modern man. The "tendencies of political centralization and social disintegration" characteristic of the modern state render attempts to restore a sense of political community close to impossible.[4] We seem consigned, in his vision, to a choice among equally nihilistic alternatives.

The manifest popularity of this pessimism should not be surprising. As we have seen, the emergence of late capitalism has seriously altered the nature of the state and the political system within which it operates. The inability of government to achieve its professed ends despite its seeming power, the separation of decision makers from the public, the eclipse of rationality and its replacement by a world of illusions and falsehoods, the bankruptcy of traditional political thought, the replacement of genuine politics by an alienated opposite, the schizophrenic nature of citizenship, the breakdown of mediating mechanisms, and the utopianization of ruling classes—all these processes operating together have contributed to a serious paralysis of the late capitalist state.

The secret, in a sense, is out; liberal democracy no longer works the way it is supposed to. While some, especially politicians, continue to proclaim that happy societies will once again exist, both popular sentiment and intellectual opinion conclude otherwise. The trend toward the exhaustion of alternatives raises the important questions of whether the capitalist state can continue to exist with minimal legitimacy and, if it cannot, what new forms it is likely to take. The legitimacy crisis of late capitalism poses questions too important to the future of Western nations to be ignored.

THE ATTACK ON LIBERAL DEMOCRACY

The everyday perception that something is amiss in the world of liberal democracy is now commonplace. One example is a poll taken by *Le Monde* in late 1970, which showed that 47 percent of the French people felt that the state defends the rich, compared to 8 percent who said it defends the poor. In addition, 42 percent felt that the state was unjust or intolerant; 24 percent said that the state leans to the right, as opposed to

3 percent who saw it leaning to the left; 69 percent indicated that the state weighed heavily on their daily lives, while only 27 percent said that it did not; and 73 percent felt that they were impotent in the face of the state, compared to 23 percent who felt that they could influence its actions.[5] A widely reported survey of American political attitudes between 1964 and 1970 showed similar sentiments, proving that the traditional French hostility toward the state is not unique. A few of the U.S. findings are worth reproducing:[6]

TABLE 2. Proportion of the Public Expressing Little Confidence in Government (Percent)

	1964	1966	1968	1970
1. How much do you think you can trust the government in Washington to do what is right?				
Only some of the time:	22.0	31.0	37.0	44.2
2. Would you say that the government is run pretty much by a few big interests looking out for themselves . . . ?				
Few big interests:	29.0	34.0	39.2	49.6
3. Do you think that almost all of the people running the government . . . don't seem to know what they are doing?				
Don't know what they are doing:	27.4	—	36.1	68.7

Moreover, alienation from government in these years cut across class and regional lines, affecting every group in the population.[7] Opinions like these seem to have intensified since 1970. A poll undertaken by Cambridge Survey Research showed that 38 percent of those interviewed in 1972 thought that their leaders regularly lied to them; this rose to 55 percent in 1974, and then to an astounding 68 percent in the spring of 1975.[8] The strongly worded conclusion of Arthur H. Miller of the University of Michigan that "a situation of widespread, basic discontent and political alienation exists in the U.S. today"[9] seems, if anything, too tame. One must wonder how long a society can continue to exist in which over half its members show strong negative feelings toward the government and toward those who occupy positions of power within it.

Survey findings like these have been responsible for a reevalution of attitudes toward liberal democracy by a number of leading social and political thinkers. Indicative of the new trend is a report of the Trilateral Commission, called *The Governability of Democracies*, which can justly be viewed as a watershed in the attitude of bourgeois social science toward liberal democracy.[10] The Trilateral Commission, an association of "private" citizens from the United States, Western Europe, and Japan, has recently come to public attention through its close connections with the Carter presidency.[11] Under the leadership of men like Zbigniew Brzezinski and other planners of what I called the Transnational State, the Commission has adopted the position that only through the cooperation of all the major capitalist powers—working in harmony with the leaders of Third World countries that control vast resources—can the stability of the present world system be maintained. Because this perspective requires some sacrifice of short-term sovereignty and self-interest in exchange for long-range global planning, the Commission is often viewed as "liberal" in contrast to the aims of the U.S. Republican Party. The Trilateral Commission—which is financed by a number of U.S. and European bankers including David Rockefeller—has come out in favor of national planning, at sharp variance with the laissez-faire rhetoric of men like former U.S. Secretary of the Treasury William Simon. This approach, also, is willing to sacrifice the short-term goals of any given corporation for their long-term benefits. Because of its links with the Carter administration the remarks of the Trilateral Commission on the "manageability" of democracy seem especially important.

The Trilateral Report is divided into four sections: one on Europe, another on Japan, a third on the United States, and some concluding remarks about structural change. The European section, written by Michel Crozier, and the American, authored by Samuel P. Huntington, are the most interesting from the perspective of this book, though the concluding recommendations, which I will discuss shortly, are the most controversial. In both Europe and the United States, all the usual agencies of "political" socialization are seen as falling apart. People are no longer deferential accepting as inviolate what established authorities tell them. The value structure has changed, and new expectations have revolutionized political life. Crozier, for example, echoes Jürgen Habermas' *Legitimation Crisis* when he notes that traditional standards of rationality in the West, such as the distinction between ends and means, have begun to disintegrate. Cut loose from ties of obedience and traditional values, people begin to make political demands on the state. The schizophrenic citizen of Chapter 9, in other words, begins to find a cure. The result is an "overload" of inputs that cannot be met by government. Consequently, in Crozier's words, "the more decisions the modern state has to handle, the more helpless it becomes." [12]

Huntington carries Crozier's pessimism further. What he calls the "democratic surge of the 1960s" was a challenge to all existing authority systems. As people became politicized, their disappointment was inevitable because democratic societies cannot work when the citizenry is not passive. The result is a substantial withering away of confidence in government, such as the University of Michigan survey cited above, of which Huntington makes extensive use. An accompanying decline of faith in the party system, combined with the inability of presidents to finish their terms, gives rise to what Huntington suggestively calls a "democratic distemper" that hinders the political system from carrying out its traditional policies, domestic and foreign. If the system is to correct itself, this "excess of democracy" must be reduced. There must be an emphasis on the fact that the "arenas where democratic procedures are appropriate are limited." Individuals and groups should be depoliticized, since a functioning system requires "some measure of apathy and non-involvement." In general, the demand is one for "balance";

> A value system which is normally good in itself is not necessarily optimized when it is maximized. We have come to recognize that there are potentially desirable limits to economic growth. There are also potentially desirable limits to the extension of political democracy. Democracy will have a longer life if it has a more balanced existence.[13]

In order to restore this balance, the authors make a number of controversial proposals. First, they strongly endorse mechanisms for economic planning. Noting that "the governability of democracy is dependent upon the sustained expansion of the economy," the Report implicitly argues that the only way to make people content with political apathy is to increase their income, and this task is too important to be left in the hands of market mechanisms. The authors' hopes for planning are as much political as they are economic, for a workable capitalist economy and acceptance of that structure are, to them, linked. Second, the Report calls for a strengthening of political leadership. Sentiments that one would have thought dead after Vietnam and Watergate are dramatically reborn: "The trend of the last decade toward the steady diminution [?] of the power of the Presidency should be stopped and reversed. The President clearly has the responsibility for insuring national action on critical matters of economic and foreign policy. He cannot discharge that responsibility if he is fettered by a chain of picayune legislative restrictions and prohibitions." Some people never seem to learn; the seeds of a new Watergate have already been planted, even before the old roots have been fully ripped out. Third, the Report calls for attempts to put some life back into dying political parties, endorsing government aid to parties, but calling for balance in the sources of campaign finance. The decision of the state to finance elections to itself, a consequence of the breakdown of mediating mechanisms discussed in Chapter 9, is worrisome to these writers. Fourth, unspecified restrictions on the freedom of the press are urged. ("But there is also the need to assure to the government the right and the ability to withhold information at the source.") Fifth, education should be cut back because the democratization of education, minimal as it has been, has raised expectations too high. Assuming that education is related to "the constructive discharge of the responsibilities of citizenship," then "a program is necessary to lower the job expectations of those who receive a college education." On the other hand, if citizenship training is not the goal of education, then colleges should be turned into vast job training centers. Sixth, the Report calls for "a more active intervention in the area of work," since alienation must be attacked at its roots. German experiences with codetermination are rejected in favor of state aid in experimenting with new forms of work organization. Finally, supranational agencies of cooperation among the major capitalist powers are encouraged, including the mobilization of private groups (just like the Trilateral Commission) to share "mutual learning experiences." [14]

The unusual bluntness of *The Governability of Democracies* violates a taboo of democratic societies, which is that no matter how much one may detest democracy, one should never violate its rhetoric in public. Consequently, this report has generated a full-scale controversy within the Trilateral Commission itself. When it was formally presented, at a conference in Kyoto, Japan, on May 30 and 31, 1975, numerous commission members from the United States and Europe denounced it as too pessimistic, and some even urged that the Trilateral Commission repudiate its own study. In a major speech Ralf Dahrendorf, now head of the London School of Economics, aligned himself with the critics, saying, "I am not, contrary to many others today, pessimistic about the future of democracy." [15] The passion of the Kyoto debates reveals that liberal democracy still has its partisans, that conservative intellectuals by no means unanimously share disdain for it. Yet in spite of the sincerity of those within the Trilateral Commission who have objected to the Crozier-Huntington analysis, one cannot escape the feeling that their commitment to democracy is as much tactical as it is principled, that they are prepared to retain democratic structures only until their breakdown becomes more complete. The seriousness with which *The Governability of Democracies* has been discussed, even by those who object to it, confers legitimacy upon its ideas because it makes reasonable what only ten years ago would have seemed to be an extremist position. Just as during the war in Indochina, the Defense Department continued to adopt "options" that it had shortly before dismissed as extreme, Western intellectuals are now calmly discussing hypotheses that they once would have associated with lunatic fringes. This tendency of social theorists to become chiliastic as the system they defend becomes untenable suggests that the issues in the debate over liberal democracy are about as deep as political issues can get.

Why should liberal democracy, after a sustained period of existence, suddenly become, not an assumption that everyone shares, but a hypothesis about which people argue? At one level, the answer lies in the polls cited above, which show the lack of positive affect toward the state characteristic of populations in the 1970s. The authors of the Trilateral Report are very much shaken by these figures. "Leadership is in disrepute in democratic societies," [16] they note, and without faith in leadership democracy as we know it can no longer exist. Huntington's section on the United States extends this preoccupation. To him, the most basic cause of the "democratic distemper" lies not so much in anything that governments have been doing lately, but in changing patterns of political participation; it is citizens, not leaders, who are responsible for the instabilities of what Maurice Duverger has recently called "plutodemocracy." [17] Huntington is particularly concerned with the increase in political participation among black Americans. Attributing it, rightly, to their increased group consciousness, he concludes that it is not greater education that makes for greater participation, but the degree to which an individual or group develops a preoccupation with political questions. The rhetoric of democratic values begins to be taken seriously. As Huntington notes:

> For much of the time, the commitment to these values is neither passionate nor intense. During periods of rapid social change, however, these democratic and egalitarian values of the American creed are reaffirmed. The intensity of belief during such creedal passion periods leads to the challenging of established authority and to major efforts to change governmental structures to accord more fully with those values.[18]

Democracy, in short, starts to work.

The decline in public faith in government and the demand that democratic values be taken seriously are interrelated. Liberal democracy loses respect because it is not democratic enough, because its liberalism is maintained at the expense of its popular component. At the same time, structural factors inherent in the capitalist mode of production bring about a crisis of disaccumulation, best reflected in the economic troubles of the 1970s. Capitalist societies seem no longer able to deliver the prosperity that has always been the main argument in their favor. With private capital no longer able to generate enough investment to keep the system afloat, the state becomes more and more involved in the economy on behalf of private capital. But this, as James O'Connor argues in *The Fiscal Crisis of the State*, merely shifts the problem from one area to another, because government assistance is, almost by definition, a confession of the failures of capitalism.[19] State aid to private capital in turn reinforces public cynicism toward government, since those who feel that the state only helps the rich are basically correct. In other words, problems of legitimacy and problems of accumulation reinforce each other. At the very moment when capitalism no longer seems to be working, democracy is just beginning to work. As one fails and the other succeeds, the inherent differences between them emerge, so that those whose main stake lies in preserving a capitalism that is no longer viable are forced to become critics of a democracy that is potentially more alive than ever, while those who consider themselves genuinely democratic increasingly become anticapitalist. The legitimacy crisis is produced by the inability of the late capitalist state to maintain its democratic rhetoric if it is to preserve the accumulation function, or the inability to spur further accumulation if it is to be true to its democratic ideology. The Trilateral Commission understands this contradiction:

> The heart of the problem lies in the inherent contradictions involved in the very phrase "governability of democracy." For, in some measure, governability and democracy are warring concepts. An excess of democracy means a deficit in governability; easy governability suggests faulty democracy. At times, in the history of democratic government the pendulum has swung too far in one direction; at other times, too far in the other.

Noting that in the late capitalist countries "the balance has tilted too far against governments," [20] the authors of the Trilateral Report make explicit their preference: accumulation is far more important than legitimation. If democracy has come to interfere with capitalism, there is no doubt which they would choose.

One need not agree with the Trilateral Commission's conclusions to be sympathetic to the analysis. What their argument boils down to is that a legitimacy crisis that can be described as *subjective*—based on the negative attitude of the population toward government—is becoming *objective*—based on structural contradictions within capitalist societies themselves. On this point, I would have to agree with them. The political conditions of late capitalist society, I have been arguing, have locked state action into contradictions from which there is no easy escape. In this situation of stalemate, it is not surprising that the inherent tensions between liberalism and democracy are beginning to surface. The temporary resolutions to this tension described in Part I have played themselves out, and in the 1970s, the problems that were not resolved in the nineteenth century have resurfaced with intensity. Capitalism and democracy do face each other as real alternatives, and at some point in the near future—one cannot tell when—one or the other will come to dominate. Thus, the dominant political issue facing late capitalism will not take place *within* the rules of the game but *over* them.

Forces are already lining up on both sides of this issue, and the willingness of the Trilateral Report to make public antidemocratic feelings that have long been in the closet is only one indication of the new political tone. As late capitalist societies are unable to develop new compromises to the tensions between liberalism and democracy, they will find themselves pushed one way or the other. Defenders of the powers that be have begun to make their prescriptions clear. Their programs involve such remedies as cutbacks in democratic expectations, attacks on the principle of participation, and, in some cases, outright proposals for authoritarian solutions. Defenders of democracy have not been as organized and articulate, but there is a growing feeling among dissenting groups that democracy has indeed become the issue. In the final sections of this book, I want to review some of the authoritarian proposals being advanced and contrast them with the possibility of the resurgence of democratic dreams. One cannot predict in advance who would win a confrontation between capitalism and democracy, but one can analyze the weapons on both sides.

AUTHORITARIAN PROCLIVITIES

The legitimacy crisis of late capitalism has placed defenders of existing social arrangements in an uneasy position, forcing them to deny once strongly asserted values. As they try to maintain control of a system that they feel is slipping away from them, their liberalism turns into social control, their concern for welfare becomes benign neglect, their faith in democracy is transformed into a penchant for hierarchy, their internationalism is reduced to a carping ethnocentrism, and their dreams of the future suddenly become the nightmares of the present. Retracing their steps, they discover that the world is not quite as they thought, and they are prepared to advocate some extreme solutions in order to bring it back into line with their prejudices and preconceptions. Having carefully admonished their antagonists to play by the rules, they wish to suspend the rules when they no longer work to their benefit. In this section, I want to look at some of the antidemocratic solutions being advocated by defenders of the capitalist mode of production. My argument will *not* be that liberal democracy is about to turn into some sort of fascist state; fascism, among other things, requires a degree of mobilization quite at odds with the depoliticized character of late capitalism.[21] Rather, I will describe three alternatives that seem to be most likely: restricting the activity of government; increasing alienated politics; and moving toward explicitly authoritarian structures. Each of these alternatives has its advocates, though no single one has yet achieved hegemony as the preferred strategy.

By far the most popular tendency, probably because it seems least radical on the surface, is the attempt to restrict the activity of government. This is a reflection of what I called in Chapter 9 the political theory of resignation, which argued that since solutions to basic problems do not exist, political action to rectify them is useless. This disenchantment with the ability of government to resolve social and economic contradictions flies in the face of the history of the capitalist state, which expanded each time a solution outside of it was not to be found. For this reason, the anti-statist urge constitutes a serious reversal of a previously held position. But more is at stake here than inconsistency. The fact is that most state spending is popular, not in the abstract (people regularly denounce big government in polls), but as it affects specific individuals (social security, hospitals, unemployment compensation, etc.). The syllogism is unalterable: welfare spending is democratic; some want to eliminate or substantially reduce it; those who do become undemocratic. The attack on government activity has become, in other words, a not particularly well disguised attack on democracy itself.

Businessmen attack big government the most, and their motive in doing so is a clear distrust of democracy. Contrary to assertions that businessmen supported the welfare state in order to buy off discontent, most corporate executives accepted government spending for social welfare only with extreme reluctance. Now that capitalist economies are in the midst of stagflation, these antidemocratic attitudes, always latent, are shooting to the surface. One study of corporate executives in the United States found that in private, businessmen were unreconciled to the ideal of one man, one vote, and all it implies; their attitudes were not much different from the laissez-faire elitism of the Harmonious State.[22] Which of the following statements were made in the nineteenth century and which in 1975? [23]

> It is one man one vote. And as the poor and the ignorant are the majority, I think it is perfectly certain—and it is only consistent with all one has heard or read of human nature—that those who have the power will use it to bring about what they consider to be a more equitable distribution of the good things of this world.

> One-man one-vote will result in the eventual failure of democracy as we know it.

> We are dinosaurs at the end of an era. There is a shift of power base from industry and commerce to masses who cannot cope with the complexities of the modern world.

> The normal end of the democratic process gives unequal people equal rights to pursue happiness in their own terms. There is a difference between the free enterprise system and a democracy which we also espouse.

> In this good, democratic country where every man is allowed to vote, the intelligence and property of the country is at the mercy of the ignorant, idle, and vicious.

The first statement was made by the Englishman J. A. Froude in 1887, and the last by an American businessman in 1868; the three in the middle, though indistinguishable in tone from the other two, were made by American corporate executives in the mid-1970s. There is a direct link between the businessman's distrust of democracy as expressed in statements like these and his distaste for social welfare programs. When the *Wall Street Journal* speaks of "putting a lid on social programs," [24] what it has in mind is a feeling that people want too much and that a democratic polity is unfortunately organized to make them believe that they can get it. The real cure to excessive spending, in their view, is to curb excessive democracy.

In the past five years this Babbitt-like prejudice of businessmen has been given a certain elegance by various European and American political scientists. Samuel Brittan, who works for both the *Financial Times* of London and Oxford University, has pointed out that "liberal representative democracy suffers from internal contradictions" that have recently made themselves felt. One endemic problem is that "democracy . . . imparts a systemic upward bias to expectations." [25] This results in what Daniel Bell has called "the revolution of rising entitlements," [26] the feeling that citizens seem to have that their dreams can come true, that economic insecurity, for example, can be abolished. But such demands make it difficult for the capitalist state to govern, since the more money ordinary people receive, the less is available for accumulation, and the more politicized the population, the less the power available to the state. As Anthony King notes for Britain:

> The reason it has become harder to govern is that, at one and the same time, the range of problems that government is expected to deal with has vastly increased, and its capacity to deal with problems, even many of the ones it had before, has decreased. It is not the increase in the number of problems alone that matters, or the reduction in capacity. It is the two coming together.[27]

According to King, the performance of government cannot be substantially altered; hence the only solution is to lower public expectations. Government is compared to an electrical system; it has become, in the favorite word of the new antidemocratic creed, "overloaded." [28] The only sensible thing to do, these writers conclude, is to reduce the current, although building new sockets would solve the problem and keep the lights on as well.

When stripped of its social science rhetoric, the theory of overload or "rising entitlements" is little more than the traditional antidemocratic biases of big businessmen. Moreover, contradictions in both positions make their sincerity suspect. Businessmen want less government, but they also support Aldo Moro's $51 billion plan to "modernize" Italian industry, Giscard's $7 billion pump priming of September 1975, and the extraordinary probusiness budget of Britain's Prime Minister James Callaghan in April 1976.[29] The only proposal to give money to business that business has opposed in recent years was former Vice President Rockefeller's $100 billion energy package, and this was more a glimmer in his eye than a serious policy option. Similarly, the neo-neo-Hamiltonian political scientists (the neo-Hamiltonians were the men around Theodore Roosevelt) speak of the necessity to streamline government, but they also desire a strong presidency, backed by a large military and foreign policy machinery, and increased expenditures for the police.[30] In short, neither the businessmen nor the social scientists are incipient anarchists; it is democracy, not government, that has aroused their ire, and their attacks on the latter are a prelude to restrictions on the former. Liberal society, in their view, can be preserved only if democracy is curtailed.[31]

This unease about democracy cannot be divorced from concern about capitalism itself. As Daniel Bell has noted:

> Though capitalism and democracy historically have arisen together, and have been commonly justified by philosophical liberalism, there is nothing which makes it either theoretically or practically necessary for the two to be yoked.[32]

There is a strong feeling in certain quarters that capitalism can be preserved only if democracy is held in check. Demands on the government are seen as a kind of "political inflation." Just as inflation is "caused" by groups pushing their self-interest at the expense of the common good, the democratic state's capacity is weakened by the too selfish pursuit of individual and group demands.[33] Controlling runaway inflation requires such noncapitalist measures as wage and price controls and state planning; controlling runaway democracy may also require control on expectations and, if necessary, state repression. As Brittan, following Schumpeter, rightly observes, the contradictions of democracy are inherently economic in nature.[34]

The recessions of the 1970s have intensified the feeling in ruling class circles that if capitalism is in trouble, democratic demands will have to be curtailed. An inadvertent rationale for this point of view has been supplied by Arthur Okun.[35] He argues that a well functioning capitalist economy produces substantial inequality, but that an inflexible pursuit of equality would be economically inefficient. While Okun, in good eclectic fashion, calls for balance, in periods of economic difficulty the argument is easy to advance that economic growth will occur when expectations about equality are lowered. High unemployment, *Business Week* noted in March 1976, "has created an economic situation that is eerily reminiscent of Karl Marx's predictions." When *Business Week* and Karl Marx agree, the situation must be serious indeed. The article also noted:

> In the Western world, something has changed radically in political economics. Economists and politicians now agree that by themselves the tradi-

tional modes of stimulating economies by government spending or increasing the money supply will not end high unemployment.[36]

Neither Democrats nor Republicans have found the answer, according to this assessment. Okun's balance, represented by full employment bills, comprehensive job training, and other government policies, is seen as a stopgap at best. Republican attempts to cut back expenditures are not measuring up to the dimensions of the crisis. Unstated but implied throughout is the feeling that drastic economic conditions require drastic changes in the political system. Democracy, in other words, is under attack because capitalism is not working, when, presumably, it is capitalism that should be under attack, for democracy is working.

Reductions in the activity of government are thus seen as one way of increasing the options of the ruling class. But there is a price. The critique of government spending stands for a disenchantment with equality, one of the key aspects of democratic theory. Citizens whose "expectations" have been reduced are citizens who have become resigned to their lot at the bottom of a hierarchy. Without a myth of opportunity, visible, articulated discontent may be the consequence. Discussing cutbacks in social services for the poor, *Business Week* quoted manpower expert Lloyd Ulman of the University of California: "I'm concerned about the young people, especially the blacks. The less they squawk now, the more of a problem we are storing for the future." [37] The image of an uprising of discontent by a population that has come to expect social welfare programs constitutes the major stumbling block of the whole strategy; cutbacks in welfare are a two-edged sword for ruling classes, enhancing immediate flexibility at the cost of longer run legitimation problems. Not surprisingly, as a result there has been some interest shown in other possible ways out of the dilemma. An increase in what I called in Chapter 9 "alienated politics," constitutes a second possible strategy for ruling classes in the late capitalist period.

Politics becomes alienated to the degree that the everyday political activity of people is used against them to reinforce passivity, instead of being used by them to advance their own collectively determined goals. Alienated politics is in many ways similar to surplus value. In order to increase surplus value and therefore his capital, an employer, when faced with a working day whose length has been agreed upon, can try to increase the "productivity" of a given worker in that period by instituting a "speedup" which, if the costs or reproducing the worker are held constant, will yield a greater proportion of the surplus product to himself. So it goes with ruling classes. An increase in alienated politics requires some way of enhancing the productivity of political action such that a smaller percentage of the collective social power produced is kept by the citizens. The most obvious method of accomplishing this task is to promote passivity by discouraging active participation in political and social life. If the strategy of cutting back government activity represented an attack on equality, the strategy of increasing alienated politics becomes little more than an attack on participation. And since, as I pointed out in the Introduction, equality and participation are the twin pillars of democratic theory, reinforcing alienated politics becomes, like lowering expectations, an attack on democracy itself.

The irony of the attack on participation is that there was not very much to begin with. Direct, informed participation in political affairs has rarely been a characteristic of the capitalist state in this country. Instead, solutions like the Franchise State instituted a system of bargaining that Lowi has called "interest group liberalism." [38] Under such a system, direct participation was sacrificed for carefully orchestrated negotiation between the leaders of variously affected interest groups. With the stagnation inherent in late capitalism, writers have begun to argue that even this minimal level of participation has become maximal, that liberal democracy can no longer afford even interest group liberalism if it is to survive unscathed. Samuel Brittan, as we have seen, finds one of the principal causes of the internal contradictions of liberal democracy to be the desire of ordinary people for social welfare, but he includes as an even more important factor the tendency of interest groups to bargain for rewards for their members.[39] The one must be cut back just as surely as the other, he concludes, or else liberal democracy will be torn apart. An even more passionate defense of a similar position took place in 1968, when *The Public Interest* sponsored a symposium on New York City. A summary of the discussion, which included many prominent officials, professors, and writers, asked whether the United States was "witnessing the ultimate, destructive working out of the telos of liberal thought." According to this symposium, New York City at one time represented the essence of a Madisonian politics of incremental interests, in which organized "subsystems" competed for public favors. Because of internal contradictions, however, these subsystems tended to break down. The conclusion, expressed in a memo that was read by President-elect Nixon, was self-evident, given the assumptions:

> That the society is breaking down means that the liberal state will no longer do. It must, on pain of anarchy or civil war, be replaced by a regime which explicitly recognizes the necessity of subsystems and which is prepared to create substitutes for those subsystems when they break down. Our problem is that informed opinion is moving in precisely the opposite direction.[40]

In this version, interest group liberalism can be preserved only if the state organizes and constitutes the interest groups. What little democratic participation there is would be reduced even more. "Informed opinion" may be moving the other way because it is not prepared to jettison even the minimal commitment to liberal democracy that exists at the moment.

Nonetheless, *The Public Interest* symposium was prophetic, because its focus was on New York City, and in the mid-1970s New York City was most directly facing the new political realities. New York's troubles have been described as a "fiscal crisis," but that is a half truth at best. What is most significant about the decisions of 1975–1977 is that they have stripped New York of its traditional political system. As *The Public Interest* pointed out, New York's politics was the most advanced form of interest group liberalism in the United States, for in this city bargaining among interest groups held the key to most public policy decisions. In this context, the decision to create agencies like the Emergency Financial Control Board represents an attempt to impose new government structures on the city, which would replace the minimal amount of democracy inherent in a bargaining system with decisions handed down from above. Nearly all the participants in these events have agreed that New York's budget as such is not at issue, but its methods of carrying out public business. Under the veritable coup d'état that has taken place there, citizens had better not only reduce their expectations, but also the idea that their participation in affairs of government would be welcome. For the immediate future, interest group leaders in New York will spend more time imposing the demands of the state on their members than they will be communicating the desires of their members to the state. *The Public Interest*'s call for the creation of new subsystems turns out to be a nightmare come true.

As New York goes, so may the rest of the world. As far as ruling classes are concerned, participation is clearly an idea whose time has passed, and we are likely to see attempts to roll back the few victories for increased participation of the postwar years. In West Germany, an attempt to obtain parity for labor unions in the system of codetermination was defeated by a coalition that wants economic growth instead. The defeat of *Paritätische Mitbestimmung* is a warning to unions that there are limits to what the capitalist class will accept in the name of participation. Yet attacks on the principle of a nonalienated politics create their own problems. Just as people have come to expect a certain level of social services, they also accept as a right the notion of participation. This does not mean that they want to participate at all times—most people, particularly in the United States, find political participation a bore—but it does mean that they reserve the right to do so when they feel aggrieved. In this sense, to restrict participation not only comes into conflict with democracy; it violates some of the basic principles of liberalism as well. Defenders of capitalist society may find that not only is democracy in contradiction with the liberal need to accumulate, but so may be aspects of liberalism itself. If both liberalism and democracy come under attack, the ability of late capitalism to reproduce itself may be upheld, but at costs so dear that they would transform the political structure into something unrecognizable.

Because restrictions on government activity are antidemocratic and limitations on participation can become illiberal, some have drawn the appropriate conclusion and suggested that capitalist societies will increasingly require explicitly authoritarian political structures. As we have seen, the Trilateral Commission's Report on *The Governability of Democracies* has suggested as much, and in an interview published after the Report was completed, Samuel Huntington was even more explicit:

> There has to be a realistic appreciation that we can't go back to a simpler world—that we're going to live in a world of big organizations, of specialization and of hierarchy. Also, there has to be an acceptance of the need for authority in various institutions in the society.[41]

Huntington's point may seem extreme, but already some of the Western capitalist societies are facing the option of authoritarianism. Italy, as so often, may be an indication of the future, for there the theory and practice of Christian Democracy are in serious trouble. The ideology of *interclassismo*, which held that all classes would reap the fruits of big business guardianship of the state, has been unable to stem the appeal of left-wing parties. As Giacomo Sani has shown, public opinion generally desires the inclusion of formerly "antisystem" parties like the Communist Party, while the leaders of the Christian Democrats remain far more cautious.[42] It seems clear that if the latter refuses to accept the former into the government, liberal democracy in Italy will fall victim, not to communism, but to a capitalist party unprepared to accept its own political logic. In this sense, in the short run, to quote P. A. Allum, "the Italian ruling class will be forced to choose between its progressive and authoritarian faces."[43] Any attempt by the Christian Democrats to rule without the left would almost necessarily be authoritarian, given current sentiment in that country.

But, to paraphrase Tolstoy, while all stable political systems resemble one another, each unstable system is different in its own way. There are as many versions of authoritarianism as there are of democracy, and to suggest that explicit authoritarian solutions are a possibility is not to answer any questions, but to raise many. What forms of authoritarian government are we likely to see if late capitalist societies start to move in that direction? Extrapolating from all the tendencies that I have been discussing, it seems that the most likely form authoritarianism would take is a neocorporatism resembling some of the features of earlier experiments tried out in the 1920s. As I pointed out in Chapter 4, early experiments with corporatism ran into difficulty because businessmen were not ideologically prepared to accept the restrictions on their freedom that were necessary to bring it into being. Experiences with the Franchise State may have changed this, and if this is the case, then the late 1970s and 1980s could be a much more fruitful period for corporatism than the 1920s. There is nothing so powerful as an idea whose time is fifty years late.

In this context it is important to make a distinction between corporatism, which characterized the Italian economy in the 1920s, and fascism, which succeeded it and then spread to Germany. Fascism contained overt state direction of the economy and a system of vigilante repression and mass mobilization that businessmen found inherently unstable, even though many supported it. Corporatism is far more compatible with the capitalist mode of production, and it also preserves a closer resemblance to the forms of a liberal democratic polity. Philippe Schmitter has described how a corporatist form could emerge out of capitalist needs:

> The more the modern state comes to serve as the indispensable and authoritative guarantor of capitalism by expanding its regulative and integrative tasks, the more it finds that it needs the professional expertise, specialized information, prior aggregation of opinion, contractive capability and deferred, participatory legitimacy which only singular, hierarchically ordered, consensually led representative monopolies can provide.[44]

The following can be considered the major aspects of a corporatist organization of the society. First, the economy would be under the domination of monopolies that would make investment decisions privately. Second, these monopolies would work closely with a state planning apparatus that would be organized to help them further their investment decisions with maximum dispatch. Third, selected representatives of "responsible" unions would be consultants to the planning agencies, charged with the task of ensuring that decisions about wages would be accepted. Fourth, a system of wage and price controls would be instituted to stymie inflation, though the controls would be more on the former than on the latter. Fifth, restrictions on freedom of assembly and speech would be designed to prevent breaks in the continuity of the system. Sixth, social welfare programs would be retained, for much the same purpose. Seventh, depoliticization would be the theme of social and political life in general. Eighth, transnational political units would extend the corporatist framework to all the capitalist countries, since it would be extremely difficult for any one of them to maintain a formal democratic system if the others were abandoning it. It should be clear how a form of neocorporatism could arise out of an extension of already existing late capitalist practices. Corporatism would not come about stealthily in the middle of the night, but would be the product of barely noticed changes in everyday practices. When all effective power has passed from representative bodies to corporate-government planning agencies, the institution of corporatism would be complete.

None of the countries described in this book could at this time be called corporatist, but each is experimenting with proposals that have a corporatist potential. My description of these experiments is not, therefore, meant to imply that the authors of them are self-conscious authoritarians, merely that their ideas could easily be adapted to conform to authoritarian proclivities. This is the case, for example, with Felix Rohatyn's proposal to reconstitute the Reconstruction Finance Corporation, one of the semi-corporatist schemes of the 1920s.[45] Rohatyn, who played a major role in New York City's Emergency Financial Control Board, is also known as one of the most articulate business spokesmen for state planning in the United States, and his sympathy for spending for social programs has led many to classify him as a "liberal." His RFC plan, as he makes quite clear, is not simply a proposal to give public money to private firms; Rohatyn wants the proposed agency to use its money as a weapon, to force firms to conform to sound planning procedures. In short, his RFC constitutes the political-economic shell for a corporatist organization of the economy. The same conclusion can also be drawn from some of the advocates of state planning in the United States. Planners seem divided into two ideological camps. Those on the left, such as John Kenneth Galbraith, Leonard Woodcock, and Wasily Leontief, support legislation like the Humphrey-Javits bill, which would retain democratic structures while trying to introduce an element of rationality into the accumulation process. But state planning is also sympathetically viewed by some on the right, such as Huntington and the Trilateral Commission, who see it as a way of ensuring social peace while at the same time allowing for rational accumulation.[46] An attempt to steer between these two approaches is a plea by Max Ways of *Fortune* for "a new political stance" for business. Ways, who praises Rohatyn and his plans, is, like all the neocorporatists, critical of traditional business laissez-faire and opposition to social spending, but at the same time he also wants to find a way to keep democratic demands under control:

> More and more voters have discovered the possibility of bettering their lives through government action. In itself, this discovery is a legitimate extension of the democratic process. But the U.S. has not yet learned to channel and restrain these exuberant pressures so that they won't be self defeating.[47]

Presumably, some kind of channeling and restraining agency will determine which actions are "legitimate" and which will have to be curbed.

Given the priorities of late capitalism, planning proposals that originate from the left could easily be adopted by the right and turned in an authoritarian direction. American advocates of planning could learn something from Britain. When a new Labour government came into power after the Conservatives were unable to settle a miners' strike, leaders toward the left of the party like Anthony Wedgwood-Benn supported a

National Enterprises Bill (NEB), which would nationalize industries that were in trouble.[48] But the NEB turned out to be something quite different, an incipient corporatist form far more compatible with the traditional Tory fascination for corporatist solutions.[49] Once created, the NEB was headed by Sir Don Ryder, an industrialist with a reputation for toughness. While it is too early at this writing to foresee how the NEB will turn out, the decision of a Labour Party position paper of 1975 to give "priority to industrial development over consumption and even over our social objectives" [50] would seem to indicate that the NEB will be more concerned with private investment decisions than with democratic control over corporations. Unless state planning agencies include active members of consumer organizations and unions, they will in all likelihood pave the way for a neocorporatism that would "reform" the polity by "streamlining" and "modernizing" it along the lines of the economy.

What would be the likely results of an explicit move toward quasi-authoritarian solutions to the political contradictions of late capitalism? There is no denying that a move in this direction could severely damage humane and democratic values. One should never underestimate the destructive potential of a ruling class that has painted itself into a corner, as every living Vietnamese peasant has come to understand. Late capitalist elites are capable of enormous wreckage before they yield their control over the state. Yet the fascination for corporatism is as much an indication of the defensiveness of late capitalist ruling classes as it is an aggressive plan to control everything in sight. Corporatism remains a solution that was tried and found wanting; an avant-garde notion in 1920, it is quite hackneyed at the present. In this sense, authoritarian solutions may intrigue ruling classes because they feel themselves becoming illegitimate, a phenomenon noted some time ago by Antonio Gramsci:

> If the ruling class has lost its consensus, i.e., is no longer "leading" but only "dominant," exercising coercive force alone, this means precisely that the great masses have become detached from their traditional ideologies, and no longer believe what they used to believe previously.[51]

As ruling classes consider authoritarian solutions like corporatism, one can question whether they would continue to be "ruling classes" at all. If the art of ruling lies in the selection of various options in order to preserve power, then the dominant forces within late capitalism are losing their ability to rule. Thus "rule by force" is a contradiction in terms. Authoritarian solutions are an expression of the inability to rule, of the replacement of choice among options with the requirement of preserving power by any means necessary. What the writers in this section symbolize, as a result, is bankruptcy and impotence, not hardheaded realism; political extremism, not moderation and civility. Those who seek to replace liberal democracy by some sort of authoritarian structure are engaged, not so much in a strategy for the ruling class, as in voicing the decline of the ruling class. This does not make authoritarianism any less of a danger to humane values, but it does indicate the desperation of a system that can no longer preserve itself in the face of the desires of the majority.

DEMOCRATIC DREAMS

The antidemocratic intellectuals discussed in this chapter base their analyses on the assumption that a historical impasse has taken place in liberal democracies, and that the next few years will consequently see a major transformation of Western society. As I have suggested, there are grounds for believing that their general analysis is correct, but I would disagree with them on some of the particulars. First, one cannot know how long the impasse will last; a historical era may be coming to an end, but historical eras generally take a long time in so doing. A postliberal democratic solution will take a long time to work itself out. In the meantime, existing structures will constitute the political framework within which the transition will take place; for that reason, they will remain important. Second, one cannot know what the future will bring. While it would be satisfying to state with precise foresight what the next stage is likely to resemble, only a fool, an astrologer, or a social scientist would try. The truth is that all possible futures will be decided by people themselves, either by ordinary people producing politics as they see fit or by elites trying to work their way out of intractable contradictions. Those who want to know what the outcome of this struggle will be should look elsewhere; those who wish to know the kinds of issues over which these struggles will be waged might consider remaining here. For as I have suggested, the immediate battles will be over the options that the state can command, and because those options are a product of the way people think and act politically, ordinary people will have much more to say about the political future of late capitalism than ruling elites.

In the long run, democratic dreams are far more important than authoritarian proclivities. Pressure from below has constituted a driving force in the adoption of new solutions to the political contradictions of capitalism and has constituted the major reason for the obsolescence of solutions once adopted. Without that pressure, no tension would be present, for then there would be nothing to prevent the capitalist state from serving as a mechanism of accumulation pure and simple. Democratic dreams have come and gone, sometimes appearing as visions of what a humane world would be like and sometimes turning into perverse nightmares as people become desperate in the search for answers to the pressures in their lives. But even though they may be suppressed momentarily, their existence can never be discounted, for the desire to be part of a meaningful community is a human urge that no historical event has yet completely overcome. What, then, is the status of the democratic dream in late capitalism? Will pressure from below be able to offset the authoritarian inclinations of dominant classes in order to make the immediate future one to which we can look forward with anticipation rather than dread? The question has no abstract answer—only political struggle can determine the result—but one can call attention to the importance of the struggle and suggest some possible forms that it might take.

The dilemmas faced by ordinary people are the opposite of those faced by ruling classes; if the latter wish somehow to expand their options, the former, particularly where class struggle is overt, wish to see them contracted. In this sense, the major objectives of democratic pressure should be to counter the directions emerging within dominant elites: increasing the number of activities in which government is engaged; decreasing the proportion of alienated politics; and thinking constructively and imaginatively about democratic solutions transcending the limitations of the capitalist mode of production.

Those who advocate less government spending on social programs know what they are doing, for given the accumulation function of the state, the only way by which government activity can be reduced is to attack the most democratic point, which is social welfare policy. But at issue is not some abstraction called "spending" or "policy" but the real needs of real people. The most immediate political strategy for ordinary people, therefore, should be directed toward both the preservation and the expansion of government services. A social democratic perspective makes perfect sense in the short run for a number of reasons. First, it is based on a historical tradition, since the welfare state has been in existence for some time. Those who wish to roll back social welfare policies become the true radicals, and their attempt to divorce themselves from the history of their own society should be pointed out. Second, however perverse government activity like welfare becomes, it is still meeting some of the needs of the poorest members of the society, and in that sense it is far preferable, by almost any human criterion, to cutbacks. But third, and most important, extensions of government activity restrict the number of options that dominant classes possess, for each increase in social spending means either a reduction in the accumulation function of the state or an intensification of fiscal and political contradictions. Implicitly understanding this, those in power are prepared to wage a battle against more spending on social programs, which makes the continuation of the welfare state essential to a strategy of realizing democratic dreams.

The most articulate presentation of this option is Piven and Cloward's notion of "exploding" the relief roles of the welfare system, in the absence of fundamental economic changes in the society.[52] Written before the fiscal crisis of the state became acute, what Piven and Cloward envisioned for welfare recipients becomes both the lot of, but also a strategy for, the majority of the population. Attempts to cut back higher education, medical care, police protection, sanitation, and just about every other aspect of domestic services puts everyone, metaphorically, on relief. For this reason, the events in New York City of 1975 and 1976, which constitute a testing ground for ruling classes in their strategy of lowering expectations and brutalizing participation, are also a testing ground for popular demands. In a period of recession, for example, there is every reason why public higher education should expand rather than contract, to absorb the unemployed and make good use of their time, if for no other reason. Similarly, "hard times" in the economy generally are times in which government spending goes up, and with it the dreams of the majority of the population for protection against depression. The fact that this is not happening, that most people seem to have accepted the "necessity" of spending cuts in New York, indicates that dominant forces are winning this particular struggle. Most people seem to have forgotten that the state owes them a decent life with all the social services that they have every right to demand, and because they have, the first step in a strategy to overcome their demoralization has been lost. In a situation of this sort, the preservation and extension of accepted social welfare programs would become a critique of the notion that business conditions are what determines the nature of public policy.

But an extension of domestic social policy, no matter how necessary in the short run, is not a strategy that by itself will bring about basic democratic changes in the nature of the late capitalist state. The power of the state, I have been arguing, is based on the way people produce and reproduce politics, and in that sense, the most meaningful long-range strategy would be one that maximized the nonalienated character of politics. What this means is that in order to fulfill democratic dreams, people must find ways to use the power generated out of political activity for their own purposes, to minimize the proportion of this power that is reimposed on them for purposes over which they have no say. It would appear that there are two general ways in which this could be accomplished: one by "hoarding" the social power that people produce; the other by expending it on activities that they themselves decide.

Hoarding constitutes a first step in the direction of a nonalienated politics, a negative refusal to have alienated power exercised over oneself.[53] It is often recognized that if workers did not work, if they withheld their labor power, no value could be produced, and therefore the capitalist mode of production would grind to a halt. Similarly, if the citizens of late capitalism were to withhold what could be called their "political production," to hoard their political power for themselves, the capitalist state could not continue to function for very long. There are degrees of political hoarding. Simple apathy toward the organized political process is one, and for this reason the authors of the Trilateral Report are so worried about the subjective decline in positive affect toward government, for such alienation represents a first step in the hoarding of political power from the state. The contradiction of depoliticization is that while it serves the need of reducing demands on the state, it also inadvertently contributes to the sense that the existing political system is unresponsive to people's needs. More organized forms of hoarding also exist. Those who engage in cooperative enterprises—such as neighborhood grocery cooperatives, daycare centers, and other social activities—are in a sense hoarding a certain amount of their power from the state, even if their expressed motive is a nonpolitical one. The same is true of those who withdraw into rural areas to produce their own means of subsistence as much as they can. Even though such activities of the "counterculture" by themselves do not pose any direct threat against the existing order, they are a form of hoarding insofar as they withdraw from the existing political system's definition of what constitutes the productive "obligations" of citizenship. When workers go on strike, they hoard their labor power for themselves; an important strategy for political change would involve a "citizens' strike," in which people would refuse to participate in the organized rituals that go under the name of politics in late capitalist society.

But hoarding is only a negative step, which, like a strike, is necessary to understand the nature of one's oppression, but which must lead in new directions or become self-defeating. Strikes, as participants in them often come to understand, are as important for the solidarity they generate as for the immediate concrete objective, and in a similar manner, citizens' strikes, leading to a hoarding of political power, become important when they release a political energy that mobilizes people to begin to make basic decisions for themselves. The difference can be expressed as a shift from unproductive citizenship to repoliticization. Economists have long made a distinction between productive and unproductive labor, in which the former contributes to surplus value and therefore the accumulation of capital, while the latter does not.[54] The same is true of citizenship. A "productive" citizen in a capitalist society is one who contributes to the political power of the state, and therefore to the imposition of an alienated power over people's lives. Hoarding involves an assertion of unproductive citizenship, which is why whenever people engage in political activity that does not conform to the "rules," their efforts are dismissed as "counterproductive," which in a real sense they are. A significant step involves the transformation of nonproductive citizenship into *repoliticization*, the attempt by people to seek genuine politics for themselves outside the formal political arena. Any kind of mobilization, even "reactionary" ones like opposition to school busing, unleashes a political energy that gives people a sense of what their liberation might be about. A repoliticized population is one that is subversive of the dominant tendencies associated with the late capitalist state.

The most compelling form of repoliticization involves the direct expenditure of political power by people on alternatives decided by themselves. Not satisfied with mere hoarding, and searching for a vehicle to express their repoliticization, people associate themselves with organized political movements whose purpose is to share social power with people rather than to hold it over them. It matters little whether this strategy is pursued within, outside, or alongside the existing electoral system, so long as the crucial component is the commitment to a nonalienated politics. Examples outside the electoral arena per se would include cultural and social activities, such as the attempts by the Italian Communist Party to create a viable cultural world within bourgeois society. Such movements, if they work, yield a sense of collective power and competence that is far more significant than winning another seat in the legislature. Examples of liberating activity within the electoral system might include attempts by public officials, generally at the local level, to develop methods of sharing their power and their information with the people who elected them, becoming power builders rather than power brokers. This is the underlying philosophy behind the decision of a number of American radicals to involve themselves in electoral activity at the local level.[55] In other words, behind strategies of this sort is an understanding that the depoliticizing needs of late capitalism must be countered with the liberation of political energy, awakening in people a feeling that they themselves are human and capable of deciding what to do with their collective power. To be avoided is a strategy that reproduces the depoliticized character of late capitalism within opposition movements, for as Gramsci once warned, "In political struggle one should not ape the methods of the ruling classes, or one will fall into easy ambushes."[56]

What I have been suggesting resolves itself into nothing other than an injunction to be political, which is not so much a strategy as an imperative. It does not tell people what to do but how to do it. Its meaning becomes apparent, not over tactics, but over conceptions. Three examples may make it clearer what the injunction to be political means. First, should the question arise as to whether the left should organize a political party, the response should depend on the recognition that no *political* parties currently exist, that the bourgeois parties are not political at all because they express an alienated politics at odds with the original meaning of politics in the West. This recognition does not answer the question (people themselves will have to do that), but it does indicate that if a genuinely political party were to be created, its role would be unique, and consequently its tasks could not be derived from existing institutions called parties. Similarly, if intellectuals are worried about whether they have a major role to play in the transition to a postcapitalist society, the answer is that they do—indeed, their role is a major one. For if struggles over conceptions of politics are as important as I have suggested, there is as great a need for conceptualizers as for organizers; to quote Gramsci one last time, " 'Popular beliefs' and similar ideas are themselves material forces." [57] Finally, the importance of being political does not settle the long dispute between reformism and militancy, but it does suggest that "reforms" depressing popular participation lead in the wrong direction while those arousing and sustaining it create a basis of politicization that can be expanded. The debates over reformism within the left have generally concerned themselves with ends—which is as it should be—but the question of means may be important also.

The ultimate objective of repoliticization, in my view, should be to resurrect the notion of democracy, which is far too important an ideal to be sacrificed to capitalism. The political contradictions of capitalist society, I have been arguing, grow out of attempts to reconcile the need for accumulation, which has been justified by philosophical liberalism, and the need to legitimate, which has given rise to democracy. Accumulation, as Daniel Bell has pointed out, will take place in any complex economy.[58] The problem is not that capitalist societies accumulate, but the way in which they do it. In order for the beneficiaries of accumulation to remain a narrow group, a boundary is established beyond which democracy is not allowed to intrude; you have the political system, or at least part of it, liberal ideology claims, but leave the accumulation of capital to us. With liberalism increasingly becoming irrelevant, even to its most articulate defenders, the time has come to think, not about demolishing accumulation, but about democratizing it. The way to eliminate the contradictions between accumulation and legitimation is to apply the principles of democracy to both—to give people the same voice in making investment and allocation decisions as they theoretically have in more directly political decisions. The democratization of accumulation can be called socialism, but it is not the name that is important but the concept behind it. To suggest that socialism can avoid the political contradictions discussed in this book is not to argue that any existing societies that are called socialist have—the degree of democratization introduced into accumulation varies greatly from one to another—but to affirm that the democratization of accumulation will prevent any nonrepresentative group of power holders from perverting the democratic process by warping it to suit their own private aggrandizement. Democracy can become reality only when its logic transcends artificial barriers and is applied to all the fundamental decisions made in a modern society, a task in many ways facilitated by the phenomenal technological capacity developed by these societies.

If a choice has to be made between liberalism and democracy, it is my hope that the overwhelming majority of people in late capitalist societies will pick the latter. Whether they do or not is beyond me or anything I can say. Neither revolutionary optimism nor quiescent cynicism are appropriate moods here. Moods do not determine the outcome of struggles; only the contrasting strengths and weaknesses of the contending parties can do that. One side has the power and control over the means of repression and consciousness, the other the weight of numbers, the flow of history, and the possession of a democratic dream. Neither has a claim to certainty. To understand, though, is to contribute, and it has been my desire in this book to illustrate to ordinary people the nature of the political contradictions of their society so that they may be able to find for themselves ways in which to resurrect the democratic dream. It is, in the long run, their vision that will determine whether authoritarianism or democracy is to be our political condition.

Notes

Introduction

1. John E. Sawyer, "As the World Turns," *New York Times*, December 30, 1974, p. 13.
2. *The Governability of Democracies* (New York: Trilateral Commission, 1975). For an analysis see Alan Wolfe, "Capitalism Shows Its Face," *The Nation*, November 29, 1975, pp. 557–63, and chap. 10 below.
3. Eric Nordlinger, *Conflict Regulation in Divided Societies* (Cambridge: Harvard Center for International Affairs, 1972).
4. Juan Linz (ed.), *The Breakdown of Democracy*, forthcoming.
5. See Frederick Pike and Thomas Stritch (eds.), *The New Corporatism* (South Bend, Ind.: University of Notre Dame Press, 1974).
6. Robert Skidelsky, "Keynes and Unfinished Business," *New York Times*, December 19, 1974, p. 45.
7. Robert Heilbroner, *An Inquiry into the Human Prospect* (New York: Norton, 1974), 90.
8. Georg Lukacs, *History and Class Consciousness* (London: Merlin Press, 1971), 101.
9. Karl Marx, "Afterword to the Second German Edition," *Capital* (New York: International Publishers, 1967), 1: 16.
10. Hannah Arendt, *The Origins of Totalitarianism* (revised edition; Cleveland: World, 1958), 137, 139.
11. C. B. Macpherson, *The Political Theory of Possessive Individualism* (London: Oxford University Press, 1964), 208, 221.
12. Carole Pateman, *Participation and Democratic Theory* (Cambridge: At the University Press, 1970), 20–22.
13. Lucio Coletti, *From Rousseau to Lenin* (New York: Monthly Review Press, 1973); Marshall Berman, *The Politics of Authenticity* (New York: Atheneum, 1972).
14. Karl Marx and Friedrich Engels, "The Communist Manifesto," in *Selected Works* (New York: International Publishers, n.d.), 52.

15. Arthur Rosenberg, *Democracy and Socialism* (Boston: Beacon Press, 1965), 138.

16. See Jürgen Habermas, *Legitimation Crisis* (Boston: Beacon Press, 1975), and the literature cited therein.

17. Karl Mannheim, *Ideology and Utopia* (New York: Harvest Books, n.d.).

18. Karl Polanyi, *The Great Transformation* (Boston: Beacon Press, 1957), 172.

19. Seymour Martin Lipset, *Political Man* (Garden City, N.Y.: Anchor Books, 1963), 297.

20. For an example, see Harry Girvetz, *The Evolution of Liberalism* (New York: Collier Books, 1966).

21. The best example of this tendency is Ronald Radosh and Murray Rothbard (eds.), *A New History of Leviathan* (New York: Dutton, 1972). For a more extended critique of this kind of approach to the capitalist state, see Alan Wolfe, "Il New Deal: Discorsi Nuovi e interpretazione vecchie," *Quaderni Storici*, 28 (January–April 1975), 294–301.

CHAPTER 1

1. Marc Bloch, *Feudal Society* (Chicago: University of Chicago Press, 1961), 2:408.

2. Jacob Burkhardt, *The Civilization of the Renaissance in Italy* (New York: New American Library, 1960), 39–120.

3. For a good study of this process see William F. Church, *Richelieu and Reason of State* (Princeton: Princeton University Press, 1973).

4. Hans Rosenberg, *Bureaucracy, Aristocracy, and Autocracy* (Boston: Beacon Press, 1966), 13.

5. Pierre Goubert, *L'Ancien Régime*, vol. 2: *La Société* (Paris: Colin, 1969).

6. Fernand Braudel, "Qu'est-ce que le XVIe siècle?," *Annales*, 8 (January–March 1953), 73. Cited in Immanuel Wallerstein, *The Modern World-System* (New York: Academic Press, 1974), 68.

7. Perry Anderson, *Lineages of the Absolutist State* (London: New Left Books, 1974), 18, 40.

8. Nicos Poulantzas, *Pouvoir politique et classes sociales* (Paris: Maspero, 1971), 1:176.

9. Anderson, p. 19.

10. Wallerstein, p. 309.

11. John U. Nef, *Industry and Government in France and England, 1540–1640* (Philadelphia: American Philosophical Society, 1940), 56.

12. Quoted in Eric Foner, *Free Soil, Free Labor, Free Men* (New York: Oxford University Press, 1970), 23.

13. William Appleman Williams, *The Contours of American History* (Chicago: Quadrangle, 1966), 41.

14. For an analysis of the consequences of this dual meaning, see Schlomo Aveneri, *Hegel's Theory of the Modern State* (Cambridge: At the University Press, 1972), 141–54.

15. Otto Hintze, "The Emergence of the Democratic Nation-State," in Heinz Lubasz (ed.), *The Development of the Modern State* (New York: Macmillan, 1964), 70.

16. R. H. Tawney, *Equality* (London: Unicorn Books, 1969), 102.

17. Alexis de Tocqueville, *The Old Regime and the French Revolution* (Garden City, N.Y.: Anchor Books, 1955), 20.

18. David Roberts, *Victorian Origins of the British Welfare State* (New Haven: Yale University Press, 1960), 14.

19. Eli F. Heckscher, *Mercantilism* (London: Allen and Unwin, 1934), 2:271.

20. Maurice Dobb, *Studies in the Development of Capitalism* (New York: International Publishers, 1963), 120.

21. Quoted in Theodor Schieder, *The State and Society in Our Times* (London: Nelson, 1962), 4.

22. Guy P. Palmade, *Capitalisme et capitalisme française au XIXe siècle* (Paris: Colin, 1961), 265.

23. William C. Lubenow, *The Politics of Governmental Growth: Early Victorian Attitudes Toward State Intervention, 1833–1848* (London: David and Charles, 1971).

24. Arthur Lewis Dunham, *The Industrial Revolution in France, 1815–1848* (New York: Exposition Press, 1955), 388–419.

25. W. O. Henderson, *The State and the Industrial Revolution in Prussia 1740–1870* (Liverpool: Liverpool University Press, 1958).

26. Louis Hartz, *Economic Policy and Democratic Thought: Pennsylvania, 1776–1860* (Cambridge: Harvard University Press, 1948).

27. Adam Smith, *The Wealth of Nations* (London: Pelican Books, 1960), 233.

28. Lubenow, pp. 10, 116, 125.

29. Dunham, pp. 409–10.

30. William Manchester, *The Arms of Krupp* (New York: Bantam Books, 1970), 158.

31. Joint-stock companies formed after legal reforms made the process easier are called "democratic" by Clapham as opposed to earlier one that he calls "aristocratic." This is similar to the distinction being made here. See Sir John Clapham, *Free Trade and Steel, 1850–1886*, vol. 2 of *An Economic History of Modern Britain* (Cambridge: At the University Press, 1952), 142–43.

32. Adolph Berle and Gardiner C. Means, "Corporation," in *Encyclopedia of the Social Sciences* (New York: Macmillan, 1931), 4:418.

33. Hartz, pp. 7, 37, 54, 71.

34. Quoted in Elie Halévy, *The Liberal Awakening, 1815–1830*, vol. 2 of A

History of the English People in the Nineteenth Century (London: Benn, 1949), 72.

35. Richard Cobb, *The People and the Police: French Popular Protest 1789–1820* (London: Oxford University Press, 1972), 19.

36. Allan Silver, "Social and Ideological Bases of British · Elite Reactions to Domestic Crisis in 1829–1832," *Politics and Society*, 1 (February 1971), 180–86.

37. F. C. Mather, *Public Order in the Age of the Chartists* (Manchester: Manchester University Press, 1959), 56. See also Allan Silver, "The Demand for Order in Civil Society," in David Bordua (ed.), *The Police* (New York: Wiley, 1967), 1–24.

38. Mather, pp. 67–68.

39. Elie Halévy, *The Growth of Philosophical Radicalism* (Boston: Beacon Press, 1960), 403.

40. Quoted in Mather, p. 124.

41. Lubenow, p. 59.

42. Quoted in David Montgomery, *Beyond Equality: Labor and the Radical Republicans, 1862–1872* (New York: Vintage Books, 1972,) 383.

43. It was an Irish peasant farmer, and not a political philosopher, who best captured the bias of the Accumulative State, when he said, "Would to God the Government would send us food instead of soldiers." Quoted in Cecil Woodham-Smith, *The Great Hunger* (New York: Signet Books, 1964), 132.

44. S. G. Checkland, *The Rise of Industrial Society in England, 1815–1885* (New York: St. Martin's Press, 1964), 329.

45. Charles Morazé, *The Triumph of the Middle Classes* (Garden City, N.Y.: Anchor Books, 1968), 316.

46. See Foner for the complete story of the rise of this ideology.

47. Incredible as it seems, this Malthusian logic never disappeared. By 1974 it was still popular, only now its scope included the whole world. For a good example of this way of thinking, see the comments of Jay Forrester in *The Boston Globe*, November 24, 1974, cited in Geoffrey Barraclough, "The Great World Crisis I," *New York Review of Books*, January 23, 1975, p. 25.

48. Lionel Robbins, *The Theory of Economic Policy in English Classical Political Economy* (New York: St. Martin's Press, 1968); Roger Warren Prouty, *The Transformation of the Board of Trade* (doctoral dissertation, Columbia University, 1954); Henry Parris, "The Nineteenth Revolution in Government: A Reappraisal Reappraised," in Peter Stansky (ed.), *The Victorian Revolution* (New York: Watts, 1973), 63; Marc Blaug, *Ricardian Economics* (New Haven: Yale University Press, 1958); J. B. Brebner, "Laissez-Faire and State Intervention in Nineteenth Century Britain," *Journal of Economic History*, 8 (1948), 59–73; and Edward R.

Kittrell, "Laissez-Faire in English Classical Political Economics," *Journal of the History of Ideas*, 27 (October–December 1966), 610–20.

49. Smith, p. 169.

50. Quoted in Lubenow, p. 177.

51. Henderson, p. 98.

52. Ibid., p. 192.

53. Prouty, *Board of Trade*; Henry Parris, *Government and the Railways* (London: Routledge and Kegan Paul, 1965).

54. Lubenow, p. 24.

55. Shepard Bancroft Clough, *France: A History of National Economics, 1789–1939* (New York: Scribner's, 1939), 147–48, 178–79, 235–36.

56. Henderson, p. 163.

57. Ibid., pp. 186–87.

58. Shepard B. Clough, *The Economic History of Modern Italy* (New York: Columbia University Press, 1964), 69.

59. Parris, pp. 205–206.

60. Thomas C. Cochran and William Miller, *The Age of Enterprise* (New York: Harper and Row, 1961), 132.

61. The position that the role of the state in America's economic development was maximal is associated with Carter Goodrich. See his *Government Promotion of American Canals and Railways, 1800–1890* (New York: Columbia University Press, 1960) and *The Government and the Economy* (Indianapolis: Bobbs-Merrill, 1967). Goodrich's position has been criticized by Douglass C. North, who has argued that he is reading the present into the past. See *Growth and Welfare in the American Past* (Englewood Cliffs, N.J.: Prentice-Hall, 1966), 98–107. Actually, this seems to be a feature of both sides in the debate, although to this reader the stronger case is clearly made by Goodrich.

62. Stephen Salsbury, *The State, The Investor, and the Railway: The Boston and Albany, 1825–1867* (Cambridge: Harvard University Press, 1967), 34.

63. An excellent exposition of Gallatin's views is contained in Williams, pp. 188–90.

64. Morazé, p. 136.

65. Clough, *France*, p. 172; Rondo E. Cameron, *France and the Economic Development of Europe, 1800–1914* (Princeton: Princeton University Press, 1961), 134.

66. Henderson, pp. 89–95.

67. Clough, *Italy*, p. 80.

68. Henderson, pp. 120–47.

69. J. H. Clapham, *The Early Railway Age, 1820–1850*, vol. 1 of *An Economic History of Modern Britain* (Cambridge: At the University Press, 1950), 521.

70. Quoted in Sir John Clapham, A *Concise Economic History of Britain* (Cambridge: At the University Press, 1963), 274.

71. Asa Briggs, *The Making of Modern England, 1783–1867* (New York: Harper Torchbooks, 1965), 339.

72. Bray Hammond, *Banks and Politics in the United States from the Revolution to the Civil War* (Princeton: Princeton University Press, 1967).

73. Williams, p. 241.

74. Cameron, p. 203.

75. Albert Soubol, *Historie de la révolution française* (Paris: Gallimard, 1962), 2:339.

76. Dunham, p. 399.

77. Quoted in Harold U. Faulkner, *Politics, Reform, and Expansion, 1890–1900* (New York: Harper Torchbooks, 1963), 140.

78. See Robert M. Stewart, *The Politics of Protection* (Cambridge: At the University Press, 1971).

79. Briggs, p. 323.

80. Ibid., p. 313.

81. Olive Anderson, *A Liberal State at War: English Politics and Economics in the Crimean War* (New York: St. Martin's Press, 1967), 93.

82. Roy F. Nichols, *American Leviathan* (New York: Harper Colophon Books, 1966), 244.

83. *Ex Parte Milligan*, 4 Wall. 2, 18 L. Ed. 281.

84. Montgomery, p. 47.

85. Hartz, *Economic Policy*; Goodrich, *Government Promotion*; Sidney Fine, *Laissez-Faire and the General Welfare State* (Ann Arbor: University of Michigan Press, 1967), 19; Henry W. Broude, "The Role of the State in American Economic Development, 1820–1890," in Harry N. Scheiber (ed.), *United States Economic History* (New York: Knopf, 1964), 118–22.

86. Clough, *France*, p. 24.

87. Clough, *Italy*, pp. 47–51.

88. Malcolm J. Rohrbough, *The Land Office Business: The Settlement and Administration of American Public Lands, 1789–1837* (New York: Oxford University Press, 1968), 300–301.

89. Olive Anderson, "The Janus-Face of Mid-Nineteenth-Century English Radicalism," *Victorian Studies*, 8 (March 1965), 231–42.

90. Hartz, p. 289.

91. Anthony Trollope, *Phineas Finn* (London: Penguin English Library, 1972).

92. Thomas Carlyle, *Chartism*, in Alan Shelston (ed.), *Thomas Carlyle: Selected Writings* (London: Penguin Books, 1971), 189, 192, 194.

93. Marx once called Carlyle a genius, but one who had gone to the devil, leaving only his cult behind him ("*Zum Teufel ist der Genius, der Kultus*

ist geblieben"). Karl Marx, *Capital* (New York: International Publishers, 1967), 1:255.

94. Carlyle, p. 187.

95. David Roberts, "Tory Paternalism and Social Reform in Early Victorian England," in Stansky, pp. 147–68.

CHAPTER 2

1. Quoted in Shepard Bancroft Clough, *France: A History of National Economics 1789–1939* (New York: Scribner's, 1939), 182.

2. R. H. Tawney, *Equality* (London: Unicorn Books, 1964), 103.

3. E. H. Carr, *The Twenty Years' Crisis* (New York: Harper Torchbooks, 1964), 48.

4. A. V. Dicey, *Lectures on the Relation Between Law and Public Opinion in England During the Nineteenth Century* (London: Macmillan, 1952), 126–210.

5. Matthew Carey, "The New Olive Branch. or. An Attempt to Establish an Identity of Interests Between Agriculture, Manufacturers, and Commerce," in *Essays in Political Economy* (Philadelphia: Carey and Lea, 1822), 261–362.

6. Matthew Carey, "Address No. 12," in ibid., p. 100, and "New Olive Branch," p. 283.

7. Adam Smith, *The Wealth of Nations* (London: Pelican Books, 1960), 181–84.

8. J. B. Say, *A Treatise on Political Economy* (Philadelphia: Grigg, Elliot, 1848), 84–85, 143.

9. Louis Say, *Etudes sur la richesse des nations, et Réfutations des principales erreurs en économie politique* (Paris: A la Librairie du Commerce, 1836), 1–23.

10. Dicey, *Law and Public Opinion;* David Roberts, *Victorian Origins of the British Welfare State* (New Haven: Yale University Press, 1960).

11. David Montgomery, *Beyond Equality: Labor and the Radical Republicans, 1862–1872* (New York: Vintage Books, 1972), 80.

12. Ibid., p. 81.

13. Karl Marx, *The Grundrisse* (New York: Vintage Books, 1973), 883–93.

14. Quoted in Montgomery, p. 343.

15. Henry Carey, *Principles of Social Science* (Philadelphia: Lippincott, 1878), 3:463.

16. Joseph Dorfman, *The Economic Mind in American Civilization, 1606–1865* (New York: Viking Press, 1946), 2:795.

17. Frédéric Bastiat, *Harmonies économiques* (Bruxelles: Meline, 1850). See also Charles Gide and Charles Rist, *A History of Economic Doctrines* (Boston: Heath, n.d.), 330.

18. Charles Morazé, *Les Bourgeois Conquérants* (Paris: Colin, 1957).

19. Asa Briggs, "The Language of Class in Early Nineteenth Century England," in Asa Briggs and John Saville (eds.), *Essays in Labor History* (revised edition; New York: St. Martin's Press, 1967), 43–73.

20. Quoted in Gide and Rust, p. 329.

21. Montgomery, pp. 230–60.

22. Ibid., p. 81.

23. John A. Scott, *Republican Ideas and the Liberal Tradition in France, 1870–1914* (New York: Columbia University Press, 1951), 159.

24. Ibid., p. 178.

25. Theodore Hamerow, *Struggles and Accomplishments* vol. 2 of *The Social Foundations of German Unification,* (Princeton: Princeton University Press, 1972), 181.

26. Quoted in ibid., p. 162.

27. Quoted in Theodore Hamerow, *Restoration, Revolution, Reaction: Economics and Politics in Germany, 1815–1871* (Princeton: Princeton University Press, 1966), 228.

28. Barbara Tuchman, *The Guns of August* (New York: Dell, 1971), 65.

29. Quoted in Carr, pp. 45–46.

30. Lawrence Gronlund, *The Cooperative Commonwealth*, ed. Stow Persons (Cambridge: Belknap Press of Harvard University Press, 1965), 74.

31. William Stanley Jevons, *The State in Relation to Labour* (London: Macmillan, 1910). See also David Harris, "European Liberalism in the Nineteenth Century," *American Historical Review*, 60 (1964–65), 502–26.

32. Quoted in Richard Hofstadter, *Social Darwinism in American Thought* (revised edition; New York: Braziller, 1959), 147.

33. Antonio Gramsci, *Selections from the Prison Notebooks* (New York: International Publishers, 1971), 160.

34. *Slaughter House Cases*, 16 Wallace 111 (1873), Mr. Justice Field, dissenting.

35. Robert G. McCloskey, *American Conservatism in the Age of Enterprise* (Cambridge: Harvard University Press, 1951), 81.

36. Quoted in H. V. Emy, *Liberals, Radicals and Social Politics, 1892–1914* (Cambridge: At the University Press, 1973), 244–45.

37. *Pollack v. Farmers' Loan and Trust Company*, 158 U.S. 601 (1895).

38. *Slaughter House Cases*, 16 Wallace 110 (1873).

39. *Lochner v. New York*, 198 U.S. 57 (1905).

40. *U.S. v. E. C. Knight Co.*, 156 U.S. 1 (1895); *In Re Debs* 158 U.S. 564 (1895).

41. William Graham Sumner, *What Social Classes Owe Each Other* (New York: Harper, 1883), 66.

42. Graham Adams, *The Age of Industrial Violence, 1900–1915* (New York: Columbia University Press, 1966).

43. Norman Pollack, *The Populist Response to Industrial America* (Cambridge: Harvard University Press, 1962).

44. *Legal Tender Cases*, 12 Wallace 680–81 (1871). Cited in McCloskey, p. 106.

45. Quoted in Sidney Fine, *Laissez-Faire and the General Welfare State* (Ann Arbor: University of Michigan Press, 1967), 180.

46. William Graham Sumner, "The Power and Beneficence of Capital," in Albert Galloway Keller and Maurice R. Davie (eds.), *Essays of William Graham Sumner* (New Haven: Yale University Press, 1934), 2:22.

47. Idem.

48. "The Concentration of Wealth: Its Economic Justification," in ibid., p. 165.

49. Harold U. Faulkner, *Politics, Reform, and Expansion, 1890–1900* (New York: Harper Torchbooks, 1963), 79.

50. Quoted in Alfred H. Kelly and Winfred Harbison, *The American Constitution: Its Origins and Development* (revised edition; New York: Norton, 1955), 565.

51. *Lochner v. New York*, 198 U.S. 59 (1905).

52. Quoted in Rondo E. Cameron, *France and the Economic Development of Europe, 1800–1914* (Princeton: Princeton University Press, 1961), 103.

53. Quoted in Fine, p. 98.

54. E. L. Godkin, *Unforeseen Tendencies of Democracy* (Boston: Houghton Mifflin, 1898).

55. See below, pp. 235–36.

56. Clough, p. 229.

57. Margot Hentze, *Pre-Fascist Italy: The Rise and Fall of the Parliamentary Regime* (New York: Octagon Books, 1972), 172, 203.

58. The classic study is still George Dangerfield, *The Strange Death of Liberal England* (New York: Capricorn Books, 1961).

59. See David Thomson, *Democracy in France since 1870* (fourth edition; New York: Oxford University Press, 1964), 139–47.

60. R. B. McCallum, "From 1852 to 1895," in Elie Halévy, (ed.), *Victorian Years 1841–1895*, vol. 4 of *A History of the English People in the Nineteenth Century* (London: Benn, 1951), 447.

61. W. L. Guttsman, *The British Political Elite* (New York: Basic Books, 1963), 80.

62. Ibid., p. 82.

63. Daniel Halévy, *La Fin des notables* (Paris: Grasset, 1930).

64. Jean Lhomme, *La grande bourgeoisie au pouvoir, 1830–1880* (Paris: Presses Universitaires de France, 1960), 275–79.

65. See Theodore Zeldin, *France: 1848–1945* (Oxford: Clarendon Press, 1973), I:570–604, for a partial correction of Lhomme's findings.

66. Hentze, p. 41.

67. Shepard B. Clough, *The Economic History of Modern Italy* (New York: Columbia University Press, 1964), 120.

68. Gaetano Salvemini, "La Piccola borghesia intellettuale del mezzogiorno d'Italia," in *Scritte sulla Questione meridionale, 1896–1955* (Milan: Einaudi, 1955), 412. Cited and analyzed in P. Allum, "The Neapolitan Politicians: A Collective Portrait," *Politics and Society*, 2 (Summer 1972), 391.

69. Arthur Rosenberg, *Imperial Germany: The Birth of the German Republic 1871–1918* (Boston: Beacon Press, 1964), 19.

70. John R. Gillis, "Aristocracy and Bureaucracy in Nineteenth Century Prussia," *Past and Present*, 41 (December 1968), 105–29.

71. See Michael Wallace, "Changing Concepts of Party in the United States: New York, 1815–1828," *American Historical Review*, 74 (December 1968), 453–91.

72. This idea is suggested by Hannah Arendt, *The Human Condition* (Chicago: University of Chicago Press, 1959).

73. Quoted in Thomas C. Cochran and William Miller, *The Age of Enterprise* (New York: Harper Torchbooks, 1961), 157.

74. Leonard D. White, *The Federalists* (New York: Macmillan, 1948); *The Jacksonians* (New York: Macmillan, 1954).

75. See Olive Anderson, "The Janus-Face of Mid-Nineteenth Century English Radicalism," *Victorian Studies*, 8 (March 1965), 231–42.

76. Quoted in Cochran and Miller, p. 166.

77. Quoted in ibid., p. 285.

78. Quoted in ibid., p. 266.

79. James G. Scott, *Comparative Political Corruption* (Englewood Cliffs, N.J.: Prentice-Hall, 1972), 26.

80. A good description of the affair is contained in Guy Chapman, *The Third Republic of France: The First Phase, 1871–1894* (New York: St. Martin's Press, 1962), 299–326.

81. Hentze, p. 188.

82. Ibid., p. 266.

83. Arthur James Whyte, *The Evolution of Modern Italy* (Oxford: Blackwell, 1944), 191–92.

84. Norman Kogan, *The Government of Italy* (New York: Crowell, 1962), 183.

85. Hannah Arendt, *The Origins of Totalitarianism* (second enlarged edition; Cleveland and New York: World, 1958), 36.

86. Elie Halévy, *Imperialism and the Rise of Labour* (second revised edition; London: Benn, 1952), 17.

87. Maurice Ostrogorski, *Democracy and the Organization of Political Parties*, 2: *The United States* (Garden City, N.Y.: Anchor Books, 1964), 299–300.

88. Quoted in Leonard D. White, *The Republican Era, 1869–1901* (New York: Macmillan, 1963), 4.

89. Quoted in ibid., p. 297.

90. Ibid., p. 387.

91. The authoritative study of this split for the United States is James Weinstein, *The Corporate Ideal in the Liberal State* (Boston: Beacon Press, 1968).

92. Thomson, p. 173.

93. Richard Hofstadter, *The Age of Reform* (New York: Knopf, 1955).

94. Gabriel Kolko, *The Triumph of Conservatism* (New York: Free Press, 1963); O. C. Moore, "The Other Face of Reform," *Victorian Studies*, 5 (September 1961), 7–34.

95. Quoted in Hentze, p. 67.

96. These distinctions are close to those used in André Gorz, *A Strategy for Labor* (Boston: Beacon Press, 1967).

97. Excerpts from Olney's letter are contained in Cochran and Miller, p. 173.

98. White, *The Republican Era*, p. 337.

99. Ibid., p. 393.

100. Maurice Bruce, *The Coming of the Welfare State* (London: Batsford, 1961).

101. Henry Pelling, *Popular Politics and Society in Late Victorian Britain* (New York: St. Martin's Press, 1968), 5.

102. Michael Katz, *The Irony of Early School Reform* (Cambridge: Harvard University Press, 1968); Samuel Bowles and Herbert Gintis, *Schooling in Capitalist America* (New York: Basic Books, 1976); and Joel Spring, *Education and the Rise of the Corporate State* (Boston: Beacon Press, 1972).

103. Bruce, p. 129.

104. Quoted in ibid., p. 131.

105. Quoted in Thomson, pp. 145–46.

106. A. M. McBriar, *Fabian Socialism and English Politics, 1884–1918* (Cambridge: At the University Press, 1962), 244–45.

107. Quoted in Emy, p. 260.

108. McBriar, p. 239.

109. A. C. Pigou, *Unemployment* (New York: Holt, 1914).

110. Emy, p. 264.

111. McBriar, p. 243.

112. Roberts, p. 77.

113. Quoted in Emy, p. 262.

114. Emy, p. 253.

115. Emy, p. 267.

116. Emy, p. 260.

117. Emy, p. 239.

118. Quoted in Theodor Schieder, *The State and Society in Our Time* (London: Nelson, 1962), 56.

CHAPTER 3

1. Joseph Schumpeter, "The Sociology of Imperialisms," in *Imperialism and Social Classes* (Cleveland: World, 1953), 89, 97.
2. For studies of this problem, see Donald Winch, *Classical Political Economy and the Colonies* (Cambridge: Harvard University Press, 1965), and Bernard Semmel, *The Rise of Free Trade Imperialism* (Cambridge: At the University Press, 1970).
3. Adam Smith, *The Wealth of Nations* (New York: Modern Library, 1937), 529, 555, 576–77.
4. David Ricardo, *On the Principles of Political Economy and Taxation*, in Piero Sraffa (ed.), *The Works and Correspondence of David Ricardo* (Cambridge: At the University Press, 1962), 1:338, 345.
5. John Stuart Mill, *Principles of Political Economy* (New York: Kelley, 1961), 748–51, 970–71, 973, 974.
6. Quoted in Mary Evelyn Townsend, *The Rise and Fall of Germany's Colonial Empire* (New York: Fertig, 1966), 60.
7. Tom E. Terrill, *The Tariff, Politics, and American Foreign Policy 1874–1901* (Westport, Conn.: Greenwood Press, 1973), 16–17, 20.
8. Ronald Robinson and John Gallagher, *Africa and the Victorians* (New York: St. Martin's Press, 1961), 15.
9. Townsend, p. 55.
10. Hans-Ulrich Wehler, "Industrial Growth and Early German Imperialism," in Roger Owen and Bob Sutcliffe (eds.), *Studies in the Theory of Imperialism* (London: Longmans, 1972), 79. See also Hans-Ulrich Wehler, *Bismarck und der Imperialismus* (Köln: Kiepenheuer and Witsch, 1969).
11. Cited in A. K. Fieldhouse, *Economics and Empire* (Ithaca, N.Y.: Cornell University Press, 1973), 22.
12. Robert V. Bruce, *1877: Year of Violence* (Indianapolis: Bobbs-Merrill, 1959).
13. Margot Hentze, *Pre-Fascist Italy* (New York: Octagon Press, 1972), 215.
14. Elie Halévy, *Imperialism and the Rise of Labour*, vol. 5 of *A History of the English People in the Nineteenth Century* (second revised edition; London: Benn, 1952), 220.
15. Thomas F. Power, Jr., *Jules Ferry and the Renaissance of French Imperialism* (New York: Octagon Books, 1966), 14.
16. Quoted in Walter LaFeber, *The New Empire* (Ithaca, N.Y.: Cornell University Press, 1963), 14.
17. Bernard Semmel, *Imperialism and Social Reform* (Cambridge: Harvard University Press, 1960), 210.

18. Quoted in D. C. M. Platt, *Finance, Trade, and Politics in British Foreign Policy, 1815–1914* (Oxford: Clarendon Press, 1968), xxiv.

19. Quoted in Robinson and Gallagher, *Africa and the Victorians*, p. 5.

20. John Gallagher and Ronald Robinson, "The Imperialism of Free Trade," *Economic History Review*, Second series, 6 (1953), 1–15.

21. Gallagher and Robinson, *Africa and the Victorians*, pp. 11, 13.

22. Semmel, *Imperialism and Social Reform*, p. 53.

23. Halévy, p. 230.

24. Quoted in Semmel, *Imperialism and Social Reform*, p. 65.

25. Quoted in Halévy, p. 337.

26. Quoted in Semmel, *Imperialism and Social Reform*, p. 94.

27. On this point Semmel pays too much attention to what Chamberlain said as opposed to what Chamberlain did.

28. See Platt, pp. xix, 83, for some evidence on this point.

29. Quoted in Terrill, p. 184.

30. Thomas J. McCormick, *China Market: America's Quest for Informal Empire, 1893–1901* (Chicago: Quadrangle, 1967), 128.

31. Quoted in LaFeber, p. 65.

32. Ibid., p. 173.

33. Ibid., p. 243.

34. William Appleman Williams, *The Tragedy of American Diplomacy* (revised and enlarged edition; New York: Delta Books, 1962), 16–50.

35. For an analysis of these trends, see H. Böhne, "Big Business, Pressure Groups and Bismarck's Turn to Protectionism, 1873–79," *Historical Journal*, 10 No. 2 (1967), 218–36.

36. Alexander Gerschenkron, *Bread and Democracy in Germany* (Berkeley and Los Angeles: University of California Press, 1943).

37. Hartmut Pogge von Strandmann, "Domestic Origins of Germany's Colonial Expansion under Bismarck," *Past and Present*, 42 (February 1969), 142.

38. Ibid., p. 158.

39. Terrill, p. 22; Halévy, p. 303.

40. Fieldhouse, p. 68.

41. Benedetto Croce, *A History of Italy, 1871–1915* (New York: Russell and Russell, 1963), 122.

42. Quoted in Hentze, p. 196.

43. Quoted in Power, pp. 182, 193.

44. Quoted in ibid., p. 57.

45. See A. S. Kanya-Forstner, *The Conquest of Western Sudan* (Cambridge: At the University Press, 1969), and "French Expansion in Africa: The Mythical Theory," in Owen and Sutcliffe, pp. 277–292.

46. Quoted in Kanya-Forstner, "French Expansion in Africa," p. 291.

47. "It is not for the commodity to decide when it should be offered for sale, to what purpose it should be used, at what price it should be allowed to change hands, and in what manner it should be consumed or destroyed."

Karl Polanyi, *The Great Transformation* (Boston: Beacon Press, 1967), 176.

48. Cecil Woodham-Smith, *The Great Hunger* (New York: New American Library, 1964), 234.

49. Theodore S. Hamerow, *Restoration, Revolution, Reaction: Economics and Politics in Germany 1815–1871* (Princeton: Princeton University Press, 1966), 83.

50. E. P. Hutchinson, *Immigrants and Their Children 1850–1950* (New York: Wiley, 1956), 2.

51. Brinley Thomas, *International Migration and Economic Development* (Paris: UNESCO, 1961), 10.

52. Philip Taylor, *The Distant Magnet: European Emigration to the U.S.A.* (London: Eyre and Spottiswoode, 1971), 118.

53. The role of the state in these matters is discussed at length in ibid., pp. 119–22.

54. Quoted in Mack Walker, *Germany and the Emigration, 1816–1885* (Cambridge: Harvard University Press, 1964), 202.

55. Ibid., p. 200.

56. Edward A. Ross, *The Old World in the New* (New York: Century, 1914), cited in Taylor, p. 239.

57. Doris Lessing, *A Proper Marriage* (London: Panther, 1966), 184.

58. Paolo Cinanni, *Emigrazione e Imperialismo* (Rome: Editori Riunti, 1968), 29. See also Stephen Castles and Godoluck Kosack, *Immigrant Workers and Class Structure in Western Europe* (London: Oxford University Press, 1973), 16.

59. Castles and Kosack, p. 18.

60. Ibid., p. 19.

61. Quoted in Michael Kraus, *Immigration: The American Mosaic* (Princeton: Van Nostrand, 1966), 64.

62. Josiah Strong, *Our Country*, ed. Jurgen Herbst (Cambridge: Belknap Press of Harvard University Press, 1963).

63. John Higham, *Strangers in the Land: Patterns of American Nativism 1860–1925* (New York: Atheneum, 1970), 52.

64. Ibid., p. 50.

65. See Castles and Kosack for an excellent analysis of this problem.

66. Fieldhouse, p. 21.

67. Polanyi, *passim*.

68. Semmel, *Imperialism and Social Reform*, p. 57. T. H. Green's place in the history of English liberalism is so confusing precisely because he wrote in a transitional period and therefore could hardly help but be ambiguous. This ambiguity makes it difficult for later writers to classify him. Thus Melvin Richter is correct to reject the influence of Dicey's distinction between polar opposite "individualist" and "collectivist" theories of the state, but incorrect to emphasize so strongly Green's attachment to Manchester liberalism, which does not follow at all. Green's theory of the state attempts

to be both individualist and collectivist, which is why it is so fascinating and why it is so filled with contradictons. See Melvin Richter, *The Politics of Conscience: T. H. Green and His Age* (London: Weidenfeld and Nicolson, 1964), *passim*.

69. Wehler, "Industrial Growth," p. 78.

70. See Herman and Julia Schwendinger, *Sociologists of the Chair* (New York: Basic Books, 1974).

71. Quoted in Hentze, p. 218.

72. Semmel, *Imperialism and Social Reform*, p. 57.

73. Halévy, pp. 18, 21.

74. Hannah Arendt, *The Origins of Totalitarianism* (second enlarged edition; Cleveland: World, 1958), 99.

75. See Semmel, *Imperialism and Social Reform*, pp. 37–52.

76. An excellent example of such polite racism, which belies the common supposition that racism is most characteristic of those at the bottom of society, is Prescott F. Hall, *Immigration and its Effects upon the United States* (New York: Holt, 1908).

77. Robinson and Gallagher, *Africa and the Victorians*, p. 470.

78. Emil Oestereicher, "Facism and the Intellectuals: The Case of Italian Futurism," *Social Research*, 41 (Autumn 1974), 515–33.

79. Arendt, p. 171.

80. Ibid., p. 93.

81. Quoted in LaFeber, p. 388.

82. Quoted in Robinson and Gallagher, *Africa and the Victorians*, p. 31.

83. Power, p. 71.

84. T. H. Green, *Lectures on the Principles of Political Obligation*, in R. C. Nettleship (ed.), *Works of Thomas Hill Green* (London: Longmans, 1906), 2:515.

85. See Richter, pp. 350–62.

86. Joel H. Spring, *Education and the Rise of the Corporate State* (Boston: Beacon Press, 1972), 114.

87. Cited in ibid., p. 75.

88. See Barry Rubin, "Marxism and Education: Radical Thought and Education Theory in the 1930s," *Science and Society*, 36 (Summer 1972), 174.

89. Halévy, p. 222.

90. Robert Malcolmson, *Popular Recreation in English Society, 1700–1850* (Cambridge: At the University Press, 1973).

91. Joel Spring, unpublished paper.

CHAPTER 4

1. Karl Polanyi, *The Great Transformation* (Boston: Beacon Press, 1957), 33.

2. Quoted in Murray Rothbard, "War Collectivism in World War I," in

Ronald Radosh and Murray Rothbard (eds.), *A New History of Leviathan* (New York: Dutton, 1972), 75.

3. See Robert Wiebe, *Businessmen and Reform* (Cambridge: Harvard University Press, 1962).

4. Robert D. Cuff, *The War Industries Board* (Baltimore: Johns Hopkins Press, 1973), 60. The following few paragraphs are indebted to this work.

5. This assertion is contained in Rothbard, "War Collectivism."

6. Samuel P. Huntington, *The Soldier and the State* (New York: Vintage Books, 1964), 270–71.

7. This distinction is discussed in detail in James Weinstein, *The Corporate Ideal in the Liberal State* (Boston: Beacon Press, 1968). While he tends to exaggerate the ideological differences between the National Civic Federation and the National Association of Manufacturers, Weinstein's book remains the best account of the twentieth-century transformation in the nature of the American ruling class.

8. Extensive evidence for this proposition is contained in Richard C. Edwards, "Capital Accumulation and Corporate Power in the Transition to Monopoly Capitalism" (Cambridge: Center for Educational Policy Research, Harvard University, n.d.).

9. Quoted in James B. Gilbert, *Designing the Industrial State* (Chicago: Quadrangle, 1972), 76.

10. Count Harry Kessler, *Walter Rathenau: His Life and Work* (New York: Harcourt Brace, 1932), 176.

11. Ibid., p. 203.

12. Ibid., p. 207.

13. Walter Struve, *Elites against Democracy* (Princeton: Princeton University Press, 1973), 149–85.

14. Robert Musil, *The Man without Qualities* (New York: Capricorn Books, 1965), 1:226–27.

15. Cited in David Felix, *Walter Rathenau and the Weimar Republic* (Baltimore: Johns Hopkins Press, 1971), 60.

16. Ibid., p. 60.

17. Charles S. Maier, *Recasting Bourgeois Europe* (Princeton: Princeton University Press, 1975), 194.

18. Roland Sarti, *Fascism and the Industrial Leadership in Italy, 1919–40* (Berkeley: University of California Press, 1971), 10.

19. Henry W. Ehrmann, *Organized Business in France* (Princeton: Princeton University Press, 1957), 20.

20. See Lord Salter, *Memoirs of a Public Servant* (London: Faber and Faber, 1961), 73–122.

21. Samuel Beer, *British Politics in the Collectivist Age* (New York: Vintage Books, 1969), 323.

22. Ehrmann, p. 33.

23. For a readable account of these revolutions see Richard M. Watt, *The Kings Depart* (London: Penguin Books, 1973).

24. See Robert K. Murray, *Red Scare* (New York: McGraw-Hill, 1964).

25. A. J. P. Taylor, *British History, 1914–45* (New York: Oxford University Press, 1965), 129–40.

26. Annie Kriegel, *Aux Origines du communisme français, 1914–20* (Paris: Mouton, 1964), 1:269–307, 359–430, 476–521. Another writer notes: "*Suite alors un défèrlement de grèves qui prennent rapidement un caractère révolutionnaire.*" Claude Fohlen, *La France de L'entre-deux-guerres (1917–39)* (Paris: Casterman, 1966), 35.

27. Maier, *passim*.

28. Philippe C. Schmitter, "Still the Century of Corporatism?", *Review of Politics*, 36 (January 1974), 85–131.

29. Quoted in Sarti, p. 32. The following account is based upon this excellent book, one of the few that avoids unnecessary generalization in discussing the meaning of fascism.

30. Ibid., p. 48.

31. Vol. 2 of *Mussolini il fascista* (Turin: Einaudi, 1968).

32. Sarti, p. 76.

33. This is the essence of the capitalist state according to the conceptualization of Nicos Poulantzas in *Political Power and Social Classes* (London: New Left Books, 1973), 190–91. Whether or not such definition has general theoretical applicability, it certainly is appropriate to this period.

34. Sarti, p. 116.

35. Maier, p. 577.

36. Herman Eugene Lebovics, *Social Conservatism and the Middle Classes in Germany, 1914–1933* (Princeton: Princeton University Press, 1969).

37. Franz Neumann, *Behemoth* (New York: Harper Torchbooks, 1966), 232–33.

38. Robert Brady, *Business as a System of Power* (New York: Columbia University Press, 1943), 39.

39. A perceptive analysis of the contradictions involved in the Whitley Council system is given by Elie Halévy, "The Policy of Social Peace in England," in *The Era of Tyrannies* (Garden City, N.Y.: Anchor Books, 1965), 159–82.

40. S. E. Finer, *Anonymous Empire* (London: Pall Mall Press, 1966), 7.

41. Beer, p. 77.

42. Arthur F. Lucas, *Industrial Reconstruction and the Control of Competition* (London: Longmans, 1937).

43. Beer, p. 297.

44. Beer, p. 283.

45. Ibid., p. 297.

46. Nigel Harris, *Competition and the Corporate Society* (London: Methuen, 1972), 56–57.

47. Matthew H. Elbow, *French Corporative Theory, 1789–1948* (New York: Columbia University Press, 1953).

48. Ehrmann, p. 23.

49. Ibid., p. 54.

50. Ibid., p. 78.

51. Elbow, p. 159.

52. Robert O. Paxton, *Vichy France* (New York: Knopf, 1972), 354–55.

53. Gilbert, p. 19.

54. Ibid., p. 58.

55. See Weinstein, pp. 92–116.

56. John D. Hicks, *The Republican Ascendency, 1921–33* (New York: Harper, 1960), the best account of this period.

57. William Appleman Williams, *The Contours of American History* (Cleveland: World, 1961), 426–32; Grant McConnell, *Private Power and American Diplomacy* (New York: Knopf, 1966), 64–69. See also Ellis W. Hawley et al., *Herbert Hoover and The Crisis of American Capitalism* (Cambridge, Mass.: Schenckman, 1973).

58. Felix Rohatyn, "A New RFC is Proposed for Business," *New York Times*, 3 (December 1, 1974), 1.

59. William E. Leuchtenberg, "The New Deal and the Analogue of War," in John Braeman, Robert H. Bremmer, and Everett Walters (eds.), *Change and Continuity in Twentieth Century America* (Columbus: Ohio State University Press, 1964), 117.

60. *The Genesis of the New Deal, 1928–32*, vol. 1 of *The Public Papers and Addresses of Franklin D. Roosevelt* (New York: Random House, 1938), 754–55. See also Daniel Fusfeld, *The Economic Thought of Franklin D. Roosevelt* (New York: Columbia University Press, 1956), 106–107.

61. See Rexford G. Tugwell, *The Industrial Discipline and Other Governmental Arts* (New York: Columbia University Press, 1933), and Bernard Sternsher, *Rexford G. Tugwell and the New Deal* (New Brunswick: Rutgers University Press, 1964), 154–55.

62. William E. Leuchtenberg, *Franklin D. Roosevelt and the New Deal* (New York: Harper and Row, 1963), 69.

63. *Schechter v. United States*, 295 U.S. 495 (1935). Besides the question of delegation, the Court also ruled against NIRA on the basis of the commerce clause.

64. Theodore J. Lowi, *The End of Liberalism* (New York: Norton, 1969), 293.

65. 321 U.S. 414 (1944).

66. Ellis W. Hawley, *The New Deal and the Problem of Monopoly* (Princeton: Princeton University Press, 1966), 130–46.

67. Robert Engler, *The Politics of Oil* (New York: Macmillan, 1961), 141.

68. Sidney Fine, *The Automobile Industry under the Blue Eagle* (Ann Arbor: University of Michigan Press, 1963).

69. Herbert Luethy, *France against Herself* (New York: Praeger, 1955), 5–27.

70. Andrew Shonfeld, *Modern Capitalism* (New York: Oxford University Press, 1965), 144.

71. Quoted in Philip M. Williams, *Crisis and Compromise* (Hamden, Conn.: Archon Books, 1968), 385.

72. Quoted in Warren C. Baum, *The French Economy and the State* (Princeton: Princeton University Press, 1958), 357.

73. Ehrmann, p. 82.

74. Quoted in ibid., pp. 134–35.

75. For a good discussion of this duality see David S. Landes, "France and the Businessman: A Social and Cultural Analysis," in Edward Meade Earle (ed.), *Modern France* (Princeton: Princeton University Press, 1951), 334–53.

76. Williams, p. 269.

77. Quoted in Baum, p. 175. See also Adolph Sturmthal, "Nationalization and Workers Control in Britain and France," *Journal of Political Economy*, 61 (February 1953), 78.

78. Adolph Sturmthal, "The Structure of Nationalized Enterprises in France," *Political Science Quarterly*, 67 (September 1952), 357–77.

79. Baum, p. 185.

80. Ibid., p. 180.

81. Williams, p. 379.

82. Baum, p. 165.

83. See Pierre Bauchet, *Economic Planning: The French Experience* (New York: Praeger, 1964), for one example.

84. Baum, p. 281.

85. Stephen Cohen, *Modern Capitalist Planning: The French Model* (Cambridge: Harvard University Press, 1969), 66–67.

86. Quoted in Philip M. Williams and Martin Harrison, *Politics and Society in deGaulle's Republic* (Garden City, N.Y.: Anchor Books, 1973), 21.

87. Ibid., p. 187. See also J. E. S. Hayward, *Private Interests and Public Policy* (London: Longmans, 1966).

88. Williams and Harrison, p. 191.

89. Ezra Suleiman, *Politics, Power and Bureaucracy in France* (Princeton: Princeton University Press, 1974), 338.

90. John H. McArthur and Bruce R. Scott, *Industrial Planning in France* (Cambridge: Harvard Business School, 1969). See also Suleiman, p. 345.

91. Sarti, p. 142.

92. LaPalombara, pp. 7–11.

93. Shonfeld, p. 240.

94. This is the main theme of John D. Montgomery, *Forced to Be Free* (Chicago: University of Chicago Press, 1957). See also Ralph Miliband, *The State in Capitalist Society* (New York: Basic Books, 1969), 95.

95. *The Economist*, December 9, 1939. Cited in Brady, p. 183.

96. *New Statesman and Nation*, April 2, 1938. Cited in ibid., p. 187.

97. S. E. Finer, "The Political Power of Private Capital: Part II," *Sociological Review*, new series, 4 (July 1956), 14.

98. Beer, p. 322.

99. Quoted in Finer, "The Political Power of Private Capital," p. 13.

100. Harris, p. 65.

101. *Anonymous Empire*, p. 41.

102. Harry Eckstein, *Pressure Group Politics* (London: Allen and Unwin, 1960), 105.

103. Harris, p. 125.

104. Irving Bernstein, *The Turbulent Years* (Boston: Houghton Mifflin, 1971), 211–317.

105. Peter Self and Herbert J. Storing, *The State and the Farmer* (Berkeley and Los Angeles: University of California Press, 1963), 24.

106. Ibid., p. 230.

107. See McConnell, pp. 235–41.

108. Ibid., p. 203.

109. Philip Selznick, *TVA and the Grass Roots* (Berkeley: University of California Press, 1949).

110. See Baum, pp. 313–42.

111. Lewis J. Edinger, *Politics in Germany* (Boston: Little Brown, 1968), 217.

112. LaPalombara, pp. 235–45.

113. Shonfeld, p. 199.

114. The complete text of the Matignon agreement is contained in Henry W. Ehrmann, *French Labor from Popular Front to Liberation* (New York: Oxford University Press, 1947), 284–85.

115. Williams and Harrison, pp. 351–58.

116. Beer, pp. 207–12.

117. Ibid., p. 215.

118. Gerald A. Dorfman, *Wage Politics in Britain, 1945–67* (Ames: Iowa State University Press, 1973), 145.

119. For details, see H. A. Clegg, *The System of Industrial Relations in Great Britain* (Oxford: Blackwell, 1972), *passim*.

120. Shonfeld, pp. 153–54.

121. Dorfman, p. 146.

122. Herbert J. Spiro, *The Politics of German Co-Determination* (Cambridge: Harvard University Press, 1958), 148–53.

123. Ralf Dahrendorf, *Society and Democracy in Germany* (Garden City, N. Y.: Anchor Books, 1969), 184.

124. Bernstein, *Turbulent Years*, p. 353, on which the following two paragraphs are based.

125. McConnell, p. 88.

126. For the British case see Graham Wootton, *The Politics of Influence* (Cambridge: Harvard University Press, 1963).

127. Lowi, p. 115.

128. Alexis de Tocqueville, *Democracy in America* (New York: Knopf, 1951), 2:281.

129. Sylvia Law and the Health Project, University of Pennsylvania, *Blue Cross: What Went Wrong?* (New Haven: Yale University Press, 1974).

130. Samuel P. Huntington, "Interservice Competition and the Political Role of the Armed Services," *American Political Science Review*, 55 (March 1961), 40–52; and Martha Derthick, "Militia Lobby in the Missile Age," in Samuel P. Huntington (ed.), *Changing Patterns of Military Politics* (New York: Free Press, 1962), 190–234.

131. Shonfeld, pp. 193–94.

132. Stuart Holland (ed.), *The State as Entrepreneur* (London: Weidenfeld and Nicolson, 1972), 243–64.

CHAPTER 5

1. Charles L. Wood, "A Co-operative Trust," *Twentieth Century* (1895). Cited in James Gilbert, *Designing the Industrial State* (Chicago: Quadrangle, 1972), 34.

2. Grant McConnell, *The Decline of Agrarian Democracy* (Berkeley and Los Angeles: University of California Press, 1959), 112.

3. William E. Leuchtenberg, *Franklin D. Roosevelt and the New Deal* (New York: Harper and Row, 1963), 141.

4. The idea that the War on Poverty represents a break with traditional conceptions of welfare legislation is put forward by Theodore Lowi in *The End of Liberalism* (New York: Norton, 1969), 233–44.

5. Dale Rogers Marshall, *The Politics of Participation in Poverty* (Berkeley and Los Angeles: University of California Press, 1971), 141.

6. Daniel Patrick Moynihan, *The Politics of a Guaranteed Income* (New York: Vintage Books, 1973), 54.

7. E. E. Schattschneider, *The Semi-Sovereign People* (New York: Holt, Rinehart and Winston, 1960).

8. The ways by which the state has had "important effects on the economics of sports" is discussed in Roger Noll, "The U.S. Team Sports Industry," in Noll (ed.), *Government and the Sports Business* (Washington: Brookings Institution, 1974), 32.

9. A perfect example of a religious group exercising state power is Italy's Catholic Action. Either the Church can be represented on public boards or its exercise of public power can be more indirect. One example of the latter is the fact that Catholic Action buys so many movie theatres in Italy that it effectively controls the distribution process and hereby acts as an

informal licensing agency. See Joseph LaPalombara, *Interest Groups in Italian Politics* (Princeton: Princeton University Press, 1964), 330–31.

10. Herbert Schiller, *Mass Communications and American Empire* (New York: Kelley, 1970), 19–29.

11. Robert Michels, *Political Parties* (New York: Free Press, 1949).

12. See LaPalombara, p. 216.

13. Ezra N. Suleiman, *Politics, Power, and Bureaucracy in France* (Princeton: Princeton University Press, 1974), 269.

14. Dean E. Mann, *The Assistant Secretaries* (Washington: Brookings Institution, 1965), 26, 34, 37, 48–51, 53–55.

15. David T. Stanley, Dean E. Mann, and Jameson W. Doig, *Men Who Govern* (Washington: Brookings Institution, 1967), 33–53.

16. Andrew Shonfeld, *Modern Capitalism* (New York: Oxford University Press, 1965). Elsewhere the elitism involved is succinctly described as follows: "The officials of the Plan seem to live in each other's pockets." Ibid., p. 138.

17. Ibid., p. 230. See also Stephen Cohen, *Modern Capitalism Planning: The French Model* (Cambridge: Harvard University Press, 1969), for a discussion of planning and participation.

18. S. E. Finer, *Anonymous Empire* (London: Pall Mall Press, 1966), 42.

19. Edward Shils, *The Torment of Secrecy* (New York: Free Press, 1956), 105–19.

20. Roy W. Sellars, *The Next Step in Democracy* (New York: Macmillan, 1916). Cited in Gilbert, p. 34.

21. Quoted in Robert Engler, *The Politics of Oil* (New York: Macmillan, 1961), 334.

22. We have already seen this expression used by Morris L. Cooke in his talk to the Taylor Society (see above, p. 112), by Neville Chamberlain in his discussion of the tariff (see above, p. 124), and by the American Federation of Labor (see above, p. 143). It will also appear in the next chapter when Maxwell Taylor uses it in his analysis of the internal affairs of Vietnam. (See below, p. 198.)

23. LaPalombara, pp. 288, 298–99.

24. Philip M. Williams and Martin Harrison, *Politics and Society in deGaulle's Republic* (Garden City, N.Y.: Anchor Books, 1933), 348.

25. Warren C. Baum, *The French Economy and the State* (Princeton: Princeton University Press, 1958), 280.

26. *United States v. American Tobacco Co.*, 221 U.S. 106 (1911).

27. James Weinstein, *The Corporate Ideal in the Liberal State* (Boston: Beacon Press, 1968), 79.

28. John Kenneth Galbraith, *The New Industrial State* (Boston: Houghton Mifflin, 1971), 298.

29. Henry Adams, *Democracy* (New York: New American Library, 1961), 92.

30. LaPalombara, p. 221.

31. Philip M. Williams, *Crisis and Compromise* (Hampden, Conn.: Archon Books, 1964), 247–48.

32. Charles O. Jones, "The Agriculture Committee and the Problem of Representation," in Robert Peabody and Nelson Polsby (eds.), *New Perspectives on the House of Representatives* (second edition; Chicago: Rand McNally, 1969), 161.

33. Williams, p. 429.

34. Senator Henry Jackson (D. Wash.), who also figures in the construction of the Dual State, described in the next chapter.

35. William S. White, *Citadel* (New York: Harper, 1957).

36. Williams, p. 429.

37. Quoted in Michael Reagan, *The Managed Economy* (New York: Oxford University Press, 1963), 85.

38. The best study of the business ideology of American labor is Michael Paul Rogin, "Voluntarism as an Organizational Ideology of the American Federation of Labor, 1886–1932" (M. A. thesis, University of Chicago, 1959).

39. Irving Bernstein, *The Turbulent Years* (Boston: Houghton Mifflin, 1971), 203.

40. See Max Kampelman, *The Communist Party versus the C.I.O.* (New York: Praeger, 1957), and Ronald Radosh, *American Labor and United States Foreign Policy* (New York: Vintage Books, 1969), 436.

41. Harry A. Millis and Emily Clark Brown, *From the Wagner Act to Taft-Hartley* (Chicago: University of Chicago Press, 1950), 655–56.

42. Bernstein, pp. 710–12.

43. See Daniel Bell, *The End of Ideology* (New York: Free Press, 1960), 159–90. The notion that Bell's data say one thing and his conclusions another is advanced by Frank Pearce, *Crimes of the Powerful* (London: Pluto Press, 1976), 131–46.

44. *The Decline of Agrarian Democracy*, and *Private Power and American Democracy* (New York: Knopf, 1966), 343–50.

45. Charles Morazé, *The Triumph of the Middle Classes* (Garden City, N.Y.: Anchor Books, 1968), 266, 277, 331.

46. Suleiman, pp. 275–81.

47. Arthur Maass, *Muddy Waters* (Cambridge: Harvard University Press, 1951).

48. Finer, p. 38.

49. Lewis Edinger, *Politics in Germany* (Boston: Little, Brown, 1968), 199.

50. Henry Ehrmann, *Organized Business in France* (Princeton: Princeton University Press, 1957), 480.

51. Engler, p. 215.

52. Leuchtenberg, p. 108.

53. Engler, p. 181.

54. The best general study is still Shonfeld, *Modern Capitalism*.

55. Engler, p. 86.

56. Shonfeld, p. 139.

57. Murray Weidenbaum, *The Modern Public Sector* (New York: Basic Books, 1969), 179–81.

58. See Richard Edwards, Michael Reich, and David Gordon, *Dual Labor Market Segmentation and American Capitalism* (Lexington, Mass.: Heath, 1976).

59. Walter Adams, "The Military Industrial Complex and the New Industrial State," *American Economic Review*, 58 (May 1968), 656.

60. The classic statement is Murray Edelman, *The Symbolic Uses of Politics* (Urbana: University of Illinois Press, 1964).

61. Reagan, p. 196; McConnell, *Private Power*, pp. 268–69.

62. Engler, p. 59.

63. Reagan, p. 309.

64. Herbert J. Spiro, *The Politics of German Co-Determination* (Cambridge: Harvard University Press, 1958).

65. H. Popitz et al., *Das Gesellschaftsbild des Arbeiters*, cited in Ralf Dahrendorf, *Society and Democracy in Germany* (Garden City, N.Y.: Anchor Books, 1969), 166.

66. Baum, p. 183.

67. LaPalombara, p. 375.

68. Ibid., p. 199.

69. The best study of the modern administrative ideology is Brian Chapman, *The Profession of Government* (London: Allen and Unwin, 1959), 273–95.

70. Ehrmann, p. 261; Suleiman, pp. 341–43.

71. The best study of one of these councils is J. E. S. Hayward, *Private Interests and Public Policy* (London: Longmans, 1966).

72. Antonio Gramsci, *Prison Notebooks* (New York: International Publishers, 1971), 302–303.

73. Charles Lindblom, *The Intelligence of Democracy* (New York: Free Press, 1966). This is a how-to-do-it text in the workings of the Franchise State. See also Charles Lindblom and Robert A. Dahl, *Politics, Economics, and Welfare* (New York: Harper Torchbooks, 1963).

74. Thurman Arnold, *The Symbols of Government* (New Haven: Yale University Press, 1935), 235.

75. Baum, p. 281.

76. Michel Crozier, *La Société Bloquée* (Paris: Editions du Seuil, 1970).

77. Suleiman, p. 384.

78. Shonfeld, pp. 121–22.

79. Cohen, pp. 131–34.

80. Nigel Harris, *Competition and the Corporate Society* (London: Methuen, 1972), 221.

81. Cited in Samuel Beer, *British Politics in The Collectivist Age* (New York: Vintage Books, 1969), 270–310.

82. Harris, p. 243.

83. H. L. Neiburg, *In the Name of Science* (Chicago: Quadrangle, 1966), 184–99.

84. Weidenbaum, p. 11.

85. Ibid., p. 11.

86. Seymour Melman, *Pentagon Capitalism* (New York: McGraw-Hill, 1970), 20, 72.

87. Weidenbaum, pp. 9–10.

88. For a case study of this process, see Richard Pious, "Policy and Public Administration: The Legal Services Program in the War on Poverty," in Ira Katznelson et al. (eds.), *The Politics and Society Reader* (New York: McKay, 1974), 101.

89. Weidenbaum, p. 41.

90. Quoted in ibid., p. 49.

91. U.S. Congress. Joint Economic Committee, Subcommittee on Economy in Government, *Economy in Governmental Procurement and Property Management* (Washington, 1968). Quoted in Melman, pp. 79–80.

92. See Charles Hitch and Roland N. McKean, *The Economics of Defense in the Nuclear Age* (New York: Atheneum, 1965), 105–33.

93. Weidenbaum, p. 48.

94. Ibid., p. 50.

95. James O'Connor, *The Fiscal Crisis of the State* (New York: St. Martin's Press, 1973), 97.

96. Ibid., p. 17.

97. Weidenbaum, p. 8.

98. Rick Deaton, "The Fiscal Crisis of the State in Canada," and B. Roy Lemoine, "The Growth of the State in Canada," in Dimitrios Roussopoulos (ed.), *The Political Economy of the State* (Montreal: Black Rose Books, 1973), 18–87.

99. David Butler and Jenna Freeman, *British Political Facts* (London: Macmillan, 1968), 174.

100. Bruce Russett et al., *World Handbook of Political and Social Indicators* (New Haven: Yale University Press, 1964), 58–68, 308.

101. O'Connor, *Fiscal Crisis.*

102. This is the formulation used by Claus Offe in "Class Rule and the Political System," mimeo, a translation of chap. 3 of *Strukturprobleme des Kapitalistischen Staates* (Frankfurt: Suhrkamp, 1972).

CHAPTER 6

1. Quoted in Sheldon Wolin, *Politics and Vision* (Boston: Little, Brown, 1960), 122.

2. Hans Rosenberg, *Bureaucracy, Aristocracy, and Autocracy* (Boston: Beacon Press, 1966), 46.

3. Emil Lederer, "Zur Soziologie des Weltkrieges," cited in Ernst Fraenkel, *The Dual State* (New York: Oxford University Press, 1941), 168.

4. Walter Bagehot, *The English Constitution* (London: Fontana, 1963), 64, 248–51.

5. Hans Gerth and C. Wright Mills (eds.), *From Max Weber* (New York: Oxford University Press, 1958), 155.

6. Karl Mannheim, *Man and Society in an Age of Reconstruction* (New York: Harvest Books, n.d.), 53.

7. Fraenkel, pp. xiii, 205–206.

8. Roger Hilsman, *To Move a Nation* (New York: Delta Books, 1968), 64.

9. David Wise and Thomas Ross, *The Invisible Government* (New York: Vintage Books, 1974), 3.

10. For example, Allen Dulles notes that both he and his brother were "deeply influenced" by Wilsonian liberalism and were "thrilled" by Wilson's plans for a postwar liberal world order. Secret intelligence is seen by him as the only realistic means to Wilson's idealistic end. See Allen Dulles, *The Craft of Intelligence* (New York: Harper and Row, 1963), 3. See also Townsend Hoopes, *The Devil and John Foster Dulles* (Boston: Little, Brown, 1973), 31.

11. Stewart Ewen, *Captains of Consciousness* (New York: McGraw-Hill, 1976).

12. Enrico Nobis, *Il Governo Invisibile* (Rome: Edizioni di Cultura Sociale, 1955).

13. Gerald Messadie, *La fin de la vie privée* (Paris: Calman-Lévy, 1974).

14. F. C. Mather, *Public Order in the Age of the Chartists* (Manchester: Manchester University Press, 1959), 182–225.

15. David Williams, *Not in the Public Interest* (London: Hutchinson, 1965).

16. Edward S. Corwin, *The President: Office and Powers* (New York: New York University Press, 1957), 238; Wise and Ross, p. 211; Paul Y. Hammond, *Organizing for Defense* (Princeton: Princeton University Press, 1961), 199.

17. Richard Barnet, *The Roots of War* (Baltimore: Penguin Books, 1973), 52–53; William E. Leuchtenberg, *Franklin D. Roosevelt and the New Deal* (New York: Harper and Row, 1963), 301.

18. Barnet, p. 68.

19. Arthur Schlesinger, Jr., *The Imperial Presidency* (Boston: Houghton Mifflin, 1973), 98.

20. *U.S. v. Curtiss Wright Export Corp.*, 299 U.S. 304 (1936).

21. *U.S. v. Belmont*, 301 U.S. 324 (1937).

22. 330 U.S. 103 (1948).

23. Corwin, p. 242.

24. Leuchtenberg, p. 125.

25. Ibid., pp. 327–28. See also Joseph I. Coffey and Vincent P. Rock, *The Presidential Staff* (Washington: National Planning Association, 1961).

26. "The prime cause for American imperialism was an immensely powerful American government motivated by New Deal ideology, which in its domestic and international forms spoke to the interests and aspirations for security of the American people, particularly its working class." Franz Schurmann, *The Logic of World Power* (New York: Pantheon Books, 1974), 42.

27. Two of the better studies, from widely different political viewpoints, are Demetrios Caraley, *The Politics of Military Unification* (New York: Columbia University Press, 1966); and Robert Borosage, "The Making of the National Security State," in Leonard S. Rodberg and Derek Shearer (eds.), *The Pentagon Watchers* (Garden City, N.Y.: Anchor Books, 1970).

28. *Unification of the War and Navy Departments and Postwar Organization for National Security* (Report to the Hon. James Forrestal, October 22, 1945) (Washington: Government Printing Office, 1945), 1. Hereafter referred to as Eberstadt Report.

29. Committee on the Organization of the Executive Branch of the Government, *National Security Organization* (Washington: Government Printing Office, 1949), 1. Hereafter referred to as Hoover Commission.

30. U.S. Senate Armed Services Committee, *National Defense Establishment* (80th Congress, 1st session, 1947), 31. Hereafter referred to as Hearings.

31. Eberstadt Report, p. 8.

32. Hilsman, p. 62.

33. Hearings, p. 176.

34. *Congressional Record*, 80th Congress, 1st session (Vol. 93, Part 7), p. 9421.

35. Hearings, p. 215. Emphasis supplied.

36. Hearings, pp. 526–28.

37. Eberstadt Report, p. 17.

38. Hoover Commission, p. 3.

39. Eberstadt Report, p. 3. Emphasis supplied.

40. Felix Gilbert (ed.), *The Historical Essays of Otto Hintze* (New York: Oxford University Press, 1975), 214.

41. Samuel P. Huntington, *The Soldier and the State* (New York: Vintage Books, 1964), 270–71.

42. Walter LaFeber, *The New Empire* (Ithaca, N.Y.: Cornell University Press, 1963).

43. Morris Janowitz, *The Professional Soldier* (New York: Free Press, 1960), 86–89.

44. Schurmann, p. 438.

45. Eberstadt Report, p. 8.

46. American Political Science Association, *Towards a More Responsible Two-Party System* (New York: Rinehart, 1950).

47. Harry S Truman, *Years of Trial and Hope*, vol. 2 of *Memoirs* (Garden City, N.Y.: Doubleday, 1956), 60. Quoted in Hammond, p. 230.

48. Hearings, p. 27.

49. Hearings, p. 22.

50. Keith L. Clark and Laurence J. Legere, *The President and the Management of National Security:* A Report by the Institute for Defense Analysis (New York: Praeger, 1969), 58.

51. U.S. Senate Armed Services Committee, *National Security Act Amendments of 1949* (81st Congress, 1st session, 1949).

52. Hoover Commission, p. 4.

53. Clark and Legere, p. 58.

54. Hearings, pp. 89–111.

55. Among its members were Robert Lovett, Vannevar Bush, Milton Eisenhower, Robert Sarnoff, Arthur Flemming, and Omar Bradley. See Hammond, pp. 263–64.

56. Peter Lyon, *Eisenhower: Portrait of a Hero* (Boston: Little Brown, 1974), 646, 669.

57. Hans Morgenthau, "Can We Entrust Defense to a Committee?", *New York Times Magazine*, June 7, 1959; Henry A. Kissinger, "The Policymaker and the Intellectuals," *The Reporter*, March 5, 1969. See also Hilsman, pp. 20–21, 25.

58. The Senator Gravel Edition, *The Pentagon Papers* (Boston: Beacon Press, 1971), 1:511.

59. Ibid., p. 593.

60. Quoted in Borosage, p. 10.

61. Eberstadt Report, p. 21.

62. See the proposed organization chart in the Eberstadt Report, which envisions one whole section of the government in charge of foreign and military policy and the other in charge of domestic and economic policy, headed by a National Security Resources Board.

63. Eberstadt Report, p. 16. Emphasis supplied.

64. On Borah, see William A. Williams, *The Tragedy of American Diplomacy* (New York: Delta Books, 1962), 118.

65. Gabriel Kolko, *The Politics of War* (New York: Random House, 1968); Gabriel and Joyce Kolko, *The Limits of Power* (New York: Harper and Row, 1972).

66. See *The Politics of War*, pp. 64–69, 356–58.

67. *Pentagon Papers*, 2:241–42.

68. Ibid., p. 128.

69. Ibid., p. 137.

70. See below, pp. 112, 124, 143.

71. *Pentagon Papers*, 2:120.

72. Maxwell Taylor memo, ibid., p. 137.

73. These stories are all told well in Wise and Ross, pp. 91–183.

74. Arthur Schlesinger, Jr., *A Thousand Days* (Boston: Houghton Mifflin, 1965), 297.

75. Schurmann, p. 419.

76. Wise and Ross, pp. 184–97.

77. *Pentagon Papers*, 2:32.

78. Hilsman, p. 21.

79. U.S. Senate. Report of the Jackson Subcommittee, *Inquiry into National Policy Machinery* (Washington: Government Printing Office, 1961); Clark and Legere, p. 70.

80. Hilsman, p. 31.

81. One of the foreign policy makers under Lyndon Johnson noted that by 1967 an "influential segment of the foreign-military bureaucracy" had become "very frustrated by their own impotence." Townsend Hoopes, *The Limits of Intervention* (New York: McKay, 1969), 116. The point is valid though it is difficult to picture the same men as impotent and influential at the same time.

82. Ralph Stavins, "Washington Determines the Fate of Vietnam: 1954–1965," in Ralph Stavins, Richard J. Barnet, and Marcus G. Raskin, *Washington Plans an Aggressive War* (New York: Random House, 1971), 59, 72.

83. In December 1974 an American television network produced a fictional account of the U.S. response to the Cuban missile crisis. As the screen pictured the Kennedy inner core of the Dual State (McNamara, Taylor, Bundy, etc.) sitting around a large table, gathered in the New York apartment of Theodore Sorensen were the very same people watching themselves being played by actors. When asked what the reaction was, Sorensen said that the TV production did not capture the spirit of the original; whether it did or not, the image of watching what political scientists call "actors" watching real actors somehow captures the fantasy world at the heart of the Dual State. See *New York Times*, December 19, 1974, p. 74.

84. Stavins, p. 98. While Stavins claims that "an increased reliance on covert activity is directly correlated with militant expansion of empire" (ibid., p. 108), I would claim the exact reverse, that the Dual State intensified with the contraction of empire.

85. Quoted in Joseph C. Goulden, *Truth Is the First Casualty* (Chicago: Rand McNally, 1969).

86. Stavins, p. 102.

87. Randolph Bourne, *War and the Intellectuals* (New York: Harper Torchbooks, 1969), 71.

88. Evidence of CIA domestic activity is contained in both the Rockefeller and Church reports on the CIA. For an analysis of the former, see Alan Wolfe, "Exercise in Gentility," *The Nation*, August 16, 1975, pp. 108–12.

89. *New York Times*, December 22, 1974, p. 1.

90. Quoted in ibid., p. 26.

91. Because I explore this problem at greater length in my book *The Seamy Side of Democracy* (New York: McKay, 1973), I am intentionally sketchy in this paragraph.

92. Jeb Stuart Magruder, *An American Life* (New York: Atheneum, 1974), 219–20.

93. Washington Post, *The Presidential Transcripts* (New York: Dell, 1974), 105.

94. Ibid., p. 444.

95. Ibid., p. 192.

96. New York Times, *The End of a Presidency* (New York: Bantam Books, 1974), 135–36.

97. The importance of "stroking" as a characteristic of alienated politics is discussed in Marcus Raskin, *Notes on the Old System* (New York: McKay, 1974), 53.

98. *The End of a Presidency*, p. 140.

99. Carl Bernstein and Bob Woodward, *All the President's Men* (New York: Simon and Schuster, 1974), 176–77, 189–91.

100. *The End of a Presidency*, p. 328.

101. Ibid., p. 347.

102. *The Presidential Transcripts*, p. 346.

103. The "Media Papers" have been published in Paul Cowan, Nick Egleson, and Nat Hentoff, *State Secrets* (New York: Holt, Rinehart and Winston, 1974), 105–217.

104. *New York Times*, December 22, 1974, p. 1.

105. Quoted in David Halberstam, *The Best and the Brightest* (Greenwich, Conn.: Fawcett, 1973), 498.

CHAPTER 7

1. David P. Calleo and Benjamin M. Rowland, *America and the World Political Economy* (Bloomington: Indiana University Press, 1973), 36.

2. Quoted in Lloyd C. Gardner, *Architects of Illusion* (Chicago: Quadrangle, 1970), 123.

3. Quoted in ibid., p. 134.

4. Ibid., p. 129.

5. Gabriel Kolko, *The Roots of War* (New York: Random House, 1968), 257.

6. Quoted in Gardner, p. 132.

7. Calleo and Rowland, p. 37.

8. Quoted in Kolko, pp. 462–63.

9. Calleo and Rowland, p. 43.

10. Cited in Richard N. Gardner, *In Pursuit of World Order* (New York: Praeger, 1966), 37.

11. Ibid., p. 38.
12. *New York Times,* May 21, 1975, pp. 1, 18.
13. George Ball, "Citizenship and the Multinational Corporation," *Social Research,* 41 (Winter 1974), 671.
14. Quoted in Kolko, p. 470.
15. Lloyd Gardner, *Architects of Illusion.*
16. U. W. Kitzinger, *The Politics and Economics of European Integration* (New York: Praeger, 1963), 6.
17. Walter Hallstein, *Europe in the Making* (New York: Norton, 1973), 45. Cited in Gordon Adams, "European Capitalism, the State, and the European Community," unpublished paper.
18. Quoted in Kitzinger, p. 11.
19. Quoted in ibid., p. 23.
20. Ibid., p. 7.
21. Leon N. Lindberg and Stuart A. Scheingold, *Europe's Would-Be Polity* (Englewood Cliffs, N.J.: Prentice-Hall, 1970), 8.
22. Nicos Poulantzas, "Internationalization of Capitalist Relations and the Nation State," *Economy and Society,* 3 (May 1974), 172.
23. Lindberg and Scheingold, p. 22.
24. See Michael Kidron, *Western Capitalism since the War* (revised edition; Baltimore: Penguin Books, 1970), 97.
25. Adams, pp. 14–15.
26. Stuart A. Scheingold, "De Gaulle v. Hallstein," *American Scholar,* 35 (Summer 1966), 478.
27. Ball, p. 657.
28. Richard J. Barnet and Ronald E. Muller, *Global Reach* (New York: Simon and Schuster, 1974), 363.
29. Stephen Hymer, "The Efficiency (Contradictions) of Multinational Corporations," *American Economic Review,* 60 (May 1970), 441.
30. Myra Wilkins, *The Emergence of Multinational Enterprise* (Cambridge: Harvard University Press, 1970).
31. Myra Wilkins, *The Maturing of Multinational Enterprise* (Cambridge: Harvard University Press, 1974), 329.
32. Raymond Vernon, *Sovereignty at Bay* (New York: Basic Books, 1971), 103.
33. U.S. Senate. Finance Committee. *The Multinational Corporations and the World Economy* (Washington: Government Printing Office, 1973).
34. This is by and large the view offered by Vernon, *Sovereignty.*
35. Ibid., p. 83. Emphasis added.
36. Robert Rowthorn and Stephen Hymer, "Multinational Corporations and International Oligarchy," in Charles P. Kindleberger (ed.), *The International Corporation* (Cambridge: MIT Press, 1970), 57–91.
37. Robert Rowthorn, *International Big Business, 1957–67* (Cambridge: At

the University Press, 1971), 84–85. See also Stephen Hymer, "The United States Multinational Corporations and Japanese Competition in the Pacific." Prepared for the Conferencia del Pacifica, Viña del Mar, Chile, 1970.

38. Stephen Hymer, "The Multinational Corporation and the Law of Uneven Development," in J. N. Bhagwati (ed.), *Economics and World Order* (New York: Macmillan, 1972), 121.

39. Ibid., p. 133.

40. The importance of "primitiveness" to an understanding of liberalism is underscored in Michael Paul Rogin, *Fathers and Children* (New York: Knopf, 1975).

41. Robert A. Packenham, *Liberal America and the Third World* (Princeton: Princeton University Press, 1973).

42. Quoted in Barnet and Muller, p. 86.

43. Quoted in ibid., p. 40.

44. Wilkins, *Maturing*, p. 50. The following paragraph is based on her book.

45. Anthony Sampson, *The Sovereign State of ITT* (Greenwich, Conn.: Fawcett Books, 1974), 45–46.

46. Jack N. Behrman, *U.S. International Business and Governments* (New York: McGraw-Hill, 1971), 12–14. The following paragraphs rely on this account.

47. Calleo and Rowland, p. 119.

48. Behrman, p. 212.

49. Alberto Martinelli and Eugenio Somaini, "Nation States and Multinational Corporations," *Kapitalistate*, 1 (1973), 74.

50. Robert Gilpin, "The Politics of Transnational Economic Relations," in Robert O. Keohane and Joseph S. Nye, Jr. (eds.), *Transnational Relations and World Politics* (Cambridge: Harvard University Press, 1973), 69.

51. Quoted in Barnet and Muller, p. 64.

52. Vernon, p. 191.

53. Quoted in Barnet and Muller, p. 56.

54. Ibid., p. 111.

55. Ibid., p. 89.

56. "CIA Covert Activities Abroad Shielded by Major U.S. Companies," *New York Times*, May 11, 1975, p. 38.

57. Behrman, p. 155.

58. Philip Agee, *Inside the Company* (London: Penguin Books, 1975), 277.

59. Ibid., p. 297.

60. Richard Eels, "Multinational Corporations: The Intelligence Function," in Courtney Brown (ed.), *World Business: Promises and Problems* (New York: Macmillan, 1970), 140–55.

61. Sampson, pp. 255–56.

62. Robin Murray, "The Internationalization of Capital and the Nation

State," in John Dunning (ed.), *The Multinational Enterprise* (London: Allen and Unwin, 1971), 285–86.

63. Charles P. Kindleberger, *American Business Abroad* (New Haven: Yale University Press, 1969), 207.

64. Lewis Turner, *Multinational Corporations and the Third World* (New York: Hill and Wang, 1973). See also Kari Levitt, *Silent Surrender: The Multinational Corporation in Canada* (New York: St. Martin's Press, 1970).

65. Kjell Skjelsbaek, "The Growth of International Nongovernmental Organization in the Twentieth Century," in Keohane and Nye, p. 75.

66. Sampson, p. 65.

67. Martinelli and Somaini, p. 74.

68. Zbigniew Brzezinski, *America in a Hostile World* (New York: Basic Books, forthcoming); for another analysis sure to influence the Carter administration, see Edward R. Fried and Philip H. Trezise, "The United States in the World Economy," in Henry Owen and Charles L. Schulze (eds.), *Setting National Priorities: The Next Ten Years* (Washington: The Brookings Institution, 1976), 167–226.

69. Karl Kaiser, "Transnational Relations as a Threat to the Democratic Process," in Keohane and Nye, p. 356.

70. Barnet and Muller, p. 113.

INTERLUDE

1. James O'Connor, *The Class Struggle*, forthcoming. O'Connor's use of the term "disaccumulation" comes from the important essay by Martin J. Sklar, "On the Proletarian Revolution and the End of Political-Economic Society," *Radical America*, 3 (May–June 1969), 1–41.

2. Ernst Mandel, *Late Capitalism* (London: New Left Books, 1975), 216. See also pp. 206–10.

3. For a clarification of the term disaccumulation, and an analysis of its relationship to politics and culture, see the work in progress on the subject by David Gold, Eli Zaretsky, and myself.

4. Jürgen Habermas, *Legitimation Crisis* (Boston: Beacon Press, 1975).

5. Robert Nozick, *Anarchy, State, and Utopia* (New York: Basic Books, 1973).

6. John Rawls, *A Theory of Justice* (Cambridge: Harvard University Press, 1973).

7. Jay Forrester, *World Dynamics* (Cambridge: Wright-Allen, 1971).

8. Daniel Bell, *The Coming of Post-Industrial Society* (New York: Basic Books, 1973).

9. Louis Althusser, *Reading Capital* (London: New Left Books, 1970).

CHAPTER 8

1. Ian Gough, "State Expenditure in Advanced Capitalism," *New Left Review*, 92 (July-August 1975), 60.
2. Ibid., p. 59.
3. For examples see Charles I. Schottland (ed.), *The Welfare State* (New York: Harper and Row, 1967).
4. Harry K. Girvetz, *The Evolution of Liberalism* (New York: Collier Books, 1966), 255.
5. Club Jean Moulin, *L'Etat et le citoyen* (Paris: Editions du Seuil, 1961), 25, 26, 95.
6. Richard Cloward and Frances Fox Piven, *Regulating the Poor* (New York: Pantheon, 1971).
7. D. C. Marsh, *The Welfare State* (London: Longmans, 1970), 20.
8. Michel Crozier, Samuel P. Huntington, and Joji Watanuki, *The Governability of Democracies* (New York: Trilateral Commission, 1975), chap. 5, p. 8.
9. James O'Connor, *The Fiscal Crisis of the State* (New York: St. Martin's Press, 1973).
10. Theodore Sorensen, *Kennedy* (New York: Harper and Row, 1965), 683–84. Cited in Graham Allison, *Essence of Decision* (Boston: Little, Brown, 1971), 124.
11. Allison, p. 61.
12. Ibid., p. 210.
13. Daniel Patrick Moynihan, *The Politics of a Guaranteed Income* (New York: Vintage Books, 1973).
14. Michel Crozier, *The Stalled Society* (New York: Viking Press, 1973), 99.
15. Guy Lord, *The French Budgetary Process* (Berkeley and Los Angeles: University of California Press, 1973), xi.
16. Michael Shanks, *The Stagnant Society* (Baltimore: Penguin Books, 1961).
17. Trevor Smith, *Anti-Politics: Consensus, Reform and Protest in Great Britain* (London: Knight, 1972), 36.
18. P. A. Allum, *Italy: Republic without Government* (New York: Norton, 1973), 246, 248.
19. Theodore Lowi, "Decision Making v. Policy Making: Toward an Antidote for Technocracy," *Public Administration Review*, 30 (May-June 1970), 314.
20. Claus Offe, "The Theory of the Capitalist State and the Problem of Policy Formation," unpublished paper, May 1974, pp. 5–15.
21. Jürgen Habermas, *Legitimation Crisis* (Boston: Beacon Press, 1975), 53–54.
22. Claus Offe, "Class Rule and the Political System: On the Selectiveness of Political Institutions," mimeo, a translation of chap. 3 of *Strukturprobleme des Kapitalistischen Staates* (Frankfurt: Suhrkamp, 1972).

23. Habermas, pp. 62–63.

24. Volker Ronge, "The Politicization of Administration in Advanced Capitalist Societies," *Political Studies*, 22 (March 1974), 86–93.

25. Hugh Heclo, "OMB and the Presidency," *The Public Interest*, Winter 1975, p. 84.

26. Ibid., pp. 94–95.

27. O'Connor, p. 24.

28. Stephan Leibfried, "U.S. Central Government Reform of the Administrative Structure during the Ash Period (1968–1971)," *Kapitalistate*, 2 (1973), 17–30.

29. Hugh Heclo and Aaron Wildavsky, *The Private Government of Public Money* (Berkeley and Los Angeles: University of California Press, 1974), 117.

30. Samuel Beer, "The Modernizing of British Politics," Epilogue to the Vintage edition of *British Politics in the Collectivist Age* (New York: Vintage Books, 1969), 390–434.

31. Gough, p. 85.

32. Ezra Suleiman, *Politics, Power, and Bureaucracy in France* (Princeton: Princeton University Press, 1974), 272.

33. Offe, "The Theory of the Capitalist State," p. 22.

34. Heclo and Wildavsky, pp. 204–205.

35. Ibid., p. 15.

36. Edward Weisband and Thomas M. Franck, *Resignation in Protest* (New York: Grossman, 1975), 72.

37. Ibid., p. 143.

38. David Halberstam, *The Best and the Brightest* (Greenwich, Conn.: Fawcett Books, 1973), 326–44.

39. Crozier, *The Stalled Society*, pp. 174–75.

40. Heclo and Wildavsky, p. 117.

41. Martin Landau, "Redundancy, Rationality, and the Problem of Duplication and Overlap," *Public Administration Review*, 34 (July–August 1969), 346–58.

42. See Aaron Wildavsky, *The Politics of the Budgetary Process* (Boston: Little, Brown, 1964), for a defense of this position.

43. For repeated examples, see Jonathan Schell, *The Time of Illusion* (New York: Knopf, 1975).

44. Aaron Wildavsky, "The Strategic Retreat on Objectives," Working Paper No. 45, Graduate School of Public Policy, University of California, Berkeley, 1976.

45. Charles L. Schultze, "Perverse Incentives and the Inefficiency of Government," in Robert H. Haveman and Robert D. Hamrin (eds.), *The Political Economy of Federal Policy* (New York: Harper and Row, 1973), 20.

46. For a political analysis of these kinds of reforms see Leibfried, "Government Reform."

47. Aaron Wildavsky, "Rescuing Policy Analysis from PPBS," *Public Administration Review*, 34 (April 1969), 189–202.

48. Heclo and Wildavsky, p. 241.

49. O'Connor, p. 77.

50. Heclo and Wildavsky, p. 188.

51. Offe, *Strukturprobleme*, p. 10.

52. See, for example, Matthew A. Crenson, *The Unpolitics of Air Pollution* (Baltimore: Johns Hopkins, 1971), and Peter Bachrach and Morton Baratz, "Decisions and Non-decisions," *American Political Science Review*, 57 (September 1963), 632–42.

53. Samuel P. Huntington, *The Soldier and the State* (New York: Vintage Books, 1964), 39.

54. Richard J. Barnet and Ronald Muller, *Global Reach* (New York: Simon and Schuster, 1974), 243.

55. Wildavsky, *Budgetary Process*, p. 60.

56. Franz Schurmann, *The Logic of World Power* (New York: Pantheon Books, 1974), 39.

57. Theodore Lowi, *The End of Liberalism* (New York: Norton, 1969), 144.

58. Ibid., p. 93.

59. Joseph LaPalombara, *Interest Groups in Italian Politics* (Princeton: Princeton University Press, 1964), 343.

60. Wildavsky, *Budgetary Process*, p. 167.

61. Ibid., p. 153.

62. Thurman Arnold, *The Symbols of Government* (New Haven: Yale University Press, 1935); Murray Edelman, *The Symbolic Uses of Politics* (Urbana: University of Illinois Press, 1964).

63. Edelman, pp. 39, 68.

64. Allison, p. 226.

65. Schurmann, p. 426.

66. Halberstam, p. 153.

67. Ibid., p. 542.

68. Jeb Stuart Magruder, *An American Life: One Man's Road to Watergate* (New York: Pocket Books, 1975), 2.

69. Dan Rather and Gary Paul Gates, *The Palace Guard* (New York: Harper and Row, 1974), 236.

70. Heclo and Wildavsky, pp. 7–8.

71. Ibid., p. 34.

72. Moynihan, pp. 10–11.

73. Wildavsky, *Budgetary Process*, p. 170.

74. Quoted in Barnet and Muller, p. 264.

75. Halberstam, p. 221.

76. Ibid., p. 349.

77. Hannah Arendt, *Crises of the Republic* (New York: Harcourt, Brace, Jovanovich, 1972), 31–36.

78. The concept of the reification of the state resembles Gramsci's notion of statolatry, except that Gramsci's concept is, for whatever reason, presented in a very confusing way. See Antonio Gramsci, *Prison Notebooks* (New York: International Publishers, 1971), 268–69.

79. Matthew Arnold, *Culture and Anarchy* (Cambridge: At the University Press, 1968), 166.

80. Heinrich von Treitschke, *Politics* (New York: Harcourt, Brace, and World, 1963), 31.

81. Emile Durkheim, *Professional Ethics and Civic Morals* (New York: Free Press, 1958), 51.

82. Ibid., p. 64.

83. Schell, p. 157.

84. Good examples include Nicholas Luhmann, *Legitimation durch Verfahren* (Neuwied: Luchterhand, 1969); the examples cited in Jean Meynaud, *Technocracy* (New York: Free Press, 1969); and David Easton, *A Systems Analysis of Political Life* (New York: Wiley, 1967).

85. Robert Kennedy, *Thirteen Days* (New York: Norton, 1969), cited in Allison, p. 133.

86. Michel Debré, *Au Service de la nation* (Paris: Stock, 1963), 228–29.

87. Michel Debré, *Une Certaine Idée de la France* (Paris: Fayard, 1972), 140.

88. Ibid., p. 146.

89. Peter Bachrach, *The Theory of Democratic Elitism* (Boston: Little, Brown, 1967).

90. Edward A. Purcell, *The Crisis of Democratic Theory* (Lexington: University of Kentucky Press, 1973).

91. Cited in Nicholas van Hoffman, "The Worshippers," *New York Post*, July 1, 1975, p. 33.

92. McGeorge Bundy, *The Strength of Government* (Cambridge: Harvard University Press, 1968), 33, 37.

93. Ibid., p. 31. A preference for efficiency over democratic procedure leads both Bundy and Debré to take a dim view of legislatures when contrasted with administrative machinery. Bundy constantly defends presidential power over congressional, and Debré noted that "the Republic, in order to be legitimate, must be governed, and government is not an affair of assemblies." *Une Certaine Idée de la France*, p. 152.

94. Wildavsky, "The Strategic Retreat on Objectives."

95. Daniel Patrick Moynihan, *Coping* (New York: Random House, 1973), 4.

96. Charles Lindblom, *The Intelligence of Democracy* (New York: Free Press, 1965).

97. Moynihan, *Coping*, p. 28.

98. Peter F. Drucker, "The Sickness of Government," *The Public Interest*, 14 (Winter 1969), 3, 17, 18.

99. Wildavsky, *Budgetary Process*, p. 102.

100. For an example see Raymond A. Bauer, Ithiel de Sola Pool, and Lewis Anthony Dexter, *American Business and Public Policy* (second edition; Chicago: Aldine-Atherton, 1972).

CHAPTER 9

1. *New York Times*, December 5, 1973, p. 58.
2. Hannah Arendt, *The Human Condition* (Chicago: Phoenix Books, 1953).
3. Carole Pateman, "Sublimation and Reification: Locke, Wolin and the Liberal-Democratic Conception of the Political," *Politics and Society* (1975), 441–68.
4. Sheldon Wolin, *Politics and Vision* (Boston: Little, Brown, 1960), 290.
5. Theodore Zeldin, *Ambition, Love, and Politics*, vol. 1 of *France: 1848–1945* (Oxford: Clarendon Press, 1973), 488.
6. Aristide Zolberg, "Moments of Madness," *Politics and Socitey*, 2 (Winter 1972), 183–207.
7. Zeldin, p. 749.
8. Ibid., p. 747.
9. For examples, see Harvey Goldberg, *The Life of Jean Juares* (Madison: University of Wisconsin Press, 1962), 169.
10. Norman Gash, *Politics in the Age of Peel* (New York: Norton, 1971).
11. Sheila Rowbothom, *Hidden from History* (New York: Vintage Books, 1976), 77–90.
12. Henry Pelling, *Popular Politics and Society in Late Victorian Britain* (New York: St. Martin's Press, 1968), 104.
13. Walter Dean Burnham, *Critical Elections and the Mainsprings of American Politics* (New York: Norton, 1970), 72.
14. Ibid., p. 73.
15. Charles Leinenweber, forthcoming article in *Science and Society*. See also Irving Howe, *World of Our Fathers* (New York: Harcourt, Brace, Jovanovich, 1976), 340–47.
16. Richard Jensen, "American Electoral Campaigns: A Theoretical and Historical Typology." Paper presented at the 1968 meetings of the Midwestern Political Science Association, cited in Burnham, p. 73.
17. Arthur Lipow, "Plebiscitarian Politics and Progressivism: The Direct Democracy Movement." Paper presented at the 1973 meetings of the American Historical Association.
18. Burnham, p. 90.
19. Samuel P. Hayes, "Political Parties and the Community-Society Continuum," in William Nisbet Chambers and Walter Dean Burnham (eds.), *The American Party Systems* (New York: Oxford University Press, 1967), 152–81.

20. T. H. Marshall, *Class, Citizenship, and Social Development* (Garden City, N.Y.: Doubleday, 1964), 87.

21. Katherine Stone, "The Origins of Job Structures in the Steel Industry," *Review of Radical Political Economics*, 6 (Summer 1974), 113–73, and Stephen A. Marglin, "What Do Bosses Do?", *Review of Radical Political Economics*, 6 (Summer 1974), 60–112.

22. Harry Braverman, *Labor and Monopoly Capital* (New York: Monthly Review Press, 1974), 319.

23. Ibid., p. 156.

24. Jürgen Habermas, *Legitimation Crisis* (Boston: Beacon Press, 1975), 58.

25. Ibid., p. 39.

26. David Easton and Jack Dennis, "The Child's Image of Government," *Annals of the American Academy of Political and Social Science*, 361 (September 1965), 42.

27. Ibid., p. 47.

28. Jack Dennis, Leon Lindberg, and Donald McCrone, "Support for Nation and Government among English Children," *British Journal of Political Science*, 1 (January 1971), 37.

29. Charles Roig and F. Billon-Grand, *La Socialisation politique des enfants* (Paris: Colin, 1968), 61.

30. Judith Gallatin and Joseph Adelson, "Individual Rights and the Public Good: A Cross National Study of Adolescents," *Comparative Political Studies*, 3 (July 1970), 239.

31. Ibid., p. 239.

32. Hayes, "Political Parties."

33. Easton and Dennis, p. 45.

34. Dean Jaros, Herbert Hirsch, and Frederick Fleron, Jr., "The Malevolent Leader: Political Socialization in an American Sub-culture," *American Political Science Review*, 62 (June 1968), 564–75. Edward Greenberg, "Black Children and the Political System," *Public Opinion Quarterly*, 34 (Fall 1970), 333–45.

35. Easton and Dennis, p. 47.

36. Greenberg, "Black Children"; Harrell Rodgers and George Taylor, "The Policeman as an Agent of Regime Legitimation," *Midwest Journal of Political Science*, 15 (February 1971), 72–86.

37. David Easton and Jack Dennis, "The Child's Acquisition of Regime Norms: Political Efficacy," *American Political Science Review*, 61 (March 1967), 33.

38. Ibid., p. 38.

39. Ibid., p. 37.

40. Gallatin and Adelson, "Individual Rights," Joseph Adelson and Robert P. O'Neil, "The Growth of Political Ideas in Adolescence: The Sense of Community," *Journal of Personality and Social Psychology*, 4 (September 1966), 295–306.

41. Philip E. Converse, "Of Time and Partisan Stability," *Comparative Political Studies*, 2 (July 1969), 139–71.

42. Philip E. Converse, "The Nature of Belief Systems in Mass Publics," in David Apter (ed.), *Ideology and Discontent* (New York: Free Press, 1964), 213.

43. Easton and Dennis, "The Child's Image of Government," p. 48.

44. Edgar Litt, "Civic Education, Community Norms, and Political Indoctrination," *American Sociological Review*, 28 (February 1963), 68–75.

45. Gabriel Almond and Sidney Verba, *The Civic Culture* (Boston: Little, Brown, 1965).

46. Ibid., pp. 339–44.

47. Ibid., p. 346.

48. For an analysis of advanced societies based on a close approximation to the accumulation-legitimation model, see Harry Eckstein, "Authority Relations and Governmental Performance: A Theoretical Framework," *Comparative Political Studies*, 2 (October 1969), 269–326.

49. Angus Campbell, Philip E. Converse, Warren E. Miller, and Donald Stokes, *The American Voter* (New York: Wiley, 1960), 541.

50. Sidney Verba and Norman Nye, *Participation in America* (New York: Harper and Row, 1972), 32. See also *The American Voter*, p. 320, where it is pointed out that only a third of those who vote for congressional candidates can remember their names shortly after the election.

51. Roger W. Cobb and Charles O. Elder. *Participation in America: The Dynamics of Agenda Building* (Boston: Allyn and Bacon, 1972).

52. Lewis Edinger, *Politics in Germany* (Boston: Little, Brown, 1968), 105–13. Sidney Verba, "Germany: The Remaking of Political Culture," in Lucian W. Pye and Sidney Verba (eds.), *Political Culture and Political Development* (Princeton: Princeton University Press, 1965), 130–70.

53. Kendall L. Baker, "Political Participation, Political Efficacy, and Socialization in Germany," *Comparative Politics*, 6 (October 1973), 73–98.

54. Philip E. Converse and Georges Dupeaux, "Politicization of the Electorate in France and the United States," in Angus Campbell, Philip E. Converse, Warren E. Miller, and Donald E. Stokes, *Elections and the Political Order* (New York: Wiley, 1966), 291.

55. Giuseppe di Palma, "Disaffection and Participation in Western Democracies: The Role of Political Oppositions," *Journal of Politics*, 31 (November 1969), 984–1015.

56. Donald McCorne, "Party Identification: A Cross National Study" (unpublished dissertation, University of North Carolina, 1966). Cited in Timothy M. Hennessey, "Democratic Attitudinal Configurations among Italian Youth," *Midwest Journal of Political Science*, 13 (May 1969), 189.

57. Ibid., pp. 189, 192.

58. Sidney Tarrow, "Economic Development and the Transformation of the Italian Party System," *Comparative Politics*, 1 (January 1969), 161–83.

59. Sidney Tarrow, "Political Dualism and Italian Communism," *American Political Science Review*, 61 (March 1967), 39–53.

60. Verba and Nye, p. 343.

61. William Kornhauser, *The Politics of Mass Society* (New York: Free Press, 1959).

62. Reinhard Bendix, *Nation-Building and Citizenship: Studies of Our Changing Social Order* (Garden City, N.Y.: Anchor Books, 1969), 128–29.

63. Burnham, pp. 94, 117, 130.

64. Stein Rokkan and Seymour Martin Lipset, *Party Systems and Voter Alignments* (New York: Free Press, 1967).

65. Otto Kirchheimer, "The Transformation of the Western European Party Systems," in Joseph LaPalombara and Myron Weiner (eds.), *Political Parties and Political Development* (Princeton: Princeton University Press, 1966), 184.

66. Ibid., pp. 189, 195.

67. Claus Offe, "Political Authority and Class Structure: An Analysis of Late Capitalist Societies," *International Journal of Social Science*, 2 (Spring 1972), 84.

68. Kirchheimer, p. 185.

69. Walter Karp, *Indispensable Enemies: The Politics of Misrule in America* (Baltimore: Penguin Books, 1973), 73.

70. Ibid., pp. 20, 37.

71. Donald Stokes, "Party Loyalty and the Likelihood of Deviating Elections," in *Elections and the Political Order*, p. 126.

72. Samuel P. Huntington, "The United States," in Trilateral Task Force on the Governability of Democracies, *The Governability of Democracies* (New York: Trilateral Commission, 1975), 34.

73. Ibid., p. 29.

74. Jack Dennis, "Trends in Public Support for the American Party System," *British Journal of Political Science*, 5 (April 1975), 222.

75. Almond and Verba, p. 148.

76. "Conclusions and Preliminary Recommendations," *The Governability of Democracies*, p. 27.

77. Almond and Verba, p. 265.

78. Offe, p. 89.

79. Huntington, p. 25.

80. Michel Crozier, "Europe," *The Governability of Democracies*, pp. 17–23.

81. Robert D. Hess and Judith V. Torney, *The Development of Basic Attitudes and Values toward Government and Citizenship during the Elementary School Years* (Washington: U.S. Office of Education, 1965), cited in M. Kent Jennings and Richard G. Niemi, "The Transmission of Political Values from Parent to Child," *American Political Science Review*, 62 (March 1968), 169–70.

82. Steven H. Chafee, L. Scott Ward, and Leonard P. Tipton, "Mass Com-

munications and Political Specialization," *Journalism Quarterly*, 47 (Winter 1970), 647–59.

83. Alan Wolfe, *The Seamy Side of Democracy* (New York: McKay, 1973), 103–105.

84. James Rule, *Private Lives and Public Surveillance* (London: Lane, 1973), 30, 270.

85. Roland Inglehart, "The Silent Revolution in Europe: Intergenerational Change in Post-Industrial Societies," *American Political Science Review*, 65 (December 1971), 911–1017.

86. This notion is discussed in Alan Wolfe, "New Directions in the Marxist Theory of Politics," *Politics and Society*, 4 (Winter 1974), 131–60.

87. Representative of this genre is Richard E. Neustadt, *Presidential Power* (New York: Wiley, 1960).

88. For an example see Anthony Downs, *An Economic Theory of Democracy* (New York: Harper and Row, 1957).

89. The operations of a system of alienated politics are fully captured in Robert A. Caro, *The Power Broker* (New York: Knopf, 1974).

90. Max Weber, "Politics as a Vocation," in Hans Gerth and C. Wright Mills (eds.), *From Max Weber* (New York: Oxford University Press, 1958), 77–128.

91. Daniel Bell, *The End of Ideology* (New York: Free Press, 1960), 269–70.

92. Bernard Crick, *In Defense of Politics* (Chicago: University of Chicago Press, 1962), 131.

93. John Bunzel, *Anti-Politics in America* (New York: Knopf, 1967), 126–28.

94. Daniel Boorstin, *The Genius of American Politics* (Chicago: Phoenix Books, 1964).

95. Most studies of this sort follow the lead of Samuel Stouffer, *Communism, Conformity, and Civil Liberties* (Gloucester, Mass.: P. Smith, 1963). For an effective critique see Robert W. Jackman, "Political Elites, Mass Publics, and Support for Democratic Principles," *Journal of Politics*, 34 (August 1972), 753–73.

96. Norman R. Luttbeg, "The Structure of Beliefs among Leaders and the Public," *Public Opinion Quarterly*, 32 (Fall 1968), 398–409.

97. P. A. Allum, "The Neapolitan Politicians: A Collective Portrait," *Politics and Society*, 2 (Summer 1972), 377–406.

98. Giorgio Galli, *Il Bipartitismo Imperfetto* (Bologna: Il Mulino, 1966), cited in Allum, p. 395.

99. Robert D. Putnam, *The Beliefs of Politicians* (New Haven and London: Yale University Press, 1973), 54.

100. Ibid., p. 105.

101. Ibid., p. 62.

102. Ibid., p. 69.

103. Frank E. Myers, "Social Class and Political Change in Western Industrial Societies," *Comparative Politics*, 2 (April 1970), 410.

104. The most utopian presentation of this position, and one that reveals a strong antipolitical bias, is Robert E. Lane, "The Decline of Politics and Ideology in a Knowledgeable Society," *American Sociological Review,* 31 (October 1966), 649–62.

105. Talcott Parsons, *Structure and Process in Modern Societies* (New York: Free Press, 1960), 181, 224.

106. Robert Boguslaw, *The New Utopians* (Englewood Cliffs, N.J.: Prentice-Hall, 1965).

107. John Goldthorpe, "Industrial Relations in Great Britain: A Critique of Reformism," *Politics and Society,* 4 (1974), 419–52.

108. See Jean Meynard, *Technocracy* (London: Faber and Faber, 1968).

109. An excellent study of some of the more bizarre of McNamara's weapons is contained in Michael Klare, *War without End* (New York: Knopf, 1972).

CHAPTER 10

1. Anthony Hartley, "The Withering Away of Western Liberal Democracy," in E. A. Goerner (ed.), *Democracy in Crisis* (Notre Dame: University of Notre Dame Press, 1971), 163.

2. Anthony King, "Overload: Problems of Governing in the 1970s," *Political Studies,* 23 (June–September 1975), 294–95.

3. See William Pfaff, "Some Questions about a Crisis," *New Yorker,* April 5, 1976, p. 100. Pfaff's point that pessimism about democracy is most of all an American phenomenon is slightly incorrect; as we shall see in this chapter, Europeans such as Michel Crozier, Giovanni Sartori, Samuel Brittan, and Anthony King all agree with the American sentiment.

4. Robert Nisbet, *Twilight of Authority* (New York: Oxford University Press, 1975), 232.

5. Alain Duhamel, "Les Français n'aiment pas l'état, mais ils en attendent tout," *Le Monde,* October 10, 1970.

6. Arthur H. Miller, "Political Issues and Trust in Government: 1964–1970," *American Political Science Review,* 68 (September 1974), 953.

7. James S. House and William M. Mason, "Political Alienation in America, 1952–68," *American Sociological Review,* 40 (April 1975), 123–47.

8. *The Cambridge Report* 3, Spring 1975, p. 118.

9. Miller, p. 951.

10. The Trilateral Task Force on the Governability of Democracies, *The Governability of Democracies* (New York: Trilateral Commission, May 1975).

11. On the Commission, see Geoffrey Barraclough, "Wealth and Power: The Politics of Food and Oil," *New York Review of Books,* 22 (August 7, 1975), 23–30.

12. Trilateral Report, chap. 2, p. 3.

13. Ibid., chap. 3, pp. 22–25, 47, 59, 60, 62.

14. Ibid., chap. 5, pp. 19, 22, 31, 34, 36, 40.

15. *Trialogue*, No. 7 (Summer 1975), pp. 7–9.

16. Trilateral Report, chap. 5, p. 7.

17. Maurice Duverger, *Janus: Les deux faces de l'Occident* (Paris: Fayard, 1972), 3.

18. Trilateral Report, chap. 3, p. 59.

19. James O'Connor, *The Fiscal Crisis of the State* (New York: St. Martin's Press, 1973).

20. Trilateral Report, chap. 5, pp. 17–18.

21. I have argued this point at greater length in "Waiting for Righty: A Critique of the 'Fascism' Hypothesis," *Review of Radical Political Economics*, 5 (Fall 1973), 46–66.

22. Leonard Silk and David Vogel, *Ethics and Profits* (New York: Simon and Schuster, 1976).

23. The first quotation was cited in Samuel Brittan, "The Economic Contradictions of Democracy," *British Journal of Political Science*, 5 (April 1975), 146. The remainder are from Silk and Vogel.

24. Jonathan Spivak, "Putting a Lid on Social Programs," *Wall Street Journal*, December 31, 1975, p. 6.

25. Brittan, pp. 129, 141.

26. Daniel Bell, *The Cultural Contradictions of Capitalism* (New York: Basic Books, 1976), 232–36.

27. King, p. 294.

28. See ibid., and also Crozier's section in *The Governability of Democracies*; another use of the term is contained in Giovanni Sartori, "Will Democracy Kill Democracy?", *Government and Opposition*, 10 (Spring 1975), 158.

29. *Wall Street Journal*, December 26, 1975, p. 6; *New York Times*, September 5, 1975, p. 35; *New York Times*, April 7, 1976, p. 1.

30. For an example see James Q. Wilson, *Thinking about Crime* (New York: Basic Books, 1975).

31. This conclusion follows from the analysis of Martin Diamond, "The Declaration and the Constitution: Liberty, Democracy, and the Founders," *The Public Interest*, 41 (Fall 1975), 39–55.

32. Bell, p. 14.

33. For an example of this reasoning see Huntington's chapter in *The Governability of Democracies*, pp. 5, 11.

34. Brittan, p. 133.

35. Arthur Okun, *Equality and Efficiency: The Big Tradeoff* (Washington: Brookings Institution, 1975).

36. "Why Recovering Economies Don't Create Enough Jobs," *Business Week*, March 22, 1976, pp. 114–15.

37. Quoted in ibid., p. 115.

38. Theodore Lowi, *The End of Liberalism* (New York: Norton, 1969), *passim*.

39. Brittan, pp. 142–46.

40. Cited in Daniel Patrick Moynihan, *The Politics of a Guaranteed Income* (New York: Vintage Books, 1973), 76–78.

41. "Is Democracy Dying?: Verdict of Leading World Scholars," *U.S. News and World Report*, March 8, 1976, p. 51.

42. Giacomo Sani, "Mass Constraints on Political Realignments: Perceptions of Anti-System Parties in Italy," *British Journal of Political Science*, 6 (January 1976), 1–32.

43. P. A. Allum, *Italy—Republic Without Government?* (New York: Norton, 1973), 250.

44. Philippe Schmitter, "Still the Century of Corporatism?", *Review of Politics*, 36 (January 1974), 111.

45. Felix Rohatyn, "A New RFC Is Proposed for Business," *New York Times*, 3 (December 7, 1974), 1.

46. See Huntington's chapter in *The Governability of Democracies*, p. 19.

47. Max Ways, "Business Needs a Different Political Stance," *Fortune*, September 1975, p. 96.

48. See Robbie Guttman, "State Intervention and the Economic Crises: The Labour Government's Economic Policy, 1974–75," *Kapitalistate*, 4–5 (1976), 225–70.

49. See Nigel Harris, *Competition and the Corporate Society* (London: Methuen, 1972).

50. Cited in *Wall Street Journal*, November 6, 1975, p. 19.

51. Antonio Gramsci, *Selections from the Prison Notebooks* (New York: International Publishers, 1971), 275–76.

52. Frances Fox Piven and Richard A. Cloward, *Regulating the Poor* (New York: Vintage Books, 1972), 345–48.

53. I have borrowed the concept of "hoarding" from James O'Connor's work in progress, provisionally called *The Class Struggle*.

54. See ibid., and James O'Connor, "Productive and Unproductive Labor," *Politics and Society*, 5 (1975), 297–336.

55. For interpretations of these movements see Manuel Castels, "Wild City," *Kapitalistate*, 4–5 (1976), 2–30.

56. Gramsci, p. 232.

57. Ibid., p. 165.

58. Bell, p. 231.

Bibliography

ADAMS, GORDON. "European Capitalism, the State, and the European Community." Unpublished paper.

ADAMS, GRAHAM. *The Age of Industrial Violence, 1900–1915.* New York: Columbia University Press, 1966.

ADAMS, HENRY. *Democracy.* New York: New American Library, 1961.

ADAMS, WALTER. "The Military Industrial Complex and the New Industrial State." *American Economic Review,* 58 (May 1968), 652–65.

ADELSON, JOSEPH, and ROBERT P. O'NEIL. "The Growth of Political Ideas in Adolescence: The Sense of Community." *Journal of Personality and Social Psychology,* 5 (September 1966), 295–306.

AGEE, PHILIP. *Inside the Company.* London: Penguin Books, 1975.

ALLARDT, ERIC, and STEIN ROKKAN, *Mass Politics.* New York: Free Press, 1970.

ALLISON, GRAHAM. *Essence of Decision.* Boston: Little, Brown, 1971.

ALLUM, P. A. "The Neapolitan Politicians: A Collective Portrait." *Politics and Society,* 2 (Summer 1972), 377–406.

———. *Politics and Society in Postwar Naples.* Cambridge: At the University Press, 1973.

———. *Italy: Republic without Government?* New York: Norton, 1973.

ALMOND, GABRIEL, and SIDNEY VERBA. *The Civic Culture.* Boston: Little, Brown, 1965.

ALTHUSSER, LOUIS. *Reading Capital.* London: New Left Books, 1970.

American Political Science Association. *Towards a More Responsible Two-Party System.* New York: Rinehart, 1950.

ANDERSON, OLIVE. "The Janus-Face of Mid-Nineteenth Century English Radicalism." *Victorian Studies,* 8 (March 1965), 231–42.

———. *A Liberal State at War: British Politics and Economics in the Crimean War.* New York: St. Martin's Press, 1967.

ANDERSON, PERRY. *Lineages of the Absolutist State.* London: New Left Books, 1974.

ARENDT, HANNAH. *The Origins of Totalitarianism.* Revised edition. Cleveland: World, 1956.

———. *The Human Condition.* Chicago: University of Chicago Press, 1959.

———. *Crises of the Republic.* New York: Harcourt, Brace, Jovanovich, 1971.

ARISTOTLE. *The Politics of Aristotle.* New York: Oxford University Press, 1962.

ARNOLD, MATTHEW. *Culture and Anarchy*. Cambridge: At the University Press, 1968.

ARNOLD, THURMAN. *The Symbols of Government*. New Haven: Yale University Press, 1935.

AVENERI, SHLOMO. *Hegel's Theory of the Modern State*. Cambridge: At the University Press, 1972.

BACHRACH, PETER. *The Theory of Democratic Elitism*. Boston: Little, Brown, 1967.

———, and MORTON BARATZ. "Decisions and Non-Decisions." *American Political Science Review*, 57 (September 1963), 632–42.

BAGEHOT, WALTER. *The English Constitution*. London: Fontana, 1963.

BAKER, KENDALL L. "Political Participation, Political Efficacy, and Socialization in Germany." *Comparative Politics*, 6 (October 1973), 73–98.

BALL, GEORGE. "Citizenship and the Multinational Corporation." *Social Research*, 41 (Winter 1974), 657–72.

BARAN, PAUL, and PAUL SWEEZY, *Monopoly Capital*. New York: Monthly Review Press, 1966.

BARNET, RICHARD. *The Roots of War*. Baltimore: Penguin Books, 1973.

———, and RONALD E. MULLER. *Global Reach*. New York: Simon and Schuster, 1974.

BARRACLOUGH, GEOFFREY. "The Great World Crisis: I." *New York Review of Books*, January 23, 1975.

———. "Wealth and Power: The Politics of Food and Oil." *New York Review of Books*, August 7, 1975.

BASTIAT, FRÉDÉRIC. *Harmonies économiques*. Brussels: Méline, 1850.

BAUCHET, PIERRE. *Economic Planning: The French Experience*. New York: Praeger, 1964.

BAUER, RAYMOND, ITHIEL DE SOLA POOL, and LEWIS ANTHONY DEXTER. *American Business and Public Policy*. Second edition. Chicago: Aldine-Atherton, 1972.

BAUM, WARREN C. *The French Economy and the State*. Princeton: Princeton University Press, 1958.

BEER, SAMUEL. *British Politics in the Collectivist Age*. New York: Vintage Books, 1969.

BEHRMAN, JACK N. *U.S. International Business and Governments*. New York: McGraw-Hill, 1971.

BELL, DANIEL. *The End of Ideology*. New York: Free Press, 1960.

———. *The Coming of Post-Industrial Society*. New York: Basic Books, 1973.

———. *The Cultural Contradictions of Capitalism*. New York: Basic Books, 1976.

BENDIX, REINHARD. *Nation-Building and Citizenship*. Garden City, N.Y.: Anchor Books, 1969.

BENJAMIN, WALTER. *Illuminations*. New York: Schocken Books, 1960.

BENTLEY, ARTHUR F. *The Process of Government.* Cambridge: Belknap Press of Harvard University Press, 1967.

BERLE, ADOLPH, and GARDNER MEANS. "Corporation." *Encyclopedia of the Social Sciences.* New York: Macmillan, 1931.

BERMAN, MARSHALL. *The Politics of Authenticity.* New York: Atheneum, 1972.

BERNSTEIN, CARL, and BOB WOODWARD. *All the President's Men.* New York: Simon and Schuster, 1974.

BERNSTEIN, IRVING. *The Turbulent Years.* Boston: Houghton Mifflin, 1971.

BIRNBAUM, NORMAN. *The Crisis of Industrial Society.* New York: Oxford University Press, 1969.

BLAUGH, MARK. *Ricardian Economics.* New Haven: Yale University Press, 1958.

BLOCH, MARC. *Feudal Society.* Chicago: University of Chicago Press, 1961.

BOGUSLAW, ROBERT. *The New Utopians.* Englewood Cliffs, N.J.: Prentice-Hall, 1965.

BÖHNE, HELMUT. "Big Business, Pressure Groups and Bismarck's Turn to Protectionism, 1873–79." *Historical Journal,* 10, No. 2 (1967), 218–36.

BOORSTIN, DANIEL. *The Genius of American Politics.* Chicago: Phoenix Books, 1964.

———. *Democracy and Its Discontents.* New York: Random House, 1974.

BOROSAGE, ROBERT. "The Making of the National Security State." In Leonard S. Rodberg and Derek Shearer (eds.), *The Pentagon Watchers* (Garden City, N.Y.: Anchor Books, 1970), 3–63.

BOURNE, RANDOLPH. *War and the Intellectuals.* New York: Harper Torchbooks, 1969.

BOWLES, SAMUEL, and HERBERT GINTIS. *Schooling in Capitalist America.* New York: Basic Books, 1976.

BRADY, ROBERT. *Business as a System of Power.* New York: Columbia University Press, 1943.

BRAUDEL, FERNAND. *The Mediterranean and the Mediterranean World in the Age of Philip II.* New York: Harper Torchbooks, 1975.

BRAUNTHAL, GERARD. *The Federation of German Industry in Politics.* Ithaca, N.Y.: Cornell University Press, 1965.

———. *The West German Legislative Process.* Ithaca, N.Y.: Cornell University Press, 1972.

BRAVERMAN, HARRY. *Labor and Monopoly Capitalism.* New York: Monthly Review Press, 1974.

BREBNER, J. B. "Laissez-Faire and State Intervention in Nineteenth Century Britain." *Journal of Economic History,* 8 (1948), 59–73.

BRIGGS, ASA. *The Making of Modern England, 1783–1864.* New York: Harper Torchbooks, 1965.

———. "The Language of Class in Early Nineteenth Century England." In

Asa Briggs and John Saville (eds.), *Essays in Labour History*. Revised edition. New York: St. Martin's Press, 1967, 43–73.

BRITTAN, SAMUEL. "The Economic Contradictions of Democracy." *British Journal of Political Science*, 5 (April 1975), 129–159.

BROUDE, HENRY. "The Role of the State in American Economic Development, 1820–1890." In Harry N. Scheiber (ed.), *United States Economic History*. New York: Knopf, 1964, 118–22.

BRUCE, MAURICE. *The Coming of the Welfare State*. London: Batsford, 1961.

BRUCE, ROBERT V. *1877: Year of Violence*. Indianapolis: Bobbs-Merrill, 1959.

BRZEZINSKI, ZBIGNIEW. *Between Two Ages*. New York: Viking Press, 1970.

BUNDY, MCGEORGE. *The Strength of Government*. Cambridge: Harvard University Press, 1968.

BUNZEL, JOHN. *Anti-Politics in America*. New York: Knopf, 1967.

BURKHARDT, JACOB. *The Civilization of the Renaissance in Italy*. New York: New American Library, 1960.

BURNHAM, WALTER DEAN. *Critical Elections and the Mainsprings of American Politics*. New York: Norton, 1970.

BUTLER, DAVID, *and* JENNA FREEMAN. *British Political Facts*. London: Macmillan, 1968.

———, and DONALD STOKES. *Political Change in Britain*. London: Macmillan, 1969.

CALLEO, DAVID P., and BENJAMIN N. ROWLAND. *America and the World Political Economy*. Bloomington: Indiana University Press, 1973.

CAMERON, RONDO E. *France and the Economic Development of Europe*. Princeton: Princeton University Press, 1961.

CAMPBELL, ANGUS et al. *The American Voter*. New York: Wiley, 1960.

———. *Elections and the Political Order*. New York: Wiley, 1966.

CARALEY, DEMETRIOS. *The Politics of Military Unification*. New York: Columbia University Press, 1966.

CAREY, HENRY. *Principles of Social Science*. Philadelphia: Lippincott, 1878.

CAREY, MATTHEW. *Essays in Political Economy*. Philadlephia: Carey and Lea, 1822.

CARLYLE, THOMAS. *Selected Writings*. London: Penguin Books, 1971.

CARO, ROBERT. *The Power Broker*. New York: Knopf, 1974.

CARR, E. H. *The Twenty Years' Crisis*. New York: Harper Torchbooks, 1964.

———. *The New Society*. Boston: Beacon Press, 1965.

CASTELS, MANUEL. "The Wild City." *Kapitalistate*, 4–5 (1976), 2–30.

CASTLES, STEPHEN, and GODOLUCK KOSACK. *Immigrant Workers and Class Structure in Western Europe*. London: Oxford University Press, 1973.

CHAFFEE, STEVEN H. et al. "Mass Communications and Political Socialization." *Journalism Quarterly*, 47 (Winter 1970), 647–59.

CHAMBERS, WILLIAM NISBET, and WALTER DEAN BURNHAM. *The American Party Systems*. New York: Oxford University Press, 1967.

CHAPMAN, BRIAN. *The Profession of Government*. London: Allen and Unwin, 1959.

CHAPMAN, GUY. *The Third Republic of France: The First Phase, 1871–1894*. New York: St. Martin's Press, 1962.

CHARLOT, MONICA. *La Persuasion politique*. Paris: Colin, 1970.

CHECKLAND, S. G. *The Rise of Industrial Society in England, 1815–1885*. New York: St. Martin's Press, 1964.

CHURCH, WILLIAM F. *Richelieu and Reason of State*. Princeton: Princeton University Press, 1973.

CINANNI, PAOLO. *Emigrazione e Imperialismo*. Rome: Editori Riuniti, 1968.

CLAPHAM, J. H. *The Early Railway Age, 1820–1850*. Vol. 1 of *An Economic History of Modern Britain*. Cambridge: At the University Press, 1950.

———. *Free Trade and Steel, 1850–1886*. Vol. 2 of *An Economic History of Modern Britain*. Cambridge: At the University Press, 1952.

———. *A Concise Economic History of Britain*. Cambridge: At the University Press, 1963.

CLARK, KEITH L., and LAURENCE J. LEGERE. *The President and the Management of National Security*. New York: Praeger, 1969.

CLEGG, H. A. *The System of Industrial Relations in Great Britain*. Oxford: Blackwell, 1972.

CLOUGH, SHEPARD B. *France: A History of National Economics, 1789–1939*. New York: Scribner's, 1939.

———. *The Economic History of Modern Italy*. New York: Columbia University Press, 1964.

CLUB JEAN MOULIN. *L'Etat et le citoyen*. Paris: Editions du Seuil, 1961.

COBB, RICHARD. *The People and the Police*. London: Oxford University Press, 1972.

COBB, ROGER W., and CHARLES O. ELDER. *Participation in America: The Dynamics of Agenda Building*. Boston: Allyn and Bacon, 1972.

COCHRAN, THOMAS C., and WILLIAM MILLER. *The Age of Enterprise*. New York: Harper and Row, 1961.

COFFEY, JOSEPH I., and VINCENT P. ROCK. *The Presidential Staff*. Washington: National Planning Association, 1961.

COHEN, STEPHEN. *Modern Capitalist Planning: The French Model*. Cambridge: Harvard University Press, 1969.

COLE, CHARLES W. *Colbert and a Century of French Mercantilism*. New York: Columbia University Press, 1939.

COLETTI, LUCIO. *From Rousseau to Lenin*. New York: Monthly Review Press, 1973.

Committee on the Organization of the Executive Branch of the Government. *National Security Organization*. Washington: Government Printing Office, 1949.

CONVERSE, PHILIP E. "The Nature of Belief Systems in Mass Publics." In David Apter (ed.), *Ideology and Discontent*. New York: Free Press, 1964, 206–61.

————. "Of Time and Partisan Stability." *Comparative Political Studies*, 2 (July 1969), 139–71.

CORWIN, EDWARD S. *The President: Office and Powers*. New York: New York University Press, 1957.

COWAN, PAUL et al. *State Secrets*. New York: Holt, Rinehart, and Winston, 1974.

CRENSON, MATTHEW A. *The Unpolitics of Air Pollution*. Baltimore: Johns Hopkins Press, 1971.

CRICK, BERNARD. *In Defense of Politics*. Chicago: University of Chicago Press, 1962.

CROCE, BENEDETTO. *A History of Italy, 1871–1915*. New York: Russell and Russell, 1963.

CROZIER, MICHEL. *The Bureaucratic Phenomenon*. Chicago: University of Chicago Press, 1964.

————. *The Stalled Society*. New York: Viking Press, 1973.

CUFF, ROBERT D. *The War Industries Board*. Baltimore: Johns Hopkins University Press, 1973.

DAHRENDORF, RALF. *Society and Democracy in Germany*. Garden City, N.Y.: Anchor Books, 1969.

DANGERFIELD, GEORGE. *The Strange Death of Liberal England*. New York: Capricorn, 1961.

DEBRÉ, MICHEL. *Au service de la nation*. Paris: Stock, 1963.

————. *Une certaine idée de la France*. Paris: Fayard, 1972.

DENNIS, JACK. "Trends in Public Support for the American Party System." *British Journal of Political Science*, 5 (April 1975), 187–230.

————, LEON LINDBERG and DONALD McCRONE. "Support for Nation and Government among English Children." *British Journal of Political Science*, 1 (January 1971), 77–101.

DERTHICK, MARTHA. "Militia Lobby in the Missile Age." In Samuel P. Huntington (ed.), *Changing Patterns of Military Politics*. New York: Free Press, 1962, 190–254.

DIAMOND, MARTIN. "The Declaration and the Constitution: Liberty, Democracy, and the Founders." *The Public Interest*, 41 (Fall 1975), 39–55.

DICEY, A. V. *Lectures on the Relation between Law and Public Opinion in England during the Nineteenth Century*. London: Macmillan, 1952.

DOBB, MAURICE. *Studies in the Development of Capitalism*. New York: International Publishers, 1963.

DOMHOFF, G. WILLIAM. *The Higher Circles*. New York: Vintage Books, 1971.

DORFMAN, GERALD A. *Wage Politics in Britain, 1945–67*. Ames: Iowa State University Press, 1973.

DORFMAN, JOSEPH. *The Economic Mind in American Civilization, 1606–1865*. New York: Viking Press, 1946.

DOWNS, ANTHONY. *An Economic Theory of Democracy*. New York: Harper and Row, 1952.

DRUCKER, PETER F. "The Sickness of Government." *The Public Interest*, 14 (Winter 1969), 3–18.

DULLES, ALLEN. *The Craft of Intelligence*. New York: Harper and Row, 1963.

DUNHAM, ARTHUR LEWIS. *The Industrial Revolution in France, 1815–1848*. New York: Exposition Press, 1955.

DURKHEIM, EMILE. *Professional Ethics and Civic Morals*. New York: Free Press, 1958.

DUVERGER, MAURICE. *Janus: Les deux faces de l'Occident*. Paris: Fayard, 1972.

EASTON, DAVID. *A Systems Analysis of Political Life*. New York: Wiley, 1967.

———, and JACK DENNIS. "The Child's Image of Government." *Annals of the American Academy of Political and Social Science*, 361 (September 1965), 40–57.

———. "The Child's Acquisition of Regime Norms: Political Efficacy." *American Political Science Review*, 61 (March 1967), 25–38.

ECKSTEIN, HARRY. *Pressure Group Politics*. London: Allen and Unwin, 1960.

———. "Authority Relations and Governmental Performance: A Theoretical Framework." *Comparative Political Studies*, 2 (October 1969), 269–326.

EDELMAN, MURRAY. *The Symbolic Uses of Politics*. Urbana: University of Illinois Press, 1964.

EDINGER, LEWIS J. *Politics in Germany*. Boston: Little, Brown, 1968.

EDWARDS, RICHARD C. "Capital Accumulation and Corporate Power in the Transition to Monopoly Capitalism." Cambridge: Center for Educational Policy Research, Harvard University, n.d.

———, MICHAEL REICH, and DAVID GORDON. *Dual Labor Market Segmentation and American Capitalism*. Lexington, Mass.: Heath, 1976.

EELS, RICHARD. "Multinational Corporations: The Intelligence Function." In Courtney Brown (ed.), *World Business: Promise and Problems*. New York: Macmillan, 1970, 140–55.

EHRMANN, HENRY. *French Labor from Popular Front to Liberation*. New York: Oxford University Press, 1947.

———. *Organized Business in France*. Princeton: Princeton University Press, 1957.

ELBOW, MATTHEW H. *French Corporative Theory, 1789–1948*. New York: Columbia University Press, 1953.

ELTON, G. R. *The Tudor Revolution in Government*. Cambridge: At the University Press, 1966.

EMY, H. V. *Liberals, Radicals and Social Politics, 1892–1914*. Cambridge: At the University Press, 1973.

ENGLER, ROBERT. *The Politics of Oil*. New York: Macmillan, 1961.

ENTREVES, ALEXANDER PASSERIN D'. *The Notion of the State*. Oxford: Clarendon Press, 1967.

ENZENSBERGER, HANS MAGNUS. *The Consciousness Industry*. New York: Seabury Press, 1974.

———. *Politics and Crime*. New York: Seabury Press, 1975.

EWEN, STEWART. *Captains of Consciousness*. New York: McGraw-Hill, 1976.

FAULKNER, HAROLD U. *Politics, Reform, and Expansion, 1890–1900*. New York: Harper Torchbooks, 1963.

FELICE, RENZO DE. *Mussolini, il fascista*. Turin: Einaudi, 1968.

FELIX, DAVID. *Walter Rathenau and the Weimar Republic*. Baltimore: Johns Hopkins University Press, 1971.

FIELDHOUSE, A. K. *Economics and Empire*. Ithaca, N.Y.: Cornell University Press, 1973.

FINE, SIDNEY. *The Automobile Industry under the Blue Eagle*. Ann Arbor: University of Michigan Press, 1963.

————. *Laissez-Faire and the General Welfare State*. Ann Arbor: University of Michigan Press, 1967.

FINER, S. E. "The Political Power of Private Capital: Part II." *Sociological Review*, new series, 4 (July 1956), 5–30.

————. *Anonymous Empire*. London: Pall Mall, 1966.

FISCHEL, JEFF. "On the Transformation of Ideology in European Political Systems: Candidates to the West German Bundestag." *Comparative Political Studies*, 4 (January 1972), 406–37.

FOHLEN, CLAUDE. *La France de l'entre-deux-guerres*. Paris: Casterman, 1966.

FONER, ERIC. *Free Soil, Free Labor, Free Men*. New York: Oxford University Press, 1970.

FORRESTER, JAY. *World Dynamics*. Cambridge: Wright-Allen, 1971.

FRAENKEL, ERNST. *The Dual State*. New York: Oxford University Press, 1941.

FUSFELD, DANIEL. *The Economic Thought of Franklin D. Roosevelt*. New York: Columbia University Press, 1956.

GALBRAITH, JOHN KENNETH. *The New Industrial State*. Boston: Houghton Mifflin, 1971.

GALLAGHER, JOHN, and RONALD ROBINSON. "The Imperialism of Free Trade." *Economic History Review*, second series, 6 (1953), 1–15.

GALLATIN, JUDITH, and JOSEPH ADELSON. "Individual Rights and the Public Good: A Cross-National Study of Adolescents." *Comparative Political Studies*, 3 (July 1970), 226–42.

GALLI, GIORGIO. *Il Bipartitismo Imperfetto*. Bologna: Il Mulino, 1966.

————. *Il Difficile Governo*. Bologna: Il Mulino, 1972.

————, and ALFONSO PRANDI. *Patterns of Political Participation in Italy*. New Haven: Yale University Press, 1970.

GARDNER, LLOYD C. *Architects of Illusion*. Chicago: Quadrangle, 1970.

GARDNER, RICHARD N. *In Pursuit of World Order*. New York: Praeger, 1966.

GASH, NORMAN. *Politics in the Age of Peel*. New York: Norton, 1971.

GERSCHENKRON, ALEXANDER. *Bread and Democracy in Germany*. Berkeley and Los Angeles: University of California Press, 1943.

GERTH, HANS, and C. WRIGHT MILLS (eds.). *From Max Weber*. New York: Oxford University Press, 1958.

GIDE, CHARLES, and CHARLES RIST. *A History of Economic Doctrines.* Boston: Heath, n.d.

GILBERT, JAMES B. *Designing the Industrial State.* Chicago: Quadrangle, 1972.

GILLIS, JOHN R. "Aristocracy and Bureaucracy in Nineteenth Century Prussia." *Past and Present,* 41 (December 1968), 105–29.

GIRVETZ, HARRY. *The Evolution of Liberalism.* New York: Collier Books, 1966.

GLYN, ANDREW, and BOB SUTCLIFFE, *British Capitalism, Workers, and the Profits Squeeze.* London: Penguin Books, 1972.

GODKIN, E. L. *Unforeseen Tendencies of Democracy.* Boston: Houghton Mifflin, 1898.

GOLDBERG, HARVEY. *The Life of Jean Juares.* Madison: University of Wisconsin Press, 1962.

GOLDTHORPE, JOHN. "Industrial Relations in Great Britain: A Critique of Reformism." *Politics and Society,* 4 (1974), 419–52.

GOODRICH, CARTER. *Government Promotion of American Canals and Railways, 1800–1890.* New York: Columbia University Press, 1960.

———. *The Government and the Economy.* Indianapolis: Bobbs-Merrill, 1967.

GOODWIN, RICHARD N. *The American Condition.* Garden City, N.Y.: Doubleday, 1974.

GORZ, ANDRÉ. *A Strategy for Labor.* Boston: Beacon Press, 1967.

GOUBERT, PIERRE. *L'Ancien Régime.* Paris: Colin, 1969.

GOUGH, IAN. "State Expenditure in Advanced Capitalism." *New Left Review,* 92 (July–August 1975), 53–92.

GOULDEN, JOSEPH C. *Truth Is the First Casualty.* Chicago: Rand McNally, 1969.

GRAHAM, OTIS L., JR. *An Encore for Reform: The Old Progressives and the New Deal.* New York: Oxford University Press, 1967.

GRAMSCI, ANTONIO. *Selections from the Prison Notebooks.* New York: International Publishers, 1971.

GREEN, THOMAS HILL. *Lectures on the Principles of Political Obligation, Works,* vol 2. London: Longmans, 1906.

GREENBERG, EDWARD. "Black Children and the Political System." *Public Opinion Quarterly,* 34 (Fall 1970), 333–45.

GRIFONE, PIETRO. *Il Capitale Finanziario in Italia.* Turin: Einaudi, 1972.

GRONLUND, LAWRENCE. *The Cooperative Commonwealth.* Cambridge: Belknap Press of Harvard University Press, 1965.

GUTTMANN, ROBBIE. "State Intervention and the Economic Crisis: The Labour Government's Economic Policy, 1974–75." *Kapitalistate,* 4–5 (1976), 225–70.

GUTTSMAN, W. L. *The British Political Elite.* New York: Basic Books, 1963.

HABERMAS, JÜRGEN. *Legitimation Crisis.* Boston: Beacon Press, 1975.

HALBERSTAM, DAVID. *The Best and the Brightest.* Greenwich, Conn.: Fawcett Books, 1973.

HALÉVY, DANIEL. *La Fin des notables.* Paris: Grasset, 1930.

HALÉVY, ELIE. *The Liberal Awakening, 1815–1830.* Vol. 2 of *A History of the English People in the Nineteenth Century.* London: Benn, 1949.

———. *Victorian Years, 1841–1895.* Vol. 4 of *A History of the English People in the Nineteenth Century.* London: Benn, 1951.

———. *Imperialism and the Rise of Labour.* Vol. 5 of *A History of the English People in the Nineteenth Century.* London: Benn, 1952.

———. *The Growth of Philosophical Radicalism.* Boston: Beacon Press, 1960.

———. *The Era of Tyrannies.* Garden City, N.Y.: Anchor Books, 1965.

HALL, PRESCOTT F. *Immigration and Its Effects upon the United States.* New York: Holt, 1908.

HALLSTEIN, WALTER. *Europe in the Making.* New York: Norton, 1973.

HAMEROW, THEODORE. *Restoration, Revolution, Reaction: Economics and Politics in Germany, 1815–1871.* Princeton: Princeton University Press, 1968.

———. *The Social Foundations of German Unification.* Princeton: Princeton University Press, 1972.

HAMMOND, BRAY. *Banks and Politics in the United States from the Revolution to the Civil War.* Princeton: Princeton University Press, 1967.

HAMMOND, PAUL Y. *Organizing for Defense.* Princeton: Princeton University Press, 1961.

HARRIS, DAVID. "European Liberalism in the Nineteenth Century." *American Historical Review,* 60 (1964–65), 502–26.

HARRIS, NIGEL. *Competition and the Corporate Society.* London: Methuen, 1972.

HARTLEY, ANTHONY. "The Withering Away of Western Liberal Democracy." In E. A. Goerner (ed.), *Democracy in Crisis.* South Bend, Ind.: University of Notre Dame Press, 1971, 153–63.

HARTZ, LOUIS. *Economic Policy and Democratic Thought: Pennsylvania, 1776–1860.* Cambridge: Harvard University Press, 1948.

———. *The Liberal Tradition in America.* New York: Harcourt, Brace, and World, 1955.

HAWLEY, ELLIS W. *The New Deal and the Problem of Monopoly.* Princeton: Princeton University Press, 1966.

———. et al. *Herbert Hoover and the Crisis of American Capitalism.* Cambridge: Schenckman, 1973.

HAYWARD, J. E. S. *Private Interests and Public Policy.* London: Longmans, 1966.

HECKSCHER, ELI. *Mercantilism.* London: Allen and Unwin, 1934.

HECLO, HUGH. *Modern Social Politics in Britain and Sweden.* New Haven: Yale University Press, 1974.

———, and AARON WILDAVSKY. *The Private Government of Public Money.* Berkeley and Los Angeles: University of California Press, 1974.

———. "OMB and the Presidency." *The Public Interest,* 38 (Winter 1975), 80–98.

HEILBRONER, ROBERT. *An Inquiry into the Human Prospect.* New York: Norton, 1974.

HENDERSON, W. O. *The State and the Industrial Revolution in Prussia, 1740–1870.* Liverpool: Liverpool University Press, 1958.

HENNESSEY, TIMOTHY M. "Democratic Attitudinal Configurations among Italian Youth." *Midwest Journal of Political Science,* 13 (May 1969), 167–93.

HENTZE, MARGOT. *Pre-Fascist Italy: The Rise and Fall of the Parliamentary Regime.* New York: Octagon Books, 1972.

HICKS, JOHN D. *The Republican Ascendancy.* New York: Harper, 1960.

HIGHAM, JOHN. *Strangers in the Land: Patterns of American Nativism, 1860–1925.* New York: Atheneum, 1970.

HIGONNET, PATRICK L. R., and TREVOR B. HIGONNET. "Class, Corruption and Politics in the French Chamber of Deputies, 1846–48." *French Historical Studies,* 5 (1967), 204–24.

HILSMAN, ROGER. *To Move a Nation.* New York: Delta Books, 1968.

HINTZE, OTTO. "The Emergence of the Democratic Nation–State." In Heinz Lubasz (ed.), *The Development of the Modern State.* New York: Macmillan, 1964, 65–71.

HITCH, CHARLES, and ROLAND N. McKEAN. *The Economics of Defense in the Nuclear Age.* New York: Atheneum, 1965.

HOFSTADTER, RICHARD. *Social Darwinism in American Thought.* Revised edition. New York: Braziller, 1959.

————. *The Age of Reform.* New York: Knopf, 1955.

HOLLAND, STUART (ed.). *The State as Entrepreneur.* London: Weidenfeld and Nicolson, 1972.

HOOPES, TOWNSEND. *The Limits of Intervention.* New York: McKay, 1969.

————. *The Devil and John Foster Dulles.* Boston: Little, Brown, 1973.

HOUSE, JAMES S., and WILLIAM M. MASON. "Political Alienation in America." *American Sociological Review,* 40 (April 1975), 123–47.

HOWE, IRVING. *World of Our Fathers.* New York: Harcourt, Brace, Jovanovich, 1976.

HUNTINGTON, SAMUEL P. "Interservice Competition and the Political Role of the Armed Services." *American Political Science Review,* 55 (March 1961), 4–52.

————. (ed.). *Changing Patterns of Military Politics.* New York: Free Press, 1962.

————. *The Soldier and the State.* New York: Vintage Books, 1964.

HUTCHINSON, E. P. *Immigrants and Their Children, 1850–1950.* New York: Wiley, 1956.

HYMER, STEPHEN. "The Efficiency (Contradictions) of Multinational Corporations." *American Economic Review,* 60 (May 1970), 441–48.

————. "The Multinational Corporation and the Law of Uneven Development." In J. N. Bhagwati (ed.), *Economics and World Order.* New York: Macmillan, 1972, 113–40.

————. "The United States Multinational Corporations and Japanese Competition in the Pacific." Prepared for the Conferencia del Pacifica, Viña del Mar, Chile, 1970.

INGLEHART, ROLAND. "The Silent Revolution in Europe: Intergenerational Change in Post-Industrial Societies." *American Political Science Review*, 65 (December 1971), 991–1017.

JACKMAN, ROBERT W. "Political Elites, Mass Publics, and Support for Democratic Principles." *Journal of Politics*, 34 (August 1972), 753–73.

JACOB, HERBERT. *German Administration since Bismarck*. New Haven: Yale University Press, 1963.

JANOWITZ, MORRIS. *The Professional Soldier*. New York: Free Press, 1960.

JAROS, DEAN et al. "The Malevolent Leader: Political Socialization in an American Sub-Culture." *American Political Science Review*, 62 (June 1968), 564–75.

JENNINGS, M. KENT, and RICHARD G. NIEMI, "The Transmission of Political Values from Parent to Child." *American Political Science Review*, 62 (March 1968), 169–84.

JEVONS, W. S. *The State in Relation to Labour*. London: Macmillan, 1910.

JONES, CHARLES O. "The Agriculture Committee and the Problem of Representation." In Robert Peabody and Nelson Polsby (eds.), *New Perspectives on the House of Representatives*. Chicago: Rand McNally, 1963, 109–20.

KAMPELMAN, MAX. *The Communist Party Versus the C.I.O.* New York: Praeger, 1957.

KANYA-FORSTNER, A. S. *The Conquest of Western Sudan*. Cambridge: At the University Press, 1969.

KARP, WALTER. *Indispensable Enemies*. Baltimore: Penguin Books, 1973.

KATZ, MICHAEL. *The Irony of Early School Reform*. Cambridge: Harvard University Press, 1968.

KELLY, ALFRED H., and WINFRED HARBISON. *The American Constitution*. Revised edition. New York: Norton, 1955.

KENNEDY, ROBERT. *Thirteen Days*. New York: Norton, 1969.

KEOHANE, ROBERT, and JOSEPH S. NYE (eds.). *Transnational Relations and World Politics*. Cambridge: Harvard University Press, 1973.

KESSLER, COUNT HARRY. *Walter Rathenau: His Life and Work*. New York: Harcourt, Brace, 1932.

KIDRON, MICHAEL. *Western Capitalism since the War*. Revised edition. Baltimore: Penguin Books, 1970.

KINDLEBERGER, CHARLES P. *American Business Abroad*. New Haven: Yale University Press, 1969.

KING, ANTHONY. "Overload: Problems of Government in the 1970s." *Political Studies*, 23 (June-September 1975), 290–95.

KIRCHHEIMER, OTTO. "The Waning of Oppositions in Parliamentary Regimes." *Social Research*, 24 (Summer 1957), 128–56.

————. "The Transformation of the Western European Party Systems." In Joseph LaPalombara and Myron Weiner (eds.), *Political Parties and*

Political Development. Princeton: Princeton University Press, 1966, 177–200.

———. "Germany: The Vanishing Opposition." In Robert A. Dahl (ed.), *Political Oppositions in Western Democracies*. New Haven: Yale University Press, 1967, 237–59.

KITTRELL, EDWARD R. "Laissez-Faire in English Classical Economics." *Journal of the History of Ideas*, 27 (October-December 1968), 610–20.

KITZINGER, UWE. *The Politics and Economics of European Integration*. New York: Norton, 1973.

KLARE, MICHAEL. *War without End*. New York: Knopf, 1972.

KOEN, ROSS Y. *The China Lobby in American Politics*. New York: Harper and Row, 1974.

KOGAN, NORMAN. *The Government of Italy*. New York: Crowell, 1962.

KOLKO, GABRIEL. *The Triumph of Conservatism*. New York: Free Press, 1963.

———. *The Politics of War*. New York: Random House, 1968.

———, and JOYCE KOLKO. *The Limits of Power*. New York: Harper and Row, 1972.

KOLKO, JOYCE. *America and the Crisis of World Capitalism*. Boston: Beacon Press, 1974.

KORNHAUSER, WILLIAM. *The Politics of Mass Society*. New York: Free Press, 1959.

KRAUS, MICHAEL. *Immigration: The American Mosaic*. Princeton: Van Nostrand, 1966.

KRIEGEL, ANNIE. *Aux Origines du communisme français, 1914–1920*. Paris: Mouton, 1964.

LADD, EVERETT CARL. *Ideology in America*. Ithaca, N.Y.: Cornell University Press, 1969.

LAFEBER, WALTER. *The New Empire*. Ithaca, N.Y.: Cornell University Press, 1963.

LANDAU, MARTIN. "Redundancy, Rationality, and the Problem of Duplication and Overlap." *Public Administration Review*, 34 (July-August 1969), 346–58.

LANDES, DAVID S. "France and the Businessman: A Social and Cultural Analysis." In Edward Meade Earle (ed.), *Modern France*. Princeton: Princeton University Press, 1951, 334–53.

———. *The Unbound Prometheus*. Cambridge: At the University Press, 1970.

LANE, ROBERT E. "The Decline of Politics and Ideology in a Knowledgeable Society." *American Sociological Review*, 31 (October 1966), 649–62.

LAPALOMBARA, JOSEPH. *Interest Groups in Italian Politics*. Princeton: Princeton University Press, 1964.

LAW, SYLVIA, and the Health Project of the University of Pennsylvania. *Blue Cross: What Went Wrong?* New Haven: Yale University Press, 1974.

LEBOVICS, HERMAN EUGENE. *Social Conservatism and the Middle Classes in Germany, 1914–1933*. Princeton: Princeton University Press, 1969.

LEIBFRIED, STEPHAN. "U.S. Central Government Reform of the Administrative Structure during the Ash Period (1968–1971)." *Kapitalistate*, 2 (1973), 17–30.

LESSING, DORIS. *A Proper Marriage*. London: Panther, 1966.

LEUCHTENBERG, WILLIAM E. *Franklin D. Roosevelt and the New Deal*. New York: Harper and Row, 1963.

————. "The New Deal and the Analogue of War." In John Braeman et al. (eds.), *Change and Continuity in Twentieth Century America*. Columbus: Ohio State University Press, 1964, 87–142.

LEVITT, KARI. *Silent Surrender: The Multinational Corporation in Canada*. New York: St. Martin's Press, 1970.

LHOMME, JEAN. *La grande bourgeoisie au pouvoir 1830–1880*. Paris: Press Universitaire de France, 1960.

LINDBERG, LEON, and STUART A. SCHEINGOLD. *Europe's Would-Be Polity*. Englewood Cliffs, N.J.: Prentice-Hall, 1970.

LINDBLOM, CHARLES. *The Intelligence of Democracy*. New York: Free Press, 1966.

————, and ROBERT A. DAHL. *Politics, Economics and Welfare*. New York: Harper Torchbooks, 1966.

LINZ, JUAN. *The Breakdown of Democracy*. Forthcoming.

LIPOW, ARTHUR. "Plebiscitarian Politics and Progressivism: The Direct Democracy Movement." Paper presented at the 1973 American Historical Association meetings.

LIPSET, SEYMOUR MARTIN. *Political Man*. Garden City, N.Y.: Anchor Books, 1963.

LITT, EDGAR. "Civic Education, Community Norms, and Political Indoctrination." *American Sociological Review*, 28 (February 1963), 68–75.

LORD, GUY. *The French Budgetary Process*. Berkeley and Los Angeles: University of California Press, 1973.

LOWI, THEODORE. *The End of Liberalism*. New York: Norton, 1969.

————. "Decision Making v. Policy Making: Toward an Antidote for Technocracy." *Public Administration Review*, 30 (May–June 1970), 314–25.

LUBASZ, HEINZ. *The Development of the Modern State*. New York: Macmillan, 1964.

LUBENOW, WILLIAM C. *The Politics of Governmental Growth: Early Victorian Attitudes Toward State Intervention, 1833–1848*. London: David and Charles, 1971.

LUCAS, ARTHUR F. *Industrial Reconstruction and the Control of Competition*. London: Longmans, 1937.

LEUTHY, HERBERT. *France against Herself*. New York: Praeger, 1955.

LUHMANN, NICHOLAS. *Legitimation durch Verfahren*. Neuwied: Luchterhand, 1969.

LUKACS, GEORG. *History and Class Consciousness*. London: Merlin, 1971.

LUTTBEG, NORMAN R. "The Structure of Beliefs among Leaders and the Public." *Public Opinion Quarterly*, 32 (Fall 1968), 398–409.

LYON, PETER. *Eisenhower: Portrait of a Hero*. Boston: Little, Brown, 1974.

MAASS, ARTHUR. *Muddy Waters*. Cambridge: Harvard University Press, 1951.

MAGDOFF, HARRY. *The Age of Imperialism*. New York: Monthly Review Press, 1969.

MAGRUDER, JEB STUART. *An American Life*. New York: Atheneum, 1974.

MAIER, CHARLES S. *Recasting Bourgeois Europe*. Princeton: Princeton University Press, 1975.

MALCOLMSON, ROBERT. *Popular Recreation in English Society, 1700–1850*. Cambridge: At the University Press, 1973.

MANCHESTER, WILLIAM. *The Arms of Krupp*. New York: Bantam Books, 1970.

MANN, DEAN E. *The Assistant Secretaries*. Washington: Brookings Institution, 1965.

MANNHEIM, KARL. *Ideology and Utopia*. New York: Harvest Books, n.d.

———. *Man and Society in an Age of Reconstruction*. New York: Harvest Books, n.d.

MARCUS, STEVEN. *Engels, Manchester, and the Working Class*. New York: Vintage Books, 1975.

MARGLIN, STEPHEN A. "What Do Bosses Do?" *Review of Radical Political Economics*, 6 (Summer 1974), 60–112.

MARSH, D. C. *The Welfare State*. London: Longmans, 1970.

MARSHALL, DALE R. *The Politics of Participation in Poverty*. Berkeley and Los Angeles: University of California Press, 1971.

MARSHALL, T. H. *Class, Citizenship, and Social Development*. Garden City, N.Y.: Doubleday, 1964.

MARTINELLI, ALBERTO, and EUGENIO SOMAINI. "Nation States and Multinational Corporations," *Kapitalistate*, 1 (1973), 69–78.

MARX, KARL. *Capital*. New York: International Publishers, 1967.

———. "Critique of Hegel's Philosophy of the State." In Kurt Guddat and Loyd Easton (eds.), *Writings of the Young Marx on Philosophy and Society*. Garden City, N.Y.: Anchor Books, 1967.

———. *The Grundrisse*. New York: Vintage Books, 1973.

———. *Selected Works*. New York: International Publishers, n.d.

———, and FREDERICK ENGELS. *The German Ideology*. New York: International Publishers, 1947.

MATHER, F. C. *Public Order in the Age of the Chartists*. Manchester: Manchester University Press, 1959.

McARTHUR, JOHN H., and BRUCE R. SCOTT. *Industrial Planning in France*. Cambridge: Harvard Business School, 1969.

McBRIAR, A. M. *Fabian Socialism and English Politics, 1884–1918*. Cambridge: At the University Press, 1962.

McCLOSKEY, ROBERT G. *American Conservatism in the Age of Enterprise*. Cambridge: Harvard University Press, 1951.

McCONNELL, GRANT. *The Decline of Agrarian Democracy*. Berkeley and Los Angeles: University of California Press, 1959.

———. *Private Power and American Democracy*. New York: Knopf, 1966.

McCORMICK, THOMAS J. *China Market: America's Quest for Informal Empire.* Chicago: Quadrangle, 1967.

MACPHERSON, C. B. *The Political Theory of Possessive Individualism.* London: Oxford University Press, 1964.

MELMAN, SEYMOUR. *Pentagon Capitalism.* New York: McGraw-Hill, 1970.

MESSADIE, GERALD. *La Fin de la vie privée.* Paris: Calman-Levy, 1974.

MEYNAUD, JEAN. *Technocracy.* New York: Free Press, 1969.

MICHELS, ROBERT. *Political Parties.* New York: Free Press, 1949.

MILIBAND, RALPH. *The State in Capitalist Society.* New York: Basic Books, 1969.

MILL, JOHN STUART. *Principles of Political Economy.* New York: Kelley, 1961.

MILLER, ARTHUR H. "Political Issues and Trust in Government." *American Political Science Review,* 68 (September 1974), 951–72.

MILLIS, HARRY A., and EMILY CLARK BROWN. *From the Wagner Act to Taft-Hartley.* Chicago: University of Chicago Press, 1950.

MOLLENKOPF, JOHN. "The Fragile Giant." *Socialist Revolution,* 29 (July–September 1976), 11–37.

MONTGOMERY, DAVID. *Beyond Equality: Labor and the Radical Republicans, 1862–1872.* New York: Vintage Books, 1972.

MONTGOMERY, JOHN D. *Forced to Be Free.* Chicago: University of Chicago Press, 1957.

MOORE, BARRINGTON. *Social Origins of Dictatorship and Democracy.* Boston: Beacon Press, 1967.

MOORE, O. C. "The Other Face of Reform." *Victorian Studies,* 5 (September 1961), 7–34.

MORAZÉ, CHARLES. *Les Bourgeois conquérants.* Paris: Armand Colin, 1957.

MOYNIHAN, DANIEL PATRICK. *The Politics of a Guaranteed Income.* New York: Vintage Books, 1973.

————. *Coping.* New York: Random House, 1973.

MUELLER, CLAUS. *The Politics of Communication.* New York: Oxford University Press, 1973.

MURRAY, ROBIN. "The Internationalization of Capital and the Nation State." In John Dunning (ed.), *The Multinational Enterprise.* London: Allen and Unwin, 1971, 265–88.

MUSIL, ROBERT. *The Man without Qualities.* New York: Capricorn, 1965.

MYERS, FRANK E. "Social Class and Political Change in Western Industrial Societies." *Comparative Politics,* 2 (April 1970), 389–412.

NEF, JOHN U. *Industry and Government in France and England, 1540–1640.* Philadelphia: American Philosophical Society, 1940.

NEIBURG, H. L. *In the Name of Science.* Chicago: Quadrangle, 1966.

NEUMANN, FRANZ. *Behemoth.* New York: Harper Torchbooks, 1966.

————. *The Democratic and the Authoritarian State.* New York: Free Press, 1967.

NEUSTADT, RICHARD E. *Presidential Power.* New York: Wiley, 1960.

NEW YORK TIMES, *The End of a Presidency.* New York: Bantam Books, 1974.

NICHOLS, ROY F. *American Leviathan.* New York: Harper Colophon Books, 1966.

NIMMO, DAN D. *Popular Images of Politics.* Englewood Cliffs, N.J.: Prentice-Hall, 1974.

NISBET, ROBERT. *Twilight of Authority.* New York: Basic Books, 1975.

NOBIS, ENRICO. *Il Governo Invisible.* Rome: Edizioni di Cultura Sociale, 1955.

NOLL, ROGER (ed.). *Government and the Sports Business.* Washington: Brookings Institution, 1974.

NORDLINGER, ERIC. *Conflict Regulation in Divided Societies.* Cambridge: Harvard Center for International Affairs, 1972.

NORTH, DOUGLASS C. *Growth and Welfare in the American Past.* Englewood Cliffs, N.J.: Prentice-Hall, 1966.

NOZICK, ROBERT. *Anarchy, State and Utopia.* New York: Basic Books, 1973.

O'CONNER, JAMES. *The Fiscal Crisis of the State.* New York: St. Martin's Press, 1973.

——. *The Class Struggle.* Forthcoming.

——. "Productive and Unproductive Labor." *Politics and Society,* 5 (1975), 297–336.

OESTEREICHER, EMIL. "Fascism and the Intellectuals: The Case of Italian Futurism." *Social Research,* 41 (Autumn 1974), 515–33.

OFFE, CLAUS. *Strukturprobleme des Kapitalistischen Staates.* Frankfurt: Suhrkamp, 1972.

——. "Political Authority and Class Structure: An Analysis of Late Capitalist Societies." *International Journal of Social Science,* 2 (Spring 1972), 73–108.

——. "The Theory of the Capitalist State and the Problem of Policy Formation." Unpublished paper, May 1974.

OKUN, ARTHUR. *Equality and Efficiency: The Big Tradeoff.* Washington: Brookings Institution, 1975.

OSTROGORSKI, MAURICE. *Democracy and the Organization of Political Parties.* Garden City, N.Y.: Anchor Books, 1964.

OWEN, ROGER, and BOB SUTCLIFFE (eds.). *Studies in the Theory of Imperialism.* London: Longmans, 1972.

PACKENHAM, ROBERT. *Liberal America and the Third World.* Princeton: Princeton University Press, 1973.

PALMA, GIUSEPPE DI (ed.). *Mass Politics in Industrial Societies.* Chicago: Markham, 1972.

PALMADE, GUY. *Capitalisme et capitalisme Français au XIXe siècle.* Paris: Colin, 1961.

PARRIS, HENRY. "The Nineteenth Century Revolution in Government: A Reappraisal Reappraised." *Historical Journal,* 3 (1960), 17–37.

——. *Government and the Railways.* London: Routledge and Kegan Paul, 1965.

PARSONS, TALCOTT. *Structure and Process in Modern Societies.* New York: Free Press, 1960.

PATEMAN, CAROLE. *Participation and Democratic Theory.* Cambridge: At the University Press, 1970.

————. "Sublimation and Reification: Locke, Wolin, and the Liberal-Democratic Conception of the Political." *Politics and Society,* 5 (1975), 441–68.

PAXTON, ROBERT O. *Vichy France.* New York: Knopf, 1972.

PEACOCK, ALAN T., and JACK WISEMAN. *The Growth of Public Expenditure in Great Britain.* Princeton: Princeton University Press, 1961.

PEARCE, FRANK. *Crimes of the Powerful.* London: Pluto Press, 1976.

PELLING, HENRY. *Popular Politics and Society in Late Victorian Britain.* New York: St. Martin's Press, 1968.

Pentagon Papers, The. Boston: Beacon Press, 1971.

PFAFF, WILLIAM. "Some Questions about a Crisis." *The New Yorker,* April 5, 1976.

PIGOU, A. C. *Unemployment.* New York: Holt, 1914.

PIKE, FREDERICK, and THOMAS STRITCH (eds.). *The New Corporatism.* South Bend, Ind.: University of Notre Dame Press, 1974.

PIOUS, RICHARD. "Policy and Public Administration: The Legal Services Program in the War on Poverty." In Ira Katznetson et al. (eds.), *The Politics and Society Reader.* New York: McKay, 1974, 101–27.

PIVEN, FRANCES FOX, and RICHARD CLOWARD. *Regulating the Poor.* New York: Vintage Books, 1972.

PLATT, D. C. M. *Finance, Trade and Politics in British Foreign Policy, 1815–1914.* Oxford: Clarendon Press, 1968.

POLANYI, KARL. *The Great Transformation.* Boston: Beacon Press, 1957.

POLLOCK, NORMAN. *The Populist Response to Industrial America.* Cambridge: Harvard University Press, 1962.

POTTER, ALLAN. *Organized Groups in British National Politics.* London: Faber and Faber, 1961.

POULANTZAS, NICOS. *Pouvoir politique et classes sociales.* Paris: Maspero, 1968.

POWELL, G. BINGHAM. *Social Fragmentation and Political Hostility: An Austrian Case Study.* Stanford, Calif.: Stanford University Press, 1970.

POWER, THOMAS F., JR. *Jules Ferry and the Renaissance of French Imperialism.* New York: Octagon Books, 1966.

PRANGER, ROBERT. *The Eclipse of Citizenship.* New York: Holt, Rinehart and Winston, 1968.

PROUTY, ROGER WARREN. *The Transformation of the Board of Trade.* Doctoral dissertation, Columbia University, 1954.

PULLEY, RAYMOND H. *Old Virginia Restored.* Charlottesville: University of Virginia Press, 1968.

PURCELL, EDWARD A. *The Crisis of Democratic Theory.* Lexington: University of Kentucky Press, 1973.

PUTNAM, ROBERT. *The Beliefs of Politicians*. New Haven and London: Yale University Press, 1969.

RADOSH, RONALD. *American Labor and United States Foreign Policy*. New York: Vintage Books, 1973.

————, and MURRAY ROTHBARD (eds.). *A New History of Leviathan*. New York: Dutton, 1972.

RASKIN, MARCUS. *Notes on the Old System*. New York: McKay, 1974.

RATHER, DAN, and GARY PAUL GATES. *The Palace Guard*. New York: Harper and Row, 1974.

RAWLS, JOHN. *A Theory of Justice*. Cambridge: Harvard University Press, 1973.

REAGAN, MICHAEL. *The Managed Economy*. New York: Oxford University Press, 1963.

RICARDO, DAVID. *Works and Correspondence*. Cambridge: At the University Press, 1962.

RICHTER, MELVIN. *The Politics of Conscience: T. H. Green and His Age*. London: Weidenfeld and Nicolson, 1964.

ROBBINS, LIONEL. *The Theory of Economic Policy in English Classical Political Economy*. New York. St. Martin's Press, 1968.

ROBERTS, DAVID. *Victorian Origins of the British Welfare State*. New Haven: Yale University Press, 1960.

ROBINSON, RONALD, and JOHN GALLAGHER. *Africa and the Victorians*. New York: St. Martin's Press, 1961.

RODGERS, HARRELL, and GEORGE TAYLOR. "The Policeman as an Agent of Regime Legitimation." *Midwest Journal of Political Science*, 15 (February 1971), 72–86.

ROGIN, MICHAEL PAUL. "Voluntarism as an Organizational Ideology of the American Federation of Labor, 1886–1932." M.A. thesis, University of Chicago, 1959.

————. *Fathers and Children*. New York: Knopf, 1975.

ROHATYN, FELIX. "A New RFC is Proposed for Business." *New York Times*, 3 (December 1, 1974), 1.

ROHRBOUGH, MALCOLM J. *The Land Office Business: The Settlement and Administration of American Public Lands, 1789–1837*. New York: Oxford University Press, 1968.

ROIG, CHARLES, and F. BILLON-GRAND. *La Socialization politique des enfants*. Paris. Colin, 1968.

ROKKAN, STEIN, and SEYMOUR MARTIN LIPSET. *Party Systems and Voter Alignments*. New York: Free Press, 1967.

RONGE, VOLKER. "The Politicization of Administration in Advanced Capitalist Societies." *Political Studies*, 23 (March 1974), 86–93.

ROSENBERG, ARTHUR. *Imperial Germany: The Birth of the German Republic, 1871–1918*. Boston: Beacon Press, 1964.

————. *Democracy and Socialism*. Boston: Beacon Press, 1965.

412   *Bibliography*

Rosenberg, Hans. *Bureaucracy, Aristocracy, and Autocracy*. Boston: Beacon Press, 1966.

Ross, Edward A. *The Old World in the New*. New York: Century, 1914.

Roussopoulos, Dimitrios (ed.). *The Political Economy of the State*. Montreal: Black Rose Books, 1973.

Rowbothom, Sheila. *Hidden from History*. New York: Vintage Books, 1976.

Rowthorn, Robert. *International Big Business*. Cambridge: At the University Press, 1971.

————, and Stephen Hymer. "Multinational Corporations and International Oligarchy." In Charles P. Kindleberger (ed.), *The International Corporation*. Cambridge: MIT Press, 1970, 57–91.

Rubin, Barry. "Marxism and Education: Radical Thought and Education Theory in the 1930s." *Science and Society*, 36 (Summer 1972), 171–201.

Rule, James. *Private Lives and Public Surveillance*. London: Lane, 1973.

Russett, Bruce et al. *World Handbook of Political and Social Indicators*. New Haven: Yale University Press, 1964.

Salsbury, Stephen. *The State, the Investor, and the Railway: The Boston and Albany, 1825–1867*. Cambridge: Harvard University Press, 1967.

Salter, Lord Arthur. *Memoirs of a Public Servant*. London: Faber and Faber, 1961.

Sampson, Anthony. *The Sovereign State of ITT*. Greenwich, Conn.: Fawcett Books, 1974.

Sani, Giacomo. "Mass Constraints on Political Realignments: Perceptions of Anti-System Parties in Italy." *British Journal of Political Science*, 6 (January 1976), 1–32.

Sarti, Roland. *Fascism and the Industrial Leadership in Italy, 1919–1940*. Berkeley and Los Angeles: University of California Press, 1971.

Sartori, Giovanni. "Will Democracy Kill Democracy?" *Government and Opposition*, 10 (Spring 1975), 131–58.

Say, J. B. A *Treatise on Political Economy*. Philadelphia: Grigg, Elliot, 1848.

Say, Louis. *Etudes sur la richesse des nations, et réfutations des principales erreurs en économie politique*. Paris. A La Librairie du Commerce, 1836.

Schaar, John. "Legitimacy in the Modern State." In Philip Green and Sanford Levinson (eds.), *Power and Community*. New York: Pantheon, 1970, 276–327.

Schell, Jonathan. *The Time of Illusion*. New York: Knopf, 1975.

Schieder, Theodor. *The State and Society in Our Times*. London: Nelson, 1962.

Schiller, Herbert. *Mass Communications and American Empire*. New York: Kelley, 1970.

Schlesinger, Arthur, Jr. A *Thousand Days*. Boston: Houghton Mifflin, 1965.

————. *The Imperial Presidency*. Boston: Houghton Mifflin, 1973.

Schmitter, Philippe. "Still the Century of Corporatism?" *Review of Politics*, 36 (January 1974), 85–131.

SCHOTTLAND, CHARLES I. (ed.). *The Welfare State.* New York: Harper and Row, 1967.

SCHUMPETER, JOSEPH. *Capitalism, Socialism and Democracy.* New York: Harper and Row, 1950.

————. *Imperialism and Social Classes.* Cleveland: World, 1953.

SCHURMANN, FRANZ. *The Logic of World Power.* New York: Pantheon, 1974.

SCHWENDINGER, HERMAN, and JULIA SCHWENDINGER. *Sociologists of the Chair.* New York: Basic Books, 1974.

SCOTT, JAMES A. *Comparative Political Corruption.* Englewood Cliffs, N.J.: Prentice-Hall, 1972.

SCOTT, JOHN A. *Republican Ideas and the Liberal Tradition in France, 1870–1914.* New York: Columbia University Press, 1951.

SELF, PETER, and HERBERT STORING. *The State and the Farmer.* Berkeley and Los Angeles: University of California Press, 1963.

SELZNICK, PHILIP. *TVA and the Grass Roots.* Berkeley and Los Angeles: University of California Press, 1949.

SEMMEL, BERNARD. *Imperialism and Social Reform.* Cambridge: Harvard University Press, 1960.

————. *The Rise of Free Trade Imperialism.* Cambridge: At the University Press, 1970.

SHANKS, MICHAEL. *The Stagnant Society.* Baltimore: Penguin Books, 1961.

SHILS, EDWARD. *The Torment of Secrecy.* New York: Free Press, 1956.

SHONFELD, ANDREW. *Modern Capitalism.* New York: Oxford University Press, 1965.

SILK, LEONARD, and DAVID VOGEL. *Ethics and Profits.* New York: Simon and Schuster, 1976.

SILVER, ALLAN. "The Demand for Order in Civil Society." In David Bordua (ed.), *The Police.* New York: Wiley, 1967, 1–24.

————. "Social and Ideological Bases of British Elite Reactions to Domestic Crises in 1829–1832." *Politics and Society,* 1 (February 1971), 179–201.

SMITH, ADAM. *The Wealth of Nations.* London: Pelican, 1960.

SMITH, TREVOR. *Anti-Politics: Consensus, Reform and Protest in Great Britain.* London: Knight, 1972.

SORENSEN, THEODORE. *Kennedy.* New York: Harper and Row, 1965.

SOUBOL, ALBERT. *Histoire de la révolution française.* Paris: Gallimard, 1962.

SPIRO, HERBERT. *The Politics of German Co-Determination.* Cambridge: Harvard University Press, 1958.

SPRING, JOEL. *Educaiton and the Rise of the Corporate State.* Boston: Beacon Press, 1972.

STANDMANN, HARTMUT POGGE VON. "Domestic Origins of Germany's Colonial Expansion under Bismarck." *Past and Present,* 42 (February 1969), 140–59.

STANLEY, DAVID T. et al. *Men Who Govern.* Washington: Brookings Institution, 1967.

STANSKY, PETER. *The Victorian Revolution.* New York: Watts, 1973.

STAVINS, RALPH et al. *Washington Plans an Aggressive War*. New York: Random House, 1971.

STEINER, GILBERT. *The State of Welfare*. Washington: Brookings Institution, 1971.

STERNSHER, BERNARD. *Rexford G. Tugwell and the New Deal*. New Brunswick: Rutgers University Press, 1964.

STEWART, ROBERT M. *The Politics of Protection*. Cambridge: At the University Press, 1971.

STONE, KATHERINE. "The Origins of Job Structures in the Steel Industry." *Review of Radical Political Economics*, 6 (Summer 1974), 60–112.

STOUFFER, SAMUEL. *Communism, Conformity and Civil Liberties*. Gloucester, Mass.: Smith, 1963.

STRONG, JOSIAH. *Our Country*. Cambridge: Belknap Press of Harvard University Press, 1963.

STRUVE, WALTER. *Elites against Democracy*. Princeton: Princeton University Press, 1973.

STURMTHAL, ADOLPH. "The Structure of Nationalized Enterprises in France." *Political Science Quarterly*, 67 (September 1952), 357–77.

———. "Nationalization and Workers Control in Britain and France." *Journal of Political Economy*, 61 (February 1953), 43–79.

SULEIMAN, EZRA. *Politics, Power and Bureaucracy in France*. Princeton: Princeton University Press, 1974.

SUMNER, WILLIAM GRAHAM. *Essays*. New Haven: Yale University Press, 1934.

SWEEZY, PAUL. *The Theory of Capitalist Development*. New York: Monthly Review Press, 1968.

TARROW, SIDNEY. "Political Dualism and Italian Communism." *American Political Science Review*, 61 (March 1967), 39–53.

———. "Economic Development and the Transformation of the Italian Party System." *Comparative Politics*, 1 (January 1969), 161–83.

TAWNEY, R. H. *Equality*. London: Unicorn Books, 1969.

TAYLOR, A. J. P. *British History, 1914–1945*. New York: Oxford University Press, 1965.

TAYLOR, PHILIP. *The Distant Magnet: European Emigration to the USA*. London: Eyre and Spottiswoode, 1971.

TERRILL, TOM E. *The Tariff, Politics, and American Foreign Policy, 1874–1901*. Westport, Conn.: Greenwood Press, 1973.

THEOHARIS, ATHAN. *The Yalta Myths: An Issue in U.S. Politics, 1945–1955*. Columbia: University of Missouri Press, 1970.

THOMAS, BRINLEY. *International Migration and Economic Development*. Paris: UNESCO, 1961.

THOMSON, DAVID. *Democracy in France since 1870*. Fourth edition. New York: Oxford University Press, 1964.

TITMUSS, RICHARD. *The Gift Relationship*. New York: Vintage Books, 1972.

TOCQUEVILLE, ALEXIS DE. *Democracy in America*. New York: Knopf, 1951.

————. *The Old Regime and the French Revolution.* Garden City, N.Y.: Anchor Books, 1955.

————. *Recollections.* Garden City, N.Y.: Anchor Books, 1971.

TOURAINE, ALAIN. *The Post-Industrial Society.* New York: Random House, 1971.

————. *Production de la société.* Paris: Editions du Seuil, 1973.

TOWNSEND, MARY EVELYN. *The Rise and Fall of Germany's Colonial Empire.* New York: Fertig, 1966.

TREITSCHKE, HEINRICH VON. *Politics.* New York: Harcourt, Brace, and World, 1963.

Trilateral Commission. *The Governability of Democracies.* New York: Trilateral Commission, 1975.

TROLLOPE, ANTHONY. *Phineas Finn.* London: Penguin Books, 1972.

TRUMAN, HARRY S. *Memoirs.* Garden City, N.Y.: Doubleday, 1956.

TUCHMAN, BARBARA. *The Guns of August.* New York: Dell, 1971.

TUGWELL, REXFORD G. *The Industrial Discipline and Other Governmental Arts.* New York: Columbia University Press, 1933.

TURNER, LEWIS. *Multinational Corporations and the Third World.* New York: Hill and Wang, 1973.

Unification of the War and Navy Departments and Postwar Organization for National Security. (Report to the Hon. James Forrestal, October 22, 1945.) Washington: Government Printing Office, 1945.

United States Senate. Committee on Armed Services. *National Defense Establishment.* (80th Congress, 1st session, 1947.) Washington: Government Printing Office, 1947.

————. Committee on Armed Services. *National Security Act Amendments of 1949.* (81st Congress, 1st session, 1949.) Washington: Government Printing Office, 1949.

————. Report of the Jackson Subcommittee. *Inquiry into National Policy Machinery.* Washington: Government Printing Office, 1961.

————. Committee on Finance. *The Multinational Corporations and the World Economy.* Washington: Government Printing Office, 1973.

VERBA, SIDNEY. "Germany: The Remaking of Political Culture." In Sidney Verba and Lucien Pye (eds.), *Political Culture and Political Development.* Princeton: Princeton University Press, 1965, 130–70.

————, and NORMAN NYE. *Participation in America.* New York: Harper and Row, 1972.

VERNON, RAYMOND. *Sovereignty at Bay.* New York: Basic Books, 1971.

WALKER, MACK. *Germany and the Emigration, 1816–1885.* Cambridge: Harvard University Press, 1964.

WALLACE, MICHAEL. "Changing Concepts of Party in the United States: New York, 1815–1828." *American Historical Review,* 74 (December 1968), 453–91.

WALLERSTEIN, IMMANUEL. *The Modern World System.* New York: Academic Press, 1974.

Washington Post. *The Presidential Transcripts.* New York: Dell, 1974.

WATT, RICHARD M. *The Kings Depart.* London: Penguin Books, 1973.

WAYS, MAX. "Business Needs a Different Political Stance." *Fortune,* September 1975.

WEBER, MAX. "Politics as a Vocation." In Hans Gerth and C. Wright Mills (eds.), *From Max Weber.* New York: Oxford University Press, 1958, 77–128.

WEHLER, HANS-ULRICH. *Bismarck und der Imperialismus.* Köln: Kiepenheuer und Witsch, 1969.

WEIDENBAUM, MURRAY. *The Modern Public Sector.* New York: Basic Books, 1969.

WEINSTEIN, JAMES. *The Corporate Ideal in the Liberal State.* Boston: Beacon Press, 1968.

WEISBAND, EDWARD, and THOMAS M. FRANCK. *Resignation in Protest.* New York: Grossman, 1975.

WENDEL, HUGO C. M. *The Evolution of Industrial Freedom in Prussia, 1845–49.* Allentown, Pa.: Haas, 1918.

WHITE, LEONARD D. *The Federalists.* New York: Macmillan, 1948.

————. *The Jacksonians.* New York: Macmillan, 1954.

————. *The Republican Era, 1869–1901.* New York: Macmillan, 1963.

WHITE, WILLIAM S. *Citadel.* New York: Harper, 1957.

WHYTE, ARTHUR JAMES. *The Evolution of Modern Italy.* Oxford: Blackwell, 1944.

WIEBE, ROBERT. *Businessmen and Reform.* Cambridge: Harvard University Press, 1962.

————. *The Search for Order, 1877–1920.* New York: Hill and Wang, 1967.

WILDAVSKY, AARON. *The Politics of the Budgetary Process.* Boston: Little, Brown, 1964.

————. "Rescuing Policy Analysis from PPBS." *Public Administration Review,* 34 (April 1969), 189–202.

————. "The Strategic Retreat on Objectives." Working Paper No. 45, Graduate School of Public Policy, University of California, Berkeley, 1976.

WILENSKY, HAROLD. *The Welfare State and Equality.* Berkeley and Los Angeles: University of California Press, 1975.

WILKINS, MYRA. *The Emergence of Multinational Enterprise.* Cambridge: Harvard University Press, 1970.

————. *The Maturing of Multinational Enterprise.* Cambridge: Harvard University Press, 1974.

WILLIAMS, DAVID. *Not in the Public Interest.* London: Hutchinson, 1965.

WILLIAMS, PHILIP M. *Crisis and Compromise.* Hamden, Conn.: Archon Books, 1968.

————, and MARTIN HARRISON. *Politics and Society in de Gaulle's Republic.* Garden City, N.Y.: Anchor Books, 1973.

WILLIAMS, RAYMOND. *Culture and Society.* New York: Columbia University Press, 1958.

————. *The Long Revolution.* London: Pelican, 1965.

————. *The Country and the City.* New York: Oxford University Press, 1975.

WILLIAMS, WILLIAM APPLEMAN. *The Tragedy of American Diplomacy.* Revised and enlarged edition. New York: Delta Books, 1962.

————. *The Contours of American History.* Chicago: Quadrangle, 1966.

WILSON, JAMES Q. *Thinking about Crime.* New York: Basic Books, 1975.

WINCH, DONALD. *Classical Political Economy and the Colonies.* Cambridge: Harvard University Press, 1965.

WISE, DAVID, and THOMAS ROSS. *The Invisible Government.* New York: Vintage Books, 1974.

WOLF, JOHN B. *France, 1814–1919: The Rise of a Liberal-Democratic Society.* New York: Harper Torchbooks, 1963.

WOLFE, ALAN. "Waiting for Righty: A Critique of the 'Fascism' Hypothesis." *Review of Radical Political Economics,* 5 (Fall 1973), 46–66.

————. *The Seamy Side of Democracy.* New York: McKay, 1973.

————. "New Directions in the Marxist Theory of Politics." *Politics and Society.* 4 (Winter 1974), 131–60.

————. "Il New Deal: Discorsi Nuovi e Interpretazione Vecchie." *Quaderni Storici,* 28 (January–April 1975), 294–301.

————. "Exercise in Gentility: The Rockefeller Report on the CIA." *The Nation,* August 16, 1975, pp. 108–12.

————. "Capitalism Shows Its Face." *The Nation,* November 29, 1975, pp. 557–63.

WOLIN, SHELDON. *Politics and Vision.* Boston: Little, Brown, 1960.

WOODHAM-SMITH, CECIL. *The Great Hunger.* New York: Signet Books, 1964.

WOOTTON, GRAHAM. *The Politics of Influence.* Cambridge: Harvard University Press, 1963.

ZELDIN, THEODORE. *Ambition, Love, and Politics.* Vol 1 of *France 1848–1945.* Oxford: Clarendon Press, 1973.

ZOLBERG, ARISTIDE. "Moments of Madness." *Politics and Society,* 2 (Winter 1972), 183–207.

Index

Absolutism, 15–16
Accumulative State, 9, 14, 19–41, 60,
    241, 247
  banking, 32–34
  corporations, 20–22
  France, 21, 22, 27–30, 33–34, 38
  Germany, 27–29, 31–32, 34
  Great Britain, 21–33, 35–36, 38
  Italy, 30, 31, 37
  land policy, 37–38
  limitations of, 39–41, 43
  preservation of order, 22–26
  public welfare, 38–39
  state aid, 28–32
  strength of, 39, 42–43
  tariff, 34–36
  United States, 21, 22, 30, 33–38
  warmaking, 36–37
Adams, Brooks, 103
Adams, Henry, 71, 156
Adams, Walter, 164
Adelson, Joseph, 299
Administrative Reform Association, 38, 66
Agee, Philip, 239
Agency for International Development
    (AID), 235
Agribusiness, 140
Agricultural Trade and Development Act
    of 1954, Cooley Amendment to, 233
Agriculture, Franchise State and, 139–
    140, 147–148, 160, 163
Agriculture Act of 1947, 139
Aldrich, Nelson, 63
Alien and Sedition Acts, 23
Alienated politics, 10, 168, 207, 288–321,
    334–337
  centrality of, 312–313
  elected officials, 315–318
  interest groups, 309–310, 312
  nationalization of legitimation function,
    311–313
  participation, 300–305
  parties, 305–309, 312
  socialization process, 296–300
  utopianization of ruling class, 318–320

Allied Maritime Transport Council, 116
Allison, Graham, 260
Allum, P. A., 63, 262, 315–316, 337
Almond, Gabriel, 300–302, 304, 308
Althusser, Louis, 253
American Economics Association, 51
American Farm Bureau Federation
    (AFBF), 139, 140, 147, 160
American Federation of Labor (AFL),
    143, 159
American Industrial League of 1867, 47
American Patriotic League, 105
American Petroleum Institute, 131
American Protective Association, 99
Amery, L. S., 124
Anarchy, ix–x, 243
Ancien régime, 38
  corruption, 67
  political heritage of, 14–20
Anderson, Olive, 36
Anderson, Perry, 15
André, Pierre, 157
Anthonioz, Marcel, 157
Anticommunism, 182–184, 204, 212,
    218–220, 224, 237, 238
Anti-Corn Law League, 35
Antipolitics: see Alienated politics
Anti-Semitism, 103
Aranda affair, 156
Arendt, Hannah, 3, 103, 104, 277, 289
Arnold, Matthew, 280
Arnold, Thurman, 169, 274
Ashley, Sir William, 84, 102
Askwith, Sir George, 78
Asquith, Herbert Henry, Earl of, 101, 103
Assistant to the President for National
    Security Affairs, 201
Associated Milk Producers, 156
Atlantic Alliance, 220, 226
Atlantic Community, 220
Australia, 145
Austria, 145
Authoritarianism, 15, 337–341
Automation, 251
Automobile industry, 131

Avis, Warren, 277

Bagehot, Walter, 177, 178
Ball, George, 222–223, 228–229, 235
Bandung Conference, 221
Banfield, Edward, 271
Bank Charter Act of 1844, 32
Bank of England, 32
Bank of France, 33
Bankhead-Jones Farm Tenancy Act of 1937, 147
Banking, 32–34, 60
Barnet, Richard, 183, 230, 244
Barres, Auguste Maurice, 104
Baruch, Bernard, 110–111, 116
Bastiat, Frederick, 47
Bay of Pigs invasion, 199, 202, 209
Beard, Charles, viii
Beer, Samuel, 116, 123, 141, 142, 265
Behrman, Jack, 233, 234, 239
Belgian Congo (Zaïre), 197
Bell, Daniel, 314, 322, 332, 333, 346
Bell, David, 173
Bendix, Reinhard, 305–306
Bentham, Jeremy, xi, 4, 25, 45, 46
Bentley, Arthur F., xii, xiii
Benton, Thomas Hart, 292
Berkshire Knitting Mills strike, 143
Berle, Adolph, 22
Berman, Marshall, 5
Bernstein, Edward, x, xii
Bernstein, Irving, 138, 158
Beuth, Peter Christian Wilhelm von, 28–29
Bismarck, Otto von, 7, 50, 63, 82, 90, 92, 96
Black Power movement, 205
Blanc, Louis, 48
Blatchford, Robert, 106
Blaug, Marc, 28
Bloch, Marc, 14
Bodin, Jean, 279
Bonomi, Paolo, 140
Boorstin, Daniel, 315
Borah, William E., 196
Borch, Fred, 232
Bosanquet, Bernard, xi, 102
Boguslaw, Robert, 319
Bourgeois, Leon, 44, 101
Bourgeois politicians, 61–64, 248
Bourne, Randolph, 205
Bowles, Samuel, 75
Bradley, Francis Herbert, 51

Brandt, Willy, 323
Braverman, Harry, 294
Brebner, J. B., 28
Bretton Woods Conference, 216–217
Briggs, Asa, 33, 35
Bright, John, 46, 51
Brittan, Samuel, 332, 333, 335
Broglie, Duc de, 62
Broude, Henry W., 37
Brownson, Orestes, 17
Bruce, Maurice, 75
Bruce, Robert V., 84
Bryce, James, 66, 89
Brzezinski, Zbigniew, 243–244, 325
Bulow, Ernst von, 42
Bundy, Harvey, 183
Bundy, McGeorge, 201, 284–285
Bureau of the Budget (BOB), 264–265
Bureaucracy, 262–271
Burgess, John W., 102
Burke, Arleigh, 200
Burke, Edmund, 64, 65
Burkhardt, Jacob, 14
Burnham, James, 126
Burnham, Walter Dean, 292, 293, 306
Business Advisory Council, 164
Business and Defense Services Administration, 164
Business pacifism, 111, 112
Butler, R. A., 171

Callaghan, James, 332
Calleo, David P., 216, 217, 234
Campbell-Bannerman, Henry, 64
Canada, 145
Capital, accumulation of, 162–163
Capitalism: see Accumulative State; Dual State; Expansionist State; Franchise State; Harmonious State; Transnational State
Carey, Henry, 42, 46–48, 52, 83
Carey, Matthew, 45, 46, 48
Carlsbad Decrees, 23
Carlyle, Thomas, 40
Carnegie, Andrew, 35, 58–59
Carr, E. H., 44
Cartels, 22
Carter, Jimmy, 213, 243, 285
Central Intelligence Agency (CIA), 179, 187–190, 198–200, 202, 205, 206, 208–210, 213, 239, 249
Centralization of bureaucracy, 265–267
Chadwick, Sir Edwin, 25, 26, 46

Chamberlain, Joseph, 64, 82, 87–88, 91, 102, 103, 200
Chamberlain, Neville, 124
Chartists, 25, 35, 181
Checkland, S. G., 27
Chevalier, Michel, 31
Chile, 203, 242
China, 221, 237–238
China Trade Act of 1922, 233
Choate, Joseph, 54
Churchill, Sir Winston, 146, 218
Civic Culture, The (Almond and Verba), 300
Civic reform, 293, 294
Civil Aeronautics Board v. Waterman S. S. (1948), 185
Civil liberties, 6
Civil service, 282
    reform, 71, 73–74
Civil Service Commission, 74
Civil War (U.S.), 36–37
Clarkson, Grosvenor, 110
Clay, Henry, 31
Clayton, Will, 217
Clemenceau, Georges, 48–49, 93, 104, 280
Clementel, Etienne, 115–116
Client state, concept of, 197
Clough, Shepard Bancroft, 62
Cloward, Richard A., 342–343
Cobb, Richard, 23
Cobb, Roger W., 303
Cobden, Richard, 28, 34, 35, 46
Coefficients, the, 87
Cohen, Stephen, 134, 170
Colbert, Jean Baptiste, 32
Cole, G. D. H., 122
Coletti, Lucio, 5
Collective bargaining, 77, 78, 159
Colonialism, 81–82, 85, 92–93, 104, 105
Committee for the Alliance for Progress (COMAP), 235
Committee for Economic Development, 234
Common Market: *see* European Economic Community (EEC)
Commune of 1871, 84
Communist Party (Great Britain), 117
Communist Party (Italy), 138, 304, 345
Communist Party (U.S.), 159
Confédération Générale de la Production Française (CGPF), 116
Confederazione Generale dell'Industria

Italiana (Confindustria), 115, 120, 155
Congress of Industrial Organizations (CIO), 159
Connally, Tom, 131
Converse, Philip E., 299–300, 303
Conwell, Russell, 56
Cooke, Jay, 37
Cooke, Morris L., 112
Cooperative Commonwealth, The (Gronlund), 51
Corn Laws, 35
Corporate liberalism, 127
Corporations, Accumulative State and, 20–22
Corporatism, 1, 113, 118–128, 129, 337–340
Corruption, 66–71, 156, 248
Corwin, Edward, 185
Covert operations, 188, 198–200, 202–206, 210
Credit, 32
Crédit Mobilier scandal, 33, 69, 71
Crimean War, 36
Crispi, Francesco, 64, 90
Critique of Capitalist Democracy (Moore), xiii
Croce, Benedetto, 90
Crozier, Michel, 261, 267, 310, 325–327
Cuba, 104, 221
    Bay of Pigs invasion, 199, 202, 209
    missile crisis, 259–260, 274

Dahl, Robert, 169
Dahrendorf, Ralf, 143, 327
Dangerfield, George, xi
D'Annunzio, Gabriele, 101
Danton, Georges Jacques, 92
Darlan, Jean François, 197
Darwin, Charles, 49, 52
Das Kapital (Marx), 250
Daudet, Alphonse, 104
Davezac, Henri, 132
De la colonisation chez les peuples modernes (Leroy-Beaulieu), 83
de Gaulle, Charles, 132, 133, 134, 197, 218, 226
Dean, Arthur H., 161
Dean, John, 207
Debré, Michel, 134, 282–283
Debs case, 89
Decentralization of bureaucracy, 267–268
Defense contracting, 163, 164, 171–173

Delafosse, Jules, 93
Democracy, defined, 4, 6
Democracy (Henry Adams), 156
Democracy and Socialism (Rosenberg), 5
Dennis, Jack, 296–300, 308
Depoliticization: *see* Alienated politics
Depression of 1873, 82–83, 90
Depretis, Agostino, 72–73
di Palma, Giuseppe, 303
Diarchy: *see* Dual State
Dicey, A. V., 44, 46
Diem, Ngo Dinh, 198
Dilke, Charles, 86
Dingley Tariff of 1897, 88
Disaccumulation, 251
Disraeli, Benjamin, 7
Dobb, Maurice, 18
Domino theory, 184
Dorfman, Gerald A., 142
Dorfman, Joseph, 47
Douglas, William O., 197–198
Dreyfus case, 103
Drucker, Peter, 257, 286
Dual labor market, 164
Dual State, 10, 176–213, 241, 249,
    275–276
  anticommunism, 182–184, 204, 212
  Central Intelligence Agency, 179, 187–
    190, 198–200, 202, 205, 206, 208–
    210, 213
  covert operations, 198–200, 202–206,
    210
  executive supremacy, 184–186, 192, 204
  France, 180–181
  Germany, 178
  Great Britain, 181
  imperialism and, 179, 180
  Italy, 180
  majoritarianism, problem of, 177, 180
  opposition to, 196
  rationality and irrationality, 178, 180,
    211–212
  United States, 179–213
  Vietnam War, 198, 200–204, 212
  Watergate, 206–211
Dubinsky, David, 159
Duchemin, René, 116
Dulles, Allen, 180, 189–190, 200
Dulles, John Foster, 183
Duncker, Max, 50
Dunham, A. L., 34
Dupeaux, Georges, 303
Durkheim, Emile, 281

Duverger, Maurice, 328

Eagleton, Thomas, 204
Easton, David, xii, 296–300
Eberstadt, Ferdinand, 187, 188, 190–193
Eckstein, Harry, 137, 302
Economic Cooperation Act of 1948, 233
Economic determinism, xiv, 56
Edelman, Murray, 274
Edge Act, 233
Edmunds, George, 54, 58
Education, 61, 327
  reforms, 75–76, 105–106
Education Act of 1921, 123
Eels, Richard, 239
Ehrmann, Henry, 116, 125, 161
Eisenhower, Dwight D., 151, 153–154,
    193
Elder, Charles O., 303
Elkins, Stephen Benton, 71
Ely, Richard T., 51, 56, 280
Emergency Relief Appropriation Act of
    1935, 186
Emigration, 94–99
Energy crisis, 162, 242
Engels, Friedrich, 5
England: *see* Great Britain
Engler, Robert, 162
Epicization of state, 282
Erhard, Ludwig, 136
Etudes sur la Richesse des Nations (Louis
    Say), 46
European Economic Community (EEC),
    224–228, 249
Evarts, William E., 80, 91
Exceptional Laws of 1899, 60
Executive Order Number 8248, 186
Executive supremacy, 184–186, 192, 204
Expansion of England, The (Seeley), 86
Expansionist State, 9, 80–107, 194, 237,
    241, 248
  colonialism, 81–82, 85, 92–93, 104
  emigration, 94–99
  France, 84, 85, 92–93, 98, 105
  free trade, 82, 85–88, 91, 100–101
  Germany, 82, 83, 90–91, 95–96, 98,
    102, 103
  Great Britain, 81–82, 85–88, 95, 102–
    105
  immigration, 97–99
  Italy, 90–91, 95, 102, 103
  liberal democratic conflict and, 81–85,
    100–107

Expansionist State (*cont.*)
  racism, 103
  tariff, 88–89, 100–101
  techniques of, 85–93
  United States, 83, 84, 88–90, 94–95,
    98–99, 103, 105, 106
  Zollverein solution, 91
Export-Import Bank, 234

Fabians, 60, 77, 78, 87, 102
Fabri, Frederick, 96
Family Assistance Plan, 261, 276
Farm Security Administration (FSA),
    140, 147–148
Fascism, 102, 121, 138, 314, 330, 338
Fashoda crisis, 93
Faulkner, Harold U., 57
Faure, Félix, 93
Federal Bureau of Investigation (FBI),
    205, 206, 208, 210
Federal Reserve Act, 233
Federal Reserve System, 33, 60
Federal Trade Commission Act, 155
Federalism, 22
Federalist Papers (Hamilton, Madison,
    and Jay), 65
Felice, Renzo de, 120
Felix, David, 115
Ferrais, Dante, 108, 115
Ferry, Jules, 64, 75–76, 80, 82, 92, 93
Feudalism, 14–15
Field, Stephen J., 53, 54, 56
Fieldhouse, A. K., 91, 100
Fine, Sidney, 37, 131
Finer, S. E., 123, 137, 153
Fino a Dogali (Oriani), 92
Fiske, John, 101
Fletcher v. Peck, 21
Follett, Mary, xi
Ford, Gerald R., 154, 288
Foreign aid, 234–235
Foreign Aid Act of 1962, 235
Forrestal, James, 183, 187, 191, 192, 194
Fouilée, Alfred, 49, 52
Fourier, François Marie Charles, 318
Fraenkel, Ernst, 178
France:
  Accumulative State, 21, 22, 27–30,
    33–34, 38
  agriculture, 140
  banking, 33–34
  civil service, 282
  colonialism, 85, 92–93, 105

corporations, early, 21, 22
corporatism, 124–126
Dual State, 180–181
education, 61, 75–76
European Economic Community, 226
Expansionist State, 84, 85, 92–93, 98,
  105
Franchise State, 131–135, 140, 141,
  145, 150–152, 155–157, 160, 166–
  168
GNP, 175, 257
Harmonious State, 44, 47–49, 61, 62,
  68, 75–76
immigration, 98
imperialism, 61
labor market, 27
labor unions, 141
managerialism, 166–168
nationalization, 133
planning, 162, 170
political corruption, 68
political leaders, 62
political participation, 303
political socialization, 297
political stagnation, 261–262
politicization, 290–291
public welfare, 38
railroads, 29, 30
reification of state, 282–283
solidarité, 48–49, 236, 280
state aid to business, 28–30
strikes, 84, 141
tariff, 34
Transnational State, 218, 226
tripartism, 133, 166
United Nations, 218
World War I, 115–116
Franchise State, 9–10, 108–175, 194,
    196–198, 218, 223, 241, 248–249
  agriculture, 139–140, 147–148, 160,
    163
  characteristics of business operation,
    146–147
  corporatism, 118–128
  corruption, 156
  defense contracting, 163, 164, 171–173
  delegation of power, 147–153
  demise of, 169–175
  extension of, 138–145
  France, 131–135, 140, 141, 145, 150–
    152, 155–157, 160, 166–168
  Germany, 135–136, 140, 142–143, 145,
    161, 166, 170

Great Britain, 136–137, 139, 141–142,
    145, 153, 160–161, 167, 168, 170–
    171, 174
  hierarchy, 150–152
  invention of, 128–138
  Italy, 135, 140, 145, 150, 155, 157,
    167, 168
  labor unions, 140–144, 158–160, 163
  managerialism, 166–168
  pluralism, 168
  self-regulation, 154–160
  tripartism, 165–166
  United States, 129–131, 139–140, 143–
    145, 147–149, 151–152, 155–165,
    167, 168, 171–175
  World War I, 108–117
Franck, Thomas M., 266–267
Franco-Prussian War, 84
Free trade, 82, 85–88, 91, 100–101,
    216–217
Freedom of the press, 327
Freedom of speech, 6
French Revolution, viii, 18
Freycinet, Charles Louis de Saulces de, 92
Freycinet Plan of 1879, 29
Frick, Henry Clay, 35
Froude, J. A., 331
Fulbright, J. W., 176, 182
Functional rationality, 178, 211, 212

Galbraith, John Kenneth, 127, 339
Gallagher, John, 83, 86, 104
Gallatin, Albert, 31, 33, 38
Galli, Giorgio, 316
Gambetta, Léon, 64
Gardner, Lloyd, 217, 224
Gardner, Richard N., 221–222
Garfield, James, 70
Gautier, Théophile, 42–43
Genocide, 103
Germany:
  Accumulative State, 27–29, 31–32, 34
  agriculture, 140
  corporatism, 121–122
  Dual State, 178
  emigration, 95–96
  Expansionist State, 82, 83, 90–91, 95–
    96, 98, 102, 103
  Franchise State, 135–136, 140, 142–
    143, 145, 161, 166, 170
  GNP, 175, 257
  Harmonious State, 44, 49–51, 63, 68
  immigration, 98

interest groups, 161
labor market, 27
labor unions, 142–143, 336
Nazism, 122, 178
planning, 162, 170
political corruption, 68
political leaders, 63
political participation, 303
political parties, 308
racism, 103
Seehandlung, 31–32
Socialist Party, 50
state aid to business, 28–29, 31
tariff, 34
tripartism, 166
welfare legislation, 50–51, 102
World War I, 112–115
Gerstacker, Carl A., 236
Gesinde Ordnungen, 27
Gibbons v. Ogdon, 31
Gignoux, Claude, 116, 124, 125
Gilbert, James B., 126
Gilpin, Robert, 235
Gintis, Herbert, 75
Gioliti, Giovanni, 60, 64, 92, 119
Giscard d'Estaing, Valéry, 318
Gladstone, Herbert, 59
Gladstone, William, 51
Glistrup, Mogens, 286
Gobineau, Joseph Arthur de, 103
Godkin, E. L., 48, 59
Goldwater, Barry, 58
Goodrich, Carter, 37
Gosnell, Harold, viii
Goubert, Pierre, 15
Gough, Ian, 265
Governability of Democracies, The (Tri-
    lateral Commission), 325–329, 337
Governmental activity, reductions in,
    330–334
Governmental Process, The (Truman),
    xiii
Grace, J. Peter, 235, 239
Gramsci, Antonio, 53, 108, 168, 340,
    345, 346
Grandval, Gilbert, 141
Grant, Ulysses S., 70
Great Britain:
  Accumulative State, 21–33, 35–36, 38
  agriculture, 139
  banking, 32–33
  bureaucracy, 266, 269
  colonialism, 81–82, 104

Great Britain (*cont.*)
  Communist Party, 117
  corporations, early, 21, 22
  corporatism, 122–124, 340
  Crimean War, 36
  Dual State, 181
  education, 61, 75, 105
  emigration, 95
  European Economic Community, 225, 227
  Expansionist State, 81–82, 85–88, 95, 102–105
  Franchise State, 136–137, 139, 141–142, 145, 153, 160–161, 167, 168, 170–171, 174
  free trade, 85–88, 216
  GNP, 175, 257
  Harmonious State, 44, 46, 51, 61, 68, 75–78
  illusion, politics of, 276
  interest groups, 153
  labor market, 27
  labor unions, 141–142
  managerialism, 167, 168
  nationalization, 133
  police, 23–26
  political corruption, 68
  political leaders, 61, 316–317
  political socialization, 297
  political stagnation, 261–262
  politicization, 291–292
  public welfare, 38
  racism, 103
  railroads, 30
  state aid to business, 28–31
  strikes, 117
  tariff, 35–36
  Transnational State, 216, 218, 225, 227
  United Nations, 218
  utilitarianism, 46
  wage and hour legislation, 76–78
  World War I, 116
Great Depression, 127, 128
Green, T. H., 51, 101, 102, 105, 236
Green, William, 158
Greenberg, Edward, 298
Gresham, Walter Quintin, 84
Grey, Sir Edward, 78
Grey, Gordon, 235
Gronlund, Lawrence, 51
Gross National Product (GNP), 174–175, 257
Gründungsschwindel, 68

Guatemala, 199, 200
Guesde, Jules, 291
Guggenheim, Daniel, 110
Guild socialism, 122
Guizot, François Pierre Guillaume, 19, 40

Habermas, Jürgen, 6, 251–252, 263–264, 295, 325
Halberstam, David, 277
Haldane, Richard Burton, 51
Haldeman, H. R., 201, 208, 275, 276
Hale, Lord, 91
Halévy, Daniel, 61
Halévy, Elie, 25, 84, 87, 102–103
Hallstein, Walter, 224
Hamerow, Theodore, 49–50
Hamilton, Alexander, 31, 33, 45
Hammond, Bray, 33
Hanna, Mark, 64
Harkins, Paul D., 277
Harmonies Economiques (Bastiat), 47
Harmonious State, 9, 42–79, 236, 241, 247–248
  education, 61
  France, 44, 47–49, 61, 62, 68, 75–76
  Germany, 44, 49–51, 63, 68
  Great Britain, 44, 46, 51, 61, 68, 75–78
  history of doctrine, 45–51
  Italy, 44, 60–63, 68
  laissez-faire: *see* Laissez-faire
  political corruption, 66–71
  political leaders, 61–64
  political theory, decline in, 64–66
  reform, 71–79
  structure of politics under, 59–71
  United States, 46–48, 51, 61, 63, 66, 68–71, 73–75
Harris, Louis, 322
Harris, Nigel, 170–171
Hartz, Louis, 22, 37, 38
Hatch Act, 73
Hawley, Ellis, 131
Hayes, Samuel, 293, 297
Heckscher, Eli, 18
Heclo, Hugh, 266, 267, 269, 276
Hegel, Georg, 5, 51, 101
Heilbroner, Robert, 2
Helms, Richard, 205, 208–209
Herring, Pendleton, viii
Hess, Robert D., 311
Hicks, John D., 126
Higham, John, 99
Hillman, Sidney, 165

Hilsman, Roger, 179
Hintze, Otto, 17, 191
Hitchcock, Ethan Allen, 71
Ho Chi Minh, 232
Hoarding, political, 343–344
Hobbes, Thomas, x–xi, 3, 279
Hobhouse, Leonard Trelawney, xi, 60
Hoffa, James, 159
Holland, 145
Holt, Felix, 291
Homeostasis, 55
Homestead strike, 84
Hoover, Herbert, 126–127
Hoover, J. Edgar, 208
Hoover Commission Task Force on Na-
    tional Security Organization, 188, 190
Hull, Cordell, 216–221, 223
Huntington, Samuel P., 111, 308, 325–
    328, 337, 339
Huston Plan, 208, 283
Hymer, Stephen, 229, 230–231

Illusion, politics of, 274–276
Immigration, 97–99
Imperialism, 61, 82, 179, 180, 237; *see
    also* Expansionist State
Indonesia, 199
Industrial bourgeoisie, 13, 14, 16–19, 21–
    22, 43, 44, 61, 67, 72
Inglehart, Roland, 312
Interest groups, 153, 160–161, 273, 309–
    310, 312, 335
International Bank for Reconstruction
    and Development (IBRD), 217
International Monetary Fund (IMF), 217
Interstate Commerce Commission (ICC),
    57
Invisible hand, 45
Iran, 199
Irrationality, 178, 180
Isolationism, 196
Italian Penal Code of 1871, 60
Italy:
    Accumulative State, 30, 31, 37
    agriculture, 140
    authoritarianism, 337
    banking, 60
    Communist Party, 138, 304, 345
    corporatism, 119–121, 338
    Dual State, 180
    emigration, 95
    European Economic Community, 227
    Expansionist State, 90–91, 95, 102, 103

fascism, 102, 121, 138, 338
Franchise State, 135, 140, 145, 150,
    155, 157, 167, 168
GNP, 175
Harmonious State, 44, 60–63, 68
imperialism, 61
land policy, 37
managerialism, 167, 168
political corruption, 68
political leaders, 62–63, 315–316
political participation, 301, 304
political parties, 308
political stagnation, 262
racism, 103
railroads, 30
state aid to business, 30, 31
Transnational State, 227
World War I, 115
Itzenplitz, Count Heinrich von, 29–30

Jackson, Andrew, 33
Jackson, Henry, 201
Jenckes Civil Service Reform Bill of 1868,
    71
Jensen, Richard, 293
Jevons, William Stanley, 51
Jews, 103
Jingoism, 7, 103
Johnson, Hugh, 162
Johnson, Lyndon B., 148, 203, 204
Joint Chiefs of Staff (JCS), 187, 201, 202
Joint-stock companies, 22
Junkers, 63, 90

Kaiser, Karl, 244
Kanya-Forstner, A. S., 93
Karp, Walter, 307
Kathedersozialisten, 102
Kattenberg, Paul, 267
Katz, Michael, 75
Katzenbach, Nicholas, 204
Kautsky, Karl Johann, xii
Kaysen, Carl, 201
Kefauver Committee (1951), 159
Kelly, Edmund, 126
Kennedy, John F., 198–201, 208, 210,
    211, 259–260, 282
Kennedy, Robert F., 159, 200, 201, 282
Key, V. O., viii, 157–158
Keynes, John Maynard, 108, 146, 216
Kidd, Benjamin, 103
Kindleberger, Charles, 240
King, Anthony, 322, 332

Kirchheimer, Otto, 306, 307
Kissinger, Henry, 193, 203, 323
Kittrell, Edward R., 28
Kitzinger, Uwe, 224, 226
Knox, Frank, 183
Kolko, Gabriel, 72, 196
Korean War, 193
Kriegel, Annie, 118
Krupp, Alfred, 21, 63
Kunth, G. J. C., 28

Labor leaders, 77, 78
Labor unions, 117–118, 336
    in Franchise State, 140–144, 158–160,
        163
LaFeber, Walter, 89
Laissez-faire, 18, 20, 22, 28, 30, 33, 35,
        37, 42, 45, 48–52, 117, 218
    liberalism and democracy, contradiction
        between, 57–58
    materialistic theory of society, 56–57
    nature and, 52–53
    offensive and defensive strategy, 58–59
    political corruption and, 68–71
    pseudoreligious quality, 56
    universalistic rhetoric and particularistic
        appeal, 53–55
    utopian and counterutopian contradic-
        tion between, 55
Lamartine, Alphonse Marie Louis de Prat
        de, 13
Lampertico, Fedele, 44
Land policy, 37–38
Landau, Martin, 268
Landrum-Griffin Act of 1959, 159
Lansing, Robert, 183
LaPalombara, Joseph, 135, 157, 273
Laski, Harold, xiii
Law, Bonar, 51, 117
Law, Sylvia, 144
Law and Opinion in the Nineteenth
        Century (Dicey), 44
Lawrence, William, 56
League of Nations, 215
LeBon, Gustave, 97
Lebovics, Herman Eugene, 122
LeChapelier Law of 1791, 27
Leinenweber, Charles, 292
Lend-lease, 197
Lenin, V. I., xii-xiii
Leontief, Wasily, 339
Leroy-Beaulieu, Paul, 83
Lessing, Doris, 97

Leuchtenberg, William, 130, 147–148,
        186
Lhomme, Jean, 62
Liautey, André, 157
Liberal democracy: see also Accumulative
        State; Dual State; Expansionist State;
        Franchise State; Harmonious State;
        Transnational State
    predicament of, 1–9
Liberalism, defined, 4
Liddy, G. Gordon, 276
Lindberg, Leon N., 226, 227
Lindblom, Charles, 169
Lindsay, John, 265
Lipow, Arthur, 293
Lipset, Seymour Martin, 1, 8
List, Friedrich, 95, 101
Litt, Edgar, 300
Livret, 27
Lloyd, Henry, 271
Lochner v. New York (1905), 54, 59
Locke, John, 4, 64
London Times, 13
Lotta Politica in Italia, La (Oriani), 92
Louis Philippe, King of France, 34
Lovett, Robert, 183
Lowi, Theodore, 130, 144, 262–263, 335
Lubenow, William C., 25–26, 29
Lucas, Arthur F., 123
Ludlow Amendment, 185
Lukacs, Georg, 2
Luttbeg, Norman, 315
Lying, 276–278
Lynd, Robert, viii

MacDonald, Ramsay, 78
MacFarland, James P., 236
Machiavelli, Niccolò, 279
MacIver, Robert, xii
Macmillan, Harold, 124, 225
Macpherson, C. B., 3
Madison, James, 13, 33, 65
Magruder, Jeb, 206–207, 209, 275
Mahan, Alfred Thayer, 103, 191
Maier, Charles, 115, 118
Maisonrouge, Jacques, 214, 215, 222
Majoritarianism, 177, 180
Malcolmson, Robert, 106
Malthus, Thomas, 253
Managerialism, 166–168
Mandel, Ernst, 250, 251
Mann, Horace, 75
Mannheim, Karl, 7, 178

Manoilesco, Mihail, 119
Mansfield, Mike, 197–198
Marchais, Georges, 318
Marglin, Stephen, 294
Marshall, John, 21, 31, 33
Marshall, T. H., 288, 294
Marshall Plan, 138, 220
Martin, Frederick Townsend, 67
Martinelli, Alberto, 243
Marx, Karl, xii, 5, 153, 250, 333
Marxism, ix, xii-xiii, xiv
Mass culture, 7, 106
Mass media, 97, 212, 311
Materialism, 56–57
Mather, F. C., 24
Matignon agreement of 1936, 141
Maturity, 155
Maurras, Charles, 104
McArthur, John H., 135
McClelland Commission (1959–60), 159
McCloskey, Robert, 53
McCloy, John, 179, 223
McCone, John, 180, 200
McConnell, Grant, 126, 160
McCormick, Thomas, 89
McCrone, Donald, 304
McNamara, Robert, 320
Means, Gardiner C., 22
"Media Papers," 210
Mediterranean system, 31
Méline, Félix Jules, 82
Mercantile bourgeoisie, 15–19
Mercantilism, 229
Merchant Shipping Act of 1906, 95
Merriam, Charles, viii
Messadie, Gerald, 181
Metaphysical Theory of the State (Hobhouse), xi
Meyer, René, 132
Michels, Robert, 150
Military unification, 187–188, 190–192
Mill, James, 4
Mill, John Stuart, 3, 44, 46, 81–82
Miller, Arthur H., 324
Milner, Alfred, 101, 103
Miners' Eight Hours Bill, 77
Minimum wage, 78
Mitchell, John, 207
Mitscher, Marc Andrew, 182
Modern State, The (MacIver), xii
Monarchy, 15–16
Mond, Alfred, 124
Monopoly, 74, 81, 163

Montgomery, David, 37, 46, 48
Moore, O. C., 72
Moore, Stanley, xiii
Morgenthau, Hans, 193
Moses, Robert, 312
Motz, Friedrich Christian Adolph von, 31
Moynihan, Daniel P., 148–149, 222, 261, 276, 286, 322
Müller, Ronald E., 230, 244
Multinational corporations, 215, 228–243, 249
Munitions Standards Board, 110
Murray, Robin, 240
Musil, Robert, 114
Mussolini, Benito, 121–122
Myers, Frank, 317–318

Napoleon III, 34
Nasser, Gamal Abdel, 221
National Civic Federation, 155
National Civil Service Reform League, 73
National Enterprises Bill (NEB), 340
National Export Expansion Committee, 234
National Farmers Union, 139
National Health Insurance Act of 1924, 123
National Industrial Recovery Act (NIRA), 130, 143
National Labor Board (NLB), 143, 144, 165
National Labor Relations Board (NLRB), 144, 165
National Planning Association, 234
National Recovery Administration (NRA), 129–131
National security, 183
National Security Act of 1947, 187, 192–194
National Security Council (NSC), 187, 188, 192, 193, 201, 202, 260
Nationalism, 224–228
Nationalization, 133
Naturalism, 104
Nature, 52–53
Naumann, Friedrich, 79, 113
Nazism, 122, 178
Neiburg, H. L., 171
Neo-Hegelianism, 51
Neomercantilism, 33
Neumann, Franz, 122
Neustadt, Richard, 284
New Deal, 129–131, 147, 186

New Left, 205
New Olive Branch, The (Carey), 45
New State, The (Follett), xi
New Utopians, The (Boguslaw), 319
Nichols, Roy, 37
Nietzsche, Friedrich Wilhelm, 113
Nisbet, Robert, 323
Nixon, Richard M., 156, 186, 205–213, 265, 271, 281–285, 289, 320–321, 335
Nobis, Enrico, 180
Nock, Albert Jay, x
Nonalignment, concept of, 221
Nye, Norman, 305

Oastler, Richard, 40
Objectification of state, 281–282
O'Connor, James, 175, 250–251, 269, 328
Offe, Claus, 6, 263, 266, 270, 303, 307, 310
Office of Management and Budget (OMB), 265
Oil industry, 131, 161–162
Okun, Arthur, 333, 334
Old regime: *see Ancien régime*
Oligarchy, iron law of, 150
Olivetti, Gino, 115, 116
Open Door Policy, 90, 237–238
Order, preservation of, 22–26
Organized Crime Control Act of 1970, 160
Oriani, Alfredo, 92
Ostrogorski, Maurice, 69
Our Country (Strong), 99
Overseas Private Investment Corporation (OPIC), 235

Packenham, Robert, 231
Paine, Thomas, 65
Palestine Liberation Organization (PLO), 211
Palmade, Guy P., 20
Palmerston, Lord, 85
Pantouflage, 151
Parris, Henry, 28, 29
Participation, political, 4–6, 300–305, 328, 335–337
Passing of the Idle Rich, The (Martin), 67
Pateman, Carole, 4, 290
Paternalism, 124
Paxton, Robert O., 125

Payne-Aldrich Tariff of 1909, 34
Pearson, Karl, 103
Pease, E. R., 78
Peel, Sir Robert, 42
Pelling, Henry, 75, 292
Pendleton Act of 1887, 73, 74
Penrose, Boise, 63
Pentagon Papers, 181, 198, 212
Penty, Arthur J., 122
Percy, Lord, 124
Périère, Emile, 58
Périère brothers, 33
Personification of state, 281
Pétain, Henri Philippe, 125
Peterloo Massacre, 23
Peters, Karl, 90
Petiet, Baron, 125
Petrie, Sir Charles, 124
Philosophical Theory of the State (Bosanquet), xi
Philosophy of Right (Hegel), 5
Pigou, A. C., 77
Pinay, Antoine, 132
Piven, Frances Fox, 342–343
Planning, 162, 170, 326, 339
Planning-programing-budgeting systems (PPBS), 268, 269
Plato, 279
Playa Girón invasion, 200
Pluralism, xii, 168, 252, 273–274
Polanyi, Karl, 7, 101, 109
Police, 23–26
Political corruption, 66–71, 156, 248
Political leaders, 61–64, 316–317
Political machines, 292
Political participation, 4–6, 300–305, 328, 335–337
Political parties, 305–309, 312
Political reform, 71–75
    rationalizing, 73–74
    repressive, 74
    responsive, 74–75
Political socialization, 296–300
Political stagnation, 257–262
Political theory, decline in, 64–66
Politicization of bureaucracy, 264–265, 270
"Politics as a Vocation" (Weber), 314
Pollock v. Farmers' Loan and Trust Company, 58, 59
Popular sovereignty, 22
Poulantzas, Nicos, 15, 226–227
Power, Thomas F., Jr., 84, 105

Pragmatism, 315
Presidency, power of, 184–186, 192, 204, 284, 326
Presidential Power (Neustadt), 284
Press, freedom of the, 327
Price competition, 162, 163
Price controls, 130, 131
Price-fixing, 131
Prince-Smith, John, 50
Principles of Social Science (Henry Carey), 47
Prison Act of 1835, 25
Problems of Greater Britain (Dilke), 86
Process of Government, The (Bentley), xiii
Profit making, 162, 163
Progressivism, 293
Protectionism: *see* Tariff
Prouty, Roger Warren, 28, 29
Public administration, 66, 69, 71
Public interest, decline of, 272–273, 275
Public welfare, 38–39
Pullman strike, 84
Purcell, Edward A., 284
Putnam, Robert, 316–317

Racism, 7, 103, 179
Racketeering, 159–160
Radical Republicanism, 46, 48
Radowitz, Joseph von, 50
Railroads, 29–30, 61
Rathenau, Walther, 112–115, 116, 121–122, 125, 127, 149, 155
Rationality, 178, 180, 211–212
Rationalization of bureaucracy, 268
Rationalizing political reforms, 73–74
Reconstruction Finance Corporation, 127, 339
Reform, 102
   civil service, 71, 73–74
   education, 75–76, 105–106
   political, 71–75
Reform Act of 1832, 291
Reification of the state, 10, 208, 278–287
Repoliticization, 344–346
Report on Manufacturers (Hamilton), 31, 45
Repressive reforms, 74
Resignation, political theory of, 279, 286–287, 330–331
Responsibility, 154–155, 161, 314, 318
Responsive reforms, 74–75

Restoration of the Guild System (Penty), 122
Rhodes, Cecil, 106
Ricardo, David, 22, 28, 45, 81
Riesman, David, 286
Riscard, Pierre, 132
Rising entitlements, theory of, 332
Risk taking, 162
Robbins, Lionel, 28
Roberts, David, 40
Robinson, Ronald, 83, 86, 104
Rockefeller, David, 232, 235, 325
Rockefeller, John D., 313
Rockefeller, Nelson, 193, 235, 332
Rodgers, Harrell, 298
Rohatyn, Felix, 339
Rohrbough, Malcolm J., 38
Romanticism, 104
Rome, Treaty of, 225
Ronge, Volker, 264
Roosevelt, Franklin Delano, 129–130, 144, 158, 182, 183
Roosevelt, Kermit, 183
Roosevelt, Theodore, 74, 101, 103
Root, Elihu, 191
Roseberry, Archibald Philip, Earl of, 86, 87, 102, 103
Rosenberg, Arthur, 5, 63
Rosenberg, Hans, 15
Ross, Edward A., 105
Rossoni, Edmundo, 120
Rostow, Walt, 201
Rousseau, Jean Jacques, 4, 290
Rowland, Benjamin M., 216, 217, 234
Rowthorn, Robert, 230, 231
Rule, James, 311
Rural Police Act of 1839, 25
Rusk, Dean, 214
Ryder, Sir Don, 340

Saint-Simon, Comte de, 253, 270, 318
Salter, Sir Arthur, 116
Salvemini, Gaetano, 63
Sampson, Anthony, 240, 242
Samuel, Herbert, 53–54, 64
Sani, Giacomo, 337
Sarti, Roland, 120, 135
Say, J. B., 45–46
Say, Leon, 62
Say, Louis, 46
Schattschneider, E. E., viii, 149
Schechter v. United States (1935), 130
Scheingold, Stuart A., 226, 227, 228

Schell, Jonathan, 281
Schlesinger, Arthur, Jr., 185, 199, 282
Schmitter, Philippe, 119, 338
Schmoller, Gustav, 102
Schultze, Charles L., 268
Schumpeter, Joseph, 81, 230, 237, 333
Schurmann, Franz, 186, 192, 272–273, 275
Scott, Bruce R., 135
Scott, James, 67
Scott, John A., 49
Securities Exchange Act, 216
Seehandlung, 31–32
Seeley, John, 86
Self, Peter, 139
Self-regulation, 154–160
Semmel, Bernard, 101
Senior, Nassau, 28, 45, 46
Seward, William E., 65
Shanks, Michael, 261
Sheehan, Neil, 212
Sherman, Forrest, 189, 190
Sherman, John, 64
Sherman Anti-Trust Act of 1890, 54, 57
Sherman Silver Purchase Act of 1890, 60
Shils, Edward, 153
Shonfeld, Andrew, 132, 142, 152–153, 163, 170
Seigfried, André, 146
Simon, William, 325
Sinclair, Upton, 185
Six Acts, 23
Skidelsky, Robert, 2
Skjelsbaek, Kjell, 241
Smith, Adam, 1–2, 22, 28, 44, 45, 48, 55, 81
Smith, J. Allen, viii
Smith, Trevor, 261
Smoot-Hawley Tariff, 34
Social Darwinism, 248
Social Democratic movement, xii
Social Evolution (Kidd), 103
Socialism, 6, 152, 153, 346
Socialists of the Chair, 102, 236, 280
Socialization, political, 296–300
Societal corporatism, 119, 127
Solidarité, 48–49, 236, 280
Somaini, Eugenio, 243
Sorel, Georges, 124
Sorensen, Theodore, 213, 260
Spahn, Othmar, 122
Speech, freedom of, 6
Speenhamland system, 26, 50

Spencer, Herbert, 44, 49, 51, 52
Spirit of American Government, The (Smith), viii
Spiro, Herbert J., 142
Spoils system, 66, 73
Sports, 106
Spring, Joel, 75, 106
Stalin, Joseph, 218, 219
Standard Oil of New Jersey, 165
Standmann, Hartmut Pogge von, 90
State: see Accumulative State; Dual State; Expansionist State; Franchise State; Harmonious State; Transnational State
State in Relation to Labour, The (Jevons), 51
State in Theory and Practice, The (Laski), xiii
Stavins, Ralph, 202
Stefani, Alberto de, 119
Steffens, Lincoln, 67
Stimson, Henry L., 182, 183, 223
Stokes, Donald, 307, 308
Stone, Katherine, 294
Storing, Herbert J., 139
Strikes, 84, 117, 118, 138, 141, 143, 144, 158, 162, 344
Strong, Josiah, 99, 105
Struve, Walter, 113
Student movement, 174
Sturmthal, Adolph, 133
Substantial rationality, 178, 211, 212
Suez crisis, 199
Suffrage, 5, 8
Sukarno, Achmed, 199
Suleiman, Ezra, 135, 150
Sumner, William Graham, 44, 51, 52–53, 55, 56, 57, 101
Supreme Court of the United States, 51, 54–55, 57, 59, 130–131, 155, 185
Sweden, 140, 145
Switzerland, 8
Swope, Gerald, 149
Syndicalists, 291

Taft, Charles P., 216–217
Taft, Robert, 186
Taft-Hartley Act of 1947, 159
Tariff, 32, 34–36, 88–89, 100–101
Tarrow, Sidney, 304
Tawney, R. H., 17, 44
Taxation, 54, 134
Taylor, George, 298

Taylor, Maxwell, 198, 200, 201
Taylor Grazing Act of 1934, 140
Teapot Dome scandal, 69
Television industry, 149–150
Tennessee Valley Authority (TVA), 140
Thiers, Louis Adolphe, 62
Thomson, David, 72
Tocqueville, Alexis de, 18, 19, 144
Tonkin Gulf Resolution, 203–204
Torney, Judith V., 311
Townsend, Mary, 83
Trade Agreements Act of 1934, 216
Trade Union Congress, 77
Transnational State, 10, 214–244, 249
  Bretton Woods Conference, 216–217
  European Economic Community, 224–228, 249
  France, 218, 226
  Great Britain, 216, 218, 225, 227
  Italy, 227
  multinational corporations, 215, 228–243, 249
  United Nations, 217–223, 249
  United States, 215–223, 229–243
Trevelyan, Sir Charles Edward, 26
Trilateral Commission, 1, 325–329, 337, 339
Tripartism, concept of, 133, 165–166
Trollope, Anthony, 39
Truman, David B., xiii
Truman, Harry S., 189, 192, 193, 288
Trusteeship, 197
Trusts, 22
Tugwell, Rexford G., 130
Tunisia, 93
Turner, Lewis, 240
Turner, Stanfield, 210, 213
Tydings, Millard, 189, 192

Ulman, Lloyd, 334
Unheavenly City, The (Banfield), 271
Union of Soviet Socialist Republics:
  Bolshevik revolution, 117
  United Nations, 218
United Nations, 217–223, 249
United States of America:
  Accumulative State, 21, 22, 30, 33–38
  agriculture, 139–140, 147, 160
  anticommunism, 182–184, 204, 212, 218–220, 224
  Atlantic Alliance, 220
  banking, 33, 60
  Bay of Pigs invasion, 199, 202, 209

bureaucracy, 262–267, 269
Central Intelligence Agency, 179, 187–190, 198–200, 202, 205, 206, 208–210, 213, 239, 249
civil service reform, 73–74
Civil War, 36–37
Communist Party, 159
Corporations, early, 21, 22
corporatism, 126–127, 339
covert operations, 198–200, 202–206, 210
Cuban missile crisis, 259–260, 274
defense contracting, 163, 164, 171–173
domino theory, 184
Dual State, 179–213
education, 75, 105
emigration, 94–95
executive supremacy, 184–186, 192, 204
Expansionist State, 83, 84, 88–90, 94–95, 98–99, 103, 105, 106
federal executives, 151–152
foreign aid, 234–235
Franchise State, 129–131, 139–140, 143–145, 147–149, 151–152, 155–165, 167, 168, 171–175
free trade, 83, 88, 216–217
GNP, 174, 175, 257
Harmonious State, 46–48, 51, 61, 63, 66, 68–71, 73–75
illusion, politics of, 276
immigration, 98–99
interest groups, 310
labor unions, 143–144, 158–160
land policy, 37–38
managerialism, 167, 168
mass culture, 106
military unification, 187–188, 190–192
multinational corporations, 229–243
national security, 183
New Deal, 129–131, 147, 186
Open Door Policy, 90, 237–238
planning, 339
political corruption, 68–70
political leaders, 63
political machines, 292
political participation, 328, 336
political parties, 307–308
public administration, 66, 71
public welfare, 38
racism, 103
Radical Republicanism, 46, 48
railroads, 30
reification of state, 281–286

United States of America (*cont.*)
state aid to business, 30
strikes, 84, 117, 138, 143, 144, 158
tariff, 34–35, 88–89
Transnational State, 215–223, 229–243
tripartism, 165
United Nations, 219–223
Venezuela boundary dispute, 89
Vietnam War, 198, 200–204, 212, 277
War on Poverty, 148–149, 261
Watergate, 206–211, 249
World War I, 110–112
U.S. v. E. C. Knight Co. (1895), 89
Utilitarianism, 49, 56
Utopianism, 55, 168, 318–320

Van Buren, Martin, 63
Vandenberg, Arthur, 219
Vandenberg, Hoyt, 189
Veblen, Thorstein, 176
Venezuela boundary dispute, 89
Verba, Sidney, 300–302, 304, 305, 308, 309
Vernon, Raymond, 230, 231, 236
Vier Jahre in Afrika (Ernst Weber), 96
Vietnam War, 198, 200–204, 212, 277
Villiers, Georges, 132
Voltaire, 31

Waddington, W. H., 64
Wage and hour legislation, 76–78
Wage restraint bargain of 1948, 141, 142
Wagner Act of 1935, 144, 158, 159
Walker, Mack, 96
Wallerstein, Immanuel, 16
Walters, Vernon, 209
Wanamaker, John, 71
War Industries Board (WIB), 111–112, 129, 165
War on Poverty, 148–149, 261
Warmaking, 36–37
Watergate, 206–211, 249
Watergate Transcripts, 181, 207

Ways, Max, 339
Wealth of Nations, The (Smith), 45
Web of Government, The (MacIver), xii
Webb, Beatrice, 87, 122, 280
Webb, Sidney, 87, 122, 280
Webb-Pomerene Act of 1918, 232–233
Weber, Ernst von, 96
Weber, Max, 80, 113, 178, 279, 314–315, 318, 320
Wedgwood-Benn, Anthony, 339
Wehler, Hans-Ulrich, 83, 101
Weidenbaum, Murray, 163, 173
Weisband, Edward, 266–267
Welfare state, xi, 46, 50, 285–286, 342–343
Wellington, Duke of, 23
Wells, David, 83
White, Leonard, 66
White, Theodore, 234
Whitney, William Collins, 71
Whyte, Arthur James, 68
Wildavsky, Aaron, 266, 267, 269, 272, 273–274, 276, 286
Wilkins, Myra, 229
Williams, David, 181
Williams, Philip, 133, 134
Williams, William Appleman, 33, 90, 126
Wilson, Woodrow, 223
Wilson-Gorman Act of 1893, 88
Wolin, Sheldon, x, xiii, 290
Woodcock, Leonard, 339
Woolsey, T. D., 26
World Bank, 233
World War I, 108–117

Yakus v. United States (1944), 130–131
Yerkes, Charles, 111
Young, Andrew, 222

Zanardelli, Giuseppe, 64
Zeldin, Theodore, 290
Zolberg, Aristide, 291
Zollverein, 31, 91